Conversion Tables

Conversion Tables
Volume 1

LC–Dewey

Third Edition

Mona L. Scott

LIBRARIES
U N L I M I T E D
A Member of the Greenwood Publishing Group

Westport, Connecticut • London

Library of Congress Cataloging-in-Publication Data

Scott, Mona L.
   Conversion tables / by Mona L. Scott.
     p. cm.
   ISBN 1-59158-348-9 (set : alk. paper) — ISBN 1-59158-315-2 (v. 1 :
alk. paper) — ISBN 1-59158-346-2 (v. 2 : alk. paper)
   —ISBN 1-59158-347-0 (v. 3 : alk. paper)
  1. Classification, Library of Congress. 2. Classification,
Dewey decimal. 3. Reclassification (Libraries) I. Title.
Z696.U4S36 2006
025.4'33—dc22   2005030846

British Library Cataloguing in Publication Data is available.

Library of Congress Catalog Card Number: 2005030846
ISBN: 1-59158-315-2 (Volume 1)
      1-59158-346-2 (Volume 2)
      1-59158-347-0 (Volume 3)
      1-59158-348-9 (Set)

First published in 2006

Libraries Unlimited, 88 Post Road West, Westport, CT 06881
A Member of Greenwood Publishing, Inc.
www.lu.com

Printed in the United States of America

The paper used in this book complies with the
Permanent Paper Standard issued by the National
Information Standards Organization (Z39.48–1984).

10 9 8 7 6 5 4 3 2 1

Contents

Introduction

The third edition of *Conversion Tables: LC–Dewey; Dewey–LC* contains extensive updates of Dewey numbers that reflect the 22nd edition of the Dewey Decimal Classification. Also included are almost one thousand additional sets of class numbers and corresponding Library of Congress (LC) subject headings. These include new subjects that reflect today's world, such as the September 11, 2001, Terrorist Attacks; the War on Terrorism; the Afghan War of 2001; and the Iraq War of 2003. There are also classification and subject sets that broaden areas that were found in the earlier editions, such as Druids and Druidism; World War, 1939–1945—Campaigns—Burma; 401(k) plans; Cosmic noise; Butterfly gardens; Anorexia; CPR (First aid); Computer art; and many ethnic groups found in Africa.

Materials referenced in the *Conversion Tables* are the 22nd edition of the Dewey Decimal Classification (DDC) and the most current editions of the various volumes of the Library of Congress classification schedules and LC Subject Headings available. Library of Congress authority files were consulted regularly to maintain the currency of country or nation names.

Conversion Tables was conceived as a cataloging tool or standard reference in any cataloging department for daily copy cataloging activities, the converting of classifications of individual MARC (machine readable cataloging) records from bibliographic utilities that include only one of the classifications. The LC subject heading table also can be used as call a number assigning tool for both LC and DDC classifications.

The LC and DDC classification schemes approach the organization of knowledge from different perspectives. This can be seen in how LC and Dewey view language and the literatures of each language. LC classes them together in the Ps, whereas Dewey separates them, placing language in the 400s and literature in the 800s. Similarly, LC places military and naval sciences in stand-alone classes, U for military science and V for naval sciences; Dewey places both in the so-called megaclass 300s, which includes virtually all of social and political sciences.

Becasue the two schemes differ so greatly in basic concepts, it was necessary to analyze the concepts of each order to select the corresponding numbers or alphanumeric notations to construct the tables. Ultimately, it involved assigning tens of thousands of class notations.

Structure of the Tables

This cataloging tool is arranged in three sections, each in its own volume: LC to Dewey, Volume 1; Dewey to LC, Volume 2; and Subject Headings with corresponding classifications, Volume 3. Thus each volume contains the same list of classifications in the two systems and corresponding subject headings but is arranged differently.

Example:

LC to Dewey tables

LC	Dewey	Subject Heading
DS79.76	956.70443	Iraq War, 2003

Dewey to LC tables

Dewey	LC	Subject Heading
956.70443	DS79.76	Iraq War, 2003

Subject Heading tables

Subject Heading	LC	Dewey
Iraq War, 2003	DS79.76	956.70443

The notation for a general concept such as Philosophy, which is 100 in Dewey and B in the Library of Congress Classification, will have divisions and subdivisions broken down into smaller concepts and thus more detailed notations ("Philosophy—Congresses" is 105 in Dewey and B20 in LC).

The differences just discussed also result in more than one notation corresponding to the other, or even a whole range of numbers and alphanumeric notations corresponding to the other. For example, 951.041 in the Dewey schedule under the history of China corresponds to seven LC notations in these tables, in the range DS773.83 to DS777.45.

Dates in the LC and Dewey schemes are a problem. The two schedules often do not agree on the date that an event occurred. For example, the LC classification indicates that the Time of Troubles in Russian history was from 1598–1613, but the Dewey scheme uses the date 1605–1613. In other places, however, the dates match perfectly, as in the history of Tunisia. To aid in the conversion, I have often used a range of dates from Table 1 in the Dewey Classification to indicate a century, rather than the single date.

The following conventions have been used:

- Diacritics have not been included in the subject headings.

- Within the class numbers and subject headings, "/" indicates a choice and is usually contained within parentheses or brackets.

- As in conventional cataloging rules, brackets [ ] contain words added by the author.

Instructions for Use of the Tables

To convert a classification from LC to Dewey or Dewey to LC, find the volume containing the table from which you wish to convert. Locate the classification from which you wish to convert in the left column. As indicated earlier, it may be included in a range of "numbers" or alphanumeric notations that correspond to the other classification, or it may fall between two classifications. In these cases, locate the class nearest in concept by using the Subject Headings. The classification to which you wish to convert is in the middle column, with the subject heading on the right.

The Subject Heading section provides a shortcut to the call-number assigning process. Using that section, you can search for the subject heading that reflects or approximates the subject matter of the item that is being cataloged and note the appropriate classifications next to it. This notation may be the classification that is needed, or it will lead you to the appropriate one in the schedules.

Subject Headings—LC and Dewey

LC	Dewey	Subject Heading	LC	Dewey	Subject Heading
AC	080	Collections	AM77-78	069.0952	Museums—Japan
AC1-8	081	American essays	AM80-91	069.096	Museums—Africa
AC16-19	083	Dutch essays	AM93-95	069.0994	Museums—Australia
AC20-25	084.1	French essays	AM96-98	069.0993	Museums—New Zealand
AC30-35	083.1	German essays	AM99-100	069.099(5-6)	Museums—Oceania
AC40-45	085.1	Italian essays	AM111-157	069.01	Museums—Methodology
AC70-75	086.(1 or 9)	Spanish and Portuguese essays	AM122	069.0681	Museum finance
AC80-85	089.945	Finno-Ugric essays	AM141-145	069.53	Museum conservation methods
AC101-102	089.924	Hebrew essays	AM200-401	069.5	Collectors and collecting
AC103-104	083.91	Yiddish essays	AM221	069.509	Collectors and collecting—History
AC105-106	089.927	Arabic essays	AM237	332.63	Collectibles as an investment
AC132-133	089.91992	Armenian essays			
AC145-146	089.956	Japanese essays	AM301-396	069.509(4-9)	Collectors and collecting—[By country]
AC149-150	089.951	Chinese essays	AM303-311	069.50973	Collectors and collecting—United States
AC168-169	089.99221	Indonesian essays			
AC177-189	089.96	African essays	AM313	069.50971	Collectors and collecting—Canada
AC195	089.97	Indian essays			
AC801-895	Varies	Dissertations, Academic	AM314	069.509728	Collectors and collecting—Mexico
AC999	Varies	Scrapbooks	AM315-322	069.509728	Collectors and collecting—Central America
AG103-190	028.7	Handbooks, vade-mecums, etc.			
AG195-196	028.7	Questions and answers	AM323-329	069.509729	Collectors and collecting—West Indies
AG240-243	030	Curiosities and wonders	AM330-341	069.5098	Collectors and collecting—South America
AI	016	Indexes			
AI11	050	Periodicals—Indexes	AM342-371	069.5094	Collectors and collecting—Europe
AI21	016.07	Newspapers—Indexes	AM343-347	069.50941	Collectors and collecting—Great Britain
AM	069	Museums			
AM	069	Collectors and collecting	AM349	069.50944	Collectors and collecting—France
AM8	069.083	Children's museums	AM350	069.50943	Collectors and collecting—Germany
AM10-101	069.09	Museums—[By region or country]			
AM11-13	069.0973	Museums—United States	AM356	069.50947	Collectors and collecting—Russia
AM21-22	069.0971	Museums—Canada			
AM23-24	069.0972	Museums—Mexico	AM362	069.50946	Collectors and collecting—Spain
AM25-27	069.09728	Museums—Central America	AM363	069.509469	Collectors and collecting—Portugal
AM33-35	069.098	Museums—South America	AM372-385	069.5095	Collectors and collecting—Asia
AM40-70	069.094	Museums—Europe			
AM41-43	069.0941	Museums—Great Britain	AM387-389	069.5096	Collectors and collecting—Africa
AM46-48	069.0944	Museums—France	AM390-391	069.50994	Collectors and collecting—Australia
AM49-51	069.0943	Museums—Germany			
AM52-53	069.09495	Museums—Greece	AM393	069.50993	Collectors and collecting—New Zealand
AM54-55	069.0945	Museums—Italy			
AM60-61	069.0947	Museums—Russia	AM395-396	069.5099(5-6)	Collectors and collecting—Oceania
AM61.5-64	069.0948	Museums—Scandinavia			
AM65	069.0946	Museums—Spain	AN	070.172	Newspapers
AM66	069.09469	Museums—Portugal			
AM69	069.09496	Museums—Balkan Peninsula			
AM71-79	069.095	Museums—Asia			
AM72	069.0951	Museums—China	AP	050	Periodicals

LC	Dewey	Subject Heading
AP2-9	051	English periodicals
AP14-17	053.931	Dutch periodicals
AP14-17	053.931	Flemish periodicals
AP20-28.7	054.1	French periodicals
AP30-36.7	053.1	German periodicals
AP37-39	055.1	Italian periodicals
AP85	059.89	Greek periodicals
AP91-93	059.924	Jewish periodicals
AP200-230	050.835	Youths' periodicals
AS	060	Academies and learned societies
AS	060	Learned institutions and societies
AS5	060.9	Learned institutions and societies—History
AS6	060	Congresses and conventions
AS7	394.268	Anniversaries
AY	030	Almanacs
AY	030	Directories
AY	050	Yearbooks
AY30-39	030.9	Almanacs—History
AY51-381	031	Almanacs—America
AY67.N5	031	Almanacs, American
AY410-425	031.0971	Almanacs—Canada
AY830-839	034.1	Almanacs—Great Britain
AY850-860	033.1	Almanacs—Germany
AY890-899	035.1	Almanacs—Italy
AY1000-1009	036.1	Almanacs—Spain
AY1010-1019	036.9	Almanacs—Portugal
AY1600-1636	032.0994	Almanacs—Australia
AY2001	011.7	Directories
AZ	001.2	Learning and scholarship
AZ101-111	001.201	Learning and scholarship—Philosophy
AZ200-361	001.2090	Learning and scholarship—History
AZ321	001.20902	Learning and scholarship—History—Medieval, 500-1500
AZ501-516	001.2097	Learning and scholarship—North America
AZ503-513	001.20973	Learning and scholarship—United States
AZ517-588	001.2098	Learning and scholarship—Latin America
AZ600-765	001.2094	Learning and scholarship—Europe
AZ770-795	001.2095	Learning and scholarship—Asia
AZ800-821	001.2096	Learning and scholarship—Africa
AZ850-881	001.2099	Learning and scholarship—Australia
AZ999	001.96	Errors, Popular
AZ999	001.96	Superstition
B	100	Philosophy
B1-8	105	Philosophy—Periodicals
B11-18	106	Philosophy—Societies, etc.
B20	106	Philosophy—Congresses
B40-48	103	Philosophy—Dictionaries
B49-50	103	Philosophy—Terminology
B52-.65	107.1	Philosophy—Study and teaching
B65	320	Political science
B69-4695	109	Philosophy—History
B104	109.22	Philosophers
B105.B64	128	Body, Human (Philosophy)
B105.D47	123	Determinism (Philosophy)
B105.D78	362.29201	Drunkenness (Philosophy)
B105.E3	128.37	Emotions (Philosophy)
B105.E5	392.4	Engagement (Philosophy)
B105.I54	121.4	Innate ideas (Philosophy)
B105.I56	128	Intentionality (Philosophy)
B105.L54	153.68	Listening (Philosophy)
B105.M4	121.68	Meaning (Philosophy)
B105.M65	573.701	Movement (Philosophy)
B105.O7	117	Order (Philosophy)
B105.P54	790.01	Play (Philosophy)
B105.Q34	119	Quantity (Philosophy)
B105.R4	324.6301	Representation (Philosophy)
B108-708	180	Philosophy, Ancient
B121-162.7	181	Philosophy, Oriental
B125-128	181.11	Philosophy, Chinese
B127.C65	181.112	Philosophy, Confucian
B127.N4	181.112	Neo-Confucianism
B130-133	181.4	Hinduism
B132.A3	181.482	Advaita
B132.Y6	181.45	Yoga
B135-138	181.12	Philosophy, Japanese
B139.1-.4	181.119	Philosophy, Korean
B140-143	181.2	Philosophy, Egyptian
B145-148	181.6	Philosophy, Babylonian
B150-153	181.5	Philosophy, Iranian
B154-157	181.06	Philosophy, Jewish
B157.C65	181.06	Jewish cosmology
B162	181.043	Philosophy, Buddhist
B162.5	181.044	Jaina philosophy
B162.6	181.09561	Philosophy, Shinto
B163	181.114	Philosophy, Taoist
B193	182	Atomism
B271	186.3	Eclecticism
B279	183	Hedonism
B285	183.6	Megarians (Greek philosophy)
B288	183.1	Sophists (Greek philosophy)
B398.C34	184	Plato's cave (Allegory)

LC	Dewey	Subject Heading	LC	Dewey	Subject Heading
B398.G6	184	God (Greek religion)	B905	141.3	Transcendentalism (New England)
B398.I3	184	Idea (Philosophy)	B981-995	191	Philosophy, Canadian
B398.L9	184	Platonic love	B1015-1019	199.72	Philosophy, Mexican
B491.R44	184	Refutation (Logic)	B1025-1026	199.728	Philosophy, Central American
B517	186.4	Neoplatonism	B1028-1029	199.729	Philosophy, West Indian
B525	186	Skeptics (Greek philosophy)	B1030-1084	199.8	Philosophy, South American
B528	188	Stoics	B1111-1674	192	Philosophy, English
B630-708	189	Philosophy, Ancient	B1801-2430	194	Philosophy, French
B645	186.4	Neoplatonism	B2521-3396	193	Philosophy, German
B720-785	189	Philosophy, Medieval	B3500-3515	199.495	Philosophy, Greek (Modern)
B728	189.5	Mysticism	B3551-3656	195	Philosophy, Italian
B734	189.4	Scholasticism	B4041-4095	199.492	Philosophy, Dutch
B740-753	181.07	Philosophy, Islamic	B4151-4175	199.493	Philosophy, Belgian
B740-753	181.92	Philosophy, Arab	B4201-4279	197	Philosophy, Russian
B755-759	181.3	Philosophy, Jewish	B4325-4395	198.9	Philosophy, Danish
B770-785	190	Philosophy, Renaissance	B4411-4445	198.1	Philosophy, Norwegian
B778	144	Humanism	B4455-4495	198.5	Philosophy, Swedish
B779	149.73	Skepticism	B4561-4568	196.1	Philosophy, Spanish
B790-5739	190	Philosophy, Modern	B4591-4598	196.9	Philosophy, Portuguese
B802	190	Enlightenment	B4628-4651	199.494	Philosophy, Swiss
B809.8	146.32	Dialectical materialism	B4687-4691	199.438	Philosophy, Polish
B812	147.4	Dualism	B4711-4800	198.8	Philosophy, Finnish
B814	148	Eclecticism	B4801-4805	199.437	Philosophy, Czech
B815	128.37	Emotions	B4811-4815	199.439	Philosophy, Hungarian
B816	146.44	Empiricism	B4821-4825	199.498	Philosophy, Romanian
B818	146.7	Evolution	B4871-4875	199.561	Philosophy, Turkish
B818.5	142.78	Existential phenomenology	B5000-5295	181	Philosophy, Oriental
B819	142.78	Existentialism	B5025-5099	181.3	Philosophy, Middle Eastern
B820	121.68	General semantics	B5025-5099	181.(6-8)	Philosophy, Middle Eastern
B820.3	121	Epistemics	B5055-5059	181.3	Philosophy, Israeli
B821	144	Humanism	B5230-5234	181.11	Philosophy, Chinese
B823	141	Idealism	B5243-5244	181.12	Philosophy, Japanese
B823	141.3	Transcendentalism	B5295	181.92	Philosophy, Arab
B823.3	145	Ideology	B5300-5320	199.6	Philosophy, African
B824	141.4	Individualism			
B824.6	146.42	Logical positivism	BC	160	Logic
B828	149.3	Mysticism	BC1	160.5	Logic—Periodicals
B828.2	146	Naturalism	BC5	160.6	Logic—Congresses
B828.36	149.94	Ordinary-language philosophy	BC11-39	160.9	Logic—History
B828.5	141.5	Personalism	BC25-32	160	Logic, Ancient
B829	149.5	Optimism	BC34-35	160	Logic, Medieval
B829	149.6	Pessimism	BC38-39	160	Logic, Modern
B829.5	142.7	Phenomenology	BC50-57	160.1	Logic—Methodology
B831	146.4	Positivism	BC59	160.71	Logic—Study and teaching
B831.5	144.3	Pragmatics	BC80-99	161	Induction (Logic)
B832	144.3	Pragmatism	BC131-135	511.3	Logic, Symbolic and mathematical
B833	149.7	Rationalism	BC137-138	006.3	Logic machines
B835	149.2	Realism	BC141	123.3	Chance
B836	111	Relationism	BC141	121.63	Probabilities
B837	149.73	Skepticism	BC171-173	121.65	Evidence
B839	149.91	Neo-Scholasticism	BC171	121	Truth
B839	149.91	Scholasticism	BC175	165	Fallacies (Logic)
B841	133.9	Spiritualism (Philosophy)			
B841.4	149.96	Structuralism			
B843	144.6	Utilitarianism			
B850-945	191	Philosophy, American			

LC	Dewey	Subject Heading	LC	Dewey	Subject Heading
BC177	160	Reasoning	BD595	123.3	Chance
BC181	121	Judgment (Logic)	BD620-655	114-115	Space and time
BC181	160	Proposition (Logic)	BD638	115	Time
BC183	167	Hypothesis	BD645	113	Harmony of the spheres
BC199.C6	165	Contradiction	BD646	146.5	Atomism
BC199.D8	160	Duality (Logic	BD493-708	117	Matter
BC199.F5	165	Fictions, Theory of			
BC199.P2	165	Paradox	BF	150	Psychology
			BF1-8	150.5	Psychology—Periodicals
BD	100	Philosophy	BF20	150.6	Psychology—Congresses
BD95-131	110	Metaphysics	BF31	150.3	Psychology—Dictionaries
BD125	149.91	Scholasticism	BF32	150.14	Psychology—Terminology
BD143-237	121	Knowledge, Theory of	BF38.5-39.8	150.1	Psychology—Methodology
BD171	121.63	Certainty	BF76.4	174.915	Psychologists—Professional ethics
BD171	121	Error			
BD181.7	128.3	Memory (Philosophy)	BF76.5-.6	150.72	Psychology—Research
BD183	121.6	Inquiry (Theory of knowledge)	BF76.6.E94	150.724	Experiential research
			BF76.7	808.066	Psychological literature
BD190	169	Analogy	BF77-80.7	150.71	Psychology—Study and teaching
BD201	121.2	Skepticism			
BD214	121.35	Senses and sensation	BF81-105	150.9	Psychology—History
BD215	121.5	Belief and doubt	BF109	150.8996073	Afro-American psychologists
BD215	121.6	Belief and doubt			
BD220	121.4	Objectivity	BF109	150.92	Psychologists
BD222	121.4	Subjectivity	BF150-172	150	Mind and body
BD232	121.8	Values	BF173-175.5	150.195	Psychoanalysis
BD236	111.82	Identity	BF175.4.C68	150.195	Psychoanalytic counseling
BD240-241	121.68	Hermeneutics	BF175.5.A33	150.1953	Adlerian psychology
BD300-450	111	Ontology	BF175.5.C37	150.195	Castration complex
BD331	110	Spiritualism (Philosophy)	BF175.5.D4	155.937	Death instinct
BD331	111.1	Substance (Philosophy)	BF175.5.E35	155.2	Ego (Psychology)
BD331	111	Reality	BF175.5.S92	154.2	Sublimation
BD331	117	Matter	BF175.5.S93	154.2	Superego
BD331	126	Personality	BF176-.5	150.287	Psychological tests
BD352	111.8	Attribute (Philosophy)	BF199	150.1943	Behaviorism (Psychology)
BD352	142.7	Phenomenalism	BF199	153.8	Motivation (Psychology)
BD373	116	Change	BF201	153	Cognitive psychology
BD394	147.4	Pluralism	BF203	150.1982	Gestalt psychology
BD396	111.82	Whole and parts (Philosophy)	BF204	150.198	Humanistic psychology
			BF204.5	150.192	Existential psychology
BD398	111.5	Nothing (Philosophy)	BF204.5	150.192	Phenomenological psychology
BD411	111.6	Finite, The			
BD411	111.6	Infinite	BF204.7	150.198	Transpersonal psychology
BD416	111.6	Absolute, The	BF205.N6	152.15	Noise
BD417	123.7	Necessity (Philosophy)	BF209.L9	154.4	LSD (Drug)
BD418-.5	128.2	Philosophy of mind	BF209.M4	154.4	Mescaline
BD419-428	128.1	Soul	BF210	153.85	Electronic behavior control
BD430-435	113.8	Life	BF231-299	152.1	Senses and sensation
BD430-435	121.8	Values	BF241	152.14	Visual perception
BD436	128.46	Love	BF251-.5	152.15	Hearing
BD450	128	Philosophical anthropology	BF261	152.167	Taste
BD493-708	113	Cosmology	BF271	152.166	Odors
BD494-497	113.09	Cosmology—History	BF271	152.166	Smell
BD495	113.0901	Cosmology, Ancient	BF275	152.182	Touch
BD495.5	113.0902	Cosmology, Medieval	BF285	152.182	Muscular sense
BD530-595	122	Causation	BF295-.5	152.3	Movement, Psychology of
BD530-595	124	Teleology	BF295-.5	152.334	Perceptual-motor learning
BD555	211.3	Theism	BF299.07	152.1882	Orientation (Psychology)
BD581	113	Philosophy of nature	BF309-499	153	Cognition

LC	Dewey	Subject Heading	LC	Dewey	Subject Heading
BF309-499	153	Consciousness	BF444	153	Human information processing
BF311	153	Cognitive styles			
BF311	152.1423	Pattern perception	BF448	153.83	Decision-making
BF315	154.2	Subconsciousness	BF455-463	153.6	Speech
BF315.5	153.44	Intuition (Psychology)	BF467-475	153.752	Space and time
BF318-319.5	153.15	Learning, Psychology of	BF468	153.753	Time perception
BF319.5.06	153.1526	Operant conditioning	BF469	153.752	Spatial behavior
BF319.5.P34	153.1526	Paired-association learning	BF469	153.752	Space perception
			BF475	153.753	Rhythm
BF319.5.R4	153.85	Reinforcement (Psychology)	BF481	158.723	Burn out (Psychology)
			BF481	158.7	Work—Psychological aspects
BF321-323	153.73	Apperception			
BF321-323	153.733	Attention	BF481	158.7	Work
BF321.I5	153.1533	Interest (Psychology)	BF482	152.1886	Fatigue
BF323.L5	153.68	Listening	BF491-493	154.4	Hallucinations and illusions
BF323.L5	153.733	Listening			
BF323.S63	302.12	Social perception	BF501-505	153.8	Achievement motivation
BF323.S8	153.736	Subliminal perception	BF505.R48	153.85	Reward (Psychology)
BF327	152.4	Attitude (Psychology)	BF511-593	152.4	Emotions
BF335-337	155.24	Adjustment (Psychology)	BF515	152.42	Pleasure
BF335-337	152.33	Habit	BF575.A3	155.232	Aggressiveness (Psychology)
BF337.B74	152.33	Habit breaking			
BF337.C62	153	Cognitive balance	BF575.A45	152.4	Ambivalence
BF353-.5	155.9	Environmental psychology	BF575.A5	152.47	Temper
BF353-.5	155.9	Man—Influence of environment	BF575.A5	152.47	Anger
			BF575.A6	152.46	Anxiety
BF353.5.N65	152.15	Noise—Psychological aspects	BF575.B3	155.232	Bashfulness
			BF575.D34	155.232	Dependency (Psychology)
BF353.5.W4	155.915	Weather—Psychological aspects	BF575.D35	155.93	Loss (Psychology)
			BF575.D57	152.4	Disappointment
BF357	153.1523	Imitation	BF575.E53	152.4	Embarrassment
BF365-395	153.123	Reproduction (Psychology)	BF575.E55	152.41	Empathy
BF365-395	153.2	Association of ideas	BF575.E6	153.1533	Enthusiasm
BF367	153.32	Eidetic imagery	BF575.F2	152.46	Fear
BF367	153.32	Imagery (Psychology)	BF575.F66	158.25	Friendship
BF370-387	153.12	Memory	BF575.F7	152.47	Frustration
BF376	153.12	Memory disorders	BF575.G8	152.4	Guilt
BF378.R4	153.124	Recognition (Psychology)	BF575.H27	152.42	Happiness
BF378.R44	153.123	Reminiscing	BF575.H3	152.4	Hate
BF378.S54	153.12	Short-term memory	BF575.H4	155.232	Helplessness (Psychology)
BF380-387	153.14	Mnemonics	BF575.H6	152.47	Hostility (Psychology)
BF408-426	153.32	Imagination	BF575.J4	152.48	Jealousy
BF408-426	153.35	Creation (Literary, artistic, etc.)	BF575.L7	155.92	Loneliness
			BF575.L8	152.41	Love
BF408-426	153.3	Creative thinking	BF575.S39	155.232	Self-confidence
BF408	153.3	Creative ability	BF575.S75	155.9042	Stress (Psychology)
BF410	153.3	Inspiration	BF575.W8	152.46	Worry
BF412-426	153.98	Genius	BF608-635	153.8	Will
BF431-433	153.93	Ability—Testing	BF611	153.8	Self-efficacy
BF431-433	153.9	Intellect	BF632	153.8	Self-control
BF431-432.5	153.93	Intelligence tests	BF633	153.853	Brainwashing
BF432.5.D53	153.94	Differential Aptitude Tests	BF636-637	158	Psychology, applied
BF432.5.M85	153.94	Multidimensional Aptitude Battery	BF637.B4	153.85	Behavior modification
			BF637.C45	158.2	Interpersonal communication
BF432.5.N64	153.93	Non-Verbal Ability Tests			
BF432.5.N65	153.93	Nonverbal intelligence tests	BF637.C56	158.3	Psychological consultation
			BF637.C6	158.35	Group counseling
BF441-449.5	153.42	Thought and thinking	BF637.C6	158.3	Counseling
BF442	153.43	Reasoning (Psychology)	BF637.L4	158.4	Leadership

LC	Dewey	Subject Heading	LC	Dewey	Subject Heading
BF637.N4	158.5	Negotiation	BF723.A4	155.41247	Temper tantrums in children
BF637.N66	153.69	Nonverbal communication (Psychology)	BF723.A5	155.41246	Anxiety in children
BF637.N66	153.69	Body language	BF723.C5	155.413	Cognition in children
BF637.S4	158.1	Self-actualization (Psychology)	BF723.C7	155.4133	Creative ability in children
			BF723.D7	155.4133	Drawing ability in children
BF637.S8	158	Success	BF723.E598	155.4	Emotional problems of children
BF637.T68	158.125	Transcendental meditation			
BF638-648	299.93	New Thought	BF723.E6	155.412	Emotions in children
BF660-685	156	Psychology, comparative	BF723.F28	155.41332	Fantasy in children
BF692-.5	155.3	Sex (Psychology)	BF723.F4	155.412	Fear in children
BF692.15	155.3	Sexual animosity	BF723.F7	155.41247	Frustration in children
BF692.2	155.334	Androgyny (Psychology)	BF723.G5	155.455	Gifted children
BF692.5	155.332	Masculinity (Psychology)	BF723.L68	155.93083	Loss (Psychology) in children
BF697-.5	155.2	Self			
BF697-.5	155.2	Individuality	BF723.M54	155.25	Moral development
BF697-.5	155.2	Self psychology	BF723.P4	155.41825	Personality development
BF697.5.S44	155	Self-presentation	BF723.S24	155.4182	Self in children
BF697.5.S46	158.1	Self-esteem	BF723.S25	155.4138	Self-control in children
BF698-.9	158.1	Personality	BF723.S4	155.3	Psychosexual development
BF698.35.A87	155.232	Authoritarianism (Personality trait)	BF723.S42	155.3	Sex role in children
			BF723.S43	155.443	Sibling rivalry
BF698.35.C45	155.232	Charisma (Personality trait)	BF723.S75	155.418	Stress in children
			BF723.T9	155.444	Twins—Psychology
BF698.35.D48	155.234	Determination (Personality trait)	BF724-.3	155.5	Adolescent psychology
			BF724-.3	155.5	Youthfulness
BF698.35.D64	155.232	Dogmatism	BF724.3.A34	155.51247	Aggressiveness (Psychology) in youth
BF698.35.I55	155.2	Inner child			
BF698.35.N44	155.232	Negativism	BF724.3.A34	155.51247	Aggressiveness (Psychology) in adolescence
BF698.35.O57	155.232	Optimism			
BF698.35.P36	155.232	Passivity (Psychology)			
BF698.35.P43	155.232	Pedantry	BF724.6-.65	155.66	Middle age—Psychological aspects
BF698.35.P47	155.232	Perfectionism (Personality trait)			
			BF724.8-.85	155.67	Aged—Psychology
BF698.35.P49	155.232	Pessimism	BF724.3.E5	155.512	Emotions in adolescence
BF698.4-.8	155.28	Personality assessment	BF761-768	158.39	Interviewing
BF698.7	155.284	Projective techniques	BF774	153.852	Influence (Psychology)
BF698.8.D9	155.283	Dynamic personality inventory	BF778	153.45	Values
			BF789.C7	535.6019	Color—Psychological aspects
BF698.8.M5	155.283	Minnesota Multiphasic Personality Inventory			
			BF789.D4	155.937	Death—Psychological aspects
BF698.8.P48	155.283	Personality questionnaires			
BF698.8.R5	155.2842	Rorschach Test	BF789.D5	155.935	Disasters—Psychological aspects
BF699-711	155.7	Genetic psychology			
BF710	155.51	Maturation (Psychology)	BF795-811	155.26	Temperament
BF712-724.85	155	Developmental psychology	BF818-839	155.2076	Character tests
BF719-720	155.422	Infant psychology	BF818-839	155.2	Character
BF720.A24	155.42239	Ability in infants	BF839.8-861	138	Physiognomy
BF720.A85	155.42221532	Attention in newborn infants	BF866-885	139	Phrenology
			BF889-905	137	Graphology
BF720.E45	155.42224	Emotions in infants	BF908-940	133.6	Hand
BF720.E45	155.412	Emotions in children	BF910-940	133.6	Palmistry
BF720.P56	155	Symbolic play	BF1001-1999	133	Supernatural
BF720.S45	155.42221	Sensory stimulation in newborn infants	BF1001-1999	001.96	Superstition
			BF1001-1389	133	Parapsychology
BF721-723	155.4	Child psychology	BF1001-1389	127	Subconsciousness
BF721-723	155.4	Child mental health	BF1001-1008	133.05	Parapsychology— Periodicals
BF723.A25	155.4139	Ability in children			
BF723.A35	155.418232	Aggressiveness in children			

LC	Dewey	Subject Heading	LC	Dewey	Subject Heading
BF1021	133.06	Parapsychology—Congresses	BF1558	133.44	Incantations
BF1025	133.03	Parapsychology—Dictionaries	BF1559	133.427	Exorcism
			BF1561	133.44	Talismans
BF1026-1027	133.092	Parapsychology—Biography	BF1562.5-1584	133.43	Witchcraft
			BF1585-1623	135.47	Cabala
BF1028-.5	133.09	Parapsychology—History	BF1585-1623	133.43	Magic
BF1040.5	133.071	Parapsychology—Study and teaching	BF1585-1623	201.44	Shamanism
			BF1623.P9	133.335	Numerology
BF1045.A48	154.4	Altered states of consciousness	BF1623.P9	133.3359	Symbolism of numbers
			BF1623.S9	133.33	Symbolism
BF1045.D42	133.3	Decision-making—Psychic aspects	BF1628	133.323	Dowisng
			BF1628	133.323	Dowsers
BF1045.D76	154.4	Drugs—Psychic aspects	BF1651-1729	133.5	Astrology
BF1045.N4	133.9013	Near-death experiences	BF1714.A6	133.593927	Astrology, Arab
BF1063.D4	133.9013	Deathbed hallucinations	BF1714.B7	133.59443	Buddhist astrology
BF1068-1073	154.6	Sleep	BF1714.H5	133.59445	Hindu astrology
BF1073.S56	154.6	Sleep positions	BF1714.J28	133.59444	Jaina astrology
BF1073.S58	154.64	Sleeptalking	BF1716-.28	133.52	Houses (Astrology)
BF1074-1099	135.3	Dreams	BF1716.28	133.52	Eighth house (Astrology)
BF1099.F34	154.63	Family in dreams	BF1718	133.5861	Medical astrology
BF1099.L82	154.63	Lucid dreams	BF1727	133.5262	Aries (Astrology)
BF1099.N53	154.63	Nightmares	BF1727.2	133.5263	Taurus (Astrology)
BF1111-1156	133.89	Hypnotism	BF1727.25	133.5264	Gemini (Astrology)
BF1111-1156	154.7	Mesmerism	BF1727.3	133.5265	Cancer (Astrology)
BF1156.S8	154.7	Mental suggestion	BF1727.35	133.5266	Leo (Astrology)
BF1161-1171	133.82	Telepathy	BF1727.4	133.5267	Virgo (Astrology)
BF1228-1389	133.9	Spiritualism	BF1727.45	133.5272	Libra (Astrology)
BF1275.G85	133.9	Guides (Spiritualism)	BF1727.5	133.5273	Scorpio (Astrology)
BF1281-1315	133.91	Channeling (Spiritualism)	BF1727.6	133.5274	Sagittarius (Astrology)
BF1335	133.322	Crystal gazing	BF1727.65	133.5275	Capricorn (Astrology)
BF1371-1389	133.88	Psychokinesis	BF1727.7	133.5276	Aquarius (Astrology)
BF1375	133.92	Table-moving (Spiritualism)	BF1727.75	133.5277	Pisces (Astrology)
			BF1729.P6	133.5832	Astrology and politics
BF1378	133.92	Materialization	BF1729.S34	133.585	Science and astrology
BF1385	133.92	Levitation	BF1745-1779	133.3248	Sibyls
BF1389.A7	133.95	Astral projection	BF1745-1779	133.3248	Oracles
BF1389.A8	133.892	Aura	BF1745-1779	133.3	Divination
BF1389.T7	133.9	Transfiguration (Spiritualism)	BF1777	133.334	Omens
			BF1779.F4	133.3337	Feng-shui
BF1404-2050	133	Occultism	BF1845-1891	133.3	Fortune-telling
BF1404	133.06	Occultism—Congresses	BF1879.T2	133.32424	Tarot
BF1407	133.03	Occultism—Dictionaries			
BF1408-.2	133.092	Occultists	BH1-8	111.8505	Aesthetics—Periodicals
BF1409	133.025	Occultism—Directories	BH19	111.8506	Aesthetics—Congresses
BF1421-1429	133.09	Occultism—History	BH56	111.8503	Aesthetics—Dictionaries
BF1434	133.09(4-9)	Occultism—[By region or country]	BH61-62	111.85071	Aesthetics—Study and teaching
BF1444-1486	133.1	Apparitions	BH81-208	111.8509	Aesthetics—History
BF1444-1486	133.1	Ghosts	BH91-116	111.850901	Aesthetics, Ancient
BF1475	133.122	Haunted houses	BH101-102	111.85095	Aesthetics, Oriental
BF1483	133.142	Poltergeists	BH131-137	111.850902	Aesthetics, Medieval
BF1501-1562	133.42	Demonology	BH151-208	111.850903	Aesthetics, Modern
BF1546-1561	133.422	Devil	BH161-168	111.8509031	Aesthetics, Modern—16th century
BF1546-1550	133.422	Satanism	BH171-178	111.8509032	Aesthetics, Modern—17th century
BF1552	398.21	Fairies			
BF1553	133.425	Evil eye	BH181-188	111.8509033	Aesthetics, Modern—18th century
BF1555	133.426	Demoniac possession			
BF1556	133.423	Vampires			

LC	Dewey	Subject Heading	LC	Dewey	Subject Heading
BH191-198	111.8509034	Aesthetics, Modern—19th century	BJ1360	171.2	Humanistic ethics
BH201-208	111.850904	Aesthetics, Modern—20th century	BJ1365-1385	171.2	Ethics, Positivist
BH221.B	111.8509495	Aesthetics, Byzantine	BJ1388	171.7	Socialist ethics
BH221.C	111.850971	Aesthetics, Canadian	BJ1390-.5	171.7	Communist ethics
BH301.A94	700.411	Avant-garde (Aesthetics)	BJ1400-1408.5	170	Good and evil
BH301.C84	153.35	Creation (Literary, artistic, etc.)	BJ1410-1418	170	Right and wrong
BH301.H3	701.8	Harmony (Aesthetics)	BJ1420-1428.3	177.3	Truthfulness and falsehood
BH301.L3	700.42	Landscape	BJ1430-1438	179.9	Compromise (Ethics)
BH301.N3	700.46	Nature (Aesthetics)	BJ1450-1458	170	Duty
			BJ1471	170	Conscience
BJ	170	Ethics	BJ1474	171.9	Egoism
BJ1-8	170.5	Ethics—Periodicals	BJ1474	171.8	Altruism
BJ10-11	170.6	Ethics—Societies, etc.	BJ1474	171.9	Self-interest
BJ10.E8	171	Ethical culture movement	BJ1475.3	171.2	Humanitarianism
BJ10.M6	267.16	Moral re-armament	BJ1476	177.7	Forgiveness
BJ19	170.6	Ethics—Congresses	BJ1477-1486	179.9	Cheerfulness
BJ37-60	170.1	Ethics—Philosophy	BJ1477	155.232	Optimism
BJ47	205	Religion and ethics	BJ1480-1486	170	Happiness
BJ63	170.3	Ethics—Dictionaries	BJ1491	171.4	Hedonism
BJ66-68	170.71	Ethics—Study and teaching	BJ1491	204.47	Asceticism
BJ71-982	170.9	Ethics—History	BJ1498	175	Leisure
BJ116-118	170.95	Ethics, Chinese	BJ1498	174	Work
BJ121-123	170.954	Ethics, Indic	BJ1500.P7	177.3	Promises
BJ136-138	170.935	Ethics, Assyro-Babylonian	BJ1518-1691	179.9	Virtue
BJ160-224	170.938	Ethics, Greek	BJ1520-1688	177.1	Courtesy
BJ231-255	170.902	Ethics, Medieval	BJ1533.A4	302.54	Ambition
BJ271-285	170.90(23-31)	Ethics, Renaissance	BJ1533.C4	176	Chastity
BJ301-982	170.903	Ethics, Modern	BJ1533.C5	179.9	Cheerfulness
BJ311	170.9033	Ethics, Modern—18th century	BJ1533.C8	179.6	Courage
BJ315	170.9034	Ethics, Modern—19th century	BJ1533.C9	177.1	Courtesy
BJ319	170.904	Ethics, Modern—20th century	BJ1533.D49	179.9	Self-control
BJ701-704	170.944	Ethics, French	BJ1533.F8	177.62	Friendship
BJ751-759	170.943	Ethics, Germanic	BJ1533.G8	179.9	Gratitude
BJ801-804	170.9495	Ethics, Greek	BJ1533.H7	179.9	Honesty
BJ847-850	170.9438	Ethics, Polish	BJ1533.K5	177.7	Kindness
BJ961-977	170.95	Ethics, Oriental	BJ1533.M73	179.9	Modesty
BJ965-968	170.951	Ethics, Chinese	BJ1533.P3	179.9	Patience
BJ969-971	170.952	Ethics, Japanese	BJ1533.P9	179.9	Prudence
BJ973-976	170.9519	Ethics, Korean	BJ1533.S27	179.9	Self-reliance
BJ991-1185	170	Ethics—Textbooks	BJ1534-1535	179.8	Vices
BJ1075-1077	170.202	Ethics—Outlines, syllabi, etc.	BJ1534-1535	179.8	Vice
BJ1188-1295	205	Religious ethics	BJ1535.A6	179.8	Anger
BJ1188.5-1278	241	Christian ethics	BJ1535.A8	178	Avarice
BJ1279-1287	296.36	Ethics, Jewish	BJ1535.C7	179	Cruelty
BJ1286.G64	296.36	Golden rule	BJ1535.G6	177.2	Gossip
BJ1289	294.35	Buddhist ethics	BJ1535.P9	179.8	Pride and vanity
BJ1289.5.Y6	294.35	Youth, Buddhist—Conduct of life	BJ1535.S6	177.3	Slander
BJ1291-1292	297.5	Islamic ethics	BJ1535.S9	179.5	Swearing
BJ1298-1335	171.7	Ethics, Evolutionary	BJ1545-1697	170.44	Conduct of life
BJ1340	171.2	Existential ethics	BJ1609-1610	646.76	Charm
			BJ1725	174	Professional ethics
			BJ1801-2195	395	Etiquette
			BJ1801	395.05	Etiquette—Periodicals
			BJ1815	395.03	Etiquette—Dictionaries
			BJ1821	395.09	Etiquette—History
			BJ1855	395.142	Etiquette for men
			BJ1856	395.144	Etiquette for women
			BJ2018-2019	395.53	Church etiquette

LC	Dewey	Subject Heading	LC	Dewey	Subject Heading
BJ2021-2078	395.3	Entertaining	BL325.M63	202.12	Mountain gods
BJ2021-2028	395.3	Hospitality	BL406.C7	203.37	Crosses
BJ2041	395.54	Table etiquette	BL435-457	202.12	Nature worship
BJ2051-2065	395.22	Wedding etiquette	BL438	202.12	Sun worship
BJ2071-2075	395.23	Mourning etiquette	BL438	202.12	Moon worship
BJ2100-2115	395.4	Letter writing	BL439-443	202.12	Animal worship
BJ2120-2128	395.59	Conversation	BL441	202.12	Serpent worship
BJ2137-2156	395.5	Travel etiquette	BL444	202.12	Tree worship
BJ2195	395.59	Telephone etiquette	BL447	202.12	Mountain worship
			BL453	202.12	Fire-worshipers
BL	200	Religion	BL458	200.8	Sexism in religion
BL1-10	200.5	Religion—Periodicals	BL465	202.13	Emperor worship
BL11-21	206	Religion—Societies or Congresses	BL467	202.13	Ancestor worship
BL35	200.25	Religion—Directories	BL473	202.1	Gods
BL41	200.71	Religion—Study and teaching	BL475	206.1	Messiah
			BL477	202.15	Angels
BL48-50	200	Religion	BL480	202.16	Devil
BL51	210	Religion—Philosophy	BL480	202.16	Satanism
BL51	210	Knowledge, Theory of (Religion)	BL480	202.16	Demonology
BL51	210	Fictions, Theory of	BL485	202.18	Idols and images—Worship
BL53	201.615	Psychology, Religious			
BL53	204.2	Experience (Religion)	BL500-547	202.3	Eschatology
BL55	201.7	Religion and civilization	BL503	202.3	Resurrection
BL60	201.7	Religion and sociology	BL515	202.37	Reincarnation
BL65.C58	201.72	Civil rights—Religious aspects	BL525	202.1	Transmigration
			BL535-547	202.3	Future life
BL65.C8	201.7	Religion and culture	BL545	202.3	Hell
BL65.E68	200.8	Equality—Religious aspects	BL550-620	203	Worship
			BL560	204.3	Prayer
BL65.J87	205.22	Religion and justice	BL560	204.3	Prayers
BL65.L33	201.72	Religion and law	BL570	203.4	Sacrifice
BL65.M4	201.7621	Medicine—Religious aspects	BL580-586	203.5	Shrines
			BL590	203.8	Fasts and feasts
BL65.P7	201.72	Religion and politics	BL600-620	203.7	Symbolism
BL65.R3	200.8	Race—Religious aspects	BL600-619	203.8	Ritual
BL65.S8	322.1	Religion and state	BL600-619	203.8	Rites and ceremonies
BL65.S8	201.72	Religion and state	BL603	203.7	Emblems
BL70-71	208.2	Sacred books	BL604.C5	203.7	Circle—Religious aspects
BL74-98	230-299	Religions	BL604.S8	203.7	Swastika
BL175-190	210	Natural theology	BL604.V2	203.7	V symbol
BL200	211.3	Theism	BL613	203.2	Divination
BL210	210	Analogy (Religion)	BL613	203.2	Oracles
BL215	211	Anthropomorphism	BL619.S3	203.6	Sacred meals
BL217	211.32	Polytheism	BL624-627	204	Religious life
BL218	211.33	Dualism (Religion)	BL625	204.47	Asceticism
BL220	211.2	Pantheism	BL625	204.22	Mysticism
BL221	211.34	Monotheism	BL626	204.2	Ecstasy
BL224-226	213	Creation	BL627	204.35	Meditation
BL239-265	201.65	Religion and science	BL632	206.5	Religious communities
BL256	202.22	Man (Theology)	BL635	206.1	Priests
BL263	213	Evolution—Religious aspects	BL640	323.442	Freedom of religion
			BL660-687	200.956	Middle East—Religion
BL290	202.22	Soul	BL689-980	201.3094	Mythology, European
BL300-325	201.3	Mythology	BL690-980	200.94	Europe—Religion
BL325.D4	222.11	Noah's ark	BL700-820	292.13	Mythology, Classical
BL325.H4	203.1	Healing gods	BL735	292.28	Hell
BL325.M6	202.114	Mother goddesses	BL740-760	299.9294	Etruscans—Religion
			BL780-795	292.08	Greece—Religion
			BL800-820	292.07	Rome—Religion

LC	Dewey	Subject Heading	LC	Dewey	Subject Heading
BL815.V4	292.61	Vestals	BL1215.M3	294.522	Man (Hinduism)
BL820.A25	292.2113	Adonis (Greek deity)	BL1215.M9	294.5422	Mysticism—Hinduism
BL820.A4	292.2113	Aesculapius (Greek deity)	BL1215.S64	294.517	Sociology, Hindu
BL820.A6	292.13	Amazons	BL1215.S8	294.522	Soul (Hinduism)
BL820.A63	292.13	Amycus (Greek mythology)	BL1216	294.52114	Goddesses, Hindu
BL820.A8	292.13	Jason (Greek mythology)	BL1225.A	294.52113	Aatimna (Hindu deity)
BL820.B2	292.2113	Dionysia	BL1225.A4	294.52114	Aditi (Hindu deity)
BL820.C	292.13	Centaurs	BL1225.A42	294.52113	Adityas (Hindu deities)
BL820.C5	292.2114	Demeter (Greek deity)	BL1225.D3	294.52113	Dattatreya (Hindu deity)
BL820.C5	292.2114	Ceres (Roman deity)	BL1225.D48	294.52113	Devanarayana (Hindu deity)
BL820.D	292.13	Dryads	BL1225.D8	294.52114	Durga (Hindu deity)
BL820.D25	292.13	Daedalus (Greek mythology)	BL1225.M	294.513	Manus (Hindu mythology)
BL820.D54	292.2114	Diktynna (Greek deity)	BL1226	294.53	Worship (Hinduism)
BL820.E5	292.2114	Eileithyia (Greek deity)	BL1226.2	294.538	Chants (Hindu)
BL820.F7	292.2114	Fortuna (Roman deity)	BL1226.82.M3	294.5441	Marriage customs and rites, Hindu
BL820.F8	292.13	Furies (Roman mythology)	BL1228	294.544	Religious life—Hinduism
BL820.F8	292.13	Erinyes (Greek mythology)	BL1236.76.S23	294.534	Sacrifice
BL820.G7	292.13	Gorgons (Greek mythology)	BL1238	294.5657	Monasticism and religious orders, Hindu
BL820.G8	292.13	Graces, The	BL1239.32	294.5351	Hindu pilgrims and pilgrimages
BL820.H5	292.13	Heracles (Greek mythology)	BL1239.72-.82	294.538	Fasts and feasts—Hinduism
BL820.J8	292.2113	Jupiter (Roman deity)	BL1241.46	294.5	Brahmans
BL820.L25	292.13	Ladon (Greek mythology)	BL1243.72-.78	294.535	Temples, Hindu
BL820.M26	292.2113	Marsyas (Greek deity)	BL1245.A1	294.55	Hindu sects
BL820.M37	292.13	Medea (Greek mythology)	BL1245.B5	294.5924	Bhagavatas
BL820.M6	292.2114	Athena (Greek deity)	BL1282.2-.292	294.5514	Shaktism
BL820.M63	292.13	Minotaur (Greek mythology)	BL1290.8	299.5145	Taoist ethics
BL820.M65	292.2114	Mother goddesses, Greek	BL1300-1365	294.4	Jainism
BL820.O6	292.2113	Ops (Roman deity)	BL1300-1365	294.4	Jains
BL820.P	292.13	Pandora (Greek mythology)	BL1310-1314.2	294.482	Jainism—Sacred books
BL820.P2	292.2113	Pan (Greek deity)	BL1355.5	294.438	Fasts and feasts—Jainism
BL820.P4	292.13	Pegasus (Greek mythology)	BL1356-1375	294.42	Jainism—Doctrines
BL820.P5	292.13	Perseus (Greek mythology)	BL1375.P	294.434	Penance (Jainism)
BL820.P7	292.2114	Persephone (Greek deity)	BL1375.Y63	294.4436	Yoga (Jainism)
BL820.T6	292.13	Titans (Mythology)	BL1376-1380	294.43	Worship (Jainism)
BL830-875	293	Germanic peoples—Religion	BL1377.3	294.437	Jaina mantras
BL870.B3	293.2113	Balder (Norse deity)	BL1378.8	294.4422	Mysticism—Jainism
BL870.F28	293.13	Fafnir (Germanic mythology)	BL1380.D	294.493	Digambara (Jaina sect)
BL870.S29	292.2113	Saturn (Roman deity)	BL1477.8.D4	294.3435	Temples, Buddhist—Dedication
BL910	299.16	Druids and Druidism	BL1477.8.F8	294.3438	Funeral rites and ceremonies, Buddhist
BL1000-2370	299.5	Mythology, Oriental	BL1478	294.3657	Profession (Buddhist monastic orders)
BL1100-1270	294.5	Hinduism	BL1493	294.3375	Zen Buddhism—Psychology
BL1100-1245	294.5	Brahmanism	BL1500-1590	295	Zorastrianism
BL1112.2	294.5921	Vedas	BL1500-1590	295	Parsees
BL1141.2-1142.6	294.5514	Tantrism	BL1510-1525	295.82	Zoroastrianism—Sacred books
BL1171	294.5213	Alvars	BL1590.R5	299.15	Rider-gods
BL1171	294.5213	Hindu saints	BL1600-1710	299.2	Semites—Religion
BL1200-1225	294.5211	God (Hinduism)	BL1616.E54	299.9295	Enki (Sumarian deity)
BL1213.32-1215	294.52	Hinduism—Doctrines	BL1620-1625	299.21	Assyro-Babylonian religion
BL1213.D87	294.536	Durga-puja (Hindu festival)			
BL1214.32.B53	294.5211	Bhakti			
BL1215.F3	294.5447	Fasting (Hinduism)			

LC	Dewey	Subject Heading	LC	Dewey	Subject Heading
BL1625.A5	299.21	Anu (Assyro-Babylonian deity)	BM1	296.67	Judaism—Societies, etc.
			BM11	296.05	Judaism—Periodicals
BL1625.M37	299.21	Marduk (Babylonian deity)	BM21-30	296.67	Judaism—Congresses
BL1625.P3	299.21	Panbabylonism	BM50	296.03	Judaism—Dictionaries
BL1671	299.26	Baal (Deity)	BM55-65	296.025	Judaism—Directories
BL1695	297.85	Druzes	BM70-135	296.68	Jews—Education
BL1800-1975	299.51	China—Religion	BM150-449	296.09	Judaism—History
BL1830-1875	299.512	Confucianism	BM165-178	296.09014	Judaism—History—To 70 A.D.
BL1900-1940	299.514	Taoism			
BL2000-2030	294.5	Hinduism	BM175	296.8	Jewish sects
BL2000-2016	294	Mythology, Indic	BM175.E8	296.814	Essenes
BL2015.K3	294.5175	Karma	BM175.P4	296.812	Pharisees
BL2017-2018.7	294.6	Sikhism	BM175.S2	296.813	Sadducees
BL2017.2-.4	294.682	Sikhism—Sacred books	BM177	296.120092	Tannaim
BL2018.7	294.69	Sikh sects	BM180-185	296.0902	Judaism—History—Medieval and early modern, 425-1789
BL2018.7.K44	294.69	Khalsa (Sect)			
BL2020.S5	294.6	Sikhs			
BL2035	299.14122	Pakistan—Religion	BM184	297.38	Judaism—Liturgy
BL2050-2150	299.5	Asia, Southeastern—Religion	BM185-.4	296.81	Karaites
			BM190-199	296.09033	Judaism—History—Modern period, 1750–
BL2200-2228	299.56	Japan—Religion			
BL2211.D33	299.56	Daikokuten (Japanese deity)	BM197.5	296.8342	Conservative Judaism
			BM197.8	296.834	Humanistic Judaism
BL2211.E24	299.56	Ebisu (Japanese deity)	BM198	296.8332	Hasidism
BL2211.E46	299.56	Emperor worship—Japanese	BM199.S3	296.82	Sabbathaians
			BM205-225	296.0973	Judaism—United States
BL2216-2227.8	299.561	Shinto	BM227-229	296.0971	Judaism—Canada
BL2217-.5	299.56182	Shinto—Sacred books	BM230-232	296.0972	Judaism—Mexico
BL2222.H5	299.5619	Hinomoto (Sect)	BM233-247	296.09728	Judaism—Central America
OBL2224.2	299.56138	Shinto—Rituals	BM248-260	296.09729	Judaism—West Indies
BL2224.3	299.56136	Shinto devotional calendars	BM261-289	296.098	Judaism—South America
			BM290-376	296.094	Judaism—Europe
BL2224.9-2225.3	299.56135	Shinto shrines	BM292-305	296.0941	Judaism—Great Britain
BL2230-2240	299.957	Korea—Religion	BM307-309	296.09436	Judaism—Austria
BL2270-2280	299.155	Iran—Religion	BM310-312	296.09493	Judaism—Belgium
BL2370.S5	201.44	Shamanism	BM313-315	296.0944	Judaism—France
BL2400-2490	299.6	Africa—Religion	BM316-318	296.0943	Judaism—Germany
BL2420-2460	299.31	Egypt—Religion	BM319-321	296.09495	Judaism—Greece
BL2450.A45	299.31	Amon (Egyptian deity)	BM322-324	296.0945	Judaism—Italy
BL2450.A89	299.31	Atum (Egyptian deity)	BM325-327	296.09492	Judaism—Netherlands
BL2450.G6	299.31	Gods, Egyptian	BM328-330	296.09469	Judaism—Portugal
BL2450.N45	299.31	Neith (Egyptian deity)	BM331-333	296.0947	Judaism—Russia
BL2450.O7	299.31	Osiris (Egyptian deity)	BM334-336	296.094897	Judaism—Finland
BL2450.S27	299.31	Satis (Egyptian deity)	BM337-339	296.09438	Judaism—Poland
BL2462	299.3	Africa, North—Religion	BM340-353	296.0948	Judaism—Scandinavia
BL2480.Y6	299.6869	Sopono (Cult)	BM342-344	296.09489	Judaism—Denmark
BL2480.Y6	299.6869	Egungun (Cult)	BM348-350	296.09481	Judaism—Norway
BL2490	299.675	Voodooism	BM351-353	296.09485	Judaism—Sweden
BL2580-2592	299.8	South America—Religion	BM354-356	296.0946	Judaism—Spain
BL2590.B7	299.891	Afro-Brazilian cults	BM357-359	296.09494	Judaism—Switzerland
BL2600-2630	299.92	Oceania—Religion	BM364-366	296.09499	Judaism—Bulgaria
BL2620.P6	299.924	Mythology, Polynesian	BM370-372	296.09498	Judaism—Romania
BL2700-2790	211.8	Atheism	BM373-375	296.094971	Judaism—Yugoslavia
BL2700-2790	211.7	Agnosticism	BM377-431	296.095	Judaism—Asia
BL2700-2790	211.6	Secularism	BM386.4-.6	296.09567	Judaism—Iraq
BL2700-2790	211.4	Skepticism	BM387-389	296.095691	Judaism—Syria
BL2700-2790	211.4	Rationalism	BM387-389	296.095694	Judaism—Palestine
			BM390-392	296.095694	Judaism—Israel
BM	296	Judaism	BM393-395	296.0953	Judaism—Arabia

LC	Dewey	Subject Heading	LC	Dewey	Subject Heading
BM396-398	296.0955	Judaism—Iran	BM720.S2	296.4391	Sabbatical year (Judaism)
BM400	296.09581	Judaism—Afghanistan	BM723	296.7	Jewish way of life
BM406-410	296.0954	Judaism—India	BM729.C6	296.72	Consolation (Judaism)
BM423-425	296.0951	Judaism—China	BM729.F3	296.32	Faith (Judaism)
BM426-428	296.0952	Judaism—Japan	BM729.S85	296.18	Summer (Jewish law)
BM432-440	296.096	Judaism—Africa	BM730	296.47	Jewish preaching
BM434-436	296.0962	Judaism—Egypt	BM746	296.4731	High Holiday sermons
BM437	296.0968	Judaism—South Africa	BM747.P3	296.4737	Passover sermons
BM443-445	296.099(3 or 4)	Judaism—[New Zealand/Australia]	BM945	296.3	Samaritan theology
BM447-449	296.099(5-6)	Judaism—Oceania	BM970	296.43	Fasts and feasts—Samaritan religion
BM495-532	296.1	Rabbinical literature			
BM500-509	296.12	Talmud	BP	297	Islam
BM511-518	296.14	Midrash	BP1-223	297	Islam
BM516-.5	296.19	Aggada	BP1-9	297.05	Islam—Periodicals
BM523.5.S53	340.18	Shaving (Jewish law)	BP10-15	297.65	Islam—Congresses
BM525	296.16	Cabala	BP40	297.03	Islam—Dictionaries
BM600-603	296.3	Judaism—Doctrines	BP42-48	297.77	Islamic religious education
BM610	296.311	God (Judaism)	BP62.N4	297.87	Muslims, Black
BM612.5	296.31172	Covenants—Judaism	BP75-77.5	297.63	Muhammad, Prophet, d. 632
BM615	296.336	Messiah—Judaism	BP75.8	297.63	Muhammad, Prophet, d. 632—Miracles
BM615	296.336	Jewish messianic movements	BP100-134	297.122	Koran
BM630	296.32	Sin (Judaism)	BP133.7.A3	297.122092	Adam (Biblical figure) in the Koran
BM650-747	296.7	Judaism—Customs and practices	BP133.7.D38	297.122092	David, King of Israel, in the Koran
BM652	296.092	Rabbis	BP133.7.M67	297.122092	Moses (Biblical leader) in the Koran
BM652.5	296.61	Pastoral counseling (Judaism)	BP134.E5	297.12209	Egypt in the Koran
BM653-655	296.65	Synagogues	BP134.F58	297.12286413	Food in the Koran
BM656-685	296.4	Worship (Judaism)	BP135	297.124	Hadith
BM657.H3	296.435	Hanukkah lamp	BP137-.5	297.18	Legends, Islamic
BM657.M35	296.435	Menorah	BP140-165	340.59	Islamic law
BM657.T6	296.4615	Torah scrolls	BP165.5-166.94	297.2	Islam—Doctrines
BM658.2	296.462	Cantors (Judaism)	BP166.2	297.211	Word of God (Islam)
BM659.S3	296.4615	Scribes, Jewish	BP166.2	297.211	God (Islam)
BM669	296.45	Prayer—Judaism	BP166.3	297.227	Predestination—Islam
BM675.A8	296.432	Yom Kippur	BP166.3	297.227	Free will and determinism (Islam)
BM675.D3	296.45	Siddurim	BP166.4	297.246	Prophets, Pre-Islamic
BM675.P3	296.437	Passover	BP166.6	297.2115	Revelation (Islam)
BM685	296.41	Sabbath	BP166.7	297.22	Man (Islam)
BM690-720	296.43	Fasts and feasts—Judaism	BP166.73	297.225	Soul (Islam)
BM690	296.43	Religious calendars—Judaism	BP166.75	297.22	Sin (Islam)
BM693.H5	296.431	High Holidays	BP166.78	297.22	Faith (Islam)
BM693.P5	296.481	Pilgrim Festivals (Judaism)	BP166.8	297.23	Eschatology, Islamic
BM695.A8	296.432	Yom Kippur	BP166.83	297.23	Resurrection (Islam)
BM695.H3	296.435	Hanukkah	BP166.85	297.23	Judgment Day (Islam)
BM695.N5	296.4315	Rosh ha-Shanah	BP166.87	297.23	Paradise (Islam)
BM695.P3	296.437	Passover	BP166.89	297.216	Devil (Islam)
BM695.P35	296.437	Seder	BP166.89	297.216	Demonology, Islamic
BM707-.4	296.4424	Confirmation (Jewish rite)	BP166.89	297.215	Angels (Islam)
BM707-.4	296.4434	Bat mitzvah	BP166.89	297.21	Spirits (Islam)
BM707.4	296.4424	Bar Mitzvah	BP166.89	297.21	Discernment of spirits (Islam)
BM710	296.73	Jews—Dietary laws			
BM712	296.445	Mourning customs, Jewish	BP170.5	297.574	Muslim converts
BM713	296.444	Marriage customs and rites, Jewish			

LC	Dewey	Subject Heading	LC	Dewey	Subject Heading
BP170.5	297.574	Muslim converts from Christianity	BQ287-296	294.30901	Buddhism—History—To ca. 100 A.D.
BP170.5	297.574092	Muslim converts from Christianity—Biography	BQ330-349	294.30954	Buddhism—India
			BQ350-379	294.3095493	Buddhism—Sri Lanka
BP170.85	297.74	Dawah (Islam)	BQ380-396	294.3095496	Buddhism—Nepal
BP173.25-.45	297.27	Sociology, Islamic	BQ416-439	294.309591	Buddhism—Burma
BP175.S8	297.81	Sunnites	BQ440-509	294.30959	Indochina—Religion
BP176	297.31	Pillars of Islam	BQ510-539	294.309598	Buddhism—Indonesia
BP178	297.382	Prayer—Islam	BQ540-549	294.309595	Buddhism—Malaysia
BP179	297.53	Fasting (Islam)	BQ550-568	294.309593	Buddhism—Thailand
BP182	297.72	Jihad	BQ570-609	294.30958	Buddhism—Asia, Central
BP183.6	297.37	Islamic sermons	BQ610-699	294.3095	Buddhism—East Asia
BP183.6	297.362	Ramadan sermons	BQ620-649	294.30951	Buddhism—China
BP184	297.61	Pastoral theology (Islam)	BQ650-669	294.309519	Buddhism—Korea
BP184.2	297.3	Worship (Islam)	BQ670-699	294.30952	Buddhism—Japan
BP184.25	297.37	Islamic preaching	BQ700-709	294.3094	Buddhism—Europe
BP184.4	297.38	Purity, Ritual—Islam	BQ710-719	294.3096	Buddhism—Africa
BP184.9.F8	297.385	Funeral rites and ceremonies, Islamic	BQ720-760	294.309(7-8)	Buddhism—America
			BQ730-739	294.30973	Buddhism—United States
BP186	297.53	Fasts and feasts—Islam	BQ740-749	294.30971	Buddhism—Canada
BP187	297.35	Muslim pilgrims and pilgrimages	BQ770-799	294.3099(3-6)	Buddhism—Oceania
			BQ840-845	294.3092	Buddhists—Biography
BP187.3	297.352	Muslim pilgrims and pilgrimages—Saudi Arabia—Mecca	BQ922	294.363	Gautama Buddha—Footprints
			BQ935	294.363	Gautama Buddha—Enlightenment
BP188	297.57	Religious life—Islam			
BP188.3.Y6	297.57	Youth, Muslim—Religious life	BQ938	294.363	Gautama Buddha—Date of death
BP189	297.4	Mysticism—Islam	BQ1100-3340	294.382	Tripitaka
BP189	297.4	Sufism	BQ1100-3340	294.382	Buddhism—Sacred books
BP189.33	297.4092	Muslim saints	BQ4050	294.342	Buddhism—Apologetic works
BP189.62	297.4382	Sufi meditations			
BP189.7.B4-.B42	297.48	Bektashi	BQ4061-4570	294.342	Buddhism—Doctrines
BP190.5.A5	297.39	Amulets (Islam)	BQ4080-4125	294.34209	Buddhism—Doctrines—History
BP190.5.A75	297.576	Asceticism—Islam			
BP190.5.S4	297.577	Sex—Religious aspects—Islam	BQ4170	294.32	Buddhism—Catechisms
			BQ4170	294.32	Buddhism—Creeds
BP193	297.82	Shiites	BQ4180	294.363	Buddha (The concept)
BP193.25-.28	297.124	Hadith (Shiites)	BQ4195-4250	294.34	Dharma (Buddhism)
BP194.6	297.35	Shiite shrines	BQ4240	294.34	Causation (Buddhism)
BP195.A8	297.822	Assassins (Ismailites)	BQ4330	294.344	Bodhisattva stages (Mahayana Buddhism)
BP221-223	297.87	Black Muslims			
BP300-395	297.93	Bahai faith	BQ4360	294.342	Compassion (Buddhism)
BP340	297.92	Babism	BQ4401-4430	294.35	Virtues (Buddhism)
BP380	297.93435	Bahai meditations	BQ4425-4430	294.35	Vice (Buddhism)
BP500-585	299.934	Theosophy	BQ4475-4525	294.3423	Eschatology, Buddhist
BP573.R5	299.934	Reincarnation	BQ4570.A4	294.3437	Amulets (Buddhism)
BP595-597	299.935	Anthroposophy	BQ4570.A4	294.3437	Charms (Buddhism)
BP605.G68	299.93	Great White Brotherhood	BQ4570.P76	294.3375	Buddhism—Psychology
BP605.N48	299.93	New Age movement	BQ4570.W6	294.3378344	Woman (Buddhism)
			BQ4600-4610	294.3372	Buddhism—Relations
BQ	294.3	Buddhism	BQ4670-4690	294.363	Buddha
BQ1-9999	294.3	Buddhism	BQ4690.M3	294.34211	Maitreya (Buddhist deity)
BQ1-10	294.305	Buddhism—Periodicals	BQ4750.D33	294.34211	Dakini (Buddhist deity)
BQ12-93	294.365	Buddhism—Societies, etc.	BQ4750.Y35	294.34211	Yama (Buddhist deity)
BQ141-209	294.375	Buddhist education	BQ4860.A4	294.34211	Acala (Buddhist deity)
BQ171-199	294.375	Buddhist education of children	BQ4890.D33-.D334	294.34211	Dam-tshig-rdo-rje (Buddhist deity)
BQ251-799	294.309	Buddhism—History			

LC	Dewey	Subject Heading
BQ4965-5030	294.344	Buddhism—Customs and practices
BQ4965-5030	294.3438	Buddhism—Rituals
BQ5005	294.3438	Confirmation (Buddhist rite)
BQ5035-5065	294.3438	Chants (Buddhist)
BQ5070-5075	294.3437	Buddhism—Liturgical objects
BQ5070-5075	294.3437	Altars, Buddhist
BQ5130-5137	294.3435	Temples, Buddhist
BQ5140-5355	294.361	Priests, Buddhist
BQ5360-5680	294.3444	Religious life—Buddhism
BQ5485-5525	294.342	Five Precepts (Buddhism)
BQ5485-5530	294.342	Buddhist precepts
BQ5485-5530	294.342	Buddhism—Doctrines
BQ5535-5594	294.34433	Buddhism—Prayer-books and devotions
BQ5595-5630	294.344	Devotion (Buddhism)
BQ5595-5630	294.3443	Prayer—Buddhism
BQ5700-5720	294.3438	Fasts and feasts—Buddhism
BQ5741-5755	294.333	Mythology, Buddhist
BQ5851-5899	294.33783	Buddhism and social problems
BQ5851-5899	294.3378	Buddhism—Charities
BQ5901-5975	294.372	Buddhism—Missions
BQ6001-6160	294.3657	Monasticism and religious orders, Buddhist
BQ6200-6240	294.34447	Asceticism—Buddhism
BQ6300-6388	294.3435	Buddhist shrines
BQ6400-6495	294.34351	Buddhist pilgrims and pilgrimages
BQ6460	294.3435	Gautama Buddha—Shrines
BQ7100-7285	294.391	Theravada Buddhism
BQ7300-7522	294.392	Mahayana Buddhism
BQ7530-7950	294.39	Dge-lugs-pa (Sect)
BQ7530-7950	294.3923	Buddhism
BQ7669	294.39	Bka'-rgyud-pa (Sect)
BQ7699.G36	294.3438	Gcod (Buddhist rite)
BQ7930	294.361	Dalai lamas
BQ7960-7989	294.39	Bonpo (Sect)
BQ7982.3	294.3438	Gcod (Bonpo rite)
BQ7982.4	294.343	Bonpo incantations
BQ8000-9800	294.39	Buddhist sects
BQ8000-8049	294.39	Abhayagiri (Sect)
BQ8500-8769	294.3926	Pure Land Buddhism
BQ9250-9519	294.3927	Zen Buddhism
BQ9288	294.3444	Spiritual life—Zen Buddhism
BR	230	Christianity
BR1-129	230	Christianity
BR1-9	270.05	Church history—Periodicals
BR21-29	270.06	Church history—Societies, etc.
BR41-43	270.06	Church history—Congresses
BR60-67	270.1092	Apostolic Fathers
BR60-67	270.092	Fathers of the church
BR95	270.03	Church history—Dictionaries
BR97-99	262.009	Ecclesiastical geography
BR138	270.01	Church history—Philosophy
BR110	248.2	Experience (Religion)
BR110	248.24	Conversion
BR112	248.2	Enthusiasm
BR114	248.2	Fanaticism
BR115.C5	230	Civilization, Christian
BR115.H5	230	History (Theology)
BR115.W2	241.3	Evil, Non-resistance to
BR127-128	261.2	Christianity and other religions
BR157	280	Christian sects
BR160-481	270.(1-8)	Church history—[By date]
BR160-270	270.3	Church history—Middle Ages, 600-1500
BR160-240	270.(1-2)	Church history—Primitive and early church, ca. 30-600
BR290-481	270.(5-8)	Church history—Modern period, 1500-
BR295	270.6	Reformation—Early movements
BR300-420	270.6	Reformation
BR307	270.6	Reformation—Causes
BR430	270.6	Counter-Reformation
BR500-1500	274-279	[By region or country]—Church history
BR513-569	277.3	United States—Religion
BR520	277.3081	Great Awakening
BR610-615	277.2	Mexico—Church history
BR620-625	277.28	Central America—Church history
BR655	277.29	Caribbean Area—Church history
BR660-730	278	South America—Church history
BR740-799	274.1	Great Britain—Church history
BR745-754	274.10902	England—Church history—1066-1485
BR748	274.4	Celtic Church
BR749	274.109021	England—Church history—449-1066
BR750	274.10903	England—Church history—1485-
BR755-757	274.109031	England—Church history—16th century
BR756	274.109032	England—Church history—17th century
BR758	274.109033	Evangelical Revival
BR759	274.10904	England—Church history—20th century
BR794	274.4	Celtic Church
BR840-849	274.4	France—Church history

LC	Dewey	Subject Heading	LC	Dewey	Subject Heading
BR850-856.35	274.3	Germany—Church history	BS580	221.092	Bible. O.T.—Biography
BR930-939	274.7	Russia—Church history	BS580.A3	225.92	Abraham (Biblical patriarch) in the New Testament
BR970-1019	274.8	Scandinavia—Church history			
BR1020-1029	274.6	Spain—Church history	BS585-613	220.071	Bible—Study and teaching
BR1060-1357	275	Asia—Church history	BS612	220.076	Bible—Examinations, questions, etc.
BR1150-1156	275.4	India—Church history			
BR1178-1261	275.9	Asia, Southeastern—Church history	BS617.8	242	Bible—Devotional use
			BS635-636	220.9	Bible—History of Biblical events
BR1280-1297	275.1	China—Church history			
BR1300-1317	275.2	Japan—Church history	BS637	220.9	Bible—Chronology
BR1320-1337	275.19	Korea—Church history	BS646	220.046	Apocalyptic literature
BR1359-1470	276	Africa—Church history	BS646	228	Revelation
BR1369-1415	276.1	Africa, North—Church history	BS647-649	220.15	Bible—Prophecies
			BS649.J5	909.04924	Jews—Restoration
BR1430	276.7	Africa, Central—Church history	BS651-652	231.7652	Creationism
			BS651-652	231.765	Creation
BR1440-1445	276.76	Africa, East—Church history	BS651-652	231.765	Biblical cosmology
			BS655	220.852	Astronomy in the Bible
BR1446-1458	276.8	Africa, Southern—Church history	BS658	222.1109505	Noah's ark
			BS658	222.11	Deluge
BR1460-1463	276.6	Africa, West—Church history	BS660-667	220.85	Nature in the Bible
			BS661	220.83058	Ethnology in the Bible
BR1480-1483	279.4	Australia—Church history	BS661	233	Man (Theology)
BR1490-1495	279.9(5-6)	Oceania—Church history	BS670	220.8301	Sociology, Biblical
BR1600-1609	272	Persecution	BS670	220.8330	Economics in the Bible
BR1610	241.4	Religious tolerance	BS680.A34	220.0846	Aged in the Bible
BR1615-1617	230.046	Liberalism (Religion)	BS680.E3	220.837	Education in the Bible
BR1644-.5	270.82	Pentecostalism	BS680.E84	220.817	Ethics in the Bible
BR1650-1653	273.7	Pietism	BS680.F3	220.830685	Family—Biblical teaching
BR1690-1725	270.092	Church history—Biography	BS680.F32	220.83638	Famines in the Bible
BR1690-1725	270.092	Christian biography	BS680.P3	226.8	Bible—Parables
BR1705	270.092	Fathers of the church	BS680.P64	242.5	Bible—Prayers
			BS680.S5	220.83067	Sex in the Bible
BS	220	Bible	BS701-1013	221.(4-5)	Bible. O.T.—Versions
BS1-3	220.51	Bible. Polyglot	BS737-765	221.48	Bible. O.T. Greek
BS135-198	220.52	Bible. English	BS767-815	221.47	Bible. O.T. Latin
BS405-408	220.5	Bible—Abridgments	BS1104	221.65	Bible. O.T.—Harmonies
BS420-429	220.(4-5)	Bible—Concordances	BS1121-1128	221.(4-5)	Bible. O.T.—Concordances
BS445-460	220.09	Bible—History			
BS450-460	220.4	Bible—Versions	BS1130-1134	221.09	Bible. O.T.—History
BS450-460	220.5	Bible—Versions	BS1143-1158	221.7	Bible. O.T.—Commentaries
BS477	220.64	Symbolism in the Bible			
BS478	220.64	Typology (Theology)	BS1160-1191.5	221.6	Bible. O.T.—Criticism, interpetation, etc.
BS480	220.13	Bible—Inspiration			
BS480	220.1	Bible—Evidences, authority, etc.	BS1181.17	220.6	D document (Biblical criticism)
BS482-498	220.7	Bible—Commentaries	BS1181.2	220.6	E document (Biblical criticism)
BS500-534.8	220.6	Bible—Criticism, interpretation, etc.			
			BS1183	221.68	Myth in the Old Testament
BS520.5	220.68	Myth in the Bible	BS1192.5	230.0411	Bible. O.T.—Theology
BS535-537	809.93522	Bible as literature	BS1193-1195	221.071	Bible. O.T.—Study and teaching
BS537	220.(4-5)	Bible—Language, style			
BS543	230.041	Bible—Theology	BS1199.E38	221.837	Education in the Bible
BS546-559	220.9505	Bible stories	BS1199.M5	231.73	Miracles
BS560	220.49	Hieroglyphic Bibles	BS1199.P7	221.92	Priests, Jewish
BS569	220.9	Genealogy in the Bible	BS1221-1285.5	222.1	Bible. O.T. Pentateuch
BS570-580	220.092	Bible—Biography	BS1225	222.106	Documentary hypothesis (Pentateuchal criticism)
BS573	222.110922	Patriarchs (Bible)			

LC	Dewey	Subject Heading	LC	Dewey	Subject Heading
BS1237	222.11	Eden	BT98-180	231	God
BS1237	222.11	Forbidden fruit	BT98-102	231.765	God—Proof, Cosmological
BS1245	222.12	Manna	BT98-101	231.042	God—Proof, Ontological
BS1281-1285.5	222.16	Ten commandments	BT98	231.09	God—History of doctrines
BS1401-1405.5	223	Hebrew poetry, Biblical	BT99	231	God—Biblical teaching
BS1419-1450	223.2	Bible. O.T. Psalms	BT109-115	231.044	Trinity
BS1445.M4	223.2	Royal Psalms	BT117-123	231.3	Holy Spirit
BS1481-1490	223.9	Bible. O.T. Song of Solomon	BT122.5	263.94	Pentecost
			BT123	234.13	Baptism in the Holy Spirit
BS1501-1675.5	224	Prophets	BT124	231	Immanence of God
BS1691-1830	229	Bible. O.T. Apocrypha	BT126-127.5	231.74	Revelation
BS1901-2970	225-228	Bible. N.T.	BT130-157	231.4	God—Attributes
BS1901	225.(4-5)	Bible. N.T.—Versions	BT131	231.4	God—Omniscience
BS2301-2308	225.(4-5)	Bible. N.T.—Concordances	BT133	231.4	God—Omnipotence
			BT135	231.5	Providence and government of God
BS2315-2318	225.09	Bible. N.T.—History			
BS2333-2348	225.7	Bible. N.T.—Commentaries	BT137	231.8	God—Goodness
			BT153.S8	231	Suffering of God
BS2350-2393	225.6	Bible. N.T.—Criticism, interpretation, etc.	BT155	231.76	Covenant theology
			BT160-162	231.8	Theodicy
BS2378	225.68	Demythologization	BT180.G6	231	Glory of God
BS2397	230	Bible. N.T.—Theology	BT198-590	232	Jesus Christ
BS2410	270.(1-2)	Christianity—Early church, ca. 30-600	BT198-590	232.8	Jesus Christ—Person and offices
BS2415-2417	232.954	Jesus Christ—Teachings	BT210	232.2	Logos
BS2440	225.92	Apostles	BT220	232.1	Incarnation
BS2525-2544	225.071	Bible. N.T.—Study and teaching	BT225	232.1	Typology (Theology)
			BT230-245	232.1	Jesus Christ—Messiahship
BS2545.M5	231.73	Miracles	BT232	232.9	Son of Man
BS2549	226	Bible. N.T. Gospels	BT263-268	234.5	Atonement
BS26S20-2628	226.6	Bible. N.T. Acts	BT300-302	232.901	Jesus Christ—Biography
BS2630-2815.5	227	Bible. N.T. Epistles	BT303	242.74	Mysteries of the Rosary
BS2640-2815.5	227	Bible. N.T. Pauline Epistles	BT304-.97	232.903	Jesus Christ—Character
BS2820-2827	228	Four Horsemen of the Apocalypse	BT306	232	Jesus Christ—Words
			BT315	232.923	Magi
BS2831-2970	229	Apocryphal books (New Testament)	BT317	232.921	Virgin birth
			BT340-500	232.95	Jesus Christ—Biography—Public life
BT	230	Doctrinal theology			
BT19-33	230	Dogma	BT363-367	232.955	Jesus Christ—Miracles
BT20-30	230.09	Theology, Doctrinal—History	BT373-378	226.8	Jesus Christ—Parables
			BT378.D5	226.8	Rich man and Lazarus (Parable)
BT20-30	262.8	Heresies, Christian			
BT40-55	230.01	Philosophical theology	BT378.G6	226.8	Good Samaritan (Parable)
BT65-84	231-239	Theology, Doctrinal	BT378.G7	226.8	Great supper (Parable)
BT82	273.9	Modernism	BT378.M8	226.8	Mustard seed (Parable)
BT82.2	270.82	Fundamentalism	BT378.P	226.8	Pearl of great price (Parable)
BT82.25	230.046	Dominion theology			
BT82.7	230.08996	Black theology	BT380-.2	226.9	Sermon on the mount
BT83.55	230.082	Feminist theology	BT382	226.93	Beatitudes
BT83.57	230.0464	Liberation theology	BT410	232.956	Jesus Christ—Transfiguration
BT88-92	262.8	Authority—Religious aspects			
			BT414	263.925	Holy Week
BT91	262.8	Church—Authority	BT414	232.96	Holy Week
BT94	231.72	Kingdom of God	BT420	232.957	Last Supper
BT95-97	241.2	Law (Theology)	BT430-470	232.96	Jesus Christ—Passion
BT95-96.2	231.5	Providence and government of God	BT465	232.963	Holy Cross
			BT587	232.966	Jesus Christ—Relics
BT97-.2	231.73	Miracles	BT587.S4	232.966	Holy Shroud

LC	Dewey	Subject Heading	LC	Dewey	Subject Heading
BT595-680	232.91	Mary, Blessed Virgin, Saint	BT919-925	236.22	Immortality
			BT919-925	236.23	Conditional immortality
BT610-660	232.91	Mary, Blessed Virgin, Saint—Theology	BT930	236.23	Annihilationism
			BT960-968	235.3	Angels
BT620	232.911	Immaculate Conception	BT960-962	235	Spirits
BT650-660	232.917	Visions	BT968.M5	235.3	Michael (Archangel)
BT650-654	232.917	Mary, Blessed Virgin, Saint—Apparitions and miracles	BT972	262.73	Communion of saints
			BT980-981	235.4	Devil
			BT985	236	Antichrist
BT683-694	235.2	Saints	BT990-1010	238	Creeds
BT700-745	233	Man (Christian theology)	BT990	238	Creeds, Ecumenical
BT700-745	233	Man (Theology)	BT1010	262	Covenants (Church polity)
BT704	233	Woman (Christian theology)	BT1029-1040	238	Catechisms
			BT1095-1255	239	Apologetics
BT708	233.5	Sex—Religious aspects—Christianity	BT1109-1115	239.09	Apologetics—History
			BT1115	230.1	Apologetics—Early church, ca. 30-600
BT710	233.14	Fall of man			
BT715-722	233.14	Sin	BT1209-1211	239.7	Rationalism
BT720	233.14	Sin, Original	BT1313-1480	270	Theology—History
BT721	241.3	Sin, Unpardonable	BT1350	273.4	Arianism
BT725	241.3	Temptation	BT1370	273.4	Donatists
BT732.5-.56	234.131	Spiritual healing	BT1390	273.1	Gnosticism
BT734-.3	270.089	Race—Religious aspects—Christianity	BT1440	281.8	Nestorians
BT734-.3	270.089	Race	BV	230	Practical theology
BT738-.5	261.5	Sociology, Christian	BV1-4	240-248	Theology, Practical
BT740-743	233.5	Soul	BV5-530	248.3	Worship
BT750-810.2	234	Salvation	BV5-25	264	Public worship
BT755	234	Salvation outside the Catholic Church	BV5-8	248.309	Worship—History
			BV6	248.30901	Worship—History—Early church, ca. 30-600
BT759	234	Salvation outside the church			
			BV30-135	263.9	Fasts and feasts
BT760-769	234	Grace (Theology)	BV30-135	263.9	Church year
BT763-764.2	234.7	Justification	BV40	252.61	Advent sermons
BT767	234.8	Holiness	BV50.A4	263.9	All Souls' Day
BT767.3	234.13	Gifts, Spiritual	BV50.A7	263.97	Feast of the Assumption of the Blessed Virgin
BT770-772	234.23	Faith			
BT773	234	Merit (Christianity)	BV50.E7	263.915	Epiphany
BT775	234.3	Redemption	BV50.H6	263.97	Feast of the Holy Innocents
BT780	248.24	Conversion			
BT790	234.4	Regeneration (Theology)	BV50.I6	263.97	Feast of the Immaculate Conception
BT795	234.5	Forgiveness of sin			
BT800	234.5	Repentance	BV53	263.92	Palm Sunday
BT809-810.2	234.9	Predestination	BV55	263.93	Paschal mystery
BT809-810.2	234	Election (Theology)	BV55	263.93	Easter
BT819-891	236	Eschatology	BV57	263.93	Ascension Day
BT830	236.4	Intermediate state	BV60	263.94	Pentecost Festival
BT834-838	236.25	Hell	BV61-63	263.94	Pentecost season
BT840-842	236.5	Purgatory	BV64.J4	263.97	Feast of Jesus Christ the King
BT844-849	236.24	Heaven			
BT844-849	236.24	Paradise	BV64.S3	263.97	Feast of the Sacred Heart
BT850-860	235.4	Limbo	BV67	263.98	All Saints' Day
BT870-872	236.8	Resurrection	BV75	263.97	Thanksgiving Day
BT875-891	236.9	End of the world	BV85-95	263.92	Lent
BT880-882	236.9	Judgment Day	BV90-95	263.925	Holy Week
BT885-886	236.9	Second Advent	BV95	263.925	Good Friday
BT890-891	236.9	Millennium	BV107-133	263.3	Sunday
BT899-940	236.2	Future life	BV150-168	246.55	Symbolism
BT910-912	236.21	Eternity	BV150-168	246.55	Signs and symbols

LC	Dewey	Subject Heading	LC	Dewey	Subject Heading
BV150-168	704.9482	Christian art and symbolism	BV675	262.14	Group ministry
			BV675.7	262.14	Clergy couples
BV150-155	246.55	Emblems	BV676	262.14	Women clergy
BV160	246.558	Crosses	BV676	262.14	Ordination of women
BV165	246.6	Colors, Liturgical	BV677	262.15	Lay readers
BV167	391.04204	Church vestments	BV680	262.14	Deacons
BV168.S7	254	Staff, Pastoral	BV685	262.14	Ordination
BV169-199	264	Liturgics	BV687	262.15	Laity
BV169-199	264	Rites and ceremonies	BV705	262.1	Church officers
BV180-181	264	Ritualism	BV710	262.(4-5)	Councils and synods
BV185	264.01	Liturgies, Early Christian	BV741	323.442	Freedom of religion
BV186.7	264	Ecumenical liturgies	BV741	323.442	Liberty of conscience
BV194.D	242.72	Doxology	BV759-763	262.9	Ecclesiastical law
BV195-196	247.1	Altars	BV761	262.90901	Canon law—Early church, ca. 30-600
BV196.C	264	Censers			
BV197.B5	264.13	Benediction	BV761.A1-.A5	255.00901	Church orders, Ancient
BV197.S5	264.9	Cross, Sign of the	BV770-777	254.8	Church finance
BV198-199	264	Liturgies	BV771	254.8	Tithes
BV199	265.9	Occasional services	BV772	254.8	Christian giving
BV199.D4	265.92	Dedication services	BV772	248.6	Stewardship, Christian
BV199.F8	265.85	Funeral service	BV772.5	254.8	Church fund raising
BV199.R5	265	Responsive worship	BV800-873	265	Sacraments
BV200	249	Family—Religious life	BV803-814	265.1	Baptism
BV205-287	264.13	Prayer—Christianity	BV813-.2	265.12	Infant baptism
BV228-284	264.13	Prayers	BV814	265.1	Baptism for the dead
BV245-283	242.8	Prayer-books	BV815	265.2	Confirmation
BV250-254	264.13	Pastoral prayers	BV820	264.36	Close and open communion
BV283.B7	242.82	Boys—Prayer-books and devotions	BV820	254.5	Church membership
BV283.G7	242.2	Grace at meals	BV823-828	264.36	Lord's Supper
BV283.S3	242.2	Schools—Prayers	BV830	262.14	Ordination
BV287	242.2	Prayer groups	BV835-838	265.5	Marriage
BV301-530	246.75	Hymns	BV840-850	265.6	Penance
BV520	246.75	Sunday schools—Hymns	BV845-847	265.62	Confessors
BV590-640	262	Church	BV845-847	265.62	Confession
BV600	262.0017	Church renewal	BV863.P4	247.1	Pews and pew rights
BV601.3	261	Church—Catholicity	BV873.E8	265.94	Exorcism
BV601.8	261	Mission of the church	BV873.F7	265.9	Foot washing (Rite)
BV625	280.042	Interdenominational cooperation	BV873.L3	265.9	Imposition of hands
			BV875-885	264.9	Sacramentals
BV626	262.5	Local church councils	BV890	235.2	Relics
BV629-631	261.7	Church and state	BV900-1450	267	Church societies
BV636	254.7	Church buildings—Interdenominational use	BV950-1220	267	Brotherhoods
			BV1000-1220	267.3	Young Men's Christian associations
BV637	250.91732	City churches			
BV637.5	262.14091732	City clergy	BV1300-1393	267.5	Young Women's Christian associations
BV637.7	250.91733	Suburban churches			
BV637.8	250	Small churches	BV1474-1475.2	268.432	Christian education of children
BV638-.8	250.91734	Rural churches			
BV652-.9	254	Church management	BV1500-1578	268	Sunday schools
BV652.1	262.1	Christian leadership	BV1518-1533	241.4	Virtues
BV652.25	254.5	Church growth	BV1531	268.3	Directors of religious education
BV652.9	250	Church controversies			
BV652.95-657	254.4	Church publicity	BV1534-1536	268.6	Religious education—Teaching methods
BV653	254.4	Advertising—Churches			
BV659-683	262.14	Priests	BV1534.4	268.67	Drama in Christian education
BV659-683	262.14	Clergy			
BV669-670.2	262.12	Episcopacy			
BV674	262.14	Associate clergy			

LC	Dewey	Subject Heading	LC	Dewey	Subject Heading
BV1535	268.635	Religious education—Audio-visual aids	BV4235.L43	251	Lectionary preaching
			BV4235.T65	251	Topical preaching
BV1580-1583	371.071	Week-day church schools	BV4239-4316	252	Sermons
BV1585	268	Vacation schools, Religious	BV4254.2	252	Occasional sermons
			BV4254.3	252.6	Festival-day sermons
BV1590	249	Religious education—Home training	BV4255	252.68	Baccalaureate addresses
			BV4257	252.615	Christmas sermons
BV1650	796.5422	Church camps	BV4257.5	252	Communion sermons
BV2000-3705	266	Missions	BV4259	252.63	Easter—Sermons
BV2082.A9	266	Aeronautics in missionary work	BV4260-4261	252.68	Election sermons
			BV4262	252.68	Execution sermons
BV2082.I6	266	Missions—Interdenominational cooperation	BV4270	252.6	Fast-day sermons
			BV4275	252.1	Funeral sermons
			BV4282	252.68	New Year sermons
BV2130-2300	266.2	Catholic Church—Missions	BV4290	252.7	Installation (Clergy)
			BV4307.D5	252	Dialogue sermons
BV2350-2595	266	Protestant churches—Missions	BV4310	252.55	Youth sermons
			BV4315	252.53	Children's sermons
BV2400-2595	266.009	Protestant churches—Missions—History	BV4327	253.2	Clergy—Political activity
			BV4335	253	Pastoral medicine
BV2617	266.0083	Youth in missionary work	BV4382	331.252912532	Clergy—Pensions
BV2619-2623	266	Missions to Jews	BV4390	253.25	Celibacy
BV2625-2626.4	266	Missions to Muslims	BV4396	253.22	Clergy—Family relationships
BV2637	266	Missions to lepers			
BV2650	266.022	Home missions	BV4395.5	253.2	Clergy—Divorce
BV2810-2820	266.00971	Missions—Canada	BV4405-4408	255.8	Monasticism and religious orders, Protestant
BV2855-3145	266.0094	Missions—Europe			
BV2860-2895	266.00941	Missions—Great Britain	BV4405-4406	262.26	Christian communities
BV2940-2945	266.00944	Missions—France	BV4423-4425	262.14	Deaconesses
BV2950-2957	266.00943	Missions—Germany	BV4427-4430	258.0835	Youth in church work
BV3120-3127	266.00946	Missions—Spain	BV4445.5	259.082	Abused women—Pastoral counseling of
BV3149-3487	266.0095	Missions—Asia			
BV3440-3457	266.00952	Missions—Japan	BV4487.E9	269.2	Evangelical academies
BV3500-3630	266.0096	Missions—Africa	BV4500-4595	248.4	Christian life
BV3640-3680	266.0099(3-6)	Missions—Oceania	BV4501	265.92	Consecration
BV3650-3660	266.00994	Missions—Australia	BV4520	248.5	Witness bearing (Christianity)
BV3700-3705	266.0092	Missionaries			
BV3750-3799	269.24	Revivals	BV4523	254.5	Church attendance
BV3750-3799	269.2	Evangelistic work	BV4530-4579	248.83	Youth—Religious life
BV3780-3785	269.2092	Evangelists	BV4560-4579	268.6	Sunday school literature
BV3793	269.2	Evangelistic invitations	BV4580	248.85	Aged—Religious life
BV3797	252.3	Evangelistic sermons	BV4593	248.88	Working class—Religious life
BV3798-3799	269.24	Camp-meetings			
BV4000-4470	253	Pastoral theology	BV4615	241.1	Conscience
BV4012-.3	253.52	Pastoral psychology	BV4618	241	Human acts
BV4012.2	253.5	Pastoral counseling	BV4625-4780	241	Christian ethics
BV4012.25	253.5	Pastoral counseling centers	BV4625-4627	241.3	Sins
			BV4625-4627	241.4	Virtues
BV4019-4180	230.071	Theology—Study and teaching	BV4625-4627	241.3	Vices
			BV4625	241.3	Sin
BV4019-4160	230.0711	Theological seminaries	BV4625.6-.7	241.31	Sin, Venial
BV4163	230.071	Pretheological education	BV4626	241.3	Deadly sins
BV4164	230.0711	Seminary extension	BV4627.B6	205.695	Blasphemy
BV4200-4317	251	Preaching	BV4627.H8	241.3	Hypocrisy
BV4207-4208	251.009	Preaching—History	BV4627.Q	241.3	Quarreling
BV4235.B56	251	Biographical preaching	BV4627.R4	241.3	Revenge
BV4235.E8	251	Extemporaneous preaching	BV4627.S6	241.3	Slander
			BV4627.S9	241.3	Swearing
BV4235.L3	251	Lay preaching	BV4630-4647	241.3	Vice

LC	Dewey	Subject Heading	LC	Dewey	Subject Heading
BV4630-4647	241.4	Virtue	BX9.5.L55	280.042	Liturgics and Christian union
BV4635-4639	241.4	Theological virtues			
BV4637	241.4	Faith	BX9.5.P29	280.042	Papacy and Christian union
BV4639	241.4	Charity			
BV4645	241.4	Cardinal virtues	BX9.5.V45	280.042	Veneration of saints and Christian union
BV4647.C5	241.66	Virginity			
BV4647.C5	241.66	Chastity	BX9.5.Y68	280.0420835	Youth in the ecumenical movement
BV4647.D6	241.4	Discretion			
BV4647.J	241.62	Justice (Virtue)	BX100-189	281.5	Eastern churches
BV4647.M2	241.4	Magnanimity	BX120-129	281.62	Armenian Church
BV4647.M3	241.4	Meekness	BX150-159	281.8	Nestorian Church
BV4647.M4	241.4	Corporal works of mercy	BX200-754	281.9	Orthodox Eastern Church
BV4647.M4	241.4	Spiritual works of mercy	BX350-376	264.019	Orthodox Eastern Church—Liturgy
BV4647.M4	241.4	Mercy			
BV4647.P5	241.4	Piety	BX377-378	264.019	Sacraments—Orthodox Eastern Church
BV4647.S4	241.4	Self-denial			
BV4647.T4	241.4	Temperance (Virtue)	BX380	235.2	Christian saints
BV4655-4710	241.52	Ten commandments	BX382.5	253.53	Spiritual direction
BV4715	241.54	Golden rule	BX385	255.819	Monasticism and religious orders
BV4720-4730	241.5	Commandments of the church			
			BX400-440	262.13	Patriarchs and patriarchate
BV4726.S2	241.3	Sacrilege			
BV4800-4897	248	Devotional exercises	BX460-605	281.947	Orthodox Eastern Church
BV4800-4895	242	Devotional literature	BX485-492	281.94709	Orthodox Eastern Church—History
BV4800-4870	248.34	Meditations			
BV4810-4812	242.3	Devotional calendars	BX520-558	262.01947	Orthodox Eastern Church—Government
BV4815	242	Devotion			
BV4900-4911	242.4	Consolation	BX560-563	264.01947	Orthodox Eastern Church—Russia
BV4912-4950	248.24	Conversion			
BV4912-4915	248.2	Experience (Religion)	BX575-577.5	235.2	Christian saints
BV4930-4935	248.24	Converts	BX576	235.24	Canonization
BV5015-5068	248.47	Asceticism	BX577	235.2	Relics
BV5023	248.470901	Asceticism—History—Early church, ca. 30-600	BX580-583	255.819	Monasticism and religious orders
BV5025	248.470902	Asceticism—History—Middle Ages, 600-1500	BX610-619	281.9495	Orthodox Eastern Church—Greece
BV5053	253.53	Spiritual direction	BX630-639	281.9436	Orthodox Eastern Church—Austria
BV5055	248.47	Fasting			
BV5068.R4	269.6	Retreats	BX630-639	281.9439	Orthodox Eastern Church—Hungary
BV5070-5095	248.22	Mysticism			
BV5083	248.29	Discernment of spirits	BX800-4795	282	Catholic Church
BV5090-5091	248.29	Trance	BX800-806	282.05	Catholic Church—Periodicals
BV5091.C7	248.34	Contemplation			
BV5091.E3	248.29	Ecstasy	BX808-816	282.06	Catholic Church—Societies, etc.
BV5091.R4	248.29	Private revelations			
BV5091.R4	248.29	Revelation	BX820-838	262.52	Councils and synods, Episcopal (Catholic)
BV5091.V6	248.29	Visions			
BV5095	248.22	Mystics	BX837.5	262.3	Episcopal conferences (Catholic)
BV5099	248.47	Quietism			
			BX838	262.3	Diocesan pastoral councils
BX	280	Christian denominations	BX841	282.03	Catholic Church—Dictionaries
BX1-9.5	280.042	Christian union			
BX6.7-.8	262.0011092	Ecumenists	BX860	262.91	Encyclicals, Papal
BX9.5.A37	280.042	Ecumenical movement—African influences	BX863	262.91	Letters, Papal
			BX895-939	268.82	Catholic Church—Education
BX9.5.E94	280.042	Evangelicalism and Christian union	BX940-1745	282.09	Catholic Church—History
			BX940-1745	270	Catholic Church—History
			BX950-961	262.13	Papacy
			BX958.A23	262.13	Popes—Abdication

LC	Dewey	Subject Heading	LC	Dewey	Subject Heading
BX958.V7	262.13	Papal visits	BX1925	391.04282	Church vestments
BX965-1263	262.13090(1-23)	Papacy—History—To 1309	BX1939.A	262.933	Absolution (Canon law)
			BX1939.A	262.932	Abbots (Canon law)
BX1001-1378	262.13	Popes	BX1939.A3	262.02	Administrators apostolic
BX1301	284.8	Schism, The Great Western, 1378-1417	BX1939.B3	262.933	Baptism (Canon law)
			BX1939.C3	262.933	Catechetics (Canon law)
BX1407.A5	282.73	Americanism (Catholic controversy)	BX1939.C665	262.932	Clergy (Canon law)
			BX1939.C72	262.933	Confirmation (Canon law)
BX1407.N4	282.08996073	Afro-American Catholics	BX1939.P47	262.932	Persons (Canon law)
BX1404-1418	282.73	Catholic Church—United States	BX1939.T65	262.934	Trial practice (Canon law)
			BX1950	254.8	Catholic Church—Finance
BX1419-1424	282.71	Catholic Church—Canada	BX1958-1968	238.2	Catholic Church—Catechisms
BX1427-1431	282.72	Catholic Church—Mexico			
BX1432-1447	282.728	Catholic Church—Central America	BX1968	268.82	Catechetics
			BX1970	264.02	Liturgical language
BX1448-1459	282.729	Catholic Church—West Indies	BX1970.A7-.Z	264.02	Catholic Church—Liturgy
			BX1999.8-2047	264.02(1-9)	Catholic Church—Liturgy—Texts
BX1460-1489	282.8	Catholic Church—South America			
			BX2000-.68	264.024	Breviaries
BX1490-1612	282.4	Catholic Church—Europe	BX2015-2016	264.023	Missals
BX1491-1514	282.41	Catholic Church—Great Britain	BX2015.5.H	264.02	Dog Mass
			BX2037	264.023	Sacramentaries
BX1528-1533	282.44	Catholic Church—France	BX2040	264.0274	Stations of the Cross
BX1534-1539	282.43	Catholic Church—Germany	BX2045.E96	264.02	Exultets (Liturgy)
			BX2045.W34	264.02085	Wake services
BX1543-1548	282.45	Catholic Church—Italy	BX2048.B5	264.13	Benediction
BX1558-1560	282.47	Catholic Church—Russia	BX2050-2155	242.802	Catholic Church—Prayer-books and devotions
BX1583-1588	282.46	Catholic Church—Spain			
BX1615-1673	282.5	Catholic Church—Asia	BX2080	242.802	Books of hours
BX1617-1636	282.56	Catholic Church—Middle East	BX2177-2198	242	Devotional literature
			BX2177-2198	248.34	Meditations
BX1662-1670.7	282.5	Catholic Church—East Asia	BX2200-2292	264.0208	Sacraments (Liturgy)
			BX2215-2239	264.02036	Lord's Supper
BX1675-1682	282.6	Catholic Church—Africa	BX2215.A1	264.02036	Eucharistic congresses
BX1685-1692	282.9(3 or 4)	Catholic Church—[New Zealand or Australia]	BX2220	264.02036	Transubstantiation
			BX2230-2234	264.02	Mass
BX1700-1745	272.2	Inquisition	BX2231.7	264.02036	Private masses
BX1746-1755	230.2	Catholic Church—Doctrines	BX2237	264.02036	First communion
			BX2240	264.02084	Ordination—Catholic Church
BX1752	230.2	Catholic Church—Apologetic works	BX2250-2254	264.02085	Marriage service
			BX2260-2283	264.02086	Penance
BX1756	252.02	Catholic Church—Sermons	BX2262-2267	264.020862	Confessors
			BX2262-2267	264.020862	Confession
BX1790-1795	261.7	Church and state—Catholic Church	BX2279-2283	264.020866	Indulgences
			BX2290	264.0207	Extreme unction
BX1800-1920	262.02	Catholic Church—Government	BX2295-2310	264.0209	Sacramentals
			BX2305	264.02092	Consecration of virgins
BX1805-1810	262.13	Popes	BX2307.3	264.02036	Baptismal water
BX1806	262.131	Popes—Infallibility	BX2310.A	264.0209	Agnus Dei (Sacramental)
BX1905	262.122	Catholic Church—Bishops	BX2310.R7	242.74	Rosary
BX1910	262.142	Vicars apostolic	BX2315	235.2	Relics
BX1910	262.142	Vicars-general	BX2320-2321	263.042	Christian shrines
BX1911	262.02	Archdeacons	BX2323	263.04	Christian pilgrims and pilgrimages
BX1912-1914.5	262.142	Priests			
BX1912-1914.5	262.142	Catholic Church—Clergy	BX2325-2333	270.092	Christian saints
BX1912	262.02	Deacons	BX2330	235.24	Canonization
BX1912.9	253.252	Catholic Church—Clergy—Sexual behavior	BX2340	264.02094	Exorcism
BX1920	262.152	Laity—Catholic Church			

LC	Dewey	Subject Heading	LC	Dewey	Subject Heading
BX2347-2348	264.02	Catholic Church—Liturgy—Theology	BX4833.5-4834	280.409728	Protestant churches—Central America
BX2350.7	253.53	Spiritual direction	BX4835	280.409729	Protestant churches—West Indies
BX2375-2376	269.6	Retreats—Catholic Church			
BX2375	269.6	Parish missions	BX4836	280.4098	Protestant churches—South America
BX2377	241.1	Conscience, Examination of	BX4837-4854	280.4094	Protestant churches—Europe
BX2400-4560	255.(1-7)	Monasticism and religious orders	BX4838-4840	280.40941	Protestant churches—Great Britain
BX2435	255.(1-7)	Monastic and religious life			
BX2436-2437	255.(1-7)06	Monasticism and religious orders—Rules	BX4843	280.40944	Protestant churches—France
BX2460-2749	255.(1-7)009	Monastic and religious life—History	BX4844-.5	280.40943	Protestant churches—Germany
BX2460-2749	255.(1-7)	Monasteries	BX4847	280.40945	Protestant churches—Italy
BX2505-2525	255.(1-7)00973	Monasticism and religious orders—United States	BX4851	280.40946	Protestant churches—Spain
BX2527-2529	255.(1-7)00971	Monasticism and religious orders—Canada	BX4857	280.4095	Protestant churches—Asia
			BX4872-4883	284.4	Waldenses
BX2530-2532	255.(1-7)00972	Monasticism and religious orders—Mexico	BX4900-4906	284.3	Lollards
			BX4913-4918	284.3	Hussites
BX2631-2676	255.(1-7)0094	Monasticism and religious orders—Europe	BX4929-4946	284.3	Anabaptists
			BX4950-4951	289.(6-7)	Plain People
BX2677-2731	255.(1-7)0095	Monasticism and religious orders—Asia	BX5001-5009	283	Anglican Communion
			BX5005	283.09	Anglican Communion—History
BX2732-2740	255.(1-7)0096	Monasticism and religious orders—Africa	BX5008	252.03	Anglican Communion—Sermons
BX2790	391.04282	Church vestments			
BX2820	255.(2-3)	Friars	BX5011-5740	283.42	Church of England
BX2901-2956	255.4	Augustinians	BX5011	283.4205	Church of England—Periodicals
BX3501-3556	255.2	Dominicans			
BX3601-3656	255.3	Franciscans	BX5031	283.42025	Church of England—Directories
BX3651-3653	255.3	Secular Franciscans			
BX4200-4556	255.9(1-7)	Sisterhoods	BX5051-5101	283.4209	Church of England—History
BX4200-4563	255.9(1-7)	Monasticism and religious orders for women	BX5115-5126	283.42	Church of England—Parties and movements
BX4337-.5	255.972	Dominican sisters			
BX4361-4364	255.973	Franciscans	BX5123	264.03	Ritualism
BX4600-4644	282.73	Catholic Church—[By region or country]	BX5127-5129.8	283.42	Church of England—Relations
BX4650-4705	282.092	Catholic Church—Biography	BX5137-5140	230.342	Church of England—Doctrines
BX4654-4662	282.0922	Martyrs—Legends	BX5140.5-5147	264.0342	Church of England—Liturgy
BX4663-4665	262.17092	Cardinals			
BX4668.2-.3	255.(1-7)	Ex-monks	BX5145	264.03	Church of England—Prayer-Books and devotions
BX4711.11-.995	281.5	Catholic Church—Byzantine rite			
BX4711.231-.2395	281.509495	Catholic Church—Byzantine rite, Greek	BX5148-5149	264.035	Sacraments—Church of England
BX4718.5-4735	284.84	Jansenists	BX5149.C5	264.03	Lord's Supper
BX4800-9999	280.4	Protestant churches	BX5149.C6	264.03562	Confession
BX4800-9890	280.4092	Protestants	BX5150-5182.5	262.0342	Church of England—Government
BX4800-4946	280.4	Protestantism			
BX4800	280.405	Protestantism—Periodicals	BX5165	248.6	Tithes
BX4804-4807	280.409	Protestantism—History	BX5175-5182.5	262.03	Priests
BX4818-.3	280.4	Protestant churches—Relations	BX5175-5182.5	262.03	Church of England—Clergy
			BX5176-5178	262.12	Episcopacy
BX4833	280.40972	Protestant churches—Mexico	BX5178	255.83	Anglican orders
			BX5179	262.12	Archdeacons
			BX5179	262.03	Archdeacons

22

LC	Dewey	Subject Heading	LC	Dewey	Subject Heading
BX5180	391.04283	Church vestments	BX6101-6193	286.7	Millerite movement
BX5185	255.983	Sisterhoods	BX6101-6193	286.7	Adventists
BX5197-5199	283.42092	Church of England—Biography	BX6115-6117	286.709	Adventists—History
			BX6123	252.067	Adventists—Sermons
BX5200-5207	280.40941	Dissenters, Religious—England	BX6124.3-.6	264.06708	Sacraments—Adventists
			BX6151-6155	286.732	Seventh-Day Adventists
BX5410-5595	283.415	Church of Ireland	BX6191-6193	286.7092	Adventists—Biography
BX5500-5510	283.41509	Church of Ireland—History	BX6195-6197	284.9	Arminianism
BX5590-5595	283.415092	Church of Ireland—Biography	BX6201-6495	286.(1-5)	Baptists
			BX6205	286.(1-5)06	Baptists—Societies, etc.
BX5596-5598	283.429	Church of England—Wales	BX6211	286.(1-5)03	Baptists—Dictionaries
BX5601-5620	283.72	Church of England—Canada	BX6219-6227	268.86(1-5)	Baptists—Education
			BX6231-6328	286.(1-5)09	Baptists—History
BX5610-5613	283.72	Church of England—Canada—History	BX6235-6249	286.(1-5)73	Baptists—United States
			BX6251-6253	286.(1-5)71	Baptists—Canada
BX5619-5620	283.0972092	Church of England—Biography	BX6271-6273	286.(1-5)8	Baptists—South America
			BX6275-6310	286.(1-5)4	Baptists—Europe
BX5661-5680.7	283.5	Church of England—Asia	BX6315-6316	286.(1-5)5	Baptists—Asia
BX5681-5700.9	283.6	Church of England—Africa	BX6320-6322	286.(1-5)6	Baptists—Africa
BX5701-5720.8	283.9(3 or 4)	Church of England—[New Zealand/Australia]	BX6325-6326	286.(1-5)94	Baptists—Australia
			BX6327-6328	286.(1-5)9(5-6)	Baptists—Oceania
BX5721-5740	283	Church of England—Oceania	BX6330-6331.2	230.6(1-5)	Baptists—Doctrines
			BX6333	252.06(1-5)	Baptists—Sermons
BX5800-6093	283.73092	Episcopalians	BX6335	238.6	Baptists—Creeds
BX5850-5876	268.8373	Episcopal Church—Education	BX6336	238.6(1-5)	Baptists—Catechisms
			BX6337	264.06(1-5)	Baptists—Liturgy
BX5879-5919	283.7309	Episcopal Church—History	BX6340-6346.3	262.06(1-5)	Baptists—Government
BX5925	269.2	Evangelicalism—Episcopal Church	BX6388.3-.38	286.1	Regular Baptists
			BX6390-6408	286.3	Seventh-Day Baptists
BX5926-5928.5	283.73	Episcopal Church—Relations	BX6475-6476	269.24	Church camps—Baptists
			BX6493-6495	286.1092	Baptists—Biography
BX5929-5930.2	230.373	Episcopal Church—Doctrines	BX6751-6793	286.63	General Convention of the Christian Church
BX5939	238.373	Episcopal Church—Creeds	BX6901-6997	289.5	Christian Science
BX5940-5948	264.03	Episcopal Church—Liturgy	BX6903	289.506	Christian Science—Societies, etc.
BX5943-5945	264.03	Episcopal Church—Prayer-books and devotions	BX6905-6907	289.506	Christian Science—Congresses
BX5949	264.035	Episcopal Church Confession	BX6917	268.895	Christian Science—Education
BX5949.C6	234.166	Confession			
BX5949.C6	265.62	Confession	BX6931-6935	289.509	Christian Science—History
BX5950-5968	262.0373	Episcopal Church—Government	BX6958	262.095	Christian Science—Government
BX5969	266.373	Episcopal Church—Missions	BX6960	264.095	Christian Science—Liturgy
BX5970-5974	255.83	Monasticism and religious orders, Anglican	BX6990-6996	289.5092	Christian Science—Biography
BX5979	283.7308996073	Afro-American Episcopalians	BX7101-7260	285.8	Congregationalism
			BX7101-7260	285.8	Congregational churches
BX5990-5995	283.73092	Episcopalians—Biography	BX7105	285.806	Congregational churches—Societies, etc.
BX6051	283.7305	Episcopal Church—Periodicals	BX7106-7109	285.806	Congregational churches—Congresses
BX6061-6064.5	268.8373	Episcopal Church—Education	BX7119-7127	268.858	Congregational churches—Education
BX6065-6069	283.7309	Episcopal Church—History	BX7131-7228	285.809	Congregational churches—History
BX6074	238.373	Episcopal Church—Creeds			
BX6075	264.03	Episcopal Church—Liturgy	BX7135-7149	285.873	Congregational churches—United States
BX6076	262.0373	Episcopal Church—Government			
BX6091-6093	283.73092	Episcopalians—Biography			

LC	Dewey	Subject Heading	LC	Dewey	Subject Heading
BX7151-7153	285.871	Congregational churches—Canada	BX8020-8023	284.143	Lutheran Church—Germany
BX7175-7210	285.84	Congregational churches—Europe	BX8041-8061	284.173	Lutheran Church—United States
BX7215-7216	285.85	Congregational churches—Asia	BX8066	252.041	Lutheran Church—Sermons
BX7220-7222	285.86	Congregational churches—Africa	BX8067	264.041	Lutheran Church—Liturgy
BX7225-7226	285.894	Congregational churches—Australia	BX8068-8070	238	Catechetics
BX7233	252.058	Congregational churches—Sermons	BX8071-.2	262.041	Lutheran Church—Clergy
BX7235-7236.2	238.58	Congregational churches—Creeds	BX8072-8073.5	264.04108	Sacraments—Lutheran Church
BX7237	264.058	Congregational churches—Liturgy	BX8079-8080	284.1092	Lutherans—Biography
BX7238-7239	264.05808	Sacraments—Congregational churches	BX8101-8143	289.7092	Mennonites
			BX8115-8119	289.709	Mennonites—History
BX7240-7246	262.058	Congregational churches—Government	BX8116-8118	289.773	Mennonites—United States
BX7259-7260	285.8092	Congregationalist—Biography	BX8118.5-.7	289.771	Mennonites—Canada
BX7301-7343	286.6	Disciples of Christ	BX8127	252.097	Mennonites—Sermons
BX7433	289.9	Dukhobors	BX8129.A1	252.097	Mennonites—Parties and movements
BX7601-7795	289.605	Society of Friends	BX8129.A5-.A6	289.73092	Amish
BX7601	289.605	Society of Friends—Periodicals	BX8129.O43	289.7092	Old Order Mennonites
BX7606.5-7608	289.606	Society of Friends—Congresses	BX8141-8143	289.7092	Mennonites—Biography
BX7619-7627	268.896	Society of Friends—Education	BX8201-8495	287	Methodist Church
			BX8201-8495	287	Methodism
BX7630-7728	289.609	Society of Friends—History	BX8207	287.06	Methodist Church—Societies, etc.
BX7635-7649	289.673	Society of Friends—United States	BX8219-8227	268.87	Methodist Church—Education
BX7650-7653	289.671	Society of Friends—Canada	BX8231-8328	287.09	Methodist Church—History
BX7671-7673	289.68	Society of Friends—South America	BX8235-8249	287.(1-8)73	Methodist Church—United States
BX7675-7710	289.64	Society of Friends—Europe	BX8251-8253	287.(1-8)71	Methodist Church—Canada
BX7676-7693	289.641	Society of Friends—Great Britain	BX8271-8273	287.(1-8)8	Methodist Church—South America
BX7715-7716	289.65	Society of Friends—Asia	BX8275-8310	287.(1-8)4	Methodist Church—Europe
BX7720-7723	289.66	Society of Friends—Africa	BX8276-8293	287.536	Methodist Church—Great Britain
BX7725-7726	289.694	Society of Friends—Australia	BX8315-8316	287.(1-8)5	Methodist Church—Asia
BX7733	252.096	Society of Friends—Sermons	BX8320-8322	287.(1-8)6	Methodist Church—Africa
BX7740-7746	262.096	Society of Friends—Government	BX8325-8326	287.(1-8)93	Methodist Church—New Zealand
BX7790-7795	289.6092	Quakers—Biography	BX8325-8326	287.(1-8)94	Methodist Church—Australia
BX7990.H6	289.9	Snake cults (Holiness churches)	BX8330-8331.2	230.7	Methodist Church—Doctrines
BX8001-8080	284.1	Lutheran Church	BX8333	252.7	Methodist Church—Sermons
BX8001	284.104	Lutheran Church—Periodicals	BX8335	238.7	Methodist Church—[Catechisms/Creeds]
BX8018-8063	284.109	Lutheran Church—History	BX8337	264.07	Methodist Church—Liturgy
BX8020-8040.5	284.14	Lutheran Church—Europe	BX8338	264.0708	Sacraments—Methodist Church
			BX8340-8345.5	262.07	Methodist Church—Government
			BX8380-8389	287.632	Methodist Episcopal Church

LC	Dewey	Subject Heading	LC	Dewey	Subject Heading
BX8380-8389	287.633	Methodist Episcopal Church	BX8905	285.(1-2)06	Presbyterian Church—Societies, etc.
BX8435-8473	287.8	Afro-American Methodists	BX8917-8925	268.85	Presbyterian Church—Education
BX8475-8476	269.24	Camp-meetings			
BX8491-8495	287.092	Methodists—Biography	BX8930-9169	285.(1-2)09	Presbyterian Church—History
BX8525-8528	289.92	Jehovah's Witnesses			
BX8551-8593	284.6	Moravians	BX8960-8968	285.1	Presbyterian Church in the U.S.
BX8553	284.606	Moravians—Societies, etc.			
BX8561-8564.5	268.846	Moravians—Education	BX8950-8958	285.1	Presbyterian Church in the U.S.A.
BX8565-8569	284.609	Moravians—History			
BX8577	252.046	Moravians—Sermons	BX8990-8998.38	285.136	Reformed Presbyterian Church
BX8591-8593	284.6092	Moravians—Biography			
BX8601-8695	289.3	Mormon Church	BX9001-9003	285.(1-2)71	Presbyterian Church—Canada
BX8610	268.893	Mormon Church—Education			
			BX9011-9043	285.(1-2)8	Presbyterian Church—Latin America
BX8611-8617	289.309	Mormon Church—History			
BX8621-8631	289.32	Mormon Church—Sacred books	BX9050-9140	285.(1-2)4	Presbyterian Church—Europe
BX8627.A3-Z	289.32	Lamanites (Mormon Church)	BX9052-9105	285.(1-2)41	Presbyterian Church—Great Britain
BX8628.A5	289.32	Doctrine and covenants stories	BX9075-9095	285.233	Church of Scotland
			BX9150-9151	285.(1-2)5	Presbyterian Church—Asia
BX8639	252.093	Mormon Church—Sermons	BX9160-9162	285.(1-2)6	Presbyterian Church—Africa
BX8643.C68	231.765	Mormon cosmology	BX9178	252.05	Presbyterian Church—Sermons
BX8643.P7	231.745	Prophets (Mormon theology)	BX9185-9187	264.05	Presbyterian Church—Liturgy
BX8643.R4	231.74	Revelation (Mormon theology)	BX9188-9189	264.05	Sacraments—Presbyterian Church
BX8643.T4	246.6	Mormon temples			
BX8643.T5	248.6	Tithes—Mormon Church	BX9190-9195	262.05	Presbyterian Church—Government
BX8655-.3	264.09308	Sacraments—Mormon Church			
			BX9220-9225	285.092	Presbyterians—Biography
BX8659.5	262.1	Aaronic Priesthood (Mormon Church)	BX9301-9359	285.9	Puritans
			BX9331-9359	285.909(4-9)	Puritans—[By region or country]
BX8661	266.93	Mormon Church—Missions	BX9401-9640	284.2	Calvinism
BX8701-8749	289.4	New Jerusalem Church	BX9401-9640	284.2	Reformed Church
BX8701	289.405	New Jerusalem Church—Periodicals	BX9401	284.205	Calvinism—Periodicals
			BX9403	284.206	Reformed Church—Societies, etc.
BX8705	289.406	New Jerusalem Church—Congresses	BX9415	284.209	Reformed Church—History
BX8714	268.894	New Jerusalem Church—Education	BX9420-9422.2	230.42	Reformed Church—Doctrines
BX8715-8719	289.409	New Jerusalem Church—History	BX9425	262.042	Reformed Church—Government
BX8724	252.094	New Jerusalem Church—Sermons	BX9426	252.042	Reformed Church—Sermons
BX8736	264.09408	Sacraments—New Jerusalem Church	BX9427-.5	264.042	Reformed Church—Liturgy
			BX9430-9480	284.24	Reformed Church—Europe
BX8737	262.094	New Jerusalem Church—Government	BX9430-9439	284.2494	Reformed Church—Switzerland
BX8747-8749	289.4092	New Jerusalem Church—Biography	BX9450-9459	284.5	Huguenots
			BX9450-9459	284.244	Reformed Church—France
BX8762-8780	289.94	Pentecostal churches	BX9470-9479	284.2492	Reformed Church—Netherlands
BX8901-9225	285	Presbyterian Church			
BX8901-9225	287	Calvinistic Methodists	BX9495-9593	284.273	Reformed Church—United States
BX8901-9225	285.(1-2)	Presbyterianism	BX9551-9593	285.733	Reformed Church in the United States

LC	Dewey	Subject Heading	LC	Dewey	Subject Heading
BX9596-9598	284.271	Reformed Church—Canada	CB19	901	Civilization—Philosophy
BX9615	284.25	Reformed Church—Asia	CB20	907.1	Civilization—Study and teaching
BX9618-9640	284.26	Reformed Church—Africa	CB155	303.44	Progress
BX9680.S3	296.82092	Sabbatarians	CB156	001.94	Civilization—Extraterrestrial influences
BX9701-9743	287.96	Salvation Army			
BX9751-9793	289.8	Shakers	CB158-161	003.2	Forecasting
BX9755	289.806	Shakers—Congresses	CB160-161	003.20904	Twentieth century—Forecasts
BX9761-9764	268.898	Shakers—Education			
BX9765-9769	289.809	Shakers—History	CB195-281	909.04	Race
BX9766-9768	289.80973	Shakers—United States	CB195-197	305.8	National characteristics
BX9766-9769	289.809(4-9)	Shakers—[By region or country]	CB203-231	940.(288-559)	Europe—Intellectual life—20th century
BX9776	262.098	Shakers—Government	CB204	940.2(7-87)	Europe—Civilization—19th century
BX9777	252.098	Shakers—Sermons			
BX9791-9793	289.8092	Shakers—Biography	CB204	940.2(7-87)	Europe—Intellectual life—19th century
BX9801-9869	289.133	Unitarianism			
BX9801-9869	289.1	Unitarian Universalist churches	CB213-214	943	Civilization, Germanic
			CB216-220	941.0042	Anglo-Saxon race
BX9805-9807	289.106	Unitarian Universalist churches—Congresses	CB245	909.09812	Civilization, Western
			CB253-256	950	Civilization, Oriental
BX9817-9823	268.891	Unitarian Universalist churches—Education	CB305	930	Protohistory
			CB311	930	Civilization, Ancient
BX9831-9835	289.109	Unitarian Universalist churches—History	CB351-369	909.08	Renaissance
			CB351-355	909.07	Civilization, Medieval
BX9833-9835	289.1(4-9)	Unitarianism—[By region or country]	CB351-355	909.07	Middle Ages
			CB353	909.1	Twelfth century
BX9833	289.173	Unitarianism—United States	CB357-430	909.08	Civilization, Modern
			CB367-401	909.5	Sixteenth century
BX9843	252.091	Unitarian Universalist churches—Sermons	CB411	940.2(526-7)	Europe—Civilization—18th century
BX9850	262.091	Unitarian Universalist churches—Government	CB415-417	909.81	Nineteenth century
			CB425-430	909.82	Twentieth century
BX9854	264.0913308	Sacraments—Unitarianism	CB481	909	War and civilization
BX9867-9869	289.1092	Unitarians			
BX9901-9969	289.134	Universalism	CC	930	Archaeology
BX9901-9996	289.134	Restorationism	CC1-15	930.105	Archaeology—Periodicals
BX9905-9907	289.13406	Universalism—Congresses	CC20-39	930.106	Archaeology—Societies, etc.
BX9917-9923	268.89134	Universalism—Education			
BX9931-9935	289.13409	Universalism—History	CC70	930.103	Archaeology—Dictionaries
BX9943	252.09134	Universalism—Sermons	CC72-81	930.101	Archaeology—Philosophy
BX9954	264.0913408	Sacraments—Universalism	CC73-75	930.101	Archaeology—Methodology
BX9967-9969	289.134092	Universalists	CC73-75	930.1028	Archaeological surveying
			CC75	930.10283	Excavations (Archaeology)
C	900	Auxiliary sciences of history	CC77.U5	930.102804	Underwater archaeology
			CC77.5	930.1028	Archaeological geology
C2	906	Auxiliary sciences of history—Societies, etc.	CC110-115	930.1092	Archaeologists
			CC120-125	930.1025	Archaeology—Directories
C3	906	Auxiliary sciences of history—Congresses	CC135-137	930.10288	Antiquities—Collection and preservation
C4	905	Auxiliary sciences of history—Periodicals	CC140	364.163	Forgery of antiquities
			CC165	930.10283	Excavations (Archaeology)
			CC200-255	786.8848	Bells
CB	900	Civilization	CC300-350	246.558	Crosses
CB3	905	Civilization—Periodicals	CC400	611.718	Fibula (Archaeology)
CB9	903	Civilization—Dictionaries	CC600-605	320.12	Boundary stones
CB13	902.22	Civilization—Pictorial works			
			CD	027	Archives
CB15-18	907.2	Civilization—Historiography	CD	327.2	Diplomatics

LC	Dewey	Subject Heading	LC	Dewey	Subject Heading
CD	737.6	Seals	CD1790-1809.5	027.04912	Archives—Iceland
CD1-724	327.2	Diplomatics	CD1810-1829.5	027.0481	Archives—Norway
CD50-79	327.2090(1-5)	Diplomatics—[By region or country]	CD1830-1849.5	027.0485	Archives—Sweden
			CD1850-1879.5	027.046	Archives—Spain
CD101-392	025.173409(4-9)	Government publications—[By region or country]	CD1880-1899.5	027.0469	Archives—Portugal
			CD1900-1929.5	027.0494	Archives—Switzerland
			CD1930-1989.5	027.0496	Archives—Balkan Peninsula
CD101-215	025.1734094	Government publications—Europe	CD2001-2291	027.05	Archives—Asia
CD221-254	025.1734095	Government publications—Asia	CD2010-2919.5	027.05694	Archives—Israel
			CD2030-2059.5	027.051	Archives—China
CD255-269	025.1734096	Government publications—Africa	CD2080-2099.5	027.054	Archives—India
CD271-272	025.1734094	Government publications—Australia	CD2160-2189.5	027.052	Archives—Japan
			CD2300-2491	027.06	Archives—Africa
CD291	025.1734099	Government publications—Oceania	CD2500-2529.5	027.094	Archives—Australia
			CD2570-2789.5	027.093	Archives—New Zealand
CD309-311	025.17340973	Government publications—United States	CD2795	027.09(5-6)	Archives—Oceania
			CD3020-3615	027.073	Archives—United States
			CD3070-3609	027.07(4-9)	Archives—[United States, By state]
CD331-332	025.17340971	Government publications—Canada	CD3620-3649.6	027.071	Archives—Canada
CD333-334	025.17340972	Government publications—Mexico	CD3650-3679.5	027.072	Archives—Mexico
			CD3690-3859.5	027.0728	Archives—Central America
CD335-350	025.173409728	Government publications—Central America	CD3860-3985	027.0729	Archives—Caribbean area
			CD4000-4279.5	027.08	Archives—South America
CD351-362	025.173409729	Government publications—Caribbean Area	CD5001-6471	737.6	Seals (Numismatics)
			CD5001	737.605	Seals (Numismatics)—Periodicals
CD365-392	025.1734098	Government publications—South America	CD5005	737.606	Seals (Numismatics)—Societies, etc.
			CD5009	737.606	Seals (Numismatics)—Congresses
CD921-4280	027	Archives	CD5017-5018	737.6074	Seals (Numismatics)—Exhibitions
CD921	027.005	Archives—Periodicals			
CD941	027.0025	Archives—Directories	CD5045	737.6071	Seals (Numismatics)—Study and teaching
CD945	027.003	Archives—Dictionaries			
CD947	027.001	Archives—Philosophy	CD5049	737.609	Seals (Numismatics)—History
CD973	027.0028	Archives—Methodology			
CD977	027.1	Personal archives	CD5051-5052	737.6092	Seals (Numismatics)—Biography
CD981-986.5	725.15	Archive buildings			
CD987-988	027.0071	Archives—Study and teaching	CD5085-5175	737.6028	Seals (Numismatics)—Techniques
CD995-4280	027.009	Archives—History	CD5592-6471	737.609(4-9)	Seals (Numismatics)—[By region or country]
CD1000-4280	027.0(4-9)	Archives—[By region or country]			
CD1000-2000	027.04	Archives—Europe	CD5601-5617	737.60973	Seals (Numismatics)—United States
CD1040-1199.5	027.041	Archives—Great Britain			
CD1120-1149.5	027.0436	Archives—Austria	CD5610	737.60973	United States—Seal
CD1150-1169.5	027.0437	Archives—Czechoslovakia	CD5619	737.0971	Seals (Numismatics)—Canada
CD1170-1189.5	027.0439	Archives—Hungary			
CD1190-1219.5	027.044	Archives—France	CD5620	737.0972	Seals (Numismatics)—Mexico
CD1220-1243.5	027.043	Archives—Germany			
CD1400-1658	027.045	Archives—Italy	CD5621-5700	737.09728	Seals (Numismatics)—Central America
CD1670-1689.5	027.0493	Archives—Belgium			
CD1690-1733.3	027.0492	Archives—Netherlands	CE	529	Chronology
CD1710-1739.5	027.047	Archives—Russia	CE1	529.05	Chronology—Periodicals
CD1740-1759.5	027.0438	Archives—Poland	CE1.5	529.06	Chronology—Congresses
CD1770-1789.5	027.0489	Archives—Denmark	CE4	529.03	Chronology—Dictionaries
			CE6	529.09	Chronology—History

LC	Dewey	Subject Heading	LC	Dewey	Subject Heading
CE31-39.5	529.325	Chronology, Oriental	CJ4801-5450	737.3	Tokens
CE33	529.0935	Calendar, Assyro-Babylonian	CJ4801	737.305	Tokens—Periodicals
			CJ4805-4808	737.3074	Tokens—Exhibitions
CE33	529.30935	Chronology, Assyro-Babylonian	CJ4805-4806	737.3074	Tokens—Museums
			CJ4901-5336	737.309(4-9)	Tokens—[By region or country]
CE35	529.326	Calendar, Jewish			
CE42	529.30938	Chronology, Greek	CJ4901-4906	737.30973	Tokens—United States
CE46	529.309376	Calendar, Roman	CJ5501-6661	737.22	Medals
CE59	529.327	Calendar, Islamic	CJ5501	737.2205	Medals—Periodicals
CE73	529.3	Calendars	CJ5525	737.22071	Medals—Study and teaching
CE75	529.42	Calendar, Julian			
CE81-83	529.44	Church calendar	CJ5581-5690	737.22093	Medals, Ancient
CE81	263.9	Fasts and feasts	CJ5625	737.220938	Medals, Greek
CE83	529.44	Easter	CJ5641-5685	737.220937	Medals, Roman
CE91-92	529.3	Perpetual calendars	CJ5793.R34	737.224	Religious medals
			CJ5795-6661	737.2209(4-9)	Medals—[By Region or country]
CJ	737	Numismatics			
CJ1-4625	737.4	Coins	CJ5801-5812	737.220973	Medals—United States
CJ1-9	737.405	Coins—Periodicals	CJ5806	737.223	Campaign insignia
CJ14-23	737.406	Coins—Societies, etc.	CJ5841-5905	737.2209728	Medals—Central America
CJ27	737.406	Coins—Congresses	CJ6091-6380	737.22094	Medals—Europe
CJ39-41	737.4074	Coins—Exhibitions	CJ6381-6485	737.22095	Medals—Asia
CJ53	737.401	Coins—Philosophy	CJ6491-6559	737.22096	Medals—Africa
CJ59	737.409	Coins—History	CJ6561-6569	737.220994	Medals—Australia
CJ101	737.4	Coins—Grading			
CJ125	737.4	Coins—Errors	CN	411.7	Inscriptions
CJ161.F3	737.4	Facing heads (Numismatics)	CN1	411.705	Inscriptions—Periodicals
			CN15	411.706	Inscriptions—Congresses
CJ201-1397	737.493	Coins, Ancient	CN25-30	411.7074	Inscriptions—Collectors and collecting
CJ301-763	737.4938	Coins, Greek			
CJ359	737.4938	Decadrachma	CN40-42	411.701	Inscriptions—Philosophy
CJ425-763	737.4938	Coins, Greek	CN50	411.7071	Inscriptions—Study and teaching
CJ517-542	737.4937	Coins, Italian			
CJ801-1147	737.4937	Coins, Roman	CN55	411.709	Inscriptions—History
CJ937	737.4937	AS (Coin)	CN70	411.703	Inscriptions—Dictionaries
CJ1021-1144	737.493	Coins, Ancient [By region or country]	CN120-730	411.7	Inscriptions, Ancient
			CN350-455	481.1	Inscriptions, Greek
CJ1021-1070	737.4937	Coins, Ancient—Italy	CN375.E6	929.50938	Epitaphs
CJ1071-1085	737.496	Coins, Ancient—Africa	CN380-455	481.109(3-9)	Inscriptions, Greek—[By region or country]
CJ1087-1099	737.49396	Coins, Ancient—Asian			
CJ1101-1147	737.4936	Coins, Ancient—Europe	CN400	481.1095	Inscriptions, Greek—Asia
CJ1101-1147	737.49398	Coins, Ancient—Europe	CN410-415	481.109561	Inscriptions, Greek—Turkey
CJ1201-1291	737.49398	Coins, Byzantine			
CJ1301-1397	737.49396	Coins, Oriental	CN420	481.1094959	Inscriptions, Greek—Crete
CJ1601-1715	737.40902	Coins, Medieval	CN430	481.1095693	Inscriptions, Greek—Cyprus
CJ1800-4625	737.49(4-9)	Coins, Medieval—[By region or country]			
			CN440-441	481.10953	Inscriptions, Greek—Middle East
CJ1800-2449	737.4973	Coins, American			
CJ1835	737.4973	Half-dollar	CN440-441	481.10932	Inscriptions, Greek—Egypt
CJ1860-1879	737.4971	Coins, Canadian	CN455	487.311	Inscriptions, Byzantine
CJ1889-2449	737.498	Coins, Latin American	CN479	499.9411	Inscriptions, Etruscan
CJ2450-3369	737.494	Coins, European	CN510-740	471	Inscriptions, Latin
CJ2484	737.4941	Guinea (Coin)	CN528.E6	929.50937	Epitaphs
CJ3188	737.4946	Doubloons	CN745	492.411	Inscriptions, Jewish
CJ3189	737.4946	Piece of eight	CN750-753	487.4	Inscriptions, Christian
CJ3370-3893	737.495	Coins, Oriental	CN870-1355	411.709	Inscriptions—[By region or country]
CJ3920-4389	737.496	Coins, African			
CJ3948	737.4968	Krugerrand (Coin)	CN870-872	411.70973	Inscriptions—United States
CJ4400-4419	737.4994	Coins, Australian			

LC	Dewey	Subject Heading	LC	Dewey	Subject Heading
CN877-878	411.70972	Inscriptions—Mexico	CR4951-5005	929.736	Orders of knighthood and chivalry—Austria
CN882-884	411.709728	Inscriptions—Central America	CR5025-5085	929.74	Orders of knighthood and chivalry—France
CN886-888	411.7098	Inscriptions—South America	CR5100-5475	929.73	Orders of knighthood and chivalry—Germany
CN900-1130	411.7094	Inscriptions—Europe	CR5351	929.8143	Iron Cross
CN910-915	411.709436	Inscriptions—Austria	CR5485-5489	929.795	Orders of knighthood and chivalry—Greece
CN945-948	411.70944	Inscriptions—France	CR5500-5580	929.75	Orders of knighthood and chivalry—Italy
CN950-957	411.70943	Inscriptions—Germany			
CN960-997	411.70941	Inscriptions—Great Britain	CR5547-5577	255.791	Papal decorations
CN1000-1005	481.1	Inscriptions, Greek	CR5547-5577	262.13	Nobility, Papal
CN1010-1015	411.70945	Inscriptions—Italy	CR5547-5575	255.7	Orders of knighthood and chivalry, Papal
CN1060-1065	411.70947	Inscriptions—Russia			
CN1090-1095	411.70946	Inscriptions—Spain	CR5657-5703	929.77	Orders of knighthood and chivalry—Russia
CN1150-1230	411.7095	Inscriptions—Asia			
CN1153	492.71	Inscriptions, Islamic	CR5713-5737	929.738	Orders of knighthood and chivalry—Poland
CN1160-1161	411.70951	Inscriptions—China			
CN1170-1175	411.70954	Inscriptions—India	CR5745-5809	929.78	Orders of knighthood and chivalry—Scandinavia
CN1180-1181	411.70952	Inscriptions—Japan			
CN1193-1194	411.7095694	Inscriptions—Israel	CR5819-5889	929.76	Orders of knighthood and chivalry—Spain
CN1300-1320	411.7096	Inscriptions—Africa			
CN1340-1345	411.70994	Inscriptions—Australia	CR5900-5925	929.769	Orders of knighthood and chivalry—Portugal
CR	929.6	Heraldry	CR6253.Y	929.8173	Young American Medal for Bravery
CR1	929.605	Heraldry—Periodicals			
CR2	929.606	Heraldry—Congresses			
CR9	929.6074	Heraldry—Exhibitions	CS	929.1	Genealogy
CR11	929.6025	Heraldry—Directories	CS1	929.105	Genealogy—Periodicals
CR13	929.603	Heraldry—Dictionaries	CS2	929.106	Genealogy—Congresses
CR14-16	929.601	Heraldry—Philosophy	CS5	929.1025	Genealogy—Directories
CR29-69	929.6	Heraldry, Ornamental	CS6	929.103	Genealogy—Dictionaries
CR41.C5	929.6	Collars in heraldry	CS42-2209	929.10720(4-9)	[By region or country]—Genealogy
CR41.F6	929.6	Flowers in heraldry			
CR55-57	929.6	Crests	CS42-71	929.1072073	United States—Genealogy
CR67-69	929.6	Badges	CS80-90	929.1072071	Canada—Genealogy
CR67-69	929.6	Devices (Heraldry)	CS100-110	929.1072072	Mexico—Genealogy
CR73-75	929.6	Mottoes	CS120-199	929.10720728	Central America—Genealogy
CR91-93	929.6	Shields			
CR101-115	929.92	Flags	CS200-261	929.10720729	West Indies—Genealogy
CR151-159	929.609	Heraldry—History	CS270-409	929.107208	South America—Genealogy
CR183-185	929.6	Heralds			
CR3499-4420	929.7	Titles of honor and nobility	CS410-1059	929.107204	Europe—Genealogy
CR3575	929.7	Precedence	CS410-479.5	929.1072041	Great Britain—Genealogy
CR4480-4485	929.9	Insignia	CS610-699	929.1072043	Germany—Genealogy
CR4480.C7	929.7	Crowns	CS780-839	929.10720492	Benelux countries—Genealogy
CR4485.07	929.7	Orbs			
CR4501-6305	929.71	Orders of knighthood and chivalry	CS840-869	929.1072047	Russia—Genealogy
			CS890-939	929.1072048	Scandinavia—Genealogy
CR4501-6305	929.81	Decorations of honor	CS1080-1549.5	929.107205	Asia—Genealogy
CR4553	929.6	Tournaments	CS1550-1779	929.107206	Africa—Genealogy
CR4571-4595	394.8	Dueling	CS2000-2009	929.1072094	Australia—Genealogy
CR4701-4731	255.791	Orders of knighthood and chivalry, Papal	CS2170-2179	929.1072093	New Zealand—Genealogy
			CS2191-2209	929.107209(5-6	Oceania—Genealogy
CR4759-4775	255.7914	Teutonic Knights	CS2300-3090	929.4	Names, Personal
CR4801-6305	929.7(2-9)	Orders of knighthood and chivalry—[By region or country]	CS2395-3090	929.409(4-9)	Names, Personal—[By region or country]
CR4801-4917	929.72	Orders of knighthood and chivalry—Great Britain			

LC	Dewey	Subject Heading	LC	Dewey	Subject Heading
CT	920	Biography	D95	359.00901	Naval history, Ancient
CT21-22	809.93592	Biography as a literary form	D101-110.5	940.2	History, Modern
			D107-110.5	920.00902	Biography—Middle Ages, 500-1500
CT25	920	Autobiography			
CT101	920	Autobiographies	D107	920.00902	Emperors
CT108	929.44	Nicknames	D111-203	940.1	Middle Ages—History
CT280-310	920.071	Canada—Biography	D115	920.00902	Biography—Middle Ages, 500-1500
CT329-448	920.0729	West Indies—Biography			
CT550-558	920.072	Mexico—Biography	D127	394.4	Coronations
CT570-638	920.0728	Central America—Biography	D128	355.009402	Military history—Medieval
			D131	321.3	Feudalism
CT640-758	920.08	South America—Biography	D134	307.760902	Cities and towns, Medieval
			D135-149	304.8	Migrations of nations
CT759-1495	920.04	Europe—Biography	D139	304.808939	Vandals
CT770-858	920.041	Great Britain—Biography	D145	304.8	Lombards
CT1050-1099.8	920.043	Germany—Biography	D151-173	940.18	Crusades
CT1240-1328	920.048	Scandinavia—Biography	D156-.5	940.18092	Crusades—Biography
CT1399-1458	920.0496	Balkan Peninsula—Biography	D156.58	940.18072	Crusades—Historiography
			D161-.5	940.182	Crusades—First, 1096-1099
CT1498-1919	920.05	Asia—Biography			
CT1870-1919	920.056	Middle East—Biography	D162-.5	940.182	Crusades—Second, 1147-1149
CT1920-2750	920.06	Africa—Biography			
CT2800-2808	920.0994	Australia—Biography	D163-.5	940.182	Crusades—Third, 1189-1192
CT2880-2888	920.0993	New Zealand—Biography			
CT2900-3090	920.099(5-6)	Oceania—Biography	D164-.5	940.184	Crusades—Fourth, 1202-1204
CT3200-3830	920.72	Women—Biography	D165	940.184	Crusades—Fifth, 1218-1221
CT9970-9971	904	Adventure and adventurers			
			D166	940.184	Crusades—Sixth, 1228-1229
D	900	History			
D1	905	History—Periodicals	D167	940.184	Crusades—Seventh, 1248-1250
D3	906	History—Congresses			
D9	903	History—Dictionaries	D168	940.184	Crusades—Eighth, 1270
D11-.5	900	Chronology, Historical	D171-173	940.19	Crusades—Later 13th, 14th, and 15th centuries
D13-15	907.2	Historiography			
D14-15	907.202	Historians	D175-195	956.944203	Jerusalem—History—Latin Kingdom, 1099-1244
D16-.18	901	History—Methodology			
D16	902.28	Historical models	D201.7-.8	909.1	Twelfth century
D16.16	901.9	Psychohistory	D204-725	909.08	History, Modern
D16.2-.5	907.1	History—Study and teaching	D205	909.0803	History, Modern—Dictionaries
D16.7-.9	901	History—Philosophy	D206	909.08072	Historiography
D16.9	901	Historicism	D214	355.00903	Military history—Modern
D17-24.5	909	World history	D217	327.112	Balance of power
D25-.4	355.009	Military history	D219-234	909.5	History, Modern—16th century
D25	355.4	Battles			
D25.5	355.0218	Guerrillas	D220-271	943.03	Counter-Reformation
D27	359.009	Naval history	D226.7	321.6	Royal houses
D27	359.4	Naval battles	D242-283.5	909.6	Seventeenth century
D31-34	909	World politics	D242-283.5	909.6	History, Modern—17th century
D51-95	930	History, Ancient			
D51	930.05	History, Ancient—Periodicals	D251-271	940.24	Thirty Years' War, 1618-1648
D54	930.03	History, Ancient—Dictionaries	D274.5-.6	940.252	Anglo-French War, 1666-1667
D55	920.00901	Biography—To 500	D277-278.5	940.252	Dutch War, 1672-1678
D56-.52	930.072	History, Ancient—Historiography	D279-280.5	940.2525	Grand Alliance, War of the, 1689-1697
D70	936.4	Celts—History			
D90.D	949.8004	Dacians			

LC	Dewey	Subject Heading	LC	Dewey	Subject Heading
D281-283.5	940.2526	Spanish Succession, War of, 1701-1714	D569	940.4(2-3)	World War, 1914-1918—Campaigns—Italy
D283.5	940.253	Hague, Treaty of, 1717	D569.C	940.432	Carzano, Battle of, 1917
D287.5	940.253	Quadruple Alliance, 1718	D580-589	940.454	World War, 1914-1918—Naval operations
D291-294	940.2532	Austrian Succession, War of, 1740-1748	D580	940.45	Freedom of the seas
D295	940.253	Neutrality, Armed	D582.D6	940.455	Dogger Bank, Battle of the, 1915
D301-309	940.27	Europe—History—1789-1815	D582.F2	940.454	Falkland Islands, Battle of the, 1914
D351-400	909.81	Nineteenth century	D589.U7	940.458	Durazzo, Battle of, 1918
D352.1	321.03094	Royal houses	D600-607	940.44	World War, 1914-1918—Aerial operations
D383	940.27	Quadruliance, 1815	D609	940.467	World War, 1914-1918—Registers of dead
D410-893	909.82	Twentieth century			
D410-893	909.82	History, Modern—20th century	D613-614	940.439	World War, 1914-1918—Peace
D412.7	321.03094	Royal houses	D625-626	940.405	World War, 1914-1918—Atrocities
D436	359.0094	Naval history, Modern—20th century	D625-626	364.13809041	War crimes
D443	940.288	Triple Entente, 1907	D627	940.472	World War, 1914-1918—Prisoners and prisons
D501-680	940.3	World War, 1914-1918	D627.R8	940.47247	World War, 1914-1918—Prisoners and prisons, Russian
D507	940.3092	World War, 1914-1918—Biography			
D507	940.3092	Generals	D642-651	940.439	World War, 1914-1918—Peace
D511	940.288	Triple Entente, 1907	D650.T4-651	940.31426	Mandates
D529-578	940.4(2-3)	World War, 1914-1918—Campaigns	D652-659	940.5(1-2)	Reconstruction (1914-1939)
D530-549.5	940.4(2-3)	World War, 1914-1918—Campaigns—Western front	D731-838	940.53	World War, 1939-1945
D531-538.5	940.4(2-3)	World War, 1914-1918—Campaigns—Germany	D736	940.53092	World War, 1939-1945—Biography
D541-542	940.4(2-3)	World War, 1914-1918—Campaigns—Belgium	D741	940.5311	World War, 1939-1945—Causes
D544-545	940.4(2-3)	World War, 1914-1918—Campaigns—France	D743.2	940.5300222	World War, 1939-1945—Pictorial works
D545.A5	940.431	Aisne, Battle of the, France, 1917	D745-.7	940.5400222	World War, 1939-1945—Caricatures and cartoons
D545.A5	940.434	Aisne, Battle of the, France, 1918	D748-754	940.532	World War, 1939-1945—Diplomatic history
D545.A6	940.424	Argonne, Battle of the, 1915	D753.2	940.531	Lend-lease operations (1941-1945)
D545.A63	940.434	Argonne, Battle of the, 1918	D755-769.87	940.542	World War, 1939-1945—Campaigns
D545.A7	940.431	Arras, Battle of, 1917	D756-763	940.5421	World War, 1939-1945—Campaigns—Western front
D545.B4	940.434	Belleau Wood, Battle of, 1918			
D545.C37	940.4(2-3)	Champagne, Battles of, 1914-1917	D756.3	940.5421	Atlantic Wall (France and Belgium)
D545.L3	940.421	Le Cateau, Battle of, 1914	D756.5.A7	940.542131	Ardennes, Battle of the, 1944-1945
D545.V25	940.421	Verdun, Battle of, 1914	D756.5.A78	940.5421	Arras, Battle of, 1940
D545.V3	940.4272	Verdun, Battle of, 1916	D756.5.C	940.542142	Calais, Battle of, 1940
D548-549.5	940.4(2-3)	World War, 1914-1918—Campaigns—France	D756.5.D5	940.54214	Dieppe Raid, 1942
D550-569.5	940.4(2-3)	World War, 1914-1918—Campaigns—Eastern front	D756.5.D8	940.5421428	Dunkerque (France), Battle of, 1940
D552.B7	940.422	Brzeziny, Battle of, 1914	D756.5.V3	940.54214	Verdun, Battle of, 1940
D557.L5	940.422	Limanova, Battle of, 1914	D757-.9	940.54213	World War, 1939-1945—Campaigns—Germany
D566-568.9	940.4(2-3)	World War, 1914-1918—Campaigns—Turkey			
D568.7	940.433	Gaza, Battles of, 1917			

LC	Dewey	Subject Heading	LC	Dewey	Subject Heading
D757.9	940.54213155	Berlin, Battle of, 1945	D772.G7	940.5428	Rio de la Plata, Battle of the, 1939
D759-760.8	940.54211	World War, 1939-1945—Campaigns—Great Britain	D774.B57	940.5426	Bismarck Sea, Battle of the, 1943
D761-762	940.54214	World War, 1939-1945—Campaigns—France	D774.C	940.5426	Coral Sea, Battle of the, 1942
D763.B42.A	940.542193222	Antwerp, Battle of, 1944	D774.J	940.5426	Java Sea, Battle of the, 1942
D763.N4	940.54219218	Arnhem, Battle of, 1944			
D764-766.7	940.5425	World War, 1939-1945—Campaigns—Eastern front	D774.M5	940.54265933	Midway, Battle of, 1942
			D780-784	940.5451	World War, 1939-1945—Naval operations—Submarine
D764.3	940.54421772	Odessa (Ukraine), Battle of, 1941			
D764.3	940.54217	Commander Islands (Russia), Battle of, 1943	D785-792	940.544	World War, 1939-1945—Aerial operations
D764.3.B73	940.542177	Brody (Ukraine), Battle of, 1944	D793	940.541	World War, 1939-1945—Tank warfare
D764.3.M	940.5421731	Moscow, Battle of, 1941-1942	D797	940.5467	World War, 1939-1945—Casualties
D764.3.S7	940.5421721	Stalingrad, Battle of, 1942-1943	D797	940.548	World War, 1939-1945—Casualties
D765-.2	940.542138	World War, 1939-1945—Campaigns—Poland	D797	940.5467	World War, 1939-1945—Registers of dead
D765.2.W3	940.5421384	Warsaw, Battle of, 1945	D802	940.5336	World War, 1939-1945—Underground movements
D766.3-.32	940.5421495	World War, 1939-1945—Campaigns—Greece	D802.A2	940.5336	World War, 1939-1945—Occupied territories
D766.6-.62	940.5421497	World War, 1939-1945—Campaigns—Yugoslavia	D802.F8	940.53440922	World War, 1939-1945—Underground movements—France—Biography
D766.82	940.5423	World War, 1939-1945—Campaigns—Africa, North			
D766.9	940.5423	El Alamein, Battle of, Egypt, 1942	D802.Y8	949.7022	Yugoslavia—History—Axis occupation, 1941-1945
D767-.99	940.5426	World War, 1939-1945—Campaigns—Pacific	D803-804.35	940.5405	World War, 1939-1945—Atrocities
D767.2-.25	940.54252	World War, 1939-1945—Campaigns—Japan	D804.S65	940.5405	Katyn Forest Massacre, 1940
D767.4	940.5425991	Bataan, Battle of, Philippines, 1942	D804.3	940.5318092	Holocaust, Jewish (1939-1945)—Personal narratives
D767.6	940.5425	World War, 1939-1945—Campaigns—Burma			
D767.7	940.542598	Biak Island (Indonesia), Battle of, 1944	D804.7.D43	940.547	Death marches
			D805	940.5472	World War, 1939-1945—Prisoners and prisons
D767.917	940.5426	Tarawa, Battle of, 1943	D805.G3	940.531853	Berga (Germany: Concentration Camp)
D767.92	940.5428	Pearl Harbor (Hawaii), Attack on, 1941			
D767.99.I9	940.5426	Iwo Jima, Battle of, 1945	D805.G3	940.53185336	Dachau (Germany: Concentration camp)
D767.99.O45	940.5425229	World War, 1939-1945—Campaigns—Japan—Okinawa Island	D805.G3	940.531853	Flossenburg (Germany: Concentration camp)
			D805.G3	940.531853515	Neuengamme (Hamburg, Germany: Concentration camp)
D767.99.W3	940.542665	Wake Island, Battle of, 1941			
D769.346	940.541273	United States. Army—Airborne troops	D805.G3	940.53185322 41	Buchenwald (Germany: Concentration camp)
D769.347	940.541273	United States. Army—Parachute troops	D805.G3	940.53185359 54	Bergen-Belsen (Germany: Concentration camp)
D770-784	940.545	World War, 1939-1945—Naval operations	D805.J3	940.547252092	Prisoners of war—Japan—Diaries
D770-784	940.5452	World War, 1939-1945—Blockades	D805.J3	940.547252	World War, 1939-1945—Prisoners and prisons, Japanese
D772.B	940.54214	Bordeaux Raid, 1942			

LC	Dewey	Subject Heading	LC	Dewey	Subject Heading
D805.P5	940.5317599	O'Donnell Camp (Philippines: Concentration camp)	DA28-.9	920.041	Great Britain—Biography
			DA28-.9	920.0361	Great Britain—Biography
			DA49-69.3	355.00941	Great Britain—History, Military
D805.P7	940.5318538	Auschwitz (Poland: Concentration camp)	DA70-89.1	359.00941	Great Britain—History, Naval
D806-807	940.5475	World War, 1939-1945—Medical care	DA86.22.D7	941.055	Lisbon Expedition, 1589
			DA87.5 1794	941.073	First of June, 1794, Battle of
D808-809	940.5308691	World War, 1939-1945—Refugees	DA87.7 1797	941.073	Spithead Mutiny, 1797
D808-809	940.5477	World War, 1939-1945—Civilian relief	DA88.5 1805	941.073	Trafalgar, Battle of, 1805
			DA89.5	358.400942	England. Royal Air force
D810.J4	940.5318	World War, 1939-1945—Jews	DA110-115	936.1	Great Britain—Civilization
			DA110-115	941	Great Britain—Civilization
D810.P6-.P7	940.5488	World War, 1939-1945—Propaganda	DA120-125	936.1004	Ethnology—Great Britain
			DA120-125	941.004	Ethnology—Great Britain
D810.S7	940.548641	World War, 1939-1945—Secret service—Great Britain	DA134-162	936.2	Great Britain—History—To 1066
D811-.5	940.548(1-2)	World War, 1939-1945—Personal narratives	DA134-162	941.01	Great Britain—History—To 1066
D812	940.5312	World War, 1939-1945—Armistice	DA140-143	941.089916	Celts
			DA150-162	941.017	Saxons
D818-819	940.531422	World War, 1939-1945—Reparations	DA150-162	941.0892	Anglo-Saxons
			DA150-162	942.017	Anglo-Saxons
D824-829	940.53144	Reconstruction (1939-1951)	DA170-260	941.0(2-46)	Great Britain—History—To 1485
D839-850	909.08	History, Modern—1945-	DA196	941.021	Hastings, Battle of, 1066
D839	909.8(24-3)05	History, Modern—1945-—Periodicals	DA300-591	941.0(5-8)	Great Britain—History—Modern period, 1485-
D847-.2	940.54217	Communist countries	DA310-360	941.05	Great Britain—History—Tudors, 1485-1603
D880-888	909.09724	Developing countries—History	DA331-339	941.052	Great Britain—History—History—Henry VIII, 1509-1547
D890-893	909.09811	Eastern Hemisphere—History			
D900-1075	940	Europe—History	DA350-360	941.055	Great Britain—History—Elizabeth, 1558-1603
D901-980	914	Europe—Description and travel	DA360	942.055	Armada, 1588
			DA370-419.5	941.06	Great Britain—History—Early Stuarts, 1603-1649
D1050-1075	940.5(5-6)	Europe—History—1945-	DA392-.1	941.061	Gunpowder Plot, 1605
D1050	940.(55-56)005	Europe—History—1945-—Periodicals	DA410-429	941.062	Great Britain—History—Civil War, 1642-1649
D1056-.2	940.55004	Ethnology—Europe	DA420-429	941.063	Fifth Monarchy Men
D1058-1065	320.94090(44-511)	Europe—Politics and government—1945-	DA430-463	941.06(6-9)	Great Britain—History—1660-1714
D1060	321.04094	European federation	DA498-499	941.072	Anglo-Spanish War, 1718-1748
D1070-1075	920.00904	Biography—20th century			
D2009	320.940948	Europe—Politics and government—1989-	DA499	941.071	Great Britain—History—George I, 1714-1727
D2009	327.4	Europe—Foreign relations—1989-	DA500	941.072	Great Britain—History—George II, 1727-1760
			DA505-522	941.073	Great Britain—History—George III, 1760-1820
DA	941	Great Britain—History	DA505-512	941.073	Anglo-Spanish War, 1762-1763
DA10-18.2	909.0971241	Commonwealth countries—History			
DA20-690	936.2	England	DA535	941.073	Luddites
DA20-690	942	England	DA537-538	941.074	Great Britain—History—George IV, 1820-1830
DA20	936.2005	England—Periodicals			
DA20	942.005	England—Periodicals	DA539-542	941.075	Great Britain—History—William IV, 1830-1837
DA28-690	936.1	Great Britain—History			
DA28-690	941	Great Britain—History			

33

LC	Dewey	Subject Heading	LC	Dewey	Subject Heading
DA550-565	941.081	Great Britain—History—Victoria, 1837-1901	DAW	943	Europe, Central
DA566-592	941.082	Great Britain—History—20th century	DAW1001	943.0005	Europe, Central—Periodicals
DA600-632	913.6204	England—Description and travel	DAW1004	943.0006	Europe, Central—Congresses
DA600-632	914.204	England—Description and travel	DAW1014-1015	914.304	Europe, Central—Description and travel
DA640	914.1003	Great Britain—Gazetteers	DAW1024	943	Europe, Central—Civilization
DA675-689	942.1	London (England)—History			
DA700-745	942.9	Wales	DAW1026-1028	943.004	Ethnology—Europe, Central
DA700	942.9005	Wales—Periodicals			
DA710	920.0429	Wales—Biography	DAW1031-1051	943	Europe, Central—History
DA711.5	942.9	Wales—Civilization			
DA714-722.1	942.9	Wales—History	DB	943.(6, 7, 9)	Austria, Czechoslovakia, Hungary
DA725-731.2	914.2904	Wales—Description and travel	DB1-879	936.3	Austria
DA750-890	936.1	Scotland	DB1-879	943.6	Austria
DA750-890	941.1	Scotland	DB1	936.3005	Austria—Periodicals
DA750	936.1005	Scotland—Periodicals	DB1	943.6005	Austria—Periodicals
DA750	941.1005	Scotland—Periodicals	DB1	936.3005	Austria—Periodicals
DA777-778.9	941.101	Scotland—History—To 1057	DB1	943.6005	Austria—Periodicals
DA779-790	941.10(2-5)	Scotland—History—1057-1603	DB14	913.63003	Austria—Gazetteers
			DB14	914.36003	Austria—Gazetteers
DA784.6	941.104	Flodden, Battle of, 1513	DB21-27.5	913.6304	Austria—Description and travel
DA803.8	941.1063	Scotland—History—1649-1660	DB21-27.5	914.3604	Austria—Description and travel
DA809-814.5	941.10(69-73)	Scotland—History—18th century	DB30	936.3	Austria—Civilization
			DB30	943.6	Austria—Civilization
DA813-814	941.10(69-72)	Jacobites	DB33-34.5	936.3004	Ethnology—Austria
DA815-818	941.1081	Scotland—History—19th century	DB33-34.5	943.6004	Ethnology—Austria
			DB36-.7	920.0363	Austria—Biography
DA821-826	941.1082	Scotland—History—20th century	DB36-.7	920.0436	Austria—Biography
			DB36.8-.9	936.30072	Austria—Historiography
DA850-878	914.1104	Scotland—Description and travel	DB36.8-.9	943.60072	Austria—Historiography
			DB42-44	355.09436	Austria—History, Military
DA900-995	936.1	Ireland—History	DB45	359.09436	Austria—History, Naval
DA900-995	941.5	Ireland—History	DB46-99.2	936.3	Austria—History
DA900	936.1005	Ireland—Periodicals	DB46-99.2	943.602	Austria—History
DA900	941.5005	Ireland—Periodicals	DB51-57	936.3	Austria—History—To 1273
DA930-932.6	936.1	Ireland—History—To 1172	DB51-57	943.602	Austria—History—To 1273
DA930-932.6	941.50(1-2)	Ireland—History—To 1172	DB51-57	943.6023	Austria—History—To 1273
DA933-937.5	941.50(3-5)	Ireland—History—1172-1603	BD57-59	943.60(25-3)	Austria—History—1273-1519
DA940-946	941.506	Ireland—History—17th century	DB65.2-77	943.60(25-31)	Austria—History—1519-1740
DA947-949.5	941.507	Ireland—History—18th century	DB72	940.2532	Austrian Succession, War of, 1740-1748
DA949.7-958	941.5081	Ireland—History—19th century	DB83	940.284	Austria—History—Revolution, 1848-1849
DA954	941.7081	Fenians	DB96-99.2	943.6051	Austria—History—1918-1938
DA959-965	941.5082	Ireland—History—20th century	DB99	943.6052	Austria—History—1938-1945
DA969-988	913.6104	Ireland—Description and travel			
DA969-988	914.1504	Ireland—Description and travel	DB99.2	943.6053	Austria—History—1955-

LC	Dewey	Subject Heading	LC	Dewey	Subject Heading
DB841-860	943.613	Vienna (Austria)	DB2003	943.7006	Czechoslovakia—Congresses
DB881-898	936.3	Liechtenstein			
DB881-898	943.648	Liechtenstein	DB2007	914.37003	Czechoslovakia—Gazetteers
DB881	936.3005	Liechtenstein—Periodicals			
DB881	943.648005	Liechtenstein—Periodicals	DB2009	943.70025	Czechoslovakia—Directories
DB888	913.6304	Liechtenstein—Description and travel	DB2018-2022	914.37(04)	Czechoslovakia—Description and travel
DB888	914.364804	Liechtenstein—Description and travel	DB2035	943.7	Czechoslovakia—Civilization
DB891-894	936.3	Liechtenstein—History	DB2040-2043	943.7004	Ethnology—Czechoslovakia
DB891-894	943.648	Liechtenstein—History			
DB901-999	939.8	Hungary	DB2044-2232	943.7	Czechoslovakia—History
DB901-999	943.9	Hungary	DB2080-2133	943.71023	Bohemia (Czech Republic)—History—To 1526
DB901	939.8005	Hungary—Periodicals			
DB901	943.9005	Hungary—Periodicals			
DB904	913.98003	Hungary—Gazetteers	DB2135-2151	943.710232	Bohemia (Czech Republic)—History—1526-1618
DB904	914.39003	Hungary—Gazetteers			
DB906.9-917.3	913.9804	Hungary—Description and travel			
			DB2155-2162	943.7102	Bohemia (Czech Republic)—History—1618-1848
DB906.9-917.3	914.3904	Hungary—Description and travel			
			DB2165-2182	943.71024	Bohemia (Czech Republic)—History—1848-1918
DB919-.2	939.8004	Ethnology—Hungary			
DB919-.2	943.9004	Ethnology—Hungary			
DB919	943.900494511	Magyars	DB2185-2232	943.7	Czechoslovakia—History
DB920.5	939.8	Hungary—Civilization	DB2195-2202	943.7032	Czechoslovakia—History—1918-1939
DB920.5	943.9	Hungary—Civilization			
DB922	920.0398	Hungary—Biography	DB2205-2211	943.7033	Czechoslovakia—History—1938-1945
DB922	920.0439	Hungary—Biography			
DB927-928.9	939.8	Hungary—History—To 896	DB2215-2232	943.704	Czechoslovakia—History—1945-1992
DB927-928.9	943.901	Hungary—History—To 896	DB2222	943.7042	Czechoslovakia—History—Coup d'etat, 1948
DB929-.9	943.902	Hungary—History—896-1301	DB2225-2232	943.7043	Czechoslovakia—History—1968-1989
DB930.2	943.903	Hungary—History—Charles Robert, 1308-1342	DB2232	943.7042	Czechoslovakia—History—Intervention, 1968
DB930.3	943.903	Hungary—History—Louis I, 1342-1382	DB2300-2421	943.72	Moravia (Czech Republic)
DB930.4	943.903	Hungary—History—Sigismund, 1387-1437	DB2335	943.72	Moravia (Czech Republic)—Civilization
DB931.94-932.4	943.9041	Hungary—History—Turkish occupation, 1529-1699	DB2340-2342	943.72004	Moravia (Czech Republic)—Ethnography
DB932.3-934	943.9043	Hungary—History—1699-1848	DB2345-2421	943.72	Moravia (Czech Republic)—History
DB940-953	943.9042	Hungary—History—Francis Joseph, 1848-1916	DB2385-2391	943.72021	Moravia (Czech Republic)—History—To 906
DB947-957	943.90(43-54)	Hungary—History—20th century	DB2600-2650	943.712	Prague (Czech Republic)
DB955	943.905(1-2)	Hungary—History—1918-1945	DB2700-3150	943.73	Slovakia
			DB2707	914.373003	Slovakia—Gazetteers
DB956-957	943.905(3-4)	Hungary—History—1945-	DB2718-2722	914.37304	Slovakia—Description and travel
DB957	943.9052	Hungary—History—Revolution, 1956			
			DB2735	943.73	Slovakia—Civilization
DB981-999	943.912	Budapest (Hungary)	DB2740-2743	943.73004	Ethnology—Slovakia
DB2000-3150	943.7	Czechoslovakia	DB2744-3000	943.73	Slovakia—History
DB2000	943.7005	Czechoslovakia—Periodicals	DB2795-2801	943.7302(34-4)	Slovakia—History—1800-1918
			DB2795-2801	943.73023	Slovakia—History—1526-1800

LC	Dewey	Subject Heading	LC	Dewey	Subject Heading
DB2795-2791	943.7302	Slovakia—History—To 1526	DC116-118	944.0(29-3)	France—History—War of the Huguenots, 1562-1598
DB2805-2841	943.730(3-5)	Slovakia—History—1918-1993	DC116-118	944.029	France—History—Charles IX, 1560-1574
DB2822	943.73033	Slovakia—History—Uprising, 1944	DC118	944.029	Saint Bartholomew's Day, Massacre of, France, 1572
DB2842	943.73042	Slovakia—History—Intervention, 1968	DC119-120	944.029	France—History—Henry III, 1574-1589
DC	944	France	DC120.8-138	944.03	France—History—Bourbons, 1589-1789
DC1	936.4005	France—Periodicals	DC122-.9	944.031	France—History—Henry IV, 1589-1610
DC1	944.005	France—Periodicals			
DC14	913.64003	France—Gazetteers	DC123-.9	944.032	France—History—Louis XIII, 1610-1643
DC14	914.4003	France—Gazetteers			
DC15	944.0025	France—Directories	DC124.45	944.033	Dunes, Battle of the, 1658
DC21-29.3	913.6404	France—Description and travel	DC124.45	944.03(2-3)	Franco-Spanish War, 1635-1659
DC21-29.3	914.404	France—Description and travel	DC124.5-130	944.033	France—History—Louis XIV, 1643-1715
DC29	914.4040904	France—Description and travel—1945-1974	DC133-135	944.034	France—History—Louis XV, 1715-1774
DC33-.9	936.4	France—Civilization	DC136-137.5	944.035	France—History—Louis XVI, 1774-1793
DC33-.9	944	France—Civilization			
DC34-.5	936.4004	Ethnology—France	DC137.15	944.035	Diamond Necklace Affair, France, 1785
DC34-.5	944.004	Ethnology—France			
DC35-423	936.4	France—History	DC139-190.8	944.04(1-2)	France—History—Revolution, 1789-1799
DC35-423	944	France—History			
DC36-.8	920.0364	France—Biography	DC167	394.2635	Bastille Day
DC36-.8	920.044	France—Biography	DC191.2-249	944.0(46-5)	France—History—Consulate and First Empire, 1799-1815
DC44-47	355.30944	France—History, Military			
DC49-53	359.30944	France—History, Naval			
DC60-81.5	944.01	France—History—To 987			
DC62-63	936.4	Gaul—History	DC222.F6	940.27	Fleurus, Battle of, 1794
DC62	936.402	Gergovie, Battle of, 52 B.C.	DC226.N5	940.27	Nile, Battle of the, 1798
DC62	936.402	Gaul—History—Gallic Wars, 58-51 B.C.	DC227.5.D8	940.27	Durnstein, Battle of, 1805
			DC227.5.E6	940.27	Elchingen, Battle of, 1805
DC96-105	944.025	Hundred Years War, 1339-1453	DC231-233.5	940.27	Peninsular War, 1807-1814
DC97.5-101.7	944.02(4-6)	France—History—14th century	DC234.65	940.27	Graz (Austria), Battle of, 1809
DC101-.7	944.026	France—History—Charles VI, 1380-1422	DC236-238.5	940.27	Wars of Liberation, 1813-1814
DC101.5.A2	944.026	Agincourt, Battle of, 1415	DC236.7.D8	940.27	Dresden, Battle of, 1813
DC101.5.C33	944.026	France—History—Cabochien Uprising, 1413	DC241-244.7	940.27	Waterloo, Battle of, 1815
DC102-105.9	944.026	France—History—Charles VII, 1422-1461	DC256-260	944.05	France—History—Louis XVIII, 1814-1824
DC106-.9	944.027	France—History—Louis XI, 1461-1483	DC261-262	944.063	France—History—July Revolution, 1830
DC107-.2	944.027	France—History—Charles VIII, 1483-1498	DC265-269	944.063	France—History—Louis Philip, 1830-1848
DC108-109	944.027	France—History—Louis XII, 1498-1515	DC271.5-274.5	944.07	France—History—Second Republic, 1848-1852
DC113-.5	944.028	France—History—Francis I, 1515-1547	DC274-.5	944.07	France—History—Coup d'etat, 1851
DC114-.5	944.028	France—History—Henry II, 1547-1559	DC275-292	944.07	France—History—Second Empire, 1852-1870
DC115	944.028	France—History—Francis II, 1559-1560	DC281-326.5	944.0812	Franco-Prussian War, 1870-1871
			DC305.22	944.0812	Belfort, Battle of, 1871

LC	Dewey	Subject Heading	LC	Dewey	Subject Heading
DC309.E8	944.0812	Epinal (France), Battle of, 1870	DD145-155	943.024	Germany—History—Hohenstaufen, 1138-1254
DC342.8-396	944.081	France—History—Third Republic, 1870-1940	DD156-174.6	943.02(6-9)	Germany—History—1273-1517
DC385	944.0814	France—History—German occupation, 1914-1918	DD176-189	943.03	Counter-Reformation
DC397	944.0816	France—History—German occupation, 1940-1945	DD188-.5	943.041	Germany—History—1618-1648
DC398-423	944.08(2-4)	France—History—1945-	DD190-.8	943.0(43-52)	Germany—History—1648-1740
DC421	944.083(6-7)	France—Politics and government—1969-1974	DD191-199	943.05	Germany—History—18th century
DC422	944.083(7-8)	France—Politics and government—1974-1981	DD197-231	943.0(57-84)	Germany—History—1789-1900
DC423	944.0838	France—Politics and government—1981-	DD206-214	943.07	Germany—History—1815-1866
DC608.1-.9	944.9	Riviera (France)	DD207-209	940.284	Germany—History—Revolution, 1848-1849
DC611.C8-.C839	944.945	Corsica (France)—History	DD214-216	943.081	Germany—History—1866-1871
DC611.P961	396.70944	Courts of love			
DC701-790	944.36	Paris (France)	DD217-231	943.08(3-4)	Germany—History—1871-1918
DC921-930	946.79	Andorra			
DC941-947	944.949	Monaco	DD223-.9	943.083	Germany—History—William I, 1871-1888
DD	943	Germany	DD224-226	943.084	Germany—History—Frederick III, 1888
DD14	913.63003	Germany—Gazetteers			
DD14	914.3003	Germany—Gazetteers	DD228-231	943.084	Germany—History—William II, 1888-1918
DD15.5	943.0025	Germany—Directories			
DD21.5-43	913.6304	Germany—Description and travel	DD232-257.4	943.08(4-79)	Germany—History—20th century
DD21.5-43	914.304	Germany—Description and travel	DD247.R56	943.086	Germany—History—Night of the Long Knives, 1934
DD60-68	936.3	Germany—Civilization			
DD60-68	943	Germany—Civilization	DD248	943.085	Germany—History—Revolution, 1918
DD73-78	943.004	Ethnology—Germany			
DD84-257.4	936.3	Germany—History	DD249	943.085	Germany—History—Kapp Putsch, 1920
DD84-257.4	943	Germany—History			
DD85-.8	920.0363	Germany—Biography	DD249	943.085	Germany—History—Beer Hall Putsch, 1923
DD85-.8	920.043	Germany—Biography			
DD86-.7	936.30072	Germany—Historiography	DD249	943.085	Germany—History—March Uprising, 1921
DD86-.7	943.0072	Germany—Historiography			
DD99-104	355.00943	Germany—History, Military	DD253-256.5	943.086	Germany—History—1933-1945
DD106	355.00943	Germany—History, Naval			
DD121-134.2	936.3	Germany—History—To 843	DD253-256.5	943.086	National socialism
			DD256.3-.4	943.086	Anti-Nazi movement
DD121-134.2	943.01	Germany—History—To 843	DD257.A2	943.085	Germany—History—Allied occupation, 1918-1930
DD125-198.7	943.02	Holy Roman Empire—History	DD257-.4	943.0881	Germany—History—Unification, 1990
DD126.5	943.0(13-25)	Donation of Pepin			
DD128	943.013	Merovingians	DD257-.4	943.087(4-5)	Germany—History—1945-1955
DD129-134.9	943.014	Carolingians			
DD134.3-135	943.021	Germany—History—843-918	DD257.4	943.088	Germany—History—1990-
DD136-140.7	943.022	Germany—History—Saxon House, 919-1024	DD258-262	943.087	Germany (West)
			DD280-289	943.1087	Germany (East)
DD141-144	943.023	Germany—History—Franconian House, 1024-1125	DD301-491	936.3	Prussia (Germany)
			DD301-491	943	Prussia (Germany)
			DD301	936.3005	Prussia (Germany)—Periodicals
			DD301	943.005	Prussia (Germany)—Periodicals

LC	Dewey	Subject Heading	LC	Dewey	Subject Heading
DD308	913.63003	Prussia (Germany)—Gazetteers	DE	938	Classical antiquities
DD308	914.3003	Prussia(Germany)—Gazetteers	DE1	937.005	Classical antiquities—Periodicals
DD314-320	913.6304	Prussia (Germany)—Description and travel	DE1	938.005	Classical antiquities—Periodicals
DD314-320	914.304	Prussia (Germany)—Description and travel	DE7	920.0937	Classical biography
DD331	936.3	Prussia (Germany)—Civilization	DE7	920.0938	Classical biography
DD331	943	Prussia (Germany)—Civilization	DE8-9	907.201822	Mediterranean Region—Historiography
DD341-454	936.3	Prussia (Germany)—History	DE15-.5	937.0071	Classical antiquities—Study and teaching
DD341-454	943	Prussia (Germany)—History	DE15-.5	938.0071	Classical antiquities—Study and teaching
DD343-.8	920.043	Prussia (Germany)—Biography	DE23-31	913.(7-8)	Classical geography
DD345	936.30072	Prussia (Germany)—Historiography	DE46-61	937	Civilization, Classical
DD345	943.0072	Prussia (Germany)—Historiography	DE46-61	938	Civilization, Classical
DD354	355.00943	Prussia (Germany)—History, Military	DF	949.5	Greece
DD358	359.00943	Prussia (Germany)—History, Naval	DF10	938.005	Greece—Periodicals
DD394-399.8	943.0(41-52)	Prussia (Germany)—History—1640-1740	DF10	949.5005	Greece—Periodicals
DD394.3	943.044	Fehrbellin, Battle of, 1675	DF27-30	913.804	Greece—Description and travel
DD399-.8	943.052	Prussia (Germany)—History—Frederick William I, 1713-1740	DF27-30	914.9504	Greece—Description and travel
DD401-413.2	943.053	Prussia (Germany)—History—Frederick II, 1740-1786	DF125	133.32480938	Oracles, Greek
			DF135	938.004	Ethnology—Greece
DD406-413.2	943.05(3-7)	Prussia (Germany)—History—1740-1789	DF135	949.5004	Ethnology—Greece
DD407.5	943.054	Dresden, Peace of, 1745	DF136.D6	938.01004	Dorians
DD409-412.8	940.2534	Seven Years' War, 1756-1763	DF218-238.9	938.0(1-8)	Greece—History—To 146 B.C.
DD414-416	943.06	Prussia (Germany)—History—Frederick William II, 1786-1797	DF221-.3	938.01	Greece—History—Dorian Invasions, ca. 1125-1025 B.C.
DD424	940.284	Prussia (Germany)—History—Revolution, 1848-1849	DF221.5	938.01	Greece—History—Geometric period, ca. 900-700 B.C.
DD424-.9	943.07	Prussia (Germany)—History—Frederick William IV, 1840-1861	DF222-224	938.01	Greece—History—Age of Tyrants, 7th-6th centuries, B.C.
DD425-446	943.0(76-83)	Prussia (Germany)—History—William I, 1861-1888	DF225-226	938.03	Greece—History—Persian Wars, 500-449 B.C.
DD436-440	943.076	Austro-Prussian War, 1866	DF225.3	938.03	Greece—History—Ionian Revolt, 499-494 B.C.
DD446-454	943.08(2-8)	Prussia (Germany)—History—1870-	DF225.4	938.03	Marathon, Battle of, 490 B.C.
DD801.S31-.S59	943.21	Saxony (Germany)—History	DF227-228	938.04	Greece—History—Athenian supremacy, 479-431 B.C.
DD851-900	943.155	Berlin (Germany)	DF229-230	938.05	Greece—History—Peloponnesian War, 431-404 B.C.
DE	937	Classical antiquities	DF231-232	938.0(5-6)	Greece—History—Spartan & Theban Supremacies, 404-362 B.C.
			DF231.32	938.05	Greece—History—Expedition of Cyrus, 401 B.C.
			DF232.5-234.9	938.07	Greece—History—Macedonian Expansion, 359-323 B.C.

LC	Dewey	Subject Heading	LC	Dewey	Subject Heading
DF233-238	938.0(1-8)	Macedonia—History—To 168 B.C.	DF565	949.5013	Byzantine Empire—History—Leo II, 474
DF233.2	938.0(1-8)	Corinthian League	DF566	949.5013	Byzantine Empire—History—Zeno, 474-491
DF233.4	938.07	Greece—History—Third Sacred War, 355-346 B.C.	DF572-.8	949.5013	Byzantine Empire—History—Justinian I, 527-565
DF234.5	938.07	Gaugamela, Battle of, 331 B.C.	DF573	949.5013	Byzantine Empire—History—Justine II, 565-578
DF235.3-.85	938.08	Greece—History—Macedonian Hegemony, 323-281 B.C.	DF573.2	949.5013	Byzantine Empire—History—Tiberius II, 578-582
DF236-238.9	938.08	Greece—History—281-146 B.C.	DF573.5	949.5013	Byzantine Empire—History—Maurice, 582-602
DF236.4	938.08	Greece—History—Galatian Invasion, 279-278 B.C.	DF574	949.5013	Byzantine Empire—History—Heraclius, 610-641
DF236.5	938.08	Greece—History—Chremonidean War, 267-262 B.C.	DF575.3	949.5013	Byzantine Empire—History—Constans II, 641-668
DF239-241	938.09	Greece—History—146 B.C.-323 A.D.			
DF239-241	949.501	Greece—History—146 B.C.-323 A.D.	DF582	949.502	Byzantine Empire—History—Leo III the Isaurian, 717-741
DF261.A2	938.3	Aetolia (Greece)			
DF261.D35	133.32480938	Delphian oracle	DF583	949.502	Byzantine Empire—History—Constantine V Copronymus, 741-775
DF261.E65	949.53	Epirus (Greece and Albania)			
DF261.05	938.8	Olympia (Greece : Ancient sanctuary)	DF586	949.502	Byzantine Empire—History—Irene, 797-802
DF501-649	949.50(13-3)	Byzantine Empire	DF589	949.502	Byzantine Empire—History—Basil I, 867-886
DF501	949.50(13-3)005	Byzantine Empire—Periodicals			
DF501.5	949.50(13-3)006	Byzantine Empire—Congresses	DF592	949.502	Byzantine Empire—History—Leo VI, 886-911
DF505-.7	949.50(13-3) + 0072	Byzantine Empire—Historiography	DF594	949.502	Byzantine Empire—History—Romanus II, 959-963
DF505.8-.82	949.50(13-3) + 0071	Byzantine Empire—Study and teaching			
DF506-.5	920.0495	Byzantine Empire—Biography	DF604-649	949.50(3-4)	Byzantine Empire—History—1081-1453
DF506-.5	949.50(13-3) + 0099	Emperors—Byzantine Empire	DF605	949.503	Byzantine Empire—Alexius I Comnenus, 1081-1118
DF518	914.95	Byzantine Empire—Geography	DF606	949.503	Byzantine Empire—History—John II Comnenus, 1118-1143
DF542-.4	949.50(13-3)004	Ethnology—Byzantine Empire			
DF543	355.009495	Byzantine Empire—History, Military	DF607	949.503	Byzantine Empire—History—Manuel I Comnenus, 1143-1180
DF544	359.009495	Byzantine Empire—History, Naval			
DF550-649	949.50(13-3)	Byzantine Empire—History	DF610-629	949.504	Latin Empire, 1204-1261
DF553.5-568	949.5013	Byzantine Empire—History—To 527	DF625	949.504	Byzantine Empire—History—Lascarid dynasty, 1208-1259
DF559	949.501	Adrianople, Battle of, 378			
DF561	949.5013	Byzantine Empire—History—Arcadius, 395-408	DF638	949.504	Byzantine Empire—History—John V Palaeologus, 1341-1391
DF562	949.5013	Byzantine Empire—History—Theodosius II, 408-450	DF701-854.32	949.50(4-9)	Greece
			DF701	949.5(4-9)005	Greece—Periodicals
			DF721-728	914.9504	Greece—Description and travel
DF564	949.5013	Byzantine Empire—History—Leo I, 457-474	DF745-747	949.50(4-9)004	Ethnology—Greece
			DF750-854.32	949.50(4-9)	Greece—History

LC	Dewey	Subject Heading	LC	Dewey	Subject Heading
DF765	355.309495	Greece—History, Military	DG247-249.4	937.04	Punic War, 2nd, 218-201 B.C.
DF801-.9	949.505	Greece—History—1453-1821	DG251	937.04	Macedonian War, 1st, 215-205 B.C.
DF802-854.32	949.50(6-76)	Greece—History—1821-	DG251	937.04	Macedonian War, 2nd, 200-196 B.C.
DF823-.7	949.5072	Greece—History—Otho I, 1832-1862	DG251.6	937.04	Macedonian War, 3rd, 171-168 B.C.
DF823.6	949.5072	Greece—History—Acarnanian Revolt, 1836	DG252.6	937.04	Punic War, 3rd, 149-146 B.C.
DF823.65	940.284	Greece—History—Revolution, 1848	DG252.9	937.05	Rome—History—Servile Wars, 135-71 B.C.
DF823.68	949.5072	Greece—History—Arta Revolt, 1854	DG263	937.05	Rome—History—First Triumvirate, 60-53 B.C.
DF825-832	949.5072	Greece—History—George I, 1863-1913	DG264	937.05	Gaul—History—Gallic Wars, 58-51 B.C.
DF831.5	949.5072	Greece—History—Coup d'etat, 1909	DG266	937.05	Durazzo, Battle of, 48 B.C.
DF837-841	949.5072	Greece—History—Constantine I, 1913-1917	DG268-269	937.05	Rome—History—Civil War, 43-31 B.C.
DF849.5-.58	949.5074	Greece—History—Civil War, 1944-1949	DG269	937.05	Actium, Battle of, 31 B.C.
DF850-852.5	949.5074	Greece—History—1950-1967	DG269.5-365	937.06	Rome—History—Empire, 30 B.C.-476 A.D.
DF853-.5	949.5075	Greece—History—1967-1974	DG270-365	937.0099	Emperors—Rome
DF853	949.5075	Greece—History—Coup d'etat, 1967 (April 21)	DG279	937.06	Rome—History—Augustus, 30 B.C.-14 A.D.
DF853	949.5075	Greece—History—Coup d'etat, 1967 (Dec. 13)	DG282.5	937.07	Rome—History—Tiberius, 14-37
DF853	949.5075	Greece—History—Coup d'etat, 1973 (May 22-23)	DG283	937.07	Rome—History—Caligula, 37-41
DF854-.32	949.5076	Greece—History—1974-	DG284	937.07	Rome—History—Claudius, 41-54
DF901.C78-.C89	949.59	Crete (Greece)—History	DG285	937.07	Rome—History—Nero, 54-68
DF901.I57-.I69	949.55	Ionian Islands (Greece)	DG286	937.07	Rome—History—Civil War, 68-69
DF915-936	949.512	Athens (Greece)	DG288	937.07	Rome—History—Revolt of Civilis, 69-70
DG	945	Italy	DG289	937.07	Rome—History—Vitellius, 69
DG11-365	937	Rome	DG290	937.07	Rome—History—Titus, 79-81
DG11	937.005	Rome—Periodicals	DG291	937.07	Rome—History—Domitian, 81-96
DG12.5	937.006	Rome—Congresses	DG292-299	937.07	Rome—History—Antonines, 96-192
DG27-31	913.7	Rome—Geography	DG294	937.07	Parthian War, 113-117
DG28-29	388.10937	Roads, Roman	DG294	937.07	Rome—History—Trajan, 98-117
DG59.D3	937.07	Dacian War, 1st, 101-102	DG295	937.07	Rome—History—Hadrian, 117-138
DG59.D3	937.07	Dacian War, 2nd, 105-106	DG300-304	937.07	Rome—History—Severan, 193-235
DG61-365	937	Rome—History	DG306	937.07	Rome—History—Maximimus, 235-238
DG75-142	937	Rome—Civilization	DG307.5	937.07	Rome—History—Gallienu, 260-268
DG124	291.2130937	Emperor worship, Rome	DG310-365	937.0(8-9)	Rome—History—Empire, 284-476
DG124	937.0099	Roman emperors			
DG203-204	920.037	Rome—Biography			
DG205	937.0072	Rome—Historiography			
DG206.5	937.0071	Rome—Study and teaching			
DG221-233.9	937.0(1-2)	Rome—History—To 510 B.C.			
DG235-269	937.0(2-5)	Rome—History—Republic, 510-30 B.C.			
DG243-244	937.04	Punic War, 1st, 264-241 B.C.			

LC	Dewey	Subject Heading	LC	Dewey	Subject Heading
DG314	937.08	Rome—History—Conference of Carnuntum, 308	DG554.5.E96	945.083	Expedition of the Thousand, Italy, 1860
DG315	937.08	Rome—History—Constantine I, the Great, 306-337	DG554.5	945.083	Italy—History—War of 1860-1861
DG315-317	937.08	Rome—History—Constantines, 306-363	DG555-569	945.0(84-91)	Italy—History—1870-1915
			DG558	945.084	Austro-Italian War, 1866
DG330-338	937.0(8-9)	Rome—History—Theodosians, 379-455	DG570-572	945.091	Italy—History—1914-1945
			DG571	945.091	Fascism
DG365	937.09	Rome—History—Romulus Augustulus, 475-476	DG571.75	945.091	Italy—History—March on Rome, 1922
DG401-583	937	Italy	DG572	945.091	Italy—History—Grand Council, 1943
DG401-583	945	Italy			
DG401	937.005	Italy—Periodicals	DG572	945.091	Italy—History—German occupation, 1943-1945
DG401	945.005	Italy—Periodicals			
DG413	945.0025	Italy—Directories	DG572	945.09(1-24)	Italy—History—Allied occupation, 1943-1947
DG415	913.7003	Italy—Gazetteers			
DG415	914.5003	Italy—Gazetteers	DG577.5-579	945.09(1-27)	Italy—History—1945-1976
DG421.5-430.2	913.704	Italy—Description and travel	DG581-583	945.092(7-9)	Italy—History—1976-
			DG600-609	945.(1-3)	Italy, Northern
DG421.5-430.2	914.504	Italy—Description and travel	DG631-645	945.182	Genoa (Italy)
			DG651-664.5	945.2	Lombardy (Italy)
DG441-453	937	Italy—Civilization	DG670-684.72	945.31	Venice (Italy)
DG441-453	945.006	Italy—Civilization	DG691-694	945.6	Italy, Central
DG455-457	937.004	Ethnology—Italy	DG731-759.3	945.5	Tuscany (Italy)
DG455-457	945.004	Ethnology—Italy	DG737.42	945.05	Medici, House of
DG461-583	937	Italy—History	DG791-800	945.6	Papal States
DG461-583	945	Italy—History	DG796-800	945.6	Papal States—History
DG463-.8	920.037	Italy—Biography	DG803-818	945.632	Rome (Italy)—History
DG463-.8	920.045	Italy—Biography	DG807.4	937.6	Catacombs
DG465-.7	937.0072	Italy—Historiography	DG807.4	945.632	Catacombs
DG465-.7	945.0072	Italy—Historiography	DG819-831	945.7	Italy, Southern
DG465.8	937.001	Italy—Study and teaching	DG845.8-851	945.73	Naples (Kingdom)—History
DG465.8	945.0071	Italy—Study and teaching			
DG480-484	355.00945	Italy—History, Military	DG861-875	945.8	Sicily (Italy)—History
DG503-514.7	945.01	Italy—History—476-774	DG975.R6	945.18	Riviera (Italy)
DG509	945.02	Italy—History—Gothic War, 535-555	DG987-999	945.85	Malta
			DG989.8-994.8	945.85	Malta—History
DG511-514.7	945.01	Lombards			
DG515-517	945.02	Italy—History—Carolingian rule, 774-887	DH	949.(2-3)	Benelux countries
			DH1	936.3005	Netherlands—Periodicals
DG515-519	945.02	Franks	DH1	949.2005	Netherlands—Periodicals
DG517.5-518	945.02	Italy— History—Period of the Italian Kings, 887-962	DH14	913.63003	Netherlands—Gazetteers
			DH14	914.92003	Netherlands—Gazetteers
DG520-529	945.0(3-4)	Italy—History—Germanic rule, 962-1268	DH31-40	913.6304	Netherlands—Description and travel
			DH31-40	914.9204	Netherlands—Description and travel
DG530-537.8	945.0(4-5)	Italy—History—1268-1492			
DG538-551.8	945.0(5-84)	Italy—History—1492-1870	DH71	936.3	Netherlands—Civilization
DG539-541.8	945.0(6-7)	Italy—History—16th century	DH71	949.2	Netherlands—Civilization
			DH91-92	936.3004	Ethnology—Netherlands
DG541	945.06	Fornovo, Battle of, 1495	DH91-92	949.2004	Ethnology—Netherlands
DG546-549	945.0(7-83)	Italy—History—1789-1815	DH95-207	936.3	Netherlands—History
DG550.5-551.8	945.0(7-8)	Italy—History—1789-1870	DH95-207	949.2	Netherlands—History
DG551	945.083	Italy—History—Uprising, 1831	DH103	920.0363	Netherlands—Biography
			DH103	920.0492	Netherlands—Biography
DG552-554.5	945.08(3-4)	Italy—History—1849-1870	DH113	355.009492	Netherlands—History, Military
DG553-.5	945.083	Austro-Sardinian War, 1848-1849	DH121	359.009492	Netherlands—History, Naval

LC	Dewey	Subject Heading	LC	Dewey	Subject Heading
DH141-162	936.3	Netherlands—History—To 1384	DH687	949.3042	Belgium—History—German occupation, 1940-1945
DH141-162	949.201	Netherlands—History—To 1384	DH690-692	949.304(3-4)	Belgium—History—Baudoiun I, 1951-
DH171-177	949.201	Netherlands—History—House of Burgundy, 1384-1477	DH802-809.95	949.332	Brussels (Belgium)
			DH901-925	949.35	Luxembourg
DH179-184	949.202	Netherlands—History—House of Habsburg, 1477-1556	DH901	949.35005	Luxembourg—Periodicals
			DH903	914.935003	Luxembourg—Gazetteers
			DH904	920.04935	Luxembourg—Biography
DH182	949.202	Netherlands—History—Charles V, 1506-1555	DH906-907	914.93504	Luxembourg—Description and travel
DH185-207	949.20(2-3)	Netherlands—History—Wars of Independence, 1556-1648	DH908-918.5	949.35	Luxembourg—History
			DH913	949.3502	Luxembourg (Luxembourg)—History—Siege, 1684
DH199.D4	949.203	Deventer, Surrender of, 1587			
DH201	949.203	Netherlands—History—Twelve Years' Truce, 1609-1621	DJ	949.2	Netherlands
			DJ1	936.3005	Netherlands—Periodicals
DH401-811	936.4	Belgium	DJ1	949.2005	Netherlands—Periodicals
DH401-811	949.3	Belgium	DJ14	913.63003	Netherlands—Gazetteers
DH401	936.4005	Belgium—Periodicals	DJ14	914.92003	Netherlands—Gazetteers
DH401	949.3005	Belgium—Periodicals	DJ33-41	913.6304	Netherlands—Description and travel
DH414	913.64003	Belgium—Gazetteers			
DH414	914.93003	Belgium—Gazetteers	DJ33-41	914.9204	Netherlands—Description and travel
DH431-435	913.6404	Belgium—Description and travel	DJ71	936.3	Netherlands—Civilization
DH431-435	914.9304	Belgium—Description and travel	DJ71	949.2	Netherlands—Civilization
			DJ91-92	936.3004	Ethnology—Netherlands
DH471	936.4	Belgium—Civilization	DJ91-92	949.2004	Ethnology—Netherlands
DH471	949.3	Belgium—Civilization	DJ95-292	936.3	Netherlands—History
DH491-492	936.4004	Ethnology—Belgium	DJ95-292	949.2	Netherlands—History
DH491-492	949.3004	Ethnology—Belgium	DJ103-106	920.0363	Netherlands—Biography
DH513-516	920.0364	Belgium—Biography	DJ103-106	920.0492	Netherlands—Biography
DH513-516	920.0493	Belgium—Biography	DJ124	355.009492	Netherlands—History, Military
DH540-545	355.009493	Belgium—History, Military			
DH551	359.009493	Belgium—History, Naval	DJ130-138	359.009492	Netherlands—History, Naval
DH571-584	936.4	Belgium—History—To 1555	DJ151-152	936.3	Netherlands—History—To 1384
DH571-584	949.30(1-2)	Belgium—History—To 1555	DJ151-152	949.201	Netherlands—History—To 1384
DH584	949.302	Belgium—History—Charles V, 1506-1555	DJ151-152	949.202	Netherlands—History—House of Habsburg, 1477-1556
DH585-606	949.302	Belgium—History—1555-1648	DJ151-152	949.202	Netherlands—History—Charles V, 1506-1555
DH607-619	949.302	Belgium—History—1648-1794	DJ170	949.203	Netherlands—History—Twelve Years' Truce, 1609-1621
DH616-618.5	949.302	Belgium—History—Revolution, 1789-1790			
DH620-631	949.302	Belgium—History—1794-1814	DJ180-209	949.204	Netherlands—History—1648-1795
DH650-665	949.303	Belgium—History—Revolution, 1830-1839	DJ180-182	949.204	Anglo-Dutch War, 1664-1667
DH671-676	949.303	Belgium—History—Leopold II, 1865-1909	DJ190-191	949.204	Dutch War, 1672-1678
DH681-685	949.3041	Belgium—History—Albert I, 1909-1934	DJ205-206	949.204	Anglo-Dutch War, 1780-1784
DH682	949.3041	Belgium—History—German occupation, 1914-1918	DJ211	949.205	Netherlands—History—Batavian Republic, 1795-1806

42

LC	Dewey	Subject Heading	LC	Dewey	Subject Heading
DJ241	949.205	Netherlands—History—1815-1830	DK1	947.005	Russia—Periodicals
			DK2.5	947.006	Russia—Congresses
DJ241-251	949.206	Netherlands—History—1830-1849	DK14	914.7003	Russia—Gazetteers
			DK19-29	914.7(04)	Russia—Description and travel
DJ251	949.206	Netherlands—History—William II, 1840-1849	DK32-.7	947	Russia—Civilization
DJ261	949.206	Netherlands—History—William III, 1849-1890	DK33-35	947.004	Ethnology—Russia (Federation)
DJ281-287	949.2071	Netherlands—History—Wilhelmina, 1898-1948	DK34.K13	947.52004	Kabardians
			DK34.K14	947.48	Kalmyks
DJ287	949.2071	Netherlands—History—German occupation 1940-1945	DK50-54	355.00947	Soviet Union—History, Military
DJ288-292	949.207(1-3)	Netherlands—History—1945-	DK55-59	359.00947	Russia—History, Naval
			DK65-290.3	947	Russia—History
DJ288-289	949.2072	Netherlands—History—Juliana, 1948-1980	DK70-104	947.0(1-42)	Russia—History—To 1533
DJ290-292	949.2073	Netherlands—History—Beatrix, 1980-	DK106-107	947.043	Russia—History—Ivan IV, 1533-1584
DJ401.F5-.F59	949.213	Frisians	DK111-112	947.045	Russia—History—Time of Troubles, 1598-1613
DJ411.A5-59	949.2352	Amsterdam (Netherlands)	DK112.8-126	947.04(6-9)	Russia—History—1613-1689
DJK	947	Europe, Eastern	DK112.8-264.8	947.0(47-83)	Russia—History—1613-1917
DJK1	947.0005	Europe, Eastern—Periodicals	DK116-122.5	947.048	Russia—History—Aleksei Mikhailovich, 1645-1676
DJK1.5	947.0006	Europe, Eastern—Congresses	DK118.5	947.048	Russia—History—Rebellion of Stenka Razin, 1667-1671
DJK6	914.70003	Europe, Eastern—Gazetteers	DK125	947.049	Russia—History—Sofia Alekseevna, 1682-1689
DJK11-18	914.7004	Europe, Eastern—Description and travel	DK128-148	947.05	Russia—History—Peter I, 1689-1725
DJK24	947	Europe, Eastern—Civilization	DK133	947.05	Russia—History—Streltsy Revolt, 1698
DJK26-28	947.0004	Ethnology—Europe, Eastern	DK168-183	947.063	Russia—History—Catherine II, 1762-1796
DJK31	920.047	Europe, Eastern—Biography	DK183	947.063	Russia—History—Rebellion of Pugachev, 1773-1775
DJK32-34	947.00072	Europe, Eastern—Historiography	DK188-264.8	947.0(72-83)	Russia—History—1801-1917
DJK35-36	947.00071	Europe, Eastern—Study and teaching	DK190-201	947.072	Russia—History—Alexander I, 1801-1825
DJK49	947.000904(1-4)	Europe, Eastern—History—1918-1945	DK209-215.97	947.073	Russia—History—Nicholas I, 1825-1855
DJK50	947.00090(44-5)	Europe, Eastern—History—1945-	DK212	947.073	Russia—History—December Uprising, 1825
DJK50	947.000904(4-8)	Europe, Eastern—History—1945-1989	DK214-215	947.0738	Crimean War, 1853-1856
DJK51	947.00090(48-5)	Europe, Eastern—History—1989-	DK219-223	947.081	Russia—History—Alexander II, 1855-1881
DJK61-66	947.7	Black Sea Coast	DK234-243	947.082	Russia—History—Alexander III, 1881-1894
DJK71-76	947.79	Carpathian Mountains	DK251-264.8	947.083	Russia—History—Nicholas II, 1894-1917
DJK76.2-.8	943.3	Danube River Valley	DK263-264.7	947.083	Russia—History—Revolution, 1905-1907
DJK77	939.8	Pannonia Region	DK265-272.7	947.084(1-2)	Soviet Union—History—1917-1936
DK	947	Russia, Soviet Union, Poland			
DK	943.8	Russia, Soviet Union, Poland			
DK1-290.3	947	Russia			

LC	Dewey	Subject Heading	LC	Dewey	Subject Heading
DK265-.95	947.0841	Soviet Union—History—Revolution, 1917-1921	DK921-929.5	958.6	Tajikistan
DK265.19	947.0841	Russia—History—February Revolution, 1917	DK931-939.5	958.5	Turkmenistan
			DK941-949.5	958.7	Uzbekistan
DK265.42.F8	947.0841	Black Sea Mutiny, 1919	DK4010-4800	943.8	Poland
DK265.8.R85	947.084	Russia (Federation)—History—Revolution, 1917-1921	DK4010	943.8005	Poland—Periodicals
			DK4018	943.8006	Poland—Congresses
			DK4030	914.38003	Poland—Gazetteers
DK266-.5	947.0841	Soviet Union—History—Allied intervention, 1918-1920	DK4047-4081	914.3804	Poland—Description and travel
			DK4110-4115	943.8	Poland—Civilization
DK266.A2	947.084005	Soviet Union—Periodicals	DK4120-4122	943.8004	Ethnology—Poland
DK266.A33	947.0840072	Soviet Union—Historiography	DK4130-4138.5	920.0438	Poland—Biography
			DK4139-.25	943.80072	Poland—Historiography
DK267-273	947.0842	Soviet Union—History—1925-1953	DK4186-4348	943.802(2-5)	Poland—History—To 1795
DK273	947.0842	Soviet Union—History—1939-1945	DK4186-4289	943.802(2-3)	Poland—History—To 1572
DK273	947.0842	Soviet Union—History—German occupation, 1941-1944	DK4210-.7	943.8022	Poland—History—To 960 (ca.)
			DK4211-4249.5	943.8022	Poland—History—Piast period, 960-1386
DK274-282	947.085	Soviet Union—History—1953-1985	DK4222	943.8022	Poland—History—Mieszko II, 1025-1034
DK285-290.3	947.0854	Soviet Union—History—1985-1991	DK4223	943.8022	Poland—History—Casimir I, 1040-1058
DK285-290.3	947.086	Soviet Union—History—Attempted coup, 1991	DK4227-4246.5	943.8022	Poland—History—1138-1305
DK502.3-.7	947.9	Baltic States	DK4245.7	943.8022	Poland—History—Mongol Invasion, 1241
DK502.7	947.9	Baltic States—History	DK4249.7-4289	943.8023	Poland—History—Jagellons, 1386-1572
DK503-.95	947.98	Estonia			
DK503.18	914.798003	Estonia—Gazetteers	DK4276	943.802(3-4)	Poland—History—16th century
DK503.75-.77	947.98	Estonia—History—1944-1991	DK4289.5-4328	943.802(4-5)	Poland—History—Elective monarchy, 1572-1763
DK503.8-.85	947.9808	Estonia—History—1991-			
DK504-.95	947.96	Latvia	DK4314.5	943.80(25-3)	Poland—History—18th century
DK504.18	914.796003	Latvia—Gazetteers			
DK504.37-.79	947.96	Latvia—History	DK4328.9-4348	943.8025	Poland—History—Parititon period, 1763-1796
DK505-.95	947.93	Lithuania			
DK505.18	914.793003	Lithuania—Gazetteers	DK4330-4348	943.8025	Poland—History—Stanislaus II Augustus, 1764-1795
DK507-.95	947.8	Belarus			
DK507.18	914.78003	Belarus—Gazetteers			
DK507.37-.78	947.8	Belarus—History	DK4338-4345	943.8025	Poland—History—Revolution of 1794
DK505.37-.79	947.93	Lithuania—History			
DK508-.95	947.7	Ukraine	DK4359-4363	943.8032	Poland—History—Revolution, 1830-1832
DK508.92-.939	947.77	Kiev (Ukraine)			
DK509.1-.95	947.(6-7)	Bessarabia (Moldova and Ukraine)	DK4363.2	943.8032	Poland—History—Partisan Campaign, 1833
DK510-651	947	Russia	DK4364	943.8032	Poland—History—Revolution, 1846
DK511.B3	947.0842	Baltic Entente, 1934-1940			
DK511.G44	947.02	Didgora Mountain (Georgia), Battle of, 1121	DK4366-4378	943.8033	Poland—History—Revolution, 1863-1864
DK588-609	947.31	Moscow (Russia)	DK4379.5-4395	943.8033	Poland—History—1864-1918
DK670-679.5	947.58	Georgia (Republic)			
DK680-689.5	947.56	Armenia (Republic)	DK4383-4389	943.8033	Poland—History—Revolution, 1905-1907
DK690-699.5	947.54	Azerbaijan			
DK751-781	957	Siberia (Russia)	DK4390-4395	943.8033	Poland—History—German occupation, 1914-1918
DK845-860	958	Asia, Central			
DK901-909.5	958.45	Kazakhstan	DK4394-4395	943.8033	Poland—History—Austrian occupation, 1915-1918
DK911-919.5	958.43	Kyrgyzstan			

LC	Dewey	Subject Heading	LC	Dewey	Subject Heading
DK4397-4420	943.804(4-53)	Poland—History—1918-1945	DL141-142	948.9004	Ethnology—Denmark
DK4404-4409	943.804	Poland—History—Wars of 1918-1921	DL162-173.8	948.9015	Denmark—History—To 1241
DK4409.4	943.804	Poland—History—Coup d'etat, 1926	DL174-183.9	948.90(1-2)	Denmark—History—1241-1397
DK4410-4415	943.8053	Poland—History—Occupation, 1939-1945	DL176	948.9015	Denmark—History—Waldemar IV, 1340-1375
DK4429-4442	943.805(4-7)	Poland—History—1945-	DL179-181.6	948.902	Denmark—History—1397-1448
DK4442	943.8057	Poland—History—1989-	DL179	948.03	Kalmar, Union of, 1397
DK4443	943.8056	Poland—History—1980-1989	DL182-192.3	948.90(2-3)	Denmark—History—1448-1660
DK4600.P77	255.7914	Teutonic Knights	DL185-192.8	948.903	Denmark—History—Frederick I, 1523-1533
DK4600.S44	943.85	Silesia, Lower (Poland and Germany)	DL187	948.903	Denmark— History—Christian III, 1534-1559
DK4600.S46	943.72	Silesia, Upper (Poland and Czech Republic) History	DL187	948.903	Denmark— History—The Count's War, 1534-1536
DK4600.S46	943.85	Silesia, Upper (Poland and Czech Republic) History	DL187	948.903	Denmark—History—Coup d'etat, 1536
DK4610-4645	943.84	Warsaw (Poland)	DL188-.8	948.903	Denmark—History—Frederick II, 1559-1588
DK4650-4685	943.82	Gdansk (Poland)	DL189-.5	948.903	Denmark—History—Christian IV, 1588-1648
DK4700-4735	943.86	Krakow (Poland)			
DL	948	Scandinavia	DL190	948.9701	Dano-Swedish War, 1643-1645
DL1	936.3005	Scandinavia—Periodicals	DL190	948.9701	Fehmarn, Battle of, 1644
DL1	948.005	Scandinavia—Periodicals	DL191.8	948.903	Denmark—History—Frederick III, 1648-1670
DL1.5	936.3006	Scandinavia—Congresses			
DL1.5	948.006	Scandinavia—Congresses	DL192	948.9701	Dano-Swedish Wars, 1657-1660
DL4	913.63003	Scandinavia—Gazetteers	DL192.3	948.903	Denmark—History—Coup d'etat, 1660
DL4	914.8003	Scandinavia—Gazetteers			
DL6.7-11.5	913.6304	Scandinavia—Description and travel	DL195-.8	948.903	Denmark—History—Christian V, 1670-1699
DL6.7-11.5	914.804	Scandinavia—Description and travel	DL196-.8	948.903	Denmark—History—Fredrick IV, 1699-1730
DL30-33	936.3	Scandinavia—Civilization	DL197-199	948.903	Denmark—History—18th century
DL30-33	948	Scandinavia—Civilization			
DL41-42	936.3004	Ethnology—Scandinavia	DL199-.8	948.903	Denmark—History—Coup d'etat, 1784
DL41-42	948.004	Ethnology—Scandinavia			
DL43-87	936.3	Scandinavia—History	DL201-249	948.904	Denmark—History—19th century
DL43-87	948	Scandinavia—History			
DL61-65	948.03	Scandinavia—History—15th century	DL205-208	948.904	Denmark—History—Frederick VI, 1808-1839
DL65	948.5014	Vikings	DL206	948.903	Denmark—History—War of 1807-1814
DL83-87	948.08	Scandinavia—History—20th century			
DL75-81	948.04	Scandinavia—History—The Count's War, 1534-1536	DL209-212	948.904	Denmark—History—Christian VIII, 1839-1848
			DL213-228	948.904	Denmark—History—Frederick VII, 1848-1863
DL101-291	936.3	Denmark—History			
DL101	948.9005	Denmark—Periodicals	DL217-241	948.904	Denmark—History—1849-1866
DL105	913.63003	Denmark—Gazetteers			
DL105	914.89003	Denmark—Gazetteers	DL234-249	948.904	Denmark—History—Christian IX, 1863-1906
DL115-120	913.6304	Denmark—Description and travel	DL248-263	948.90(4-6)	Denmark—History—1900-
DL115-120	914.8904	Denmark—Description and travel			
DL131-133	936.3	Denmark—Civilization	DL255-257	948.9051	Denmark—History—Christian X, 1912-1947
DL131-133	948.9	Denmark—Civilization			
DL141-142	936.3004	Ethnology—Denmark			

LC	Dewey	Subject Heading	LC	Dewey	Subject Heading
DL256.5-257	948.9051	Denmark—History—German occupation, 1940-1945	DL525	948.1041	Norway—History—Separation from Sweden, 1905
DL276	948.913	Copenhagen (Denmark)	DL530-532	948.1041	Norway—History—1905-1940
DL301-398	949.12	Iceland			
DL301	949.12005	Iceland—Periodicals	DL532	948.1041	Norway—History—German Occupation, 1940-1945
DL304	914.912003	Iceland—Gazetteers			
DL309-315	914.91204	Iceland—Description and travel	DL533	948.10(43-5)	Norway—History—1945-
			DL601-991	936.3	Sweden—History
DL331-334	949.12004	Ethnology—Iceland	DL601-991	948.5	Sweden—History
DL351-380	949.12	Iceland—History	DL601	936.3005	Sweden—Periodicals
DL357-360	949.1201	Iceland—History—To 1262	DL601	948.5005	Sweden—Periodicals
			DL605	913.63003	Sweden—Gazetteers
DL375	949.1205	Iceland—History—1918-1945	DL605	914.85003	Sweden—Gazetteers
			DL614.55-619.5	913.6304	Sweden—Description and travel
DL401-596	936.3	Norway—History			
DL401-596	948.1	Norway—History	DL614.55-619.5	914.8504	Sweden—Description and travel
DL401-403	948.1005	Norway—Periodicals			
DL401-403	936.3005	Norway—Periodicals	DL631-635	936.3	Sweden—Civilization
DL405	913.63003	Norway—Gazetteers	DL631-635	948.5	Sweden—Civilization
DL405	914.81003	Norway—Gazetteers	DL639-641	936.3004	Ethnology—Sweden
DL415-419.2	913.6304	Norway—Description and travel	DL639-641	948.5004	Ethnology—Sweden
			DL644	920.0363	Sweden—Biography
DL415-419.2	914.8104	Norway—Description and travel	DL644	920.0485	Sweden—Biography
			DL645	936.30072	Sweden—Historiography
DL431-433	936.3	Norway—Civilization	DL645	948.50072	Sweden—Historiography
DL431-433	948.1	Norway—Civilization	DL660-700.9	936.3	Sweden—History—To 1397
DL441-442	936.3004	Ethnology—Norway			
DL441-442	948.1004	Ethnology—Norway	DL660-700.9	948.501	Sweden—History—To 1397
DL444	920.0363	Norway—Biography			
DL444	920.0481	Norway—Biography	DL689	948.501	Sweden— History—Magnus II Ericksson, 1319-1363
DL445	936.30072	Norway—Historiography			
DL445	948.10072	Norway—Historiography			
DL460-478	936.3	Norway—History—To 1030	DL694	948.5018	Kalmar, Union of, 1397
			DL696-700.9	948.5018	Sweden—History—1397-1523
DL460-478	948.101	Norway—History—To 1030			
			DL701-879	948.503(2-4)	Sweden—History—1523-1718
DL480-502	948.101	Norway—History—1030-1397			
			DL703	948.5032	Sweden—History—Gustavus I Vasa, 1523-1560
DL485-502	948.10(1-2)	Norway—History—1397-1814			
DL485	948.03	Kalmar, Union of, 1397	DL703.8	948.5032	Sweden—History—Eric XIV, 1560-1568
DL490	948.102	Norway—History—Frederick III, 1648-1670			
			DL704.6-.7	948.503	Sweden—History—17th century
DL490	948.102	Norway—History—Hannibal's War, 1644-1645			
			DL704.8	948.5032	Sweden—History—Charles IX, 1604-1611
DL490	948.102	Norway—History—Scottish Expedition, 1612	DL705.A2-715	948.5034	Sweden—History—Gustavus II, Adolphus, 1611-1632
DL490	948.102	Norway—History—Christian IV, 1588-1648			
			DL710	948.5034	Kalmar War, 1611-1613
DL495-.8	948.102	Norway—History—Christian V, 1670-1699	DL725.7	948.5034	Sweden—History—Charles X Gustavus, 1654-1660
DL499	948.102	Norway—History—War of 1807-1814			
DL500-502	948.10(2-3)	Norway—History—Christian Frederick, 1814	DL727-729	948.5034	Sweden—History—Charles XI, 1660-1697
			DL730-743	948.5034	Sweden—History—Charles XII, 1697-1718
DL503-526	948.103	Norway—History—1814-1905			
			DL733-743	947.05	Northern War, 1700-1721

LC	Dewey	Subject Heading	LC	Dewey	Subject Heading
DL747-805	948.50(36-4)	Sweden—History—1718-1814	DP	946	Spain
			DP	946.9	Portugal
DL753	948.5036	Sweden—History—Ulrika Eleonora, 1718-1720	DP1-402	936.6	Spain
			DP1-402	946	Spain
DL755-759	948.5036	Sweden—History—Frederick I, 1720-1751	DP1	936.6005	Spain—Periodicals
			DP1	946.005	Spain—Periodicals
DL757	948.5036	Sweden—History—Insurrection, 1743	DP2	936.6006	Spain—Congresses
			DP2	946.006	Spain—Congresses
DL766-770	948.503(6-8)	Sweden—History—Gustavus III, 1771-1792	DP11	946.0025	Spain—Directories
			DP12	913.66003	Spain—Gazetteers
DL766	948.503(6-8)	Sweden—History—Revolution, 1772	DP12	914.6003	Spain—Gazetteers
DL807-859	948.50(3-4)	Sweden—History—1814-1905	DP27-43.2	913.6604	Spain—Description and travel
DL860-879	948.505	Sweden—History—20th century	DP27-43.2	914.604	Spain—Description and travel
DL867-870	948.505(1-3)	Sweden—History—Gustavus V, 1907-1950	DP48-.9	936.6	Spain—Civilization
			DP48-.9	946	Spain—Civilization
DL868	948.5051	Sweden—History—Farmers' Demonstration, 1914	DP52-53	936.6004	Ethnology—Spain
			DP52-53	946.004	Ethnology—Spain
			DP58	920.0366	Spain—Biography
DL872-876	948.505(3-4)	Sweden—History—Gustavus VI Adolphus, 1950-1973	DP58	920.046	Spain—Biography
			DP63-.83	936.60072	Spain—Historiography
			DP63-.83	946.0072	Spain—Historiography
DL877-879	948.50(54-6)	Sweden—History—Carl XVI Gustav, 1973-	DP76-78	355.00946	Spain—History, Military
			DP80-81	359.00946	Spain—History, Naval
DL976	948.73	Stockholm (Sweden)	DP91-96	936.6	Spain—History—To 711
DL1002-1180	948.97	Finland	DP91-96	946.01	Spain—History—To 711
DL1002	948.97005	Finland—Periodicals	DP94-95	936.603	Spain—History—Roman period, 218 B.C.-414 A.D.
DL1004	948.97006	Finland—Congresses			
DL1007	914.897003	Finland—Gazetteers	DP96	946.01	Spain—History—Gothic period, 414-711
DL1015-.4	914.89704	Finland—Description and travel	DP97.3-160.8	946.0(2-3)	Spain—History—711-1516
DL1017	948.97	Finland—Civilization	DP115-118	946.82	Granada (Kingdom)—History
DL1018-1020	948.97004	Ethnology—Finland			
DL1024	920.04897	Finland—Biography	DP161.5-166	946.03	Spain—History—Ferdinand and Isabella, 1479-1516
DL1025	948.970072	Finland—Historiography			
DL1050-1052.9	948.9701	Finland—History—To 1523	DP170-189	946.04	Spain—History—House of Austria, 1516-1700
DL1055-1141.6	948.9701	Finland—History—1523-1611	DP172-175	946.042	Spain—History—Charles I, 1516-1556
DL1058-1063	948.9701	Finland—History—Gustavus II Adolphus, 1611-1632	DP176-181	946.043	Spain—History—Philip II, 1556-1598
DL1060-.5	948.9701	Finland—History—Charles X Gustavus, 1654-1660	DP182-183.9	946.051	Spain—History—Philip III, 1598-1621
DL1063-.9	948.9701	Finland—History—18th century	DP184-185.9	946.052	Spain—History—Philip IV, 1621-1665
DL1065-.8	948.9702	Finland—History—1809-1917	DP186-189	946.053	Spain—History—Charles II, 1665-1700
DL1066-1141.6	948.970(2-3)	Finland—History—20th century	DP192-200.8	946.054	Spain—History—Bourbon, 1700-
DL1070-1075	948.97031	Finland—History—Revolution, 1917-1918	DP194-200.8	946.054	Spain—History—18th century
DL1084	948.97031	Finland—History—1918-1939	DP194	946.055	Anglo-Spanish War, 1718-1748
DL1090-1105	948.9703(2-4)	Finland—History—1939-	DP195	946.055	Spain—History—Louis I, 1724
DL1095-1105	948.97032	Russo-Finnish War, 1939-1940	DP196	940.2526	Spanish Succession, War of, 1701-1714
DL1175-.95	948.971	Helsinki			

LC	Dewey	Subject Heading	LC	Dewey	Subject Heading
DP198-.7	946.056	Spain—History—Ferdinand VI, 1746-1759	DP532-.7	936.6	Portugal—Civilization
			DP532-.7	946.9	Portugal—Civilization
DP199-.9	946.057	Spain—History—Charles III, 1759-1788	DP533-534.5	936.6004	Ethnology—Portugal
			DP533-534.5	946.9004	Ethnology—Portugal
DP199	946.057	Anglo-Spanish War, 1762-1763	DP536	920.0366	Portugal—Biography
			DP536	920.0469	Portugal—Biography
DP200-.8	946.058	Spain—History—Charles IV, 1788-1808	DP536.8-.96	936.60072	Portugal—Historiography
			DP536.8-.96	946.90072	Portugal—Historiography
DP201-232.6	946.0(58-7)	Spain—History—19th century	DP547	355.009469	Portugal—History, Military
			DP550-551	359.009469	Portugal—History, Naval
DP204-208	940.27	Spain—History—Napoleonic Conquest, 1808-1813	DP558-618	936.6	Portugal—History—To 1385
			DP558-618	946.90(1-2)	Portugal—History—To 1385
DP212-220	946.072	Spain—History—Bourbon Restoration, 1814-1868	DP570	946.90(1-2)	Portugal—History—Alfonso Henriques, 1139-1185
DP214-215.9	946.072	Spain—History—Ferdinand VII, 1813-1833	DP571	946.902	Portugal—History—Sancho I, 1185-1211
DP215	946.072	Spain—History—Revolution, 1820-1823	DP572	946.902	Portugal—History—Alfonso II, 1211-1223
DP216-220	946.072	Spain—History—Isabella II, 1833-1868	DP573	946.902	Portugal—History—Sancho II, 1223-1248
DP217	946.072	Spain—History—Revolution, 1854	DP574	946.902	Portugal—History—Alfonso III, 1248-1279
DP219-.2	946.072	Spain—History—Carlist War, 1833-1840	DP575-.3	946.902	Portugal—History—Denis, 1279-1325
DP222-232.6	946.073	Spain—History—Revolutionary period, 1868-1875	DP576	946.902	Portugal—History—Alfonso IV, 1325-1357
DP228-231.5	946.07(3-4)	Spain—History—Carlist War, 1873-1876	DP577	946.902	Portugal—History—Pedro I, 1357-1367
DP230-231.5	946.073	Spain—History—Republic, 1873-1875	DP578	946.902	Portugal—History—Fernando, 1367-1383
DP232-.6	946.074	Spain—History—Alfonso XII, 1875-1885	DP580	946.902	Portugal—History—Interregnum, 1383-1385
DP233-272.4	946.074	Spain—History—Alfonso XIII, 1886-1931	DP582-618	946.902	Portugal—History—Period of discoveries, 1385-1580
DP247	946.074	Spain—History—Dictatorship, 1923-1930	DP585-590	946.902	Portugal—History—John I, 1385-1433
DP250-269.9	946.081	Spain—History—Republic, 1931-1939	DP592-594	946.902	Portugal—History—Edward, 1433-1438
DP250	946.08	Spain—History—Revolution, 1931	DP596-598	946.902	Portugal—History—Alfonso V, 1438-1481
DP269.A1-.9	946.081	Spain—History—Civil War, 1936-1939	DP600-602	946.902	Portugal—History—John II, 1481-1495
DP270-271	946.082	Spain—History—1939-1975	DP604-606	946.902	Portugal—History—Manual, 1495-1521
DP272-.4	946.083	Spain—History—1975-	DP608-610	946.902	Portugal—History—John III, 1521-1557
DP272	946.083	Spain—History—Coup d'etat, 1981	DP612-616	946.902	Portugal—History—Sebastian, 1557-1578
DP350-374	946.41	Madrid (Spain)	DP614	946.902	Kassr-el-Kebir, Battle of, 1578
DP501-900	936.6	Portugal—History			
DP501-900	946.9	Portugal—History	DP618	946.902	Portugal—History—Henry I, 1578-1580
DP501	936.6005	Portugal—Periodicals			
DP501	946.9005	Portugal—Periodicals	DP620-682.2	946.90(2-4)	Portugal—History—Modern, 1580-
DP514	913.66003	Portugal—Gazetteers			
DP514	914.69003	Portugal—Gazetteers	DP622-629	946.902	Portugal—History—Spanish dynasty, 1580-1640
DP520-526.5	913.6604	Portugal—Description and travel			
DP520-526.5	914.6904	Portugal—Description and travel			

LC	Dewey	Subject Heading	LC	Dewey	Subject Heading
DP628	946.902	Portugal—History—Revolution, 1640	DQ36-39	936.4	Switzerland—Civilization
			DQ36-39	949.4	Switzerland—Civilization
DP634-.8	946.9032	Portugal—History—John IV, 1640-1656	DQ48-49	936.4004	Ethnology—Switzerland
			DQ48-49	949.4004	Ethnology—Switzerland
DP635	946.9032	Portugal—History—Alfonso VI, 1656-1683	DQ52-.7	920.0364	Switzerland—Biography
			DQ52-.7	920.0494	Switzerland—Biography
DP635	946.9032	Elvas, Linhas de, Battle of, 1659	DQ52.8-.95	936.40072	Switzerland—Historiography
DP636-.8	946.9032	Portugal—History—Peter II, 1683-1706	DQ52.8-.95	949.40072	Switzerland—Historiography
DP638	946.9032	Portugal—History—John V, 1706-1750	DQ59	355.009494	Switzerland—History, Military
DP639-641.9	946.9033	Portugal—History—Joseph I, 1750-1777	DQ79-84	936.4	Switzerland—History—To 1648
DP642-644.9	946.903(3-4)	Portugal—History—Maria I, 1777-1816	DQ79-84	949.40(1-3)	Switzerland—History—To 1648
DP650-651	946.903(4-5)	Portugal—History—John VI, 1816-1826	DQ85-87	936.4	Switzerland—History—To 1032
DP650	946.9034	Portugal—History—Conspiracy of 1817	DQ85-87	949.401	Switzerland—History—To 1032
DP650	946.9035	Portugal—History—Revolution, 1820	DQ85-87	949.401	Carolingians
			DQ88-110	949.40(1-2)	Switzerland—History—1032-1499
DP653-660	946.903(5-6)	Portugal—History—1826-1853	DQ90-91	949.402	Switzerland—History—Perpetual League, 1291
DP659	946.9035	Portugal—History—Civil War, 1846-1847	DQ104-118	949.403	Switzerland—History—1499-1648
DP659	946.9035	Portugal—History—Uprising, 1846	DQ107.S8	949.403	Dornach, Battle of, 1499
DP662	946.9036	Portugal—History—Revolution, 1891	DQ111-123	949.404	Switzerland—History—1648-1798
DP665-.5	946.9036	Portugal—History—Peter V, 1853-1861	DQ124	949.40(5-6)	Switzerland—History—19th century
DP668-669	946.9036	Portugal—History—Charles I, 1889-1908	DQ131-151	949.405	Switzerland—History—Helvetic Republic, 1798-1803
DP670-682.2	946.904	Portugal—History—20th century	DQ131-151	949.40(4-5)	Switzerland—History—1789-1815
DP674-682.2	946.9041	Portugal—History—Revolution, 1910	DQ154-191	949.40(6-74)	Switzerland—History—1815-
DP675-680.5	946.904(1-3)	Portugal—History—1910-1974	DQ154	949.4062	Switzerland—History—1815-1830
DP680	946.9042	Portugal—History—Revolution, 1926	DQ156	949.4062	Switzerland—History—1830-1848
DP680	946.9044	Portugal—History—1974-	DQ158-161	949.4062	Switzerland—History—Sonderbund, 1845-1847
DP681	946.9044	Portugal—History—Revolution, 1974	DQ171-210	949.40(63-74)	Switzerland—History—1848-
DP681	946.9044	Portugal—History—Coup d'etat, 1975	DQ201-210	949.407	Switzerland—History—20th century
DP752-776	946.9425	Lisbon (Portugal)	DQ458	949.451	Geneva (Switzerland)—History—1536-1603
DQ	949.4	Switzerland			
DQ1	936.4005	Switzerland—Periodicals	DQ820-829	949.47	Alps
DQ1	949.4005	Switzerland—Periodicals			
DQ2	936.4006	Switzerland—Congresses	DR	949.6	Balkan Peninsula
DQ2	949.4006	Switzerland—Congresses	DR	949.9	Bulgaria
DQ14	913.64003	Switzerland—Gazetteers	DR	949.8	Romania
DQ14	914.94003	Switzerland—Gazetteers	DR	956.1	Turkey
DQ20-26	913.6404	Switzerland—Description and travel	DR1	949.6005	Balkan Peninsula—Periodicals
DQ20-26	914.9404	Switzerland—Description and travel			

LC	Dewey	Subject Heading	LC	Dewey	Subject Heading
DR1.5	949.6006	Balkan Peninsula—Congresses	DR207-210	914.9804	Romania—Description and travel
DR5	914.96003	Balkan Peninsula—Gazetteers	DR212	939.8	Romania—Civilization
DR11-16	914.9604	Balkan Peninsula—Description and travel	DR212	949.8	Romania—Civilization
			DR213-214	939.8004	Ethnology—Romania
DR22-23	949.6	Balkan Peninsula—Civilization	DR213-214	949.8004	Ethnology—Romania
			DR215-267.5	939.8	Romania—History
DR24-27	949.6004	Ethnology—Balkan Peninsula	DR215-267.5	949.8	Romania—History
			DR216.7-.92	939.80072	Romania—Historiography
DR32-48.5	949.6	Balkan Peninsula—History	DR216.7-.92	949.80072	Romania—Historiography
DR33	920.0496	Balkan Peninsula—Biography	DR219	355.009498	Romania—History, Military
			DR225	359.009498	Romania—History, Naval
DR50-.84	949.61	Thrace	DR238-241	939.8	Romania—History—To 1711
DR51-98	939.8	Bulgaria			
DR51-98	949.9	Bulgaria	DR238-241	949.801	Romania—History—To 1711
DR51	939.8005	Bulgaria—Periodicals			
DR51	949.9005	Bulgaria—Periodicals	DR241	949.8016	Romania—History—Revolution, 1821
DR53	913.98003	Bulgaria—Gazetteers			
DR53	914.99003	Bulgaria—Gazetteers	DR241	949.8015	Romania—History—1711-1821
DR53.7	949.90025	Bulgaria—Directories			
DR57-61	913.9804	Bulgaria—Description and travel	DR242-250	949.8016	Romania—History—1821-1859
			DR244	940.284	Romania—History—Revolution, 1848
DR57-61	914.9904	Bulgaria—Description and travel			
			DR244	949.80(16-2)	Romania—History—1859-1866
DR63	939.8	Bulgaria—Civilization			
DR63	949.9	Bulgaria—Civilization	DR248	949.802	Romania—History—War of Independence, 1876-1878
DR64	939.8004	Ethnology—Bulgaria			
DR64	949.9004	Ethnology—Bulgaria			
DR65-93.34	939.8	Bulgaria—History	DR250-266	949.802	Romania—History—Charles I, 1866-1914
DR65-93.34	949.9	Bulgaria—History			
DR66	920.0398	Bulgaria—Biography	DR256	949.802	Romania—History—Peasants' Uprising, 1888
DR66	920.0499	Bulgaria—Biography			
DR66.7-.97	939.80072	Bulgaria—Historiography	DR263	949.802	Romania—History—1914-1918
DR66.7-.97	949.90072	Bulgaria—Historiography			
DR70	355.009499	Bulgaria—History, Military	DR264-266	949.802	Romania—History—Uprising, 1941
DR74.3	939.8	Bulgaria—History—To 681			
			DR267-.5	949.8032	Romania—History—1989-
DR74.3	949.9013	Bulgaria—History—To 681	DR267	949.80(2-31)	Romania—History—1944-1989
DR74.5	949.9013	Bulgaria—History—681-1018	DR269.5-.6	949.8032	Romania—History—Revolution, 1989
DR79	949.9014	Bulgaria—History—1018-1185	DR279-280.74	949.84	Transylvania (Romania)
			DR343	949.71014	Serbia—History—Insurrection, 1804-1813
DR82-.5	949.9015	Bulgaria—History—1393-1878			
			DR343	949.71	Serbia—History
DR84.9-.8	949.902	Bulgaria—History—1878-1944	DR414	939.2003	Turkey—Gazetteers
			DR414	956.1003	Turkey—Gazetteers
DR89.9-93.34	949.90(2-3)	Bulgaria—History—1944-	DR421-429.4	913.9204	Turkey—Description and travel
DR97	949.99	Sofia (Bulgaria)			
DR201-296	939.8	Romania	DR421-429.4	915.6104	Turkey—Description and travel
DR201-296	949.8	Romania			
DR201	939.8005	Romania—Periodicals	DR432	939.2	Turkey—Civilization
DR201	949.8005	Romania—Periodicals	DR432	956.1	Turkey—Civilization
DR204	914.98003	Romania—Gazetteers	DR434-435	939.2004	Ethnology—Turkey
DR204	914.98003	Romania—Gazetteers	DR434-435	956.1004	Ethnology—Turkey
DR207-210	913.9804	Romania—Description and travel	DR436-603	939.2	Turkey—History
			DR436-603	956.1	Turkey—History
			DR438.8-.95	939.20072	Turkey—Historiography

LC	Dewey	Subject Heading	LC	Dewey	Subject Heading
DR438.8-.95	956.10072	Turkey—Historiography	DR573.7-584.5	956.10154	Turkey—History—1878-1909
DR448	355.009561	Turkey—History, Military			
DR451	359.009561	Turkey—History, Naval	DR583-588	956.10154	Turkey—History—Mehmed V, 1909-1918
DR481	939.2	Turkey—History—To 1453			
DR481	956.101	Turkey—History—To 1453	DR583	956.10154	Turkey—History—Revolution, 1909
DR485-486	956.101(4-5)	Turkey—History—Ottoman Empire, 1288-1918	DR589-590	956.10(23-36)	Turkey—History—1918-1960
DR493-502	956.101(4-5)	Turkey—History—1288-1453	DR589	956.1023	Turkey—History—Revolution, 1918-1923
DR496	956.1015	Turkey—History—Bayezid I, 1389-1403	DR589	956.1023	Turkey—History—Mehmed VI, 1918-1922
DR496	956.1015	Turkey—History—Invasion of Timur, 1402	DR593-603	956.10(36-4)	Turkey—History—1960-
DR501-.7	956.10152	Turkey—History—Mehmed II, 1451-1481	DR593	956.1036	Turkey—History—Revolution, 1960
DR502-536	956.1015(2-3)	Turkey—History—1453-1683	DR600	956.1037	Turkey—History—Coup d'etat, 1971
DR503	956.10152	Turkey—History—Bayezid II, 1481-1512	DR601	956.1038	Turkey—History—Coup d'etat, 1980
DR505-506	956.10152	Turkey—History—Suleyman I, 1520-1566	DR701.M13-.M14	949.76	Macedonia—History
			DR716-741	949.618	Istanbul (Turkey)—History
DR523	956.10153	Turkey—History—Wars with Persia, 1576-1639	DR901-998	939.8	Albania
			DR901-998	949.65	Albania
DR525	956.10153	Turkey—History—Mehmed III, 1595-1603	DR901	949.65005	Albania—Periodicals
			DR901	939.8005	Albania—Periodicals
DR529	956.10153	Turkey—History—Murad IV, 1623-1640	DR903.5	939.8006	Albania—Congresses
			DR903.5	949.65006	Albania—Congresses
DR534-536.5	956.10153	Turkey—History—Mehmed IV, 1648-1687	DR907	913.98003	Albania—Gazetteers
			DR907	914.965003	Albania—Gazetteers
DR534.5.D3	956.10153	Dardanelles, Battle of the, 1656	DR914-918	913.9804	Albania—Description and travel
DR536-562	956.1015(3-4)	Turkey—History—1683-1829	DR914-918	914.96504	Albania—Description and travel
DR537	956.10153	Turkey—History—Suleyman II, 1687-1691	DR922	939.8	Albania—Civilization
			DR922	949.65	Albania—Civilization
DR541.3	956.10153	Turkey—History—Mustafa II, 1695-1703	DR923-925	939.8004	Ethnology—Albania
			DR923-925	949.65004	Ethnology—Albania
DR542-545	956.10153	Turkey—History—Ahmed III, 1703-1730	DR927-977.25	939.8	Albania—History
			DR927-977.25	949.65	Albania—History
DR542	956.10153	Turkey—History—Rebellion, 1703	DR928-934	920.0398	Albania—Biography
			DR928-934	920.04965	Albania—Biography
DR545	956.10153	Austro-Turkish War, 1716-1718	DR954-960.5	939.8	Albania—History—To 1501
DR547-548	956.10153	Turkey—History—Mahmud I, 1730-1754	DR954-960.5	949.6501	Albania—History—To 1501
DR548	956.10153	Austro-Turkish War, 1737-1739	DR959-960.5	949.6501	Albania—History—Turkish War, 15th century
DR551-553	956.10153	Turkey—History—Mustafa III, 1757-1773	DR961-969	949.6501	Albania—History—1501-1912
DR555	956.10154	Turkey—History—Abdul Hamid I, 1774-1789	DR965.9-969	949.6501	Albania—History—1840-1912
DR559-.5	956.10154	Turkey—History—Selim III, 1789-1807	DR966	949.6501	Albania—History—1878-1912
DR562-564	956.10154	Turkey—History—Mahmud II, 1808-1839	DR969	949.6502	Albania—History—Uprising, 1912
DR564-573.7	956.10154	Turkey—History—1829-1878	DR970-975	949.6502	Albania—History—1912-1944
DR565	956.10154	Turkey—History—Tanzimat, 1839-1876	DR972	949.6502	Albania—History—Peasant Uprising, 1914-1915
DR567	956.10154	Crimean War, 1853-1856			

LC	Dewey	Subject Heading	LC	Dewey	Subject Heading
DR973	949.6502	Albania—History—June Revolution, 1924	DR1827-1928	949.745	Montenegro—History
			DR1932-2125	949.71	Serbia
DR975	949.6502	Albania—History—Axis occupation, 1939-1944	DR1977-1999.5	949.71013	Serbia—History—To 1456
			DR2000-2005	949.71013	Serbia—History—1456-1804
DR976-977.25	949.6503	Albania—History—1944-1990	DR2004.8	949.71013	Serbia—History—Great Emigration, 1690
DR976-977.25	949.650(3-4)	Albania—History—1990-	DR2005	949.71013	Serbia—History—Insurrection, 1788
DR1202-2285	939.8	Yugoslavia	DR2006-2032	949.7101(4-5)	Serbia—History—1804-1918
DR1202-2285	949.7	Yugoslavia			
DR1202	939.8005	Yugoslavia—Periodicals	DR2016	949.71014	Serbia—History—Milos Obrenovic, 1814-1839
DR1202	949.7005	Yugoslavia—Periodicals			
DR1205	939.8006	Yugoslavia—Congresses	DR2026.8	949.71015	Serbia—History—Revolt, 1883
DR1205	949.7006	Yugoslavia—Congresses			
DR1209	913.98003	Yugoslavia—Gazetteers	DR2033-2047	949.710(2-3)	Serbia—History—1918-
DR1209	914.97003	Yugoslavia—Gazetteers	DR2033-2040	949.7102	Serbia—History—1918-1945
DR1218-1224	913.9804	Yugoslavia—Description and travel	DR2041-2047	949.710(2-3)	Serbia—History—1945-1992
DR1218-1224	914.9704	Yugoslavia—Description and travel	DR2047	949.7103	Serbia—History—1992-
DR1228	939.8	Yugoslavia—Civilization	DR2152-2285	949.76	Macedonia
DR1228	949.7	Yugoslavia—Civilization	DR2211	949.98	Macedonia—Karpos Uprising, 1689
DR1229-1230	939.8004	Ethnology—Yugoslavia			
DR1229-1230	949.7004	Ethnology—Yugoslavia			
DR1232-1321	939.8	Yugoslavia—History	DS	950	Asia
DR1232-1321	949.7	Yugoslavia—History	DS1	950.05	Asia—Periodicals
DR1233-1235	920.0398	Yugoslavia—Biography	DS4	915.03	Asia—Gazetteers
DR1233-1235	920.0497	Yugoslavia—Biography	DS5.95-10	915.04	Asia—Description and travel
DR1239-1243	939.80072	Yugoslavia—Historiography			
DR1239-1243	949.70072	Yugoslavia—Historiography	DS11	950	Oriental antiquities
DR1250-1251	355.009497	Yugoslavia—History, Military	DS13-28	950.04	Ethnology—Asia
			DS19-23	950.04942	Mongols
DR1252-1253	359.009497	Yugoslavia—History, Naval	DS22.7	950.04942	Golden Horde
DR1281-1312	949.70(2-3)	Yugoslavia—History—1918-1945	DS25	950.04	Hsiung-nu
			DS25	950.0494387	Tatars
DR1297-1298	949.7022	Yugoslavia—History—Coup d'etat, 1941	DS31-35.2	950	Asia—History
			DS35-.2	950.4	Asia—History—20th century
DR1300	949.7023	Yugoslavia—History—1945-1980	DS35.2	950.4(2-3)	Asia—History—1945-
DR1306-1313.8	949.7024	Yugoslavia—History—1980-1992	DS35.62	909.0976701	Civilization, Islamic
			DS35.74.U6	327.7301767 + 090511	Islamic countries—Relations—United States
DR1306-1312	949.7103	Yugoslavia—History—1992-	DS36-39.2	909.04927	Arab countries
DR1352-1485	939.8	Slovenia	DS36.77-.88	909.04927	Arab countries—Civilization
DR1352-1485	949.73	Slovenia			
DR1376-1450	939.8	Slovenia—History	DS36.77-.88	909.04927	Civilization, Arab
DR1376-1450	949.73	Slovenia—History	DS36.88 .B36	909.04927082	Civilization, Arab—20th century
DR1444-1450	949.7302	Slovenia—History—1945-1990	DS37-39.2	909.04927	Arab countries—History
DR1452-1457.5	949.7303	Slovenia—History—1990-	DS38	939.4	Middle East—History—To 622
DR1502-1645	939.8	Croatia			
DR1502-1645	949.72	Croatia	DS38	320.5409 + 174927	Panarabism
DR1547-1598	939.8	Croatia—History			
DR1547-1598	949.72	Croatia—History	DS38.1	956.013	Dhat al-Sawari, Battle of, 655
DR1652-1785	939.8	Bosnia and Hercegovina			
DR1652-1785	949.742	Bosnia and Hercegovina	DS38.5	956.013	Islamic Empire—History—661- 750
DR1697-1785	949.742	Bosnia and Hercegovina—History			
DR1802-1928	949.745	Montenegro			

52

LC	Dewey	Subject Heading	LC	Dewey	Subject Heading
DS38.6	956.01(3-4)	Islamic Empire—History—750- 1258	DS80.7-87.53	956.92	Lebanon—History
			DS81-89	939.44	Phoenicians
DS38.7	956.01(4-5)	Islamic Empire—History—1258- 1517	DS83	939.44	Lebanon—History—635-1516
DS38.8	909.09749270 (5-821)	Arab countries—History—1517-1918	DS83	956.9203	Lebanon—History—635-1516
DS38.9	909.09749270 + 8	Arab countries—History—1798-	DS84	956.92034	Lebanon—History—1516-1918
DS39	909.09749270 + 821	Arab countries—History—Arab Revolt, 1916-1918	DS87.2.C4	956.92044092	Hostages—Lebanon—Biography
DS39	909.09749270 + 82	Arab countries—History—20th century	DS87.5	956.92044	Lebanon—History—Civil War, 1975-
DS41-66	939.4	Middle East	DS87.53	956.92044	Lebanon—History—Israeli intervention, 1982-1984
DS41-66	956	Middle East			
DS43	913.94003	Middle East—Gazetteers	DS92.6	913.943003	Syria—Gazetteers
DS43	915.6003	Middle East—Gazetteers	DS92.6	915.691003	Syria—Gazetteers
DS44.98-49.7	913.9404	Middle East—Description and travel	DS94	913.94304	Syria—Description and travel
DS44.98-49.7	915.604	Middle East—Description and travel	DS94	915.69104	Syria—Description and travel
DS54.A4-Z	913.93704	Cyprus—Description and travel	DS94.6	939.43	Syria—Civilization
			DS94.6	956.91	Syria—Civilization
DS54.A4-Z	915.69304	Cyprus—Description and travel	DS94.7-.8	939.43004	Ethnology—Syria
			DS94.7-.8	956.91004	Ethnology—Syria
DS54.35	939.37	Cyprus—Civilization	DS94.9-98.3	939.43	Syria—History
DS54.35	956.93	Cyprus—Civilization	DS94.9-98.3	956.91	Syria—History
DS54.4-.44	939.37004	Ethnology—Cyprus	DS101-151	933	Jews
DS54.4-.44	956.93004	Ethnology—Cyprus	DS101-151	956.94	Jews
DS54.5-.9	939.37	Cyprus—History	DS101-151	933	Israel
DS54.5-.9	956.93	Cyprus—History	DS101-151	956.94	Israel
DS67.8	913.5003	Iraq—Gazetteers	DS103-108.5	913.304	Israel—Description and travel
DS67.8	915.67003	Iraq—Gazetteers			
DS69-70.5	935	Iraq—Antiquities	DS103-108.5	915.69404	Israel—Description and travel
DS70.7	935	Iraq—Civilization			
DS70.7	956.7	Iraq—Civilization	DS109-.94	933	Jerusalem
DS70.7	935	Civilization, Assyro-Babylonian	DS109-.94	956.9442	Jerusalem
			DS109.85-.94	933	Jerusalem—History
DS70.8	935.004	Ethnology—Iraq	DS109.85-.94	956.9442	Jerusalem—History
DS70.8	956.7004	Ethnology—Iraq	DS123.5	956.9402	Palestine—History—70-638
DS70.82-79.66	935	Iraq—History			
DS70.82-79.66	956.7	Iraq—History	DS110.S3	933	Samaria Region
DS72	935.01	Sumerians	DS110.S3	956.953	Samaria Region
DS79.72	956.70442	Persian Gulf War, 1991	DS112-113	933	Jews—Civilization
DS79.74	956.704427	Persian Gulf War, 1991—Prisoners and prisons	DS112-113	956.94	Jews—Civilization
			DS113.2-.8	933.004	Ethnology—Israel
			DS113.2-.8	956.94004	Ethnology—Israel
DS79.76	956.70443	Iraq War, 2003	DS114-128.19	933	Israel—History
DS80.A5	913.944003	Lebanon—Gazetteers	DS114-128.19	956.94	Israel—History
DS80.A5	915.692003	Lebanon—Gazetteers	DS119.7-.76	956.04	Arab-Israeli conflict
DS80.2	913.94404	Lebanon—Description and travel	DS119.7	956.94054	Entebbe Airport Raid, 1976
DS80.2	915.69204	Lebanon—Description and travel	DS121	933.01	Jews—History—To 1200 B.C.
DS80.3	939.44	Phoenician antiquities	DS121	933.02	Jews—History—To 953 B.C.
DS80.4	939.44	Lebanon—Civilization			
DS80.4	956.92	Lebanon—Civilization	DS121	933.0(3-5)	Jews—History—586 B.C.-70 A.D.
DS80.5	939.44004	Ethnology—Lebanon			
DS80.5	956.92004	Ethnology—Lebanon	DS121.4	933.004926	Canaanites
DS80.7-87.53	939.44	Lebanon—History	DS121.4	956.004926	Canaanites

LC	Dewey	Subject Heading	LC	Dewey	Subject Heading
DS121.55	933.02	Jews—History—1200-953 B.C.	DS153.4	956.95	Jordan—Civilization
			DS153.5-.55	933.004	Ethnology—Jordan
DS121.6	933.03	Jews—History—953-586 B.C.	DS153.5-.55	956.95004	Ethnology—Jordan
			DS153.7-154.55	933	Jordan—History
DS121.65	933.03	Jews—History—Babylonian captivity, 598-515 B.C.	DS153.7-154.55	956.95	Jordan—History
DS121.7-.8	933.0(4-5)	Jews—History—168 B.C.-135 A.D.	DS154.5-.55	956.950(3-44)	Jordan—History—20th century
DS121.7-.8	956.9402	Jews—History—168 B.C.-135 A.D.	DS154.55	956.95043	Jordan—History—Intervention, 1958
DS122.8	933.05	Jews—History—Rebellion, 66-73	DS161-195.5	947.56	Armenia
DS122.8	956.9402	Jews—History—Rebellion, 66-73	DS165	914.75604	Armenia—Description and travel
DS122.8	956.9402	Jerusalem—History—Siege, 70 A.D.	DS171	947.56	Armenia—Civilization
			DS172	947.56004	Ethnology—Armenia
DS122.9	956.9402	Jews—History—Bar Kokhba Rebellion, 132-135	DS173-195.5	947.56	Armenia—History
			DS181-184	947.56	Armenia—History—To 428
DS123.5	956.9402	Jews—History—70-638	DS181-184	947.56	Armenia—History—Arsacid (Arshakuni) dynasty, 66-428
DS124-125.5	956.9403	Palestine—History—638-1917	DS186-188	947.56	Armenia—History—428-640
DS124-126	956.940(3-4)	Jews—History—1789-1945	DS186-188	947.56	Armenia—History—Turkic Mongol Domination, 1045-1522
DS125	956.94034	Palestine—History—1799-1917			
DS125.5-126.4	956.9404	Palestine—History—1917-1948	DS186-188	947.56	Armenia—History—428-1522
			DS186-188	947.56	Armenia—History—Arab period, 640-885
DS126	956.9404	Palestine—History—Arab riots, 1920	DS191-193	947.5607	Armenia—History—1522-1800
DS126.4	956.9404	Palestine—History—Partition, 1947	DS194-.5	947.560(7-83)	Armenia—History—1801-1900
DS126-.4	956.9404	Palestine—History—1929-1948	DS195-.3	947.5608(3-6)	Armenia—History—1901-
DS126	956.9404	Palestine—History—Arab riots, 1929	DS195.5	947.560(83-841)	Armenian massacres, 1915-1923
DS126	956.9404	Palestine—History—Arab rebellion, 1936-1939	DS195.5	947.560841	Armenia (Republic)—History—Uprising, 1921
DS2126	956.9404	Palestine—History—Proposed partition, 1937	DS195.5	947.560841	Armenia—History—Revolution, 1917-1920
DS126.5-126.99	956.94052	Israel—History—1948-1949	DS201-248	939.49	Saudi Arabia
			DS201-248	953.8	Saudi Arabia
DS126.5	956.9405	Israel—History—Declaration of Independence, 1948	DS204.5-208	913.94904	Saudi Arabia—Description and travel
			DS204.5-208	915.3804	Saudi Arabia—Description and travel
DS126.9-.99	956.042	Israel-Arab War, 1948-1949	DS215	939.49	Saudi Arabia—Civilization
			DS215	953.8	Saudi Arabia—Civilization
DS127-.9	956.046	Israel-Arab War, 1967	DS218-219	939.49004	Ethnology—Saudi Arabia
DS135.G33	940.531842	Kristallnacht, 1938	DS218-219	953.8004	Ethnology—Saudi Arabia
DS145-146	305.8924	Antisemitism	DS221-244.63	939.49	Saudi Arabia—History
DS128.1-.19	956.048	Israel-Arab War, 1973	DS221-244.63	953.8	Saudi Arabia—History
DS149-151	320.54095694	Zionism	DS232	953.802	Ditch, Battle of the, 627
DS153-154.9	933	Jordan	DS234-238	953.80099	Abbasids
DS153-154.9	956.95	Jordan	DS234-238	953.80099	Caliphs
DS153.2	913.304	Jordan—Description and travel	DS251-326	935	Iran
			DS251-326	955	Iran
DS153.2	915.69504	Jordan—Description and travel	DS253	913.5003	Iran—Gazetteers
DS153.4	933	Jordan—Civilization	DS253	915.5003	Iran—Gazetteers

LC	Dewey	Subject Heading
DS255-259.2	913.504	Iran—Description and travel
DS255-259.2	915.504	Iran—Description and travel
DS268-269	935.004	Ethnology—Iran
DS268-269	955.004	Ethnology—Iran
DS270-318.85	935	Iran—History
DS270-318.85	955	Iran—History
DS276	935	Iran—History—To 640
DS276	935.06	Iran—History—Macedonian Conquest, 334-325 B.C.
DS281-284.7	935.05	Achaemenid dynasty, 559-330 B.C.
DS287.8-288.9	955.02	Iran—History—640-1256
DS288-290	955.02	Iran—History—640-1500
DS288.95-289.8	955.02	Iran—History—1256-1500
DS292-297	955.03	Iran—History—16th-18th centuries
DS298-316	955.0(4-51)	Iran—History—Qajar dynasty, 1794-1925
DS307.5	955.04	Iran—History—War with Great Britain, 1856-1857
DS313	955.051	Iran—History—1905-1911
DS316.2-318.7	955.05(2-3)	Iran—History—Paklavi dynasty, 1925-1979
DS318-.7	955.053	Iran—History—Mohammed Reza Pahlavi, 1941-1979
DS318.72-.85	955.054	Iran—History—Revolution, 1979
DS318.72-.85	955.054	Iran—History—1979-
DS318.85	955.0542	Iran-Iraq War, 1980-1988
DS327-329.4	939.6	Asia, Central
DS327-329.4	958	Asia, Central
DS351	913.96003	Afghanistan—Gazetteers
DS351	915.81003	Afghanistan—Gazetteers
DS352	913.9604	Afghanistan—Description and travel
DS352	915.8104	Afghanistan—Description and travel
DS354	939.6	Afghanistan—Civilization
DS354	958.1	Afghanistan—Civilization
DS354.5-.6	939.6004	Ethnology—Afghanistan
DS354.5-.6	958.1004	Ethnology—Afghanistan
DS355-371.2	939.6	Afghanistan—History
DS355-371.2	958.1	Afghanistan—History
DS371.2	958.1045	Afghanistan—History—Soviet occupation, 1979-1989
DS371.3	958.104(5-6)	Afghanistan—History—1989-
DS371.414	958.1047	Afghan War, 2001—Prisoners and prisons, American
DS376.8	934.003	Pakistan—Gazetteers
DS376.8	915.491003	Pakistan—Gazetteers
DS377	913.404	Pakistan—Description and travel

LC	Dewey	Subject Heading
DS377	915.49104	Pakistan—Description and travel
DS379	934	Pakistan—Civilization
DS379	954.91	Pakistan—Civilization
DS380.A1-.A2	934.004	Ethnology—Pakistan
DS380.A1-.A2	954.91004	Ethnology—Pakistan
DS381.7-388.2	934	Pakistan—History
DS381.7-388.2	954.91	Pakistan—History
DS385.9	954.9042	India-Pakistan Conflict, 1947-1949
DS393.3	934.003	Bangladesh—Gazetteers
DS393.3	915.492003	Bangladesh—Gazetteers
DS393.8	934	Bangladesh—Civilization
DS393.8	954.92	Bangladesh—Civilization
DS393.82-.83	934.004	Ethnology—Bangladesh
DS393.82-.83	954.92004	Ethnology—Bangladesh
DS394.5-395.7	934	Bangladesh—History
DS394.5-395.7	954.92	Bangladesh—History
DS395.5	954.92051	Bangladesh—History—Revolution, 1971
DS421-486.8	934	India
DS421-486.8	954	India
DS421-428.2	934	India—Civilization
DS421-428.2	954	India—Civilization
DS422.C3	305.51220954	Caste
DS423-425	909.097645	Civilization, Hindu
DS425	934.02	Indo-Aryans
DS430-432.5	934.004	Ethnology—India
DS430-432.5	954.004	Ethnology—India
DS432.B4	954.0049144	Bengali (South Asian people)
DS451-.9	934	India—History—324 B.C-1000 A.D.
DS451-.9	954.0(2-223)	India—History—324 B.C-1000 A.D.
DS451.8	954.02	Gurjara-Pratihara dynasty
DS452-462.8	954.02(23-96)	India—History—1000-1765
DS457-460	954.02(23-45)	India—History—1000-1526
DS459.2	954.0234	Khilji dynasty
DS461-.9	954.025	Mogul Empire
DS463-480.83	954.0(296-4)	India—History—British occupation, 1765-1947
DS473	954.0298	Maratha War, 1775-1782
DS474.1	954.0311	India—History—Mysore War, 1790-1792
DS475.3	954.0312	India—History—Mysore War, 1799
DS475.5	954.0313	India—History—Mutiny, 1809
DS475.6	954.0313	Maratha War, 1816-1818
DS478-.3	954.0317	India—History—Sepoy Rebellion, 1857-1858
DS480.5	954.0357	Massacres—India—Amritsar
DS480.82	954.0359	India—History—Quit India movement, 1942
DS480.832-481	954.0(4-5)	India—History—1947-

LC	Dewey	Subject Heading	LC	Dewey	Subject Heading
DS480.85	954.042	Sino-Indian Border Dispute, 1957-	DS554.34-.382	915.9604	Cambodia—Description and travel
DS485.N4	954.0313	Nepalese War, 1814-1816	DS554.42	959.6	Cambodia—Civilization
DS488-490	954.93	Sri Lanka	DS554.44-.46	959.6004	Ethnology—Cambodia
DS488.9	915.493003	Sri Lanka—Gazetteers	DS554.5-.842	959.6	Cambodia—History
DS489-.15	915.49304	Sri Lanka—Description and travel	DS554.6-.64	959.601	Cambodia—History—To 800
DS489.2-.25	954.93004	Ethnology—Sri Lanka	DS554.6-.64	959.602	Cambodia—History—800-1444
DS489.5-490	954.93	Sri Lanka—History	DS554.6-.64	959.603	Cambodia—History—1444-1863
DS489.6-.63	954.9301	Sri Lanka—History—To 1505	DS554.7-.73	959.60(3-41)	Cambodia—History—1863-1953
DS489.7-.73	954.930(1-2)	Sri Lanka—History—1505-1948	DS554.8-.83	959.604(1-2)	Cambodia—History—1953-1975
DS489.7	954.9302	Sri Lanka—History—Rebellion, 1848	DS554.84-.842	959.6042	Cambodia—History—1975-
DS489.7	954.9302	Sri Lanka—History—Rebellion, 1818	DS554.84	959.6042	Cambodia—History—Civil War, 1970-1975
DS489.8-.86	954.9303	Sri Lanka—History—1948-	DS555.25	915.94003	Laos—Gazetteers
DS489.8	954.93031	Sri Lanka—History—Rebellion, 1971	DS555.34-.382	915.9404	Laos—Description and travel
DS491.5	915.49804	Bhutan—Description and travel	DS555.42	959.4	Laos—Civilization
DS493.3	915.496	Nepal—Gazetteers	DS555.44-.45	959.4004	Ethnology—Laos
DS493.5-.53	915.49604	Nepal—Description and travel	DS555.5-86	959.4	Laos—History
DS493.7	954.96	Nepal—Civilization	DS555.84-.86	959.4042	Laos—History—1975-
DS493.8-.9	954.96004	Ethnology—Nepal	DS556-559.916	959.7	Vietnam
DS494.4-495.59	954.96	Nepal—History	DS556.25	915.97003	Vietnam—Gazetteers
DS495	954.96	Nepal—History—To 1768	DS556.34-.39	915.9704	Vietnam—Description and travel
DS495.3	954.96	Nepal—History—1768-1951	DS556.42	959.7	Vietnam—Civilization
DS501-519	950	East Asia	DS556.44-.45	959.7004	Ethnology—Vietnam
DS516-517.9	952.031	Russo-Japanese War, 1904-1905	DS556.6-.63	959.703	Vietnam—History—To 939
DS518.1	950.4(2-3)	East Asia—History—1945-	DS556.7-.73	959.703	Vietnam—History—Later Le dynasty, 1428-1787
DS524-526.7	959	Asia, Southeastern—History	DS556.8-.83	959.70(3-4)	Vietnam—History—19th century
DS527.2-.3	959.102	Burma—History—To 1824	DS556.815	959.703	Vietnam—History—August Revolution, 1945
DS527.5-.7	915.9104	Burma—Description and travel	DS556.9-.93	959.704(2-44)	Vietnamese reunification question (1954-1976)
DS527.9	959.1	Burma—Civilization	DS557-559.8	959.7043	Vietnamese Conflict, 1961-1975
DS528-.2	959.1004	Ethnology—Burma	DS557.8.E23	959.704342	Easter Offensive, 1972
DS529.7-530.32	959.10(2-4)	Burma—History—1824-1948	DS557.8.I	959.704342	Ia Drang Valley (Vietnam), Battle of, 1965
DS530	959.104	Burma—History—Japanese occupation, 1942-1945	DS557.8.K5	959.704342	Khe Sanh, Battle of, 1968
DS530	959.104	Burma—History—Peasant Uprising, 1931	DS557.8.S6	959.704342	Sontay Raid, 1970
DS530.4	959.105	Burma—History—1948-	DS559.4	959.70437	Vietnamese Conflict, 1961-1975—Prisoners and prisons
DS538-539	959.1004	Ethnology—Burma	DS563	915.93003	Thailand—Gazetteers
DS553.3	959.7041	Dong Khe (Vietnam), Battle of, 1950	DS564-566.2	915.9304	Thailand—Description and travel
DS553.3.D5	959.7042	Dien Bien Phu (Vietnam), Battle of, 1954	DS568	959.3	Thailand—Civilization
DS554.25	915.96003	Cambodia—Gazetteers	DS569-570	959.3004	Ethnology—Thailand
			DS570.95-586	959.3	Thailand—History

LC	Dewey	Subject Heading	LC	Dewey	Subject Heading
DS558.4	959.7043	Vietnamese Conflict, 1961-1975—Regimental histories—United States	DS674-.9	959.90(22-312)	Philippines—History—1521-1898
DS591.5	915.95003	Malaysia—Gazetteers	DS674	959.902	Philippines—History—1521-1812
DS592.4-.6	915.9504	Malaysia—Description and travel	DS675	959.902	Philippines—History—1812-1898
DS594	959.5	Malaysia—Civilization	DS675.5	959.902	Philippines—History—Cavite Mutiny, 1872
DS595-.2	959.5004	Ethnology—Malaysia	DS676	959.9027	Philippines—History—Insurrection, 1896-1898
DS595.8-597.21	959.5	Malaya—History			
DS596.6	959.503	Malaya—History—Japanese occupation, 1942-1945	DS679	959.9031	Philippines—History—Insurrection, 1899-1901
DS597	959.504	Malaya—History—Malayan Emergency, 1948-1960	DS685	959.9032	Dajo, Mount, Battle of, 1906
DS614	915.98003	Indonesia—Gazetteers	DS686.4	959.9035	Philippines—History—Japanese occupation, 1942-1945
DS617-620	915.9804	Indonesia—Description and travel			
DS625	959.8	Indonesia—Civilization	DS686.5-.6	959.904(1-6)	Philippines—History—1946-1986
DS631-632	959.8004	Ethnology—Indonesia	DS686.6	959.9047	Philippines—History—Attempted coup, 1987
DS632.B25	959.80049922	Balinese (Indonesia people)			
DS633-644.4	959.8	Indonesia—History	DS686.6	959.9047	Philippines—History—Coup d'etat, 1989
DS641	959.8012	Indonesia—History—To 1478	DS686.614	959.904(7-8)	Philippines—History—1986-
DS641.5-642.22	959.80(15-21)	Indonesia—History—1478-1798	DS686.62	959.9047	Philippines—History—Revolution, 1986
DS643-.22	959.8022	Indonesia—History—1798-1942	DS701-799.9	931	China
DS643	959.8022	Indonesia—History—British occupation, 1811-1816	DS701-799.9	951	China
			DS705	931.003	China—Gazetteers
			DS705	915.1003	China—Gazetteers
DS643	959.8022	Indonesia—History—Java War, 1825-1830	DS707-712	913.104	China—Description and travel
DS643	959.8022	Indonesia—History—Achinese War, 1873-1904	DS707-712	915.104	China—Description and travel
DS643.5	959.8022	Indonesia—History—Japanese occupation, 1942-1945	DS721-727	931	China—Civilization
			DS721-727	951	China—Civilization
			DS730-731	931.004	Ethnology—China
			DS730-731	951.004	Ethnology—China
DS644-.1	959.803(5-6)	Indonesia—History—1950-1966	DS740.6-.63	950.(3-41)	Eastern question (Far East)
DS644	959.8035	Indonesia—History—Revolution, 1945-1949	DS741-747.23	931.0(1-3)	China—History—To 221 B.C.
DS644.32	959.8036	Indonesia—History—Coup d'etat, 1965	DS747.15	931.01	China—History—Spring and Autumn period, 722-481 B.C.
DS644.4	959.8036	Indonesia—History—1966-	DS747.2	931.01	China—History—Warring States, 403-221 B.C.
DS650.2	915.955003	Brunei—Gazetteers			
DS650.35	915.95504	Brunei—Description and travel	DS747.28-749.7	931.04	China—History—221 B.C.-960 A.D.
DS650.4	959.55	Brunei—Civilization	DS747.28-749.7	951.01	China—History—221 B.C.-960 A.D.
DS650.42-.43	959.55004	Ethnology—Brunei	DS747.5-.9	931.04	China—History—Ch'in dynasty, 221-207 B.C.
DS650.44-.83	959.55	Brunei—History			
DS651-689	959.9	Philippines	DS748-.164	931.04	China—History—Han dynasty, 202 B.C.-220 A.D.
DS654	915.99003	Philippines—Gazetteers			
DS658-660	915.9904	Philippines—Description and travel	DS748.17-.76	931.04	China—History—220-589
DS663-664	959.9	Philippines—Civilization	DS748.2-.29	931.04	China—History—Three Kingdoms, 220-265
DS673.8	959.901	Philippines—History—To 1521			

57

LC	Dewey	Subject Heading	LC	Dewey	Subject Heading
DS748.4-.44	931.04	China—History—Chin dynasty, 265-419	DS763.65	951.03(4-5)	China—History—Self-strengthening movement, 1861-1895
DS748.45-.48	931.04	China—History—Five Hu and the Sixteen kingdoms, 304-439	DS764.4-767.6	951.035	Chinese-Japanese War, 1894-1895
DS748.5-.76	951.015	China—History—Northern and Southern dynasties, 386-589	DS770-772.3	951.035	China—History—Boxer Rebellion, 1899-1901
DS748.6-.66	951.015	China—History—Ch'i dynasty, 479-502	DS771.5	951.035	German Expedition to China, 1900-1901
DS748.6-.66	951.015	China—History—Liang dynasty, 502-557	DS773-.6	951.035	China—History—Hsuan t'ung, 1908-1912
DS748.6-.66	951.015	China—History—Liu Sung dynasty, 420-479	DS773.32-.6	951.036	China—History—Revolution, 1911-1912
DS748.7-.76	951.015	China—History—Ch'en dynasty, 557-589	DS773.83-777.5	951.04	China—History—Republic, 1912-1949
DS748.7-.76	951.015	China—History—Northern Chou dynasty, 557-581	DS774	951.0(35-59)	China—History—20th century
DS748.7-.76	951.015	China—History—Northern Ch'i dynasty, 550-577	DS775	951.042	China—History—December Ninth Movement, 1935
DS748.7-.76	931.04	China—History—Northern Wei dynasty, 386-534	DS775.4	355.30951	China—History, Military—1912-1949
DS748.7-.76	951.015	China—History—Northern Wei dynasty, 386-534	DS776.4-777.46	951.041	China—History—1912-1928
DS749.46	951.017	China—History—An Lu shan Rebellion, 755-763	DS777.2	951.041	China—History—Revolution, 1913
DS749.47	951.017	China—History—Huang Ch'ao Rebellion, 874-884	DS777.25	951.041	China—History—Revolution, 1915-1916
DS749.5-.76	951.0(18-24)	China—History—Five dynasties and the Ten kingdoms, 907-979	DS777.36	951.041	China—History—Warlord period, 1916-1928
DS749.7-.76	951.018	China—History—Later Shu kingdom, 934-965	DS777.43	951.041	China—History—May Fourth movement, 1919
DS749.7-.76	951.0(18-24)	China—History—Southern T'ang kingdom, 937-975	DS777.45	951.041	China—History—May Thirtieth movement, 1925
DS749.7-.76	951.018	China—History—Earlier Shu kingdom, 907-925	DS777.462	951.042	China—History—Tsinan Incident, 1928
DS749.7-.76	951.0(18-24)	China—History—Southern Han kingdom, 917-971	DS777.47-.514	951.042	China—History—1928-1937
DS751.72-.78	951.0(18-24)	China—History—Liao dynasty, 947-1125	DS777.5132-.51	951.042	China—History—Long March, 1934-1935
DS751.82-.88	951.024	China—History—Hsi Hsia dynasty, 1038-1227	DS777.51393	951.042	China—History—December Ninth Movement, 1935
DS751.92-.98	951.024	China—History—Chin dynasty, 1115-1234	DS777.514	951.042	China—History—Sian Incident, 1936
DS753.65	951.026	China—History—Li Tzu ch'eng Rebellion, 1628-1645	DS777.518-.531	951.042	China—History—1937-1945
DS753.82-773.6	951.03	Manchus	DS777.534	951.042	China—History—Southern Anhui Incident, 1941
DS756.3-.37	951.033	China—History—White Lotus Rebellion, 1796-1804	DS777.535-.544	951.042	China—History—Civil War, 1945-1949
DS757.4-.7	951.033	China—History—Opium War, 1840-1842	DS777.545-779	951.0 (5-6)	China—History—1949-
DS758.7-759.4	951.034	China—History—Taiping Rebellion, 1850-1864	DS777.55	951.05(5-7)	China—History—1949-1976
DS759.5	951.034	China—History—Nien Rebellion, 1853-1868	DS777.65	355.00951090 (45-5)	China—History, Military
DS763.5-773.6	951.03(4-6)	China—History—1861-1912	DS777.7	359.00951090 (45-5)	China—History, Naval—1949-
			DS778.4	951.055	China—History—Hundred Flowers Campaign, 1956

LC	Dewey	Subject Heading	LC	Dewey	Subject Heading
DS778.5	951.055	China—History—Antirightist Campaign, 1957-1958	DS855.7-.73	952.01	Japan—History—Nara period, 710-794
DS778.7	951.056	China—History—Cultural Revolution, 1966-1969	DS855.87-856.7	952.01	Japan—History—Heian period, 794-1185
DS779.15-.29	951.0(57-6)	China—History—1976-	DS856.3	952.01	Japan—History—Later Three Years' War, 1083-1087
DS779.32	951.058	China—History—Tiananmen Square Incident, 1989	DS856.75-869.6	952.02(1-4)	Japan—History—1185-1600
DS781-784.2	951.8	Manchus			
DS781-784.2	951.8	Manchuria (China)	DS858-861	952.021	Japan—History—Kamakura period, 1185-1333
DS785	915.15	Tibet (China)—Description and travel	DS861	952.021	Japan—History—Jokyu Revolt, 1221
DS793.G6	915.17304	Gobi Desert (Mongolia and China)—Description and travel	DS861	952.021	Japan—History—Attempted Mongol Invasions, 1274-1281
DS795.23-.3	951.156	Beijing (China)—History	DS861	952.021	Japan—History—Genko Incident, 1331-1333
DS796.N2	951.042	Nanking Massacre, Nanjing, Jiangsu Sheng, China, 1937	DS863	952.02(1-2)	Japan—History—Kenmu Restoration, 1333-1336
DS798.96	931.003	Taiwan—Gazetteers	DS863.75-869.6	952.02(2-3)	Japan—History—Muromachi period, 1336-1573
DS798.96	915.1249003	Taiwan—Gazetteers			
DS799.15-.24	913.104	Taiwan—Description and travel	DS868-869.6	952.02(3-4)	Japan—History—Period of civil wars, 1480-1603
DS799.15-.24	915.124904	Taiwan—Description and travel	DS870-881.84	952.025	Japan—History—Tokugawa period, 1600-1868
DS799.4	931	Taiwan—Civilization	DS871.5	952.025	Japan—History—Keicho Peasant Uprising, 1614-1615
DS799.4	951.249	Taiwan—Civilization			
DS799.42-.43	931.004	Ethnology—Taiwan	DS871.5	952.025	Japan—History—Ako Vendetta, 1703
DS799.42-.43	951.249004	Ethnology—Taiwan			
DS799.64-.66	931	Taiwan—History—To 1895	DS881-.84	952.025	Japan—History—19th century
DS799.64-.66	951.2490(2-3)	Taiwan—History—To 1895	DS881.2-.84	952.025	Japan—History—Restoration, 1853-1870
DS799.69-.72	951.2490(3-4)	Taiwan—History—1895-1945	DS881.4	952.031	Japan—History—Kobe Incident, 1868
DS799.69	951.24904	Taiwan—History—Insurrection, 1895	DS881.4	952.025	Japan—History—Sakai Incident, 1868
DS799.77-.833	951.24905	Taiwan—History—1945-	DS881.83-.84	952.025	Japan—History—Civil War, 1868
DS799.823	951.24905	Taiwan—History—February Twenty Eighth Incident, 1947	DS881.85-890.3	952.0(3-5)	Japan—History—1868-
DS799.83-.833	951.24905	Taiwan—History—1975-	DS881.98-884	952.031	Japan—History—Meiji period, 1868-1912
DS799.834	951.24905	Taiwan—History—Kaohsiung Incident, 1979	DS882.5	952.031	Japan—History—Takehashi Incident, 1878
DS799.99-.833	931	Taiwan—History	DS882.5	952.031	Japan—History—Kioizaka Incident, 1878
DS799.99-.833	951.249	Taiwan—History	DS884.5-890.3	952.0(31-49)	Japan—History—20th century
DS801-897	952	Japan			
DS805	915.2003	Japan—Gazetteers	DS885.8-888	952.032	Japan—History—Taisho period, 1912-1926
DS807-811	915.204	Japan—Description and travel	DS888.15-890.3	952.033	Japan—History—Showa period, 1926-1989
DS820.8-827	952	Japan—Civilization			
DS830-832	952.004	Ethnology—Japan	DS888.4-.5	952.033	Japan—History—February Incident, 1936 (February 26)
DS832	952.004946	Ainu			
DS850-856.72	952.01	Japan—History—To 1185			
DS854	952.01	Japan—History—Earlier Nine Years' War, 1051-1062	DS888.4-.5	952.033	Japan—History—1926-1945
DS855-.73	952.01	Japan—History—To 794			
DS855.6	952.01	Japan—History—Taika Reform, 645-710			

LC	Dewey	Subject Heading	LC	Dewey	Subject Heading
DS888.5	952.033	Japan—History—March and October Incidents, 1931	DS921.7	951.90422	Korean Demilitarized Zone (Korea)
DS888.5	952.033	Japan—History—May Incident, 1932 (May 15)	DS921.7	951.90422	Korean War, 1950-1953—Armistices
DS888.84-890.3	952.0(33-5)	Japan—History—1945-	DS922-.42	951.95043	Korea (South)—History—April Revolution, 1960
DS889.16	952.04(4-5)	Japan—History—Allied occupation, 1945-1952			
DS890.3	952.0(48-5)	Japan—History—Heisei period, 1989-	DS922.44	951.95043	Korea (South)—May Revolution, 1961
DS895.R97	952.29	Ryukyu Islands—History	DS922.445	951.95043	Kwangju Uprising, Kwangju-si, Korea, 1980
DS901.8	915.19003	Korea—Gazetteers	DS930-937	951.93	Korea (North)
DS902.2-.4	915.1904	Korea—Description and travel			
DS904	951.9	Korea—Civilization	DT	960	Africa
DS904.5-.7	951.9004	Ethnology—Korea	DT2	916.003	Africa—Gazetteers
DS911-.78	951.901	Korea—History—To 935	DT6.5-12.25	916.04	Africa—Description and travel
DS912-.43	951.901	Korea—History—Koryo period, 935-1392	DT14	960	Africa—Civilization
DS912.4-.43	951.901	Korea—History—Mongolian Invasions, 1231-1270	DT15-16	960.04	Ethnology—Africa
			DT17-39	960	Africa—History
DS913-915.5	951.902	Korea—History—Yi dynasty, 1392-1910	DT24-28	960.(1-23)	Africa—History—To 1884
			DT25	960.(1-21)	Africa—History—To 1498
DS913-.45	951.902	Korea—History—Japanese Invasions, 1592-1598	DT29-30.2	960.(23-326)	Africa—History—1884-1960
DS913.615-.675	951.902	Korea—History—Manchu Invasions, 1627-1637	DT29	960.(23-314)	Africa—History—1884-1918
DS915-.5	951.902	Korea—History—1864-1910	DT30.5	960.3(26-3)	Africa—History—1960-
			DT43-154	932	Egypt—History
DS915.56-922.4	951.90(2-4s)	Korea—History—20th century	DT43-154	962	Egypt—History
			DT45	913.2003	Egypt—Gazetteers
DS916.525-.58	951.903	Korea—History—Japanese occupation, 1910-1945	DT45	916.2003	Egypt—Gazetteers
DS916.6-922.42	951.904	Korea—History—1945-	DT49.98-56	913.204	Egypt—Description and travel
DS917.5-.55	951.9041	Korea—History—Allied occupation, 1945-1948	DT49.98-56	916.204	Egypt—Description and travel
DS918-921.8	951.9042	Korean War, 1950-1953	DT57-154	932	Egyptology
DS918.2	951.904242	Korean War, 1950-1953—Campaigns	DT63-.5	932.01	Pyramids
			DT70	932	Egypt—Civilization
DS918.2	951.904242	Naktong River (Korea), Battle of, 1950	DT70	962	Egypt—Civilization
			DT71-72	932.004	Ethnology—Egypt
DS920.2	951.904248	Korean War, 1950-1953—Aerial operations.	DT71-72	962.004	Ethnology—Egypt
			DT83-93	932	Egypt—History—To 640 A.D.
DS920.8-.9	951.90428	Korean War, 1950-1953—Atrocities	DT83-91	932.0(1-2)	Egypt—History—To 332 B.C.
DS921-.2	951.90427	Korean War, 1950-1953—History—Prisoners and prisons	DT87-.5	932.014	Egypt—History—Eighteenth dynasty, 1570-1320
DS921	951.90427	Korean War, 1950-1953—Prisoners and prisons, American	DT92-93	932.02	Egypt—History—Greco Roman period, 332 B.C.-640 A.D.
DS921.5.S4	951.90428	Korean War, 1950-1953—Search and rescue operations—Korea (North)	DT92-.7	932.021	Egypt—History—332 - 30 B.C.
			DT92-.7	932.021	Alexandrine War, 48-47 B.C.
			DT93	932.02(2-3)	Egypt—History—30 B.C.-640 A.D.
DS921.6	951.9042092	Korean War, 1950-1953—Personal narratives, American	DT95-107.4	962.0(2-3)	Egypt—History—640-1882
			DT95-.88	962.02	Egypt—History—640-1250

LC	Dewey	Subject Heading	LC	Dewey	Subject Heading
DT95.8-.88	962.02	Egypt—History—Saladin, 1171-1193	DT172	961.0(22-45)	Africa, North—History—647-1517
DT95.8	962.02	Egypt—History—Invasion of Saint Louis, 1249	DT176	961.0(3-5)	Africa, North—History—1882-
DT96-.7	962.02	Egypt—History—1250-1517	DT179.2-.9	939.7	Africa, Northwest
			DT179.2-.9	964	Africa, Northwest
DT97-107.4	962.03	Egypt—History—1517-1882	DT193.5.B45	961.004933	Berbers
			DT211-239	939.74	Libya
DT100-107.87	962.0(3-55)	Egypt—History—1798-	DT211-239	961.2	Libya
DT103	962.03	Egypt—History—French occupation, 1798-1801	DT218-220.2	913.97404	Libya—Description and travel
DT104	962.03	Egypt—History—Mohammed Ali, 1805-1849	DT218-220.2	916.1204	Libya—Description and travel
DT106	962.03	Egypt—History—Ismail, 1863-1879	DT222	939.74	Libya—Civilization
			DT222	961.2	Libya—Civilization
DT107-.4	962.0(3-4)	Egypt—History—Tewfik, 1879-1892	DT223-.2	961.2004	Ethnology—Libya
			DT223.2-236	939.74	Libya—History
DT107.3-.8	962.0(4-51)	Egypt—History—British occupation, 1882-1936	DT223.2-236	961.2	Libya—History
			DT228	939.74	Libya—History—To 642
DT107.8-.87	962.0(4-55)	Egypt—History—1919-	DT229	961.2022	Libya—History—642-1551
DT107.8	962.0(4-51)	Egypt—History—Fuad, 1917-1936	DT231	961.2024	Libya—History—1551-1912
DT107.8	962.04	Egypt—History—Insurrection, 1919	DT235	961.203	Libya—History—1912-1951
DT107.82	962.052	Egypt—History—Revolution, 1952	DT235.5	961.204	Libya—History—1951-1969
DT107.821-.87	962.05(3-5)	Egypt—History—1952-	DT236	961.2042	Libya—History—1969-
DT107.83	962.053	Egypt—History—Intervention, 1956	DT236	961.2042	Libya—History—Coup d'etat, 1969
DT154.1-159.9	962.4	Sudan	DT236	961.2042	Libya—History—Bombardment, 1986
DT154.4	916.24003	Sudan—Gazetteers			
DT154.7-.75	916.2404	Sudan—Description and travel	DT241-269	939.73	Tunisia
			DT241-269	961.1	Tunisia
DT154.9	962.4	Sudan—Civilization	DT244	913.973003	Tunisia—Gazetteers
DT155-.2	962.4004	Ethnology—Sudan	DT244	916.11003	Tunisia—Gazetteers
DT155.2.A35	962.4004965	Acoli (African people)	DT248-250.2	913.97304	Tunisia—Description and travel
DT155.2.D56	962.4004965	Dinka (African people)			
DT155.3-157.67	962.4	Sudan—History	DT248-250.2	916.1104	Tunisia—Description and travel
DT156-.3	962.40(1-2)	Sudan—History—To 1820			
DT156.4-157.67	962.40(3-4)	Sudan—History—1820-	DT252	939.73	Tunisia—Civilization
DT156.6	962.403	Sudan—History—1862-1899	DT252	961.1	Tunisia—Civilization
			DT253-.2	939.73004	Ethnology—Tunisia
DT156.6	962.403	Fashoda Crisis, 1898	DT253-.2	961.1004	Ethnology—Tunisia
DT156.7-157.67	962.403	Sudan—History—1899-1956	DT253.4-264.49	939.73	Tunisia—History
			DT253.4-264.49	961.1	Tunisia—History
DT156.7	962.4043	Sudan—History—Coup d'etat, 1985	DT258	939.73	Tunisia—History—To 647
DT157.67	962.4041	Sudan—History—Civil War, 1955-1972	DT259	961.102	Tunisia—History—647-1516
DT160-177	939.7	Africa, North	DT261-263.76	961.103	Tunisia—History—1516-1881
DT160-177	961	Africa, North			
DT160-176	939.7	Africa, North—History	DT262	961.103	Tunisia—History—Expedition of Charles V, 1535
DT160-176	961	Africa, North—History			
DT163-165.2	913.9704	Africa, North—Description and travel	DT262	961.103	Tunisia—History—Conquest, 1573
DT163-165.2	916.104	Africa, North—Description and travel	DT263.9-264.3	961.104	Tunisia—History—French occupation, 1881-1956
DT168-171	939.701	Africa, North—History—To 647	DT264.35-.49	961.105	Tunisia—History—1956-
			DT271-299	939.71	Algeria
			DT271-299	965	Algeria

LC	Dewey	Subject Heading	LC	Dewey	Subject Heading
DT274	913.971003	Algeria—Gazetteers	DT324-325.92	964.0(4-5)	Morocco—History—20th century
DT274	916.5003	Algeria—Gazetteers	DT324	964.03	Morocco—History—19th century
DT277.8-280.2	913.97104	Algeria—Description and travel	DT331-346	966	Sahara
DT277.8-280.2	916.504	Algeria—Description and travel	DT333	916.604	Sahara—Description and travel
DT282	939.71	Algeria—Civilization	DT352.65	967.0(1-2)	Africa, Central—History—To 1884
DT282	965	Algeria—Civilization	DT352.7	967.03(1-26)	Africa, Central—History—1884-1960
DT283-299	939.71	Algeria—History	DT363	967.0312	Emin Pasha Relief Expedition, 1887-1889
DT283-299	965	Algeria—History			
DT283-.6	939.71004	Ethnology—Algeria	DT365-469	967.6	Africa, East
DT283-.6	965.004	Ethnology—Algeria	DT365.5-.8	967.6	Africa, East—History
DT288	939.71	Algeria—History—To 647	DT365.65	967.601	Africa, East—History—To 1886
DT289	965.022	Algeria—History—647-1516	DT371-398	963	Ethiopia
DT291-292	965.024	Algeria—History—1516-1830	DT371.5	916.3003	Ethiopia—Gazetteers
			DT375-378.3	916.304	Ethiopia—Description and travel
DT291	965.024	Algeria—History—English Expedition, 1620-1621	DT379.5	963	Ethiopia—Civilization
DT291	965.024	Algeria—History—Spanish Expedition, 1775	DT380-.4	963.004	Ethnology—Ethiopia
			DT380.5-387.95	963	Ethiopia—History
DT291	965.024	Algeria—History—English Expedition, 1816	DT383	963.0(1-2)	Ethiopia—History—To 1490
DT291	965.024	Algiers, Battle of, 1816	DT384-386.73	963.0(2-4)	Ethiopia—History—1490-1889
DT292	965.024	Algeria—History—Expedition of Charles V, 1541	DT386.3	963.041	Abyssinian Expedition, 1867-1868
DT294-295.3	965.03	Algeria—History—1830-1962	DT387-.92	963.0(43-6)	Ethiopia—History—1889-1974
DT294	965.03	Algeria—History—French Expedition, 1830	DT387.7-.8	963.054	Ethiopia—History—Rebellion, 1928-1930
DT295-.3	965.04	Algeria—History—1945-1962	DT387.9	963.06	Ethiopia—History—Coup d'etat, 1960
DT295	965.046	Algeria—History—Revolution, 1954-1962	DT397	963.5071	Eritrea—History—1962-1993
DT295.5-.55	965.05	Algeria—History—1962-	DT397.3	963.5072	Eritrea—History—1993-
DT301-330	939.71	Morocco	DT401-409	967.73	Somalia
DT301-330	964	Morocco	DT401.2	916.773003	Somalia—Gazetteers
DT304	913.971003	Morocco—Gazetteers	DT401.8	916.77304	Somalia—Description and travel
DT304	916.4003	Morocco—Gazetteers	DT402.2	967.73	Somalia—Civilization
DT307-310.2	913.97104	Morocco—Description and travel	DT402.3-.45	967.73004	Ethnology—Somalia
DT307-310.2	916.404	Morocco—Description and travel	DT402.5-407.3	967.73	Somalia—History
DT312	939.71	Morocco—Civilization	DT407-.3	967.7305(1-2)	Somalia—History—1960-1991
DT312	964	Morocco—Civilization	DT407	967.73053	Somalia—History—1991-
DT313-.6	939.71004	Ethnology—Morocco	DT407.42	967.73053	Operation Restore Hope, 1992-1993
DT313-.6	964.004	Ethnology—Morocco			
DT313.7-325.92	939.71	Morocco—History	DT411-.9	967.71	Djibouti
DT313.7-325.92	964	Morocco—History	DT411.15	916.771003	Djibouti—Gazetteers
DT318	939.71	Morocco—History—To 647	DT411.27	916.77104	Djibouti—Description and travel
DT319	964.02(1-3)	Morocco—History—647-1516	DT411.4	967.71	Djibouti—Civilization
DT321-323.5	964.025	Morocco—History—1516-1830	DT411.42-.45	967.71004	Ethnology—Djibouti
			DT411.5-.83	967.71	Djibouti—History
DT322	964.025	Kassr-el-Kebir, Battle of, 1578	DT433.215	916.761003	Uganda—Gazetteers

LC	Dewey	Subject Heading	LC	Dewey	Subject Heading
DT433.227	916.76104	Uganda—Description and travel	DT469.M34	969.103	Madagascar—History—Menalamba Rebellion, 1895-1899
DT433.24	967.61	Uganda—Civilization	DT469.M34	969.103	Madagascar—History—Revolution, 1947
DT433.242-.245	967.61004	Ethnology—Uganda			
DT433.252-.287	967.61	Uganda—History	DT469.M39	969.8	Mascarene Islands
DT433.265-.267	967.6101	Uganda—History—To 1890	DT469.M415	916.982003	Mauritius—Gazetteers
DT433.27-.273	967.610(1-3)	Uganda—History—1890-1962	DT469.M429	916.98204	Mauritius—Description and travel
DT433.282	967.61042	Uganda—History—1971-1979	DT469.M44	969.82	Mauritius—Civilization
DT433.284-.286	967.6104(2-4)	Uganda—History—1979-	DT469.M442 -.M445	969.82004	Ethnology—Mauritius
DT433.515	916.762003	Kenya—Gazetteers	DT469.M45-.M495	969.82	Mauritius—History
DT433.527	916.76204	Kenya—Description and travel	DT469.M463	969.8201	Mauritius—History—To 1810
DT433.54	967.62	Kenya—Civilization	DT469.R32	916.981003	Reunion—Gazetteers
DT433.542-.545	967.62004	Ethnology—Kenya	DT469.R35	916.98104	Reunion—Description and travel
DT433.552-.584	967.62	Kenya—History			
DT433.565-.567	967.6201	Kenya—History—To 1895	DT469.R37	969.81	Reunion—Civilization
DT433.565-.577	967.620(1-3)	Kenya—History—To 1963	DT469.R38-.R39	969.81004	Ethnology—Reunion
DT433.57-.577	967.6203	Kenya—History—1895-1963	DT469.R42-.R5	969.81	Reunion—History
			DT469.R44-.R443	969.8102	Reunion—History—To 1764
DT433.58-.584	967.6204	Kenya—History—1963-			
DT437	916.78003	Tanzania—Gazetteers	DT469.R45-.R453	969.8102	Reunion—History—1764-1946
DT439-440.5	916.7804	Tanzania—Description and travel	DT469.R45	969.8102	Reunion—History—British occupation, 1810-1815
DT442.5	967.8	Tanzania—Civilization			
DT443-.3	967.8004	Ethnology—Tanzania	DT469.R455-.R458	969.8104	Reunion—History—1946-
DT443.5-448.25	967.8	Tanzania—History	DT469.S415	916.96003	Seychelles—Gazetteers
DT443.5-448.25	967.80(1-3)	Tanzania—History—To 1964	DT469.S427	916.9604	Seychelles—Description and travel
DT450.115	916.7571003	Rwanda—Gazetteers	DT469.S44	969.6	Seychelles—Civilization
DT450.2	916.757104	Rwanda—Description and travel	DT469.S442-.S43	969.6004	Ethnology—Seychelles
			DT469.S452-.S49	969.6	Seychelles—History
DT450.22	967.571	Rwanda—Civilization	DT469.S48	969.6	Seychelles—History—Coup d'etat, 1977
DT450.24-.25	967.571004	Ethnology—Rwanda			
DT450.26-.437	967.571	Rwanda—History	DT469.S48	969.6	Seychelles—History—Coup d'etat, 1981
DT450.435	967.571043	Rwanda—History—Civil War, 1994	DT470-671	966	Africa, West
DT450.515	916.7572003	Burundi—Gazetteers	DT476	966.02	Africa, West—History—To 1884
DT450.6	916.757204	Burundi—Description and travel	DT476.2-.23	966.03(12-26)	Africa, West—History—1884-1960
DT450.63	967.572	Burundi—Civilization			
DT450.64-.65	967.572004	Ethnology—Burundi	DT476.5-.523	966.03(26-3)	Africa, West—History—1960-
DT450.66-.855	967.572	Burundi—History	DT507	966.23	Ashanti War, 1822-1831
DT469.M24	916.91003	Madagascar—Gazetteers	DT507	966.23	Ashanti War, 1873-1874
DT469.M274	969.1	Madagascar—Civilization	DT507	966.31	Ashanti War, 1895-1896
DT469.M276-.M2	969.1004	Ethnology—Madagascar	DT509.27	916.65104	Gambia—Description and travel
DT469.M282 -.M277	969.1	Madagascar—History	DT509.4	966.51	Gambia—Civilization
			DT509.42-.45	966.51004	Ethnology—Gambia
DT469.M31	969.101	Madagascar—History—To 1810	DT509.5-.83	966.51	Gambia—History
DT469.M32	969.101	Madagascar—History—Hova rule, 1810-1885	DT509.8	966.51031	Gambia—History—Coup d'etat, 1981
DT469.M34	969.10(1-3)	Madagascar—History—1885-1960	DT510.2	916.6704	Ghana—Description and travel
DT469.M34	969.103	Madagascar—History—French Invasion, 1895	DT510.4	966.7	Ghana—Civilization

LC	Dewey	Subject Heading	LC	Dewey	Subject Heading
DT510.42-.43	966.7004	Ethnology—Ghana	DT541.4	966.83	Benin—Civilization
DT510.43.E94	966.7004 + 963374	Ewe (African people)	DT541.42-.45	966.83004	Ethnology—Benin
			DT541.5-.845	966.83	Benin—History
DT510.5-512.34	966.7	Ghana—History	DT541.65-.67	966.8301	Benin—History—To 1894
DT511-.3	966.70(1-3)	Ghana—History—To 1957	DT541.845	966.83051	Benin—History—Coup
DT511	966.7016	Ghana—History—Portuguese rule, 1469-1637			d'etat, 1977
			DT543.27	916.65204	Guinea—Description and travel
DT511	966.701(6-8)	Ghana—History—Danish Settlements, 1659-1850	DT543.4	966.52	Guinea—Civilization
			DT543.42-.45	966.52004	Ethnology—Guinea
DT512-.34	966.705	Ghana—History—1957-	DT543.5-.827	966.52	Guinea—History
DT512	966.7051	Ghana—History—Coup d'etat, 1966	DT543.8	966.52051	Guinea—History—Portuguese Invasion, 1970
DT512	966.7051	Ghana—History—Coup d'etat, 1972			
DT512.32	966.7052	Ghana—History—Coup d'etat, 1979	DT543.822	966.52052	Guinea—History—Coup d'etat, 1984
DT512.32	966.7052	Ghana—History—Coup d'etat, 1981	DT545.15	916.668003	Cote d'Ivoire—Gazetteers
			DT545.27	916.66804	Cote d'Ivoire—Description and travel
DT515.15	916.69003	Nigeria—Gazetteers	DT545.4	966.68	Cote d'Ivoire—Civilization
DT515.27	916.6904	Nigeria—Description and travel	DT545.42-.45	966.68004	Ethnology—Cote d'Ivoire
			DT545.45.D85	966.68004 + 96345	Dyula (African people)
DT515.4	966.9	Nigeria—Civilization			
DT515.42-.45	966.9004	Ethnology—Nigeria	DT545.52-.83	966.68	Cote d'Ivoire—History
DT515.45.E34	966.9004 + 963642	Efik (African people)	DT546.115	916.721003	Gabon—Gazetteers
			DT546.127-.128	916.72104	Gabon—Description and travel
DT515.45.E35	966.900496333	Egba (African people)			
DT515.53-.84	966.9	Nigeria—History	DT546.14	967.21	Gabon—Civilization
DT515.65-.67	966.901	Nigeria—History—To 1851	DT546.142-.145	967.21004	Ethnology—Gabon
			DT546.15-.183	967.21	Gabon—History
DT515.7-.72	966.90(1-3)	Nigeria—History—1851-1899	DT546.165	967.2101	Gabon—History—To 1839
			DT546.165-.175	967.2102	Gabon—History—1839-1960
DT515.7-.77	966.903	Nigeria—History—1900-1960			
DT515.8-.84	966.905	Nigeria—History—1960-	DT546.18-.183	967.2104	Gabon—History—1960-
DT515.832	966.9051	Nigeria—History—Coup d'etat, 1966 (January 15)	DT546.215	916.724003	Congo (Brazzaville)—Gazetteers
DT515.832	966.9051	Nigeria—History—Coup d'etat, 1966 (July 29)	DT546.24	967.24	Congo (Brazzaville)—Civilization
DT515.836	966.9052	Nigeria—History—Civil War, 1967-1970	DT546.242-.245	967.24004	Ethnology—Congo (Brazzaville)
DT515.84	966.9053	Nigeria—History—Coup d'etat, 1983	DT546.25-.283	967.24	Congo (Brazzaville)—History
DT516.15	916.64003	Sierra Leone—Gazetteers	DT546.265-.275	967.240(1-3)	Congo (Brazzaville)—History—To 1960
DT516.2	916.6404	Sierra Leone—Description and travel	DT546.315	916.741003	Central African Republic—Gazetteers
DT516.4	966.4	Sierra Leone—Civilization	DT546.34	967.41	Central African Republic—Civilization
DT516.42-.45	966.4004	Ethnology—Sierra Leone			
DT516.5-.82	966.4	Sierra Leone—History	DT546.342-.345	967.41004	Ethnology—Central African Republic
DT516.65-.72	966.40(1-2)	Sierra Leone—History—To 1896	DT546.348-.384	967.41	Central African Republic—History
DT530.5.D64	966.004963	Dogon (African people)			
DT532.12	966.68	Denkyira (Kingdom)	DT546.365-.37	967.410(1-3)	Central African Republic—History—To 1960
DT532.128	966.3	Fuladu (Kingdom)	DT546.37	967.4103	Kongo Wars, 1928-1931
DT532.128	966.51	Fuladu (Kingdom)	DT546.375-.384	967.4105	Central African Republic—History—1960-
DT532.23	966.3	Niumi (Kingdom)			
DT532.23	966.51	Niumi (Kingdom)	DT546.38	967.4105	Central African Republic—History—Coup d'etat, 1979
DT541.27	916.68304	Benin—Description and travel			

LC	Dewey	Subject Heading	LC	Dewey	Subject Heading
DT546.427	916.74304	Chad—Description and travel	DT571.D68	967.11004 + 96361	Doyayo (African people)
DT546.44	967.43	Chad—Civilization	DT571.D83	967.11004 + 963962	Duala (African people)
DT546.422-.445	967.43004	Ethnology—Chad	DT572-578.4	967.11	Cameroon—History
DT546.457-.483	967.43	Chad—History	DT578	967.1102	Cameroon—History—Coup d'etat, 1984
DT546.48-.483	967.4304	Chad—History—1960-			
DT546.48	967.4304(1-4)	Chad—History—Civil War, 1965-	DT582.15	916.681003	Togo—Gazetteers
			DT582.27	916.68104	Togo—Description and travel
DT547.27	916.62604	Niger—Description and travel	DT582.4	966.81	Togo—Civilization
DT547.4	966.26	Niger—Civilization	DT582.42-.45	966.81004	Ethnology—Togo
DT547.42-.45	966.26004	Ethnology—Niger	DT582.45.E93	966.81004 + 963374	Ewe (African people)
DT547.5-.83	966.26	Niger—History			
DT547.65-.75	966.260(1-3)	Niger—History—To 1960	DT582.5-.82	966.81	Togo—History
DT549.15	916.63003	Senegal—Gazetteers	DT582.75	966.8103	Togo—History—1922-1960
DT549.27	916.6304	Senegal—Description and travel	DT613.2	916.65704	Guinea-Bissau—Description and travel
DT549.4	966.3	Senegal—Civilization	DT613.4	966.57	Guinea-Bissau—Civilization
DT549.42-.45	966.3004	Ethnology—Senegal			
DT549.45.D56	966.30049632	Diola (African people)	DT613.42-.45	966.57004	Ethnology—Guinea-Bissau
DT549.47-.83	966.3	Senegal—History	DT613.5-.83	966.57	Guinea-Bissau—History
DT549.7-.73	966.30(1-3)	Senegal—History—To 1960	DT613.78	966.5702	Guinea-Bissau—History—Revolution, 1963-1974
DT549.8-.83	966.305	Senegal—History—1960-	DT613.8	966.5703	Guinea-Bissau—History—Coup d'etat, 1980
DT549.8	966.3051	Senegal—History—Coup d'etat, 1962			
			DT615.42-.45	967.15004	Ethnology—Sao Tome and Principe
DT551.15	916.623003	Mali—Gazetteers	DT615.5-.8	967.15	Sao Tome and Principe—History
DT551.27	916.62304	Mali—Description and travel			
DT551.4	966.23	Mali—Civilization	DT620.15	916.718003	Equatorial Guinea—Gazetteers
DT551.42-.45	966.23004	Ethnology—Mali			
DT551.45.D64	966.23004963	Dogon (African people)	DT620.27	967.1804	Equatorial Guinea—Description and travel
DT551.45.S	966.23	Songhai Empire			
DT551.5-.82	966.23	Mali—History	DT620.4	967.18	Equatorial Guinea—Civilization
DT551.8	966.23051	Mali—History—Coup d'etat, 1968	DT620.42-.45	967.18004	Ethnology—Equatorial Guinea
DT554.15	916.61003	Mauritania—Gazetteers			
DT554.27	916.6104	Mauritania—Description and travel	DT620.46-.83	967.18	Equatorial Guinea—History
			DT623	916.662003	Liberia—Gazetteers
DT554.4	966.1	Mauritania—Civilization	DT625-627	916.66204	Liberia—Description and travel
DT554.42-.45	966.1004	Ethnology—Mauritania			
DT554.52-.83	966.1	Mauritania—History	DT629	966.62	Liberia—Civilization
DT554.8-.83	966.105	Mauritania—History—1960-	DT630-.5	966.62004	Ethnology—Liberia
			DT630.8-636.53	966.62	Liberia—History
DT555.15	916.625003	Burkina Faso—Gazetteers	DT633-.3	966.6201	Liberia—History—To 1847
DT555.27	916.62504	Burkina Faso—Description and travel	DT634-.3	966.6202	Liberia—History—1847-1944
DT555.4	966.25	Burkina Faso—Civilization			
DT555.42-.45	966.25004	Ethnology—Burkina Faso	DT635-636	966.62031	Liberia—History—1944-1971
DT555.52-.83	966.25	Burkina Faso—History			
DT555.8	966.25053	Burkina Faso—History—Coup d'etat, 1987	DT636.2-.4	966.62031	Liberia—History—1971-1980
			DT636.5-.53	966.6203(2-3)	Liberia—History—1980-
DT563	916.711003	Cameroon—Gazetteers	DT636.5	966.62032	Liberia—History—Coup d'etat, 1980
DT566-568	916.71104	Cameroon—Description and travel			
DT569.5	967.11	Cameroon—Civilization	DT636.5	966.62032	Liberia—History—Civil War, 1989-
DT570-571	967.11004	Ethnology—Cameroon			
			DT639	916.75104	Congo River—Description and travel

LC	Dewey	Subject Heading	LC	Dewey	Subject Heading
DT645-647.5	916.75104	Zaire—Description and travel	DT1638-1648	968.8103	Namibia—History—1946-1990
DT649	967.51	Zaire—Civilization	DT1648	968.8104	Namibia—History—1990-
DT649.5-650	967.51004	Ethnology—Zaire	DT1714	916.8003	South Africa—Gazetteers
DT650.2-663	967.51	Zaire—History	DT1730-1738	916.804	South Africa—Description and travel
DT654-655.2	967.510(1-22)	Zaire—History—To 1908	DT1752	968	South Africa—Civilization
DT657-.2	967.51024	Zaire—History—1908-1960	DT1754-1770	968.004	Ethnology—South Africa
DT658-.25	967.5103	Zaire—History— 1960-	DT1760	968.29	Homelands (South Africa)
DT658	967.51031	Zaire—History—Civil War, 1960-1965	DT1772-1969	968	South Africa—History
DT658.25	967.51033	Zaire—History— Shaba Invasion, 1977	DT1807-1845	968.0(2-42)	South Africa—History—To 1836
DT658.25	967.51033	Zaire—History— Shaba Uprising, 1978	DT1837	968.0(3-45)	South Africa—History—Frontier Wars, 1811-1878
DT671.C22	916.65804	Cape Verde—Description and travel	DT1848-1922	968.04(2-9)	South Africa—History—1836-1909
DT671.C23	966.58	Cape Verde—Civilization	DT1853	968.044	South Africa—History—Great Trek, 1836-1840
DT671.C242-.C2	966.58004	Ethnology—Cape Verde	DT1863	968.045	South Africa—History—Xhosa Cattle-Killing, 1856-1857
DT671.C25-.C28	966.58	Cape Verde—History			
DT671.C265	966.580(1-2)	Cape Verde—History—To 1975	DT1875-1882	968.045	Zulu War, 1879
DT671.C28	966.5803	Cape Verde—History—1975-	DT1888	968.045	South Africa—History—Usutu Uprising, 1888
DT1123	968.0009034	Africa, Southern—History—Mfecane period, 1816-ca. 1840	DT1889	968.045	Jameson's Raid, 1895-1896
DT1264	916.73003	Angola—Gazetteers	DT1924-1941	968.0(49-58)	South Africa—History—1906-1961
DT1282-1286	916.7304	Angola—Description and travel	DT1933	968.052	South Africa—History—Rebellion, 1914-1915
DT1302	967.3	Angola—Civilization	DT1945-1970	968.06	South Africa—History—1961-
DT1304-1308	967.3004	Ethnology—Angola			
DT1314-1436	967.3	Angola—History	DT1959	968.0627	South Africa—History—Soweto Uprising, 1976
DT1357-1369	967.301	Angola—History—1482-1648	DT2434	916.883003	Botswana—Gazetteers
DT1357	967.301	Angola—History—To 1482	DT2448	968.8304	Botswana—Description and travel
DT1373-1382	967.302	Angola—History—1648-1885	DT2452	968.83	Botswana—Civilization
			DT2454-2458	968.83004	Ethnology—Botswana
DT1385-1396	967.30(2-3)	Angola—History—1885-1961	DT2464-2502	968.83	Botswana—History
			DT2483-2493	968.830(1-2)	Botswana—History—To 1966
DT1398-1417	967.303	Angola—History—Revolution, 1961-1975	DT2496-2502	968.8303	Botswana—History—1966-
DT1428	967.304	Angola—History—Civil War, 1975-	DT2554	916.885003	Lesotho—Gazetteers
DT1514	916.881003	Namibia—Gazetteers	DT2572	916.88504	Lesotho—Description and travel
DT1532-1536	916.88104	Namibia—Description and travel	DT2582	968.85	Lesotho—Civilization
DT1552	968.81	Namibia—Civilization	DT2592-2596	968.85004	Ethnology—Lesotho
DT1554-1558	968.81004	Ethnology—Namibia	DT2604-2660	968.85	Lesotho—History
DT1564-1648	968.81	Namibia—History	DT2630-2648	968.850(1-2)	Lesotho—History—To 1966
DT1587-1601	968.8101	Namibia—History—To 1884	DT2652-2660	968.8503	Lesotho—History—1966-
DT1603-1622	968.8102	Namibia—History—1884-1915	DT2714	916.887003	Swaziland—Gazetteers
DT1618	968.8103	Namibia—History—Herero Revolt, 1904-1907	DT2732	916.88704	Swaziland—Description and travel
DT1625-1636	968.8103	Namibia—History—1915-1946	DT2742	968.87	Swaziland—Civilization
			DT2744-2746	968.87004	Ethnology—Swaziland
			DT2754-2806	968.87	Swaziland—History

LC	Dewey	Subject Heading	LC	Dewey	Subject Heading
DT2884	916.891003	Zimbabwe—Gazetteers	DT3345-3348	967.901	Mozambique—History—To 1505
DT2886	916.8910451	Zimbabwe—Guidebooks			
DT2900-2904	916.89104	Zimbabwe—Description and travel	DT3350-3359	967.90(1-2)	Mozambique—History—1505-1698
DT2908	968.91	Zimbabwe—Civilization	DT3361-3374	967.902	Mozambique—History—1698-1891
DT2910-2913	968.91004	Ethnology—Zimbabwe			
DT2914-3000	968.91	Zimbabwe—History	DT3376-3387	967.90(2-3)	Mozambique—History—1891-1975
DT2959-2979	968.910(2-4)	Zimbabwe—History—1890-1965			
DT2968	968.9102	Zimbabwe—History—Ndebele Insurrection, 1896	DT3381	967.902	Mozambique—History—War of 1894-1895
			DT3387	967.903	Mozambique—History—Revolution, 1964-1975
DT2970	968.9102	Zimbabwe—History—Shona Insurrection, 1896-1897	DT3389-3398	967.905	Mozambique—History—1975-
DT2981-2994	968.9104	Zimbabwe—History—1965-1980	DU	990	Oceania
			DU10	919.(5-6)003	Oceania—Gazetteers
DT2988	968.9104	Zimbabwe—History—Chimurenga War, 1966-1980	DU19-23.5	919.(5-6)04	Oceania—Description and travel
			DU28.11-66	995-996	Oceania—History
DT2996-3000	968.9105	Zimbabwe—History—1980-	DU90	919.4003	Australia—Gazetteers
DT3037	916.894003	Zambia—Gazetteers	DU97-5-105.2	919.404	Australia—Description and travel
DT3050	916.89404	Zambia—Description and travel	DU98.1	994.01	Australia—History—To 1788
DT3052	968.94	Zambia—Civilization	DU108-117.2	994	Australia—History
DT3054-3058	968.94004	Ethnology—Zambia	DU114-115.2	994.0(2-3)	Australia—History—1788-1900
DT3064-3119	968.94	Zambia—History			
DT3079-3089	968.9401	Zambia—History—To 1890	DU115	994.02	Australia—History—1788-1851
DT3091-3101	968.9402	Zambia—History—1890-1924	DU116-117.2	994.04	Australia—History—20th century
DT3103-3106	968.9402	Zambia—History—1924-1953	DU120-125	994.004	Ethnology—Australia
			DU125.D59	994.0049915	Diyari (Australian people)
DT3108-3111	968.9403	Zambia—History—1953-1964	DU405	919.3003	New Zealand—Gazetteers
			DU409-413	919.304	New Zealand—Description and travel
DT3113-3119	968.9404	Zambia—History—1964-			
DT3169	916.897003	Malawi—Gazetteers	DU418	993	New Zealand—Civilization
DT3182	916.89704	Malawi—Description and travel	DU419-422	993	New Zealand—History
			DU420.12-.14	993.01	New Zealand—History—To 1840
DT3187	968.97	Malawi—Civilization	DU420.16-.18	993.02(1-2)	New Zealand—History—1840-1876
DT3189-3192	968.97004	Ethnology—Malawi			
DT3194-3237	968.97	Malawi—History			
DT3211-3214	968.9701	Malawi—History—To 1891	DU420.16	993.021	New Zealand—History—Maori War, 1845-1847
DT3216-3225	968.9702	Malawi—History—1891-1953	DU420.22-.34	993.022	New Zealand—History—Taranaki War, 1860-1861
DT3225	968.9702	Malawi—History—Chilembwe Rebellion, 1915	DU420.22-.24	993.0(23-31)	New Zealand—History—1876-1918
DT3227-3230	968.9703	Malawi—History—1953-1964	DU420.26-.28	993.032	New Zealand—History—1918-1945
DT3232-3240	968.9704	Malawi—History—1964-	DU420.32-.34	993.0(35-4)	New Zealand—History—1945-
DT3294	916.79003	Mozambique—Gazetteers			
DT3308-3312	916.7904	Mozambique—Description and travel	DU422.5-424.5	993.004	Ethnology—New Zealand
			DU490	995	Melanesia
DT3320	967.9	Mozambique—Civilization	DU500	996.5	Micronesia
DT3324-3328	967.9004	Ethnology—Mozambique	DU510	996	Polynesia
DT3330-3398	967.9	Mozambique—History	DU560-568	996.6	Caroline Islands
			DU565-567	996.6	Caroline Islands—History

LC	Dewey	Subject Heading	LC	Dewey	Subject Heading
DU600	996.11	Fiji	E78	978.9004974	Pueblo Indians— Antiquities
DU615	996.81	Kiribati			
DU622	919.69003	Hawaii—Gazetteers	E78.I5	976.603004973	Five Civilized Tribes
DU624.5	996.9	Hawaii—Civilization	E78.I5	976.603004975	Five Civilized Tribes
DU624.6-.7	996.9004	Ethnology—Hawaii	E78.045	976.604004973	Five Civilized Tribes
DU625-629	996.9	Hawaii—History	E78.045	976.604004975	Five Civilized Tribes
DU640-648	996.7	Mariana Islands	E81-83.895	973.(1-8)	Indians of North America—Wars
DU650	996.4	Line Islands			
DU700-701	996.31	Marquesas Islands	E82	973.(1-26)	Indians of North America—Wars—1600-1750
DU710	996.83	Marshall Islands			
DU720	995.97	New Caledonia			
DU739-747	995	New Guinea	E83.655	974.702	Esopus Indians—Wars, 1655-1660
DU740	995.3	Papua New Guinea			
DU760	995.95	Vanuatu	E83.663	974.702	Esopus Indians—Wars, 1663-1664
DU790	996.81	Phoenix Islands (Kiribati)			
DU800	996.18	Pitcairn Island	E83.67	974.402	Falls Fight, 1676
DU810-819	996.1(3-4)	Samoan Islands	E83.72	974.02	Eastern Indians, Wars with, 1722-1726
DU817	996.1(3-4)	Samoan question			
DU819.A1	996.13	American Samoa	E83.(759-813)	973.(26-53)	Indians of North America—Wars—1750-1815
DU819.A2	996.14	Western Samoa			
DU850	995.93	Solomon Islands			
DU870	996.21	Society Islands	E83.77	975.502	Dunmore's Expedition, 1774
DU870	996.211	Tahiti			
DU880	996.12	Tonga	E83.775	975.402	Indians of North America—Wars—1775-1783
DU910	996.15	Tokelau			
DU920	996.16	Wallis and Futuna Islands			
			E83.79	973.41	Indians of North America—Wars—1790-1794
DX	909.0491497	Gypsies			
DX125-127	920.009291497	Gypsies—Biography	E83.812	973.52	Indians of North America—Wars—1812-1815
DX135-145	909.0491497	Gypsies—History			
			E83.813	975.803	Creek War, 1813-1814
E	970	America	E83.8(17-75)	973.(53-82)	Indians of North America—Wars—1815-1875
E	980	America			
E11	970.005	America—Periodicals			
E11	980.005	America—Periodicals	E83.817	975.903	Seminole War, 1st, 1817-1818
E14	917.003	America—Gazetteers			
E14	918.003	America—Gazetteers	E83.83	977.303	Black Hawk War, 1832
E16-18.85	970	America—History	E83.835	975.904	Seminole War, 2nd, 1835-1842
E16-18.85	980	America—History			
E17	920.07	America—Biography	E83.836	975.803	Creek War, 1836
E17	920.08	America—Biography	E83.84	979.02	Pacific Coast Indians, Wars with, 1847-1865
E31-45	970	North America			
E31	970.005	North America— Periodicals	E83.86	978.302	Dakota Indians—Wars, 1862-1865
E35	917.003	North America— Gazetteers	E83.86	978.402	Dakota Indians—Wars, 1862-1865
E36	920.07	North America—Biography	E83.863	973.7	Indians of North America—Wars—1862-1865
E40	970	North America— Civilization			
			E83.863	978.802	Sand Creek Massacre, Colo., 1864
E41	917.04	North America— Description and travel			
			E83.863	978.701	Shoshoni Indians—Wars, 1863-1865
E45-46	970	North America—History			
E51-73	970.00497	Indians			
E58	970.00497	Indians—History	E83.863	979.202	Shoshoni Indians—Wars, 1863-1865
E59.C6	391.08997	Indians—Costume			
E59.F6	398.08997	Indians—Folklore	E83.863	979.602	Shoshoni Indians—Wars, 1863-1865
E75-99	973.1	United States—Antiquities			
E75-99	973.0497	Indians of North America			

LC	Dewey	Subject Heading	LC	Dewey	Subject Heading
E83.863	979.60(1-2)	Bear River Massacre, Idaho, 1863	E99.D1	978.303	Wounded Knee Massacre, S.D., 1890
E83.866	973.8(1-7)	Indians of North America—Wars—1866-1895	E99.D2	974.00497345	Delaware Indians
			E99.D5	979.40049757	Diegueno Indians
E83.869	973.81	Indians of North America—Wars—1868-1869	E99.E7	979.8004971	Eskimos
			E99.E7	979.8004971	Nunamiut Eskimos
			E99.E7	979.8004971	Yupik Eskimos
E83.868	978.802	Beecher Island, Battle of, 1868	E99.E7	979.8004971	Koniagmiut Eskimos
			E99.H7	979.100497458	Hopi Indians
E83.876	978.602	Little Bighorn, Battle of the, Mont., 1876	E99.I7	974.80049755	Iroquois Indians
			E99.M12	974.70049734	Mahican Indians
E83.876	978.302	Dakota Indians—Wars, 1876	E99.M44	977.500497313	Menominee Indians
			E99.M77	979.004975722	Mohave Indians
E83.876	978.402	Dakota Indians—Wars, 1876	E99.M8	974.7004 + 9755	Mohawk Indians
E83.89	978.303031	Dakota Indians—Wars, 1890-1891	E99.M83	974.600497344	Mohegan Indians
			E99.M95	975.0049738	Muskogean Indians
E83.876	978.403031	Dakota Indians—Wars, 1876	E99.N3	979.10049726	Navajo Indians
E83.89	978.3031	Wounded Knee Massacre, S.D., 1890	E99.N5	979.7004 + 9741	Nez Perce Indians
E98.C8	391.413008997	Moccasins	E99.O3	978.0049752	Oglala Indians
E98.D2	299.74	Indian dance—North America	E99.O8	977.8004 + 9752	Osage Indians
E98.D2	299.7138	Eagle dance	E99.P244	976.481	Panhandle culture
E98.D2	299.7138	Sun dance	E99.P3	978.200497933	Pawnee Indians
E98.E6	331.125008997	Indians of North America—Employment	E99.P6	979.1004974 + 5529	Pima Indians
E98.M7	332.4089973	Wampum	E99.P9	978.9004974	Pueblo Indians
E98.P6	497	Picture-writing, Indian	E99.P9	978.9004974	Cliff-dwellers
E98.P86	394.2608997	Powwows	E99.P9	978.9004974	Pueblo Indians
E98.P95	155.8497	Indians of North America—Psychology	E99.S28	975.9004 + 9738	Seminole Indians
E98.R2	299.7138	Wolf ritual	E99.S35	976.800497317	Shawnee Indians
E98.R3	299.7	Indians of North America—Religion	E99.S39	979.0049745	Shoshonean Indians
E98.S5	419	Sign language	E99.S4	979.6004 + 9745	Shoshoni Indians
E98.S7	973.0497	Indians of North America—Social life and customs	E99.T2	978.9004 + 9749	Taos Indians
			E99.T34	978.0049752	Teton Indians
E98.S7	390.08997	Indians of North America—Social life and customs	E99.U8	978.8004 + 9745	Ute Indians
			E99.Z9	979.100497994	Zuni Indians
E98.W2	399.08997	Scalping	E101-135	970.01	America—Discovery and exploration
E99.A12	974.004971	Abitibi Indians			
E99.A13	974.0049734	Abenaki Indians	E101-135	980.01	America—Discovery and exploration
E99.A34	979.80049719	Aleuts			
E99.A349	974.004973	Algonquin Indians	E120	394.264	Columbus Day
E99.A35	970.00497	Algonquian Indians	E151-887	973	United States
E99.A6	979.0049725	Apache Indians	E151	973.05	United States—Periodicals
E99.A7	978.00497354	Arapaho Indians	E154	917.3003	United States—Gazetteers
E99.C5	975.00497557	Cherokee Indians	E154.5-.7	973.025	United States—Directories
E99.C53	978.00497353	Cheyenne Indians	E159.5	973.1	United States—Antiquities
E99.C6	977.00497333	Ojibwa Indians	E160	333.780973	National parks and reserves—United States
E99.C8	976.00497387	Choctaw Indians			
E99.C85	976.4004 + 9745	Comanche Indians	E161.5-169.04	917.304	United States—Description and travel
E99.C92	978.004975272	Crow Indians	E162-168	973	United States—Civilization
E99.D1	978.004975243	Dakota Indians	E169.1-.12	973	United States—Civilization

69

LC	Dewey	Subject Heading	LC	Dewey	Subject Heading
E171-183.9	973	United States—History	E185.86	305.2308996 + 073	Afro-American children
E175-.7	973.072	United States—Historiography	E185.86	973.04	Afro-Americans—Social life and customs
E176	920.073	United States—Biography	E185.86	390.089 + (96073)	Afro-Americans—Social life and customs
E176.4	321.80420973	Presidents—United States—Mistresses	E185.86	973.0496073	Afro-Americans—Social conditions
E179.5	973	United States—Territorial expansion	E185.96-.97	920.009296073	Afro-Americans—Biography
E181	355.00973	United States—History, Military	E186-199	973.(1-2)	United States—History—Colonial period, ca. 1600-1775
E181	355.00973	United States. Army—History	E196	973.25	United States—History—King William's War, 1689-1697
E182	359.00973	United States. Navy—History			
E182	359.00973	United States—History, Naval	E196	974.702	New York(State)—History—King William's War, 1689-1697
E183.8.I55	327.730550947	Iran Hostage Crisis, 1979-1981	E197	973.25	United States—History—Queen Anne's War, 1702-1713
E184-185.98	973.04	Ethnology—United States			
E184-185.98	305.8073	United States—Race relations	E197	974.403	Massachusetts—History—Queen Anne's War, 1702-1713
E184.A1	305.8073	United States—Ethnic relations	E197	974.702	New York (State)—History—Queen Anne's War, 1702-1713
E184.D6	973.04687293 + 073	Dominican Americans			
E184.D9	973.043931073	Dutch Americans	E197	975.702	South Carolina—History—Queen Anne's War, 1702-1713
E184.E17	973.04917073	East European Americans			
E184.E2	973.04914073	East Indian Americans	E198	973.26	United States—History—King George's War, 1744-1748
E184.E95	973.04(2-8)073	European Americans			
E184.F4	973.049921073	Filipino Americans	E198	974.202	New Hampshire—History—King George's War, 1744-1748
E184.F5	973.0494541 + 073	Finnish Americans			
E184.M5	973.046872073	Mexican Americans	E198	974.502	Rhode Island—History—King George's War, 1744-1748
E184.S19	973.043981073	Danish Americans			
E184.S75	973.0468073	Hispanic Americans	E198	974.402	Massachusetts—History—King George's War, 1744-1748
E185	973.0496073	Afro-Americans			
E185.18-.98	973.0496073	Afro-Americans—History	E199	973.26	United States—History—French and Indian War, 1755-1763
E185.18	973.(1-7) + 0496073	Afro-Americans—History—To 1863			
E185.2	973.(7-82) + 0496073	Afro-Americans—History—1863-1877	E199	973.26	Braddock's Campaign, 1755
E185.6	973.(83-923) + 0496073	Afro-Americans—History—1877-1964	E199	973.26	Fort William Henry (N.Y.)—Capture, 1757
E185.61	305.896073	Afro-Americans—Segregation	E199	973.26	Forbes Expedition against Fort Duquesne, 1758
E185.61	323.1196073	Afro-Americans—Civil rights	E199	973.26	Ticonderoga, Battle of, 1758
E185.615	973.92(3-9) + 0496073	Afro-Americans—History—1964-	E199	973.26	Fort Oswego (Oswego, N.Y.)—Capture, 1756
E185.62	306.846	Miscegenation	E199	973.26	Necessity, Fort, Battle of, 1754
E185.625	155.8496073	Afro-Americans—Psychology			
E185.63	355.30089960 + 73	United States—Armed Forces—Afro-Americans			
E185.8	338.790896073	Afro-Americans in business			
E185.8	330.9730896 + 073	Afro-Americans—Economic conditions			
E185.86	306.850896073	Afro-American families			

70

LC	Dewey	Subject Heading	LC	Dewey	Subject Heading
E199	974.402	Massachusetts—History—French and Indian War, 1755-1763	E263.G3	975.80(2-3)	Georgia—History—Revolution, 1775-1783
E199	974.02	New England—History—French & Indian War, 1755-1763	E263.L	976.30(2-3)	Louisiana—History—Revolution, 1775-1783
E201-298	973.3	United States—History—Revolution, 1775-1783	E263.M3	975.20(2-3)	Maryland—History—Revolution, 1775-1783
E215.3	973.3112	Non-importation agreements, 1768-1769	E263.M4	974.40(2-3)	Massachusetts—History—Revolution, 1775-1783
E215.4	973.3113	Boston Massacre, 1770	E263.N4	974.20(2-3)	New Hampshire—History—Revolution, 1775-1783
E215.7	973.3115	Tea tax (American colonies)	E263.N5	974.90(2-3)	New Jersey—History—Revolution, 1775-1783
E215.7	973.3115	Boston Tea Party, 1773	E263.N6	974.70(2-3)	New York (State)—History—Revolution, 1775-1783
E230-241	973.33	United States—History—Revolution—1775-1783—Campaigns	E263.N8	975.60(2-3)	North Carolina—History—Revolution, 1775-1783
E231	973.33(1-2)	Canadian Invasion, 1775-1776	E263.O	977.102	Ohio—History—Revolution, 1775-1783
E231	394.26973	Patriots' Day	E263.R4	974.50(2-3)	Rhode Island—History—Revolution, 1775-1783
E234	973.334	Clark's Expedition to the Illinois, 1778-1779	E263.S7	975.70(2-3)	South Carolina—History—Revolution, 1775-1783
E235	973.335	Sullivan's Indian Campaign, 1779	E263.V5	974.30(2-3)	Vermont—History—Revolution, 1775-1783
E239	973.339	Evacuation Day, Nov. 25, 1783	E263.V8	975.50(2-3)	Virginia—History—Revolution, 1775-1783
E241.B4	973.333	Bennington, Battle of, 1777	E263.W5	972.972	Virgin Islands of the United States—History—1775-1783
E241.B8	973.333	Brandywine, Battle of, 1777	E263.W5	972.972	Virgin Islands of the United States—History—1775-1793
E241.B9	973.3312	Bunker Hill, Battle of, 1775	E271	973.35	Dominica, Battle of, 1782
E241.C56	973.337	Claps Mill, Battle of, N.C., 1781	E277	973.314	American loyalists
E241.C7	973.3311	Concord, Battle of, 1775	E301-655	973.3	United States—History—1783-1865
E241.E	973.337	Eutaw Springs, Battle of, 1781	E303-309	973.318	United States—History—Confederation, 1783-1789
E241.G9	973.337	Guilford Court House, Battle of 1781	E310-337	973.4	United States—History—Constitutional period, 1789-1809
E241.K48	973.335	Kettle Creek (Ga.), Battle of, 1779	E312.6	394.26973	Washington's Birthday
E241.L6	973.3311	Lexington, Battle of, 1775	E315	973.43	Whiskey Rebellion, Pa., 1794
E241.M7	973.334	Monmouth, Battle of, 1778	E326	973.44	Fries Rebellion, 1798-1799
E241.P2	973.333	Paoli Massacre, 1777	E328	973.44	Kentucky and Virginia resolutions of 1798
E356.C	973.523	Champlain, Lake, Battle of, 1814	E333	973.46	Louisiana Purchase
E356.C4	973.523	Chateauguay, Battle of, 1813	E334	973.48	Burr Conspiracy, 1805-1807
E356.C8	973.523	Crane Island, Battle of, 1813	E335	973.47	United States—History—Tripolitan War, 1801-1805
E259	973.34(4-5)	United States. Continental Army—History			
E263.D3	975.210(2-3)	Delmarva Peninsula—History—Revolution, 1775-1783			
E263.D3	975.10(2-3)	Delaware—History—Revolution, 1775-1783			

LC	Dewey	Subject Heading	LC	Dewey	Subject Heading
E336.5	973.48	Embargo, 1807-1809	E423	973.64	Compromise of 1850
E331-337	973.4(6-8)	United States—History—1801-1809	E423	973.7113	Compromise of 1850
E338	973.(51-68)	United States—History—1815-1861	E441-453	973.711	Slavery
			E450	973.7115	Underground railroad
E341-370	973.5(1-4)	United States—History—1809-1817	E461-656	973.7	United States—History—Civil War, 1861-1865
E351-364.9	973.52	United States—History—War of 1812	E457	973.7	Lincoln, Abraham, 1809-1865
E356.B2	973.523	Baltimore, Battle of, 1814	E458-459	973.713	Secession—Southern States
E356.B5	973.523	Bladensburg, Battle of, 1814	E468.9	373.70223	United States—History—Civil War, 1861-1865—Cartography
E356.D4	973.523	Detroit (Mich.)—Surrender to the British, 1812	E470.2	955.00975	Confederate States of America—History, Military
E356.D8	973.523	Dudley's Defeat, 1813			
E356.E6	973.5254	Erie, Lake, Battle of, 1813	E470.9	978	West (U.S.)—History—Civil War, 1861-1865
E356.N5	973.5239	New Orleans (La.), Battle of, 1815	E471.1	975.703	South Carolina—History—Civil War, 1861-1865
E356.W3	975.302	Washington (D.C.)—History—Capture by the British, 1814	E472.14	973.731	Big Bethel, Battle of, 1861
E357-359	974.03	New England—History—War of 1812	E472.18	973.731	Bull Run, 1st Battle of, Va., 1861
E357.2-.3	973.525	Impressment	E472.28	973.731	Belmont (Mo.), Battle of, 1861
E359.5.D3	975.103	Delaware—History—War of 1812	E472.63	973.731	Ball's Bluff, Battle of, 1861
E359.5.G4	975.803	Georgia—History—War of 1812	E472.96	973.731	Fort Henry (Tenn.), Battle of, 1862
E359.5.L8	976.304	Louisiana—History—War of 1812	E473.2	973.752	Hampton Roads (Va.), Battle of, 1862
E359.5.M2	975.203	Maryland—History—War of 1812	E473.54	973.731	Shiloh, Battle of, 1862
E359.5.M3	974.403	Massachusetts—History—War of 1812	E473.55	973.731	Chattanooga Railroad Expedition, 1862
E359.5.N6	974.703	New York (State)—History—War of 1812	E473.6-.68	973.73(1-3)	Peninsular Campaign, 1862
E359.5.O2	977.103	Ohio—History—War of 1812	E473.68	973.732	Seven Days' Battles, 1862
E359.5.V3	974.303	Vermont—History—War of 1812	E473.7	973.732	Shenandoah Valley Campaign, 1862
E359.5.V8	975.503	Virginia—History—War of 1812	E473.77	973.732	Bull Run, 2nd Battle of, Va., 1862
E365	973.53	United State—History—War with Algeria, 1815	E473.77	973.732	Chantilly (Va.), Battle of, 1862
E371-375	973.54	United States—History—1817-1825	E474.61	973.7336	Maryland Campaign, 1862
E373	973.7113	Missouri compromise	E474.65	973.733	Antietam, Battle of, Md., 1862
E376-380	973.55	United States—History—1825-1829	E474.85	973.733	Fredericksburg (Va.), Battle of, 1862
E384.3	973.561	Nullification	E474.9	973.734	Chalk Bluff (Ark. and Mo), Battle of, 1863
E398	973.57	Aroostock War, 1839			
E401-415.2	973.62	Mexican War, 1846-1848	E475.3	973.734	Kelly's Ford (Va.), Battle of, 1863
E405.2	973.6242	Doniphan's Expedition, 1846-1847	E475.35	973.733	Chancellorsville (Va.), Battle of, 1863
E405.2	973.6242	Kearny's Expedition, 1846	E475.53	973.7349	Gettysburg (Pa.), Battle of, 1863
E406.M7	973.6242	Monterrey (Mexico), Battle of, 1846			
E415.6-680	973.(63-82)	United States—History—1849-1877	E475.76	973.735	Droop Mountain (W. Va.), Battle of, 1863
E415.7	973.711	Squatter sovereignty			

LC	Dewey	Subject Heading	LC	Dewey	Subject Heading
E475.81	973.73(4-5)	Chickamauga (Ga.), Battle of, 1863	E516	976.205	Mississippi—History—Civil War, 1861-1865
E475.97	973.7359	Chattanooga (Tenn.), Battle of, 1863	E517	977.803	Missouri—History—Civil War, 1861-1865
E476.52	973.736	Spotsylvania Court House, Battle of, Va., 1864	E520	974.203	New Hampshire—History—Civil War, 1861-1865
E476.65	973.736	Lynchburg (Va.), Battle of, 1864	E521	974.903	New Jersey—History—Civil War, 1861-1865
E476.66	973.737	Maryland Campaign, 1864	E522	978.904	New Mexico—History—Civil War, 1861-1865
E476.66	973.73(6-7)	Shenandoah Valley Campaign, 1864 (May-August)	E524	975.603	North Carolina—History—Civil War, 1861-1865
E476.69	973.7378	Sherman's March to the Sea	E525	977.103	Ohio—History—Civil War, 1861-1865
E476.7	973.7371	Atlanta Campaign, 1864	E528	974.503	Rhode Island—History—Civil War, 1861-1865
E476.85	973.75	Mobile Bay (Ala.), Battle of, 1864	E529	975.703	South Carolina—History—Civil War, 1861-1865
E477.16	973.737	Big Blue, Battle of the, Mo., 1864	E531	976.804	Tennessee—History—Civil War, 1861-1865
E477.21	973.737	Fort Harrison (Va.), Battle of, 1864	E532	976.405	Texas—History—Civil War, 1861-1865
E477.33	973.737	Shenandoah Valley Campaign, 1864 (August-November)	E532.95	979.202	Utah—History—Civil War, 1861-1865
E477.33	973.737	Cedar Creek (Va.), Battle of, 1864	E533	974.303	Vermont—History—Civil War, 1861-1865
E477.65	973.738	Shenandoah Valley Campaign, 1865	E534	975.503	Virginia—History—Civil War, 1861-1865
E477.67	973.738	Dinwiddie Court House, Battle of, Dinwiddie, Va.1865	E536	975.403	West Virginia—History—Civil War, 1861-1865
E477.67	973.738	Appomattox Campaign, 1865	E537	977.503	Wisconsin—History—Civil War, 1861-1865
E482-489	973.713	Confederate States of America	E545	355.00975	Confederate States of America—History, Military
E482-489	975	Confederate States of America	E558.1-.9	975.905	Florida—History—Civil War, 1861-1865
E487-488	973.713	Confederate States of America—History	E559	975.803	Georgia—History—Civil War, 1861-1865
E487-488	975	Confederate States of America—History	E565	976.305	Louisiana—History—Civil War, 1861-1865
E487	973.713	Confederate States of America—Social conditions	E568	976.205	Mississippi—History—Civil War, 1861-1865
E487	975	Confederate States of America—Social conditions	E569	977.803	Missouri—History—Civil War, 1861-1865
E500	975.103	Delaware—History—Civil War, 1861-1865	E571	978.904	New Mexico—History—Civil War, 1861-1865
E503	975.803	Georgia—History—Civil War, 1861-1865	E573	975.603	North Carolina—History—Civil War, 1861-1865
E507	977.702	Iowa—History—Civil War, 1861-1865	E577	975.703	South Carolina—History—Civil War, 1861-1865
E508	978.1031	Kansas—History—Civil War, 1861-1865	E579	976.804	Tennessee—History—Civil War, 1861-1865
E510	976.305	Louisiana—History—Civil War, 1861-1865	E580	976.405	Texas—History—Civil War, 1861-1865
E513	974.403	Massachusetts—History—Civil War, 1861-1865	E581	975.503	Virginia—History—Civil War, 1861-1865
			E582	975.403	West Virginia—History—Civil War, 1861-1865

LC	Dewey	Subject Heading	LC	Dewey	Subject Heading
E591-600	359.00975	Confederate States of America—History, Naval	F23	974.102	Maine—History—King William's War, 1689-1697
E591-600	359.00975	Confederate States of America. Navy—History	F23	974.102	Maine—History—King George's War, 1744-1748
E611-612	973.771	Confederate States of America. Army—Prisons	F24	974.10(1-3)	Maine—History—1775-1865
E642	394.26973	Memorial Day	F24	974.103	Maine—History—War of 1812
E645	394.26975	Confederate Memorial Day			
E660-887	973.(8-9)	United States—History—1865-	F31-45	974.2	New Hampshire—History
E660-783	973.(8-913)	United States—History—1865-1921	F31	974.2005	New Hampshire—Periodicals
E660-735	973.8(1-8)	United States—History—1865-1898	F32	917.42003	New Hampshire—Gazetteers
E671-680	973.(63-82)	United States—History—1849-1877	F37	974.20(1-2)	New Hampshire—History—Colonial period, ca. 1600-1775
E717.1	973.893	El Caney, Battle of, 1898	F38	974.203	New Hampshire—History—1775-1865
E717.7	973.895	Manila Bay, Battle of, 1898	F40	974.2043	New Hampshire—History—1951-
E740-887	973.91	United States—History—20th century	F46-60	974.3	Vermont—History
E740-760	973.911	United States—History—1901-1909	F46	974.3005	Vermont—Periodicals
			F47	917.43003	Vermont—Gazetteers
E761-765	973.912	United States—History—1909-1913	F52	974.303	Vermont—History—To 1791
E766-783	973.913	United States—History—1913-1921	F61-75	974.4	Massachusetts—History
E784-805	973.91(3-6)	United States—History—1919-1933	F61	974.4005	Massachusetts—Periodicals
E806-812	973.917	United States—History—1933-1945	F62	917.44003	Massachusetts—Gazetteers
E813-816	973.918	United States—History—1945-1953	F67	974.40(1-2)	Massachusetts—History—Colonial period, ca. 1600-1775
E835-837.7	973.921	United States—History—1953-1961	F68	974.402	Massachusetts—History—New Plymouth, 1620-1691
E838-851	973.92(2-3)	United States—History—1961-1969			
E841.W49	973.922	Cuban Missile Crisis, 1962	F68	974.402008 + 825	Pilgrims (New Plymouth Colony)
E860	973.924	Watergate Affair, 1972-1974	F69	974.40(2-3)	Massachusetts—History—1775-1865
E865	973.925	Mayaguez Incident, 1975	F70-71	974.404	Massachusetts—History—1865-
F	970-989	America—History	F73-.9	974.461	Boston (Mass.)
F1-15	974	New England—History	F76-90	974.5	Rhode Island—History
F1	974.005	New England—Periodicals	F76	974.5005	Rhode Island—Periodicals
F2	917.4003	New England—Gazetteers	F77	917.45003	Rhode Island—Gazetteers
F7-.75	974.0(1-2)	New England—History—Colonial period, ca. 1600-1775	F82	974.50(1-2)	Rhode Island—History—Colonial period, ca. 1600-1775
F7	974.02008825	Puritans	F83.4	974.503	Dorr Rebellion, 1842
F8	974.0(2-3)	New England—History—1775-1865	F91-105	974.6	Connecticut—History
			F91	974.6005	Connecticut—Periodicals
F8	974.0(2-3)	New England—History—Revolution, 1775-1783	F92	917.46003	Connecticut—Gazetteers
F16-30	974.1	Maine—History	F97	974.60(1-2)	Connecticut—History—Colonial period, ca. 1600-1775
F16	974.1005	Maine—Periodicals			
F17	917.41003	Maine—Gazetteers	F99	974.60(2-3)	Connecticut—History—1775-1865
F23	974.10(1-2)	Maine—History—Colonial period, ca. 1600-1775			

LC	Dewey	Subject Heading	LC	Dewey	Subject Heading
F100	974.604(1-3)	Connecticut—History—1865-1950	F176-190	975.2	Maryland—History
F101	974.604(3-4)	Connecticut—History—1951-	F176	975.2005	Maryland—Periodicals
			F179	917.52003	Maryland—Gazetteers
F106	974	Middle Atlantic States	F184	975.20(1-2)	Maryland—History—Colonial period, ca. 1600-1775
F116-130	974.7	New York (State)—History	F189.A6	975.256	Annapolis (Md.)
F116	974.7005	New York (State)—Periodicals	F189.B1	975.26	Baltimore (Md.)
F117	917.47003	New York (State)—Gazetteers	F191-205	975.3	Washington (D.C.)
			F191	975.3005	Washington (D.C.)—Periodicals
F122-.1	974.70(1-2)	New York (State)—History—Colonial period, ca. 1600-1775	F192	917.53003	Washington (D.C.)—Gazetteers
F123	974.702	New York (State)—History—French and Indian War, 1755-1763	F206-220	975	Southern States—History
			F221-235	975.5	Virginia—History
			F221	975.5005	Virginia—Periodicals
			F224	917.55003	Virginia—Gazetteers
F123	974.70(2-3)	New York (State)—History—1775-1865	F229	975.50(1-2)	Virginia—History—Colonial period, ca. 1600-1775
			F229	975.502	Bacon's Rebellion, 1676
F124-125	974.74	New York (State)—History—1865-	F230	975.50(2-3)	Virginia—History—1775-1865
F128.44	974.703	Draft Riot, New York, N.Y., 1863	F234.E	975.503	Emporia (Va.)—History—Civil War, 1861-1865
F128-.9	974.71	New York (N.Y.)			
F128.44	322.4.099747	Draft Riot, New York, N.Y., 1863	F236-250	975.4	West Virginia
			F236	975.4005	West Virginia—Periodicals
F131-145	974.9	New Jersey—History	F239	917.54003	West Virginia—Gazetteers
F131	974.9005	New Jersey—Periodicals	F245-.42	975.404(3-4)	West Virginia—History—1951-
F132	917.49003	Now Jersey—Gazetteers			
F137	974.90(1-2)	New Jersey—History—Colonial period, ca. 1600-1775	F251-265	975.6	North Carolina
			F251	975.6005	North Carolina—Periodicals
F138	974.90(2-3)	New Jersey—History—1775-1865	F252	917.56003	North Carolina—Gazetteers
F138	974.903	New Jersey—History—War of 1812	F257	975.60(1-2)	North Carolina—History—Colonial period, ca. 1600-1775
F139-140.22	974.904	New Jersey—History—1865-			
F146-160	974.8	Pennsylvania—History	F257	975.602	North Carolina—History—Regulator Insurrection, 1766-1771
F146	974.8005	Pennsylvania—Periodicals			
F147	917.48003	Pennsylvania—Gazetteers	F258	975.60(2-3)	North Carolina—History—1775-1865
F152-.2	974.80(1-2)	Pennsylvania—History—Colonial period, ca. 1600-1775	F259-260.42	975.604	North Carolina—History—1865-
F153	974.803	Buckshot War, Harrisburg, Pa., 1838	F266-280	975.7	South Carolina—History
			F266	975.7005	South Carolina—Periodicals
F154-155.3	974.804	Pennsylvania—History—1865-	F267	917.57003	South Carolina—Gazetteers
F158.1-.9	974.811	Philadelphia (Pa.)	F272	975.70(1-2)	South Carolina—History—Colonial period, ca. 1600-1775
F160.G3	974.8004310 + 748	Pennsylvania Dutch			
			F273	975.70(2-3)	South Carolina—History—1775-1865
F161-175	975.1	Delaware—History			
F161	975.1005	Delaware—Periodicals	F274-275.42	975.704	South Carolina—History—1865-
F162	917.51003	Delaware—Gazetteers			
F169	975.14(1-3)	Delaware—History—1865-1950	F281-295	975.8	Georgia
			F281	975.8005	Georgia—Periodicals
F170	975.104(3-4)	Delaware—History—1951-	F284	917.58003	Georgia—Gazetteers

LC	Dewey	Subject Heading	LC	Dewey	Subject Heading
F290	975.80(2-3)	Georgia—History—1775-1865	F390	976.403	Texas—History—Revolution, 1835-1836
F291-.3	975.804	Georgia—History—1865-	F390	976.404	Texas—History—Republic, 1836-1846
F294.A8	975.8231	Atlanta (Ga.)	F391	976.40(5-63)	Texas—History—1846-1950
F296	976	Gulf States—History			
F306-320	975.9	Florida—History	F391.2-.4	976.406(3-4)	Texas—History—1951-
F306	975.9005	Florida—Periodicals	F394.D21	976.42812	Dallas (Tex.)
F309	917.59003	Florida—Gazetteers	F394.H8	976.41411	Houston (Tex.)
F314	975.901	Florida—History—To 1565	F396	976	Southwest, Old
F314	975.903	Florida—History—Cession to the United States, 1819	F406-420	976.7	Arkansas
			F406	976.7005	Arkansas—Periodicals
F314	975.90(1-3)	Florida—History—To 1821	F409	917.67003	Arkansas—Gazetteers
F314	975.901	Florida—History—Huguenot colony, 1562-1565	F431-445	976.8	Tennessee
			F431	976.8005	Tennessee—Periodicals
F314	975.901	Florida—History—Spanish colony, 1565-1763	F434	917.68003	Tennessee—Gazetteers
			F446-460	976.9	Kentucky—History
F314	975.90(2-3)	Florida—History—English colony, 1763-1784	F446	976.9005	Kentucky—Periodicals
			F449	917.69003	Kentucky—Gazetteers
F314	975.903	Florida—History—Spanish colony, 1784-1821	F454	976.90(1-2)	Kentucky—History—To 1792
F315	975.90(4-5)	Florida—History—1821-1865	F454	976.902	Estill's Defeat, 1782
			F454	973.338	Blue Licks, Battle of the, Ky., 1782
F316-.23	975.906	Florida—History—1865-			
F316.2-.23	975.906(3-4)	Florida—History—1951-	F455	976.903	Kentucky—History—1792-1865
F321-355	976.1	Alabama			
F321	976.1005	Alabama—Periodicals	F456-.26	976.904	Kentucky—History—1865-
F324	917.61003	Alabama—Gazetteers			
F326	976.105	Alabama—History—To 1819	F456	976.9041	Black Patch War, 1906-1909
F326	976.10(5-63)	Alabama—History—1819-1950	F461-475	977.8	Missouri
			F461	977.8005	Missouri—Periodicals
F330-.3	976.106(3-4)	Alabama—History—1951-	F464	917.78003	Missouri—Gazetteers
F336-350	976.2	Mississippi	F474.S2	977.866	Saint Louis (Mo.)
F336	976.2005	Mississippi—Periodicals	F476-485	977	Northwest, Old
F339	917.62003	Mississippi—Gazetteers	F486-500	977.1	Ohio
F341	976.20(1-4)	Mississippi—History—To 1803	F486	977.1005	Ohio—Periodicals
			F489	917.71003	Ohio—Gazetteers
F347.A25	976.202	Ackia, Battle of, 1736	F495	977.10(1-2)	Ohio—History—To 1787
F350.5-358.2	977	Mississippi River Valley	F495	977.103	Ohio—History—1787-1865
F351-353	976.204	Louisiana Purchase			
F366-380	976.3	Louisiana	F496-.2	977.104	Ohio—History—1865-
F366	976.3005	Louisiana—Periodicals	F516-520	977	Ohio River Valley
F367	917.63003	Louisiana—Gazetteers	F521-535	977.2	Indiana
F372-373	976.30(1-3)	Louisiana—History—To 1803	F521	977.2005	Indiana—Periodicals
			F524	917.72003	Indiana—Gazetteers
F374	976.30(4-5)	Louisiana—History—1803-1865	F526	977.20(1-2)	Indiana—History—To 1787
F375	976.306(1-3)	Louisiana—History—1865-1950	F530-.22	977.204(3-4)	Indiana—History—1951-
			F534.I3	977.252	Indianapolis (Ind.)
F376-.3	976.306(3-4)	Louisiana—History—1951-	F536-550	977.3	Illinois
			F536	977.3005	Illinois—Periodicals
F379.N5	976.335	New Orleans (La.)	F539	917.73003	Illinois—Gazetteers
F381-395	976.4	Texas	F544	977.30(1-2)	Illinois—History—To 1778
F381	976.4005	Texas—Periodicals	F545	977.30(2-3)	Illinois—History—1778-1865
F384	917.64003	Texas—Gazetteers			
F389-390	976.40(1-4)	Texas—History—To 1846	F546-.4	977.304	Illinois—History—1865-
F389	976.402	Texas—History—1810-1821	F546.2-.4	977.304(3-4)	Illinois—History—1951-
			F548-.9	977.311	Chicago (Ill.)

LC	Dewey	Subject Heading	LC	Dewey	Subject Heading
F551	977	Northern boundary of the United States	F685	978.102	Kansas—History—1854-1861
F561-575	977.4	Michigan	F691-705	976.6	Oklahoma
F561	977.4005	Michigan—Periodicals	F691	976.6005	Oklahoma—Periodicals
F564	917.74003	Michigan—Gazetteers	F692	917.66003	Oklahoma—Gazetteers
F566	977.40(1-3)	Michigan—History—To 1837	F699	976.604	Oklahoma—History—Land Rush, 1889
F566	977.40(3-4)	Michigan—History—1837-1950	F699	976.604	Oklahoma—History—Land Rush, 1893
F570-.2	977.404(3-4)	Michigan—History—1951-	F721-722	978	Rocky Mountains
F574.D4	977.434	Detroit (Mich.)	F722	978.752	Yellowstone National Park
F576-590	977.5	Wisconsin	F726-740	978.6	Montana
F576	977.5005	Wisconsin—Periodicals	F726	978.6005	Montana—Periodicals
F579	917.75003	Wisconsin—Gazetteers	F729	917.86003	Montana—Gazetteers
F584	977.50(1-3)	Wisconsin—History—To 1848	F735-.2	978.603(3-4)	Montana—History—1951-
F586-.42	977.50(3-4)	Wisconsin—History—1848-	F741-755	979.6	Idaho
F589.M6	977.595	Milwaukee (Wi.)	F741	979.6005	Idaho—Periodicals
F590.3-596.3	978	West(U.S.)—History	F744	917.96003	Idaho—Gazetteers
F592-.7	978.0(1-2)	West(U.S.)—History—To 1848	F750-.22	979.603(3-4)	Idaho—History—1951-
F593	978.02	West(U.S.)—History—1848-1860	F756-770	978.7	Wyoming
			F756	978.7005	Wyoming—Periodicals
F594	978.02	West(U.S.)—History—1860-1890	F759	917.87003	Wyoming—Gazetteers
F595	978.0(2-32)	West(U.S.)—History—1890-1945	F761	978.701	Fetterman Fight, Wyo., 1866
F595-.3	978.033	West(U.S.)—History—1945-	F771-785	978.8	Colorado
			F771	978.8005	Colorado—Periodicals
F596	636.213092	Cowboys	F774	917.88003	Colorado—Gazetteers
F596	636.213092	Cowgirls	F780	978.80(1-2)	Colorado—History—To 1876
F598	978	Missouri River	F781	978.803(1-3)	Colorado—History—1876-1950
F601-615	977.6	Minnesota			
F601	977.6005	Minnesota—Periodicals	F781.2-.3	978.803(3-4)	Colorado—History—1951-
F604	917.76003	Minnesota—Gazetteers	F784.D4	978.883	Denver (Colo.)
F606	977.60(1-4)	Minnesota—History—To 1858	F786-790	979	Southwest, New
			F791-805	978.9	New Mexico
F606	977.60(4-5)	Minnesota—History—1858-	F791	978.9005	New Mexico—Periodicals
			F794	917.89003	New Mexico—Gazetteers
F614.M5	977.6579	Minneapolis (Minn.)	F799-800	978.90(1-3)	New Mexico—History—To 1848
F616-630	977.7	Iowa			
F616	977.7005	Iowa—Periodicals	F801-.2	978.90(4-5)	New Mexico—History—1848-
F619	917.77003	Iowa—Gazetteers			
F625-.42	977.703(3-4)	Iowa—History—1951-	F806-820	979.1	Arizona
F631-645	978.4	North Dakota	F806	979.1005	Arizona—Periodicals
F631	978.4005	North Dakota—Periodicals	F809	917.91003	Arizona—Gazetteers
F634	917.84003	North Dakota—Gazetteers	F811	979.10(1-4)	Arizona—History—To 1912
F646-660	978.3	South Dakota			
F646	978.3005	South Dakota—Periodicals	F811	979.105(2-3)	Arizona—History—1912-1950
F649	917.83003	South Dakota—Gazetteers			
F661-675	978.2	Nebraska—History	F815-.3	979.105(3-4)	Arizona—History—1951-
F661	978.2005	Nebraska—Periodicals	F819.P57	979.173	Phoenix (Ariz.)
F664	917.82003	Nebraska—Gazetteers	F821-835	979.2	Utah
F676-690	978.1	Kansas—History	F821	979.2005	Utah—Periodicals
F676	978.1005	Kansas—Periodicals	F824	917.92003	Utah—Gazetteers
F679	917.81003	Kansas—Gazetteers	F826	979.202	Morrisite War, 1862
			F836-850	979.3	Nevada
			F836	979.3005	Nevada—Periodicals
			F839	917.93003	Nevada—Gazetteers
			F851.7	979.5	Cascade Range

LC	Dewey	Subject Heading	LC	Dewey	Subject Heading
F853	979.7	Columbia River Valley	F1032	971.02(2-49)	Canada—History—1763-1867
F856-870	979.4	California			
F856	979.4005	California—Periodicals	F1032	971.024	Canada—History—1775-1783
F859	917.94003	California—Gazetteers			
F864	979.40(1-3)	California—History—To 1846	F1032	971.03	Canada—History—1791-1841
F865	979.40(3-4)	California—History—1846-1850	F1032	971.038	Canada—History—Rebellion, 1837-1838
F866	979.40(4-53)	California—History—1850-1950	F1032	971.04(2-8)	Canada—History—1841-1867
F866.2-.4	979.405(3-4)	California—History—1950-	F1033	971.049	Canada—History—Fenian Invasions, 1866-1870
F867	979.49	California, Southern	F1033	971.05	Canada—History—Confederation, 1867
F869.L8	979.494	Los Angeles (Calif.)			
F869.S3	979.461	San Francisco (Calif.)	F1034	971.06(12-32)	Canada—History—1914-1945
F871-885	979.5	Oregon			
F871	979.5005	Oregon—Periodicals	F1034.2-.3	971.0(632-7)	Canada—History—1945-
F874	917.95003	Oregon—Gazetteers	F1035.8	971.5	Maritime Provinces—History
F879-880	979.50(1-3)	Oregon—History—To 1859			
F880	979.503	Oregon Trail	F1036-1040	971.6	Nova Scotia—History
F881-.35	979.504	Oregon—History—1859-	F1036	971.6005	Nova Scotia—Periodicals
F881.2-.35	979.504(3-4)	Oregon—History—1951-	F1036.4	917.16003	Nova Scotia—Gazetteers
F886-900	979.7	Washington (State)	F1041	971.51005	New Brunswick—Periodicals
F886	979.7005	Washington (State)—Periodicals			
			F1041.4	917.151003	New Brunswick—Gazetteers
F889	917.97003	Washington (State)—Gazetteers	F1046-1049.7	971.7	Prince Edward Island—History
F891	979.70(1-3)	Washington (State)—History—To 1889			
			F1046	971.7005	Prince Edward Island—Periodicals
F891	979.704	Washington (State)—History—1889-			
			F1051-1055	971.4	Quebec (Province)—History
F899.S4	979.7772	Seattle (Wash.)			
F901-951	979.8	Alaska	F1051	971.4005	Quebec (Province)—Periodicals
F901	979.8005	Alaska—Periodicals			
F902	917.98008	Alaska—Gazetteers	F1051.4	917.14003	Quebec (Province)—Gazetteers
F907	979.80(1-2)	Alaska—History—To 1867			
F908-909	979.80(3-4)	Alaska—History—1867-1959	F1056-1059.7	971.3	Ontario—History
			F1056	971.3005	Ontario—Periodicals
F910-.7	979.805	Alaska—History—1959-	F1056.4	917.13003	Ontario—Gazetteers
F951	979.84	Aleutian Islands (Alaska)	F1060-.97	971.92	Northwest, Canadian
F1001-1040	971	Canada	F1061-1065	971.27	Manitoba—History
F1001	971.005	Canada—Periodicals	F1061	971.27005	Manitoba—Periodicals
F1004	917.1003	Canada—Gazetteers	F1061.4	917.127003	Manitoba—Gazetteers
F1012-1017	917.104	Canada—Description and travel	F1070-1074.7	971.24	Saskatchewan—History
			F1070	971.24005	Saskatchewan—Periodicals
F1021-.2	971	Canada—Civilization			
F1027	971.004114	French-Canadians	F1070.4	917.124003	Saskatchewan—Gazetteers
F1028	355.00971	Canada—History, Military			
F1028.5	359.00971	Canada—History, Naval	F1075-1080	971.23	Alberta—History
F1030-.9	971.01	Canada—History—To 1763 (New France)	F1075	971.23005	Alberta—Periodicals
			F1075.4	917.123003	Alberta—Gazetteers
F1030	971.018	Lake of the Woods Massacre, 1736	F1086-1089.7	971.1	British Columbia—History
			F1086	971.1005	British Columbia—Periodicals
F1030.9	971.0188	Canada—History—1755-1763	F1086.4	917.11003	British Columbia—Gazetteers
F1031	971.02	Canada—History—1763-1791	F1091-1095.5	971.91	Yukon Territory—History
			F1091.A1	971.91005	Yukon Territory—Periodicals

LC	Dewey	Subject Heading	LC	Dewey	Subject Heading
F1092	917.191003	Yukon Territory—Gazetteers	F1409-.3	918.04	Latin America—Description and travel
F1106-1110.5	971.94	Keewatin—History	F1421-1577	972.8	Central America
F1106.A1	971.94005	Keewatin—Periodicals	F1421	972.8005	Central America—Periodicals
F1121-1124	971.8	Newfoundland—History			
F1121	971.8005	Newfoundland—Periodicals	F1424	917.28003	Central America—Gazetteers
F1121.4	917.18003	Newfoundland—Gazetteers	F1430	972.8	Central America—Civilization
F1135-1139	971.82	Labrador (Nfld.)—History	F1431-1433.2	917.2804	Central America—Description and travel
F1135	971.82005	Labrador (Nfld.)—Periodicals	F1434-1435.3	972.800497	Indians of Central America
F1135.4	917.182003	Labrador (Nfld.)—Gazetteers	F1435.4-1439.5	972.8	Central America—History
			F1441-1457	972.82	Belize
F1201-1392	972	Mexico	F1441	972.82005	Belize—Periodicals
F1201	972.005	Mexico—Periodicals	F1443.8	972.82	Belize—Civilization
F1204	917.2003	Mexico—Gazetteers	F1444-.3	917.28204	Belize—Description and travel
F1210	972	Mexico—Civilization			
F1211-1216.5	917.204	Mexico—Description and travel	F1445.5-1448	972.82	Belize—History
			F1461-1477	972.81	Guatemala
F1219-1221	972.00497	Indians of Mexico	F1461	972.81005	Guatemala—Periodicals
F1219.73-.75	972.00497452	Aztecs	F1462	917.281003	Guatemala—Gazetteers
F1219.73-.75	972.00497452	Nahuas	F1463.5	972.81	Guatemala—Civilization
F1219.76.R45	299.78452013	Aztec mythology	F1464-.3	917.28104	Guatemala—Description and travel
F1228.98	972.018	Mexico—History—To 1519	F1465-1466.7	972.81	Guatemala—History
F1229-1231	972.0(1-2)	Mexico—History—To 1810	F1466.4	972.810(1-3)	Guatemala—History—To 1821
F1230	972.02	Mexico—History—Conquest, 1519-1540	F1466.45	972.810(4-52)	Guatemala—History—1821-1945
F1231	972.02	Mexico—History—Spanish colony, 1540-1810	F1466.5	972.81052	Guatemala—History—1945-1985
F1231.5-1236.6	972.0(3-84)	Mexico—History—1810-	F1466.7	972.8105(2-3)	Guatemala—History—1985-
F1232	972.03	Mexico—History—Wars of Independence, 1810-1821	F1481-1497	972.84	El Salvador
			F1481	972.84005	El Salvador—Periodicals
F1232-.5	972.0(3-6)	Mexico—History—1821-1861	F1482	917.284003	El Salvador—Gazetteers
			F1483.8	972.84	El Salvador—Civilization
F1233	972.07	Mexico—History—European intervention, 1861-1867	F1484-.3	917.28404	El Salvador—Description and travel
			F1485.5-1488.53	972.84	El Salvador—History
F1233.5	972.081	Mexico—History—1867-1910	F1487	972.840(1-42)	El Salvador—History—To 1838
F1234	972.08(16-21)	Mexico—History—Revolution, 1910-1920	F1487.5	972.840(4-52)	El Salvador—History—1838-1944
F1234	972.0816	El Ebano, Battle of, 1915	F1487.5	972.84052	El Salvador—History—Revolution, 1944
F1234	972.08(16-26)	Mexico—History—1910-1946	F1488	972.84052	El Salvador—History—1944-1979
F1234	972.0816	Mexico—History—Decena Tragica, 1913	F1488	972.84052	El Salvador—History—Revolution of 1948
F1234	972.0822	Mexico—History—Revolution, 1923-1924	F1488	972.84052	El Salvador-Honduras Conflict, 1969
F1235-.5	972.08(27-31)	Mexico—History—1946-1970	F1488.3-.53	972.8405(3-4)	El Salvador—History—1979-
F1236	972.083(2-4)	Mexico—History—1970-1988	F1488.3	972.84053	El Salvador—History—1979-1992
F1236	972.08(35-41)	Mexico—History—1988-	F1488.5-.53	972.8405(3-4)	El Salvador—History—1992-
F1401	980.005	Latin America—Periodicals			
F1406	918.003	Latin America—Gazetteers	F1501-1517	972.83	Honduras
F1408.3-.4	980	Latin America—Civilization			

LC	Dewey	Subject Heading	LC	Dewey	Subject Heading
F1501	972.83005	Honduras—Periodicals	F1544	917.28604	Costa Rica—Description and travel
F1502	917.283003	Honduras—Gazetteers	F1547	972.860(1-3)	Costa Rica—History—To 1821
F1503.8	972.83	Honduras—Civilization			
F1504	917.28304	Honduras—Description and Travel	F1547.5	972.8604	Costa Rica—History—1821-1948
F1505.5-1508.33	972.83	Honduras—History	F1547.5	972.86044	Costa Rica—History—Uprising, 1932
F1507	972.830(1-4)	Honduras—History—To 1838			
F1507.5	972.8305(1-2)	Honduras—History—1838-1933	F1548	972.86051	Costa Rica—History—1948-1986
F1507.5	972.83051	Honduras—History—Coup d'etat, 1904	F1548.2-.23	972.86052	Costa Rica—History—1986-
F1507.5	972.83051	Honduras—History—Revolution, 1919	F1561-1577	972.87	Panama
F1508-.22	972.8305(2-3)	Honduras—History—1933-1982	F1561	972.87005	Panama—Periodicals
			F1562	917.287003	Panama—Gazetteers
F1508.3-.33	972.83053	Honduras—History—1982-	F1563.8	972.87	Panama—Civilization
F1521-1537	972.85	Nicaragua	F1564-.3	917.28704	Panama—Description and travel
F1521	972.85005	Nicaragua—Periodicals			
F1522	917.285003	Nicaragua—Gazetteers	F1565.5-1567	972.87	Panama—History
F1523.8	972.85	Nicaragua—Civilization	F1566.45	972.870(1-3)	Panama—History—To 1903
F1524-.3	917.28504	Nicaragua—Description and travel			
F1525.5-1528.22	972.85	Nicaragua—History	F1566.5	972.87051	Panama—History—Revolution, 1903
F1526.25	972.850(1-42)	Nicaragua—History—To 1838	F1566.5	972.87051	Panama—History—1903-1946
F1526.25	972.8503	Nicaragua—History—English Invasion, 1780-1781	F1566.5-1567	972.8705(1-3)	Panama—History—1946-1981
F1526.27	972.850(44-51)	Nicaragua—History—1838-1909	F1566.5	972.87051	Panama—History—Coup d'etat, 1968
F1526.27	972.85044	Nicaragua—History—Filibuster War, 1855-1860	F1567	972.87053	Panama—History—1981-
			F1567	972.87053	Panama—History—American Invasion, 1989
F1526.3	972.85051	Nicaragua—History—Revolution, 1909-1910	F1601-1629	972.9	West Indies
F1526.3	972.8505(1-2)	Nicaragua—History—1909-1937	F1601	972.9005	West Indies—Periodicals
			F1604	917.29003	West Indies—Gazetteers
F1526.3	972.85051	Nicaragua—History—Revolution of 1912	F1609.5	972.9	West Indies—Civilization
F1526.3	972.85051	Nicaragua—History—Revolution, 1926-1929	F1610-1613	917.2904	West Indies—Description and travel
F1527	972.85052	Nicaragua—History—1937-1979	F1619	972.900497	Indians of the West Indies
			F1620-1623	972.9	West Indies—History
F1527	972.85052	Nicaragua—San Carlos Barracks Attack, 1977	F1621	972.903	English West Indian Expedition, 1793-1794
F1527	972.85052	Nicaragua—History—Uprising, 1978	F1621	972.903	English West Indian Expedition, 1654-1655
F1528	972.85052	Nicaragua—History—Revolution, 1979	F1621	972.903	English West Indian Expedition, 1695
F1528	972.85053	Nicaragua—History—1979-1990	F1621	972.903	English West Indian Expedition, 1795-1796
F1528	972.85054	Nicaragua—History—1990-	F1630-1640	972.99	Bermuda Islands
			F1630	972.99005	Bermuda Islands—Periodicals
F1541-1557	972.86	Costa Rica	F1630.7	917.299003	Bermuda Islands—Gazetteers
F1541	972.86005	Costa Rica—Periodicals	F1631	917.29904	Bermuda Islands—Description and travel
F1542	917.286003	Costa Rica—Gazetteers	F1633	972.99	Bermuda Islands—Civilization
F1543.8	972.86	Costa Rica—Civilization	F1635-1637	972.99	Bermuda Islands—History
			F1650-1660	972.96	Bahamas
			F1650	972.96005	Bahamas—Periodicals

LC	Dewey	Subject Heading	LC	Dewey	Subject Heading
F1650.7	917.296003	Bahamas—Gazetteers	F1886	972.92034	Jamaica—History—Slave Insurrection, 1831
F1651	917.29604	Bahamas—Description and travel	F1886	972.9204	Jamaica—History—Insurrection, 1865
F1654	972.96	Bahamas—Civilization	F1887	972.9206	Jamaica—History—1962-
F1655.3-1657.2	972.96	Bahamas—History	F1900-1930	972.94	Haiti
F1741-1991	972.9(1-5)	Antilles, Greater	F1900	972.94005	Haiti—Periodicals
F1751-1854.9	972.91	Cuba	F1913	917.294003	Haiti—Gazetteers
F1751-1849	972.91	Cuba—History	F1916	972.94	Haiti—Civilization
F1751	972.91005	Cuba—Periodicals	F1917	917.29404	Haiti—Description and travel
F1754	917.291003	Cuba—Gazetteers	F1918-1939	972.94	Haiti—History
F1760	972.91	Cuba—Civilization	F1923	972.940(1-3)	Haiti—History—To 1791
F1761-1765.3	917.29104	Cuba—Description and travel	F1923	972.9403	Haiti—History—Revolution, 1791-1804
F1779	972.910(1-4)	Cuba—History—To 1810	F1924	972.9404	Haiti—History—1804-1844
F1781	972.9103	Cuba—History—British occupation, 1762-1763	F1924	972.9404	Haiti—History—Revolution, 1843
F1783	972.9105	Cuba—History—1810-1899	F1926	972.9404	Haiti—History—1844-1915
F1783	972.9105	Cuba—History—Black Eagle Conspiracy, 1830	F1927	972.9405	Haiti—History—American occupation, 1915-1934
F1783	972.9105	Cuba—History—Negro Conspiracy, 1844	F1927-1928	972.940(6-72)	Haiti—History—1934-1986
F1783	972.9105	Cuba—History—Insurrection, 1849-1851	F1928.2-.23	972.94073	Haiti—History—1986-
F1785	972.9105	Cuba—History—Insurrection, 1868-1878	F1928.2	972.94073	Haiti—History—Coup d'etat, 1991
F1785	972.9105	Cuba—History—1878-1895	F1931-1941	972.93	Dominican Republic
F1785	972.9105	Cuba—History—Revolution, 1879-1880	F1931	972.93005	Dominican Republic—Periodicals
F1786-1788.22	972.910(5-6)	Cuba—History—1895-	F1932	917.293003	Dominican Republic—Gazetteers
F1786	972.9105	Cuba—History—Revolution, 1895-1898	F1935	972.93	Dominican Republic—Civilization
F1787	972.9106(1-2)	Cuba—History—1899-1906	F1936-.3	917.29304	Dominican Republic—Description and travel
F1787	972.91062	Cuba—History—American occupation, 1906-1909	F1937-1938.58	972.93	Dominican Republic—History
F1787	972.91062	Cuba—History—1909-1933	F1938.3	972.930(1-4)	Dominican Republic—History—To 1844
F1787.5	972.91063	Cuba—History—Revolution, 1933	F1938.4	972.930(4-52)	Dominican Republic—History—1844-1930
F1787.5	972.91063	Cuba—History—Moncada Barracks Attack, 1953	F1938.45	972.93052	Dominican Republic—History— American occupation, 1916-1924
F1787.5	972.91063	El Jigue (Cuba), Battle of, 1958	F1938.5	972.93053	Dominican Republic—History—1930-1961
F1788	972.91064	Cuba—History—Revolution, 1959	F1938.5-.58	972.9305(3-5)	Dominican Republic—History—1930-
F1788	972.91064	Cuba—History—Invasion, 1961	F1938.5	972.93053	Dominican-Haitian Conflict, 1937
F1861-1896	972.92	Jamaica	F1938.5	972.93053	Dominican Republic—History—Invasion, 1959
F1861-1896	972.92005	Jamaica—Periodicals	F1938.55-.58	972.9305(4-5)	Dominican Republic—History—1961-
F1864	917.292003	Jamaica—Gazetteers			
F1870-1872.2	917.29204	Jamaica—Description and travel			
F1874	972.92	Jamaica—Civilization			
F1878-1887	972.92	Jamaica—History			
F1884-1886	972.920(1-5)	Jamaica—History—To 1962			
F1884	972.92034	Jamaica—History—Maroon War, 1795-1796			

LC	Dewey	Subject Heading	LC	Dewey	Subject Heading
F1938.55	972.93054	Dominican Republic—History—Coup d'etat, 1963	F2136	972.9722	Virgin Islands of the United States
F1938.55	972.93054	Dominican Republic—History—Revolution, 1965	F2151	972.903	English West Indian Expedition, 1759
F1938.55	972.93054	Dominican Republic—History—Revolution, 1973	F2155-2191	972.9	Caribbean Area
			F2161	910.45092	Buccaneers
F1938.55	972.93054	Dominican Republic—History—Uprising, 1984	F2173-2191	972.9	Caribbean Area—History
			F2201-3799	980	South America
F1951-1983	972.95	Puerto Rico	F2201-2239	980	South America—History
F1951	972.95005	Puerto Rico—Periodicals	F2217	980.0099	Gauchos
F1954	917.295003	Puerto Rico—Gazetteers	F2229-2290	980.00498	Indians of South America
F1960	972.95	Puerto Rico—Civilization	F2251-2299	986.1	Colombia
F1961-1965.3	917.29504	Puerto Rico—Description and travel	F2251	986.1005	Colombia—Periodicals
			F2254	918.61003	Colombia—Gazetteers
F1970-1976.3	972.95	Puerto Rico—History	F2259.5	918.6104	Colombia—Guidebooks
F1973	972.950(1-4)	Puerto Rico—History—To 1898	F2260	986.1	Colombia—Civilization
			F2261-2264.2	918.6104	Colombia—Description and travel
F1973	972.9504	Puerto Rico—History—Insurrection, 1868	F2270.3-2279.22	986.1	Colombia—History
F1975	972.950(4-52)	Puerto Rico—History—1898-1952	F2272	986.10(1-2)	Colombia—History—To 1810
F1975	972.95052	Puerto Rico—History—Nationalist Insurrection, 1950	F2272	986.102	Colombia—History—Insurrection of the Comuneros, 1781
F1976-.3	972.95053	Puerto Rico—History—1952-	F2272.5	986.102	English West Indian Expedition, 1739-1742
F2001-2151	972.9(7-8)	Antilles, Lesser	F2273	986.105	Colombia—History—19th century
F2006	972.97	Leeward Islands (West Indies)	F2273	986.10(3-6)	Colombia—History—1810-
F2011	972.98	Windward Islands	F2274	986.10(3-4)	Colombia—History—War of Independence, 1810-1822
F2033	972.973	Anguilla			
F2035	972.974	Antigua			
F2041	972.981	Barbados	F2275	986.104	Colombia—History—1822-1832
F2048	972.986	Bonaire			
F2048.5	972.921	Cayman Islands	F2276	986.105(2-61)	Colombia—History—1832-1886
F2049	972.986	Curacao			
F2050	972.976	Desirade (Guadeloupe)	F2276	986.1053	Colombia—History—Civil War, 1860-1862
F2051	972.9841	Dominica			
F2056	972.9845	Grenada	F2276.5	986.1062	Colombia—History—1886-1903
F2061	972.9844	The Grenadines			
F2066	972.976	Guadeloupe	F2276.5	986.1062	Colombia—History—Revolution, 1899-1903
F2070	972.976	Saintes Islands (Guadeloupe)	F2277	986.106(2-31)	Colombia—History—1903-1946
F2076	972.976	Marie Galante			
F2081	972.982	Martinique	F2278	986.1063(2-3)	Colombia—History—1946-1974
F2082	972.975	Montserrat			
F2088	972.977	Saba (Netherlands Antilles)	F2278	986.10632	Colombia—History—Coup d'etat, 1953
F2091	972.973	Saint Kitts and Nevis	F2279-.22	986.1063(4-5)	Colombia—History—1974-
F2096	972.9722	Saint Croix (V.I.)			
F2097	972.977	Saint Eustatius (Netherlands Antilles)	F2301-2349	987	Venezuela
			F2301	987.005	Venezuela—Periodicals
F2098	972.9722	Saint John (V.I.)	F2304	918.7003	Venezuela—Gazetteers
F2100	972.9843	Saint Lucia	F2310	987	Venezuela—Civilization
F2103	972.976	Saint Martin	F2311-2315	918.704	Venezuela—Description and travel
F2105	972.9722	Saint Thomas (V.I.)			
F2116-2123	972.983	Trinidad and Tobago	F2319.5-2328.52	987	Venezuela—History
F2129	972.9725	British Virgin Islands	F2322	987.0(1-3)	Venezuela—History—To 1556

LC	Dewey	Subject Heading	LC	Dewey	Subject Heading
F2322	987.0(1-3)	Venezuela—History—To 1810	F2409.8	988.3	Surinam—Civilization
F2322	987.03	Venezuela—History—1556-1810	F2410-2413	918.8304	Surinam—Description and travel
F2322	987.03	Venezuela—History—Insurrection of the Comuneros, 1781	F2420.3-2425.23	988.3	Surinam—History
			F2423	988.301	Surinam—History—To 1814
F2322	987.03	Venezuela—History—Miranda's Expedition, 1806	F2424	988.30(1-31)	Surinam—History—1814-1950
F2322.8	987.0(4-6)	Venezuela—History—1810-	F2425-.23	988.303(1-2)	Surinam—History—1950-
F2324	987.0(4-5)	Venezuela—History—War of Independence, 1810-1823	F2425	988.3032	Surinam—History—Coup d'etat, 1980
			F2425	988.3032	Surinam—History—Coup d'etat, 1982
F2324	987.0(4-5)	Venezuela—History—1810-1830	F2441-2471	988.2	French Guiana
F2324	973.54	Carabobo, Battle of, 1821	F2441	988.2005	French Guiana—Periodicals
F2325	987.061	Venezuela—History—1830-1935	F2444	918.82003	French Guiana—Gazetteers
F2325	987.062	Venezuela—History—Federal Wars, 1858-1863	F2449.8	988.2	French Guiana—Civilization
F2325	987.0631	Venezuela—History—Anglo German Blockade, 1902	F2450-2452	918.8204	French Guiana—Description and travel
			F2460.3-2464	988.2	French Guiana—History
F2325	987.0631	Venezuela—History—Revolution, 1902-1903	F2501-2656	981	Brazil
			F2501	981.005	Brazil—Periodicals
F2325	987.06313	Venezuela—History—1908-1935	F2504	918.1003	Brazil—Gazetteers
			F2510	981	Brazil—Civilization
F2326-2327	987.063(1-3)	Venezuela—History—1935-1974	F2511-2517	918.104	Brazil—Description and travel
F2326	987.063(14-2)	Venezuela—History—1935-1958	F2520.3-2538.5	981	Brazil—History
			F2526-2534	981.0(1-33)	Brazil—History—To 1822
F2326	987.0632	Venezuela—History—Revolution, 1945	F2526	981.03(1-2)	Brazil—History—1500-1548
F2326	987.0632	Venezuela—History—Coup d'etat, 1948	F2528	981.032	Brazil—History—1548-1580
F2326	987.0633	Venezuela—History—Revolution, 1958	F2528	981.032	Brazil—History—1549-1762
F2328-.52	987.063(3-4)	Venezuela—History—1974-	F2528	981.032	Brazil—History—War of the Emboabas, 1707-1709
F2328	987.064	Venezuela—History—Attempted coup, 1992 (February 4)	F2529	981.032	Brazil—History—French colony, 1555-1567
			F2530	981.032	Brazil—History—1580-1640
F2328	987.064	Venezuela—History—Attempted coup, 1992 (November 27)	F2532	981.032	Brazil—History—Dutch Conquest, 1624-1654
F2361-2391	988.1	Guyana	F2534	981.033	Brazil—History—1763-1822
F2361	988.1005	Guyana—Periodicals			
F2364	918.81003	Guyana—Gazetteers	F2534	981.033	Brazil—History—United Kingdom, 1815-1822
F2369.8	988.1	Guyana—Civilization			
F2380.3-2391	988.1	Guyana—History	F2535-2538.5	981.0(4-6)	Brazil—History—1822-
F2383	988.101	Guyana—History—To 1803	F2536	981.033	Brazil—History—Declaration of Independence, 1822
F2384	988.10(1-31)	Guyana—History—1803-1966	F2536	981.04	Brazil—History—Empire, 1822-1889
F2385	988.1032	Guyana—History—1966-	F2536	981.04	Brazil—History—Revolution, 1842
F2401-2431	988.3	Surinam			
F2401	988.3005	Surinam—Periodicals	F2536	981.04	Brazil—History—Quebra Quilos' Revolt, 1874
F2404	918.83003	Surinam—Gazetteers			

LC	Dewey	Subject Heading	LC	Dewey	Subject Heading
F2537	981.05	Brazil—History—1889-1930	F2689	989.207(1-3)	Paraguay—History—1938-1989
F2537	981.05	Brazil—History—Naval Revolt, 1893-1894	F2689	989.2072	Paraguay—History—Revolution, 1947
F2537	981.05	Brazil—History—Canudos Campaign, 1893-1897	F2689.2-.23	989.2073	Paraguay—History—1989-
F2537	981.05	Brazil—History—Naval Revolt, 1910	F2689.2	989.2073	Paraguay—History—Coup d'etat, 1989
F2537	981.05	Brazil—History—Contestado Insurrection, 1912-1916	F2701-2799	989.5	Uruguay
			F2701	989.5005	Uruguay—Periodicals
			F2704	918.95003	Uruguay—Gazetteers
F2537	981.05	Brazil—History—Revolution, 1922	F2710	989.5	Uruguay—Civilization
F2537	981.05	Brazil—History—Revolution, 1924-1925	F2711-2715	918.9504	Uruguay—Description and travel
F2538	981.05	Brazil—History—Revolution, 1930	F2720-2729.52	989.5	Uruguay—History
			F2723	989.50(1-3)	Uruguay—History—To 1810
F2538	981.061	Brazil—History—1930-1945	F2725	989.504	Uruguay—History—1810-1830
F2538	981.061	Brazil—History—Uprising, 1935	F2726	989.505	Uruguay—History—1830-1875
F2538	981.061	Brazil—History—Revolution, 1938	F2726	989.505	Uruguay—History—Great War, 1843-1852
F2538	981.061	Brazil—History—1945-1954	F2726	989.50(5-61)	Uruguay—History—1875-1904
F2538.2-.22	981.062	Brazil—History—1954-1964	F2726	989.5061	Uruguay—History—Revolution, 1886
F2538.2	981.063	Brazil—History—Revolution, 1964	F2726	989.5061	Uruguay—History—Revolution, 1897
F2538.25-.27	981.063	Brazil—History—1964-1985	F2728	989.506(1-5)	Uruguay—History—1904-1973
F2538.3-.5	981.064	Brazil—History—1985-	F2728	989.5063	Uruguay—History—Revolution, 1935
F2661-2699	989.2	Paraguay			
F2661	989.2005	Paraguay—Periodicals	F2729	989.5066	Uruguay—History—Coup d'etat, 1973
F2664	918.92003	Paraguay—Gazetteers			
F2670	989.2	Paraguay—Civilization	F2729	989.5066	Uruguay—History—1973-1985
F2671-2676	918.9204	Paraguay—Description and travel	F2729	989.5067	Uruguay—History—1985-
F2679.35-2689.23	989.2	Paraguay—History	F2801-3021	982	Argentina
F2683-2684	989.20(1-3)	Paraguay—History—To 1811	F2801	982.005	Argentina—Periodicals
			F2804	918.2003	Argentina—Gazetteers
F2683	989.203	Paraguay—History—Revolution of the Comuneros, 1721-1735	F2810	982	Argentina—Civilization
			F2811-2817	918.204	Argentina—Description and travel
F2683	989.203	Paraguay—History—War of Independence, 1810-1811	F2827-2849.22	982	Argentina—History
			F2841	982.0(1-24)	Argentina—History—To 1810
F2686-2687	989.20(4-5)	Paraguay—History—1811-1870	F2841	982.0(1-22)	Argentina—History—1515-1535
F2688-.5	989.20(6-71)	Paraguay—History—1870-1938	F2841	982.02(2-3)	Argentina—History—1535-1617
F2688	989.207	Paraguay—History—20th century	F2841	982.023	Argentina—History—1617-1776
F2688	989.2071	Paraguay—History—Revolution, 1904	F2841	982.023	Argentina—History—1776-1810
F2688	989.2071	Paraguay—History—Revolution, 1922-1923	F2843	982.04	Argentina—History—19th century
F2688	989.2071	Paraguay—History—Revolution, 1936	F2843	982.0(3-7)	Argentina—History—1810-

LC	Dewey	Subject Heading	LC	Dewey	Subject Heading
F2845	982.024	Argentina—History—English Invasions, 1806-1807	F3099	983.06(3-45)	Chile—History—1920-1970
F2845	982.03	Argentina—History—War of Independence, 1810-1817	F3099	983.0641	Chile—History—Naval Revolt, 1931
F2846	982.0(3-4)	Argentina—History—1817-1860	F3099	983.0642	Chile—History—Uprising, 1938
F2846	982.04	Argentina—History—Revolution, 1833	F3100	983.0646	Chile—History—1970-1973
F2847	982.0(4-5)	Argentina—History—1860-1910	F3100	983.065	Chile—History—Coup d'etat, 1973
F2847	982.05	Argentina—History—Revolution, 1890	F3100	983.065	Chile—History—1973-1988
F2848	982.061	Argentina—History—1910-1943	F3100	984.06(5-6)	Chile—History—1988-
F2848	982.061	Argentina—History—Revolution, 1930	F3169	996.18	Easter Island
F2849-.22	982.0(61-7)	Argentina—History—1943-	F3301-3359	984	Bolivia
			F3301	984.005	Bolivia—Periodicals
F2849	982.06(1-2)	Argentina—History—1943-1955	F3304	918.4003	Bolivia—Gazetteers
			F3310	984	Bolivia—Civilization
F2849.2	982.063	Argentina—History—Revolution, 1955	F3311-3315	918.404	Bolivia—Description and travel
F2849.2	982.06(3-4)	Argentina—History—1955-1983	F3320.3-3327	984	Bolivia—History
			F3322	984.0(1-3)	Bolivia—History—To 1809
F2849.2	982.063	Argentina—History—Peronist Revolt, 1956	F3323	984.041	Bolivia—History—Wars of Independence, 1809-1825
F2849.2	982.063	Argentina—History—Coup d'etat, 1966	F3324-3325	984.0(45-51)	Bolivia—History—1879-1938
F2849.2	982.0(64-7)	Argentina—History—1983-	F3324	984.04(2-5)	Bolivia—History—1825-1879
F3051-3285	983	Chile	F3326-3327	984.05(1-2)	Bolivia—History—1938-
F3051	983.005	Chile—Periodicals	F3326	984.05(1-2)	Bolivia—History—1938-1982
F3054	918.3003	Chile—Gazetteers			
F3060	983	Chile—Civilization	F3326	984.051	Bolivia—History—Coup d'etat, 1943
F3061-3065	918.304	Chile—Description and travel	F3326	984.051	Bolivia—History—Revolution, 1946
F3081-3098	983	Chile—History	F3326	984.052	Bolivia—History—Revolution, 1952
F3091	983.0(1-3)	Chile—History—To 1565			
F3091	983.0(1-3)	Chile—History—To 1810	F3326	984.052	Bolivia—History—Revolution, 1964
F3091	983.03	Chile—History—1565-1810	F3326	984.052	Bolivia—History—Coup d'etat, 1979
F3093	983.0(4-6)	Chile—History—1810-	F3326	984.052	Bolivia—History—Coup d'etat, 1980
F3094	983.04	Chile—History—War of Independence, 1810-1824	F3327	984.052	Bolivia—History—1982-
			F3401-3619	985	Peru
F3095	983.0(4-63)	Chile—History—1824-1920	F3401	985.005	Peru—Periodicals
			F3404	918.5003	Peru—Gazetteers
F3095	983.05	Chile—History—Insurrection, 1851	F3410	985	Peru—Civilization
F3095	983.05	Chile—History—Insurrection, 1859	F3410.5-3425	918.504	Peru—Description and travel
F3095	983.061	Chile—History—War with Spain, 1865-1866	F3430.3-3448.4	985	Peru—History
			F3442-3444	985.0(1-4)	Peru—History—To 1820
F3098	983.062	Chile—History—Revolution, 1891	F3442	985.0(1-2)	Peru—History—To 1548
			F3442	985.02	Peru—History—Conquest, 1522-1548
F3099	983.064	Chile—History—20th century	F3444	985.0(2-4)	Peru—History—1548-1820

85

LC	Dewey	Subject Heading	LC	Dewey	Subject Heading
F3444	985.033	Peru—History—Insurrection of Tupac Amaru, 1780-1781	G86	530.8	Mile, Roman
			G87	913.(7-8)	Classical geography
			G89-95	911.0902	Geography, Medieval
F3446	985.0(4-5)	Peru—History—War of Independence, 1820-1829	G109-110	910.21	Distances—Tables
			G128	910	Geography
			G141	911	Historical geography
F3447	985.0(5-631)	Peru—History—1829-1919	G149-922	910	Voyages and travels
			G149-180	910	Travel
F3447	985.05	Peru—History—Spanish question, 1864	G153	910.202	Travel—Guidebooks
			G154.9	338.4791	Tourist trade
F3447	985.061	Peru—History—Revolution of 1872	G156.5.Y6	910.83	Youth—Travel
			G200-336	910.9	Discoveries in geography
F3448	985.063(1-2)	Peru—History—1919-1968	G200-336	910.92	Travelers
			G420-445	910.41	Voyages around the world
F3448	985.0632	Peru—History—Revolution, 1930	G445	910.41	Flights around the world
			G516	916.04	Safaris
F3448.2	985.0633	Peru—History—Coup d'etat, 1968	G521-539	904	Adventure and adventurers
			G521-539	910.452	Shipwrecks
F3448.2	985.0633	Peru—History—1968-1980	G530.H82	910.45209164	Shipwrecks—Pacific Ocean
			G535-537	910.45092	Buccaneers
F3448.2	985.06(4-5)	Peru—History—1980-	G535-537	910.45092	Pirates
F3701-3799	986.6	Ecuador	G539	355.354	Soldiers of fortune
F3701	986.6005	Ecuador—Periodicals	G540-550	910.45	Seafaring life
F3704	918.66003	Ecuador—Gazetteers	G540-550	910.45	Ocean travel
F3710	986.6	Ecuador—Civilization	G545	910.45	Whaling
F3711-3716	918.6604	Ecuador—Description and travel	G575-597	910.0211	Polar regions
			G600-839	919.8	Arctic regions
F3723.3-3738.4	986.6	Ecuador—History	G640-665	910.0216327	Northwest Passage
F3733	986.60(1-2)	Ecuador—History—To 1809	G680-700	910.021811	Eastern Hemisphere
			G725-770	917.98(6-7)	Arctic regions—American
F3734	986.60(2-4)	Ecuador—History—Wars of Independence, 1809-1830	G778-787	914.843	Arctic regions—Norwegian
			G820-839	915.7	Arctic regions—Siberian
			G845-890	919.89	Antarctica
F3736	986.60(5-6)	Ecuador—History—1830-1895	G850	919.890409034	Expedition antarctique belge, 1897-1899
F3736	986.606	Ecuador—History—Revolution, 1895	G905-910	910.0213	Tropics
F3737	986.60(6-72)	Ecuador—History—1895-1944	G912-916	910.021813	Northern Hemisphere
			G918-922	910.021814	Southern Hemisphere
F3737	986.6071	Ecuador—History—20th century	G1000.3-.5	912.991	Moon—Maps
			G1001-1046	912	World maps
F3737	986.6072	Ecuador—History—Coup d'etat, 1925	G1046.C813	912.1954	Deserts—Maps
			G1050	912.19813	Northern Hemisphere—Maps
F3737	986.6072	Ecuador-Peru Conflict, 1941	G1052	912.19814	Southern Hemisphere—Maps
F3738	986.607(2-5)	Ecuador—History—1944-	G1053	912.193	Tropics—Maps
F3738	986.6072	Ecuador—History—Coup d'etat, 1944	G1054-1055	912.191	Polar regions—Maps
			G1059-1061	912.1962	Nautical charts
F3738	986.6074	Ecuador-Peru Conflict, 1981	G1100-1779	912.19812	Western Hemisphere—Maps
			G1105-1692	912.7	North America—Maps
G	910	Geography	G1110-1114	912.982	Greenland—Maps
G2-55	910.6	Geography—Societies, etc.	G1115-1193	912.71	Canada—Maps
			G1200-1534.24	912.73	United States—Maps
G67-69	910.92	Geographers—Biography	G1535-1537	912.729	Caribbean Area—Maps
G70-.4	910.01	Geography—Methodology	G1545-1549	912.72	Mexico—Maps
G72-76.5	910.71	Geography—Study and teaching	G1550-1594	912.728	Central America—Maps
			G1600-1692	912.729	West Indies—Maps
G80-99	910.9	Geography—History	G1700-1779	912.8	South America—Maps
G83-88	913	Geography, Ancient			

LC	Dewey	Subject Heading	LC	Dewey	Subject Heading
G1780-2799	912.19811	Eastern Hemisphere—Maps	G2750-2793	912.94	Australia—Maps
G1791-1799	911.4	Europe—Historical geography—Maps	G2795-2799	912.93	New Zealand—Maps
			G2805-2839	912.1963	Atlantic Ocean—Maps
G1805-1829.24	912.41	Great Britain—Maps	G2860-2867	912.1964	Pacific Ocean—Maps
G1837-1844.24	912.44	France—Maps	G2870-2894	912.95	Melanesia—Maps
G1850-1874	912.492	Benelux countries	G2905-2934	912.965	Micronesia—Maps
G1895-1899	912.494	Switzerland—Maps	G2970-2984	912.96	Polynesia—Maps
G1907-1924	912.43	Germany—Maps	G3055-3064	912.19632	Arctic Ocean—Maps
G1935-1939	912.436	Austria—Maps	G3100-3102	912.989	Antarctica—Maps
G1940-1944	912.439	Hungary—Maps	G3195-3199	912.991	Moon—Maps
G1945-1949	912.437	Czechoslovakia—Maps	G3200-9980	912	Maps
G1950-1954	912.438	Poland—Maps	G3210-3212	912.19813	Northern Hemisphere—Maps
G1965-1969	912.46	Spain—Maps			
G1975-1979	912.469	Portugal—Maps	G3220-3222	912.19814	Southern Hemisphere—Maps
G1983-1989.53	912.45	Italy—Maps			
G2000-2004	912.495	Greece—Maps	G3240-3241	912.193	Tropics—Maps
G2015-2017	912.4971	Serbia—Maps	G3260-3272	912.191	Polar regions—Maps
G2020-2022	912.49745	Montenegro—Maps	G3290-5669	912.7	America—Maps
G2025-2027	912.4972	Dalmatia (Croatia)—Maps	G3300-4884	912.7	North America—Maps
G2030-2032	912.4972	Croatia—Maps	G3380-3384	912.982	Greenland—Maps
G2035-2039	912.498	Romania—Maps	G3400-3612	912.71	Canada—Maps
G2040-2044	912.499	Bulgaria—Maps	G3410-3444	912.715	Maritime Provinces—Maps
G2055-2059	912.489	Denmark—Maps	G3420-3424	912.716	Nova Scotia—Maps
G2060-2064	912.4912	Iceland—Maps	G3430-3434	912.7151	New Brunswick—Maps
G2065-2069	912.481	Norway—Maps	G3440-3444	912.717	Prince Edward Island—Maps
G2070-2074	912.485	Sweden—Maps			
G2075-2079	912.4897	Finland—Maps	G3450-3454	912.714	Quebec (Province)—Maps
G2110-2193	912.47	Russia—Maps	G3460-3464	912.713	Ontario—Maps
G2200-2444	912.5	Asia—Maps	G3470-3504	912.712	Prairie Provinces—Maps
G2210-2214	912.561	Turkey—Maps	G3480-3484	912.7127	Manitoba—Maps
G2215-2219	912.5693	Cyprus—Maps	G3490-3494	912.7124	Saskatchewan—Maps
G2220-2224	912.5691	Syria—Maps	G3500-3504	912.7123	Alberta—Maps
G2225-2229	912.5692	Lebanon—Maps	G3510-3514	912.711	British Columbia—Maps
G2235-2239	912.5694	Israel—Maps	G3520-3524	912.7191	Yukon Territory—Maps
G2240-2244	912.5695	Jordan—Maps	G3530-3564	912.7192	Northwest Territories—Maps
G2249.3-.34	912.538	Saudi Arabia—Maps			
G2250-2254	912.567	Iraq—Maps	G3600-3604	912.718	Newfoundland—Maps
G2255-2259	912.55	Iran—Maps	G3610-3612	912.7182	Labrador (Nfld.)—Maps
G2265-2269	912.581	Afghanistan—Maps	G3690-3691	912.73	United States—Territories and possessions—Maps
G2270-2274	912.5491	Pakistan—Maps			
G2275-2279	912.5492	Bangladesh—Maps	G3690-4383	912.73	United States—Maps
G2280-2284	912.54	India—Maps	G3701	911.73	United States—Historical geography—Maps
G2285-2289	912.591	Burma—Maps			
G2290-2294	912.5493	Sri Lanka—Maps	G3709.3-3933	912.7(4-5)	Atlantic States—Maps
G2295-2299	912.5496	Nepal—Maps	G3720-3784	912.74	New England—Maps
G2305-2321	912.51	China—Maps	G3730-3734	912.741	Maine—Maps
G2330-2334.34	912.519	Korea—Maps	G3740-3744	912.742	New Hampshire—Maps
G2340-2344	912.51249	Taiwan—Maps	G3750-3754	912.743	Vermont—Maps
G2355-2359	912.52	Japan—Maps	G3760-3764	912.744	Massachusetts—Maps
G2370-2374	912.597	Vietnam—Maps	G3770-3774	912.745	Rhode Island—Maps
G2374.3-.34	912.596	Cambodia—Maps	G3780-3784	912.746	Connecticut—Maps
G2374.5-.54	912.594	Laos—Maps	G3790-3854	912.74	Middle Atlantic States—Maps
G2375-2379	912.593	Thailand—Maps			
G2445-2739	912.6	Africa—Maps	G3800-3804	912.747	New York (State)—Maps
G2455-2499	912.61	Africa, North—Maps	G3810-3814	912.749	New Jersey—Maps
G2500-2559	912.676	Africa, East—Maps	G3820-3824	912.748	Pennsylvania—Maps
G2590-2639	912.67	Africa, Central—Maps	G3830-3834	912.751	Delaware—Maps
G2640-2714	912.66	Africa, West—Maps	G3840-3844	912.752	Maryland—Maps
			G3850-3854	912.753	Washington (D.C.)—Maps

LC	Dewey	Subject Heading	LC	Dewey	Subject Heading
G3870-3933	912.75	South Atlantic States—Maps	G4960-4964	912.7292	Jamaica—Maps
			G4965-4969	912.72921	Cayman Islands—Maps
G3880-3884	912.755	Virginia—Maps	G4970-4974	912.7295	Puerto Rico—Maps
G3890-3894	912.754	West Virginia—Maps	G4980-4984	912.7296	Bahamas—Maps
G3900-3904	912.756	North Carolina—Maps	G5010-5014	912.729722	Virgin Islands of the United States—Maps
G3910-3914	912.757	South Carolina—Maps			
G3920-3924	912.758	Georgia—Maps	G5020-5024	912.729725	British Virgin Islands—Maps
G3930-3934	912.759	Florida—Maps			
G3950-3954	912.769	Kentucky—Maps	G5030-5059	912.7297	Leeward Islands (West Indies)—Maps
G3960-3964	912.768	Tennessee—Maps			
G3970-3974	912.761	Alabama—Maps	G5040-5044	912.72973	Saint Kitts (Island)—Maps
G3980-3984	912.762	Mississippi—Maps	G5045-5049	912.72973	Anguilla—Maps
G4000-4004	912.767	Arkansas—Maps	G5050-5054	912.72974	Antigua—Maps
G4010-4014	912.763	Louisiana—Maps	G5055-5059	912.72975	Montserrat—Maps
G4020-4024	912.766	Oklahoma—Maps	G5070-5074	912.72976	Guadeloupe—Maps
G4030-4034	912.764	Texas—Maps	G5080-5084	912.72982	Martinique—Maps
G4050-4052	912.78	West (U.S.)—Maps	G5090-5184	912.7298	Windward Islands—Maps
G4080-4084	912.771	Ohio—Maps	G5100-5104	912.729841	Dominica—Maps
G4090-4094	912.772	Indiana—Maps	G5110-5114	912.729843	Saint Lucia—Maps
G4100-4104	912.773	Illinois—Maps	G5120-5124	912.729844	Saint Vincent—Maps
G4110-4114	912.774	Michigan—Maps	G5130-5134	912.729845	Granada—Maps
G4120-4124	912.775	Wisconsin—Maps	G5140-5144	912.72981	Barbados—Maps
G4140-4144	912.776	Minnesota—Maps	G5150-5162	912.72983	Trinidad and Tobago—Maps
G4150-4154	912.777	Iowa—Maps			
G4160-4164	912.778	Missouri—Maps	G5170-5174	912.72986	Aruba—Maps
G4170-4174	912.784	North Dakota—Maps	G5175-5179	912.72986	Bonaire—Maps
G4180-4184	912.783	South Dakota—Maps	G5180-5184	912.72986	Curacao—Maps
G4190-4194	912.782	Nebraska—Maps	G5200-5668	912.8	South America—Maps
G4200-4204	912.781	Kansas—Maps	G5250-5254	912.881	Guyana—Maps
G4230-4232	912.79	Pacific States—Maps	G5260-5264	912.883	Surinam—Maps
G4250-4254	912.786	Montana—Maps	G5270-5274	912.882	French Guiana—Maps
G4260-4264	912.787	Wyoming—Maps	G5280-5284	912.87	Venezuela—Maps
G4270-4274	912.796	Idaho—Maps	G5290-5294	912.861	Colombia—Maps
G4280-4284	912.797	Washington (State)—Maps	G5300-5304	912.866	Ecuador—Maps
			G5310-5314	912.85	Peru—Maps
G4290-4294	912.795	Oregon—Maps	G5320-5324	912.84	Bolivia—Maps
G4310-4314	912.788	Colorado—Maps	G5330-5334	912.83	Chile—Maps
G4320-4324	912.789	New Mexico—Maps	G5350-5354	912.82	Argentina—Maps
G4330-4334	912.791	Arizona—Maps	G5370-5374	912.895	Uruguay—Maps
G4340-4344	912.792	Utah—Maps	G5380-5384	912.892	Paraguay—Maps
G4350-4354	912.793	Nevada—Maps	G5400-5404	912.81	Brazil—Maps
G4360-4364	912.794	California—Maps	G5700-7153	912.4	Europe—Maps
G4370-4374	912.798	Alaska—Maps	G5740-5814	912.41	Great Britain—Maps
G4380-4384	912.969	Hawaii—Maps	G5741	911.41	Great Britain—Historical geography—Maps
G4390-4392	912.729	Caribbean Area—Maps			
G4410-4414	912.72	Mexico—Maps	G5750-5754	912.42	England—Maps
G4800-4884	912.728	Central America—Maps	G5760-5764	912.429	Wales—Maps
G4810-4814	912.7281	Guatemala—Maps	G5770-5774	912.411	Scotland—Maps
G4820-4824	912.7282	Belize—Maps	G5780-5784	912.415	Ireland—Maps
G4830-4834	912.7283	Honduras—Maps	G5790-5794	912.416	Northern Ireland—Maps
G4840-4844	912.7284	El Salvador—Maps	G5830-5834	912.44	France—Maps
G4850-4854	912.7285	Nicaragua—Maps	G5980-5984	912.44949	Monaco—Maps
G4860-4864	912.7286	Costa Rica—Maps	G6000-6004	912.492	Netherlands—Maps
G4870-4874	912.7287	Panama—Maps	G6010-6014	912.493	Belgium—Maps
G4900-5184	912.729	West Indies—Maps	G6020-6024	912.4935	Luxemburg—Maps
G4920-4924	912.7291	Cuba—Maps	G6035-6036	912.4947	Alps—Maps
G4940-4944	912.7294	Haiti—Maps	G6040-6044	912.494	Switzerland—Maps
G4950-4954	912.7293	Dominican Republic—Maps	G6050-6054	912.43648	Liechtenstein—Maps
			G6080-6428	912.43	Germany—Maps

LC	Dewey	Subject Heading	LC	Dewey	Subject Heading
G6490-6494	912.436	Austria—Maps	G8025-8029	912.593	Thailand—Maps
G6500-6504	912.439	Hungary—Maps	G8030-8034	912.595	Malaysia—Maps
G6510-6514	912.437	Czechoslovakia—Maps	G8040-8044	912.5957	Singapore—Maps
G6520-6524	912.438	Poland—Maps	G8060-8064	912.599	Philippines—Maps
G6560-6564	912.46	Spain—Maps	G8070-8074	912.598	Indonesia—Maps
G6690-6694	912.469	Portugal—Maps	G8140-8142	912.95	New Guinea—Maps
G6710-6714	912.45	Italy—Maps	G8200-8202	912.6	Africa—Maps
G6760-6763	912.458	Sicily (Italy)—Maps	G8220-8222	912.61	Africa, North—Maps
G6810-6814	912.495	Greece—Maps	G8230-8234	912.64	Morocco—Maps
G6840-6844	912.497	Yugoslavia—Maps	G8240-8244	912.65	Algeria—Maps
G6850-6853	912.4971	Serbia—Maps	G8250-8254	912.611	Tunisia—Maps
G6860-6863	912.49742	Bosnia and Herzegovina—Maps	G8260-8264	912.612	Libya—Maps
G6870-6873	912.4972	Croatia—Maps	G8300-8304	912.62	Egypt—Maps
G6875-6878	912.4973	Slovenia—Maps	G8330-8334	912.63	Ethiopia—Maps
G6880-6884	912.498	Romania—Maps	G8350-8354	912.6773	Somalia—Maps
G6890-6894	912.499	Bulgaria—Maps	G8410-8414	912.6762	Kenya—Maps
G6910-6963	912.48	Scandinavia—Maps	G8420-8424	912.6761	Uganda—Maps
G6920-6924	912.489	Denmark—Maps	G8430-8434	912.67571	Rwanda—Maps
G6930-6934	912.4912	Iceland—Maps	G8435-8439	912.67572	Burundi—Maps
G6940-6944	912.481	Norway—Maps	G8440-8444	912.678	Tanzania—Maps
G6950-6954	912.485	Sweden—Maps	G8450-8454	912.679	Mozambique—Maps
G6960-6964	912.4897	Finland—Maps	G8460-8464	912.691	Madagascar—Maps
G7030-7033	912.4798	Estonia—Maps	G8500-8504	912.68	South Africa—Maps
G7040-7043	912.4796	Latvia—Maps	G8530-8533	912.684	Natal (South Africa)—Maps
G7060-7342	912.47	Russia—Maps	G8540-8543	912.682	Transvaal—Maps
G7400-8198.54	912.5	Asia—Maps	G8580-8584	912.6885	Lesotho—Maps
G7420-7624	912.56	Middle East—Maps	G8590-8594	912.6887	Swaziland—Maps
G7430-7434	912.561	Turkey—Maps	G8600-8604	912.6883	Botswana—Maps
G7450-7454	912.5693	Cyprus—Maps	G8610-8614	912.6897	Malawi—Maps
G7460-7464	912.5691	Syria—Maps	G8620-8624	912.6881	Namibia—Maps
G7470-7474	912.5692	Lebanon—Maps	G8640-8644	912.673	Angola—Maps
G7500-7504	912.5694	Israel—Maps	G8650-8654	912.6751	Zaire—Maps
G7510-7514	912.5695	Jordan—Maps	G8660-8664	912.6718	Equatorial Guinea—Maps
G7530-7534	912.538	Saudi Arabia—Maps	G8675-8679	912.6715	Sao Tome and Principe—Maps
G7550-7554	912.533	Yemen—Maps	G8690-8694	912.6721	Gabon—Maps
G7560-7564	912.5353	Oman—Maps	G8700-8704	912.6724	Congo (Brazzaville)—Maps
G7580-7584	912.5363	Qatar—Maps	G8710-8714	912.6741	Central African Republic—Maps
G7590-7594	912.5365	Bahrain—Maps	G8720-8724	912.6743	Chad—Maps
G7600-7604	912.5367	Kuwait—Maps	G8730-8734	912.6711	Cameroon—Maps
G7610-7614	912.567	Iraq—Maps	G8750-8754	912.6683	Benin—Maps
G7620-7624	912.55	Iran—Maps	G8760-8764	912.6681	Togo—Maps
G7630-7634	912.581	Afghanistan—Maps	G8770-8774	912.6626	Niger—Maps
G7640-7644	912.5491	Pakistan—Maps	G8780-8784	912.6668	Cote d'Ivoire—Maps
G7645-7649	912.5492	Bangladesh—Maps	G8790-8794	912.6652	Guinea—Maps
G7650-7654	912.54	India—Maps	G8800-8804	912.6623	Mali—Maps
G7720-7724	912.591	Burma—Maps	G8805-8809	912.6625	Burkina Faso—Maps
G7750-7754	912.5493	Sri Lanka—Maps	G8810-8814	912.663	Senegal—Maps
G7760-7764	912.5496	Nepal—Maps	G8820-8824	912.661	Mauritania—Maps
G7780-7784	912.5498	Bhutan—Maps	G8840-8844	912.669	Nigeria—Maps
G7820-7824	912.51	China—Maps	G8850-8854	912.667	Ghana—Maps
G7895-7899	912.517	Mongolia—Maps	G8860-8864	912.664	Sierra Leone—Maps
G7940-7944	912.5125	Hong Kong—Maps	G8870-8874	912.6651	Gambia—Maps
G7945-7947	912.5126	Macao—Maps	G8880-8884	912.6662	Liberia—Maps
G7960-7964	912.52	Japan—Maps	G8890-8894	912.6657	Guinea-Bissau—Maps
G8000-8198.54	912.59	Indochina—Maps	G8960-8964	912.94	Australia—Maps
G8010-8014	912.596	Cambodia—Maps	G9080-9084	912.93	New Zealand—Maps
G8015-8019	912.594	Laos—Maps			
G8020-8024	912.597	Vietnam—Maps			

LC	Dewey	Subject Heading	LC	Dewey	Subject Heading
G9130-9134	912.4699	Azores—Maps	GB448	551.43	Slopes (Physical geography)
G9140-9144	912.4698	Madeira Islands—Maps			
G9150-9154	912.649	Canary Islands—Maps	GB450-460	551.457	Coasts
G9160-9164	912.6658	Cape Verde—Maps	GB451-460	551.458	Seashore
G9170-9174	912.973	Saint Helena—Maps	GB454.F5	551.44	Fjords
G9175-9179	912.9711	Falkland Islands—Maps	GB454.I54	551.44	Inlets
G9185-9189	912.6982	Mauritius—Maps	GB461-468	551.424	Reefs
G9190-9194	912.6981	Reunion—Maps	GB461-468	551.424	Coral reefs and islands
G9200-9204	912.696	Seychelles—Maps	GB471-478	551.42	Islands
G9210-9214	912.694	Comoro Islands—Maps	GB501-555	551.432	Mountains
G9215-9219	912.5495	Maldives—Maps	GB561-568	551.442	Arroyos
G9260-9262	912.95	Melanesia—Maps	GB561-568	551.442	Floodplains
G9280-9284	912.9593	Solomon Islands—Maps	GB561-568	551.442	Valleys
G9295-9297	912.9595	Vanuatu—Maps	GB561-568	551.45	Watersheds
G9340-9344	912.9597	New Caledonia—Maps	GB561-568	551.453	Savannas
G9380-9384	912.9611	Fiji—Maps	GB571-578	551.434	Plateaus
G9400-9494	912.965	Micronesia—Maps	GB571-578	551.453	Prairies
G9410-9414	912.967	Mariana Islands—Maps	GB571-578	551.434	Mesas
G9420-9424	912.966	Caroline Islands—Maps	GB571-578	551.453	Plains
G9460-9464	912.9683	Marshall Islands—Maps	GB571-578	551.453	Steppes
G9480-9484	912.9681	Kiribati—Maps	GB581-588	551.315	Glacial landforms
G9500-9652	912.96	Polynesia—Maps	GB591-598	551.453	Alluvial plains
G9515-9517	912.9616	Wallis and Futuna Islands—Maps	GB591-598	551.456	Deltas
			GB599-609.2	551.447	Karst
G9530-9534	912.964	Line Islands—Maps	GB601-608	551.447	Caves
G9550-9554	912.9615	Tokelau—Maps	GB601.52.M34	796.525	Cave mapping
G9555-9557	912.961(3-4)	Samoan Islands—Maps	GB609.2	551.447	Sinkholes
G9570-9574	912.9612	Tonga—Maps	GB611-618	551.415	Arid regions
G9600-9604	912.9623	Cook Islands—Maps	GB611-618	551.415	Desertification
G9620-9624	912.9631	Marquesas Islands—Maps	GB611-618	551.415	Desertification—Control
G9640-9644	912.9621	Society Islands—Maps	GB611-618	551.415	Deserts
G9660-9664	912.9618	Pitcairn Island—Maps	GB621-628	551.41	Bogs
G9800-9804	912.989	Antarctica—Maps	GB621-628	551.41	Swamps
			GB631-638	551.375	Sand dunes
GA	526	Mathematical geography	GB641-648	551.312	Rock glaciers
GA	526	Cartography	GB649.S3	551.375	Sand waves
GA1-87	526	Mathematical geography	GB651-2998	551.48	Hydrology
GA4	526.021	Mathematical geography—Tables	GB651-2998	551.48	Water
			GB651-2998	551.48	Water-supply
GA23	526.3	Area measurement	GB656.2.A37	551.48028	Aerial photography in hydrology
GA51-87	526.9	Surveys			
GA101-1999	526	Cartography	GB855	546.22	Water chemistry
GA101-130	912	Outline maps	GB1001-1199.8	551.49	Groundwater
GA109.8	310.0223	Maps, Statistical	GB1198-.4	551.23	Hot springs
GA110-115	526.8	Map projection	GB1198-.4	551.498	Springs
GA130	526	Map drawing	GB1198.5-.8	551.23	Geysers
GA139	526.0285	Digital mapping	GB1201-1399.5	551.483	Rivers
GA201-246	526.09	Cartography—History	GB1201-1398	551.4830287	Stream measurements
GA405	526.0973	Cartography—United States	GB1203	551.489	Flood routing
			GB1207	551.483	Streamflow
GA409-460	526.097(4-9)	Cartography—[United States, By state]	GB1399-.5	551.489	Floods
			GB1399.2	551.4890112	Flood forecasting
			GB1401-1597	551.484	Waterfalls
GB	910.02	Physical geography	GB1601-1798.9	551.482	Lakes
GB400-649	551.41	Geomorphology	GB2201-2398	551.482	Lagoons
GB400-649	551.41	Landforms	GB2401-2598	551.343	Sea ice drift
GB400.42.A35	551.41028	Aerial photography in geomorphology	GB2401-2598	551.312	Glaciers
			GB2401-2598	551.31	Ice sheets
			GB2401-2597	551.31	Ice

LC	Dewey	Subject Heading	LC	Dewey	Subject Heading
GB2401-2597	551.342	Icebergs	GE140-160	363.7	Environmental degradation
GB2401.72.A37	551.31028	Aerial photography in glaciology	GE140-160	363.7	Environmental indicators
			GE140-160	363.7	Environmental quality
GB2801-2998	551.57	Hydrometeorology	GE195-199	333.72	Green movement
GB5018	904	Natural disasters	GE195-199	333.72	Environmentalism
			GE300-350	333.7	Environmental management
GC	551.46	Oceanography			
GC41	551.460284	Oceanographic instruments	GF	304.2	Human ecology
			GF1-900	304.2	Human ecology
GC57-59	551.46072	Oceanography—Research	GF24	304.2	Applied human geography
GC65-78	551.4607	Underwater exploration	GF70-90	333.7071	Environmental education
GC66	551.46072	Manned undersea research stations	GF71	304.25	Man—Influence of climate
GC67	387.2045	Oceanographic submersibles	GF101-127	307.14	Human settlements
			GF125	910.021732	Urban geography
GC83-87.6	551.4683	Submarine topography	GF127	910.021734	Rural geography
GC87-.6	551.4683	Ocean bottom	GF500-895	304.209(4-9)	Human ecology—[By region or country]
GC87.6	551.468	Submarine trenches			
GC96-97.8	551.4618	Estuarine oceanography	GF503-504	304.20973	Human ecology—United States
GC96-97.8	551.4618	Estuaries			
GC100-103	551.465	Seawater	GF895	304.20913	Human ecology—Tropics
GC109-149	551.465	Chemical oceanography			
GC121-127	551.4664	Salinity	GN	301	Anthropology
GC160-177	551.4653	Ocean temperature	GN20-21	301.092	Anthropologists
GC175	551.4653	Deep-sea temperature	GN33-34.3	301.01	Anthropology—Methodology
GC190-.5	551.5246	Ocean-atmosphere interaction	GN33.5	304.6	Demographic anthropology
			GN34.3.A35	301.028	Aerial photography in anthropology
GC205-226	551.463	Ocean waves			
GC211-222	551.463	Waves	GN35-41	305.80074	Ethnological museums and collections
GC211.2	551.463	Waves			
GC225-226	551.463	Storm surges	GN42-46	301.072	Anthropology—Research
GC228.5-.6	551.462	Ocean circulation	GN49-298	599.9	Physical anthropology
GC229-299	551.462	Ocean currents	GN51-59	599.94	Anthropometry
GC296.8.E	551.462	El Nino Current	GN59.A35	599.940846	Aged—Anthropometry
GC296.G9	551.462	Gulf Stream	GN63	612.65	Child development
GC300-376	551.464	Tides	GN63	599.90835	Adolescence
GC308-309	551.464	Tidal currents	GN63.6	306.875	Quintuplets
GC376	551.464	Bores (Tidal phenomena)	GN63.6	306.875	Quadruplets
GC380-399	551.4686	Marine sediments	GN63.6	306.875	Twins
GC401-455	551.46132	Oceanography—Arctic Ocean	GN63.6	306.875	Triplets
			GN66-69	599.949	Proportion (Anthropometry)
GC461-462	551.4617	Oceanography—Antarctic Ocean			
			GN66	599.949	Somatotypes
GC481-711	551.4613	Oceanography—Atlantic Ocean	GN69.3-.5	599.949	Midgets
			GN69.3-.5	599.949	Dwarfs
GC721-761	551.4615	Oceanography—Indian Ocean	GN70	599.947	Skeleton
			GN70	599.947	Ribs
GC771-871	551.4614	Oceanography—Pacific Ocean	GN71-131	599.948	Craniology
			GN71-131	599.948	Skull
GC1000-1023	333.9164	Marine resources	GN131	599.948	Eye-sockets
GC1018	333.916416	Marine resources conservation	GN181-190.5	599.948	Brain
			GN191-199	599.945	Skin
GC1080-1581	363.7394	Marine pollution	GN192	599.945	Dermatoglyphics
			GN192	599.945	Fingerprints
GE	333.7 363.7	Environmental sciences	GN197	599.945	Color of man
GE45.S25	363.7064	Environmental sampling	GN199	599.945	Albinos and albinism
GE51-71	304.2	Man—Influence of environment	GN209	599.943	Dental anthropology
GE70-90	333.7071	Environmental education	GN209	599.943	Teeth

LC	Dewey	Subject Heading	LC	Dewey	Subject Heading
GN231-232	599.947	Posture	GN468	305.8001	Ethnophilosophy
GN254	306.846	Miscegenation	GN470-474	203	Worship
GN270-279	155.82	Ethnopsychology	GN471	202.1	Animism
GN281-289	599.938	Human evolution	GN472	202.1	Fetishism
GN281-.4	599.938	Man—Origin	GN473	203.8	Rites and ceremonies
GN282-286.7	569.9	Fossil man	GN475.3	203	Magic
GN282.5	569.9	Missing link	GN475.3	133.43	Magic
GN283.9	569.9	Homo habilis	GN475.6	133.425	Evil eye
GN284-.7	569.97	Homo erectus	GN476.1	513	Arithmetic
GN284.4	569.9	Solo man	GN476.4	910	Geography
GN284.6	569.97	Java man	GN477-.7	615.88	Traditional medicine
GN284.7	569.97	Peking man	GN477.5-.7	617.0901	Surgery, Primitive
GN285	569.986	Neanderthals	GN478-491.7	305	Social structure
GN286.3	569.98	Cro-Magnon man	GN479.6	321.1	Patriarchy
GN301-673	305.8	Ethnology	GN480-.65	306.85	Family
GN307-499	569.9	Man, Primitive	GN480-.65	306.83	Kinship
GN325	305.8	Ethnology	GN480	306.83	Double descent (Kinship)
GN345.2	305.8009	Ethnohistory	GN480	306.81	Marriage
GN345.6	303.482	Intercultural communication	GN480.1	392.4	Bridal price
			GN480.3	306.82	Endogamy and exogamy
GN345.65	303.482	Cross-cultural orientation	GN480.3	306.877	Incest
GN365.9	304.5	Sociobiology	GN480.33-.36	306.8423	Polygamy
GN370	304.8	Man—Migrations	GN480.4	306.81	Cross-cousin marriage
GN372	305.48969	Wild women	GN480.6	306.8423	Polyandry
GN372	305.3899	Wild men	GN482.1	392.12	Birth customs
GN372	155.4567	Feral children	GN483-484	305.235	Adolescence
GN380	305.8	Indigenous peoples	GN484	392.1	Circumcision
GN387	305.906918	Nomads	GN484.3	392.6	Sex customs
GN395	307.76	Urban anthropology	GN484.43	392.4	Betrothal
GN400-406	306	Culture	GN486	393.1	Burial
GN406-498	301.7	Society, Primitive	GN486	393	Funeral rites and ceremonies
GN407-411.5	641.592	Food			
GN407.4-.8	630	Traditional farming	GN486.3	302.34	Friendship
GN407.6-.7	636	Domestic animals	GN489	202.11	Totemism
GN414	722	Architecture, Primitive	GN491	202.11	Totems
GN415.C8	645.4	Cradles	GN491.4	305.5122	Caste
GN418-419	391	Clothing and dress	GN492-495	306.2	Political anthropology
GN419.15	391.65	Body marking	GN492.3	398.27	Political customs and rites
GN419.2	391.65	Mutilation	GN492.5	305.8	Tribes
GN419.25	391.7	Body piercing	GN492.6	320.11	State, The—Origin
GN419.5	391.434	Masks	GN492.7	352.23	Kings and rulers
GN431	746.412	Basket making	GN493.3	306	Social norms
GN432	641.812	Tapa	GN494	390	Taboo
GN432	677.028242	Weaving	GN495.2	366.(1-5)	Secret societies
GN432	677.028242092	Weavers	GN495.4	305.8	Ethnic groups
GN432	677.02822	Spinning	GN495.5	321.60901	Kings and rulers, Ancient
GN435.7-450.5	332.4	Shell money	GN495.6	305.8	Ethnicity
GN436.2	332.4	Stone money	GN496-498	305.8	Ethnic relations
GN436.8-437	621.9	Tools	GN496-498	305.8	Race relations
GN440.1	387.2	Ships	GN497.5	306.859	Matriarchy
GN440.2	386.229	Outrigger canoes	GN498	623.441	Spears
GN440.2	386.229	Dugout canoes	GN498.B78	623.441	Arrowheads
GN440.2	386.229	Canoes and canoeing	GN498.B78	623.441	Bow and arrow
GN448-450.7	306.3	Economic anthropology	GN498.S5	623.441	Shields
GN451-477.7	306.42	Intellectual life	GN498.S55	623.441	Slings
GN454-455	306.483	Sports	GN502-517	155.82	Ethnopsychology
GN454-456	394.3	Toys	GN510	303.32	Socialization
GN454.6	306.482	Gambling	GN537	305.8034	Caucasian race
GN454.8-455	394.3	Games	GN547	305.8924	Jews

92

LC	Dewey	Subject Heading	LC	Dewey	Subject Heading
GN547	305.892	Semites	GR74-76	398.2	Tales
GN548	305.8942	Mongols	GR75.L56	398.245	Little Red Riding Hood (Tale)
GN549.G4	305.83	Germanic peoples	GR75.S6	398.21	Snow White (Tale)
GN549.T4	305.83	Teutonic race	GR81	398.41	Superstition
GN550-560	305.80097	Ethnic groups—North America	GR100-390	398.09(4-9)	Folklore—[By region or country]
GN562-564	305.80098	Ethnic groups—South America	GR101-118	398.097	Folklore—North America
GN575-585	305.80094	Ethnic groups—Europe	GR103	394.308996073	Afro-American children's games
GN625-635	305.80095	Ethnic groups—Asia	GR130-133	398.098	Folklore—South America
GN643-661	305.80096	Ethnic groups—Africa	GR135-263	398.094	Folklore—Europe
GN645	305.8044	Mulattoes	GR265-345	398.095	Folklore—Asia
GN662-671	305.80099(5-6)	Ethnic groups—Oceania	GR350-360	398.096	Folklore—Africa
GN664.N3	305.8096	Negritos	GR365-370	398.0993	Folklore—Australia
GN664.P2	305.89912	Papuans	GR375-376	398.0994	Folklore—New Zealand
GN666	305.89915	Australian aborigines—Ethnic identity	GR380-385	398.0996	Folklore—Oceania
			GR455	393	Dead
GN669	305.89952	Micronesians	GR455	393	Death
GN671.B5	305.8995	Gunantuna (Melanesian people)	GR462	398.354	Sex—Folklore
			GR465	392.5	Marriage
GN700-890	569.9	Man, Prehistoric	GR480-485	394.3	Games
GN700-890	930.1	Archaeology	GR485	398.8	Counting-out rhymes
GN750-751	001.94	Lost continents	GR490-497	392.36	Dwellings
GN771	930.12	Paleolithic period, Lower	GR500-510	398.45	Supernatural
GN775-776	930.11	Eoliths	GR525	398.45	Ghouls and ogres
GN775-768	930.1(2-4)	Stone age	GR530	398.45	Witchcraft
GN777-778	930.15	Bronze age	GR540	398.45	Demonology
GN777-778	930.15	Copper age	GR540	398.45	Exorcism
GN783-784	930.1	Cave dwellings	GR540	398.45	Incantations
GN783-.5	930.1	Caves	GR549-552	398.45	Fairies
GN785-786	569.9	Lake-dwellers and lake-dwellings	GR550-552	398.2	Fairy tales
			GR555	398.45	Trolls
GN789	930.1028	Earthworks (Archaeology)	GR560	398.45	Ghouls and ogres
GN795-796	930.1	Mounds	GR580	398.47	Ghosts
GN799.A	700.901	Art, Prehistoric	GR600	398.45	Amulets
GN799.A4	630.901	Agriculture—Origin	GR600	398.45	Charms
GN799.A4	630.901	Agricultural implements, Prehistoric	GR660	398.3209143	Mountains
			GR600	398.45	Talismans
GN799.A8	520.901	Astronomy, Prehistoric	GR625	398.362	Sun
GN799.B62	623.821	Boats, Prehistoric	GR625	398.362	Stars
GN799.C49	623.8620901	Cordage, Prehistoric	GR630	398.363	Lightning
GN799.H84	639.0901	Hunting, Prehistoric	GR630	398.363	Thunderstorms
GN799.P5	646.2040284	Pins and needles, Prehistoric	GR650-690	398.32	Geographical myths
			GR680	398.32091693	Rivers
GN799.R4	201.42	Religion, Prehistoric	GR690	398.364	Springs—Folklore
GN799.S4	732	Sculpture, Prehistoric	GR690	398.364	Wells
GN799.T73	302.2	Communication, Prehistoric	GR720	398.3699772	Dogs
			GR740	398.36979	Reptiles
GN799.T75	790.1330901	Toys	GR745	398.3697	Fishes—Folklore
GN799.W3	623.441	Weapons, Prehistoric	GR750	398.36957	Insects
GN799.W66	569.9	Women, Prehistoric	GR780	398.368	Botany—Folklore
GN871-875	994.01	Australian aborigines—Antiquities	GR780-790	302.222	Flower language
			GR780-790	398.368	Plants
GR	398	Folklore	GR785	398.368216	Trees—Folklore
GR50	398.092	Folklorists	GR800	398.365	Rocks
GR72-390	398.2	Folk literature	GR820-830	398.369	Animals, Mythical
GR72.3	398	Folklore—Performance	GR825-830	398.45	Monsters
GR72.3	808.543	Storytelling	GR830.D7	398.469	Dragons

LC	Dewey	Subject Heading	LC	Dewey	Subject Heading
GR830.U6	398.469	Unicorns	GT331-341	392.3609496	Dwellings—Balkan Peninsula
GR830.V3	398.45	Vampires	GT343-372	392.36095	Dwellings—Asia
GR880	615.88	Traditional medicine	GT344-.2	392.36095691	Dwellings—Syria
GR890-910	398.355	Occupations—Folklore	GT345-346	392.3609561	Dwellings—Turkey
GR910	398.45	Mermaids	GT346.5-.6	392.3609567	Dwellings—Iraq
GR930	398.33	Days	GT347-348	392.360955	Dwellings—Iran
GR930	398.33	Seasons	GT349-350	392.36095	Dwellings—Asia
GR933	398.41	Thirteen (The number)	GT351-352	392.360954	Dwellings—India
GR940-941	398.32	Geographical myths	GT352.5-.6	392.36095493	Dwellings—Sri Lanka
GR950.L4	398.355	Lanterns	GT355-356	392.3609593	Dwellings—Thailand
			GT357-358	392.3609595	Dwellings—Malaysia
GT	390	Manners and customs	GT359-360	392.3609598	Dwellings—Indonesia
GT49	391	Beauty, Personal	GT361-362	392.3609599	Dwellings—Philippines
GT165-476	392.36	Dwellings	GT365-366	392.360951	Dwellings—China
GT170	392.36	Dwellings—Social aspects	GT367-368	392.360952	Dwellings—Japan
GT201-384	392.3609(4-9)	Dwellings—[By region or country]	GT369-370	392.3609519	Dwellings—Korea
GT205-227	392.360973	Dwellings—United States	GT373-377	392.36096	Dwellings—Africa
GT228-229	392.360971	Dwellings—Canada	GT375-376	392.360962	Dwellings—Egypt
GT231-232	392.360972	Dwellings—Mexico	GT379-380	392.360994	Dwellings—Australia
GT235-236	392.36097282	Dwellings—Belize	GT381-382	392.360993	Dwellings—New Zealand
GT237-238	392.36097286	Dwellings—Costa Rica	GT383-384	392.36099(5-6)	Dwellings—Oceania
GT239-240	392.36097281	Dwellings—Guatemala	GT420-425	392.36	Heating
GT241-242	392.36097283	Dwellings—Honduras	GT440-445	392.36	Lighting
GT243-244	392.36097285	Dwellings—Nicaragua	GT445	392.36	Lanterns
GT245-.5	392.36097287	Dwellings—Panama	GT445	392.36	Lamps
GT246-.5	392.36097284	Dwellings—El Salvador	GT450	392.36	Furniture
GT249-250	392.36097296	Dwellings—Bahamas	GT472	392.36	Sanitation, Household
GT251-252	392.36097291	Dwellings—Cuba	GT476	392.36	Toilets
GT253-254	392.36097294	Dwellings—Haiti	GT500-2350	391	Clothing and dress
GT255-256	392.36097292	Dwellings—Jamaica	GT500-2370	391	Fashion
GT257-.5	392.36097295	Dwellings—Puerto Rico	GT500-2370	391	Costume
GT261-262	392.360982	Dwellings—Argentina	GT525	391	Clothing and dress—Social aspects
GT263-264	392.360984	Dwellings—Bolivia			
GT265-266	392.360981	Dwellings—Brazil	GT529	391	Cold weather clothing
GT267-268	392.360983	Dwellings—Chile	GT530-596	391.0090(1-5)	Costume—History
GT269-270	392.3609861	Dwellings—Colombia	GT530-560	391.00901	Costume—History—To 500
GT271-272	392.3609866	Dwellings—Ecuador			
GT275-276	392.3609892	Dwellings—Paraguay	GT540	391.0088296	Costume, Jewish
GT277-278	392.360985	Dwellings—Peru	GT575	391.00902	Costume—History—Medieval, 500-1500
GT279-280	392.3609895	Dwellings—Uruguay			
GT281-282	392.360987	Dwellings—Venezuela	GT585	391.009031	Costume—History—16th century
GT285-294	392.360941	Dwellings—Great Britain			
GT294.5-.6	392.3609415	Dwellings—Ireland	GT585	391.009032	Costume—History—17th century
GT295-296	392.3609436	Dwellings—Austria			
GT296.5-.6	392.3609439	Dwellings—Hungary	GT585	391.009033	Costume—History—18th century
GT297-298	392.360944	Dwellings—France			
GT298.9-300.5	392.360943	Dwellings—Germany	GT601-1605	391.009(4-9)	Costume—[By region or country]
GT301-302	392.3609495	Dwellings—Greece			
GT303-304	392.360945	Dwellings—Italy	GT603-648	391.0097	Costume—North America
GT307-308	392.3609492	Dwellings—Netherlands	GT675-716	391.0098	Costume—South America
GT311-312	392.360947	Dwellings—Russia	GT720-1330	391.0094	Costume—Europe
GT315-316	392.3609489	Dwellings—Denmark	GT1370-1570	391.0095	Costume—Asia
GT317-318	392.36094912	Dwellings—Iceland	GT1560	391.00952	Kimonos
GT319-320	392.3609481	Dwellings—Norway	GT1580-1589	391.0096	Costume—Africa
GT321-322	392.3609485	Dwellings—Sweden	GT1590-1593	391.00993	Costume—Australia
GT323-324	392.360946	Dwellings—Spain	GT1595	391.00994	Costume—New Zealand
GT325-326	392.3609469	Dwellings—Portugal	GT1597-1599	391.00996	Costume—Oceania
GT327-328	392.3609494	Dwellings—Switzerland	GT1747-1748	391	Disguise

LC	Dewey	Subject Heading	LC	Dewey	Subject Heading
GT1747-1748	391.434	Masks	GT2955	394.15	Picnicking
GT1850	391.024	Peasantry	GT2995	394.12	Lying down position
GT2073	391.42	Underwear	GT3000.3-.5	392	Sleeping customs
GT2075	391.42	Crinolines	GT3005.3-.4	392	Sitting customs
GT2075	391.42	Corsets	GT3010	394.14	Narcotics
GT2110	391.43	Head-gear	GT3020-3030	394.14	Tobacco
GT2110	391.43	Hats	GT3020	394.14	Smoking
GT2112	391.43	Veils	GT3030	394.14	Snuff
GT2120	391.44	Neckties	GT3050	394	Salutations
GT2128	391.413	Hosiery	GT3050	394	Gifts
GT2150	391.44	Fans	GT3080	394	Swearing
GT2170	391.412	Gloves	GT3085	394	Oaths
GT2190	391.412	Muffs	GT3150-3390.5	393.1	Burial
GT2210	391.44	Umbrellas and parasols	GT3150-3390.5	393	Death
GT2220	391.44	Staffs (Sticks, canes, etc.)	GT3150-3390.5	393	Funeral rites and ceremonies
GT2250-2281	391.7	Jewelry			
GT2250-2280	391.7	Gems	GT3150-3390	393	Dead
GT2260	391.7	Necklaces	GT3170	393.0901	Funeral rites and ceremonies, Ancient
GT2265	391.7	Earrings			
GT2270	391.7	Rings	GT3320	393.1	Cemeteries
GT2280	391.44	Pins and needles	GT3330	393.2	Cremation
GT2310	391.5	Wigs	GT3340	393.3	Embalming
GT2318	391.5	Mustache	GT3350	393.4	Scaffold burial
GT2320	391.5	Beard	GT3353	393	Body snatching
GT2340-2341	391.63	Cosmetics	GT3370	393.9	Sati
GT2340	391.63	Perfumes	GT3370	393.9	Widow suicide
GT2370	391.44	Eyeglasses	GT3380	393.1	Ship burial
GT2420	392	Family	GT3412	390.0952	Geishas
GT2420	392.3	Home	GT3470	390.091734	Country life
GT2460-2465	392.12	Birth customs	GT3490	390.09143	Mountain life
GT2520-2540	390.082	Women	GT3510-3530	390.23	Courts and courtiers
GT2540	390.08342	Girls	GT3650	390.478	Minstrels
GT2600-2640	392.4	Love	GT3650	390.478	Troubadours
GT2620	392.4	Courtly love	GT3770-3896	395.53	Hotels
GT2640	394	Kissing	GT3920-4995	394.2	Fasts and feasts
GT2650	392.4	Betrothal	GT3930-4995	394.26	Festivals
GT2660-2800	392.5	Marriage customs and rites	GT3930-4995	394.26	Holidays
			GT3980-4096	394.5	Parades
GT2680	392.50902	Marriage customs and rites, Medieval	GT3980-4099	394.5	Processions
			GT3980-4099	394.5	Pageants
GT2695.M8	392.50882971	Marriage customs and rites, Islamic	GT4180-4299	394.26	Carnivals
			GT4380-4499	394.26	Harvest festivals
GT2701-2796	392.509(4-9)	Marriage customs and rites—[By country]	GT4403	394.26	Kwanzaa
			GT4504-.995	394.262	Spring festivals
GT2797	392.5	Wedding cakes	GT4580-4699	394.6	Fairs
GT2800	394.2	Wedding anniversaries	GT4905-4908	394.2614	New Year
GT2810	392.5	Chastity belts	GT4930	394.2667	Holy Week
GT2850-2960	394.1	Food habits	GT4935	394.2667	Easter
GT2850-2930	394.1	Drinking customs	GT4945	394.2627	May Day
GT2865-2866	394.12	Food of animal origin	GT4945	394.2627	May-pole
GT2870	394.12	Condiments	GT4965	394.2646	Halloween
GT2870	394.12	Salt	GT4975	394.2649	Thanksgiving Day
GT2870	394.12	Spices	GT4985	394.2663	Christmas
GT2905-2916	394.12	Tea	GT4987.5	394.2667	Advent calendars
GT2910-2916	394.120952	Japanese tea ceremony	GT4989	394.2663	Christmas trees
GT2918	394.12	Coffee	GT4995.A4	394.264	All Souls' Day
GT2940-2947	394.12	Drinking cups	GT4995.A6	394.262	April Fools' Day
GT2940-2947	394.13	Drinking cups	GT4995.A8	394.266	Ascension Day
GT2952	394.12	Toothpicks	GT4995.G	394.261	Groundhog Day

LC	Dewey	Subject Heading	LC	Dewey	Subject Heading
GT4995.P3	394.262	Saint Patrick's Day	GV403-405	796.068	Gymnasiums
GT4995.P45	394.266	Pentecost Festival	GV411-416	796.068	Athletic fields
GT5010-5090	390.23	Nobility—Social life and customs	GV415-416	796.068	Stadiums
			GV421-433	796.068	Playgrounds
GT5020	394.23	Heralds	GV426-.5	796.0680284	Playgrounds—Equipment and supplies
GT5050	394.4	Coronations			
GT5220-5285	394.53	Travel	GV428-433	613.706	Physical fitness centers
GT5220	394.53	Transportation	GV436	613.70287	Physical fitness—Testing
GT5350-5490	390.23	Nobility—Social life and customs	GV443	613.7042	Physical education for children
			GV450	613.194	Nudism
GT5650-5680	390.24	Peasantry—Social life and customs	GV451-.4	613.19406	Nudist camps
			GV454.B3	796.53	Beaches
GT5810-5895	395.5	Hunting	GV461-475	796.44	Gymnastics
GT5810-5850	394.3	Hunting customs	GV460-548	613.71	Exercise
GT5810-5856.995	390.463	Harvesting	GV464	613.714	Musico-calisthenics
GT5870-5899	392.3	Domestication	GV481-510	613.714	Calisthenics
GT5904-5905	394.3	Fishing	GV482.5	613.71081	Exercise for men
GT6010-6070	395.52	Commerce	GV501.5	613.71	Step aerobics
GT6110-6390	395.52	Professions	GV512	796.44	Balance beam
GT6550-6710	390.406927	Criminals	GV536	613.714	Uneven parallel bars
			GV539	613.714	Rings (Gymnastics)
GV	790	Recreation	GV546.3	613.713	Weight lifting
GV	790	Leisure	GV546.5-.56	613.713	Bodybuilding
GV1-200	790.1	Leisure	GV547.4	613.7130284	Dumbbells
GV14.5	790.092	Recreation leadership	GV551-553	796.47	Acrobatics
GV33	798	Chariot racing	GV561-1198.995	796	Sports
GV35	796.8092	Gladiators	GV561-749.5	796	Athletics
GV182-.5	790.068	Recreation centers	GV563	796.068	Athletic clubs
GV182.8	790.191	Family recreation	GV697	796.092	Athletes
GV184	790.1926	Aged—Recreation	GV709.3	796.087	Sports for the handicapped
GV191.2-200.56	796.5	Outdoor life			
GV191.67.F6	333.784	Forest reserves— Recreational use	GV710	796.042	Intramural sports
			GV711	796.077	Coaching (Athletics)
GV191.68-198.9	796.54	Camping	GV713	796.06	Sports administration
GV192-198	796.54	Camps	GV716	796.0681	Sports—Economic aspects
GV197.D3	796.5423	Day camps			
GV197.H3	796.542087	Camps for the handicapped	GV721.8	796.48	Olympics—Records
			GV743-749	796.0284	Sporting goods
GV198.9	796.54	Snow camping	GV743-749	796.0284	Athletics—Equipment and supplies
GV198.945-.975	796.56	Dude ranches			
GV198.95	796.54	Swamp camping	GV749.B34	796.30284	Balls (Sporting goods)
GV198.L3	796.54	Camp sites, facilities, etc.	GV749.M6	796.0284	Mouth protectors
GV199-.5	796.51	Hiking	GV749.5	796.425	Endurance sports
GV199.6	796.51	Backpacking	GV750-770	797.5	Aeronautical sports
GV199.7	796.54	Packhorse camping	GV761.5	796.154	Model airplane racing
GV199.8-200.3	796.522	Mountaineering	GV762-763	797.51	Ballooning
GV200.19.R34	796.522	Rappelling	GV763	797.51	Balloon racing
GV200.2	796.5223	Rock climbing	GV764-766	797.55	Gliding and soaring
GV200.3	796.52	Snow and ice climbing	GV769.5-770	797.56	Skydiving
GV200.4	796.58	Orienteering	GV769.5-770.2	797.56	Parachuting
GV200.5-.56	796.5	Wilderness survival	GV770.27	797.5	Bungee jumping
GV200.6-.66	796.525	Caving	GV771-840	797	Aquatic sports
GV201-555	796.07	Physical education and training	GV771-836.15	797.1	Boats and boating
			GV775	797.14	Regattas
GV346-350	796.043	College sports	GV777.7	643.2	Boat living
0GV346	796.042	School sports	GV781-790.3	797.1224	Kayaking
GV350.5	796.043	College athletes— Recruiting	GV781-785	797.122	Canoes and canoeing
			GV786	797.14	Canoe racing
GV401-433	796.068	Sports facilities			

LC	Dewey	Subject Heading	LC	Dewey	Subject Heading
GV788.5	797.1224	Sea kayaking	GV881-.4	796.3578	Softball
GV790.9-807.5	797.123	Rowing	GV881.5	796.3578	T-ball
GV811	797.124	Sailing, Single-handed	GV884	796.323092	Basketball players
GV811	797.124	Sailing	GV885	796.323	Basketball
GV811.53-.58	797.1246	Multihull sailboats	GV891-899	794.733	Pool (Game)
GV811.57	797.1246	Catamarans	GV891	794.72	Billiards
GV811.63.W56	797.33	Windsurfing	GV901-909	794.6	Bowling
GV811.65	643.2	Sailboat living	GV907	794.6	Bowling alleys
GV811.8-833	797.1246	Yachting	GV910.5.D8	794.6	Duckpin bowling
GV826.5-832	797.14	Yacht racing	GV911-929.3	796.358	Cricket
GV832	797.14091631	Fastnet Yacht Race	GV931-933	796.354	Croquet
GV833.5-835.9	797.125	Motorboats	GV937-960	796.332	Football
GV835	797.125	Launches	GV939	796.332092	Football players
GV836	797.129	Houseboats	GV942.7	796.3343	Soccer referees
GV837	797.24	Diving	GV943-944	796.334	Soccer
GV837	797.21	Swimming	GV943.45-.54	796.33464	Soccer—Tournaments
GV837.9-838	797.23092	Skin divers	GV943.5	796.33466	Europa Cup (Soccer)
GV838.5	797.21	Swimming—Records	GV945	796.333	Rugby football
GV838.52.C73	797.21	Swimming—Crawl stroke	GV948	796.33	Canadian football
GV838.53.E94	613.716	Aquatic exercises	GV951.18	796.3322	Football—Defense
GV838.53.L65	797.21	Long distance swimming	GV951.25	796.3322	End play (Football)
GV838.62.M45	797.24081	Diving for men	GV951.8	796.3322	Football—Offense
GV838.62.W65	797.24082	Diving for women	GV955	796.33202022	Football—Rules
GV838.65.J32	797.24	Diving—Jackknife dive	GV959.55.C45	796.332083	Football for children
GV838.65.S84	797.24	Diving—Swan dive	GV961-987	796.352	Golf
GV838.67.S65	797.24	Springboard diving	GV975-.5	796.35206	Driving ranges
GV838.68-.76	797.21	Life-saving	GV989	796.347	Lacrosse
GV838.76	797.21	Survival swimming	GV990-1005	796.342	Tennis
GV840.S5	797.35	Water skiing	GV1003	796.342	Court tennis
GV840.S78	797.23	Deep diving	GV1003.2	796.34	Paddleball
GV841-857	796.9	Winter sports	GV1005	796.346	Table tennis
GV843	796.97	Ice-boats	GV1006	796.346	Paddle tennis
GV847	796.962	Hockey	GV1015-.57	796.325	Volleyball
GV848.9-852	796.91	Skating	GV1015.5.B43	796.325	Beach volleyball
GV853	796.92	Snowshoes and snowshoeing	GV1018	796	Racing
GV854	796.93	Skis and skiing	GV1021-1025	796.7	Automobile travel
GV854-.87	796.935	Downhill skiing	GV1029	796.73	Grand Prix racing
GV854.B5	796.932	Biathlon	GV1029.2	796.73	Automobile rallies
GV854.35	796.93068	Ski resorts	GV1029.3	796.72	Drag racing
GV854.9.D78	796.93	Dry slope skiing	GV1029.7	796.6	Soap box derbies
GV854.9.R3	796.935	Downhill ski racing	GV1029.9.D8	796.72	Dune buggy racing
GV854.9.R3	796.935	Ski racing	GV1032	796.72092	Automobile racing drivers
GV856	796.95	Bobsledding	GV1033.5.D	796.72068759	Daytona International Speedway Race
GV856	796.95	Tobogganing			
GV855-.5	796.932	Cross-country skiing	GV1040-1058	796.6(2-4)	Bicycles
GV855.5.R33	796.932	Cross-country ski racing	GV1040-1058	796.6(2-4)	Tricycles
GV857.S57	796.95	Snowboarding	GV1040-1059	796.6	Cycling
GV857.S6	796.94	Snowmobiling	GV1044-1046	796.64	Bicycle touring
GV858.2-859.7	796.21	Roller-skating	GV1049	796.62	Bicycle racing
GV861	796.3	Ball games	GV1056	796.63	All terrain cycling
GV862-880.6	796.357	Baseball	GV1060.14	796.75	Sidecar motorcycle racing
GV865	796.357092	Baseball players	GV1060.5-1098	796.42	Track-athletics
GV870	796.35724	Fielding (Baseball)	GV1061-1069	796.42	Running
GV875.3	796.357075	Baseball cards	GV1063	796.428	Cross-country running
GV877	796.357	Baseball—Records	GV1065-.23	796.4252	Marathon running
GV879.5	976.357068	Baseball fields	GV1071	796.51	Walking (Sports)
GV880.5	796.357083	Little League baseball	GV1077	796.432	Broad jump
GV881	796.3578	Slow pitch softball	GV1079-1080	796.434	Vaulting
			GV1099	796.2	Shuffleboard

LC	Dewey	Subject Heading	LC	Dewey	Subject Heading
GV1107-1108.6	791.82	Bullfights	GV1491-1507	793.73	Puzzles
GV1111-1141	796.81	Hand-to-hand fighting	GV1493	790.138	Literary recreations
GV1111	613.66	Self-defense	GV1507.A5	793.734	Anagrams
GV1113	796.8092	Martial artists	GV1507.C7	793.732	Crossword puzzles
GV1114	796.8152	Judo	GV1541-1561	793.8	Conjuring
GV1114.3	796.8153	Karate	GV1541-1561	793.8	Tricks
GV1114.35	796.8154	Aikido	GV1545	793.8092	Magicians
GV1114.7	796.8159	Kung fu	GV1549	793.85	Card tricks
GV1115-1137	796.83	Boxing	GV1557	793.89	Ventriloquism
GV1143-1150.6	796.86	Fencing	GV1559	793.8	Coin tricks
GV1143-1150.6	796.86	Swordplay	GV1564-1565	794.3	Darts (Game)
GV1144-.2	796.86092	Fencers	GV1570	796.156	Model car racing
GV1151-1181.3	799.31	Shooting	GV1580-1799.4	792.8	Dance
GV1167-1172	799.31	Shooting contests	GV1580-1799	793.31	Folk dancing
GV1175	799.31	Pistol shooting	GV1600	792.809	Dance criticism
GV1175.5	799.31	Fast draw pistol shooting	GV1746-1750	793.38	Balls (Parties)
GV1177	799.31	Rifle practice	GV1747	793.38	Court dances
GV1181-.3	799.3132	Trapshooting	GV1751	793.33	Ballroom dancing
GV1181.3	799.3132	Skeet shooting	GV1757	793.38	Balls (Parties)
GV1185-1189	799.32	Archery	GV1761	793.33	Waltz
GV1191-.75	790.134	Tournaments	GV1763	793.3	Country-dance
GV1195	796.812	Wrestling	GV1783	792.8	Modern dance
GV1196.5	796.812	Arm wrestling	GV1785	792.8092	Dance—Biography
GV1199-1570	790.1	Games	GV1787	792.84	Ballet
GV1201	790.13	Hobbies	GV1788	792.84	Ballet dancing
GV1201.42	790.102022	Games—Rules	GV1789.2	792.8026	Ballet—Costume
GV1205	793.21	Children's parties	GV1789.2	792.8028	Ballet slippers
GV1213	796.2	Marbles (Game)	GV1794	792.78	Tap dancing
GV1215	782.42083	Children's songs	GV1796.B74	793.3	Break dancing
GV1219	790.133	Dolls	GV1796.C2	793.33	Cha-cha (Dance)
GV1220	790.133	Dollhouses	GV1796.C4	793.33	Charleston (Dance)
GV1220.7	790.133	Teddy bears	GV1796.C68	793.3	Country swing (Dance)
GV1221-1229	793	Indoor games	GV1796.D57	793.33	Disco dancing
GV1232-1299	795.4	Card games	GV1796.H8	792.319969	Hula (Dance)
GV1251-1255	795.412	Poker	GV1796.J6	793.33	Jitterbug (Dance)
GV1281	795.415	Bridge whist	GV1796.L5	793.33	Lindy (Dance)
GV1282	795.414	Auction bridge	GV1796.M5	793.3	Minuet
GV1282.8.D86	795.415	Duplicate contract bridge	GV1796.P55	793.31	Polka (Dance)
GV1283	795.413	Duplicate whist	GV1796.S9	793.35	Sword-dance
GV1295.P6	795.416	Double pinochle	GV1799	793.083	Dance for children
GV1295.R8	795.418	Rummy (Game)	GV1799.2	793.087	Dance for the handicapped
GV1299.M3	795.34	Mah jong			
GV1301-1311	795	Gambling	GV1799.3	793.0846	Dance for the aged
GV1302	795	Gambling systems	GV1800-1831	791.3	Circus
GV1303	795.1	Dice	GV1811	791.33	Clowns
GV1303	795.1	Dice games	GV1829-1831	791.32	Animal training
GV1309	795.23	Roulette	GV1834	791.84	Rodeos
GV1311.B5	795.3	Bingo	GV1834.45.B35	791.84	Barrel racing
GV1312-1469	794	Board games	GV1834.7-1835.56	791.1	Carnivals
GV1313-1457	794.1	Chess	GV1835	791.1	Carnivals
GV1449.3	794.172	Computer chess	GV1838	791.3	Amateur circus
GV1461-1463	794.2	Checkers	GV1851-186	791.068	Amusement parks
GV1462.7.B33	392.5	Bachelorette parties			
GV1467	795.32	Dominoes	H	300	Social sciences
GV1469.15-.25	794.8	Computer games	H1-8	300.5	Social sciences—Periodicals
GV1469.2	794.8	Electronic games			
GV1469.3	794.8	Video games	H21-29	300.6	Social sciences—Congresses
GV1470-1521	793.2	Entertaining			
GV1472.7.B33	392.5	Bachelor parties			

LC	Dewey	Subject Heading	LC	Dewey	Subject Heading
H51-53	300.9	Social sciences—History	HA1011-1020	318.61	Colombia—Census
H57-59	300.92	Social sciences—Biography	HA1021-1030	318.66	Ecuador—Census
			HA1033	318.81	Guyana—Census
H61-.4	300.1	Social sciences—Methodology	HA1035	318.83	Surinam—Census
			HA1037	318.82	French Guiana—Census
H61.28	361.322	Focused group interviewing	HA1041-1050	318.92	Paraguay—Census
			HA1051-1070	318.5	Peru—Census
H62-.5	300.71	Social sciences—Study and teaching	HA1071-1090	318.95	Uruguay—Census
			HA1091-1100	318.7	Venezuela—Census
H62-.5	300.72	Social sciences—Research	HA1107-1650	314	Europe—Census
			HA1121-1170	314.1	Great Britain—Census
H62	300.724	Social sciences—Experiments	HA1141-1150	314.16	Northern Ireland—Census
			HA1151-1160	314.11	Scotland—Census
			HA1161-1170	314.29	Wales—Census
HA	310	Statistics	HA1170.1-.5	314.15	Ireland—Census
HA1	310.5	Statistics—Periodicals	HA1171-1190	314.36	Austria—Census
HA19	310.9	Statistics—History	HA1191-1200	314.37	Czechoslovakia—Census
HA29-32	310.1	Statistics—Methodology	HA1201-1210	314.39	Hungary—Census
HA30.6	310.1	Spatial analysis (Statistics)	HA1210.5	314.3648	Liechtenstein—Census
HA31	001.4226	Statistics—Graphic methods	HA1211-1230	314.4	France—Census
			HA1231-1349	314.3	Germany—Census
HA31.2	310.0723	Sampling (Statistics)	HA1351-1359	314.95	Greece—Census
HA31.3	310.72	Correlation (Statistics)	HA1361-1379	314.5	Italy—Census
HA35	310.72	Statistics—Research	HA1381-1390	314.92	Netherlands—Census
HA154-4737	310	Vital statistics	HA1391-1410	314.93	Belgium—Census
HA175-4737	310	Census	HA1411-1420	314.935	Luxembourg—Census
HA201-730	317.3	United States—Census	HA1431-1450.12	314.7	Russia—Census
HA201-214	317.3	United States—Statistics, Vital	HA1450.5	314.897	Finland—Census
			HA1451-1460	314.38	Poland—Census
HA201-214	317.3	United States—Statistics	HA1471-1490	314.89	Denmark—Census
HA221-730	317.7(4-9)	[United States, By state]—Census	HA1491-1500	314.912	Iceland—Census
			HA1501-1520	314.81	Norway—Census
HA740	319.82	Greenland—Census	HA1521-1540	314.85	Sweden—Census
HA741-750	317.1	Canada—Census	HA1541-1560	314.6	Spain—Census
HA761-770	317.2	Mexico—Census	HA1571-1580	314.69	Portugal—Census
HA791-800	317.282	Belize—Census	HA1591-1610	314.94	Switzerland—Census
HA801-810	317.286	Costa Rica—Census	HA1620.5	314.965	Albania—Census
HA811-820	317.281	Guatemala—Census	HA1621-1630	314.99	Bulgaria—Census
HA821-830	317.283	Honduras—Census	HA1631-1635	314.97	Yugoslavia—Census
HA831-840	317.285	Nicaragua—Census	HA1641-1650	314.98	Romania—Census
HA841-850	317.284	El Salvador—Census	HA2280	314.699	Azores—Census
HA851-854	317.287	Panama—Census	HA2285	314.698	Madeira Islands—Census
HA865	317.2981	Barbados—Census	HA2287	316.49	Canary Islands—Census
HA866-.9	317.297	Leeward Islands (West Indies)—Census	HA2289	316.658	Cape Verde—Census
			HA2291	319.73	Saint Helena—Census
HA867	317.2983	Trinidad and Tobago—Census	HA2295	319.71	Falkland Islands—Census
			HA2300	315.495	Maldives—Census
HA901-910	317.295	Puerto Rico—Census	HA2301	316.96	Seychelles—Census
HA911-915	317.29722	Virgin Islands of the United States—Census	HA2303	316.94	Comoro Islands—Census
			HA2305	316.982	Mauritius—Census
HA917-.78	317.2986	Netherlands Antilles—Census	HA2307	316.981	Reunion—Census
			HA2309	316.99	Kerguelen Islands—Census
HA918.7	317.2976	Guadeloupe—Census			
HA918.9	317.2982	Martinique—Census	HA3001-3010	319.4	Australia—Census
HA921-930	317.299	Bermuda Islands—Census	HA3171-3190	319.3	New Zealand—Census
HA941-960	318.2	Argentina—Census	HA4012	319.67	Guam—Census
HA961-970	318.4	Bolivia—Census	HA4013	319.53	Papua New Guinea—Census
HA971-990	318.1	Brazil—Census			
HA991-1010	318.3	Chile—Census	HA4014	319.593	Solomon Islands—Census

LC	Dewey	Subject Heading	LC	Dewey	Subject Heading
HA4015	319.597	New Caledonia—Census	HA4698	316.79	Mozambique—Census
HA4015.5	319.595	Vanuatu—Census	HA4699	316.91	Madagascar—Census
HA4016	319.611	Fiji—Census	HA4701	316.8	South Africa—Census
HA4016.7	319.681	Kiribati—Census	HA4702	316.89	Zimbabwe—Census
HA4017	319.612	Tonga—Census	HA4703	316.894	Zambia—Census
HA4017.5	319.623	Cook Islands—Census	HA4704	316.885	Lesotho—Census
HA4018.5	319.613	American Samoa—Census	HA4705	316.887	Swaziland—Census
HA4020-.5	319.89	Antarctica	HA4706	316.883	Botswana—Census
HA4556.5	315.61	Turkey—Census	HA4707	316.897	Malawi—Census
HA4557	315.693	Cyprus—Census	HA4708	316.881	Namibia—Census
HA4558	315.691	Syria—Census	HA4710	316.73	Angola—Census
HA4559	315.692	Lebanon—Census	HA4711	316.751	Zaire—Census
HA4560	315.694	Israel—Census	HA4712	316.718	Equatorial Guinea—Census
HA4561	315.695	Jordan—Census			
HA4563	315.38	Saudi Arabia—Census	HA4713	316.715	Sao Tome and Principe—Census
HA4564	315.33	Yemen—Census			
HA4565	315.353	Oman—Census	HA4715	316.721	Gabon—Census
HA4566	315.357	United Arab Emirates—Census	HA4716	316.724	Congo (Brazzaville)—Census
HA4567	315.363	Qatar—Census	HA4717	316.741	Central African Republic—Census
HA4568	315.365	Bahrain—Census			
HA4569	315.67	Iraq—Census	HA4718	316.743	Chad—Census
HA4570.2	315.5	Iran—Census	HA4719	316.711	Cameroon—Census
HA4570.6	315.81	Afghanistan—Census	HA4722	316.683	Benin—Census
HA4570.7	315.91	Burma—Census	HA4723	316.681	Togo—Census
HA4570.8	315.493	Sri Lanka—Census	HA4724	316.626	Niger—Census
HA4570.9	315.496	Nepal—Census	HA4725	316.668	Cote d'Ivoire—Census
HA4581-4590	315.4	India—Census	HA4726	316.652	Guinea—Census
HA4590.3	315.498	Bhutan—Census	HA4727	316.623	Mali—Census
HA4590.5	315.491	Pakistan—Census	HA4728	316.625	Burkina Faso—Census
HA4590.6	315.492	Bangladesh—Census	HA4729	316.63	Senegal—Census
HA4600.3	315.96	Cambodia—Census	HA4730	316.61	Mauritania—Census
HA4600.4	315.94	Laos—Census	HA4731	316.69	Nigeria—Census
HA4600.5	315.97	Vietnam—Census	HA4732	316.67	Ghana—Census
HA4600.55	315.93	Thailand—Census	HA4733	316.64	Sierra Leone—Census
HA4600.6	315.95	Malaysia—Census	HA4734	316.651	Gambia—Census
HA4601-4610	315.98	Indonesia—Census	HA4735	316.662	Liberia—Census
HA4611-4620	315.99	Philippines—Census	HA4736	316.657	Guinea-Bissau—Census
HA4621-4630	315.2	Japan—Census	HA4737	316.48	Western Sahara—Census
HA4630.5-.6	315.19	Korea—Census			
HA4630.8	315.17	Mongolia—Census	HB	330	Economics
HA4631-4640	315.1	China—Census	HB	304.6	Demography
HA4641-4645	315.126	Macao—Census	HB1-130	330	Economics
HA4646-4650	315.1249	Taiwan—Census	HB1-9	330.05	Economics—Periodicals
HA4651-4655	315.125	Hong Kong—Census	HB21	330.06	Economics—Congresses
HA4682	316.4	Morocco—Census	HB61	330.03	Economics—Dictionaries
HA4683	316.5	Algeria—Census	HB63	330.025	Economics—Directories
HA4684	316.11	Tunisia—Census	HB75-130	330.09	Economics—History
HA4685	316.12	Libya—Census	HB77-83	330.090(1-33)	Economics—History—To 1800
HA4686	316.2	Egypt—Census			
HA4687	316.24	Sudan—Census	HB85	330.09034	Economics—History—19th century
HA4689	316.3	Ethiopia—Census			
HA4690	316.773	Somalia—Census	HB87	330.0904	Economics—History—20th century
HA4691	316.771	Djibouti—Census			
HA4693	316.762	Kenya—Census	HB91	330.1513	Mercantile system
HA4694	316.761	Uganda—Census	HB95	330.122	Free enterprise
HA4695	316.7571	Rwanda—Census	HB97.5	335.4	Marxian economics
HA4696	316.7572	Burundi—Census	HB137	330.0727	Economics—Statistical methods
HA4697	316.78	Tanzania—Census			

LC	Dewey	Subject Heading	LC	Dewey	Subject Heading
HB139-141	330.015195	Econometrics	HB1335-1526	304.645(4-9)	Mortality—[By region or country]
HB141	330.011	Econometric models			
HB142	339.23	Input-output analysis	HB1528	304.6451724	Mortality—Developing countries
HB143	338.52	Shadow prices			
HB145	339.5	Equilibrium (Economics)	HB1531-1738	305.2	Age distribution (Demography)
HB201-205	330.157	Marginal utility			
HB201-206	338.521	Value	HB1541-1737	305.209(4-9)	Age distribution—[By region or country]
HB201-206	338.521	Supply and demand			
HB206	335.412	Labor theory of value	HB1545-1567	305.20973	Age distribution (Demography)—United States [By state]
HB221-236	338.52	Prices			
HB225	338.528	Consumer price indexes			
HB236	338.526	Prices—Government policy	HB1565	305.2097(4-9)	Age distribution (Demography)—United States
HB238	338.6048	Competition, Imperfect			
HB241	330.15	Supply-side economics			
HB401	333.5	Rent	HB1741-1948	305.3	Sex distribution (Demography)
HB401	339.21	Rent			
HB501	332.041	Capital	HB1755-1777	305.30973	Sex distribution (Demography)—[United States, By state]
HB501	330.122	Capitalism			
HB522-715	331.21	Income			
HB531-549	332.6323	Interest rates	HB1775	305.3097(4-9)	Sex distribution (Demography—[United States, By city]
HB551	332.83	Usury			
HB601	338.516	Profit			
HB615	338.04	Entrepreneurship	HB1777	305.3097(4-9)	Sex distribution (Demography)—United States
HB615	338.5	Risk			
HB701-715	330.17	Property			
HB801-843	339.47	Consumption (Economics)	HB1953	304.61	Population density
HB848-3697	304.6	Demography	HB1955	307.24	Rural-urban migration
HB848-3697	304.6	Population	HB1956-2157	307.26	Urban-rural migration
HB848	304.605	Demography—Periodicals	HB1965-1987	304.60973	Population geography—United States
HB849.49	304.60723	Demographic surveys			
HB850-.5	304.6072	Population Research	HB1985	304.6097(4-9)	Population geography—[United States, By state]
HB851-853	304.609	Population—History			
HB855-865	304.6092	Demography—Biography	HB1987	304.6097(4-9)	Population geography—[United States, By city]
HB883.5	363.9	Population policy			
HB884	304.6091724	Developing countries—Population	HB1989-1990	304.60971	Population geography—Canada
HB884.5	363.96091724	Population assistance	HB1991-1992	304.60972	Population geography—Mexico
HB887	304.6	Demographic transition			
HB901-1108	304.632	Fertility, Human	HB1995-1996	304.6097282	Population geography—Belize
HB901-1108	304.63209(4-9)	Fertility, Human—[By region or country]			
			HB1997-1998	304.6097286	Population geography—Costa Rica
HB1108	304.632091724	Fertility, Human—Developing countries	HB1999	304.6097281	Population geography—Guatemala
HB1111-1317	306.81021	Marital status—Statistics			
HB1121-1317	306.8109	Marital status—[By region or country]	HB2000	304.6097283	Population geography—Honduras
			HB2001	304.6097285	Population geography—Nicaragua
HB1125-1126	306.810973	Marital status—United States			
HB1145	306.81097(4-9)	Marital status—[United States, By state]	HB2002-2003	304.6097287	Population geography—Panama
			HB2004	304.6097284	Population geography—El Salvador
HB1147	306.81097(4-9)	Marital status—[United States, By city]			
			HB2007-2008	304.6097296	Population geography—Bahamas
HB1321-1528	304.64	Mortality			
HB1322	304.64021	Mortality—Tables	HB2009-2010	304.6097291	Population geography—Cuba
HB1323.B5	304.64089960 + 73	Afro-Americans—Mortality			
			HB2011	304.6097294	Population geography—Haiti
HB1323.C5	304.64083	Children—Mortality			
HB1323.S8	362.28021	Suicide—Statistics	HB2012	304.6097293	Population geography—Dominican Republic

LC	Dewey	Subject Heading	LC	Dewey	Subject Heading
HB2013-2014	304.6097292	Population geography—Jamaica	HB2037-2038	304.609895	Population geography—Uruguay
HB2016.57	304.60972981	Population geography—Barbados	HB2039-2040	304.60987	Population geography—Venezuela
HB2016.72	304.60972973	Population geography—Anguilla	HB2045-2046	304.60942(9)	Population geography—England and Wales
HB2016.74	304.60972974	Population geography—Antigua	HB2047-2048	304.609411	Population geography—Scotland
HB2016.76	304.60972975	Population geography—Montserrat	HB2048.5	304.609416	Population geography—Northern Ireland
HB2016.78	304.60972973	Population geography—St. Kitts and Nevis	HB2049-2050	304.609415	Population geography—Ireland
HB2016.93	304.609729841	Population geography—Dominica	HB2051-2052	304.609436	Population geography—Austria
HB2016.95	304.609729845	Population geography—Grenada	HB2052.3	304.609437	Population geography—Czechoslovakia
HB2016.97	304.609729843	Population geography—Saint Lucia	HB2052.5	304.609439	Population geography—Hungary
HB2016.99	304.609729844	Population geography—Saint Vincent	HB2052.9	304.60943648	Population geography—Liechtenstein
HB2017	304.60972983	Population geography—Trinidad and Tobago	HB2053-2054	304.60944	Population geography—France
HB2017.35	304.60972986	Population geography—Aruba	HB2055-2056	304.60943	Population geography—Germany
HB2017.36	304.60972986	Population geography—Bonaire	HB2059-2060	304.60945	Population geography—Italy
HB2017.37	304.60972986	Population geography—Curacao	HB2063-2064	304.609493	Population geography—Belgium
HB2017.385	304.60972977	Population geography—Saint Eustatius (Netherlands Antilles)	HB2065-2066	304.609492	Population geography—Netherlands
HB2017.39	304.60972977	Population geography—Saint Martin	HB2066.5	304.6094935	Population geography—Luxembourg
HB2017.7	304.60972976	Population geography—Guadeloupe	HB2067-2068.2	304.60947	Population geography—Russia
HB2017.9	304.60972982	Population geography—Martinique	HB2068.3	304.6094897	Population geography—Finland
HB2019-2020	304.60982	Population geography—Argentina	HB2068.7	304.609438	Population geography—Poland
HB2021-2022	304.60984	Population geography—Bolivia	HB2071-2072	304.609489	Population geography—Denmark
HB2023-2024	304.60981	Population geography—Brazil	HB2073-2074	304.6094912	Population geography—Iceland
HB2025-2026	304.60983	Population geography—Chile	HB2075-2076	304.609481	Population geography—Norway
HB2027-2028	304.609861	Population geography—Colombia	HB2077-2078	304.609485	Population geography—Sweden
HB2029-2030	304.609866	Population geography—Ecuador	HB2079-2080	304.60946	Population geography—Spain
HB2032.3	304.609881	Population geography—Guyana	HB2081-2082	304.609469	Population geography—Portugal
HB2032.5	304.609883	Population geography—Surinam	HB2083-2084	304.609494	Population geography—Switzerland
HB2032.7	304.609882	Population geography—French Guiana	HB2086.5	304.6094965	Population geography—Albania
HB2033-2034	304.609892	Population geography—Paraguay	HB2087-2088	304.609499	Population geography—Bulgaria
HB2035-2036	304.60985	Population geography—Peru	HB2088.5	304.609497	Population geography—Yugoslavia
			HB2091-2092	304.609498	Population geography—Romania

LC	Dewey	Subject Heading	LC	Dewey	Subject Heading
HB2092.5	304.609495	Population geography—Greece	HB2111-2112	304.60952	Population geography—Japan
HB2093.4	304.609561	Population geography—Turkey	HB2112.5-.6	304.609519	Population geography—Korea
HB2093.5	304.6095693	Population geography—Cyprus	HB2112.8	304.609517	Population geography—Mongolia
HB2093.7	304.6095691	Population geography—Syria	HB2114	304.60951	Population geography—China
HB2093.9	304.6095692	Population geography—Lebanon	HB2115	304.6095126	Population geography—Macao
HB2094	304.6095694	Population geography—Israel	HB2116	304.60951249	Population geography—Taiwan
HB2094.3	304.6095695	Population geography—Jordan	HB2117	304.6095125	Population geography—Hong Kong
HB2094.7	304.609538	Population geography—Saudi Arabia	HB2121.3	304.60964	Population geography—Morocco
HB2094.9-2095	304.609533	Population geography—Yemen	HB2121.4	304.60965	Population geography—Algeria
HB2095.3	304.6095353	Population geography—Oman	HB2121.5	304.609611	Population geography—Tunisia
HB2095.7	304.6095363	Population geography—Qatar	HB2121.6	304.609612	Population geography—Libya
HB2095.9	304.6095365	Population geography—Bahrain	HB2121.7	304.60962	Population geography—Egypt
HB2096	304.6095367	Population geography—Kuwait	HB2121.8	304.609624	Population geography—Sudan
HB2096.3	304.609567	Population geography—Iraq	HB2122	304.60963	Population geography—Ethiopia
HB2096.4	304.60955	Population geography—Iran	HB2122.2	304.6096773	Population geography—Somalia
HB2096.6	304.609581	Population geography—Afghanistan	HB2122.3	304.6096771	Population geography—Djibouti
HB2096.7	304.609591	Population geography—Burma	HB2122.5	304.6096762	Population geography—Kenya
HB2096.8	304.6095493	Population geography—Sri Lanka	HB2122.6	304.6096761	Population geography—Uganda
HB2096.9	304.6095496	Population geography—Nepal	HB2122.7	304.60967571	Population geography—Rwanda
HB2099-2100	304.60954	Population geography—India	HB2122.8	304.60967572	Population geography—Burundi
HB2100.3	304.6095498	Population geography—Bhutan	HB2122.9	304.609678	Population geography—Tanzania
HB2100.5	304.6095491	Population geography—Pakistan	HB2123	304.609679	Population geography—Mozambique
HB2100.6	304.6095492	Population geography—Bangladesh	HB2123.2	304.609691	Population geography—Madagascar
HB2104.3	304.609596	Population geography—Cambodia	HB2123.4	304.60968	Population geography—South Africa
HB2104.4	304.609594	Population geography—Laos	HB2123.6	304.6096894	Population geography—Zambia
HB2104.5	304.609597	Population geography—Vietnam	HB2123.7	304.6096885	Population geography—Lesotho
HB2104.55	304.609593	Population geography—Thailand	HB2123.8	304.6096887	Population geography—Swaziland
HB2104.6	304.609595	Population geography—Malaysia	HB2123.9	304.6096883	Population geography—Botswana
HB2107-2108	304.609598	Population geography—Indonesia	HB2124	304.6096897	Population geography—Malawi
HB2109-2110	304.609599	Population geography—Philippines	HB2124.2	304.6096881	Population geography—Namibia

LC	Dewey	Subject Heading	LC	Dewey	Subject Heading
HB2124.4	304.609673	Population geography—Angola	HB2130.5	304.609973	Population geography—Tristan da Cunha
HB2124.5	304.6096751	Population geography—Zaire	HB2131	304.6099711	Population geography—Falkland Islands
HB2124.6	304.6096718	Population geography—Equatorial Guinea	HB2131.5	304.6095495	Population geography—Maldives
HB2124.9	304.6096721	Population geography—Gabon	HB2132	304.609696	Population geography—Seychelles
HB2125	304.6096724	Population geography—Congo (Brazzaville)	HB2132.5	304.609694	Population geography—Comoro Islands
HB2125.2	304.6096741	Population geography—Central African Republic	HB2133	304.6096982	Population geography—Mauritius
HB2125.3	304.6096743	Population geography—Chad	HB2133.5	304.6096981	Population geography—Reunion
HB2125.4	304.6096711	Population geography—Cameroon	HB2134	304.609699	Population geography—Kerguelen Islands
HB2125.7	304.6096683	Population geography—Benin	HB2135-2136	304.60994	Population geography—Australia
HB2125.8	304.6096681	Population geography—Togo	HB2152.5	304.60993	Population geography—New Zealand
HB2125.9	304.6096626	Population geography—Niger	HB2152.7	304.609967	Population geography—Guam
HB2126	304.6096668	Population geography—Cote d'Ivoire	HB2152.8	304.609953	Population geography—Papua New Guinea
HB2126.2	304.6096652	Population geography—Guinea	HB2152.9	304.6099681	Population geography—Kiribati
HB2126.3	304.6096623	Population geography—Mali	HB2153	304.6099593	Population geography—Solomon Islands
HB2126.4	304.6096625	Population geography—Burkina Faso	HB2153.3	304.6099597	Population geography—New Caledonia
HB2126.5	304.609663	Population geography—Senegal	HB2153.4	304.6099595	Population geography—Vanuatu
HB2126.6	304.609661	Population geography—Mauritania	HB2153.5	304.6099611	Population geography—Fiji
HB2126.7	304.609669	Population geography—Nigeria	HB2153.6	304.6099612	Population geography—Tonga
HB2126.8	304.609667	Population geography—Ghana	HB2153.65	304.6099623	Population geography—Cook Islands
HB2126.9	304.609664	Population geography—Sierra Leone	HB2153.7	304.6099613	Population geography—American Samoa
HB2127	304.6096651	Population geography—Gambia	HB2153.8	304.6099614	Population geography—Western Samoa
HB2127.2	304.6096662	Population geography—Liberia	HB2153.9	304.609962	Population geography—French Polynesia
HB2127.3	304.6096657	Population geography—Guinea-Bissau	HB2155	304.60998(1-8)	Population geography—Arctic regions
HB2127.4	304.609648	Population geography—Western Sahara	HB2156	304.609982	Population geography—Greenland
HB2127.5	304.6094699	Population geography—Azores	HB2371-2578	304.6091734	Rural population
HB2128	304.6097299	Population geography—Bermuda Islands	HB2581-2787	331.7	Occupations—Statistics
HB2128.5	304.6094698	Population geography—Madeira Islands	HB3505-3527	304.60973	Demography—United States
HB2129	304.609649	Population geography—Canary Islands	HB3525	304.6097(4-9)	Demography—[United States, By State]
HB2129.5	304.6096658	Population geography—Cape Verde	HB3527	304.6097(4-9)	Demography—[United States, By City]
HB2130	304.609973	Population geography—Saint Helena	HB3529-3530	304.60971	Demography—Canada
			HB3531-3532	304.60972	Demography—Mexico
			HB3535-3536	304.6097282	Demography—Belize

LC	Dewey	Subject Heading	LC	Dewey	Subject Heading
HB3537-3538	304.6097286	Demography—Costa Rica	HB3588.5	304.609416	Demography—Northern Ireland
HB3539	304.6097281	Demography—Guatemala	HB3589-3590	304.609415	Demography—Ireland
HB3540	304.6097283	Demography—Honduras	HB3591-3592	304.609436	Demography—Austria
HB3541	304.6097285	Demography—Nicaragua	HB3592.3	304.609437	Demography—Czechoslovakia
HB3542-3543	304.6097287	Demography—Panama	HB3592.5	304.609439	Demography—Hungary
HB3544	304.6097284	Demography—El Salvador	HB3592.9	304.60943648	Demography—Liechtenstein
HB3547-3548	304.6097296	Demography—Bahamas	HB3593-3594	304.60944	Demography—France
HB3549-3550	304.6097291	Demography—Cuba	HB3594.5	304.60944949	Demography—Monaco
HB3551	304.6097294	Demography—Haiti	HB3595-3596.5	304.60943	Demography—Germany
HB3552	304.6097293	Demography—Dominican Republic	HB3599-3600	304.60945	Demography—Italy
HB3553-3554	304.6097292	Demography—Jamaica	HB3603-3604	304.609493	Demography—Belgium
HB3556.3	304.609729722	Demography—Virgin Islands of the United States	HB3605-3606	304.609492	Demography—Netherlands
HB3556.57	304.60972981	Demography—Barbados	HB3606.5	304.6094935	Demography—Luxembourg
HB3556.72	304.60972973	Demography—Anguilla	HB3607-3608.2	304.60947	Demography—Russia
HB3556.74	304.60972974	Demography—Antigua	HB3608.3	304.6094897	Demography—Finland
HB3556.76	304.60972975	Demography—Montserrat	HB3608.7	304.609438	Demography—Poland
HB3556.78	304.60972973	Demography—Saint Kitts and Nevis	HB3611-3612	304.609489	Demography—Denmark
HB3556.93	304.609729841	Demography—Dominica	HB3613-3614	304.6094912	Demography—Iceland
HB3556.95	304.609729845	Demography—Grenada	HB3615-3616	304.609481	Demography—Norway
HB3556.97	304.609729843	Demography—Saint Lucia	HB3617-3618	304.609485	Demography—Sweden
HB3556.99	304.609729844	Demography—Saint Vincent	HB3619-3620	304.60946	Demography—Spain
HB3557	304.60972983	Demography—Trinidad and Tobago	HB3621-3622	304.609469	Demography—Portugal
HB3557.35	304.60972986	Demography—Aruba	HB3623-3624	304.609494	Demography—Switzerland
HB3557.36	304.60972986	Demography—Bonaire	HB3626.5	304.6094965	Demography—Albania
HB3557.37	304.60972986	Demography—Curacao	HB3627-3628	304.609499	Demography—Bulgaria
HB3557.38	304.60972977	Demography—Saba (Netherlands Antilles)	HB3628.5	304.609497	Demography—Yugoslavia
HB3557.385	304.60972977	Demography—Saint Eustatius (Netherlands Antilles)	HB3631-3632	304.609498	Demography—Romania
			HB3632.5	304.609495	Demography—Greece
HB3557.39	304.60972977	Demography—Saint Martin	HB3633.4	304.609561	Demography—Turkey
HB3557.7	304.60972976	Demography—Guadeloupe	HB3633.5	304.6095693	Demography—Cyprus
			HB3633.7	304.6095691	Demography—Syria
HB3557.9	304.60972982	Demography—Martinique	HB3633.9	304.6095692	Demography—Lebanon
HB3559-3560	304.60982	Demography—Argentina	HB3634	304.6095694	Demography—Israel
HB3561-3562	304.60984	Demography—Bolivia	HB3634.3	304.6095695	Demography—Jordan
HB3563-3564	304.60981	Demography—Brazil	HB3634.7	304.609538	Demography—Saudi Arabia
HB3565-3566	304.60983	Demography—Chile			
HB3567-3568	304.609861	Demography—Colombia	HB3634.9-3635	304.609533	Demography—Yemen
HB3569-3570	304.609866	Demography—Ecuador	HB3635.3	304.6095353	Demography—Oman
HB3572.3	304.609881	Demography—Guyana	HB3635.5	304.6095357	Demography—United Arab Emirates
HB3572.5	304.609883	Demography—Surinam			
HB3572.7	304.609882	Demography—French Guiana	HB3635.7	304.6095363	Demography—Qatar
			HB3635.9	304.6095365	Demography—Bahrain
HB3573-3574	304.609892	Demography—Paraguay	HB3636	304.6095367	Demography—Kuwait
HB3575-3576	304.60985	Demography—Peru	HB3636.3	304.609567	Demography—Iraq
HB3577-3578	304.609895	Demography—Uruguay	HB3636.4	304.60955	Demography—Iran
HB3579-3580	304.60987	Demography—Venezuela	HB3636.6	304.609581	Demography—Afghanistan
HB3585-3586	304.60942(9)	Demography—England and Wales	HB3636.7	304.609591	Demography—Burma
			HB3636.8	304.6095493	Demography—Sri Lanka
			HB3636.9	304.6095496	Demography—Nepal
HB3587-3588	304.609411	Demography—Scotland	HB3639-3640	304.60954	Demography—India
			HB3640.3	304.6095498	Demography—Bhutan
			HB3640.5	304.6095491	Demography—Pakistan
			HB3640.6	304.6095492	Demography—Bangladesh
			HB3644.3	304.609596	Demography—Cambodia

LC	Dewey	Subject Heading	LC	Dewey	Subject Heading
HB3644.4	304.609594	Demography—Laos	HB3666.5	304.609663	Demography—Senegal
HB3644.5	304.609597	Demography—Vietnam	HB3666.6	304.609661	Demography—Mauritania
HB3644.55	304.609593	Demography—Thailand	HB3666.7	304.609669	Demography—Nigeria
HB3644.6	304.609595	Demography—Malaysia	HB3666.8	304.609667	Demography—Ghana
HB3647-3648	304.609598	Demography—Indonesia	HB3666.9	304.609664	Demography—Sierra Leone
HB3649-3650	304.609599	Demography—Philippines			
HB3651-3652	304.60952	Demography—Japan	HB3667	304.6096651	Demography—Gambia
HB3652.5-.6	304.609519	Demography—Korea	HB3667.2	304.6096662	Demography—Liberia
HB3652.8	304.609517	Demography—Mongolia	HB3667.3	304.6096657	Demography—Guinea-Bissau
HB3654	304.60951	Demography—China			
HB3655	304.6095126	Demography—Macao	HB3667.4	304.609648	Demography—Western Sahara
HB3656	304.60951249	Demography—Taiwan			
HB3657	304.6095125	Demography—Hong Kong	HB3667.5	304.6094699	Demography—Azores
HB3661.3	304.60964	Demography—Morocco	HB3668	304.6097299	Demography—Bermuda Islands
HB3661.4	304.60965	Demography—Algeria			
HB3661.5	304.609611	Demography—Tunisia	HB3668.5	304.6094698	Demography—Madeira Islands
HB3661.6	304.609612	Demography—Libya			
HB3661.7	304.60962	Demography—Egypt	HB3669	304.609649	Demography—Canary Islands
HB3661.8	304.609624	Demography—Sudan			
HB3662	304.60963	Demography—Ethiopia	HB3669.5	304.6096658	Demography—Cape Verde
HB3662.2	304.6096773	Demography—Somalia	HB3670	304.609973	Demography—Saint Helena
HB3662.3	304.6096771	Demography—Djibouti			
HB3662.5	304.6096762	Demography—Kenya	HB3670.5	304.609973	Demography—Tristan da Cunha
HB3662.6	304.6096761	Demography—Uganda			
HB3662.7	304.60967571	Demography—Rwanda	HB3671	304.6099711	Demography—Falkland Islands
HB3662.8	304.60967572	Demography—Burundi			
HB3662.9	304.609678	Demography—Tanzania	HB3671.5	304.6095495	Demography—Maldives
HB3663	304.609679	Demography—Mozambique	HB3672	304.609696	Demography—Seychelles
HB3663.2	304.609691	Demography—Madagascar	HB3672.5	304.609694	Demography—Comoro Islands
HB3663.4	304.60968	Demography—South Africa			
			HB3673	304.6096982	Demography—Mauritius
HB3663.6	304.6096894	Demography—Zambia	HB3673.5	304.6096981	Demography—Reunion
HB3663.7	304.6096885	Demography—Lesotho	HB3674	304.609699	Demography—Kerguelen Islands
HB3663.8	304.6096887	Demography—Swaziland			
HB3663.9	304.6096883	Demography—Botswana	HB3675-3676	304.60994	Demography—Australia
HB3664	304.6096897	Demography—Malawi	HB3692.5	304.60993	Demography—New Zealand
HB3664.2	304.6096881	Demography—Namibia			
HB3664.4	304.609673	Demography—Angola	HB3692.7	304.609967	Demography—Guam
HB3664.5	304.6096751	Demography—Zaire	HB3692.8	304.609953	Demography—Papua New Guinea
HB3664.6	304.6096718	Demography—Equatorial Guinea			
			HB3692.9	304.6099681	Demography—Kiribati
HB3664.7	304.6096715	Demography—Sao Tome and Principe	HB3693	304.6099593	Demography—Solomon Islands
HB3664.9	304.6096721	Demography—Gabon	HB3693.3	304.6099597	Demography—New Caledonia
HB3665	304.6096724	Demography—Congo (Brazzaville)			
			HB3693.4	304.6099595	Demography—Vanuatu
HB3665.2	304.6096741	Demography—Central African Republic	HB3693.5	304.6099611	Demography—Fiji
			HB3693.6	304.6099612	Demography—Tonga
HB3665.3	304.6096743	Demography—Chad	HB3693.65	304.6099623	Demography—Cook Islands
HB3665.4	304.6096711	Demography—Cameroon			
HB3665.7	304.6096683	Demography—Benin	HB3693.7	304.6099613	Demography—American Samoa
HB3665.8	304.6096681	Demography—Togo			
HB3665.9	304.6096626	Demography—Niger	HB3693.8	304.6099614	Demography—Western Samoa
HB3666	304.6096668	Demography—Cote d'Ivoire			
			HB3693.9	304.609962	Demography—French Polynesia
HB3666.2	304.6096652	Demography—Guinea			
HB3666.3	304.6096623	Demography—Mali	HB3695	304.60998	Demography—Arctic Regions
HB3666.4	304.6096625	Demography—Burkina Faso			
			HB3696	304.609982	Demography—Greenland

LC	Dewey	Subject Heading	LC	Dewey	Subject Heading
HB3711-3840	338.542	Business cycles	HC240-407	330.94	Europe—Economic conditions
HB3711-3840	338.542	Depressions			
HB3722-3725	338.542	Financial crises	HC241.2-.25	341.2422	European Economic Community literature
HB3729	338.542	Long waves (Economics)			
HB3730	330.0112	Economic forecasting	HC246	330.917241	Commonwealth countries—Economic conditions
HB3732	339.5	Economic stabilization			
HB3741-3840	338.54209(4-9)	Business cycles—[By region or country]	HC251-260	330.942	England—Economic conditions
			HC261-270	330.9436	Austria—Economic conditions
HC	330.9	Economic history			
HC41-42	330.0902	Economic history—Medieval, 500-1500	HC270.2-.295	330.9437	Czechoslovakia—Economic conditions
			HC271-280	330.944	France—Economic conditions
HC54-60.5	330.0904	Economic history—20th century			
HC59-60.5	330.09044	Economic history—1945-	HC275	330.944	Famine compact, 1765
HC79.C3	332.041	Capital	HC281-290.795	330.943	Germany—Economic conditions
HC79.C6	339.47092	Consumers			
HC79.C6	339.47	Consumption (Economics)	HC291-300	330.9495	Greece—Economic conditions
HC79.D5	338.7	Business relocation			
HC79.F3	363.8	Famines	HC301-310	330.945	Italy—Economic conditions
HC79.I55	303.4833	Information technology			
HC79.P6	339.46	Poverty	HC311-320	330.9493	Belgium—Economic conditions
HC79.P7	338.516	Profit			
HC101-110	330.973	United States—Economic conditions	HC321-329.5	330.9492	Netherlands—Economic conditions
HC110.5	330.9982	Greenland—Economic conditions	HC330	330.94935	Luxembourg—Economic conditions
HC111-120	330.971	Canada—Economic conditions	HC331-340	330.947	Russia—Economic conditions
HC131-140	330.972	Mexico—Economic conditions	HC340.3	330.9438	Poland—Economic conditions
HC141-148	330.9728	Central America—Economic conditions	HC341-380	330.948	Scandinavia—Economic conditions
HC151-158.6	330.9729	West Indies—Economic conditions	HC351-360	330.9489	Denmark—Economic conditions
HC161-239.5	330.98	South America—Economic conditions	HC361-370	330.9481	Norway—Economic conditions
HC171-180	330.982	Argentina—Economic conditions	HC371-380	330.9485	Sweden—Economic conditions
HC181-185	330.984	Bolivia—Economic conditions	HC381-390	330.946	Spain—Economic conditions
HC186-190	330.981	Brazil—Economic conditions	HC391-394.5	330.9469	Portugal—Economic conditions
HC191-195	330.983	Chile—Economic conditions	HC395-400	330.9494	Switzerland—Economic conditions
HC196-200	330.9861	Colombia—Economic conditions	HC401-407	330.9496	Balkan Peninsula—Economic conditions
HC201-204.5	330.9866	Ecuador—Economic conditions	HC402	330.94965	Albania—Economic conditions
HC221-225	330.9892	Paraguay—Economic conditions	HC403	330.9499	Bulgaria—Economic conditions
HC226-230	330.985	Peru—Economic conditions	HC405	330.9498	Romania—Economic conditions
HC231-235	330.9895	Uruguay—Economic conditions	HC407	330.9497	Yugoslavia—Economic conditions
HC236-239.5	330.987	Venezuela—Economic conditions	HC411-495	330.95	Asia—Economic conditions
			HC415.23	330.95691	Syria—Economic conditions

LC	Dewey	Subject Heading	LC	Dewey	Subject Heading
HC415.24	330.95692	Lebanon—Economic conditions	HC585-595.5	330.997	Islands of the Atlantic—Economic conditions
HC415.25	330.95694	Israel—Economic conditions	HC601-610	330.994	Australia—Economic conditions
HC415.26	330.95695	Jordan—Economic conditions	HC661-670	330.993	New Zealand—Economic conditions
HC415.33	330.9538	Saudi Arabia—Economic conditions	HC681-688	330.99(5-6)	Islands of the Pacific—Economic conditions
HC415.34	330.9533	Yemen—Economic conditions	HC731-740	330.998(1-8)	Arctic regions
HC415.35	330.95353	Oman—Economic conditions	HC800-1085	330.96	Africa—Economic conditions
HC415.36	330.95357	United Arab Emirates—Economic conditions	HC810	330.964	Morocco—Economic conditions
HC415.37	330.95363	Qatar—Economic conditions	HC815	330.965	Algeria—Economic conditions
HC415.38	330.95365	Bahrain—Economic conditions	HC820	330.9611	Tunisia—Economic conditions
HC415.39	330.95367	Kuwait—Economic conditions	HC825	330.9612	Libya—Economic conditions
HC415.4	330.9567	Iraq—Economic conditions	HC830	330.962	Egypt—Economic conditions
HC416-420	330.9581	Afghanistan—Economic conditions	HC835	330.9624	Sudan—Economic conditions
HC422	330.9591	Burma—Economic conditions	HC845	330.963	Ethiopia—Economic conditions
HC424	330.95493	Sri Lanka—Economic conditions	HC850	330.96773	Somalia—Economic conditions
HC425	330.95496	Nepal—Economic conditions	HC865	330.96762	Kenya—Economic conditions
HC426-430	330.951	China—Economic conditions	HC870	330.96761	Uganda—Economic conditions
HC430.5	330.951249	Taiwan—Economic conditions	HC875	330.967571	Rwanda—Economic conditions
HC431-440	330.954	India—Economic conditions	HC880	330.967572	Burundi—Economic conditions
HC440.5	330.95491	Pakistan—Economic conditions	HC885	330.9678	Tanzania—Economic conditions
HC440.8	330.95492	Bangladesh—Economic conditions	HC890	330.9679	Mozambique—Economic conditions
HC442	330.9596	Cambodia—Economic conditions	HC895	330.9691	Madagascar—Economic conditions
HC443	330.9594	Laos—Economic conditions	HC905	330.968	South Africa—Economic conditions
HC444	330.9597	Vietnam—Economic conditions	HC910	330.9689	Zimbabwe—Economic conditions
HC445	330.9593	Thailand—Economic conditions	HC915	330.96894	Zambia—Economic conditions
HC446-450	330.9598	Indonesia—Economic conditions	HC925	330.96887	Swaziland—Economic conditions
HC451-460	330.9599	Philippines—Economic conditions	HC950	330.9673	Angola—Economic conditions
HC461-465	330.952	Japan—Economic conditions	HC955	330.96751	Zaire—Economic conditions
HC466-470.2	330.9519	Korea—Economic conditions	HC975	330.96721	Gabon—Economic conditions
HC471-480	330.955	Iran—Economic conditions	HC980	330.96724	Congo (Brazzaville)—Economic conditions
HC491-495	330.9561	Turkey—Economic conditions			

LC	Dewey	Subject Heading	LC	Dewey	Subject Heading
HC990	330.96743	Chad—Economic conditions	HD72-88	338.9	Economic development
			HD82-85	338.9	Autarchy
HC995	330.96711	Cameroon—Economic conditions	HD87-88	338.9	Economic policy
			HD101-1131	333.73	Land use
HC1020	330.96626	Niger—Economic conditions	HD101-1131	333.76	Land capability for agriculture
HC1025	330.96668	Cote d'Ivoire—Economic conditions	HD108-.8	338.901	Economic development— Methodology
HC1030	330.96652	Guinea—Economic conditions	HD113-156	333.7309	Land use—History
			HD170-279	333.730973	Land use—United States
HC1055	330.9669	Nigeria—Economic conditions	HD241	333.740973	Grazing
			HD242.5	333.850973	Mineral lands
			HD251-279	333.30973	Real property
HD	338	Production (Economic theory)	HD311-320	333.730971	Land use—Canada
			HD321-330	333.730972	Land use—Mexico
HD28-70	658	Management	HD336-340	333.73097282	Land use—Belize
HD30.22	338.068	Managerial economics	HD341-350	333.73097286	Land use—Costa Rica
HD30.23	658.403	Decision-making	HD351-360	333.73097281	Land use—Guatemala
HD30.27	338.544	Business forecasting	HD361-370	333.73097283	Land use—Honduras
HD30.28	658.4012	Strategic planning	HD371-380	333.73097285	Land use—Nicaragua
HD38.2-.25	658.409	Executive ability	HD381-385	333.73097287	Land use—Panama
HD38.5	658.5	Business logistics	HD386-390	333.730972875	Land use—Panama Canal Zone
HD38.7	658.47	Business intelligence			
HD39-40.7	658.152	Capital	HD391-400	333.73097284	Land use—El Salvador
HD39.5	658.72	Industrial procurement	HD406-410	333.73097296	Land use—Bahamas
HD41	338.6048	Competition	HD411-420	333.73097291	Land use—Cuba
HD47.25	658.1554	Break-even analysis	HD421-425	333.73097294	Land use—Haiti
HD47.3	658.1552	Cost control	HD426-430	333.73097293	Land use—Dominican Republic
HD47.4	658.1554	Cost effectiveness			
HD49-.6	658.4056	Crisis management	HD431-440	333.73097292	Land use—Jamaica
HD49	658.477068	Emergency management	HD441-450	333.73097295	Land use—Puerto Rico
HD50-.5	658.402	Delegation of authority	HD450.3	333.7309 + 729722	Land use—Virgin Islands of the United States
HD50	658.402	Decentralization in management			
			HD451.5	333.730972981	Land use—Barbados
HD51	338.6	Division of labor	HD453.2	333.730972973	Land use—Anguilla
HD56-57.5	338.06	Industrial productivity	HD453.4	333.730972974	Land use—Antigua
HD57.7	658.4	Leadership	HD453.6	333.730972975	Land use—Montserrat
HD58.6	658.4052	Negotiation in business	HD453.8	333.730972973	Land use—Saint Kitts and Nevis
HD58.7	658.019	Organizational behavior			
HD58.8	658.406	Organizational change	HD454.3	333.7309 + 729841	Land use—Dominica
HD58.85	658.406	Downsizing of organizations			
			HD454.5	333.7309 + 729845	Land use—Grenada
HD59	338.74	Corporations—Investor relations			
			HD454.7	333.7309 + 729843	Land use—Saint Lucia
HD59-.6	659.2	Public relations			
HD59.2	338.74	Corporate image	HD454.9	333.7309 + 729844	Land use—Saint Vincent
HD59.3	659.1	Advocacy advertising			
HD60-.5	658.408	Social responsibility of business	HD455	333.730972983	Land use—Trinidad and Tobago
HD61	658.155	Risk management	HD456.5	333.730972986	Land use—Aruba
HD62	658.562	Standardization	HD456.6	333.730972986	Land use—Bonaire
HD62.15	658.4013	Total quality management	HD456.7	333.730972986	Land use—Curacao
HD62.25	338.7	Family-owned business enterprises	HD456.8	333.730972977	Land use—Saba (Netherlands Antilles)
HD62.27	338.7	Couple-owned business enterprises	HD456.85	333.730972977	Land use—Saint Eustatius (Netherlands Antilles)
HD66-.2	658.4013	Quality circles	HD456.9	333.730972977	Land use—Saint Martin
HD66-.2	658.402	Work groups	HD458	333.730972976	Land use—Guadeloupe
HD69.C6	658.46	Business consultants	HD459	333.730972982	Land use—Martinique

LC	Dewey	Subject Heading	LC	Dewey	Subject Heading
HD471-480	333.730982	Land use—Argentina	HD860.2	333.730955	Land use—Iran
HD481-490	333.730984	Land use—Bolivia	HD860.6	333.7309581	Land use—Afghanistan
HD491-500	333.730981	Land use—Brazil	HD860.7	333.7309591	Land use—Burma
HD501-510	333.730983	Land use—Chile	HD860.8	333.73095493	Land use—Sri Lanka
HD511-520	333.7309861	Land use—Colombia	HD860.9	333.73095496	Land use—Nepal
HD521-530	333.7309866	Land use—Ecuador	HD871-880	333.730954	Land use—India
HD540.3	333.7309881	Land use—Guyana	HD880.3	333.73095498	Land use—Bhutan
HD540.5	333.7309883	Land use—Surinam	HD880.5	333.73095491	Land use—Pakistan
HD540.7	333.7309882	Land use—French Guiana	HD880.6	333.73095492	Land use—Bangladesh
HD541-550	333.7309892	Land use—Paraguay	HD890.3	333.7309596	Land use—Cambodia
HD551-560	333.730985	Land use—Peru	HD890.4	333.7309594	Land use—Laos
HD561-570	333.7309895	Land use—Uruguay	HD890.5	333.7309597	Land use—Vietnam
HD571-580	333.730987	Land use—Venezuela	HD890.55	333.7309593	Land use—Thailand
HD601-610	333.730942	Land use—England	HD890.6	333.7309595	Land use—Malaysia
HD611-620	333.7309411	Land use—Scotland	HD891-900	333.7309598	Land use—Indonesia
HD620.5	333.7309416	Land use—Northern Ireland	HD901-910	333.7309599	Land use—Philippines
			HD911-920	333.730952	Land use—Japan
HD621-630	333.7309415	Land use—Ireland	HD920.5-.6	333.7309519	Land use—Korea
HD631-640	333.7309436	Land use—Austria	HD920.8	333.7309517	Land use—Mongolia
HD640.3	333.7309437	Land use—Czechoslovakia	HD921-930	333.730951	Land use—China
HD640.5	333.7309439	Land use—Hungary	HD931-935	333.73095126	Land use—Macao
HD640.9	333.730943648	Land use—Liechtenstein	HD936-940	333.730951249	Land use—Taiwan
HD641-650	333.730944	Land use—France	HD941-945	333.73095125	Land use—Hong Kong
HD650.5	333.730944949	Land use—Monaco	HD972	333.730964	Land use—Morocco
HD651-660.5	333.730943	Land use—Germany	HD973	333.730965	Land use—Algeria
HD671-680	333.730945	Land use—Italy	HD974	333.7309611	Land use—Tunisia
HD691-700	333.7309493	Land use—Belgium	HD975	333.7309612	Land use—Libya
HD701-710	333.7309492	Land use—Netherlands	HD976	333.730962	Land use—Egypt
HD710.5	333.73094935	Land use—Luxembourg	HD977	333.7309624	Land use—Sudan
HD711-720	333.730947	Land use—Russia	HD979	333.730963	Land use—Ethiopia
HD721-725	333.73094897	Land use—Finland	HD980	333.73096773	Land use—Somalia
HD726-729.5	333.7309438	Land use—Poland	HD981	333.73096771	Land use—Djibouti
HD731-740	333.7309489	Land use—Denmark	HD983	333.73096762	Land use—Kenya
HD741-750	333.73094912	Land use—Iceland	HD984	333.73096761	Land use—Uganda
HD751-760	333.7309481	Land use—Norway	HD985	333.730967571	Land use—Rwanda
HD761-770	333.7309485	Land use—Sweden	HD986	333.730967572	Land use—Burundi
HD771-780	333.730946	Land use—Spain	HD987	333.7309678	Land use—Tanzania
HD781-790	333.7309469	Land use—Portugal	HD988	333.7309679	Land use—Mozambique
HD791-800	333.7309494	Land use—Switzerland	HD989	333.7309691	Land use—Madagascar
HD810.5	333.73094965	Land use—Albania	HD991	333.730968	Land use—South Africa
HD811-820	333.7309499	Land use—Bulgaria	HD992	333.7309689	Land use—Zimbabwe
HD821-825	333.7309497	Land use—Yugoslavia	HD993	333.73096894	Land use—Zambia
HD831-840	333.7309498	Land use—Romania	HD994	333.73096885	Land use—Lesotho
HD840.5	333.7309495	Land use—Greece	HD995	333.73096887	Land use—Swaziland
HD846.5	333.7309561	Land use—Turkey	HD996	333.73096883	Land use—Botswana
HD847	333.73095693	Land use—Cyprus	HD997	333.73096897	Land use—Malawi
HD848	333.73095691	Land use—Syria	HD998	333.73096881	Land use—Namibia
HD849	333.73095692	Land use—Lebanon	HD1000	333.7309673	Land use—Angola
HD850	333.73095694	Land use—Israel	HD1001	333.73096751	Land use—Zaire
HD851	333.73095695	Land use—Jordan	HD1002	333.73096718	Land use—Equatorial Guinea
HD853	333.7309538	Land use—Saudi Arabia			
HD854-.5	333.7309533	Land use—Yemen	HD1003	333.73096715	Land use—Sao Tome and Principe
HD855	333.73095353	Land use—Oman			
HD856	333.73095357	Land use—United Arab Emirates	HD1005	333.73096721	Land use—Gabon
			HD1006	333.73096724	Land use—Congo (Brazzaville)
HD857	333.73095363	Land use—Qatar			
HD858	333.73095365	Land use—Bahrain	HD1007	333.73096741	Land use—Central African Republic
HD859	333.73095367	Land use—Kuwait			
HD860	333.7309567	Land use—Iraq	HD1008	333.73096743	Land use—Chad

LC	Dewey	Subject Heading	LC	Dewey	Subject Heading
HD1009	333.73096711	Land use—Cameroon	HD1301-1339	333.14	Land, Nationalization of
HD1012	333.73096683	Land use—Benin	HD1332-1333.5	333.31	Land reform
HD1013	333.73096681	Land use—Togo	HD1334-1335	333.33	Consolidation of land holdings
HD1014	333.73096626	Land use—Niger			
HD1015	333.73096668	Land use—Cote d'Ivoire	HD1336-1339	333.32	Peasantry
HD1016	333.73096652	Land use—Guinea	HD1361-1395.5	333.33	Real estate business
HD1017	333.73096623	Land use—Mali	HD1393	333.76	Farms—Valuation
HD1018	333.73096625	Land use—Burkina Faso	HD1393.5	333.77	Industrial districts
HD1019	333.7309663	Land use—Senegal	HD1401-2210	338.16	Farms
HD1020	333.7309661	Land use—Mauritania	HD1428-1431	338.181	Agriculture—International cooperation
HD1021	333.7309669	Land use—Nigeria			
HD1022	333.7309667	Land use—Ghana	HD1439-1440	332.71	Agricultural credit
HD1023	333.7309664	Land use—Sierra Leone	HD1443	332.72	Mortgages
HD1024	333.73096651	Land use—Gambia	HD1447	338.13	Agricultural prices
HD1025	333.73096662	Land use—Liberia	HD1470-1476	338.16	Farms, Size of
HD1026	333.73096657	Land use—Guinea Bissau	HD1471	333.335	Haciendas
HD1027	333.7309648	Land use—Western Sahara	HD1478	333.335563	Sharecropping
			HD1483-1491.5	334.683	Agriculture, Cooperative
HD1028	333.73094699	Land use—Azores	HD1492-.5	334.683	Collective farms
HD1028.3	333.73097299	Land use—Bermuda Islands	HD1492-.5	334.683	Collectivization of agriculture
HD1028.5	333.73094698	Land use—Madeira Islands	HD1493-.5	334.683	State farms
			HD1521-1542	331.763	Agricultural laborers
HD1028.7	333.7309649	Land use—Canary Islands	HD1521-1542	331.544	Migrant agricultural laborers
HD1028.9	333.73096658	Land use—Cape Verde			
HD1029	333.7309973	Land use—Saint Helena	HD1521-1542	331.763	Peasantry
HD1029.3	333.7309973	Land use—Tristan da Cunha	HD1549	338.163	Gleaning
			HD1665-1671	333.73137	Waste lands
HD1029.5	333.7309971	Land use—Falkland Islands	HD1690-1702	333.91	Water resources development
HD1029.7	333.73095495	Land use—Maldives	HD1711-1741	333.736153	Desert reclamation
HD1029.9	333.7309696	Land use—Seychelles	HD2321-4730.9	338	Industries
HD1030	333.7309694	Land use—Comoro Islands	HD2329	338	Industrialization
			HD2331-2336.35	338.634	Home labor
HD1030.3	333.73096982	Land use—Mauritius	HD2331-2336.35	338.634	Home-based businesses
HD1030.5	333.73096981	Land use—Reunion	HD2331-2336.35	658.3128	Telecommuting
HD1030.7	333.7309699	Land use—Kerguelen Islands	HD2337-2339	331.117	Sweatshops
			HD2336.2-.25	338.634	Cottage industries
HD1031-1040	333.730994	Land use—Australia	HD2350.8-2356	338.644	Big business
HD1120.5	333.730993	Land use—New Zealand	HD2350.8-2356	338.65	Factory system
HD1121.5	333.7309967	Land use—Guam	HD2365-2385	331.542	Contracting out
HD1122	333.7309953	Land use—Papua New Guinea	HD2709-2932	338.82	Monopolies
			HD2709-2932	338.86	Stock companies
HD1122.3	333.73099681	Land use—Kiribati	HD2709-2932	338.74	Corporations
HD1123	333.73099593	Land use—Solomon Islands	HD2741-2749	658.4	Corporate governance
			HD2745	658.422	Directors of corporations
HD1124	333.73099597	Land use—New Caledonia	HD2746.5-.55	338.83	Consolidation and merger of corporations
HD1125	333.73099595	Land use—Vanuatu			
HD1126	333.73099611	Land use—Fiji	HD2746.6	658.164	Corporate divestiture
HD1127	333.73099612	Land use—Tonga	HD2747	658.1	Liquidation
HD1127.5	333.73099623	Land use—Cook Islands	HD2753	336.207	Corporations—Taxation
HD1128	333.73099613	Land use—American Samoa	HD2756-.2	338.6	Diversification in industry
			HD2756-.2	338.8042	Conglomerate corporations
HD1129.5	333.7309962	Land use—French Polynesia	HD2757-2768	338.82	Oligopolies
HD1130	333.730998(1-8)	Land use—Arctic regions	HD2757.5	338.87	Cartels
HD1130.5	333.7309982	Land use—Greenland	HD2763-2768	363.6	Public utilities
HD1241-1339	333.3	Land tenure	HD2770-2930.7	338.7409	Corporations—[By region or country]
HD1286-1289	333.2	Commons			

LC	Dewey	Subject Heading	LC	Dewey	Subject Heading
HD2771-2798.5	338.740973	Corporations—United States	HD3881-4420.8	352.2660973	Corporations, Government—United States
HD2807-2810	338.740971	Corporations—Canada	HD4001-4420.7	352.26609(4-9)	Corporations, Government—[Other countries]
HD2811	338.740972	Corporations—Mexico			
HD2813.5-2819	338.7409728	Corporations—Central America	HD4421-4730.9	352.266	Municipal ownership
HD2820.5-2825.9	338.7409729	Corporations—West Indies	HD4801-8943	331.11	Proletariat
HD2827-2843	338.74098	Corporations—South America	HD4801-8943	331	Work
			HD4801-8943	331	Labors
HD2844-2891.84	338.74094	Corporations—Europe	HD4801-8943	331.11	Working class
HD2845-2847.5	338.740941	Corporations—Great Britain	HD4801-4854	331.8	Labor movement
HD2853-2856	338.740944	Corporations—France	HD4861-4865	331.11734	Slave labor
HD2857-2860.5	338.740943	Corporations—Germany	HD4871-4875	331.542	Contract labor
HD2862-2865	338.740945	Corporations—Italy	HD4871-4875	331.1173	Service, Compulsory non-military
HD2865.5-2873.5	338.7409492	Corporations—Benelux countries	HD4871-4875	306.363	Indentured servants
HD2874-2877	338.740947	Corporations—Russia	HD4881-4885	331.55	Apprentices
HD2885-2888	338.740946	Corporations—Spain	HD4903-.5	331.702	Free choice of employment
HD2889	338.7409469	Corporations—Portugal			
HD2891.83	338.7409495	Corporations—Greece	HD4903-.5	331.133	Discrimination in employment
HD2891.93	338.7409561	Corporations—Turkey			
HD2892.2	338.74095694	Corporations—Israel	HD4903-.5	331.8892	Right to labor
HD2892.55	338.7409567	Corporations—Iraq	HD4904.7	331.11	Human capital
HD2892.56	338.740955	Corporations—Iran	HD4905-.3	306.3613	Work ethic
HD2897-2900	338.740954	Corporations—India	HD4905.5	331.1173	Service, Compulsory non-military
HD2904	338.7409598	Corporations—Indonesia			
HD2905	338.7409599	Corporations—Philippines	HD4909-5100.7	331.21	Wages
HD2907	338.740952	Corporations—Japan	HD4917-4924	331.23	Minimum wage
HD2910	338.740951	Corporations—China	HD4918-4924	331.2309(4-9)	Minimum wage—[By region or country]
HD2917-2929.3	338.74096	Corporations—Africa			
HD2930	338.740994	Corporations—Australia	HD4928.A5	331.236	Guaranteed annual wage
HD2951-3575	334	Cooperation	HD4928.B6	331.2164	Bonus system
HD2952	334.06	Cooperation—Societies, etc.	HD4928.D5	331.216	Severance pay
			HD4928.E4	331.255	Employee discounts
HD2956	334.09	Cooperation—History	HD4928.G34	331.2164	Gain sharing
HD2970-3110.9	331.2164	Profit-sharing	HD4928.H	331.2576	Holiday pay
HD2981-3110.9	331.216409(4-9)	Profit-sharing—[By region or country]	HD4928.N6	331.255	Cafeteria benefit plans
			HD4928.N6	331.255	Employee fringe benefits
HD3120-3260.9	334.6	Producer cooperatives	HD4928.P5	331.2164	Piece-work
HD3131-3260.9	334.609(4-9)	Producer cooperatives—[By region or country]	HD4928.S74	331.2164	Employee stock options
			HD4928.T93	331.216	Two-tier wage payment systems
HD3271-3575	334.5	Consumers' leagues	HD4966.A29	331.283	Agricultural wages
HD3271-3575	334.5	Consumer cooperatives	HD4966.C82	331.287482	Coopers and cooperage
HD3281-3410.9	334.509	Consumer cooperatives—[By region or country]	HD4967	331.291724	Wages—Developing countries
			HD4973-4976	331.2973	Wages—United States
HD3611-4730.9	321.94	Corporate state	HD4977-4980	331.2971	Wages—Canada
HD3656-3790.9	658.568	Factory inspection	HD4981	331.2972	Wages—Mexico
HD3661-3790.9	658.56809(4-9)	Factory inspection—[By region or country]	HD4983-4989	331.29728	Wages—Central America
			HD4990-4995.9	331.29729	Wages—West Indies
HD3840-4420.8	352.266	Government ownership	HD4996-5013	331.298	Wages—South America
HD3840-4420.8	338.749	Government ownership	HD5014-5061.84	331.294	Wages—Europe
HD3840-4420.8	363	Public works	HD5106-5267	331.25723	Eight-hour movement
HD3850	338.749	Corporations, Government	HD5106-5267	331.257	Hours of labor
HD3850	352.266	Corporations, Government	HD5108-.2	331.25724	Hours of labor, Staggered
HD3860-3861	346.023	Public contracts	HD5109-.2	331.25724	Hours of labor, Flexible
			HD5110-.2	331.25727	Part-time employment

LC	Dewey	Subject Heading	LC	Dewey	Subject Heading
HD5110.5-.6	331.257277	Work sharing	HD5733-5739	331.1209728	Labor market—Central America
HD5111	331.2572	Overtime	HD5740-5745.9	331.1209729	Labor market—West Indies
HD5111.5-.6	331.25725	Shift systems	HD5746-5763	331.12098	Labor market—South America
HD5112	331.2576	Rest periods			
HD5113-.2	331.2574	Night work	HD5764-5811.84	331.12094	Labor market—Europe
HD5114	331.2576	Weekly rest-day	HD5765-5767.5	331.120941	Labor market—Great Britain
HD5115.5-.6	331.25762	Sick leave			
HD5255-5257.3	331.25763	Leave of absence	HD5773-5776	331.120944	Labor market—France
HD5257-.2	331.25763	Educational leave	HD5777-5780.5	331.120943	Labor market—Germany
HD5260-5267	331.2576	Vacations, Employee	HD5782-5785	331.120945	Labor market—Italy
HD5306-5474	331.892	Strikes and lockouts	HD5785.5-5793.5	331.1209492	Labor market—Benelux countries
HD5306-5474	331.894	Strikes and lockouts			
HD5307	331.8925	General strikes	HD5794-5797	331.120947	Labor market—Russia
HD5309	331.892	Strikes and lockouts, Sympathetic	HD5805-5808	331.120946	Labor market—Spain
			HD5810	331.1209494	Labor market—Switzerland
HD5311	331.892	Wildcat strikes			
HD5321-5450.7	331.8929 + (4-9)	Strikes and lockouts—[By region or country]	HD5811.83	331.1209495	Labor market—Greece
			HD5811.93	331.1209561	Labor market—Turkey
HD5366	331.89250941	General strike, Great Britain, 1926	HD5812.2	331.12095694	Labor market—Israel
			HD5812.55	331.1209567	Labor market—Iraq
HD5368	331.892509416	General strike, Northern Ireland, 1974	HD5812.56	331.120955	Labor market—Iran
			HD5812.6	331.1209581	Labor market—Afghanistan
HD5379.C6	331.89280943	Eles (Firm) Strike, Bleidenstadt, Ger., 1975			
			HD5817-5820	331.120954	Labor market—India
HD5427	331.89280952	Daiichi Togyo Kabushiki Kaisha Strike, 1970-1975	HD5825	331.1209599	Labor market—Philippines
			HD5827	331.120952	Labor market—Japan
HD5461	331.893	Boycotts	HD5830	331.120951	Labor market—China
HD5468	331.8927	Picketing	HD5837-5849.3	331.12096	Labor market—Africa
HD5473	331.893	Sabotage	HD5850	331.120994	Labor market—Australia
HD5481-5630.7	331.89143	Arbitration, Industrial	HD5855-5856	331.544	Casual labor
HD5501-5630.7	331.8914309 + (4-9)	Arbitration, Industrial—[By region or country]	HD5855-5856	331.544	Migrant labor
			HD5855-5856	331.137044	Seasonal unemployment
HD5650-5660	338.69	Employee ownership	HD5860-6000.7	331.128	Employment agencies
HD5650-5660	331.0112	Management—Employee participation	HD5871-6000.7	331.12809(4-9)	Employment agencies—[By region or country]
HD5701-5852	331.123	Labor demand	HD6060-.5	331.4133	Sex discrimination in employment
HD5701-5852	331.12	Labor market			
HD5701-5852	331.12	Labor supply	HD6061-.2	331.2153	Pay equity
HD5701.5-.75	331.125	Employment (Economic theory)	HD6065-.5	331.25763	Parental leave
			HD6072-.2	640.46	Domestics
HD5701.55	331.1250112	Employment forecasting	HD6073.M7	746.92092	Models (Persons)
HD5707.5-5710.2	331.137	Unemployed	HD6091-6220.7	331.409(4-9)	Working class women—[By region or country]
HD5707.5-5710.2	331.137	Unemployment			
HD5708.4-.45	331.2596	Job security	HD6228-6250.5	331.31	Children—Employment
HD5708.46-.47	331.137041	Structural unemployment	HD6270-6276	331.34	Youth—Employment
HD5708.5-.55	338.6042	Plant shutdowns	HD6271-.2	331.137044	Summer employment
HD5708.7-.75	331.137	Disguised unemployment	HD6276.5-.52	331.34	College students—Employment
HD5708.8-.85	331.137	Hard-core unemployed			
HD5709-.2	331.13	Underemployment	HD6279-6283	331.398	Aged—Employment
HD5710.5	331.124	Job vacancies	HD6300	331.62	Alien labor
HD5713.5-.6	352.63	Public service employment	HD6304	331.6	Minorities—Employment
HD5715-.2	331.2598	Absenteeism (Labor)	HD6331-.2	331.137042	Technological unemployment
HD5715-.5	370.113	Occupational training			
HD5723-5851	331.1209(4-9)	Labor market—[By region or country]	HD6350-6940.7	331.88	Trade-unions
			HD6451-6481.2	331.8809	Trade-unions—History
HD5723-5726	331.120973	Labor market—United States	HD6477	335.82	Syndicalism
HD5727-5729	331.120971	Labor market—Canada	HD6479	335.15	Guild socialism
HD5731	331.120972	Labor market—Mexico			

113

LC	Dewey	Subject Heading	LC	Dewey	Subject Heading
HD6488-.2	331.8892	Open and closed shop	HD7357.5	363.509495	Housing—Greece
HD6490.07	331.8912	Trade-unions—Organizing	HD7358.25	363.509561	Housing—Turkey
HD6490.R4	331.8912	Trade-unions—Recognition	HD7358.45	363.5095694	Housing—Israel
			HD7359	363.509567	Housing—Iraq
HD6500-6940.7	331.8809(4-9)	Trade-unions—[By region or country]	HD7359.2	363.50955	Housing—Iran
			HD7359.6	363.5095	Housing—Asia
HD6500-6519	331.880973	Trade-unions—United States	HD7361	363.50954	Housing—India
			HD7366	363.509599	Housing—Philippines
HD6951-6957	306.36	Industrial sociology	HD7367	363.50952	Housing—Japan
HD6951-6957	306.361	Quality of work life	HD7368	363.50951	Housing—China
HD6958.5-6976	331	Industrial relations	HD7372-7378.4	363.5096	Housing—Africa
HD6971.5-.65	331.89	Collective bargaining	HD7379	363.50994	Housing—Australia
HD6971.8	331.011	Employee rights	HD7391	363.5091724	Housing—Developing countries
HD6972.5	331.8896	Grievance procedures			
HD6977-7080	339.42	Cost and standard of living	HD7395.C5	363.1172	Protective clothing
HD6977-7080	338.52	Prices	HD7406-7510	338.4767	Factories
HD7088-7250.7	368.4	Social security	HD7651-7780.8	613.6209(4-9)	Industrial hygiene—[By region or country]
HD7095-7096	331.2550973	Insurance, Unemployment			
HD7105-7108.4	331.252	Retirement age	HD7795-8013	331.12042	Labor policy
HD7105.2-.25	368.382	Insurance, Disability	HD8001-8013	352.63	Civil service
HD7105.2-.25	306.38	Disability retirement	HD8038	331.71	Professional employees
HD7105.3-.35	331.252	Old age pensions	HD8039.A425	629.1366092	Air traffic controllers
HD7105.4-.45	332.0240145	401(k) plans	HD8039.B2	641.815	Bakers and bakeries
HD7110-.5	306.38	Early retirement	HD8039.B7-.B72	685.310092	Shoemakers
HD7121-7250.7	368.4009	Social security—[By region or country]	HD8039.D5	640.46	Domestics
			HD8039.D7	615.1092	Drugstore employees
HD7123-7126	368.400973	Social security—United States	HD8039.F65	639.2092	Fishers
			HD8039.G5	666.1092	Glass-workers
HD7255-7256	362.0425	Rehabilitation counselors	HD8039.L8	387.5092	Stevedores
HD7260-7780.8	331.25	Work environment	HD8039.M39	381.1092	Clerks (Retail trade)
HD7262-.5	363.11	Industrial accidents	HD8039.M39	331.792	White collar workers
HD7273	363.107	Safety appliances	HD8039.M6-.M7	331.7622	Miners
HD7285-7391	363.5	Housing	HD8039.M9	338.47355092	Defense industries—Employees
HD7287.7-.72	334.1	Housing, Cooperative			
HD7287.8-.82	363.506	Homeowners' associations	HD8039.P496	630.92	Plantation workers
HD7287.8-.82	363.5	Home ownership	HD8039.R1-.R45	385.092	Railroads—Employees
HD7288.72U	363.5908996 + 073	Afro-Americans—Housing	HD8039.S4	387.5092	Sailors
			HD8039.T4	677.028242092	Weavers
HD7288.75-.76	363.51	Discrimination in housing	HD8045-8942.5	331.09(4-9)	Labor—[By region or country]
HD7289	363.5091734	Housing, Rural			
HD7289.4-.42	363.5091732	Urban homesteading	HD8051-8085	331.0973	Labor—United States
HD7291-7391	363.509(4-9)	Housing—[By region or country]	HD8101-8110	331.0971	Labor—Canada
			HD8111-8120	331.0972	Labor—Mexico
HD7293-7304	363.50973	Housing—United States	HD8126-8190	331.09728	Labor—Central America
HD7305	363.50971	Housing—Canada	HD8191-8250	331.09729	Labor—West Indies
HD7306	363.50972	Housing—Mexico	HD8251-8370	331.098	Labor—South America
HD7307-7313	363.509728	Housing—Central America	HD8371-8650.7	331.094	Labor—Europe
HD7314-7319.9	363.509729	Housing—West Indies	HD8381-8400	331.0941	Labor—Great Britain
HD7320-7331	363.5098	Housing—South America	HD8421-8440	331.0944	Labor—France
HD7332-7357.7	363.5094	Housing—Europe	HD8441-8460.5	331.0943	Labor—Germany
HD7333-7335.5	363.50941	Housing—Great Britain	HD8471-8490	331.0945	Labor—Italy
HD7338	363.50944	Housing—France	HD8491-8520.5	331.09492	Labor—Benelux countries
HD7339-.5	363.50943	Housing—Germany	HD8521-8530	331.0947	Labor—Russia
HD7341	363.50945	Housing—Italy	HD8581-8590	331.0946	Labor—Spain
HD7342-7344.5	363.509492	Housing—Benelux countries	HD8601-8610	331.09494	Labor—Switzerland
			HD8650.5	331.09495	Labor—Greece
HD7345	363.50947	Housing—Russia	HD8656-8669	331.0956	Labor—Middle East
HD7351	363.50946	Housing—Spain	HD8660	331.095694	Labor—Israel
HD7353	363.509494	Housing—Switzerland	HD8670	331.09567	Labor—Iraq

LC	Dewey	Subject Heading	LC	Dewey	Subject Heading
HD8670.2	331.0955	Labor—Iran	HD9705-9705.5	338.476218	Machinery industry
HD8670.6	331.09581	Labor—Afghanistan	HD9705.5.F35-.F354	338.4762161	Fans (Machinery) industry
HD8681-8690	331.0954	Labor—India			
HD8711-8720	331.09599	Labor—Philippines	HD9709.5	388.341	Wagons
HD8721-8730	331.0952	Labor—Japan	HD9710-.37	381.45388342	Automobiles—Marketing
HD8731-8740	331.0951	Labor—China	HD9711-.2	338.4738773	Aircraft industry
HD8771-8837	331.096	Labor—Africa	HD9711.5	338.4762912	Aerospace industries
HD8841-8850	331.0994	Labor—Australia	HD9715-9717.5	338.47624	Construction industry
HD9000-9019	338.17	Farm produce	HD9716 .C3-.C33	338.47694	Carpentry
HD9000-9019	363.8	Food supply	HD9720-9739	338.4767	Manufactures
HD9000-9019	381.41	Farm produce—Marketing	HD9743-9744	338.47355	Defense industries
HD9000.9	363.192	Food adulteration and inspection	HD9744.F55-.F554	338.476834	Firearms industry and trade
HD9019.A43-A434	338.173577	Agave products industry	HD9750-9769	338.17498	Forest products
HD9030-9049	381.4131	Grain trade	HD9750-9769	338.4767482	Coopers and cooperage
HD9049.W3-.W5	338.17311	Durum wheat industry	HD9778-.5	338.176	Hides and skins
HD9057-9058	338.47641815	Bakers and bakeries	HD9801	338.476816	Electronic office machine industry
HD9070-9093	338.17351	Cotton growing	HD9870-9889	381.41351	Cotton trade
HD9070-9089	381.41351	Cotton trade	HD9929.5.A274	338.476774742	Acrylic fiber industry
HD9130-9149	336.27863371	Tobacco industry	HD9939	338.476453	Drapery industry
HD9210-9211	381.41383	Spice trade	HD9940-9949.5	381.45391	Fashion merchandising
HD9220-9235	381.415	Vegetable trade	HD9948.3	338.4739142	Lingerie industry
HD9275-9283.7	381.417	Dairy products—Marketing	HD9971.5.T32-.T324	338.4767634	Disposal tableware industry
HD9275-9283.7	338.47637143	Dairy products industry	HD9980-9990	338.4	Service industries
HD9282	338.7637143	Dried milk industry	HD9993 .D65-.D654	338.476887221	Doll industry
HD9330.B2-.B23	338.4766468	Baking powder	HD9995 .D54-.D544	338.47681761	Diagnostic equipment industry
HD9390-9395	338.4766316	Distilling industries			
HD9433	381.4162	Cattle trade	HD9999.A4-.A44	338.476683	Adhesives industry
HD9486-.6	338.76313	Agricultural machinery industry	HD9999.C36	338.2768	Chalk
			HD9999.C6	338.4768111	Clocks and watches
HD9490-.5	338.476655	Oil industries	HD9999.T34-.T344	338.4765173	Telephone answering services
HD9502-.5	333.79	Energy policy	HD9999.U5-.U54	363.75	Undertakers and undertaking
HD9506-9624	381.424	Metal trade			
HD9536	339.27421	Silver mines and mining			
HD9536	338.2741	Gold mines and mining	HE	388	Transportation
HD9540-9559	381.422	Coal trade	HE1-8	388.05	Transportation—Periodicals
HD9540-9559	338.2724	Coal			
HD9579.D5-.D54	338.47 + 6655384	Diesel fuels industry	HE11	388.06	Transportation—Congresses
HD9585.B67-.B674	338.27633	Borax	HE147.5-149	388.01	Transportation—Theory
HD9650-9660	338.4766	Chemical industry	HE151.4-.5	388.092	Transportation—Biography
HD9660.D84-.D844	338.4754786	Dye industry	HE159-181	388.09	Transportation—History
			HE191.4-.5	388.021	Transportation—Statistics
HD9660.G58-.G6	338.476682	Glycerin	HE191.9-192	388.071	Transportation—Study and teaching
HD9662.E42-.E423	338.47678	Elastomer industry			
HD9665-9675	338.476151	Nonprescription drug industry	HE195.4-.5	388.049	Transportation—Rates
			HE199-.5	388.044	Freight and freightage
HD9675.A7-.A74	338.476153137	Aspirin	HE305-311	388.4	Urban transportation
HD9677	332.63	Diamonds as an investment	HE331-380	388.1	Roads
			HE331-380	388.411	Streets
HD9681	333.7923	Solar energy industries	HE336.B8	388.12	Bus lanes
HD9685-9695	333.7932	Electric utilities	HE336.B8	388.12	High occupancy vehicle lanes
HD9696.D36-.D364	338.4702504	Database industry			
HD9696.D54-.D544	338.47004	Digital computer industry	HE336.C64	388.314	Traffic congestion
HD9697	381.456213121	Electric industries	HE336.E94	388.122	Beltways
HD9698-.5	333.7924	Nuclear industry			

LC	Dewey	Subject Heading	LC	Dewey	Subject Heading
HE336.E94	388.122	Express highways	HE1003	385.06	Railroads—Societies, etc.
HE336.H48	388.314	Highway capacity	HE1009	385.025	Railroads—Directories
HE336.R68	388.1	Route choice	HE1021	385.09	Railroads—History
HE336.R85	388.12091734	Rural roads	HE1062	385.0979	Pacific railroads
HE336.T64	388.122	Toll roads	HE1613-1614	385.314	Railroad stations
HE369-373	388.312	Traffic regulations	HE1617-1618	385.312	Railroads—Crossings
HE369-373	388.310723	Traffic surveys	HE1621-1813	385.068	Railroads—Management
HE374-377	388.132	Bridges	HE1741-1759	331.761385	Railroads—Employees
HE380.8-560	386	Waterways	HE1779-1795	363.122	Railroad accidents
HE392.8-398	386.0973	Waterways—United States	HE1811	385.092	Railroad conductors
HE399-401.25	386.0971	Waterways—Canada	HE1821-2591	385.2	Railroads—Traffic
HE401.5-402	386.098	Waterways—Latin America	HE1826	385.22	Demurrage (Car service)
HE403.5-520.9	386.09(4-9)	Waterways—[Other countries]	HE1830	385.37	Railroads—Cars
			HE1831-2220	388.042	Transportation—Rates
HE526	386.4	Canals	HE1951-2100	385.22	Railroads—Fares
HE528-545	386.42	Canals, Interoceanic	HE2231-2261	385.1	Railroads—Finance
HE550-560	387.1	Harbors	HE2271-2273	385.021	Railroads—Statistics
HE550-560	387.15	Docks	HE2301-2547	385.24	Freight and freightage
HE561-971	387.5	Shipping	HE2301-2547	385.24	Railroads—Freight
HE561	387.505	Shipping—Periodicals	HE2321.E8	385.24	Explosives—Transportation
HE562	387.506	Shipping—Congresses	HE2321.L7	385.24	Railroads—Livestock transportation
HE564	387.506	Shipping—Societies, etc.			
HE565-566	387.20216	Ship registers	HE2321.L7	385.24	Cattle—Transportation
HE565	387.2	Tonnage	HE2556	385.22	Railroads—Baggage handling
HE566.P3	387.2044	Paddle steamers			
HE566.R64	387.5442	Roll-on/roll-off ships	HE2561-2591	385.22	Railroads—Passenger traffic
HE566.T3	387.245	Tankers			
HE593-597	387.544	Freight and freightage	HE2701-3560	385.09(4-9)	Railroads—[By region or country]
HE594	387.54	Shipping—Rates			
HE595.L7	387.5448	Cattle—Transportation	HE2704-2791	385.0973	Railroads—United States
HE599-601	387.2044	Steamboats—Passenger accommodation	HE2763	385.0979	Pacific railroads—Early projects
HE603-605	387.54	Shipping—Finance	HE2763	385.0979	Pacific railroads
HE617-720	623.89229	Inland navigation	HE2801-2810	385.0971	Railroads—Canada
HE623-720	623.89229(4-9)	Inland navigation—[By region or country]	HE2811-2820	385.0972	Railroads—Mexico
			HE2825.5	385.097282	Railroads—Belize
HE623-633	623.8922973	Inland navigation—United States	HE2831-2835	385.097286	Railroads—Costa Rica
			HE2836-2840	385.097281	Railroads—Guatemala
HE635-720	623.89229(4-9)	Inland navigation—[Other countries]	HE2841-2845	385.097283	Railroads—Honduras
			HE2846-2850	385.097285	Railroads—Nicaragua
HE730-943	387.5	Merchant marine	HE2851-2855	385.097284	Railroads—El Salvador
HE730-943	387.524	Coastwise shipping	HE2856-2889	385.09729	Railroads—West Indies
HE740-743	387.50681	Shipping bounties and subsidies	HE2891-3000	385.098	Railroads—South America
			HE2901-2910	385.0982	Railroads—Argentina
HE745-943	387.509(4-9)	Merchant marine—[By region or country]	HE2911-2920	385.0984	Railroads—Bolivia
			HE2921-2930	385.0981	Railroads—Brazil
HE745-767	387.50973	Merchant marine—United States	HE2931-2940	385.0983	Railroads—Chile
			HE2941-2950	385.09861	Railroads—Colombia
HE769-937	387.509(4-9)	Merchant marine—[Other countries]	HE2951-2960	385.09866	Railroads—Ecuador
			HE2962	385.09881	Railroads—Guyana
HE943	387.5091724	Merchant marine—Developing countries	HE2963	385.09883	Railroads—Surinam
			HE2964	385.09882	Railroads—French Guiana
HE945	387.2044	Steamboat lines	HE2966-2970	385.09892	Railroads—Paraguay
HE951-953	387.15	Docks	HE2971-2980	385.0985	Railroads—Peru
HE961-971	368.22	Insurance, Marine	HE2981-2990	385.09895	Railroads—Uruguay
HE961-971	368.23	Insurance, Marine	HE2991-3000	385.0987	Railroads—Venezuela
HE971	387.55	Salvage	HE3011-3040	385.0941	Railroads—Great Britain
HE1001-5600	385	Railroads	HE3041-3050	385.09415	Railroads—Ireland
HE1001	385.05	Railroads—Periodicals	HE3051-3059.2	385.09436	Railroads—Austria

LC	Dewey	Subject Heading	LC	Dewey	Subject Heading
HE3059.3	385.09437	Railroads—Czechoslovakia	HE3436	385.096715	Railroads—Sao Tome and Principe
HE3059.5	385.09439	Railroads—Hungary			
HE3060.5	385.09438	Railroads—Poland	HE3438	385.096721	Railroads—Gabon
HE3061-3070	385.0944	Railroads—France	HE3439	385.096724	Railroads—Congo (Brazzaville)
HE3071-3080.5	385.0943	Railroads—Germany			
HE3091-3100	385.0945	Railroads—Italy	HE3441	385.096743	Railroads—Chad
HE3111-3120	385.09493	Railroads—Belgium	HE3442	385.096711	Railroads—Cameroon
HE3121-3130	385.09492	Railroads—Netherlands	HE3444	385.096683	Railroads—Benin
HE3131-3140.2	385.0947	Railroads—Russia	HE3445	385.096681	Railroads—Togo
HE3151-3160	385.09489	Railroads—Denmark	HE3446	385.096626	Railroads—Niger
HE3161-3170	385.094912	Railroads—Iceland	HE3447	385.096668	Railroads—Cote d'Ivoire
HE3171-3180	385.09481	Railroads—Norway	HE3448	385.096652	Railroads—Guinea
HE3181-3190	385.09485	Railroads—Sweden	HE3449	385.096623	Railroads—Mali
HE3191-3200	385.0946	Railroads—Spain	HE3450	385.096625	Railroads—Burkina Faso
HE3201-3210	385.09469	Railroads—Portugal	HE3451	385.09663	Railroads—Senegal
HE3211-3220	385.09494	Railroads—Switzerland	HE3452	385.09661	Railroads—Mauritania
HE3231-3240	385.09499	Railroads—Bulgaria	HE3453	385.09669	Railroads—Nigeria
HE3241-3245	385.09497	Railroads—Yugoslavia	HE3454	385.09667	Railroads—Ghana
HE3251-3260	385.09498	Railroads—Romania	HE3455	385.09664	Railroads—Sierra Leone
HE3281-3290	385.0951	Railroads—China	HE3456	385.096651	Railroads—Gambia
HE3291-3300	385.0954	Railroads—India	HE3457	385.096662	Railroads—Liberia
HE3300.3	385.095493	Railroads—Sri Lanka	HE3458	385.096657	Railroads—Guinea-Bissau
HE3300.5	385.095491	Railroads—Pakistan	HE3458.2	385.09648	Railroads—Western Sahara
HE3300.6	385.095492	Railroads—Bangladesh			
HE3320.3	385.09597	Railroads—Vietnam	HE3461-3550	385.0994	Railroads—Australia
HE3320.4	385.09594	Railroads—Laos	HE3550.5	385.0993	Railroads—New Zealand
HE3321-3330	385.09595	Railroads—Malaysia	HE3601-4043	388.42	Railroads, Local and light
HE3331-3340	385.09598	Railroads—Indonesia	HE3601	388.4205	Railroads, Local and light—Periodicals
HE3341-3350	385.09599	Railroads—Philippines			
HE3351-3360	385.0952	Railroads—Japan	HE3651-4043	388.4209(4-9)	Railroads, Local and light—[By region or country]
HE3360.5	385.09519	Railroads—Korea			
HE3380.3	385.09538	Railroads—Saudi Arabia			
HE3401-3410	385.0962	Railroads—Egypt	HE4051-4071	385.6	Mountain railroads
HE3411	385.0964	Railroads—Morocco	HE4201-5300	388.44	Railroads, Elevated
HE3412	385.0965	Railroads—Algeria	HE4341-4345	388.46	Street-railroads—Fares
HE3413	385.09611	Railroads—Tunisia	HE4351	388.46	Street-railroads—Finance
HE3414	385.09612	Railroads—Libya	HE4401-5260	388.4409(4-9)	Railroads, Elevated—[By region or country]
HE3415	385.09624	Railroads—Sudan			
HE3416	385.0963	Railroads—Ethiopia	HE4401-4491	388.440973	Railroads, Elevated—United States
HE3417	385.096773	Railroads—Somalia			
HE3419	385.096762	Railroads—Kenya	HE4500-5260	388.4409(4-9)	Railroads, Elevated—[Other countries]
HE3420	385.096761	Railroads—Uganda			
HE3421	385.0967571	Railroads—Rwanda	HE5351-5600	388.42	Electric railroads
HE3422	385.0967572	Railroads—Burundi	HE5601-5725	388.322	Bus lines
HE3423	385.09678	Railroads—Tanzania	HE5601-5725	388.413214	Cab and omnibus service
HE3424	385.09679	Railroads—Mozambique	HE5601-5725	388.34232	Taxicabs
HE3425	385.09691	Railroads—Madagascar	HE5601-5725	388.324	Trucking
HE3426	385.0968	Railroads—South Africa	HE5613.5-5614.6	363.125	Traffic safety
HE3428	385.096894	Railroads—Zambia	HE5620.B87	388.33	Bus stops
HE3429	385.096885	Railroads—Lesotho	HE5620.C3	388.413212	Car pools
HE3430	385.096887	Railroads—Swaziland	HE5620.D65	364.147	Drugged driving
HE3431	385.096883	Railroads—Botswana	HE5620.D7	364.147	Drunk driving
HE3432	385.096897	Railroads—Malawi	HE5620.D7	363.12514	Drinking and traffic accidents
HE3432.3	385.096881	Railroads—Namibia			
HE3433	385.09673	Railroads—Angola	HE5620.R53	388.413212	Ridesharing
HE3434	385.096751	Railroads—Zaire	HE5623-5725	388.32409(4-9)	Trucking—[By region or country]
HE3435	385.096718	Railroads—Equatorial Guinea			
			HE5736-5739	388.3472	Bicycles
			HE5746-5749	388.228	Coaching

117

LC	Dewey	Subject Heading	LC	Dewey	Subject Heading
HE5751-5870	386.6	Ferries	HE8660-8688	384.52	Telegraph, Wireless
HE5880-5990	388.044	Express service	HE8689.7.F34	384.54	Fairness doctrine (Broadcasting)
HE5893-5990	388.04409(4-9)	Express service—[By region or country]	HE8690-8699	384.54	Radio broadcasting
HE5893-5904.5	388.0440973	Express service—United States	HE8697.P57	384.54	Pirate radio broadcasting
			HE8700-.95	384.55	Television broadcasting
HE5905-5990	388.04409(4-9)	Express service—[Other countries]	HE8700.65-.66	384.5532	Television programs—Rating
HE5999	383.1	Mail receiving and forwarding services	HE8700.7-.72	384.555	Satellite master antenna television
HE6000-7500	383.1	Postal service	HE8700.7-.72	384.55	Low power television
HE6031	383.1025	Postal service—Directories	HE8701-9685	384.6	Telephone companies
HE6036	383.1071	Postal service—Study and teaching	HE8701-9685	384.6	Telephone
			HE8801-9685	384.609(4-9)	Telephone companies—[By region or country]
HE6041-6055	383.49	Postal service—History			
HE6061	383.492	Postal service—Biography	HE8801-8846	384.60973	Telephone companies—United States
HE6125-6148	383.23	Postal rates			
HE6148	383.1202	Franking privilege	HE8861-9685	384.609(4-9)	Telephone companies—[Other countries]
HE6149	383.1	Postal service—Unclaimed mail			
			HE9713-9715	384.53	Cellular radio
HE6171-6173	383.125	Parcel post	HE9719-9721	384.51	Artificial satellites
HE6175-.5	383.143	Railway mail service	HE9723-9737	384	Signals and signaling
HE6182-6228	383.1	Postmarks	HE9751-9756	651.3743	Messengers
HE6182-6228	383.23	Postage stamps	HE9761-9900	387.7	Aeronautics, Commercial
HE6184.A35	383.144	Aerogrammes	HE9761-9990	387.7	Airlines
HE6184.D4	769.56	Essays and proofs (Philately)	HE9761-.9	387.705	Aeronautics, Commercial—Periodicals
HE6184.D56	769.56	Disinfection markings (Philately)	HE9774-9775	387.709	Aeronautics, Commercial—History
HE6184.F57	769.56	First day covers (Philately)	HE9783-.75	387.712	Airlines—Rates
HE6184.P65	383.122	Postcards	HE9785	387.7	Local service airlines
HE6187-6230	769.56	Stamp collecting	HE9787-.5	387.742	Aeronautics, Commercial—Passenger traffic
HE6221	769.56075	Postage-stamp albums			
HE6238	383.144	Air mail service			
HE6300-7496	383.49(4-9)	Postal service—[By region or country]	HE9795-9796	387.7	Airplanes, Company
			HE9797-.5	387.736	Airports
HE6300-6500	383.4973	Postal service—United States	HE9797.4.S56	387.7364	Airport slot allocation
			HE9801-9900	387.709(4-9)	Aeronautics, Commercial—[By region or country]
HE6448	383.12020973	Franking privilege—United States			
HE6455-6456	383.1450973	Rural free delivery—United States	HE9803-9814	387.70973	Aeronautics, Commercial—United States
HE6471-6473	383.1250973	Parcel post—United States			
			HE9815	387.70971	Aeronautics, Commercial—Canada
HE6475-.3	383.1430973	Railway mail service—United States	HE9816	387.70972	Aeronautics, Commercial—Mexico
HE6651-7496	383.49(4-9)	Postal service—[Other countries]	HE9817-9823	387.709728	Aeronautics, Commercial—Central America
HE7551	384.34	Electronic mail systems			
HE7601-8635	384.1	Telegraph	HE9824-9829.9	387.709729	Aeronautics, Commercial—West Indies
HE7603	384.106	Telegraph—Societies, etc.			
HE7621	384.1025	Telegraph—Directories	HE9830-9841	387.7098	Aeronautics, Commercial—South America
HE7669-7679	384.14	Cipher and telegraph codes			
HE7681-7691	384.13	Telegraph—Rates	HE9842-9867.7	387.7094	Aeronautics, Commercial—Europe
HE7709-7741	384.1	Cables, Submarine			
HE7761-8630.7	384.109(4-9)	Telegraph—[By region or country]	HE9843-9845.5	387.70941	Aeronautics, Commercial—Great Britain
HE7761-7798	384.10973	Telegraph—United States			

LC	Dewey	Subject Heading	LC	Dewey	Subject Heading
HE9848	387.70944	Aeronautics, Commercial—France	HF1140-1165	650.07104	Business education—Europe
HE9849-.5	387.70943	Aeronautics, Commercial—Germany	HF1171	650.07105	Business education—Asia
HE9851	387.70945	Aeronautics, Commercial—Italy	HF1176	650.07106	Business education—Africa
HE9855	387.70947	Aeronautics, Commercial—Russia	HF1181-1182	650.071094	Business education—Australia
HE9861	387.70946	Aeronautics, Commercial—Spain	HF1351-1532.935	337	International economic relations
HE9863	387.709494	Aeronautics, Commercial—Switzerland	HF1371-1385	382	International trade
			HF1410-1411	381.3	Commercial policy
HE9867.5	387.709495	Aeronautics, Commercial—Greece	HF1413.5	327.117	Economic sanctions
			HF1414	338.6048	Competition
HE9868.2-.95	387.70956	Aeronautics, Commercial—Middle East	HF1414.4-1417.3	382.6	Exports
			HF1414.5-.55	382.64	Export controls
HE9868.45	387.7095694	Aeronautics, Commercial—Israel	HF1417.5	382	Foreign trade promotion
			HF1418-.5	387.13	Free ports and zones
HE9869	387.709567	Aeronautics, Commercial—Iraq	HF1419-1420	382.5	Imports
			HF1425	382.6	Dumping (International trade)
HE9869.2	387.70955	Aeronautics, Commercial—Iran	HF1430	382.9	Nontariff trade barriers
HE9869.22-9869.27	387.7095	Aeronautics, Commercial—Asia	HF1451-1647	337.(4-9)	International economic relations—[By region or country]
HE9871	387.70954	Aeronautics, Commercial—India	HF1701-2701	382.7	Tariff
			HF1715-1718	382.7	Drawbacks
HE9876	387.709599	Aeronautics, Commercial—Philippines	HF1721-1733	382.7	Tariff preferences
			HF1721-1733	382.9	Reciprocity
HE9877	387.70952	Aeronautics, Commercial—Japan	HF1745-2580.9	382.709(4-9)	Tariff—[By region or country]
HE9878	387.70951	Aeronautics, Commercial—China	HF1750-1757	382.70973	Tariff—United States
HE9882-9888.4	387.7096	Aeronautics, Commercial—Africa	HF1761-2580.9	382.709(4-9)	Tariff—[Other regions or countries]
HE9889	387.70994	Aeronautics, Commercial—Australia	HF2651.G8	381.41331	Grain trade
			HF2701	382.63	Export subsidies
HF	381	Commerce	HF3000-3163	381.0973	United States—Commerce
HF1-53	381.05	Commerce—Periodicals	HF3021-3031	381.0973(1-9)	United States—Commerce—History
HF54	381.025	Commerce—Directories			
HF294-343	381.06	Commercial associations	HF3221-3230	381.0971	Canada—Commerce
HF294-343	381.06	Boards of trade	HF3231-3240	381.0972	Mexico—Commerce
HF351-499	381.0609	Boards of trade—History	HF3241-3310	381.09728	Central America—Commerce
HF370	381.093944	Phoenicians	HF3311-3369	381.09729	West Indies—Commerce
HF1001-1002.5	381.03	Commerce—Encyclopedias	HF3371-3480	381.098	South America—Commerce
HF1014	382.17	Balance of trade	HF3491-3750.7	381.094	Europe—Commerce
HF1016-1017	381.7021	Commercial statistics	HF3501-3530.5	381.0941	Great Britain—Commerce
HF1021-1027	381.09	Commercial geography	HF3551-3560	381.0944	France—Commerce
HF1021-1027	330.9	Economic geography	HF3561-3570.5	381.0943	Germany—Commerce
HF1040-1054	381.4	Primary commodities	HF3581-3590	381.0945	Italy—Commerce
HF1040-1044	381.4	Commercial products	HF3591-3620.5	381.09492	Benelux countries—Commerce
HF1051-1054	381.43	Raw materials	HF3621-3630	381.0947	Russia—Commerce
HF1101-1186	650.071	Business education	HF3681-3690	381.0946	Spain—Commerce
HF1131-1186	650.0710(4-9)	Business education—[By region or country]	HF3701-3710	381.09494	Switzerland—Commerce
			HF3750.5	381.09495	Greece—Commerce
HF1131-1134	650.071073	Business education—United States	HF3756-3770.2	381.0956	Middle East—Commerce
			HF3760	381.095694	Israel—Commerce
HF1135	650.07108	Business education—Latin America	HF3770	381.09567	Iraq—Commerce

LC	Dewey	Subject Heading	LC	Dewey	Subject Heading
HF3770.2	381.0955	Iran—Commerce	HF5446-5456	381	Canvassing
HF3770.22-.27	381.0958	Asia, Central—Commerce	HF5457-5459	381.092	Peddlers and peddling
HF3781-3790	381.0954	India—Commerce	HF5460-5469.5	381.141	Department stores
HF3811-3820	381.09599	Philippines—Commerce	HF5465.5-5467	381.142	Mail-order business
HF3821-3830	381.0952	Japan—Commerce	HF5468	381.12	Chain stores
HF3831-3840	381.0951	China—Commerce	HF5468.2	381.45004	Computer stores
HF3871-3937	381.096	Africa—Commerce	HF5469.25-.55	381.147	Convenience stores
HF3941-3950	381.0994	Australia—Commerce	HF5469.7-5481	381.18	Markets
HF4050	382	East-West trade	HF5469.7-5481	381.1	Fairs
HF5001-6182.2	338.7	Business	HF5476-5477	381.17	Auctions
HF5371	651.29	Business—Forms	HF5481	381.1	Fairs
HF5381-5382.5	650.1	Career development	HF5482.15	381.192	Flea markets
HF5381-5382.5	331.702	Vocational guidance	HF5482.3	381.195	Garage sales
HF5382.7-.75	650.14	Job hunting	HF5484-5495	381	Warehouses
HF5383	650.142	Applications for positions	HF5495	381.1	Stores or stock-room keeping
HF5383	650.14	Resumes (Employment)			
HF5384.5	650.1	Career plateaus	HF5546-5548	651.3	Office Management
HF5384	650.14	Career changes	HF5548-.115	651.2	Office equipment and supplies
HF5386	650.1	Success in business			
HF5387	174.4	Business ethics	HF5548	651.74	Dictating machines
HF5389	395.52	Business etiquette	HF5548	651.74	Dictograph
HF5410-5417.5	381.1	Marketing	HF5548.125-.6	651.8	Office practice—Automation
HF5415	381.3	Rationing			
HF5415.126	381.1	Direct marketing	HF5548.115	005.52	Word processing
HF5415.126	381.1	Database marketing	HF5548.33	651.8	Electronic data interchange
HF5415.126	381.1	Multilevel marketing			
HF5415.1265	381.142	Telemarketing	HF5548.7-.85	158.7	Psychology, Industrial
HF5415.15-.157	658.5	Product management	HF5548.85	158.72	Job stress
HF5415.2-5415.34	658.83	Marketing research	HF5549-.5	658.3	Personnel management
HF5415.3	658.83	Market surveys	HF5549.12	658.302	Supervision of employees
HF5415.5-.55	658.812	Customer relations	HF5549.5.A34	331.133	Affirmative action programs
HF5415.5	381.3	Consumer affairs departments	HF5549.5.A4	658.3822	Alcoholism and employment
HF5415.5	658.812	Consumer satisfaction	HF5549.5.C35	658.3	Career development
HF5415.6-.9	381.1	Physical distribution of goods	HF5549.5.C8	658.3151	Employees—Counseling of
HF5415.9	363.19	Product recall	HF5549.5.D39	658.3	Employer-supported day care
HF5416	381	Product coding	HF5549.5.D55	658.3134	Downsizing of organizations
HF5416.5-5417	658.816	Pricing			
HF5417	658.816	Price maintenance	HF5549.5.D7	658.3822	Drugs and employment
HF5417	658.816	Price fixing	HF5549.5.D7	658.3112	Employees—Drug testing
HF5417	338.52	Price cutting	HF5549.5.E42	331.255	Employee assistance programs
HF5419-5422	381.2092	Brokers			
HF5419-5422	381.2	Wholesale trade	HF5549.5.E43	658.473	Employee theft
HF5422	381.2092	Commission merchants	HF5549.5.E5	658.3112	Employment tests
HF5428-5429.6	381.1	Retail trade	HF5549.5.G7	658.3155	Grievance procedures
HF5429.2-.215	381.149	Discount houses (Retail trade)	HF5549.5.I5	658.3142	Incentives in industry
			HF5549.5.I53	658.31242	Employee orientation
HF5429.2-.215	381.15	Outlet stores	HF5549.5.I6	658.31124	Employment interviewing
HF5429.7-5430.6	381.11	Shopping centers	HF5549.5.J6	658.306	Job analysis
HF5429.7-5430.6	381.11	Shopping malls	HF5549.5.J613	658.306	Job descriptions
HF5438-5439	381.1	Selling	HF5549.5.M3	658.301	Manpower planning
HF5438.8.M4	658.8106	Sales meetings	HF5549.5.M5	658.3008	Diversity in the workplace
HF5438.8.P74	658.82	Sales presentations	HF5549.5.M6	658.314	Employee morale
HF5439.25-.8	381.092	Sales executives	HF5549.5.M63	658.314	Employee motivation
HF5439.25-.8	381.092	Sales personnel	HF5549.5.P7	658.31424	Promotions
HF5439.A8	381.45388342	Selling—Automobiles	HF5549.5.R3	658.3125	Employees-Rating of
HF5439.D75	381.456151	Selling—Drugs	HF5549.5.R44	658.3111	Employees—Recruiting
HF5441-5444	381.092	Traveling sales personnel			

LC	Dewey	Subject Heading	LC	Dewey	Subject Heading
HF5549.5.R45	650.14	Employment references	HF5833	343.082	Advertising laws
HF5549.5.S38	658.3112	Employee selection	HF5843-.5	659.132	Posters
HF5549.5.S4	658.312	Seniority, Employee	HF5843	659.1342	Billboards
HF5549.5.T8	331.126	Labor turnover	HF5845-5849	659.152	Display of merchandise
HF5601-5689.8	657	Accounting	HF5845-5849	659.157	Show-windows
HF5601-5689.8	657.2	Bookkeeping	HF5851	659.132	Advertising cards
HF5630	657.071	Accounting—Study and teaching (Internship)	HF5861-5863	659.133	Commercial catalogs
			HF5861-5863	659.133	Advertising, Direct-mail
HF5657.4	658.1511	Managerial accounting	HF5871-6141	659.132	Advertising, Newspaper
HF5667-5668.25	657.45	Auditing	HF5901-6097	659.13209(4-9)	Advertising, Newspaper—[By region or country]
HF5667.65	657.3	Financial statements, Unaudited	HF6125.5	659.19658311	Help-wanted advertising
HF5668-.25	657.458	Auditing, Internal	HF6146.D75	659.19	Advertising drinking glasses
HF5679	657.0284	Accounting machines			
HF5680-5681	657	Account books	HF6146.P75	659.17	Prize contests in advertising
HF5681.A2	657.72	Accounts current			
HF5681.A27	657.74	Accounts payable	HF6146.T42	659.143	Television advertising
HF5681.A3	657.72	Accounts receivable	HF6161.A38	659.193877	Advertising—Airlines
HF5681.B2	657.3	Funds-flow statements	HF6178-6182	659.1125	Advertising agencies
HF5681.B2	657.3	Financial statements	HG	332	Finance
HF5681.D39	657.46	Deferred tax	HG1-9999	332	Financial institutions
HF5681.D5	657.73	Depreciation	HG1-61	332.05	Finance—Periodicals
HF5681.G55	657	Going concern (Accounting)	HG63	332.06	Finance—Congresses
			HG64-96	332.025	Finance—Directories
HF5681.N65	657.742	Employee fringe benefits—Accounting	HG151	332.03	Finance—Encyclopedias
			HG152-.5	332.071	Finance—Study and teaching
HF5681.V3	657.73	Valuation			
HF5686.C7	657.95	Corporations—Accounting	HG171	332.09	Finance—History
HF5686.C8	657.42	Cost accounting	HG176-.5	332.021	Finance—Statistics
HF5686.C8	657.42	Direct costing	HG177-.5	658.15224	Fund raising
HF5686.C8	657.42	Activity-based costing	HG179	332.024	Finance, Personal
HF5688-5689	681.145	Calculators	HG179.5	332.024092	Financial planners
HF5691-5716	650.01513	Business mathematics	HG201-1496	332.4	Money
HF5705-5707	658.32021	Wages—Tables	HG223	332.41	Value
HF5717-5734.7	651.7	Business communication	HG226.5	332.414	Demand for money
HF5718.3-5734	651.74	Business writing	HG226.6	332.401	Quantity theory of money
HF5719	651.74	Business report writing	HG229-.5	332.41	Purchasing power
HF5721-5734	651.75	Commercial correspondence	HG229-.5	332.41	Prices
			HG229-.5	332.41	Deflation (Finance)
HF5734.5	658.456	Business meetings	HG235	332.4	Shell money
HF5735-5746	651	Filing systems	HG258-312	332.4042	Precious metals
HF5735-5746	651.53	Card system in business	HG261-315	332.4042	Coinage
HF5738	651.53	Electronic filing systems	HG289	332.4042	Gold
HF5761-5780	658.788	Delivery of goods	HG297	332.4222	Gold standard
HF5761-5780	658.788	Shipment of goods	HG301-309	332.4223	Silver
HF5770	658.7884	Cartons	HG321-329	332.4	Mints
HF5801-6182	659.1	Advertising	HG321	332.4042	Gold—Minting
HF5801-5802	659.105	Advertising—Periodicals	HG325-329	669.92	Assaying
HF5803	659.103	Advertising—Encyclopedias	HG335-341	332.90973	Counterfeits and counterfeiting
HF5804-5808	659.1122	Advertising departments	HG348-353.5	332.4044	Paper money
HF5804-5808	659.1025	Advertising—Directories	HG348-353.5	332.4044	Bank notes
HF5811-5813	659.109	Advertising—History	HG353.5	332.4	Military currency
HF5814-5815	659.1071	Advertising—Study and teaching	HG361-363	332.42	Legal tender
			HG381-421	332.45	Coinage, International
HF5825	659.132	Advertising layout and typography	HG393	332.404	Decimal system
			HG451-1496	332.49(4-9)	Money—[By region or country]
HF5826.5	659.111	Advertising media planning			
HF5828	659.157	Advertising, Point-of-sale	HG451-645	332.4973	Money—United States

LC	Dewey	Subject Heading	LC	Dewey	Subject Heading
HG551-566	332.40420973	Coinage	HG2070-2106	332.34	Pawnbroking
HG551	332.40420973	Gold	HG2121-2156	332.32	Savings and loan associations
HG604	332.40440973	Greenbacks			
HG607-610	332.40440973	Bank notes	HG2251-2256	332.178	Safe-deposit boxes
HG641-645	332.490973	Counterfeits and counterfeiting	HG2301-2351	332.12	Clearinghouses (Banking)
			HG2401-3542.7	332.109(4-9)	Banks and banking—[By region or country]
HG1501-3550	332.1	Banks and banking			
HG1616.C34	332.1	Bank capital	HG2401-2626	332.10973	Banks and banking— United States
HG1616.C87	332.17	Banks and banking— Customer services			
			HG2559-2565	332.110973	Federal Reserve banks
HG1616.I5	332.1754	Bank investments	HG3691-3769	332.7	Credit
HG1621-1623	332.8	Interest rates	HG3705-3711	332.75	Credit control
HG1641-1643	332.1753	Commercial loans	HG3745	332.77	Letters of credit
HG1641-1643	332.1753	Bank loans	HG3746	332.7	Documentary credit
HG1641-1643	332.1753	Term loans	HG3751-3754.5	332.742	Commercial credit
HG1643	332.178	Bank credit cards	HG3751.5-.9	332.7	Credit ratings
HG1643	332.178	Affinity credit cards	HG3752	658.82	Cash discounts
HG1643	332.178	Check credit plans	HG3752.3	332.7	Accounts receivable loans
HG1651-1654	332.84	Discount houses (Finance)	HG3753-3754	332.742	Export credit
HG1651-1654	332.84	Discount	HG3755-3756	332.743	Consumer credit
HG1655	332	Acceptances	HG3755-3756	332.743	Loans, Personal
HG1656	332.1	Bank reserves	HG3755.5	332.743	Installment plan
HG1660	332.1752	Bank deposits	HG3760-3769	332.75	Bankruptcy
HG1660	332.1752	Bank accounts	HG3760-3769	332.75	Business failures
HG1660	332.1752	Savings accounts	HG3773	332.75	Receivers
HG1662	368.854	Deposit insurance	HG3810-4000	332.45	Foreign exchange
HG1685-1704	332.55	Drafts	HG3810.5	332.4503	Foreign exchange— Encyclopedias
HG1689	332.77	Bills of exchange			
HG1691-1704	332.1752	Checking accounts	HG3811-3815	332.4509	Foreign exchange—History
HG1692	332.76	Check collection systems	HG3853	332.6452	Foreign exchange futures
HG1692	332.76	Check float	HG3854-3858	332.4021	Money—Tables
HG1696-1698	332.9	Forgery	HG3879-4000	332.042	International finance
HG1706-1708	657.8333	Banks and banking— Accounting	HG3882-3890	332.152	Balance of payments
			HG3891	332.042	Capital movements
HG1709	332.10285	Banks and banking— Computer programs	HG3896	337.14	Euro-bond market
			HG3901-4000	332.4509(4-9)	Foreign exchange—[By region or country]
HG1710-.5	332.10285	Electronic funds transfer			
HG1710.5	332.76	Debit cards	HG4001-4285	338.6041	Business enterprises— Finance
HG1711-1712	332.17	Home banking services			
HG1722	332.16	Bank mergers	HG4001-4285	338.74	Corporations—Finance
HG1723	332.6722	Bank stocks	HG4027.7	338.6420681	Small business—Finance
HG1725-1778	346.082	Banking law	HG4028.B6	332.6323	Bond transfer
HG1881-1966	332.21	Savings banks	HG4028.C4	332.0414	Capital investments
HG1951-1956	332.22	Postal savings banks	HG4028.C45	658.15244	Cash management
HG1970-1971	332.37	Merchant banks	HG4028.D5	332.63221	Dividend reinvestment
HG1975-1976	332.28	Development banks	HG4028.M4	338.83	Consolidation and merger of corporations
HG1978-2031	332.123	Private banks			
HG2032-2039	334.22	Credit unions	HG4028.S7	658.15224	Going public (Securities)
HG2032-2039	334.2	Banks and banking, Cooperative	HG4028.T4	332.6322	Tender offers (Securities)
			HG4028.V3	332.63221	Valuation
HG2039.5-2040.5	332.32	Mortgage banks	HG4301-4480.9	332.26	Trust companies
HG2039.5-2040.5	332.72	Mortgage loans, Reverse	HG4307	332.26025	Trust companies— Directories
HG2040.2	332.72	Discrimination in mortgage loans			
			HG4311	332.2609	Trust companies—History
HG2040.4	332.722	Home improvement loans	HG4341-4480.9	332.2609(4-9)	Trust companies—[By region or country]
HG2040.45	332.722	Home equity loans			
HG2041-2051	332.31	Agricultural cooperative credit associations	HG4341-4356	332.260973	Trust companies—United States
HG2041-2051	332.31	Land banks			

LC	Dewey	Subject Heading	LC	Dewey	Subject Heading
HG4357-4480.9	332.2609(4-9)	Trust companies—[Other countries]	HG8901-8914	346.08632	Insurance, Life—Law and legislation
HG4501-6051	332.6	Investments	HG8941-9200.5	368.32009(4-9)	Insurance, Life—[By region or country]
HG4529.5	332.6	Portfolio management	HG9201-9245	334.7	Friendly societies
HG4530	332.6	Investment clubs	HG9251-9262	368.362	Industrial life insurance
HG4530	332.6327	Mutual funds	HG9271	368.32	Insurance, Child
HG4538	332.673	Investments, Foreign	HG9291-9295	368.424	Insurance, Maternity
HG4551-4598	332.642	Stock-exchanges	HG9301-9343	368.384	Insurance, Accident
HG4571-4575.3	332.64273	Wall Street	HG9371-9399	368.382	Insurance, Health
HG4621	332.62	Discount brokers	HG9389	368.3827	Insurance, Hospitalization
HG4621	332.642	Floor traders (Finance)	HG9466-9479	368.366	Insurance, Burial
HG4621	332.62	Stockbrokers	HG9651-9899	368.11	Insurance, Fire
HG4651	332.6323	Bonds	HG9660	368.11009	Insurance, Fire—History
HG4650-4930.5	332.632	Securities	HG9663	368.110021	Insurance, Fire—Statistics
HG4655	332.63244	Mortgages	HG9711-9715	368.11014	Fire insurance claims adjusters
HG4661	332.6322	Stocks	HG9733-9735	346.086	Insurance, Fire—Law and legislation
HG4701-4726	332.63232	Government securities	HG9751-9899	368.11009(4-9)	Insurance, Fire—[By region or country]
HG4726	332.63233	Municipal bonds	HG9751-9780	368.1100973	Insurance, Fire—United States
HG4901-5993	332.609(4-9)	Investments—[By region or country]	HG9781-9866	368.11009(4-9)	Insurance, Fire—[Other countries]
HG4905-5131	332.60973	Investments—United States	HG9903-9905	368.23	Insurance, Inland marine
HG4931-4955	332.632320 + 973	Government securities—United States	HG9956-9969	368.5	Insurance, Casualty
HG4951-4953	379.130973	School bonds	HG9966-9969	368.121	Insurance, Agricultural
HG5151-5993	332.609(4-9)	Investments—[Other countries]	HG9968	368.121	Crop insurance
HG6001-6051	332.645	Speculation	HG9970	368.092	Insurance, Automobile
HG6024-6051	332.6452	Futures	HG9970.A4-.A68	368.5728	Insurance, No-fault automobile
HG6024.3-.9	332.6452	Financial futures	HG9972	368.093	Insurance, Aviation
HG6042	332.63228	Stock options	HG9979	368.122	Insurance, Disaster
HG6043	332.63228	Stock index futures	HG9981	368.1226	Insurance, Earthquake
HG6046-6051	332.6328	Commodity futures	HG9983	368.1222	Insurance, Flood
HG6046-6051	332.644	Commodity exchanges	HG9986	368.096	Homeowner's insurance
HG6105-6270.9	336.17	Lotteries	HG9990	368.5	Insurance, Liability
HG6126-6134	336.170973	Lotteries—United States	HG9992	368.852	Mortgage guarantee insurance
HG7920-7933	332.0415	Saving and thrift	HG9995	368.562	Insurance, Products liability
HG8011-9999	368	Insurance	HG9997	368	Insurance, Surety and fidelity
HG8053.5-8054.45	368.564	Insurance, Malpractice	HG9999	368.88	Insurance, Title
HG8054	368.5642	Insurance, Physicians' liability	HJ	336	Finance, Public
HG8054.5	368	Risk (Insurance)	HJ9-99.8	336.005	Finance, Public—Periodicals
HG8058	368.3	Insurance, Group	HJ210-240	336.090(1-5)	Finance, Public—History
HG8059	368.094	Insurance, Business	HJ241-785	336.73	Finance, Public—United States
HG8075-8107	368.0065	Insurance companies	HJ285-785	336.7(4-9)	Finance, Public—[United States, By state]
HG8082	368	Self-insurance	HJ2005-2216	352.48	Budget
HG8205-8220	368.4	Insurance, Government	HJ2050-2053	352.530973	United States—Appropriations & expenditure
HG8501-8745	368.9(4-9)	Insurance—[By region or country]			
HG8501-8540	368.973	Insurance—United States			
HG8550-8740.5	368.9(4-9)	Insurance—[Other regions or countries]	HJ2240-7395	336	Taxation
HG8751-9271	368.32	Insurance, Life			
HG8779-8793	368.3200151	Insurance, Life—Mathematics			
HG8783-8785	368.3201	Mortality—Tables			
HG8790-8793	368.37	Annuities			

LC	Dewey	Subject Heading	LC	Dewey	Subject Heading
HJ2240-7395	336.02	Revenue	HJ7663-7977	336.3909(4-9)	Expenditures, Public—[Other countries]
HJ2250-2279	336.2009	Taxation—History			
HJ2321-2323	336.294	Tax incidence	HJ8001-8899	336.34	Debts, Public
HJ2326-2327	336.293	Progressive taxation	HJ8003-8899	336.34	Debts, External
HJ2336-2337	336.206	Tax exemption	HJ8052	336.363	Sinking-funds
HJ2351.4	336.20015195	Tax revenue estimating	HJ8061	336.368	State bankruptcy
HJ2361-3192.7	336.2009(4-9)	Taxation—[By region or country]	HJ8101-8899	336.3409(4-9)	Debts, Public—[By region or country]
HJ2361-2442	336.200973	Taxation—United States	HJ9103-9695	336.014	Local finance
HJ2361	336.200973	Internal revenue—United States	HJ9103	336.01405	Local finance—Periodicals
			HJ9115-9123	336.2014	Municipal revenue
HJ2391-2442	336.20097(4-9)	Taxation—[United States, By state]	HJ9141-9695	336.014(4-9)	Local finance—[By region or country]
HJ2449-3192.7	336.2009(4-9)	Taxation—[Other regions or countries]	HJ9141-9343	336.01473	Local finance—United States
HJ3241	336.2	Tax assessment	HJ9350-9695	336.014(4-9)	Local finance—[Other countries]
HJ3863-3925	336.294	Direct taxation			
HJ3925.A-.Z	336.29409(4-9)	Direct taxation—[By region or country]	HJ9701-9995	657.61	Finance, Public—Accounting
HJ4101-4936	336.22	Property tax	HM	301	Sociology
HJ4120-4460	336.2309(4-9)	Property tax—[By region or country]	HM1-7	301.05	Sociology—Periodicals
			HM13	301.06	Sociology—Congresses
HJ4581-4601	336.23	Taxation of personal property	HM17	301.03	Sociology—Dictionaries
			HM19-22	301.09	Sociology—History
HJ4621-4830	336.24	Income tax	HM24-37	301.01	Sociology—Methodology
HJ4639	336.2424	Capital gains tax	HM24	305.8001	Ethnomethodology
HJ4653.C3	336.24240973	Capital gains tax	HM33	320	Political science
HJ4653.E8	336.24320973	Excess profits tax	HM35	306.3	Economics—Sociological aspects
HJ5250-5255	336.294	Indirect taxation			
HJ5301-5508	336.16	Licenses	HM45-47	301.071	Sociology—Study and teaching
HJ5315	336.272	Revenue-stamps			
HJ5321-5510	336.1609(4-9)	Licenses—[By region or country]	HM101	909	Civilization
			HM101-121	303.4	Social change
HJ5321-5374	336.160973	Licenses—United States	HM101-121	306	Culture
HJ5711-5721	336.2713	Sales tax	HM101-121	303.44	Progress
HJ5711-5715	336.27	Turnover tax	HM104	301.09	Historical sociology
HJ5711-5715	336.2714	Value-added tax	HM121	304.5	Heredity
HJ5730-5731	336.271	Excise tax	HM131-134	307	Community life
HJ5771-5797	336.271	Luxuries—Taxation	HM131-134	305	Social groups
HJ5801-5823	336.276	Inheritance and transfer tax	HM132	302	Interpersonal relations
			HM132.5	302.34	Friendship—Sociological aspects
HJ6603-7390	352.448	Customs administration			
HJ6619	364.133	Smugglers	HM136-146	302.54	Individualism
HJ6622-7390	352.44809(4-9)	Customs administration—[By region or country]	HM141	303.34	Leadership
			HM146	305	Equality
			HM206-208	304.2	Social ecology
HJ6622-6731	352.4480973	Customs administration—United States	HM213	306.42	Intellectuals
			HM216	303.372	Social ethics
HJ6690-6710	364.1330973	Smugglers—United States	HM221	306.46	Technology—Sociological aspects
HJ6750-7390	352.44809(4-9)	Customs administration—[Other countries]			
			HM251-291	302	Social psychology
HJ7461-7977	336.39	Expenditures, Public	HM253	302.015195	Sociometry
HJ7537-7977	336.3909(4-9)	Expenditures, Public—[By region or country]	HM258	303.482	Intercultural communication
HJ7537-7654	336.390973	Expenditures, Public—United States	HM259	303.34	Social influence
			HM261	303.380723	Public opinion polls
HJ7543	336.39	Entitlement spending	HM261	303.38	Public opinion
			HM263	303.375	Propaganda

LC	Dewey	Subject Heading	LC	Dewey	Subject Heading
HM271-276	303.36	Authority	HQ71	306.877	Incest
HM281-283	302.33	Crowds	HQ74-.2	306.765	Bisexuality
HM281-283	303.623	Riots	HQ75-76.95	306.766	Homosexuality
HM281-283	302.33	Mobs	HQ75.3-.6	306.7663	Abused lesbians
HM281-283	303.64	Revolutions	HQ75.3-.6	306.7663	Lesbianism
HM281-283	303.6	Violence	HQ75.8	306.7662	Gay men
HM291	302.3	Social interaction	HQ76.5-.8	306.766	Gay liberation movement
HM291	302.4	Social interaction	HQ76.97-77.2	306.778	Transvestites
			HQ77.7-.95	305.3	Transsexualism
HN	361.1	Social problems	HQ79	306.775	Sadism
HN1	361.105	Social problems—Periodicals	HQ79	306.77	Fetishism (Sexual behavior)
HN3	361.106	Social problems—Congresses	HQ79	306.775	Sadomasochism
HN8-19	361.109	Social problems—History	HQ101-440.7	306.74	Prostitution
HN25	306	Quality of life	HQ111-117	306.7409	Prostitution—History
HN29	361.10723	Social surveys	HQ141-270.7	306.7409(4-9)	Prostitution—[By region or country]
HN29.5	360	Applied sociology			
HN30-39	261.83	Church and social problems	HQ301-440.7	362.809(4-9)	Church work with prostitutes
HN41-46	790.068	Community centers	HQ447	306.772	Masturbation
HN43-46	790.068(4-9)	Community centers—[By region or country]	HQ450-472	809.933538	Erotic literature
			HQ471-472	363.47	Pornography
HN43-45	790.06873	Community centers—United States	HQ471	363.47	Pornography—Social aspects
HN49.C6	307.14	Community development	HQ503-1064	306.81	Marriage
HN49.V64	302.14	Voluntarism	HQ503-1064	306.8	Family
HN51-90	973	United States—Social conditions	HQ503-1064	306.8	Home
			HQ503-518	306.8109	Marriage—History
			HQ531-727.9	306.8109(4-9)	Marriage—[By region or country]
HQ	306.7	Sex	HQ535-557	306.810973	Marriage—United States
HQ	306.81	Marrlage	HQ559-560	306.810971	Marriage—Canada
HQ	306.85	Family	HQ561-562	306.810972	Marriage—Mexico
HQ12-449	306.7	Sex	HQ563-574	306.8109728	Marriage—Central America
HQ12-18	306.73	Sex customs			
HQ19-30.7	306.7	Sexual instinct	HQ575-587.9	306.8109729	Marriage—West Indies
HQ27-.5	306.70835	Young adults—Sexual behavior	HQ588-610	306.81098	Marriage—South America
			HQ611-662.7	306.81094	Marriage—Europe
HQ27	306.7088375	Students—Sexual behavior	HQ613-618.5	306.810941	Marriage—Great Britain
			HQ623-624	306.810944	Marriage—France
HQ29	306.7082	Women—Sexual behavior	HQ625-626.5	306.810943	Marriage—Germany
HQ30	306.70846	Aged—Sexual behavior	HQ629-630	306.810945	Marriage—Italy
HQ30.5	306.70816	Handicapped—Sexual behavior	HQ631-636.5	306.8109492	Marriage—Benelux Countries
HQ31-64	176	Sexual ethics	HQ637-638	306.810947	Marriage—Russia
HQ35	176.0835	Sexual ethics for teenagers	HQ649-650	306.810946	Marriage—Spain
			HQ653-654	306.8109494	Marriage—Switzerland
HQ46	176.082	Sexual ethics for women	HQ662.5	306.8109495	Marriage—Greece
HQ51	613.9071	Sex instruction for girls	HQ663-690.5	306.81095	Marriage—Asia
alphaHQ53	613.9071	Sex instruction for children	HQ664	306.81095694	Marriage—Israel
HQ41	613.9071	Sex instruction for boys	HQ666.3	306.8109567	Marriage—Iraq
HQ54-.4	613.9071	Sex instruction for the handicapped	HQ666.4	306.810955	Marriage—Iran
			HQ669-670	306.810954	Marriage—India
HQ55	613.9071	Sex instruction for the aged	HQ679-680	306.8109599	Marriage—Philippines
			HQ681-682	306.810952	Marriage—Japan
HQ56-59	613.9071	Sex instruction	HQ684	306.810951	Marriage—China
HQ60	613.9072	Sexology—Research	HQ691-697.4	306.81096	Marriage—Africa
HQ71-72	364.153	Sex offenders	HQ705-706	306.810994	Marriage—Australia
HQ71-72	364.153	Sex crimes	HQ734	306.85	Family

LC	Dewey	Subject Heading	LC	Dewey	Subject Heading
HQ745	392.5	Marriage service	HQ799	305.23509(4-9)	Youth—[By region or country]
HQ750-755.5	363.92	Eugenics	HQ799.15	306.874	Parent and teenager
HQ755.7-759.92	306.874	Parenting	HQ799.5-.9	305.235	Young adults
HQ755.7-759.92	306.874	Parenthood	HQ799.95-.97	305.24	Adulthood
HQ755.85	306.874	Abused parents	HQ800-.4	306.815	Single people
HQ755.86	306.874084	Parent and adult child	HQ800.15	306.732	Celibacy
HQ756-.7	306.8742	Fatherhood	HQ800.2	306.8153	Single women
HQ756-.7	306.8742	Fathers	HQ800.3	305.8152	Bachelors
HQ756	306.874208653	Divorced fathers	HQ801-.83	306.7	Man-woman relationships
HQ756	306.8742	Stepfathers	HQ801.8	306.73	Interracial dating
HQ756.6	640.92	Househusbands	HQ801.83	306.73	Dating violence
HQ759-.6	306.8743	Motherhood	HQ803	306.84	Temporary marriage
HQ759-.6	306.8743	Mothers	HQ803	306.84	Marriage, Companionate
HQ759.2	394.2628	Mother's Day	HQ805	306.88	Desertion and non-support
HQ759.3	306.8743	Absentee mothers	HQ806	306.736	Adultery
HQ759.4	306.87430835	Teenage mothers	HQ811-960.7	306.89	Divorce
HQ759.48	306.8743	Working mothers	HQ831-960.7	306.8809(4-9)	Divorce—[By region or country]
HQ759.5	306.8743	Surrogate mothers	HQ833-836	306.880973	Desertion—United States
HQ759.64	306.8740835	Teenage parents	HQ837-960.9	306.8809(4-9)	Desertion—[Other countries]
HQ759.9	306.8745	Grandparenting	HQ961-967	306.73	Free love
HQ759.912	306.874087	Handicapped parents	HQ970-975.7	307.774	Communal living
HQ759.913	306.8740879	Parents of exceptional children	HQ981-996	306.842	Group marriage
HQ759.913	306.874087	Parents of handicapped children	HQ981-996	306.8423	Polygamy
			HQ998-999	306.874	Illegitimacy
HQ759.98	304.63	Family demography	HQ1017	392.4	Dowry
HQ760-767.7	304.63	Family size	HQ1018-1019	306.84	Remarriage
HQ762	304.6309(1-9)	Family size—[By region or country]	HQ1028	306.84	Marriage with deceased wife's sister
HQ763-767.52	304.666	Birth control	HQ1031	306.843	Interfaith marriage
HQ766.2-.4	363.96	Birth control—Moral and ethical aspects	HQ1031	306.846	Interracial marriage
HQ767-.52	363.46	Abortion	HQ1036-1043	306.81087	Handicapped—Marriage
HQ767.8-792.2	305.23	Children	HQ1040	306.810872	Deaf—Marriage
HQ767.87	305.2309	Children—History	HQ1058-.5	306.882	Widowers
HQ768-777.95	649.1	Child rearing	HQ1058-.5	306.883	Widows
HQ769.5	649.10248	Babysitting	HQ1059.4-.5	305.244	Middle age
HQ770.4	364.67	Corporal punishment	HQ1060-1064	305.26091734	Rural aged
HQ770.4	649.64	Discipline of children	HQ1060-1064	305.26	Aged
HQ773.5	649.155	Gifted children	HQ1073-.5	306.9	Thanatology
HQ773.65	599.949083	Dwarf children	HQ1073-.5	306.9	Death
HQ774	305.232	Infants	HQ1075-.5	305.3	Sex role
HQ774	305.232	Infants—Development	HQ1088-1090.7	305.31	Men's studies
HQ774.5	305.233	Preschool children	HQ1101-2030.7	305.4	Women
HQ774.5	305.232	Toddlers	HQ1121-1870.5	305.42	Women—Social conditions
HQ775	649.132	Boys			
HQ777.2	306.87	First-born children	HQ1121-1172	305.409	Women—History
HQ777.22	306.87	Second-born children	HQ1139	305.409	Amazons
HQ777.9	306.843083	Children of interracial marriage	HQ1170	305.486971	Muslim women
HQ778.5-.7	362.712	Day care centers	HQ1172	305.48696	Jewish women
HQ778.5-.7	649.1	Child care	HQ1180-1186	305.407	Women's studies
HQ778.6	305.234	School-age child care	HQ1190	305.42	Feminist theory
HQ779-.5	305.232	Baby books	HQ1201-1216	302.32082	Women—Socialization
HQ783	303.32	Socialization	HQ1206-1216	155.633	Women—Psychology
HQ784.F7	302.34083	Friendship in children	HQ1229	155.533	Young women—Psychology
HQ784.S45	306.7083	Children—Sexual behavior			
HQ793-799.9	305.235	Youth	HQ1236-.5	323.34	Women's rights
HQ798	305.235	Teenage girls			

LC	Dewey	Subject Heading	LC	Dewey	Subject Heading
HQ1400-1870.5	305.409(4-9)	Women—[By region or country]	HS2321-2330	369.1	Patriotic societies—United States
HQ1402-1439	305.40973	Women—United States	HS2501-3371	367	Clubs
HQ1871-2030.7	367.082	Women—Societies and clubs	HS2501-2503	367.05	Clubs—Periodicals
			HS2507-2515	367.025	Clubs—Directories
HS	366	Societies	HS2721-3200	367.9(4-9)	Clubs—[By region or country]
HS1	366.005	Societies—Periodicals	HS2721-2725	367.973	Clubs—United States
HS5	366.006	Societies—Congresses	HS2731-3200	367.9(4-9)	Clubs—[Other regions or countries]
HS12	366.003	Societies—Encyclopedias			
HS17	366.0025	Societies—Directories	HS3250-3270	367.4	Youth—Societies and clubs
HS25-35	366.009	Societies—History, organization, etc.	HS3301-3325	369.42	Boys—Societies and clubs
HS101-330.7	366.(1-5)	Secret societies	HS3312-3316	369.43	Boy Scouts
HS101-106	366.(1-5)05	Secret societies—Periodicals	HS3353.G5	369.463	Girl Scouts
			HS3359	369.463	Daisy Girl Scouts
HS110	366.(1-5)06	Secret societies—Congresses			
			HT	307	Communities
HS121-123	366.(1-5)03	Secret societies—Directories	HT	305.5	Social classes
			HT	305.8	Race
HS125-148	366.(1-5)09	Secret societies—History	HT51-65	307	Human settlements
HS155-158	366.(1-5)	Secret societies—Rituals	HT101-395	307	Cities and towns
HS159-160	366.6027	Insignia	HT101-395	307.76	Sociology, Urban
HS201-330.7	366.(1-5)09 (4-9)	Secret societies—[By region or country]	HT110	307.76072	Sociology, Urban—Research
HS203-206	366.(1-5)0973	Secret societies—United States	HT111-150	307.7609	Sociology, Urban—History
			HT114	307.76093	Cities and towns, Ancient
HS207-330.7	366.(1-5)09 (4-9)	Secret societies—[Other countries]	HT115	307.760902	Cities and towns, Medieval
			HT123-.5	307.760973	Sociology, Urban—United States
HS351-929	366.1	Freemasons			
HS351-929	366.1	Freemasonry	HT127	307.760971	Sociology, Urban—Canada
HS351-359	366.105	Freemasons—Periodicals	HT127.7	307.760972	Sociology, Urban—Mexico
HS381-390	366.1025	Freemasons—Directories	HT128	307.7609728	Sociology, Urban—Central America
HS403-420	366.109	Freemasons—History			
HS455-459	366.12	Freemasonry—Rituals	HT129	307.76098	Sociology, Urban—South America
HS501-680.7	366.109(4-9)	Freemasons—[By region or country]	HT131-145	307.76094	Sociology, Urban—Europe
HS503-539	366.10973	Freemasons—United States	HT133	307.760941	Sociology, Urban—Great Britain
HS557-680.7	366.109(4-9)	Freemasons—[Other countries]	HT135	307.760944	Sociology, Urban—France
			HT137	307.760943	Sociology, Urban—Germany
HS875-895	366.108996073	Afro-American freemasonry	HT147	307.76095	Sociology, Urban—Asia
HS951-1179	366.3	Independent Order of Odd Fellows	HT148	307.76096	Sociology, Urban—Africa
			HT149	307.760994	Sociology, Urban—Australia
HS951-953	366.305	Independent Order of Odd Fellows—eriodicals	HT149.5	307.76091724	Sociology, Urban—Developing countries
HS963-975	366.3025	Independent Order of Odd Fellows—Directories			
HS987-991	366.309	Independent Order of Odd Fellows—History	HT156	307.76	Inner cities
			HT161-165	307.76	Garden cities
HS1019-1021	366.3	Independent Order of Odd Fellows—Rituals	HT165.5-169.5	307.1216	City planning
HS1041-1051	366.309(4-9)	Independent Order of Odd Fellows—[By region or country]	HT167-169.54	307.121609 (4-9)	City planning—[By region or country]
HS1041-1045	366.30973	Independent Order of Odd Fellows—United States	HT167-168	307.12160973	City planning—United States
			HT169.55-.57	307.768	Planned communities
HS1501-1510	334.7	Friendly societies	HT169.55-.57	307.768	New towns
HS2301-2460.7	369	Patriotic societies	HT169.6-.9	333.7717	Zoning
			HT170-178	307.3416	Urban renewal

LC	Dewey	Subject Heading	LC	Dewey	Subject Heading
HT175-177	307.34160973	Urban renewal—United States	HT1276	306.3620952	Slavery—Japan
HT178	307.341609 (4-9)	Urban renewal—[Other countries]	HT1321-1427	306.362096	Slavery—Africa
			HT1431	306.3620994	Slavery—Australia
HT206	305.23091732	City children	HT1501-1595	305.8	Race
HT241-243	577.56	Urban ecology	HT1501-1595	305.8	Race relations
HT321-325	330.91732	Urban economics	HT1507	305.8009	Race relations—History
HT351-352	307.74	Suburban life	HT1575-1577	305.8034	Caucasian race
HT381	307.26	Urban-rural migration			
HT392-395	307.1209(4-9)	Regional planning—[By region or country]	HV	361.6	Public welfare
			HV	364	Criminology
HT392-394	307.120973	Regional planning—United States	HV1-4959	361.7	Charities
			HV1-4630	362.5	Poverty
HT401-485	307.72	Sociology, Rural	HV1-696	361	Social service
HT415	307.72090(1-5)	Sociology, Rural—History	HV6	361.006	Social service—Societies, etc.
HT421	305.963	Farm life			
HT601-1444	305.5	Social classes	HV7	361.025	Social service—Directories
HT607	305.509	Social classes—History	HV10.5	361.3023	Social service—Vocational guidance
HT608	305.5072	Social classes—Research			
HT647-653	305.52	Aristocracy (Social class)	HV11-.8	361.3071	Social work education
HT647-653	305.522	Nobility	HV16-25	361.709	Social service—History
HT657	305.5232	Gentry	HV40-69	361.7	Charity organization
HT680-690	305.55	Middle class	HV40.54	361.3092	Social workers—Supervision of
HT690	305.5509(4-9)	Middle class—[By region or country]	HV41.2-.9	361.70681	Fund raising
			HV45	361.4	Social group work
HT713-725	305.5122	Caste	HV59-63	361.05	Institutional care
HT751-815	306.365	Serfdom	HV61	362.585	Almshouses
HT781-815	306.36509(4-9)	Serfdom—[By region or country]	HV67	361.91734	Social service, Rural
			HV85-520.5	361.9(4-9)	Social service—[By region or country]
HT781	306.3650941	Serfdom—Great Britain			
HT785	306.3650944	Serfdom—France	HV85-99	361.973	Social service—United States
HT791-801	306.3650943	Serfdom—Germany			
HT803	306.36509436	Serfdom—Austria	HV98-99	361.97(4-9)	Social service—[United States, By state or city]
HT807-809	306.3650947	Serfdom—Russia			
HT851-1444	306.362	Slavery	HV101-520.5	361.9(4-9)	Social service—[Other countries]
HT863-867	306.362090 (1-5)	Slavery—History			
			HV530	361.75	Church charities
HT910-921	261.8	Slavery and the church	HV544	361.7	Bazaars (Charities)
HT975-1445	381.44	Slave-trade	HV547	361.4	Self-help groups
HT1025-1037	326.8	Slaves—Emancipation	HV551.2-639	363.34068	Emergency management
HT1051-1052	306.3620971	Slavery—Canada	HV553-639	363.348	Disaster relief
HT1053-1054	306.3620972	Slavery—Mexico	HV555	363.34809(4-9)	Disaster relief—[By region or country]
HT1055-1056	306.36209728	Slavery—Central America			
HT1071-1119	306.36209729	Slavery—West Indies	HV560-583	361.77	Red Cross
HT1121-1152	306.362098	Slavery—South America	HV575-580	361.7709(4-9)	Red Cross—[By region or country]
HT1155-1240	306.362094	Slavery—Europe			
HT1161-1165	306.3620941	Slavery—Great Britain	HV599-600	363.3495	Earthquakes
HT1176-1180	306.3620944	Slavery—France	HV609-610	363.34938	Floods
HT1181	306.3620943	Slavery—Germany	HV620	363.37	Fires
HT1191-1194	306.3620945	Slavery—Italy	HV625-626	363.34929	Droughts
HT1196-1203	306.36209492	Slavery—Benelux countries	HV630-635	363.8	Famines
			HV635.5-636	363.3492	Storms
HT1206-1209	306.3620947	Slavery—Russia	HV639	363.34988	War relief
HT1216-1220	306.3620946	Slavery—Spain	HV640-.5	362.87	Refugees
HT1227-1228	306.36209494	Slavery—Switzerland	HV640-.5	362.87	Refugees, Political
HT1234	306.36209495	Slavery—Greece	HV675-677	363.107	Accidents—Prevention
HT1240.5-1315	306.362095	Slavery—Asia	HV687-694	361.7	Charities, Medical
HT1241-1244	306.3620951	Slavery—China	HV687-694	362.1	Sick
HT1271	306.36209599	Slavery—Philippines	HV687-688	362.10425	Medical social work

LC	Dewey	Subject Heading	LC	Dewey	Subject Heading
HV689-690	362.20425	Psychiatric social work	HV1551-3024	362.(3-4)	Handicapped
HV694	363.883	Diet kitchens	HV1568.2-.25	362.4072	Disability studies
HV696.F6	363.883	Food relief	HV1568.7-.8	362.48	Day care centers for the
HV696.F6	363.882	Food stamps			handicapped
HV697-700	362.713	Aid to families with	HV1570-.5	362.1968	Developmentally disabled
		dependent children	HV1571-2349	362.41	Blind
HV697-700	362.83	Maternal and infant	HV1597-.2	362.41	Blind-deaf—Services for
		welfare	HV1597.5	362.6	Blind aged
HV697-700.5	362.8292	Abused wives—Services	HV1618-1782	371.911	Blind—Education
		for	HV1631.5	362.418	Visually
HV699-700	362.829209	Abused wives—Services			handicapped—Means of
	(4-9)	for—[By region or country]			communication
HV700.5	362.8394	Unmarried mothers	HV1652-1658	331.1250871	Blind—Employment
HV700.7	362.8294	Unmarried fathers	HV1701	362.418	Blind, Apparatus for the
HV701-1420.5	362.7	Child welfare	HV1780-.6	362.418071	Guide dog schools
HV701	362.705	Child welfare—Periodicals	HV1783-2220.5	362.4109(4-9)	Blind—[By region or
HV741-804	362.709(4-9)	Child welfare—[By region			country]
		or country]	HV1783-1796	362.410973	Blind—United States
HV741-743	362.70973	Child welfare—United	HV1801-2220.5	362.4109(4-9)	Blind—[Other regions or
		States			places]
HV745-804	362.709(4-9)	Child welfare—[Other	HV2350-2990.5	362.42	Deaf
		countries]	HV2350-2990.5	362.42	Hearing impaired
HV835-847	362.73	Foundlings	HV2402	362.4283	Interpreters for the deaf
HV862-866	362.732	Group homes for children	HV2417-2500	371.912	Deaf—Education
HV868	363.83	Milk programs	HV2477-2480	419	Finger spelling
HV873-887	362.70869	Street children	HV2503	362.4283	Video recordings for the
HV873-875.7	362.73	Abandoned children			hearing impaired
HV874.8-875.7	362.734	Adoption	HV2510-2990.5	362.4209(4-9)	Deaf—[By region or
HV875.5	362.734	Intercountry adoption			country]
HV877-878	369.42	Boys	HV2510-2561	362.420973	Deaf—United States
HV878	369.42	Boys—Societies and clubs	HV3004-3009	362.3	Mental retardation
HV879-887	369.46	Girls	HV3004-3008	362.385	Mental retardation
HV880-887	362.7309(4-9)	Abandoned children—[By			facilities
		region or country]	HV3006-3008	362.30973	Mentally handicapped—
HV880-885	362.730973	Abandoned			[By region or country]
		children—United States	HV3011-3024	362.48	Physically handicapped—
HV888-907	362.(3-4)	Handicapped			Services for
		children—Services for	HV3023-3024	362.4809(4-9)	Physically handicapped—
HV891-901	362.1968	Developmentally disabled			[By region or country]
		children	HV3023	362.480973	Physically handicapped—
HV903-907	362.4083	Disfigured children			United States
HV959-1420.5	362.732	Orphanages	HV3024	362.4809(4-9)	Physically handicapped—
HV959-1420.5	362.73	Orphans			[Other countries]
HV971-1420.5	362.73209(4-9)	Orphanages—[By region	HV3025-3163	362.858	Sailors—Services for
		or country]	HV3181-3185	362.8496073	Afro-Americans—Services
HV971-995	362.7320973	Orphanages—United			for
		States	HV4023-4170.7	307.3364	Slums
HV1423	362.7083	Young men	HV4023-4470.7	362.5091732	Urban poor
HV1425	362.7083	Young women	HV4023-4470.7	362.5	Poor
HV1442-1448	362.83	Women—Services for	HV4041-4173	362.509(4-9)	Poor—[By region or
HV1449	361.308664	Social work with gays			country]
HV1450-1494	362.6091734	Rural aged	HV4043-4046	362.50973	Poor—United States
HV1450-1494	362.6	Aged	HV4047-4050	362.50971	Poor—Canada
HV1450-1493	362.6	Old age	HV4051	362.50972	Poor—Mexico
HV1454-.2	362.16	Old age homes	HV4053-4059	362.509728	Poor—Central America
HV1455-.2	362.68	Day care centers for the	HV4060-4065.9	362.509729	Poor—West Indies
		aged	HV4066-4083	362.5098	Poor—South America
HV1457-1494	362.609(4-9)	Aged—[By region or	HV4084-4131.84	362.5094	Poor—Europe
		country]	HV4085-4087.5	362.50941	Poor—Great Britain

LC	Dewey	Subject Heading	LC	Dewey	Subject Heading
HV4093-4096	362.50944	Poor—France	HV5800-5840	362.29(3-8)	Drug abuse
HV4097-4100.5	362.50943	Poor—Germany	HV5800-5840	362.29(3-8)7	Drug abuse—Prevention
HV4102-4105	362.50945	Poor—Italy	HV5800-5840	362.293	Narcotic habit
HV4105.5-4113.5	362.509492	Poor—Benelux countries	HV5810	362.298	Cocaine habit
HV4114-4117	362.50947	Poor—Russia	HV5810	362.298	Crack (Drug)
HV4125-4128	362.50946	Poor—Spain	HV5813	362.293	Morphine habit
HV4131.85-4156.5	362.5095	Poor—Asia	HV5816	362.293	Opium habit
HV4137-4140	362.50954	Poor—India	HV5822.G5	362.299	Glue-sniffing
HV4147	362.50952	Poor—Japan	HV5822.H4	362.293	Heroin
HV4150	362.50951	Poor—China	HV5822.M3	362.295	Marihuana
HV4157-4169.3	362.5096	Poor—Africa	HV5822.5.L9	362.294	LSD (Drug)
HV4170	362.50994	Poor—Australia	HV5823-.5	362.29363	Drug testing
HV4173	362.5091724	Poor—Developing countries	HV5825-5840	362.29(3-8) 09 + (4-9)	Drug abuse—[By region or country]
HV4330-4470.7	287.96	Salvation Army	HV5825-5833	362.29(3-8) + 0973	Drug abuse—United States
HV4480-4630.7	364.148	Vagrancy			
HV4480-4630	362.5	Tramps	HV5840	362.29(3-8) 09 + (4-9)	Drug abuse—[Other countries]
HV4701-4959	636.0832	Animal welfare			
HV4701-4890.7	179.3	Animal rights	HV6001-7220.5	364	Criminology
HV4746	636.0832	Dog rescue	HV6001-7220.5	364	Crime
HV4749-4755	364.187	Horses	HV6001-7220.5	364.3	Criminals
HV4905-4959	590.724	Animal experimentation	HV6001-6197	364.2	Criminal anthropology
HV4975-4977	362.2	Insanity	HV6001-6006	364.05	Criminology—Periodicals
HV4997-5840	362.29	Substance abuse	HV6021-6023	364.09	Criminology—History
HV4999.2-5000	362.2909(4-9)	Substance abuse—[By region or country]	HV6024	364.071	Criminology—Study and teaching
HV4999.C45	362.290834	School children—Substance use	HV6024.5	364.072	Criminology—Research
			HV6047	364.24	Criminal behavior—Genetic aspects
HV4999.Y68	362.29083	Youth—Substance use			
HV5001-5722	362.292	Alcoholism	HV6049	364.3	Recidivism
HV5001-5720	362.2926	Temperance	HV6053	364.1	Crimes of passion
HV5001-5002	362.29205	Alcoholism—Periodicals	HV6065-6079	363.258	Criminals—Identification
HV5006	362.292606	Temperance—Societies, etc.	HV6071	363.24	Legal photography
			HV6074	363.24	Fingerprints
HV5020-5025	362.292609	Temperance—History	HV6080-6113	364.3	Criminal psychology
HV5045	616.8610019	Alcoholism—Psychological aspects	HV6089	155.962	Prison psychology
			HV6121-6125	364.24	Heredity
HV5053-5055	362.292	Alcoholism and crime	HV6133	364.24	Insane, Criminal and dangerous
HV5132	362.2923	Children of alcoholics			
HV5132	362.2923	Alcoholics' spouses	HV6163	364.24	Crime and age
HV5132	362.2923	Alcoholics—Family relationships	HV6166	364.25	Education and crime
			HV6166	364.25	Reading disability and crime
HV5132	362.2923	Adult children of alcoholics			
			HV6174	364.256	Begging
HV5275-5283	362.29286	Alcoholism counseling	HV6177	364.22	Cities and towns
HV5285-5722	362.29209(4-9)	Alcoholism—[By region or country]	HV6189	364.2	War and crime
			HV6250-.4	362.88	Victims of crimes
HV5285-5298	362.2920973	Alcoholism—United States	HV6250	362.880723	Victims of crimes surveys
HV5301-5722	362.29209(4-9)	Alcoholism—[Other countries]	HV6250.4.A34	362.880846	Aged—Crimes against
			HV6250.4.E75	362.88089960 + 73	Afro-Americans—Crimes against
HV5725-5770	362.296	Smoking			
HV5725-5770	362.296	Ex-smokers	HV6250.4.S78	362.88088375	Students—Crimes against
HV5725-5770	362.296	Tobacco habit	HV6250.4.W65	362.88082	Women—Crimes against
HV5740-5745	362.296	Cigarette habit	HV6250.4.Y68	362.88083	Youth—Crimes against
HV5755-5770	362.29609(4-9)	Smoking—[By region or country]	HV6252	364.135	Transnational crime
			HV6254-6322.7	364.131	Political crimes and offenses
HV5755-5768	362.2960973	Smoking—United States			
HV5770	362.29609(4-9)	Smoking—[Other countries]	HV6275	364.1	Conspiracies
			HV6275	364.131	Treason

LC	Dewey	Subject Heading	LC	Dewey	Subject Heading
HV6278	364.1524	Assassination	HV6631	364.156	Libel and slander
HV6285	364.131	Sedition	HV6635-6700	364.16	Offenses against property
HV6301-6321	364.1323	Bribery	HV6638-.5	364.164	Arson
HV6303-6321	364.132309(4-9)	Bribery—[By region or country]	HV6638.5	364.16409(4-9)	Arson—[By region or country]
HV6306-6316	364.13230973	Bribery—United States	HV6640	364.164	Bombings
HV6322-.7	362.87	Disappeared persons	HV6646-6665	364.162	Burglary
HV6322.7	364.151	Genocide	HV6646-6665	364.1552	Cattle stealing
HV6326	364.134	Perjury	HV6646-6665	364.1552	Mugging
HV6419-6433	364.142	Offenses against public safety	HV6653	364.162	Thieves
			HV6666-6669	364.164	Vandalism
HV6422-6425	364.147	Traffic violations	HV6675-6685	364.163	Forgery
HV6430.B55	303.62509538	Terrorists—Saudi Arabia—Biography	HV6675-6685	364.162	Embezzlement
HV6431	363.32	Terrorism—Prevention	HV6679	364.1630973	Identification cards—Forgeries—United States
HV6432	303.625073	Nuclear terrorism—United States	HV6688	364.165	Extortion
HV6432	303.6250973	Terrorism—United States—Prevention	HV6691-6699	364.163	Fraud
			HV6705-6738	364.1	Crimes without victims
HV6432	364.154092273	Victims of terrorism—United States—Biography	HV6708-6722	364.172	Gambling
HV6432.7	973.931	September 11 Terrorist Attacks, 2001	HV6711	364.17206	Casinos
			HV6763-6771	364.168	Corporations—Corrupt practices
HV6432.7	363.320973	War on Terrorism, 2001-	HV6763-6771	364.168	Insurance crimes
HV6335.C	323.0440951	Red Brigades	HV6763-6771	364.168	Securities theft
HV6437-6439	364.106	Gangs	HV6763-6771	364.168	Securities fraud
HV6441-6453	364.1552	Brigands and robbers	HV6772-6773.3	364.168	Computer crimes
HV6441-6453	364.106	Mafia	HV6774-7220.5	364.309(4-9)	Criminals—[By region or country]
HV6441-6453	364.3	Outlaws			
HV6441-6453	364.256	Vendetta	HV6774-6795	364.30973	Criminals—United States
HV6448	364.10660973	Black Hand (United States)	HV6801-7220.5	364.309(4-9)	Criminals—[Other countries]
HV6455-6471	364.134	Lynching	HV7231-9960	345.05	Criminal Justice, Administration of
HV6474-6485	364.143	Riots	HV7231-9960	364.6	Punishment
HV6474-6485	364.143	Mobs	HV7245-7400	364.09(4-9)021	Criminal statistics—[By region or country]
HV6486-6491	364.143	Disorderly conduct			
HV6493-6633	364.15	Offenses against the person	HV7245-7300	364.0973021	Criminal statistics—United States
HV6499-6535	364.1524	Assassination	HV7250-7300	364.097(4-9) + 021	Criminal statistics—[United States, By state]
HV6499-6542	364.1523	Murder			
HV6518-6535	364.152309 (4-9)	Murder—[By region or country]	HV7315	364.0971021	Criminal statistics—Canada
HV6518-6534	364.15230973	Murder—United States	HV7316	364.0972021	Criminal statistics—Mexico
HV6535	364.152309 (4-9)	Murder—[Other regions or countries]	HV7317-7323	364.09728021	Criminal statistics—Central America
HV6537-6541	364.1523	Infanticide	HV7324-7329.9	364.09729021	Criminal statistics—West Indies
HV6543-6548	364.1522	Suicide			
HV6547	364.1522	Mass suicide	HV7330-7341	364.098021	Criminal statistics—South America
HV6549-6555	364.1791	Poisoning			
HV6558-6569	364.1532	Gang rape	HV7342-7367.7	364.094021	Criminal statistics—Europe
HV6558-6569	364.1532	Rape			
HV6558-6569	364.153	Sex crimes	HV7343-7345.5	364.0941021	Criminal statistics—Great Britain
HV6571-6574	364.154	Abduction			
HV6584-6589	364.153	Seduction	HV7348	364.0944021	Criminal statistics—France
HV6595-6604	364.154	Kidnapping	HV7349-.5	364.0943021	Criminal statistics—Germany
HV6618	364.1555	Assault and battery			
HV6626-.23	364.1555(3-4)	Family violence	HV7351	364.0945021	Criminal statistics—Italy
HV6626-.23	364.15553	Wife abuse	HV7355	364.0947021	Criminal statistics—Russia
HV6626.5-.54	364.15554	Child abuse			

LC	Dewey	Subject Heading	LC	Dewey	Subject Heading
HV7361	364.0946021	Criminal statistics—Spain	HV8079.C48	363.2595554	Child sexual abuse—Investigation
HV7368-7381	364.0995021	Criminal statistics—Asia			
HV7371	364.0954021	Criminal statistics—India	HV8079.C65	363.25968	Computer crimes—Investigation
HV7377	364.0952021	Criminal statistics—Japan			
HV7378	364.0951021	Criminal statistics—China	HV8079.D76	363.25947	Drunk driving—Investigation
HV7382-7388.4	364.096021	Criminal statistics—Africa			
HV7389	364.0994021	Criminal statistics—Australia	HV8079.F7	363.25963	Fraud investigation
			HV8079.N3	363.25977	Drug traffic—Investigation
HV7428	361.3	Social work with criminals	HV8079.O73	363.25906	Organized crime investigation
HV7431	364.4	Crime prevention			
HV7435-7439	363.33	Gun control	HV8079.R35	363.259532	Rape—Investigation
HV7551-8280.7	363.2	Police	HV8079.R62	363.259552	Robbery investigation
HV7551-8077	363.25092	Detectives	HV8079.S48	363.25953	Sex crimes—Investigation
HV7900	363.2025	Police—Directories	HV8079.S67	363.2595553	Wife abuse—Investigation
HV7903-7909	363.209	Police—History	HV8079.W47	363.25968	White collar crime investigation
HV7923	363.2071	Police—Study and teaching			
			HV8080.A6	363.232	Arrest (Police methods)
HV7935-8025	353.36	Police administration	HV8080.D54	363.22	Police divers
HV7936.C58	364.4	Crime stoppers programs	HV8080.P2	363.232	Police patrol—Field interrogation
HV7936.C8	363.24	Police communication systems			
			HV8080.P2	363.232	Police patrol—Surveillance operations
HV7936.C88	363.256	Crime analysis			
HV7936.D78	363.2	Police—Drug testing	HV8081-8099	363.289	Private investigators
HV7936.E7	363.20284	Handcuffs	HV8130-8280.7	363.209(4-9)	Police—[By region or country]
HV7936.E7	363.20284	Riot helmets			
HV7936.E7	363.20284	Nonlethal weapons	HV8130-8148	363.20973	Police—United States
HV7936.E7	363.20284	Tear gas munitions	HV8157-8160	363.20971	Police—Canada
HV7936.E7	363.20284	Truncheons	HV8161	363.20972	Police—Mexico
HV7936.E85	363.24	Evidence preservation	HV8163-8169	363.209728	Police—Central America
HV7936.J63	363.22019	Police—Job stress	HV8170-8175.9	363.209729	Police—West Indies
HV7936.P75	363.22	Police psychiatrists	HV8176-8193	363.2098	Police—South America
HV7936.P75	363.22	Police psychologists	HV8194-8261.84	363.2094	Police—Europe
HV7936.R53	363.24	Police reports	HV8195-8197.5	363.20941	Police—Great Britain
HV7961	363.283	Secret service	HV8203-8206	363.20944	Police—France
HV7965-7985	363.2091734	Police, Rural	HV8207-8210	363.20943	Police—Germany
HV7981	363.2	Constables	HV8212-8215	363.20945	Police—Italy
HV8012	363.22	Police chiefs	HV8215.5-8223.5	363.209492	Police—Benelux countries
HV8023	363.22082	Policewomen	HV8224-8227	363.20947	Police—Russia
HV8025	636.70886	Police dogs	HV8235-8238	363.20946	Police—Spain
HV8059	683.4	Firearms ownership	HV8239	363.209469	Police—Portugal
HV8067	364	Vice control	HV8241.83	363.209495	Police—Greece
HV8073-8079.3	363.25	Criminal investigation	HV8241.85-8263	363.2095	Police—Asia
HV8073-8077.5	363.25	Chemistry, Forensic	HV8241.9-8242.56	363.20956	Police—Middle East
HV8073-.8	363.258	Identification	HV8247-8250	363.20954	Police—India
HV8073.4	363.258	Police artists	HV8255	363.209599	Police—Philippines
HV8074-8076	363.2565	Writing—Identification	HV8257	363.20952	Police—Japan
HV8077	363.2562	Forensic ballistics	HV8260	363.20951	Police—China
HV8077	363.2565	Firearms—Identification	HV8267-8279.3	363.2096	Police—Africa
HV8077.5.F6	363.2562	Footprints	HV8280	363.20994	Police—Australia
HV8078-.5	363.254	Lie detectors and detection	HV8290-8291	363.289	Police, Private
			HV8290-8291	363.289	Campus police
HV8078	363.254092	Polygraph operators	HV8290-8291	363.289	Private security services
HV8079.2-.3	363.22	Police social work	HV8290-8291	363.289	Watchmen
HV8079.5-.55	363.2332	Traffic police	HV8301-9960	365	Prisons
HV8079.5	363.23320284	Radar in speed limit enforcement	HV8482-8488	365.021	Prisons—Statistics
			HV8497-8654	365.09	Prisons—History
HV8079.A98	363.25962	Automobile theft investigation	HV8551-8586	364.66	Executions and executioners
HV8079.C46	363.2595554	Child abuse—Investigation	HV8552-8555	364.66	Beheading

LC	Dewey	Subject Heading	LC	Dewey	Subject Heading
HV8555	364.66	Guillotine	HV9511-9515	365.972	Prisons—Mexico
HV8569	364.66	Crucifixion	HV9516-9550	365.9728	Prisons—Central America
HV8579-8581	364.66	Hanging	HV9551-9575.95	365.9729	Prisons—West Indies
HV8593-8599	364.67	Torture	HV9576-9635	365.98	Prisons—South America
HV8609	364.67	Branding (Punishment)	HV9636-9775.7	365.94	Prisons—Europe
HV8609-8621	364.67	Corporal punishment	HV9641-9650	365.941	Prisons—Great Britain
HV8613-8621	364.67	Flagellation	HV9661-9670	365.944	Prisons—France
HV8647-8649	365.3	Galleys	HV9671-9680.5	365.943	Prisons—Germany
HV8652-8654	323.631	Asylum, Right of	HV9686-9695	365.945	Prisons—Italy
HV8657-8658	365.641	Escapes	HV9696-9710.5	365.9492	Prisons—Benelux
HV8692	364.65	Pardon			countries
HV8696	364.66	Electrocution	HV9711-9715	365.947	Prisons—Russia
HV8705-8749	365	Imprisonment	HV9715.15	364.130947	Prisoners—Russia
HV8708-8719	365	Prison sentences			(Federation)
HV8738	365.34082	Reformatories for women	HV9715.7	365.9438	Prisons—Social
HV8748-8749	365.34	Workhouses			aspects—Poland
HV8756-8763	365.068	Prison administration	HV9741-9745	365.946	Prisons—Spain
HV8766-8778	365.643	Prison discipline	HV9776-831	365.9495	Prisons—Greece
HV8833-8844	365.66	Prison physicians	HV9776.5-9785.2	365.956	Prisons—Middle East
HV8833-8844	365.66	Prison nurses	HV9791-9795	365.954	Prisons—India
HV8884	365.6	Prison visits	HV9806-9810	365.9599	Prisons—Philippines
HV8888-8931	365.65	Convict labor	HV9811-9815	365.952	Prisons—Japan
HV8888-8931	365.65	Prison industries	HV9816-9820	365.951	Prisons—China
HV8935-8962	365.64	Prisoners, Transportation	HV9836-9868.5	365.96	Prisons—Africa
		of	HV9871-9875	365.994	Prisons—Australia
HV8935-8962	365.34	Penal colonies	HV9950-9960	345 0509(4-9)	Criminal justice,
HV8971-8978	365.7	Prison reformers			Administration of—[By
HV9025	365.6	Prison violence			region or country]
HV9025	365.64	Prison homicide	HV9950	345.050973	Criminal justice,
HV9051-9230.7	364.36	Juvenile delinquency			Administration of
HV9051-9230.7	365.34	Reformatories			
HV9051-9230.7	364.36	Juvenile delinquents	HX	335	Collectivism
HV9051-9230.7	364.6	Social work with juvenile	HX	335	Socialism
		delinquents	HX	321.07	Utopias
HV9051-9230.7	365.6	Status offenders	HX1-780.9	335.43	Communism
HV9068	364.36071	Juvenile delinquency—	HX1-550	335	Socialism
		Study and teaching	HX19-.2	335.0071	Socialism—Study and
HV9101-9230.7	364.3609(4-9)	Juvenile delinquency—[By			teaching
		region or country]	HX21-54	335.009	Socialism—History
HV9103-9106	364.360973	Juvenile	HX51-54	335.7	Socialism, Christian
		delinquency—United	HX77	335.43	Democratic centralism
		States	HX80-517.5	335.009(4-9)	Socialism—[By region or
HV9107-9230.7	364.3609(4-9)	Juvenile			country]
		delinquency—[Other	HX518.L4	335.43092	Communist leadership
		countries]	HX546	306.73	Free love
HV9261-9430.7	364.601	Criminals—Rehabilitation	HX550.A37	334.683	Communism and
HV9276.5	364.68	Alternatives to			agriculture
		imprisonment	HX626-632	335.1209	Utopian socialism—History
HV9277	364.68	Fines (Penalties)	HX651-780.7	335.1209(4-9)	Utopian socialism—[By
HV9277.5	364.68	Community service			region or country]
		(Punishment)	HX742.2	335.1209694	Kibbutzim
HV9278	364.63	Parole	HX806-811	321.07	Utopias
HV9278	364.63	Probation	HX821-970.7	335.83	Anarchism
HV9279	365.34	Community-based	HX841-970.7	335.8309(4-9)	Anarchism—[By region or
		corrections			country]
HV9441-9649	365.9(4-9)	Prisons—[By region or	HX914-917	149.8	Nihilism
		country]			
HV9456-9481	365.973	Prisons—United States	J	320	Political science
HV9501-9510	365.971	Prisons—Canada	J80-82	352.238	Presidents—Messages

LC	Dewey	Subject Heading	LC	Dewey	Subject Heading
J82	352.2380973	Presidents—United States—Messages	JC391	321.6	Coronations
			JC393	371.82621	Education of princes
			JC419	321.5	Oligarchy
JA	320	Political science	JC421-423	321.8	Democracy
JA1-26	320.05	Political science—Periodicals	JC421-458	321.86	Republics
			JC474	321.92	Communist state
JA27-34	320.06	Political science—Societies, etc.	JC478	321.94	Corporate state
			JC481	320.533	Fascism
JA35.5	320.06	Political science—Congresses	JC480-481	321.9	Totalitarianism
			JC478	321.94	Corporate state
JA51	320.05	Political science—Periodicals	JC491	321.094	Revolutions
			JC492	321.09	Counterrevolutions
JA75.8	333.72	Green movement	JC494	321.09	Coups d'etat
JA81-84	320.09	Political science—History	JC495	321.9092	Dictators
JA81-84	320.11	Social contract	JC571-628	323	Human rights
JA86-88	320.071	Political science—Study and teaching	JC571-628	323	Civil rights
			JC571-605	323	Individualism
			JC575-578	323.42	Equality
JC	320.011	State, The	JC578	320.011	Justice
JC20-89	321.5	Theocracy	JC585-599	323.044	Political persecution
JC66	320.932	Egypt—Politics and government	JC585-599	323.44	Liberty
			JC609	323.48	Petition, Right of
JC67	320.933	Jews—Politics and government			
			JF	350	Public administration
JC71-75	320.938	Greece—Politics and government—To 146 B.C.	JF71-99	342.0292	Constitutional conventions
			JF195	322.5	Civil-military relations
JC75.D	320.938	Deme	JF225	352.283	Delegation of powers
htJC75.S8	324.620938	Suffrage	JF229	320.404	Separation of powers
JC81-89	320.9376	Rome—Politics and government	JF247.R4	324.68	Recall
			JF251-289	352.23	Heads of state
JC85.S8	324.6209376	Suffrage	JF251-289	352.235	Executive power
JC91-93	320.9495	Byzantine Empire—Politics and government	JF255	352.23	Presidents
			JF285	324.63	Presidents—Election
JC109-121	321.3	Feudalism	JF285	321.8042	Heads of state—Succession
JC312	323.1	Minorities			
JC311-314	320.54	Nationalism	JF286	352.23	Heads of state—Term of office
JC319-323	320.12	Political geography			
JC319-323	320.12	Geopolitics	JF331-341	352.24	Cabinet system
JC323	320.12	Boundaries	JF341	352.293	Ministerial responsibility
JC327	320.15	Sovereignty	JF491-619	328	Legislation
JC328	323.6	Allegiance	JF491-497	328.23	Referendum
JC328	323.6	Treason	JF501-619	328	Legislative bodies
JC328.3	323.044	Government, Resistance to	JF518	328.369	Opposition (Political science)
JC328.3	322.4	Civil disobedience	JF519	328.34	Filibusters (Political science)
JC328.5	322.42	Insurgency			
JC336	320.11	Social contract	JF525	328.373	Bill drafting
JC345-347	929.(82 or 92)	Seals (Numismatics)	JF538	328.34	Cloture
JC352	321.06	City-states	JF541-549	328.31	Legislative bodies—Upper chambers
JC355	321.02	Federal government			
JC359	321.030944	Bonapartism	JF601-619	328.32	Legislative bodies—Lower chambers
JC359	325.32	Imperialism			
JC361-363	327.17	Internationalism	JF711	347.012	Judicial review
JC362	327.17	International cooperation	JF781	345.052	Extradition
JC365	321.06	States, Small	JF801	323.6	Citizenship
JC374-408	321	Kings and rulers	JF825-1141	324.62	Voting
JC375-393	321.6	Monarchy	JF831-851	324.62	Suffrage
JC375-392	321.6	Despotism	JF841	324.62	Voting age
JC389	321.6	Divine right of kings	JF847-855	324.623	Women—Suffrage

LC	Dewey	Subject Heading	LC	Dewey	Subject Heading
JF1001-1048	324	Elections	JK765-770	352.63	Civil service—Personnel management
JF1031	324.62	Voting, Compulsory	JK771-794	352.630973	United States—Officials and employees—Salaries, etc.
JF1033	324.65	Absentee voting			
JF1051-1075	324.63	Representative government and representation			
			JK1012-1432	328.73	United States. Congress
JF1051-1075	324.63	Majorities	JK1012	328.73025	United States. Congress—Directories
JF1071-1075	328.3347	Proportional representation			
			JK1033-1059	342.730509	United States. Congress—History
JF1081-1083	324.66	Elections—Corrupt practices			
			JK1118	328.380973	Lobbying
JF1081-1083	324.66	Political corruption	JK1154-1259	328.310973	United States. Congress. Senate
JF1091-1177	324.65	Ballot			
JF1125	324.65	Polling places	JK1308-1432	328.320973	United States. Congress. House
JF1128	324.65	Voting-machines			
JF1501-1521	351	Civil service	JK1347-1343	328.33455	Gerrymander
JF1525.D4	352.33	Public administration—Decision making	JK1533	324.680973	Recall
			JK1543	364.1340973	Contempt of court
JF1525.I6	327.1209	Espionage—History	JK1548.P8	345.7301	Public defenders
JF1525.P7	352.5	Government property	JK1606	347.7301	Courts—United States
JF1621	352.35	Administrative responsibility	JK1717-2217	323.0973	Political rights—United States
JF1621	352.885	Government liability	JK1731	323.480973	Petition, Right of
JF1671	353.549	Civil service—Pensions	JK1758-1759	323.60973	Patriotism—United States
JF2011-2112	324.2	Political parties	JK1758	323.60973	Americanization
JF2085	324.54	Primaries	JK1761	394.26973	Flag Day
JF2085	324.5	Nominations for office	JK1846-1929	324.60973	Suffrage—United States
JF2085	324.52	Caucus	JK1924-1929	324.6208 + 996073	Afro-Americans—Suffrage
JF2101	324.3	Political clubs			
			JK1965-2217	324.620973	Elections
JK	320.973	United States—Politics and government	JK1991-.5	324.780973	Campaign funds
			JK1994	324.66	Elections—Corrupt practices
JK4	353.00074	Freedom Train			
JK54-103	320.9730903	United States—Politics and government—To 1775	JK2063-2075	324.273015	Nominations for office
			JK2071-2077	324.2730154	Primaries
			JK2214-2217	324.650973	Ballot
JK301	342.73024	Constitutional conventions	JK2249	324.660973	Elections—Corrupt practices
JK305	342.73044	Separation of powers			
JK311-325	342.73042	States rights	JK2255-2261	324.2730156	Political conventions
JK310-331	342.73042	Secession	JK2251-2391	324.70973	Campaign literature
JK318	346.043	Squatter sovereignty	JK2403-9593	352.130973	State governments—United States
JK320	320.97309034	United States—Politics and government—1861-1865			
			JK2413-2428	342.0297(4-9)	Constitutions, State
			JK2441	352.133	Interstate agreements
JK321	320.97309034	United States—Politics and government—1865-1877	JK2443-2525	352.1309(4-9)	Public administration—[United States, By state]
			JK2447-2454	352.232130973	Governors—United States
JK371.P7-.P8	342.0418	Police power	JK2459	352.2390973	Lieutenant governors—United States
JK404-1685	353	Public administration—United States			
JK511-609	352.230973	Presidents—United States	JK2498	328.38097(4-9)	Lobbying
JK524-529	324.0973	Presidents—United States—Election	JK2556	320.120973	United States—Territories and possessions
			JK2701-9593	352.1309(4-9)	State governments—[United States, By state]
JK536	394.40973	Inauguration Day			
JK609.5	352.2390973	Vice-Presidents—United States	JK9661-9993	320.0975	Confederate States of America—Politics and government
JK610-616	352.240973	Cabinet officers			
JK631-868	351.73063	Civil service			
JK681	352.630973	Civil service reform			

LC	Dewey	Subject Heading	LC	Dewey	Subject Heading
JK9720-9770	351.75	Executive departments—Confederate States of America	JL830-839	320.972982	Martinique—Politics and government
JL	320.971	Canada—Politics and government	JL1000-1019	320.97291	Cuba—Politics and government
JL	320.9728	Central America—Politics and government	JL1040-1059	320.97295	Puerto Rico—Politics and government
JL	320.98	South America—Politics and government	JL1080-1099	320.97294	Haiti—Politics and government
JL	320.9729	Caribbean Area—Politics and government	JL1120-1139	320.97293	Dominican Republic—Politics and government
JL1-500	351.71	Public administration—Canada	JL1200-1299	320.972	Mexico—Politics and government
JL1-500	320.971	Canada—Politics and government	JL1440-1459	320.97286	Costa Rica—Politics and government
JL41-45	320.971090 + (1-33)	Canada—Politics and government—To 1763	JL1480-1499	320.97281	Guatemala—Politics and government
JL48	320.97109033	Canada—Politics and gunmen—1763-1791	JL1520-1539	320.97283	Honduras—Politics and government
JL53	320.9710903 + (3-4)	Canada—Politics and government—1791-1841	JL1560-1579	320.97284	El Salvador—Politics and government
JL55	320.97109034	Canada—Politics and government—1841-1867	JL1600-1619	320.97285	Nicaragua—Politics and government
JL65	320.971090 + (34-511)	Canada—Politics and government—1867-	JL2000-2099	320.982	Argentina—Politics and government
JL87-111	347.71	Executive departments—Canada	JL2200-2299	320.984	Bolivia—Politics and government
JL106-111	352.630971	Civil service—Canada	JL2400-2499	320.981	Brazil—Politics and government
JL131-179	354.7299	Canada. Parliament	JL2600-2699	320.983	Chile—Politics and government
JL590-599	320.97299	Bermuda Islands—Politics and government	JL2800-2899	320.9861	Colombia—Politics and government
JL610-619	320.97296	Bahamas—Politics and government	JL3000-3099	320.9866	Ecuador—Politics and government
JL629.5	320.972921	Cayman Islands—Politics and government	JL3200-3299	320.9892	Paraguay—Politics and government
JL629.6	320.9729845	Grenada—Politics and government	JL3400-3499	320.985	Peru—Politics and government
JL630-639	320.97292	Jamaica—Politics and government	JL3600-3699	320.9895	Uruguay—Politics and government
JL640-649.7	320.97297	Leeward Islands (West Indies)—Politics and government	JL3800-3899	320.987	Venezuela—Politics and government
JL650-659	320.972983	Trinidad and Tobago—Politics and government	JN	354.094	Europe—Politics and government
JL670-679	320.97282	Belize—Politics and government	JN12	320.94	Europe—Politics and government—20th century
JL680-689	320.9881	Guyana—Politics and government	JN15	321.04094	European federation
JL690-699	320.99711	Falkland Islands—Politics and government	JN101-1371	320.941	Great Britain—Politics and government
JL770-779	320.972986	Curacao—Politics and government	JN137-158	320.9410902 + (1-4)	Great Britain—Politics and government—1066-1485
JL780-789	320.9883	Surinam—Politics and government	JN175-231	320.941090 + (3-511)	Great Britain—Politics and government—1485-
JL810-819	320.9882	French Guiana—Politics and government	JN309-678	351.41	Public administration—Great Britain
JL820-829	320.972976	Guadeloupe—Politics and government			

LC	Dewey	Subject Heading	LC	Dewey	Subject Heading
JN331-389	352.2330941	Great Britain—Kings and rulers	JN9600-9689	320.9496	Balkan Peninsula—Politics and government
JN500-678	328.41	Great Britain. Parliament			
JN900-1088	323.0941	Political rights—Great Britain	JQ	320.95	Asia—Politics and government
JN1088	324.660941	Elections—Corrupt practices	JQ	320.956	Middle East—Politics and government
JN1111-1129	324.241	Political parties—Great Britain	JQ	320.96	Africa—Politics and government
JN1129.T7	324.24102	Tories, English	JQ21-1825	320.95	Asia—Politics and government
JN1150-1159	320.9429	Wales—Politics and government	JQ200-620	320.954	India—Politics and government
JN1187-1371	320.9411	Scotland—Politics and government	JQ629	320.95491	Pakistan—Politics and government
JN1405-1571.5	320.9415	Ireland—Politics and government	JQ630-639	320.95492	Bangladesh—Politics and government
JN1572	320.9416	Northern Ireland—Politics and government	JQ650-659	320.95493	Sri Lanka—Politics and government
JN1601-2041	320.9436	Austria—Politics and government	JQ751	320.9595	Burma—Politics and government
JN2210-2229	320.9437	Czechoslovakia—Politics and government	JQ760-779	320.9598	Indonesia—Politics and government
JN2301-3007	320.944	France—Politics and government	JQ800-899	320.9597	Vietnam—Politics and government
JN3201-4944	320.943	Germany—Politics and government	JQ930-939	320.9596	Cambodia—Politics and government
JN3250.C83	324.630943	Electors (Kurfursten)	JQ950-959	320.9594	Laos—Politics and government
JN5001-5191	320.9495	Greece—Politics and government			
JN5201-5690	320.954	Italy—Politics and government	JQ1250-1419	320.9599	Philippines—Politics and government
JN5701-5999	320.9492	Netherlands—Politics and government	JQ1500-1519	320.951	China—Politics and government
JN6101-6371	320.9493	Belgium—Politics and government	JQ1520-1539	320.951249	Taiwan—Politics and government
JN6500-6598	320.947	Russia—Politics and government	JQ1600-1699	320.952	Japan—Politics and government
JN6750-6769	320.9438	Poland—Politics and government	JQ1720-1729.5	320.9519	Korea—Politics and government
JN7011-7066	320.948	Scandinavia—Politics and government	JQ1740-1749	320.9593	Thailand—Politics and government
JN7101-7367	320.9489	Denmark—Politics and government	JQ1760-1769	320.9581	Afghanistan—Politics and government
JN7370-7379	320.94912	Iceland—Politics and government	JQ1780-1789	320.955	Iran—Politics and government
JN7380-7389	320.9982	Greenland—Politics and government	JQ1800-1809	320.9561	Turkey—Politics and government
JN7390-7399	320.94897	Finland—Politics and government	JQ1811	320.95693	Cyprus—Politics and government
JN7401-7695	320.9481	Norway—Politics and government	JQ1826	320.95691	Syria—Politics and government
JN7721-7995	320.9485	Sweden—Politics and government	JQ1828	320.95692	Lebanon—Politics and government
JN8101-8399	320.946	Spain—Politics and government	JQ1830	320.95694	Israel—Politics and government
JN8423-8661	320.9469	Portugal—Politics and government	JQ1833	320.95695	Jordon—Politics and government
JN8701-9599	320.9494	Switzerland—Politics and government	JQ1841	320.9538	Saudi Arabia—Politics and government

LC	Dewey	Subject Heading
JQ1842	320.9533	Yemen—Politics and government
JQ1843	320.95353	Oman—Politics and government
JQ1844	320.95357	United Arab Emirates—Politics and government
JQ1845	320.95363	Qatar—Politics sand government
JQ1846	320.95365	Bahrain—Politics and government
JQ1848	320.95367	Kuwait—Politics and government
JQ1849	320.9567	Iraq—Politics and government
JQ1850	320.9174927	Arab countries—Politics and government
JQ1870-3981	320.96	Africa—Politics and government
JQ5995-6651	320.9(5-6)	Oceania—Politics and government
JS	320.85	Local government
JS42	352.1406	Local government—Societies, etc.
JS49	352.14071	Local government—Study and teaching
JS55-67	352.1409	Local government—History
JS113	352.283	Decentralization in government
JS113	320.85	Municipal home rule
JS143-163	352.23216	Mayors
JS148-155	352.16092	Municipal officials and employees
JS148-153	352.63	Civil service
JS215	324.62	Suffrage
JS261	352.16	Boroughs
JS300-1583	351.7(4-9)	Local government—United States
JS342-343	352.250973	Municipal government by commission
JS344.R4	324.680973	Recall
JS411	352.150973	County government—United States
JS422	352.16097(4-9)	Metropolitan government—United States
JS426	324.973	Special districts—United States
JS504-1583	352.16097(4-9)	Municipal government—[United States, By city]
JS1701-1800	351.71	Local government—Canada
JS1840-2058	351.729	Local government—West Indies
JS2101-2143	351.72	Local government—Mexico
JS2145-2219	351.728	Local government—Central America
JS2300-2778	351.8	Local government—South America
JS3000-6949.8	351.4	Local government—Europe
JS3001-4295	351.41	Local government—Great Britain
JS4501-4655	351.436	Local government—Austria
JS4661-4696	351.439	Local government—Hungary
JS4801-5250	351.44	Local government—France
JS5301-5598	351.43	Local government—Germany
JS5701-5925	351.45	Local government—Italy
JS5931-5998	351.492	Local government—Netherlands
JS6001-6048	351.493	Local government—Belgium
JS6051-6109	351.47	Local government—Russia
JS6151-6185	351.489	Local government—Denmark
JS6251-6285	351.485	Local government—Sweden
JS6301-6335	351.46	Local government—Spain
JS6341-6375	351.469	Local government—Portugal
JS6401-6889	351.494	Local government—Switzerland
JS6899.5-6949.8	351.496	Local government—Balkan Peninsula
JS6950-7520	351.5	Local government—Asia
JS7001-7090	351.54	Local government—India
JS7301-7335	351.599	Local government—Philippines
JS7351-7365	351.51	Local government—China
JS7371-7385	351.52	Local government—Japan
JS7435-7520	351.056	Local government—Middle East
JS7525-7819	351.6	Local government—Africa
JS8001-8310	351.94	Local government—Australia
JS8331-8399	351.93	Local government—New Zealand
JS8450-8490	351.9(5-6)	Local government—Oceania
JV	321.08	Colonies
JV1-5399	325.3	Colonization
JV61-151	325.309	Colonies—History
JV221-231	325.(7-8)	America—Colonization
JV246	325.6	Africa—Colonization
JV412-461	353.15	Colonies—Administration
JV431	353.15092	Viceroyalty
JV443	353.15	Civil service, Colonial
JV500-599	325.373	United States—Territories and possessions
JV1000-1099	325.341	Great Britain—Colonies

LC	Dewey	Subject Heading	LC	Dewey	Subject Heading
JV1800-1899	325.344	France—Colonies	JV7510-7519	325.(285) or (85)	Peru—Emigration and immigration
JV2200-2299	325.345	Italy—Colonies	JV7520-7529	325.(2895) or (895)	Uruguay—Emigration and immigration
JV2500-2899	325.3492	Benelux countries—Colonies	JV7530-7539	325.(287) or (87)	Venezuela—Emigration and immigration
JV3300-3399	325.3489	Denmark—Colonies			
JV4000-4099	325.346	Spain—Colonies	JV7600-7699	325.(241) or (41)	Great Britain—Emigration and immigration
JV4200-4299	325.3469	Portugal—Colonies			
JV5200-5299	325.352	Japan—Colonies	JV7700-7709	325.(2411) or (411)	Scotland—Emigration and immigration
JV6001-9500	325.(2 or 1)	Emigration and immigration	JV7710-7719	325.(2415) or (415)	Ireland—Emigration and immigration
JV6021-6032	325.(2 or 1) + 090(1-5)	Emigration and immigration—History	JV7800-7899	325.(2436) or (436)	Austria—Emigration and immigration
JV6118	325.(2 or 1)	Emigration and immigration—Economic aspects	JV7900-7999	325.(244) or (44)	France—Emigration and immigration
JV6342	303.482	Assimilation (Sociology)	JV8000-8099	325.(243) or (43)	Germany—Emigration and immigration
JV6403-7127	325.(273) or (73)	United States—Emigration and immigration	JV8110-8119	325.(2495) or (495)	Greece—Emigration and immigration
JV7200-7299	325.(271) or (71)	Canada—Emigration and immigration	JV8130-8139	325.(245) or (45)	Italy—Emigration and immigration
JV7320-7397	325.(2729) or (729)	West Indies—Emigration and immigration	JV8150-8159	325.(2492) or (492)	Netherlands—Emigration and immigration
JV7370-7379	325.(27291) or (7291)	Cuba—Emigration and immigration	JV8160-8169	325.(2493) or (493)	Belgium—Emigration and immigration
JV7380-7389	325.(27295) or (7295)	Puerto Rico—Emigration and immigration	JV8175	325.(24935) or (4935)	Luxembourg—Emigration and immigration
JV7393	325.(27294) or (7294)	Haiti—Emigration and immigration	JV8180-8189	325.(247) or (47)	Russia—Emigration and immigration
JV7395	325.(27293) or (7293)	Dominican Republic—Emigration and immigration	JV8195	325.(2438) or (438)	Poland—Emigration and immigration
JV7400-7409	325.(272) or (72)	Mexico—Emigration and immigration	JV8200-8209	325.(2489) or (489)	Denmark—Emigration and immigration
JV7413	325.(27286) or (7286)	Costa Rica—Emigration and immigration	JV8210-8219	325.(2481) or (481)	Norway—Emigration and immigration
JV7416	325.(27281) or (7281)	Guatemala—Emigration and immigration	JV8220-8229	325.(2485) or (485)	Sweden—Emigration and immigration
JV7419	325.(27283) or (7283)	Honduras—Emigration and immigration	JV8250-8259	325.(246) or (46)	Spain—Emigration and immigration
JV7423	325.(27284) or (7284)	El Salvador—Emigration and immigration	JV8260-8269	325.(2469) or (469)	Portugal—Emigration and immigration
JV7426	325.(27285) or (7285)	Nicaragua—Emigration and immigration	JV8280-8289	325.(2494) or (494)	Switzerland—Emigration and immigration
JV7429	325.(27287) or (7287)	Panama—Emigration and immigration	JV8490-8758	325.(25) or (5)	Asia—Emigration and immigration
JV7440-7449	325.(282) or (82)	Argentina—Emigration and immigration	JV8500-8509	325.(254) or (54)	India—Emigration and immigration
JV7450-7459	325.(284) or (84)	Bolivia—Emigration and immigration	JV8685	325.(2599) or (599)	Philippines—Emigration and immigration
JV7460-7469	325.(281) or (81)	Brazil—Emigration and immigration	JV8700-8709	325.(251) or (51)	China—Emigration and immigration
JV7470-7479	325.(283) or (83)	Chile—Emigration and immigration	JV8710-8719	325.(251249) or (51249)	Taiwan—Emigration and immigration
JV7480-7489	325.(2861) or (861)	Colombia—Emigration and immigration	JV8720-8729	325.(252) or (52)	Japan—Emigration and immigration
JV7490-7499	325.(2866) or (866)	Ecuador—Emigration and immigration	JV8739-8751	325.(256) or (56)	Middle East—Emigration and immigration
JV7500-7509	325.(2892) or (892)	Paraguay—Emigration and immigration	JV8790-9024.5	325.(26) or (6)	Africa—Emigration and immigration

LC	Dewey	Subject Heading	LC	Dewey	Subject Heading
JV9100-9199	325.(294) or (94)	Australia—Emigration and immigration	K3285	321.02	Federal government
			K3290-3304	342.08	People (Constitutional law)
JV9260-9269	325.(293) or (93)	New Zealand—Emigration and immigration	K3332-3351	342.062	Executive power
			K3367	347.012	Judicial power
JV9290-9470	325.29(5-6) or 9(5-6)	Oceania—Emigration and immigration	K3375	341.28	Colonies—Law and legislation
			K3400-3431	342.066	Administrative law
K	340-349	Law	K3440-3460	342.068	Civil service
K50-54	340.03	Law—Dictionaries	K3476-3558	343.02	Public domain
K100-103	340.071	Law—Study and teaching	K3478-3486	346.044	Natural resources—Law and legislation
K140-165	340.09	Law—History			
K170	340.092	Law—Biography	K3492	343.0942	Highway law
K183-184.7	340.0207	Law—Humor	K3496-3501	343.0924	Water-supply—Law and legislation
K190-195	340.52	Law, Primitive			
K280-286	340.11	Law—Sources	K3511-3512	343.0252	Eminent domain
K368-380	340.115	Sociological jurisprudence	K3531-3544	346.045	Regional planning—Law and legislation
K540-5570	341	International law			
K540-546	347.07	Trials	K3550-3553	344.063635	Public housing—Law and legislation
K583-591	340.2	Comparative law			
K623-968	346	Civil law	K3558-3560	343.02	Government property
K670-709	346.015	Domestic relations	K3566-3597	344.04	Public health laws
K783-793	346.047	Personal property	K3615-3617	344.049	Veterinary hygiene—Law and legislation
K805-821	346.052	Inheritance and succession			
			K3626-3633	344.04232	Food law and legislation
K830-968	346.02	Obligations (Law)	K3651-3654	344.042	Alcohol—Law and legislation
K840-917	346.02	Contracts			
K920	346.029	Quasi contracts	K3661	344.0533	Weapons—Law and legislation
K923-968	346.03	Torts			
K970	342.03288	Reparation	K3740-3762	344.07	Educational law and legislation
K1001-1388	346.07	Commercial law			
K1010-1014	346.07	Business law	K3770	344.09	Research—Law and legislation
K1024-1132	346.02	Contracts			
K1054-1065	346.096	Negotiable instruments	K3840-4375	343.07	Commercial law
K1066-1088	346.082	Banking law	K3842-3862	343.08	Trade regulation
K1100-1108	346.092	Security (Law)	K3978-3990	343.09	Public utilities—Law and legislation
K1112-1116	346.092	Investments—Law and legislation			
			K4021-4025	343.093	Transportation—Law and legislation
K1241-1287	346.086	Insurance law			
K1401-1578	346.048	Intellectual property	K4028-4042	343.0942	Highway law
K1411-1485	346.0482	Copyright	K4061-4070	343.095	Railroad law
K1500-1578	346.048	Industrial property	K4080	343.098	Local transit—Law and legislation
K1701-2000	344	Social legislation			
K1701-1841	344.01	Labor laws and legislation	K4091-4124	343.097	Aeronautics—Law and legislation
K1861-1929	344.05242	Social security—Law and legislation			
			K4135	341.47	Space law
K1960-2000	344.0316	Public welfare—Law and legislation	K4182-4194	343.0967	Inland navigation—Law and legislation
			K4198-4200	343.0967	Harbors—Law and legislation
K2100-2385	347.05	Procedure (Law)			
K2201-2385	347.05	Civil procedure	K4245-4254	343.0992	Postal service—Law and legislation
K2320	344.01893	Injunctions			
K3150	342	Public law	K4301-4339	343.0994	Telecommunication—Law and legislation
K3154-3367	342	Constitutional law			
K3161	342.029	Constitutional history	K4360-4375	344.01712	Professions—Law and legislation
K3220-3225	342.041	Public policy (Law)			
K3224-3229	342.08	People (Constitutional law)	K4430-4675	343.03	Finance, Public—Law and legislation
K3236-3268	342.085	Civil rights			
K3236-3268	342.085	Human rights	K4456-4590	343.04	Taxation—Law and legislation
K3252	342.085	Right to life			
K3280-3282	322.1	Church and state			

LC	Dewey	Subject Heading	LC	Dewey	Subject Heading
K4501-4550	343.052	Income tax—Law and legislation	K7470	340.986	Conflict of laws—Insurance
K4560-4564	343.054	Property tax—Law and legislation	K7490-7495	340.966	Conflict of laws—Corporations
K4568	343.053	Inheritance and succession	K7550-7582	340.948	Conflict of laws—Intellectual property
K4572-4580	343.0553	Excise tax—Law and legislation	K7555-7557	340.9482	Conflict of laws—Copyright licenses
K4600-4640	343.056	Tariff—Law and legislation	K7570-7582	340.948	Conflict of laws—Industrial property
K4650-4675	343.03	Local finance—Law and legislation	K7680	340.9	Judgments, Foreign
K4720-4760	343.01	Military readiness—Law and legislation	K7690	347.09	Conflict of laws—Arbitration and award
K5011-5316	345	Criminal law			
K5036-5048	345.01	Criminal jurisdiction	KD	349.42	Law—England
K5064-5083	345.04	Criminal liability	KD125-180	328.3742	Legislation—England
K5401-5570	345.05	Criminal procedure	KD125-150	348.42022	Statutes—England
K5423	345.01	Criminal jurisdiction	KD187-291	348.42041	Law reports, digests, etc.—England
K5425	345.072	Indictments			
K5460-5492	345.075	Trials	KD313	349.4203	Law—England—Dictionaries
K5465-5490	345.06	Evidence, Criminal			
K5492	345.075	Jury	KD318	347.42055	Forms (Law)—England
K5495	347.035	Appellate procedure	KD327-332	347.42013	Judicial statistics—England
K5510-5560	345.0772	Sentences (Criminal procedure)	KD370-379.5	347.4207	Trials—England
K5575-5582	345.08	Juvenile courts	KD392-400	349.42072	Legal research—England
K7000-7720	342.042	Conflict of laws	KD419-452	349.42071	Law—Study and teaching—England
K7010-7011	348.022	Statutes			
K7051-7054	341.7	Law—International unification	KD460-472	349.42	Lawyers—England
K7120-7197	340.912	Conflict of laws—Persons	KD530-632	349.4209	Law—England—History
K7145-7148	340.913	Conflict of laws—Juristic persons	KD674	346.42004	Equity—England
			KD680-685	342.42042	Conflict of laws—England
K7155-7197	340.915	Conflict of laws—Domestic relations	KD720-721	347.42	Civil law—England
			KD723-785	346.42012	Persons (Law)—England
K7181-7197	340.917	Conflict of laws—Parent and child	KD750-785	346.42015	Domestic relations—England
K7197	340.918	Conflict of laws—Guardian and ward	KD810-815	346.420437	Possession (Law)—England
K7200-7218	340.94	Conflict of laws—Property	KD821-1195	346.42043	Real property—England
K7230-7245	340.952	Conflict of laws—Inheritance and succession	KD833-960	346.420432	Land tenure—Law and legislation—England
			KD834-839	340.550942	Feudal law—England
K7260-7335	340.92	Conflict of laws—Obligations	KD841-960	346.420432	Estates (Law)—England
			KD1010-1016	346.4204364	Mortgages—England
K7265-7305	340.92	Conflict of laws—Contracts	KD1034-1107	343.4202	Government property—England
K7310	340.929	Conflict of laws—Quasi contracts	KD1035	346.42046	Natural resources—Law and legislation—England
K7315-7335	340.93	Conflict of laws—Torts	KD1040-1048	343.420942	Highway law—England
K7340-7512	340.97	Conflict of laws—Commercial law	KD1070	346.4204691	Water—Law and legislation—England
K7350-7444	340.97	Conflict of laws—Contracts	KD1125-1162	346.42045	Zoning law—England
			KD1185-1189	343.420252	Eminent domain—England
K7350	340.972	Conflict of laws—Sales	KD1195	343.420256	Public works—Law and legislation—England
K7360-7370	340.996	Conflict of laws—Negotiable instruments			
			KD1205-1465	346.42047	Personal property—England
K7380-7384	340.982	Conflict of laws—Banking			
K7449-7460	343.096	Conflict of laws—Maritime law			

LC	Dewey	Subject Heading	LC	Dewey	Subject Heading
KD1238-1450	346.42048	Intangible property—England	KD2405-2430	343.4207833 + 847664	Food law and legislation—England
KD1261-1450	346.42048	Intellectual property—England	KD2435	343.42078624	Construction industry—Law and legislation
KD1281-1325	346.420482	Copyright—England			
KD1345	346.420484	Design protection—England	KD2455-2530	343.4207	Commercial law—England
KD1361-1413.3	346.420486	Patent laws and legislation—England	KD2535-2560	343.4209	Public utilities—Law and legislation—England
KD1450	346.42048	Business names—England	KD2571-2838	343.42093	Transportation—Law and legislation—England
KD1497	346.4205	Estate planning—England	KD3000-3315	344.42	Social legislation—England
KD1500-1534	346.42052	Inheritance and succession—England	KD3001-3177	344.4201	Labor laws and legislation—England
KD1554-1920	346.4202	Contracts—England			
KD1638-1642	344.4201542	Labor contract—England	KD3241-3250	343.4205242	Social security—Law and legislation—England
KD1679-1685	346.42025	Bailments—England			
KD1695-1699	346.42096	Negotiable instruments—England	KD3291-3315	344.420316	Public welfare—Law and legislation
KD1715-1737	346.42082	Banking law—England	KD3351-3375	344.4204	Public health laws—England
KD1740-1742	346.42073	Loans—Law and legislation—England	KD3395-3413	344.4204	Medical laws and legislation—England
KD1752	346.42074	Suretyship and guaranty—England	KD3420-3422	344.42049	Veterinary hygiene—Law and legislation—England
KD1774-1787	346.42092	Investments—Law and legislation—England	KD3460-3462	344.4204233	Drugs—Law and legislation—England
KD1800-1847	343.42093	Carriers—Law and legislation—England	KD3466-3480	344.42042	Alcohol—Law and legislation—England
KD1845-1847	346.420862	Insurance, Marine—England	KD3492	344.420533	Weapons—Law and legislation—England
KD1851-1913	346.42086	Insurance law—England	KD3510	344.42047	Accident law—England
KD1924	346.42029	Quasi contracts—England	KD3523	344.42099	Amusements—Law and legislation—England
KD1941-1980	346.4203	Torts—England			
KD2022	346.42029	Power of attorney—England	KD3525	344.42099	Sports—Law and legislation—England
KD2046-2054	346.42064	Unincorporated societies—England	KD3527	344.42099	Gambling—Law and legislation—England
KD2049-2054	346.420682	Partnership—England	KD3600-3689	344.4207	Educational law and legislation
KD2057-2127	346.42066	Corporation law—England	KD3720-3731	344.42097	Performing arts—Law and legislation—England
KD2061-2062	346.42064	Nonprofit organizations—Law and legislation	KD3736	344.42093	Museums—Law and legislation—England
KD2141-2164	346.42078	Bankruptcy—England			
KD2204-2231	343.4208	Trade regulation—England	KD3746	344.42092	Library legislation—England
KD2206	343.42082	Advertising laws—England	KD3753-3755	344.42092	Archives—Law and legislation—England
KD2208-2209	343.42082	Labels—Law and legislation—England	KD3931-4645	342.42	England—Constitutional law
KD2215	343.42083	Price regulation—England	KD3931-3966	342.42029	England—Constitutional history
KD2218-2220	343.420721	Antitrust law—England			
KD2225-2226	343.42072	Competition, Unfair—England	KD4000-4010	342.42044	Separation of powers—England
KD2228	346.4206	Trade associations—Law and legislation—England	KD4030	342.420412	England—Foreign relations—Law and legislation
KD2230-2231	343.42075	Containers—Law and legislation—England			
KD2241-2295	343.42076	Agricultural laws and legislation—England	KD4050-4058	342.42083	Citizenship—England
KD2310-2315	343.4207692	Fishery law and legislation—England	KD4080-4119	342.42085	Civil rights—England
			KD4130-4139	342.42083	Aliens—England
KD2331-2370	343.42077	Mining law—England	KD4190-4381	342.4105	Great Britain. Parliament.

LC	Dewey	Subject Heading	LC	Dewey	Subject Heading
KD4430-4531	342.4106	Monarchy—Great Britain	KDC462-470	346.411052	Inheritance and succession—Scotland
KD4462	342.4106	Prime ministers—Great Britain	KDC635-674	344.411	Social legislation—Scotland
KD4645	347.4201	Courts—England	KDC690-695	344.411041	Medical laws and legislation—Scotland
KD4650	344.4209	Emblems, National—England	KDC750-785	342.411	Scotland—Constitutional law
KD4746-4840	342.4209	Local government—Law and legislation—England	KDC807-825	343.41103	Finance, Public—Law and legislation—Scotland
KD5020-5025	349.42	Commonwealth countries	KDC840-915	347.41105	Procedure (Law)—Scotland
KD5280-5752	343.4203	Finance, Public—Law and legislation—England	KDC910-920	345.411	Criminal law—Scotland
KD5284-5286	343.42032	Money—Law and legislation—England	KDE	349.416	Law—Northern Ireland
KD5288	343.42032	Foreign exchange—Law and legislation—England	KDE42-50	328.37416	Legislation—Northern Ireland
KD5292	343.42034	Budget—Law and legislation—England	KDE55-60	348.416041	Law reports, digests, etc.—Northern Ireland
KD5300	343.42037	Debts, Public—Law and legislation—England	KDE90-98	346.416012	Persons (Law)—Northern Ireland
KD5351-5605	343.4204	Taxation—Law and legislation—England	KDE145-151	346.416052	Inheritance and succession—Northern Ireland
KD5641-5694	343.42056	Tariff—Law and legislation—England	KDE235-282	343.41607	Commercial law—Northern Ireland
KD5710-5752	343.42(1-9)03	Local finance—Law and legislation—England	KDE320-348	344.416	Social legislation—Northern Ireland
KD6000-6355	343.4201	Military readiness—Law and legislation—England	KDE410-462	342.416	Northern Ireland—Constitutional law
KD6340	344.420535	Civil defense—Law and legislation—England	KDE510-530	347.41605	Procedure (Law)—Northern Ireland
KD6850-7640	347.4205	Procedure (Law)—England	KDE550-557	345.41675	Criminal procedure—Northern Ireland
KD7132-7216	347.4203	Appellate courts—England			
KD7645-7647	347.4209	Arbitration and award—England	KDG	349.4234	Law—Channel Islands
KD7850-8090	345.42	Criminal law—England	KDG26-170	349.4279	Law—Isle of Man
KD8220-8464	345.4205	Criminal procedure—England	KDG220-380	349.42341	Law—Jersey (Channel Islands)
KD8850-9355	349.42	Statutes—England	KDG421-440	349.42342	Law—Guernsey (Channel Islands)
KD8996-9142	342.421	Statutes—London			
KD9400-9500	349.429	Law—Wales	KDK	349.415	Law—Ireland
KD9407	348.429022	Statutes—Wales	KDK38-50	328.37415	Legislation—Ireland
KD9410-9417	348.429041	Law reports, digests, etc.—Wales	KDK61-80	348.41504	Law reports, digests, etc.—Ireland
KD9420	349.42903	Law—Wales—Dictionaries	KDK84	349.41503	Law—Ireland—Dictionaries
KD9423	345.42907	Trials—Wales	KDK102-106	347.41507	Trials—Ireland
KD9460	344.429071	Law—Wales—Study and teaching	KDK120-134	349.415	Lawyers—Ireland
KD9480-9484	347.42901	Courts—Wales	KDK185-205	346.415012	Persons (Law)—Ireland
KD9490	345.429	Criminal law—Wales	KDK360-365	346.415052	Inheritance and succession—Ireland
KDC	349.411	Law—Scotland	KDK370-437	346.41502	Contracts—Ireland
KDC70-90	328.37411	Legislation—Scotland	KDK450-469	346.41503	Torts—Ireland
KDC110-113	347.41103	Appellate courts—Scotland	KDK550-769	343.41507	Commercial law—Ireland
KDC152	349.411003	Law—Scotland—Dictionaries	KDK800-895	344.415	Social legislation—Ireland
KDC184-188	347.41107	Trials—Scotland	KDK926-932	344.415041	Medical laws and legislation—Ireland
KDC225-247	349.411	Lawyers—Scotland			
KDC350-378	346.411012	Persons (Law)—Scotland			

LC	Dewey	Subject Heading	LC	Dewey	Subject Heading
KDK1200-1350	342.415	Ireland—Constitutional law	KE1915	343.71078624	Construction industry—Law and legislation
KDK1430-1526	343.41503	Finance, Public—Law and legislation—Ireland	KE1935-1999	343.7107	Commercial law—Canada
KDK1580-1713	347.41505	Procedure (Law)—Ireland	KE2020-2061	343.7109	Public utilities—Law and legislation—Canada
KDK1750-1782	345.415	Criminal law—Ireland	KE2071-2649	343.71093	Transportation—Law and legislation—Canada
KE	349.71	Law—Canada	KE2771-2998	346.71048	Intellectual property—Canada
KE78-125	328.3771	Legislation—Canada	KE3098-3542	344.71	Social legislation—Canada
KE132-156	348.71041	Law reports, digests, etc.—Canada	KE3575-3635	344.71041	Public health laws—Canada
KE198-206	347.71013	Judicial statistics—Canada	KE3646-3660	344.71041	Medical laws and legislation—Canada
KE225-237	347.7107	Trials—Canada	KE3714-3725	344.7104233	Drugs—Law and legislation—Canada
KE250-259	349.71072	Legal research—Canada	KE3805-3917	344.7107	Educational law and legislation—Canada
KE273-322	349.71071	Law—Study and teaching—Canada	KE3968	344.71097	Law and art—Canada
KE335-355	349.71	Lawyers—Canada	KE4125-4775	342.71	Canada—Constitutional law
KE457	346.71004	Equity—Canada	KE4310	342.710412	Canada—Foreign relations—Law and legislation
KE470-474	342.71042	Conflict of laws—Canada			
KE495	347.71	Civil law—Canada	KE4381-4430	342.71085	Civil rights—Canada
KE498-606	346.71012	Persons (Law)—Canada	KE4533-4665	342.7105	Canada. Parliament
KE531-606	346.71015	Domestic relations—Canada	KE4730	342.7106	Prime ministers—Canada
KE625-754	346.71043	Real property—Canada	KE4775	347.7101	Courts—Canada
KE765-781	346.71047	Personal property—Canada	KE4900-4995	342.7109	Local government—Law and legislation—Canada
KE806-833	346.71052	Inheritance and succession—Canada	KE5006-5010	342.710418	Police power—Canada
KE850-1225	346.7102	Contracts—Canada	KE5105-5420	343.7102	Government property—Canada
KE928-936	344.710189	Labor contract—Canada			
KE970-972	346.71025	Bailments—Canada	KE5258-5284	346.71045	Regional planning—Law and legislation—Canada
KE980-986	346.71096	Negotiable instruments—Canada	KE5600-6328	343.7103	Finance, Public—Law and legislation—Canada
KE991-1026	346.71082	Banking law—Canada			
KE1030-1034	346.71073	Loans—Law and legislation—Canada	KE6800-7240	343.7101	Military readiness—Law and legislation—Canada
KE1042-1056	346.71092	Securities—Canada	KE8200-8605	347.7101	Courts—Canada
KE1060-1089	346.71092	Investments—Law and legislation—Canada	KE8341-8605	347.7105	Procedure (Law)—Canada
KE1099-1135	343.71093	Carriers—Law and legislation—Canada	KE8618	347.7109	Arbitration and award—Canada
KE1141-1220	346.71086	Insurance law—Canada	KE8801-9112	345.71	Criminal law—Canada
KE1232-1309	346.7103	Torts—Canada			
KE1328-1332	346.7102	Agency (Law)—Canada	KEA	349.7123	Law—Alberta
KE1351-1361	346.71064	Unincorporated societies—Canada	KEB	349.711	Law—British Columbia
KE1369-1465	346.71066	Corporation law—Canada	KEM	349.7127	Law—Manitoba
KE1491-1506	346.71078	Bankruptcy—Canada	KEN0-599	349.7151	Law—New Brunswick
KE1591-1660	343.7108	Trade regulation—Canada	KEN1200-1799	349.718	Law—Newfoundland
KE1610-1614	343.71082	Advertising laws—Canada	KEN7400-7999	349.716	Law—Nova Scotia
KE1616-1618	343.71082	Labels—Law and legislation—Canada	KEO	349.713	Law—Ontario
KE1671-1745	343.71076	Agricultural laws and legislation—Canada	KEP	349.717	Law—Prince Edward Island
KE1760-1765	343.7107692	Fishery law and legislation—Canada	KEQ	349.714	Law—Quebec
KE1790-1802	343.71077	Mining law—Canada	KES	349.7124	Law—Saskatchewan
KE1867-1906	344.7104232	Food law and legislation—Canada	KEY	349.7191	Law—Yukon Territory
			KEZ	349.71(1-9)	Law—[Canada, By city]

LC	Dewey	Subject Heading	LC	Dewey	Subject Heading
KF	349.73	Law—United States	KF1035-1040	346.73073	Loans—Law and legislation—United States
KF16-22	348.7301	Bills, Legislative—United States	KF1045	346.73074	Suretyship and guaranty—United States
KF50-70	348.73022	Statutes—United States	KF1046-1062	346.73092	Security (Law)—United States
KF101-153	347.7301	Courts—United States			
KF156	349.7303	Law—United States—Dictionaries	KF1066-1084	346.73092	Investments—Law and legislation—United States
KF165	348.7(4-9)	Uniform state laws	KF1085-1087	343.7308	Commodity exchanges—Law and legislation—United States
KF180-185	347.73013	Judicial statistics—United States			
KF219-224	345.7307	Trials—United States	KF1091-1137	343.73093	Carriers—Law and legislation—United States
KF221.B74	345.7302	Trials (Bribery)—United States	KF1146-1238	346.73086	Insurance law—United States
KF221.C6	345.730207	Trials (Conspiracy)—United States	KF1241	344.730542	Contracts, Aleatory—United States
KF224.W	345.730231	Watergate Trial, Washington, D.C., 1973	KF1244-.5	346.73029	Quasi contracts—United States
KF240-247	349.73072	Legal research—United States	KF1246-1329	346.7303	Torts—United States
KF255	348.73041	Law reporting—United States	KF1341-1348	346.73029	Agency (Law)—United States
KF261-292	349.73071	Law—United States—Study and teaching	KF1355-1480	346.7306	Associations, institutions, etc.—Law and legislation—United States
KF285	341.0711	Law School Admission Test	KF1361-1381	346.73064	Unincorporated societies—United States
KF297-338	349.73	Lawyers—United States	KF1384-1480	346.73066	Corporation law—United States
KF299.A35	349.730899 + 6073	Afro-American lawyers			
KF338	340.0973	Lawyer referral service—United States	KF1388-1390	346.73064	Nonprofit organizations—Law and legislation
KF350-374	349.7309	Law—United States—History	KF1396-1477	346.73066	Corporations—Law and legislation—United States
KF382	340.11	Rule of law—United States	KF1480	346.73067	Corporations, Government—Law and legislation—United States
KF398-400	346.73004	Equity—United States			
KF410-418	342.73042	Conflict of laws—United States	KF1501-1548	346.73078	Bankruptcy—United States
KF465-553	346.73012	Persons (Law)—United States	KF1600-2940	343.7307	Commercial law—United States
KF501-553	346.73015	Domestic relations—United States	KF1601-1611	343.73072	Competition, Unfair—United States
KF566-698	346.73043	Real property—United States	KF1614-1617	343.73082	Advertising laws—United States
KF701-720	346.73047	Personal property—United States	KF1619-1620	343.73082	Labels—Law and legislation
KF753-780	346.73052	Inheritance and succession—United States	KF1631-1657	343.73072	Monopolies—United States
KF801-1241	346.7302	Contracts—United States	KF1659-.1	343.7307	Small business—Law and legislation—United States
KF898-905	344.7301542	Contracts for work and labor—United States	KF1661	346.73064	Trade associations—Law and legislation—United States
KF939-951	346.73025	Bailments—United States			
KF956-962	346.73096	Negotiable instruments—United States	KF1665-1666	343.73075	Weights and measures—Law and legislation—United States
KF966-1032	346.73082	Banking law—United States	KF1681-1755	343.73076	Agricultural laws and legislation—United States
			KF1770-1773	343.7307692	Fishery law and legislation—United States

LC	Dewey	Subject Heading	LC	Dewey	Subject Heading
KF1801-1873	343.73077	Mining law—United States	KF3992	344.730542	Lotteries—Law and legislation—United States
KF1875-1893	343.73078	United States—Manufactures—Law and legislation	KF4101-4257	344.7307	Educational law and legislation—United States
KF1900-1944	344.7304232	Food law and legislation—United States	KF4125-4143	344.73076	Education—Finance—Law and legislation—United States
KF1950	343.73078624	Construction industry—Law and legislation—United States	KF4150-4166	344.73079	Students—Legal status, laws, etc.—United States
KF1970-2105	346.7307	Business law—United States	KF4175-4190	344.73078	Teachers—Legal status, laws, etc.—United States
KF2161-2654	343.73093	Transportation—Law and legislation—United States	KF4192-.5	344.7307	School employees—Legal status, laws, etc.—United States
KF2900-2940	344.7301712	Professions—Law and legislation—United States	KF4195-4223	344.7307	Educational law and legislation—United States
KF2971-3193	346.73048	Intellectual property—United States	KF4225-4257	344.73074	Education, Higher—Law and legislation—United States
KF2986-3080	346.730482	Copyright—United States	KF4305	344.73093	Museums—Law and legislation—United States
KF3084	070.520973	Authors and publishers—United States	KF4310-4312	344.73094	Historic buildings—Law and legislation—United States
KF3086	346.730484	Design protection—United States	KF4315-4319	344.73092	Library legislation—United States
KF3091-3193	346.730486	Patent laws and legislation—United States	KF4325	344.73092	Archives—Law and legislation—United States
K3195-3198	343.73072	Competition, Unfair—United States	KF4501-5130	342.73	Constitutional law—United States
KF3300-3771	344.73	Social legislation—United States	KF4555-4558	342.73032	Constitutional amendments—United States
KF3301-3580	344.7301	Labor laws and legislation—United States	KF4565-4579	342.73044	Separation of powers—United States
KF3641-3664	343.7305242	Social security—United States	KF4600-4629	342.73042	Federal government—United States
KF3720-3745	344.730316	Public welfare—Law and legislation–United States	KF4635	342.730413	Law—United States—Territories and possessions
KF3750	344.7305348	Disaster relief—Law and legislation—United States	KF4695	342.730418	Police power—United States
KF3775-3816	344.7304	Public health laws—United States	KF4700-4720	342.73083	Citizenship—United States
KF3821-3829	344.73041	Medical laws and legislation—United States	KF4788	342.73087	Political parties—United States
KF3832	344.73048	Sterilization, Eugenic—Law and legislation—United States	KF4794-.5	342.73082	Passports—United States
			KF4800-4848	342.73083	Aliens—United States
KF3835-3838	344.73049	Veterinary hygiene—Law and legislation—United States	KF4850-4856	344.7305	Internal security—United States
KF3901-3925	344.7305	Alcohol—Law and legislation—United States	KF4865-4869	342.730852	Church and state—United States
KF3941-3942	344.730533	Weapons—Law and legislation—United States	KF4881-4921	342.7308	People (Constitutional law)—United States
KF3945-3965	344.73042	Product safety—Law and legislation—United States	KF4930-5005	342.7305	Legislative bodies—United States
KF3970	344.73047	Accident law—United States	KF5050-5125	342.7306	Executive departments—United States
KF3975-3977	344.7305377	Fire prevention—Law and legislation—United States	KF5130	347.73012	Judicial power—United States
KF3987	344.73099	Amusements—Law and legislation—United States			
KF3989	344.73099	Sports—Law and legislation—United States			

LC	Dewey	Subject Heading	LC	Dewey	Subject Heading
KF5150	344.7309	Emblems, National—United States	KF6525-6558	343.73054	Property tax—Law and legislation—United States
KF5300-5332	342.7309	Local government—Law and legislation—United States	KF6598-6609	343.730526	Indirect taxation—Law and legislation—United States
KF5336-5398	342.73068	Civil service—United States	KF6651-6708	343.73056	Tariff—Law and legislation—United States
KF5399-.5	342.730418	Police power—United States	KF6770-6795	343.73043	Local finance—Law and legislation—United States
KF5401-5425	342.73066	Administrative law—United States	KF7625-7659	343.730143	Courts-martial and courts of inquiry—United States
KF5500-5865	343.7302	Government property—United States	KF7685	344.730535	Civil defense—Law and legislation–United States
KF5505-5510	346.73044	Conservation of natural resources—United States	KF8201-8228	342.730872	Indians of North America—Legal status, laws, etc.
KF5521-5536	343.730942	Highway law—United States	KF8700-9075	347.7305	Procedure (Law)—United States
KF5551-5590	346.7304691	Water resources development—Law and legislation—United States	KF8741-8752	347.7305	Appellate procedure—United States
KF5594	344.730655168	Weather control—Law and legislation—United States	KF8771-8807	347.731(4-6)	Courts—United States—Officials and employees
KF5599	343.730252	Eminent domain—United States	KF8810-9075	347.7305	Civil procedure—United States
KF5670-5673	343.730253	Homestead law—United States	KF8816-8821	347.73051	Court rules—United States
KF5675-5677	343.730253	Land grants—Law and legislation—United States	KF8858-8861	347.73051	Jurisdiction—United States
KF5691-5710	346.73045	City planning and redevelopment law—United States	KF8863-8865	347.73053	Actions and defenses—United States
			KF8866-8885	347.73072	Pleading—United States
KF5721-5740	344.73063635	Housing—Law and legislation—United States	KF8890-8896.5	347.73052	Parties to actions—United States
KF5865	344.7306	Public works—Law and legislation—United States	KF8900-8902	347.73072	Pre-trial procedure—United States
KF5900-6075.5	343.7301	War and emergency legislation—United States	KF8910-8986	347.7307	Trials—United States
			KF8911-8925	347.73075	Trial practice—United States
KF6200-6795	343.7303	Finance, Public—Law and legislation—United States	KF8931-8969	347.7306	Evidence (Law)—United States
KF6201-6219	343.73032	Money—Law and legislation—United States	KF8971-8984	347.730752	Jury—United States
			KF8990-9002	347.73077	Judgments—United States
KF6221-6227	343.73034	Budget—Law and legislation—United States	KF9085-9086	347.7309	Arbitration and award—United States
KF6231-6239	343.73034	Finance, Public—Auditing—Law and legislation—United States	KF9201-9479	345.73	Criminal law—United States
KF6241-6245	343.73037	Debts, Public—Law and legislation—United States	KF9304-9329	345.73025	Offenses against the person—United States
KF6251-6708	343.73036	Internal revenue law—United States	KF9350-9379	345.73026	Offenses against property—United States
KF6271-6636	343.7304	Taxation—Law and legislation—United States	KF9625	345.730527	Arrest—United States
KF6329-6330	343.7304	Tax exemption—Law and legislation—United States	KF9630	345.730522	Searches and seizures—United States
KF6334	345.730233	Tax evasion—United States	KF9632	345.73056	Bail—United States
			KF9635	345.73052	Extradition—United States
			KF9640-9642	345.73072	Indictments—United States
KF6351-6499	343.73052	Income tax—Law and legislation—United States	KF9645-9650	345.73072	Arraignment—United States
			KF9660-9678	345.7306	Evidence, Criminal—United States

LC	Dewey	Subject Heading	LC	Dewey	Subject Heading
KF9680	345.73075	Jury—United States	KFZ8600-9199	349.75	Law—Confederate States of America
KF9695	345.73077	Pardon—United States			
KF9725	345.730773	Capital punishment—United States	KGA	349.7282	Law—Belize
KF9763	344.7303288	Victims of crimes—United States	KGB	349.7286	Law—Costa Rica
			KGC	349.7284	Law—El Salvador
			KGD	349.7281	Law—Guatemala
KFA0-599	349.761	Law—Alabama	KGE	349.7283	Law—Honduras
KFA1200-1799	349.798	Law—Alaska	KGF	349.72	Law—Mexico
KFA2400-2999	349.791	Law—Arizona	KGG	349.7285	Law—Nicaragua
KFA3600-4199	349.767	Law—Arkansas	KGH	349.7287	Law—Panama
KFC0-1199	349.794	Law—California	KGJ	349.729	Law—West Indies
KFC1800-2399	349.788	Law—Colorado	KGJ7000-7499	349.72973	Law—Anguilla
KFC3600-4199	349.746	Law—Connecticut	KGK0-499	349.72974	Law—Antiguilla
KFD0-599	349.751	Law—Delaware	KGK1000-1499	349.72986	Law—Aruba
KFD1200-1799	349.753	Law—Washington, D.C.	KGL0-499	349.7296	Law—Bahamas
KFF0-599	349.759	Law—Florida	KGL1000-1499	349.72981	Law—Barbados
KFG0-599	349.758	Law—Georgia	KGL2000-2499	349.72986	Law—Bonaire
KFH0-599	349.969	Law—Hawaii	KGL4000-4499	349.729725	Law—British Virgin Islands
KFI0-599	349.796	Law—Idaho	KGN	349.7291	Law—Cuba
KFI1200-1799	349.773	Law—Illinois	KGP0-499	349.72986	Law—Curacao
KFI4200-4799	349.777	Law—Iowa	KGP2000-2499	349.729841	Law—Dominica
KFK0-599	349.781	Law—Kansas	KGQ	349.7293	Law—Dominican Republic
KFK1200-1799	349.769	Law—Kentucky	KGR1000-1499	349.72986	Law—Netherlands Antilles
KFL0-599	349.763	Law—Louisiana	KGR3000-3499	349.72976	Law—West Indies, French
KFM0-599	349.741	Law—Maine	KGR4000-4499	349.729845	Law—Grenada
KFM1200-1799	349.752	Law—Maryland	KGR5000-5499	349.72976	Law—Guadeloupe
KFM2400-2999	349.744	Law—Massachusetts	KGS	349.7294	Law—Haiti
KFM4200-4799	349.774	Law—Michigan	KGT0-499	349.7292	Law—Jamaica
KFM5400-5999	349.776	Law—Minnesota	KGT1000-1499	349.72982	Law—Martinique
KFM6600-7199	349.762	Law—Mississippi	KGT2000-2499	349.72975	Law—Montserrat
KFM7800-8399	349.778	Law—Missouri	KGV	349.7295	Law—Puerto Rico
KFM9000-9599	349.786	Law—Montana	KGW0-499	349.72977	Law—Saba (Netherlands Antilles)
KFN0-599	349.782	Law—Nebraska			
KFN 600-1199	349.793	Law—Nevada	KGW2000-2499	349.72973	Law—Saint Kitts and Nevis
KFN1200-1799	349.742	Law—New Hampshire			
KFN1800-2399	349.749	Law—New Jersey	KGW3000-3499	349.729843	Law—Saint Lucia
KFN3600-4199	349.789	Law—New Mexico	KGW5000-5499	349.729844	Law—Saint Vincent
KFN5000-6199	349.747	Law—New York (State)	KGW7000-7499	349.72977	Law—Saint Eustatius (Netherlands Antilles)
KFN7400-7999	349.756	Law—North Carolina			
KFN8600-9199	349.784	Law—North Dakota	KGW8000-8499	349.72977	Law—Saint Martin
KFO0-599	349.771	Law—Ohio	KGX0-499	349.72983	Law—Trinidad and Tobago
KFO1200-1799	349.766	Law—Oklahoma	KGZ0-499	349.729722	Law—Virgin Islands of the United States
KFO2400-2999	349.795	Law—Oregon			
KFP0-599	349.748	Law—Pennsylvania			
KFR0-599	349.745	Law—Rhode Island	KH	349.8	Law—South America
KFS1800-2399	349.757	Law—South Carolina	KHA	349.82	Law—Argentina
KFS3000-3599	349.783	Law—South Dakota	KHC	349.84	Law—Bolivia
KFT0-599	349.768	Law—Tennessee	KHD	349.81	Law—Brazil
KFT1200-1799	349.764	Law—Texas	KHF	349.83	Law—Chile
KFU0-599	349.792	Law—Utah	KHH	349.861	Law—Columbia
KFV0-599	349.743	Law—Vermont	KHK	349.866	Law—Ecuador
KFV2400-2999	349.755	Law—Virginia	KHL	349.9711	Law—Falkland Islands
KFW0-599	349.797	Law—Washington	KHM	349.882	Law—French Guiana
KFW1200-1799	349.754	Law—West Virginia	KHP	349.892	Law—Paraguay
KFW2400-2999	349.775	Law—Wisconsin	KHQ	349.85	Law—Peru
KFW4200-4799	349.787	Law—Wyoming	KHS	349.883	Law—Surinam
KFX	349.7(4-9)	Law—[United States, By city]	KHU	349.895	Law—Uruguay
			KHW	349.87	Law—Venezuela

LC	Dewey	Subject Heading	LC	Dewey	Subject Heading
			L451-466	370.947	Education—Russia
KJA3210	343.37604	Taxation (Roman law)	L471-476	370.9489	Education—Denmark
KJG	349.4965	Law—Albania	L481	370.94912	Education—Iceland
KJJ	349.436	Law—Austria	L491-496	370.9481	Education—Norway
KJK	349.493	Law—Belgium	L501-506	370.9485	Education—Sweden
KJM	349.499	Law—Bulgaria	L511-516	370.946	Education—Spain
KJN	349.5645	Law—Cyprus	L521-526	370.9469	Education—Portugal
KJP	349.437	Law—Czechoslovakia	L531-536	370.9494	Education—Switzerland
KJR	349.489	Law—Denmark	L539-540	370.9561	Education—Turkey
KJT	349.4897	Law—Finland	L541-542	370.9499	Education—Bulgaria
KJV	349.44	Law—France	L545-546	370.9498	Education—Romania
KK	349.43	Law—Germany	L549-550	370.9497	Education—Yugoslavia
KKE	349.495	Law—Greece	L561-642	370.95	Education—Asia
KKF	349.439	Law—Hungary	L571-573	370.951	Education—China
KKG	349.4912	Law—Iceland	L577-578	370.954	Education—India
KKH	349.45	Law—Italy	L578.5-.6	370.95491	Education—Pakistan
KKJ	349.43648	Law—Liechtenstein	L585-586	370.959(4-7)	Education—Indochina
KKK0-499	349.4935	Law—Luxembourg	L597-598	370.9598	Education—Indonesia
KKK1000-1499	349.4585	Law—Malta	L611-612	370.952	Education—Japan
KKL	349.44949	Law—Monaco	L613-614	370.9519	Education—Korea
KKM	349.492	Law—Netherlands	L615-616	370.955	Education—Iran
KKN	349.481	Law—Norway	L617-620	370.957	Education—Siberia
KKP	349.438	Law—Poland	L627-628	370.9567	Education—Iraq
KKQ	349.469	Law—Portugal	L631-632	370.95694	Education—Israel
KKR	349.498	Law—Romania	L651-742	370.96	Education—Africa
KKT	349.46	Law—Spain	L750-792,	370.994	Education—Australia
KKV	349.485	Law—Sweden	757-775		
KKW	349.494	Law—Switzerland	L754-755	370.993	Education—New Zealand
KKX	349.561	Law—Turkey	L777-791	370.99(5-6)	Education—Oceania
KKZ	349.497	Law—Yugoslavia	L797-898	370.74	Education—Museums
			L900-991	370.25	Education—Directories
L	370	Education			
L	371	Schools	LA	370.9	Education—History
L7-101	370.5	Education—Periodicals	LA23	370.207	Humor in education
L106-107	370.6	Education—Congresses	LA31-81	370.901	Education, Ancient
L111-791	370.9(4-9)	Education—[By region or	LA37	370.932	Education, Egyptian
		country]	LA75	370.938	Education, Greek
L111-219	370.973	Education—United States	LA77	370.938	Education, Minoan
L116-219	370.97(4-9)	Education—[United	LA91-98	370.902	Education, Medieval
		States, By state]	LA106-108	370.11209024	Education, Humanistic
L221-223	370.971	Education—Canada	LA173-186	378.009	Education, Higher
L227-229	370.972	Education—Mexico	LA177	378.00902	Education, Medieval
L231-249	370.9728	Education—Central	LA186	371.81	Student movements
		America	LA190-2284	370.9 (4-9)	Education—History
L251-267	370.9729	Education—West Indies	LA2301-2397	370.92	Educators
L291-335	370.98	Education—South	LA2301-2397	370.92	Teachers
		America			
L341-359	370.941	Education—Great Britain	LB	370	Education
L341-551	370.94	Education—Europe	LB	371	Schools
L346-348	370.9415	Education—Ireland	LB	371.102	Teaching
L361-366	370.9436	Education—Austria	LB41	370.1	Education—Aims and
L381-383	370.9439	Education—Hungary			objectives
L385-387	370.9437	Education—Czechoslovakia	LB41.5	370.112	Education—Forecasting
L391-396	370.944	Education—France	LB45	306.43	Educational anthropology
L401-410	370.943	Education—Germany	LB51-875	370.92	Educators
L411-416	370.9495	Education—Greece	LB125-875	370.1	Education—Philosophy
L421-426	370.945	Education—Italy	LB1025-1050.7	371.1	Teaching
L431-436	370.9493	Education—Belgium	LB1027	371.3	Educational innovations
L441-446	370.9492	Education—Netherlands			

LC	Dewey	Subject Heading	LC	Dewey	Subject Heading
LB1027.25	371.3	Creative activities and seat work	LB1050	372.4	Reading
LB1027.3	371.3	Education—Experimental methods	LB1050.37	372.40284	Reading machines
			LB1050.43	372.414	Reading readiness
			LB1050.45	372.47	Reading comprehension
LB1027.5-.8	371.4	Educational counseling	LB1050.46	372.48	Reading—Ability testing
LB1027.5	371.4047	Peer counseling of students	LB1050.5	372.43	Reading—Remedial teaching
LB1027.55	371.713	School psychology	LB1050.5	371.9144	Dyslexia
LB1027.9	379.111	School choice	LB1050.53	418.4	Developmental reading
LB1028-.25	370.72	Education—Research	LB1050.55	418.4	Silent reading
LB1028.24	370.72	Action research in education	LB1051-1091	370.15	Educational psychology
			LB1059	153.154	Transfer of training
LB1028.4	371.33	Media programs (Education)	LB1060-1091	153.15	Learning, Psychology of
			LB1060	153.15	Learning
LB1028.43	371.334	Education—Data processing	LB1060.2	370.1528	Behavior modification
			LB1062	370.157	Creative thinking
LB1028.5-.7	371.334	Computer-assisted instruction	LB1063-1064	370.1522	Memory
			LB1065	153.1533	Interest (Psychology)
LB1028.5	371.334	Programmed instruction	LB1065	153.1532	Attention
LB1028.75	371.334	Interactive video	LB1067	153.73	Apperception
LB1029.A85	371.334	Teaching machines	LB1067.5	153.152	Visual learning
LB1029.F7	371.04	Free schools	LB1071	153.8	Will
LB1029.G3	371.337	Educational games	LB1075	152.1886	Mental fatigue
LB1029.L3	371.382	Dalton laboratory plan	LB1101-1139	155.4	Child development
LB1029.M7	371.39	Monitorial system of education	LB1123	152.335	Left- and right-handedness
LB1029.M75	371.392	Montessori method of education	LB1134	153.9	Learning ability
			LB1135	155.5	Adolescence
LB1029.N6	371.255	Nongraded schools	LB1139.2-.4	372.21	Early childhood education
LB1029.06	371.256	Open plan schools	LB1139.L3	153.6	Speech
LB1029.R4	374.012	Remedial teaching	LB1139.S88	370.158	Student adjustment
LB1029.S5	371.397	Simulated environment (Teaching method)	LB1140-.5	372.21	Education, Preschool
			LB1140.35.C74	371.3	Creative activities and seat work
LB1029.S53	371.397	Education—Simulation methods	LB1140.5.R4	372.4	Reading (Preschool)
LB1029.T6	371.337	Educational toys	LB1141-1499	372.218	Kindergarten
LB1029.U6	371.36	Unit method of teaching	LB1181.2	372.4	Reading (Kindergarten)
LB1032	371.148	Team learning approach in education	LB1501-1547	372	Education, Primary
			LB1525-.8	372.4	Reading (Primary)
LB1033	371.1023	Teacher-student relationships	LB1525	372.4	Reading (Elementary)
			LB1536	372.634	Penmanship
LB1033.5	370.14	Nonverbal communication in education	LB1537	372.11	Education, Primary—Activity programs
LB1039	371.37	Recitation (Education)	LB1537	371.3	Creative activities and seat work
LB1042	372.677	Storytelling			
LB1043-1044.9	371.335	Audio-visual education	LB1555-1601	372	Education, Elementary
LB1043.5-1044	371.335	Visual aids	LB1570-1571	375	Education—Curricula
LB1043.5	371.335	Overhead projection	LB1573	372.4	Reading (Elementary)
LB1043.6	371.33	Displays in education	LB1573.3	372.465	Reading—Phonetic method
LB1043.67	371.3352	Pictures in education			
LB1043.8	371.3352	Filmstrips in education	LB1573.37	372.462	Reading (Elementary)—Whole-word method
LB1044.5-.6	371.3331	Radio in education			
LB1044.7	371.3358	Television in education	LB1573.5	372.452	Oral reading
LB1044.75	371.33523	Video tapes in education	LB1574	372.632	Spelling ability
LB1044.75	371.33523	Video tapes	LB1576	372.6	Language arts (Elementary)
LB1047	371.384	School field trips			
LB1047	371.384	Outdoor education	LB1590	372.634	Penmanship
LB1048	371.30281	Homework	LB1590.3-.5	153.42	Thought and thinking
LB1049	371.3943	Independent study	LB1595-1599	372.5	Manual training

LC	Dewey	Subject Heading	LC	Dewey	Subject Heading
LB1603-1694	373.238	High schools	LB2361-2365	378.199	Universities and colleges—Curricula
LB1623	373.236	Middle schools	LB2366-2367	378.241	Examinations
LB1623	373.236	Junior high schools	LB2367	378.1662	Universities and colleges—Examinations
LB1627.7	373.238	High school equivalency certificates	LB2369	378.242	Dissertations, Academic
LB1705-2286	370.711	Teachers—Training of	LB2371	378.155	Universities and colleges—Graduate work
LB1731	370.711	Teachers—In-service training	LB2372.E3	378.155	Education—Graduate work
LB1755-1779	371.11	Teachers	LB2375-2378	378.016	Student exchange programs
LB1762-1765	370.711	Examinations	LB2375-2378	378.016	Educational exchanges
LB1771-1773	371.12	Teachers—Certification	LB2381-2391	378.2	Degrees, Academic
LB1775-1785	371.1	Teaching	LB2383	378.2	Bachelor of arts degree
LB1775.5	372.21	Preschool teachers	LB2385	378.2	Master of arts degree
LB1775.6	372.11	Early childhood educators	LB2386	378.2	Doctor of philosophy degree
LB1776	372.11	Elementary school teachers	LB2389	378.28	Academic costume
LB1777-.4	373.11	High school teachers	LB2393	378.1796	Lecture method in teaching
LB1778	378.12	College teachers	LB2393.5	378.177	Seminars
LB1805-2151	370.711	Teachers colleges	LB2395	378.170281	Note-taking
LB2157	370.71	Student teachers	LB2801-2997	378.1	School management and organization
LB2283-2286	370.116	Educational exchanges			
LB2283-2285	370.1163	Teacher exchange programs	LB2806.2	371.393	Performance contracts in education
LB2300-2411	378	Universities and colleges	LB2806.22	379.158	Educational accountability
LB2328	378.1543	Junior colleges	LB2806.3	371.2	School management teams
LB2328	378.1543	Community colleges			
LB2328.4	378.052	Urban universities and colleges	LB2806.4	371.203	School supervision
LB2329	378.052	Municipal universities and colleges	LB2809	379.152	State departments of education
LB2329.5	378.053	State universities and colleges	LB2810-.5	379.158	Accreditation (Education)
LB2331.5	378.104	University cooperation	LB2813	379.123	County school systems
LB2331.6-.615	353.88284	Universities and colleges—Accreditation	LB2817-.5	379.1535	School districts
			LB2818	373.241	Magnet schools
LB2331.7-.74	378.12	Universities and colleges—Faculty	LB2822.5	372.12	Elementary school administration
LB2335.95-2337	378.106	Educational fund raising	LB2822.75	379.158	Educational evaluation
LB2336-2337	378.106	Endowments	LB2823	370.723	Educational surveys
LB2337.2-2340.8	378.3	Student aid	LB2823.2	379.1535	School closings
LB2338-2339	378.34	Scholarships	LB2824-2830	371.206	Education—Finance
LB2340-.4	378.362	Student loan funds	LB2824-2830	379.13	School bonds
LB2341	378.111	College administrators	LB2825-2826.6	379.121	Federal aid to education
LB2341	378.161	Student registration	LB2828	379.32	State aid to private schools
LB2341	371.4	Deans (Education)			
LB2342	378.106	Universities and colleges—Finance	LB2831	379.1531	School boards
			LB2831.5-2844.4	371.201	School personnel management
LB2342-.2	378.38	College costs			
LB2343	378.194	Faculty advisors	LB2831.5-.585	371.201	School employees
LB2351-2359	378.161	Universities and colleges—Admission	LB2831.7-.776	371.2011	School superintendents
			LB2831.8-.876	371.2011	School administrators
LB2351-2360	378.1617	Universities and colleges—Entrance requirements	LB2831.9-.976	371.2012	School principals
			LB2831.9-.976	373.12012	High school principals
			LB2831.9-.976	372.12012	Elementary school principals
LB2351.5-.52	378.1616	College applications	LB2832-2844.47	371.1	Teachers
LB2353	378.1662	Universities and colleges—Examinations	LB2832.2	379.1535	Public school closings
LB2359.5	378.1618	College credits	LB2836	371.104	Teachers—Tenure

LC	Dewey	Subject Heading	LC	Dewey	Subject Heading
LB2844.1.W6	371.1412	Teachers—Workload	LB3251	371.61	School grounds
LB2842-2844	331.2813711	Teachers—Salaries, etc.	LB3253	371.61	Campus parking
LB2843.L4	371.104	Teachers—Leaves of absence	LB3261-3281	371.63	Schools—Furniture, equipment, etc.
LB2844.1	371.14	Teachers, Part-time	LB3401-3495	371.71	School hygiene
LB2844.1.P7	371.144	Teachers, Probationary	LB3401-3495	371.71	School health services
LB2844.52-.53	331.88113711	Teachers' unions	LB3473-3479	371.716	School children—Food
LB2846	370.21	Educational statistics	LB3473-3479	371.716	School milk programs
LB2848-2849	371.223	Scholarships	LB3473-3479	371.716	School breakfast programs
LB2861	379.1535	Schools—Centralization	LB3602-3618	371.8	Students
LB2862	379.1535	Schools—Decentralization	LB3604-3615	371.8	Hazing
LB2864	371.872	School children—Transportation	LB3604	371.8	Students—Language
			LB3605	371.8	Student activities
LB2864.6.A25	363.119371	School accidents	LB3609	174.9375	Student ethics
LB2865	363.1257	School safety patrols	LB3613.M3	371.82655	Married students
LB3011-3095	371.5	School discipline	LB3618	371.8	Class reunions
LB3011-3095	371.2	School management and organization	LB3621	371.897	Student publications
			LB3635	791.64	Cheerleading
LB3013	371.1024	Classroom management			
LB3013.2	371.251	Class size	LC	371.01	Public schools
LB3013.3	371.78	School violence	LC40	371.042	Home schooling
LB3013.4	371.46	School social work	LC41	371.394	Tutors and tutoring
LB3013.5	371.46	Visiting teachers	LC46-.8	371.04	Alternative schools
LB3025	371.5	Discipline of children	LC47-57	371.02	Private schools
LB3034	371.23	School year	LC58-.7	373.222	Preparatory schools
LB3044.7-.74	027.7	Instructional materials centers	LC71-188	379	Education and state
			LC71.2	371.207	Educational planning
LB3045-3048	371.32	Textbooks	LC72-.5	371.104	Academic freedom
LB3045.6	371.32	Textbook bias	LC72-.5	371.104	Teaching, Freedom of
LB3045.66	379.156	Sexism in textbooks	LC107-120	379.28	Religion in the public schools
LB3050-3060	371.271	Examinations			
LB3051-3059	371.271	Examinations—Questions	LC129-139	379.23	Education, Compulsory
LB3051-3060.87	371.271	Educational tests and measurements	LC130-139	371.219	School enrollment
			LC142-145	371.2913	Dropouts
LB3051-3063	371.272	Grading and marking (Students)	LC142-148.5	371.294	School attendance
			LC145.5-.8	372.12913	Elementary school dropouts
LB3060.3	371.271	Achievement tests			
LB3060.32.D65	371.271	Domain-referenced tests	LC146	373.1219	High school enrollment
LB3060.32.M85	371.271	Multiple-choice examinations	LC146.5-.8	373.12913	High school dropouts
			LC149-160	379.24	Literacy
LB3060.32.N67	371.271	Norm-referenced tests	LC189-214.53	306.43	Educational sociology
LB3060.32.O35	371.271	Objective tests	LC201.5-.7	370.117	Native language and education
LB3060.57	371.27	Examinations—Study guides	LC212-.863	379.26	Discrimination in education
LB3060.65	371.27	Examinations—Design and construction	LC212.5-.73	379.26	Segregation in education
			LC212.6-.63	379.263	De facto school segregation
LB3060.77	371.27	Examinations—Scoring			
LB3061	371.254	Ability grouping in education	LC212.8-.83	379.26	Sex discrimination in education
LB3061.8	371.25	Track system (Education)	LC213-.3	379.26	Educational equalization
LB3064	371.2914	Students, Transfer of	LC213-.3	370.111	Compensatory education
LB3081-3087	371.294	School attendance	LC214-.3	379.263	School integration
LB3089-.4	371.543	Student suspension	LC214.5-.53	379.263	Busing for school integration
LB3092-3095	371.59	Student government			
LB3205-3295	371.6	School buildings	LC225.5	371.103	Parent-teacher conferences
LB3205-3325	371.6	School facilities			
LB3226-3228	371.871	Student housing	LC230-235	371.19206	Parents' and teachers' associations
LB3226-3229	371.871	Dormitories			
LB3249	371.58	School vandalism			

LC	Dewey	Subject Heading	LC	Dewey	Subject Heading
LC241-245	371.206	Educational fund raising	LC4201-4580	371.91	Physically handicapped children—Education
LC251-301	370.114	Character	LC4219.7	370.113087	Physically handicapped children—Vocational education
LC251-318	370.114	Moral education			
LC427-629	371.071	Church schools			
LC427-629	378.071	Church colleges			
LC487	378.07122	Catholic universities and colleges	LC4601-4700	371.92	Mentally handicapped children—Education
LC905.T42	371.100882971	Muslim teachers	LC4604	371.9573	Mentally handicapped children—Education (Secondary)
LC1001-1024	370.112	Education, Humanistic			
LC1001-1021	373.242	Classical education			
LC1035-.8	370	Basic education	LC4661-4700.4	371.926	Slow learning children
LC1037-.8	370.113	Career education	LC4704-4706	371.9	Learning disabilities
LC1041-1047	370.113	Vocational education	LC4708-4710	371.9144	Dyslexic children
LC1041-1047	370.113	Technical education	LC4818-.53	371.9	Learning disabled
LC1049-.8	371.28	Educational acceleration	LC5001-5060	371.82623	Working class—Education
LC1051-1071	378.013	Professional education	LC5101-5143	370.91732	Education, Urban
LC1070-1071	378.013076	Examinations	LC5101-5143	370.91732	Urban schools
LC1099-.5	370.117	Multicultural education	LC5144-.3	371.826942	Homeless students
LC1101-1261	340.0711	Law schools	LC5146-5148	370.91734	Education, Rural
LC1401-2571	371.822	Women—Education	LC5161-5163	370.111	Fundamental education
LC1500-1506	370.113082	Women—Vocational education	LC5201-6660	374	Adult education
			LC5201-6660	374	Continuing education
LC1551-1651	378.19822	Women—Education (Higher)	LC5225.L42	374	Adult learning
			LC5451-5493	371.8246	Aged—Education
LC1660-1666	374.1822	Adult education of women	LC5501-5560	374.8	Evening and continuation schools
LC2601-2611	370.91724	Education—Developing countries			
			LC5701-5760	371.232	Summer schools
LC2667-2688	370.8968073	Hispanic Americans—Education	LC5800-5808	371.35	Distance education
			LC6201-6401	378.175	University extension
LC2699-2913	371.82996073	Blacks—Education	LC6501-6560.4	080	Lectures and lecturing
LC2701-2853	371.82996073	Afro-Americans—Education	LC6501-6560	371.396	Forums (Discussion and debate)
LC2707	371.22308996 + 073	Afro-Americans—Scholarships, fellowships, etc.			
			LD	371.00973	Schools—United States
			LD13-7251	378.73	Universities and colleges—United States
LC2771	372.182996 + 073	Afro-Americans—Education (Elementary)	LD6501	378.15430973	Junior colleges—United States
LC2779	373.182996 + 073	Afro-Americans—Education (Secondary)	LD7501	373.73	High schools—United States
LC2780	370.11308996 + 073	Afro-Americans—Vocational education			
LC2781	378.1982996 + 073	Afro-Americans—Education (Higher)	LE3-5	378.7	Universities and colleges—Canada
L2785	378.01308996 + 073	Afro-Americans—Professional education	LE7-9	378.72	Universities and colleges—Mexico
LC3001-3501	371.82995	Asians—Education	LE11-13	378.728	Universities and colleges—Central America
LC3503-3520	371.82991497	Gypsies—Education			
LC3701-3743	370.1175	Education, Bilingual	LE15-17	378.729	Universities and colleges—Caribbean Area
LC3701-3740	371.829	Minorities—Education			
LC3800-3806	371.829	Ethnic schools	LE21-78	378.8	Universities and colleges—South America
LC3950-3990.4	371.9	Special education			
LC3991-4000	371.8279	Gifted children			
LC4001-4100	371.91	Handicapped children—Education	LF	378	Universities and colleges—Europe
LC4051-4100	371.82694	Socially handicapped children—Education	LG21-320	378.5	Universities and colleges—Asia
LC4165-4184	371.94	Mentally ill children—Education	LG331-370	378.56	Universities and colleges—Middle East

LC	Dewey	Subject Heading	LC	Dewey	Subject Heading
LG401-690	378.6	Universities and colleges—Africa	M140-141	787.83	Lute music
LG715-720	378.94	Universities and colleges—Australia	M142.A7	787.75	Appalachian dulcimer music
LG741-745	378.93	Universities and colleges—New Zealand	M142.B2	787.875	Balalaika music
			M142.C44	787.95	Celtic harp music
LG961	378.9(5-6)	Universities and colleges—Oceania	M142.D8	787.74	Dulcimer music
			M142.E4	787.87	Electric guitar music
			M142.S5	787.82	Sitar music
			M142.U5	787.89	Ukulele music
LJ	371.85	Greek letter societies	M145	788.49	Bagpipe music
LT	371.32	Textbooks	M146	786.873	Cymbal music
			M146	786.93	Tabla music
M	780	Music	M146	786.94	Snare drum music
M5-1459	784	Instrumental music	M146	786.93	Timpani music
M6-14	786.5	Organ music	M146	786.8	Percussion music
M14.8	786.59	Electronic organ music	M147	786.843	Glockenspiel music
M15-17	786.55	Reed-organ music	M147	786.88485	Handbell music
M20-39	786.3	Clavichord music	M154	788.84	Concertina music
M20-39	786.2	Piano music	M172	786.64	Carillon music
M20-39	786.4	Harpsichord music	M172	786.848	Chime music
M20-32	786.4	Electronic harpsichord music	M175.5	785	Solo instrument music
			M175.A4	788.86	Accordion music
M20-32	786.66	Player-piano music	M175.A8	787.75	Autoharp music
M40-44	787.2	Violin music	M175.B2	788.84	Bandonion music
M45-49	787.3	Viola music	M175.C35	786.873	Castanet music
M50-54	787.4	Violoncello music	M175.C44	786.83	Celesta music
M55-58	787.5	Double-bass music	M175.H9	787.69	Hurdy-gurdy music
M59	787.6	Hardanger fiddle music	M175.M38	788.863	Melodeon music
M59	787.6	Baryton music	M175.M8	788.82	Harmonica music
M59	787.6	Viol music	M175.T	786.8842	Triangle music
M59.5	787	String instrument music	M175.T	786.95	Tambourine music
M59.V	787.66	Violetta d'amore music	M175.X6	786.843	Vibraphone music
M60-64	788.3	Flute music	M175.X6	786.843	Marimba music
M60-62	788.33	Fife music	M175.X6	786.843	Xylophone music
M65-69	788.52	Oboe music	M176	781.542	Silent film music
M70-74	788.62	Clarinet music	M176.5	781.544	Radio music
M70-74	788.65	Bass clarinet music	M177-990	785	Chamber music
M75-79	788.58	Bassoon music	M177-298.5	785.12	Duets
M85-89	788.92	Trumpet music	M300-386	785.13	Trios
M85-89	788.96	Cornet music	M349-353	785.13	String trios
M90-94	788.93	Trombone music	M400-486	785.14	Quartets
M90-94	788.975	Baritone music	M450-454	784.4	String quartets
M90-94	788.974	Alto trombone music	M500-586	785.15	Quintets
M95-99	788.98	Tuba music	M600-686	785.16	Sextets
M105-109	788.7	Saxophone music	M700-786	785.17	Septets
M110	788.974	Alto horn music	M800-886	785.18	Octets
M110	788.92	Alpenhorn music	M900-986	785.19	Nonets
M110.B33	788.975	Euphonium music	M955-959	785.43	Wind ensembles
M110.E5	788.53	English-horn music	M955-959	785.8	Woodwind ensembles
M110.P5	788.33	Piccolo music	M955-959	785.9	Brass ensembles
M110.R4	788.36	Recorder music	M1000-1075	784.2	Orchestral music
M111	788	Wind instrument music	M1001	784.184	Symphonies
M111	788.9	Brass instrument music	M1004	784.18926	Overtures
M115-119	787.9	Harp music	M1100-1160	784.7	String-orchestra music
M120-122	787.88	Banjo Music	M1200-1268	784	Band music
M125-129	787.87	Guitar music	M1200-1269	784.9	Brass band music
M125-129	787.87	Bass guitar music	M1247	784.1897	Marches (Band)
M130-134	787.84	Mandolin music	M1260	784.1897	Marches (Band)
M135-137	787.7	Zither music	M1270	781.599	Military music

LC	Dewey	Subject Heading	LC	Dewey	Subject Heading
M1270	788.92	Trumpet-calls	ML155	784.190294	Musical instruments—Catalogs, Manufacturers'
M1350	784.4	Salon-orchestra music			
M1356	784.48	Dance-orchestra music	ML159-3799	780.9	Music—History and criticism
M1365	791.12	Minstrel music			
M1366	781.65	Jazz	ML162-169	784.1901	Musical instruments, Ancient
M1366	781.645	Ragtime music			
M1366	784.48	Big band music	ML196	780.9034	Romanticism in music
M1366	781.653	Dixieland music	ML385-403	780.92	Musicians
M1470	781.3	Chance compositions	ML385-429	780.92	Music—Bio-bibliography
M1473	786.74	Synthesizer music	ML430-455	781.309	Composition (Music)
M1495-5000	782	Vocal music	ML457	780.7809	Music—Performance
M1500-1527.8	782.1	Dramatic music	ML457	781.4409	Performance practice (Music)
M1500-1508	782.14	Musicals			
M1500-1508	782.14	Revues	ML459-1093	784.1909	Musical instruments
M1500-1508	782.1	Operas	ML475-1354	784.19(4-9)	Musical instruments—[By region or country]
M1528-1529.5	782.0438	Vocal ensembles			
M1530-1546.5	782.48	Cantatas, Secular	ML476	784.1973	Musical instruments—United States
M1547-1610	782.5	Choruses, Secular			
M1578-1600	783.1	Part-songs	ML478	784.1971	Musical instruments—Canada
M1580.4	783.14	Barbershop quartets			
M1594	783.14	Barbershop quartets	ML480	784.19729	Musical instruments—West Indies
M1604	783.14	Barbershop quartets			
M1609	782.5	Cantatas, Secular (Unison)	ML482	784.1972	Musical instruments—Mexico
M1621.4	782.47	Song cycles	ML484	784.19728	Musical instruments—Central America
M1627-1853	781.599	National music			
M1627-1844	781.63	Popular music	ML486	784.198	Musical instruments—South America
M1627	782.42162	Folk songs			
M1627	782.43	Ballads	ML489-522	784.194	Musical instruments—Europe
M1670-1671	782.253	Spirituals (Songs)			
M1977.C5	782.42	Songbooks	ML491	784.19436	Musical instruments—Austria
M1977.P75	781.592	Protest songs			
M1977.S2	782.421595	Sea songs	ML493	784.19437	Musical instruments—Czechoslovakia
M1990-1998	782.42083	Children's songs			
M1999-2199	782.3	Sacred vocal music	ML494	784.19439	Musical instruments—Hungary
M2000-2007	782.23	Oratorios			
M2010-2014	782.3238	Requiems	ML496	784.19493	Musical instruments—Belgium
M2018-2019.5	782.221438	Sacred vocal ensembles			
M2020-2036	782.24	Cantatas, Sacred	ML497	784.1944	Musical instruments—France
M2038-2099	782.265	Anthems			
M2099.5	781.76	Synagogue music	ML499-500	784.1943	Musical instruments—Germany
M2114.3	781.76	Synagogue music			
M2115-2145	782.27	Hymns	ML501	784.1941	Musical instruments—Great Britain
M2186-2187	781.76	Synagogue music			
M2198-2199	782.254	Gospel music	ML503	784.1945	Musical instruments—Italy
M3516	783.14	Barbershop singing	ML505	784.19492	Musical instruments—Netherlands
ML	780.72	Musicology	ML513-516	784.1948	Musical instruments—Scandinavia
ML25-28	780.6	Music—Societies, etc.			
ML35-38	780.79	Music festivals	ML514	784.19489	Musical instruments—Denmark
ML48-49	780	Librettos			
ML93-98	780.262	Musicians—Autographs	ML515	784.19481	Musical instruments—Norway
ML93-98	780	Music—Manuscripts			
ML100-110	780.3	Music—Dictionaries	ML516	784.19485	Musical instruments—Sweden
ML105-107	780.12	Music—Bio-bibliography			
ML108	780.14	Music—Terminology	ML518	784.1946	Musical instruments—Spain
ML111-158	016.78	Music—Bibliography			
			ML519	784.19469	Musical instruments—Portugal

LC	Dewey	Subject Heading	LC	Dewey	Subject Heading
ML520	784.19494	Musical instruments—Switzerland	ML1900	782.1209	Operetta
ML525-541	784.195	Musical instruments—Asia	ML2500-2862	782.4209	Songs—History and criticism
ML527	784.19538	Musical instruments—Saudi Arabia	ML2900-3275	782.2209	Sacred vocal music
			ML3000-3190	781.71009	Church music
ML531	784.195	Musical instruments—China	ML3001	782.3209	Music in churches
			ML3002-3051	782.3222009	Church music—Catholic Church
ML533	784.1954	Musical instruments—India			
ML535	784.1952	Musical instruments—Japan	ML3060	782.32215009	Church music—Catholic Church (Byzantine rite)
ML537	784.19519	Musical instruments—Korea	ML3100-3188	782.3224009	Church music—Protestant churches
ML539	784.1955	Musical instruments—Iran	ML3166	782.3223009	Church music—Episcopal Church
ML544	784.196	Musical instruments—Africa	ML3166	782.3223009	Church music—Church of England
ML547	784.1994	Musical instruments—Australia	ML3300-3354	781.5609	Program music
ML547	784.1993	Musical instruments—New Zealand	ML3400-3451	781.55409	Dance music—History and criticism
ML547	784.199(5-6)	Musical instruments—Oceania	ML3460	781.55609	Ballet
ML550-649	786.509	Organ	ML3469-3541	781.6309	Popular music
ML597	786.5509	Reed-organ	ML3469-3541	784.16309	Popular instrumental music
ML597	786.509	Hammond organ	ML3505.8-3509	784.165309	Dixieland music
ML649.8-747	786.209	Piano	ML3518	784.4809	Dance-orchestra music
ML649.8-747	786.309	Clavichord	ML3519-3520	784.164209	Bluegrass music
ML750-927	787.09	Stringed instruments	ML3521	784.164309	Blues (Music)
ML800-897	787.209	Violin	ML3523-3524	784.164209	Country music
ML929-990	788.09	Wind instruments	ML3533.8-3534	784.16609	Rock music
ML935-937	788.3309	Piccolo	ML3535	784.16609	Rockabilly music
ML953	788.5807	Bassoon	ML3541	784.16409	Western swing (Music)
ML980	788.4909	Gaita	ML3545	781.59909	National music—History and criticism
ML990.E	788.97509	Euphonium	ML3795	331.28178	Musicians—Salaries, etc.
ML1015-1018	787.7409	Dulcimer	ML3797.7-3799	780.89	Ethnomusicology
ML1030-1040	786.809	Percussion instruments	ML3800-3920	780.1	Music—Philosophy and aesthetics
ML1035	786.909	Drum			
ML1038.S	786.9409	Snare drum	ML3800	780.9	Music, Origin of
ML1055	788.3609	Music recorder	ML3807-3809	781.232	Musical pitch
ML1055	780.26609	Phonograph	ML3809	784.1928	Musical temperament
ML1058	786.6609	Mechanical organs	ML3809	781.246	Musical intervals and scales
ML1065-1066	786.6509	Music box			
ML1083	788.8609	Accordion	ML3815	781.25	Harmony
ML1087	786.88709	Jew's harp	ML3830-3838	781.11	Music—Psychology
ML1088	788.8209	Harmonica	ML3834	781.24	Melody
ML1092	786.7409	Electronic keyboard (Synthesizer)	ML3836	781.25	Harmony
			ML3845	781.825	Variation (Music)
ML1100-1165	785.009	Chamber music—History and criticism	ML3849	780.0398	Music and mythology
			ML3850	781.22(4 or 6)	Musical Meter and rhythm
ML1158	784.18509	Suite (Music)	ML3851	781.24	Melody
ML1200-1251	784.209	Orchestra	ML3852	781.25	Harmony
ML1258	784.18509	Suite (Music)	ML3855	781.56	Program music
ML1300-1354	784.09	Bands (Music)	ML3857-3862	781.552	Dramatic music
ML1400-3275	782.009	Vocal music—History and criticism	ML3858	782.1	Opera
			ML3869	781.71017	Church music
ML1500-1554	782.509	Choral music	ML3919-3920	615.85154	Music therapy
ML1699-2100	782.109	Dramatic music	ML3920	780.0365	Music in prisons
ML1700-1751	782.1409	Musicals—History and criticism			

LC	Dewey	Subject Heading
MT	780.7	Music—Instruction and study
MT6-7	781	Music—Theory
MT9	780.76	Music—Examinations, questions, etc.
MT35	780.1407	Musical shorthand
MT35	781.424	Ear training
MT35	780.14	Musical dictation
MT35	780.148	Musical notation
MT38	780.87107	Blind, Music for the
MT40-67	781.307	Composition (Music)
MT42	781.2207	Tempo (Music)
MT47	781.2407	Melody
MT62	784.18307	Sonata
MT68	781.4707	Songs—Accompaniment
MT68	781.4707	Musical accompaniment
MT80	781.247	Embellishment (Music)
MT80	781.247	Embellishment (Vocal music)
MT82	781.426	Music—Memorizing
MT85	781.4507	Conducting
MT88	782.507	Choirs (Music)
MT90-145	781.17	Music appreciation
MT125	784.117	Band music—Analysis, appreciation
MT125	784.2117	Orchestral music—Analysis, appreciation
MT170-805	784.1907	Musical instruments
MT180-258	786.07	Keyboard instruments
MT180	786.507	Organ—Instruction and study
MT190	786.14707	Musical accompaniment
MT208	786.5507	Reed-organ—Methods—Self-instruction
MT220-255	786.207	Piano—Instruction and study
MT236	781.42307	Sight-reading (Music)
MT239	786.214707	Musical accompaniment
MT259-338	787.07	Stringed instruments
MT320-334	787.5107	Double bass
MT340-348	788.307	Flute
MT356	788.3307	Fife
MT360-378	788.5207	Oboe
MT380-388	788.6207	Clarinet
MT418	788.907	Brass instruments
MT493	788.9707	Flugelhorn
MT560-570	787.8807	Banjo
MT580-588	787.8707	Guitar
MT620-634	787.707	Zither—Instruction and study
MT700	786.607	Musical instruments (Mechanical)
MT710	786.8848507	Handbell ringing
MT724	786.707	Musical instruments, Electronic
MT728	785.143807	Ensemble playing
MT733.4	784.8307	Marching bands
MT737	781.54207	Silent films—Musical accompaniment
MT825-850	782.001	Singing—Methods
MT870	782.042307	Sight-singing
MT875	782.507	Choral singing
MT882	782.001	Singing—Methods
MT949.5	782.98	Whistling
N	700	Art
N1-9.9	705	Art—Periodicals
N10-17	706	Art—Societies, etc.
N21	706	Art—Congresses
N33	703	Art—Dictionaries
N40-43	709.2	Art—Biography
N40	700.92	Artists
N50-55	702.5	Art—Directories
N61-79	701.17	Aesthetics
N61-79	701.15	Imagination
N61-75	701	Art—Philosophy
N61	701.1709031	Aesthetics, Modern—16th century
N61	701.1709032	Aesthetics, Modern—17th Century
N61	701.1709033	Aesthetics, Modern—18th century
N61	701.170902	Aesthetics, Medieval
N61	701.1709034	Aesthetics, Modern—19th century
N61	701.170904	Aesthetics, Modern—20th century
N70	709.0342	Romanticism in art
N72.P5	770	Art and photography
N72.T4	700.105	Art and technology
N81-390	707.1	Art—Study and teaching
N325-335	707.1	Art schools
N328-330	707.1073	Art schools—United States
N332	707.104	Art schools—Europe
N400-3990	708	Art museums
N510-880	708.1(3-9)	Art museums—United States
N1010-3690	708.(2-9)	Art museums—Europe
N1020-1560	708.2	Art museums—Great Britain
N1750-1850	708.93	Art museums—Belgium
N2010-2180	708.4	Art museums—France
N2210-2406	708.3	Art museums—Germany
N2410-2430	708.95	Art museums—Greece
N2450-2505	708.92	Art museums—Netherlands
N2510-3065	708.5	Art museums—Italy
N3310-3382	708.7	Art museums—Russia
N3410-3499	708.6	Art museums—Spain
N4000-4042	779.074	Photograph collections
N4390-5098	707.4	Art—Exhibitions
N5198-5299	708	Art—Private collections
N5215-5220	708.1(3-9)	Art—Private collections—United States
N5240-5280	708.(2-8)	Art—Private collections—Europe
N5300-7418	709	Art—History

LC	Dewey	Subject Heading
N5310-5313	709.011	Art, Primitive
N5310-5313	709.011	Art, Prehistoric
N5312-5313	745	Folk art
N5315-5899	709.01	Art, Ancient
N5343-5345	709.31	Oriental antiquities
N5350-5351	709.32	Art, Egyptian
N5370	709.35	Art, Sumerian
N5460	709.3943	Art, Syrian
N5470	709.394	Art, Arab
N5480-5560	709.392	Art, Turkish
N5603-5896.3	709.38	Art, Classical
N5630-5720	709.38	Art, Greek
N5760-5763	709.37	Art, Roman
N5940-6320	709.02	Art, Medieval
N6280	709.0216	Art, Romanesque
N6350-6494	709.03	Art, Modern
N6370-6375	709.024	Art, Renaissance
N6410-6415	709.032	Art, Modern—17th century
N6420-6425	709.033	Art, Modern—18th century
N6410	709.0332	Art, Rococo
N6450-6465	709.034	Art, Modern—19th century
N6465.N44	709.0345	Neo-impressionism (Art)
N6480-6494	709.04	Art, Modern—20th century
N6490	700.4112	Modernism (Art)
N6490	709.04052	Art, Abstract
N6494.A7	709.04012	Art deco
N6494.D3	709.04062	Dadaism
N6538.N5	700.08996073	Afro-American artists
N6540-6545.5	709.71	Art—Canada—History
N6555-.5	709.72	Art—Mexico—History
N6573.2-6582.5	709.728	Art—Central America—History
N6635-6735.5	709.8	Art—South America—History
N6805-6808.5	709.436	Art—Austria—History
N6819-6820.5	709.439	Art—Hungary—History
N6828-6831.5	709.437	Art—Czechoslovakia—History
N6897-6898.5	709.495	Art—Greece—History
N6915-6923	709.45	Art—Italy—History
N6967-6973	709.493	Art—Belgium—History
N7007-7088	709.48	Art—Scandinavia—History
N7105-7108.5	709.46	Art—Spain—History
N7125-7128.5	709.469	Art—Portugal—History
N7260-7355.5	709.5	Art, Oriental
N7429.7-7433	701.8	Composition (Art)
N7429.7-7433	702.8	Art—Technique
N7433.8	776	Computer art
N7436.5-.53	745.8	Panoramas
N7475-7485	701.18	Art criticism
N7572	704.9421	Nude in art
N7574	702.8	Artists' models
N7575-7649	704.942	Portraits
N7616	704.942	Portrait miniatures
N7720	700.4548	Dance of death

LC	Dewey	Subject Heading
N7740-7745	704.946	Symbolism in art
N7740	704.946	Emblems
N7760-7763	704.947	Art and mythology
N7810-8189.6	704.9482	Christian art and symbolism
N7832	704.9482	Art, Early Christian
N8205	700.421734	Pastoral art
N8217.D3	704.9497928	Dance in art
N8217.E6	704.9428	Erotic art
N8530-8540	700.284	Artists' materials
N8543	702.84	Artists' tools
N8550-8553	684	Picture frames and framing
N8554-8585	702.88	Art—Conservation and restoration
N8580	702.872	Pictures—Copying
N8600	332.63	Art as an investment
N8610-8660	381.457(3-6)	Art dealers
N8665	707.4	Sidewalk art exhibitions
N8795	364.162	Art thieves
NA	720	Architecture
NA1-9	720.5	Architecture—Periodicals
NA10-17	720.6	Architecture—Societies, etc.
NA31	720.3	Architecture—Encyclopedias
NA40	720.92	Architecture—Biography
NA50-60	720.25	Architecture—Directories
NA105-112	720.288	Architecture—Conservation and restoration]
NA190-1555.5	722-724	Architecture—History
NA205-207	722	Architecture, Primitive
NA210-340	722	Architecture, Ancient
NA215-216	722.2	Architecture, Egyptian
NA220-221	722.51	Architecture, Assyro-Babylonian
NA270-290	722.8	Architecture, Greek
NA277	728.820938	Palaces
NA295-340	722.70937	Architecture, Italian
NA300-301	722.62	Architecture, Etruscan
NA310-340	722.7	Architecture, Roman
NA313	725.827	Amphitheaters
NA320	728.8209376	Palaces
NA350-497	723	Architecture, Medieval
NA390-419	723.4	Architecture, Romanesque
NA423-429	723.4	Architecture, Norman
NA440-489	723.5	Architecture, Gothic
NA490-497	725.18	Military architecture
NA500-680	724	Architecture, Modern
NA510-575	724.12	Architecture, Renaissance
NA590	724.16	Architecture, Baroque
NA590	724.19	Architecture, Rococo
NA600	724.2	Neoclassicism (Architecture)
NA627-640	724.19	Architecture, Modern—18th century
NA630	720.94209033	Architecture, Queen Anne

LC	Dewey	Subject Heading	LC	Dewey	Subject Heading
NA640	724.19	Architecture, Georgian	NA1281-1293.3	720.9485	Architecture—Sweden
NA645-670	724.5	Architecture, Modern—19th century	NA1301-1313.3	720.946	Architecture, Spanish
			NA1301-1313.3	720.946	Architecture—Spain
NA673-682	724.6	Architecture, Modern—20th century	NA1321-1333.3	720.9469	Architecture—Portugal
			NA1341-1353.3	720.9494	Architecture—Switzerland
NA702.5-939	720.9(7-8)	Architecture, American	NA1361-1375	720.9561	Architecture—Turkey
NA705-738	720.973	Architecture—United States	NA1381-1393.3	720.9499	Architecture—Bulgaria
			NA1421-1433.3	720.9498	Architecture—Romania
NA707	724.1	Architecture, Colonial	NA1441-1453.3	720.9497	Architecture—Yugoslavia
NA740-749.5	720.971	Architecture—Canada	NA1455.F5	720.94897	Architecture—Finland
NA750-759	720.972	Architecture—Mexico	NA1460-1579	720.95	Architecture, Oriental
NA760-790	720.9728	Architecture—Central America	NA1466.P6	720.9438	Architecture—Poland
			NA1467-1469	720.9567	Architecture—Iraq
NA773-775	720.97286	Architecture—Costa Rica	NA1470-1472	720.9538	Architecture—Saudi Arabia
NA776-778	720.97281	Architecture—Guatemala			
NA779-781	720.97283	Architecture—Honduras	NA1476.6-.8	720.95692	Architecture—Lebanon
NA782-784	720.97285	Architecture—Nicaragua	NA1477-1479	720.95694	Architecture—Israel
NA785-787	720.97287	Architecture—Panama	NA1479.6-.8	720.95695	Architecture—Jordan
NA788-790	720.97284	Architecture—El Salvador	NA1480-1489	720.955	Architecture—Iran
NA791-815	720.9729	Architecture—West Indies	NA1489.6-.8	720.95691	Architecture—Syria
NA800-802	720.97296	Architecture—Bahamas	NA1492-.3	720.9581	Architecture—Afghanistan
NA803-805	720.97291	Architecture—Cuba	NA1492.6-1499	720.957	Architecture—Asiatic Russia
NA806-808	720.97294	Architecture—Haiti			
NA809-811	720.97292	Architecture—Jamaica	NA1501-1510.3	720.954	Architecture—India
NA812-814	720.97295	Architecture—Puerto Rico	NA1510.6-.63	720.95493	Architecture—Sri Lanka
NA820-939	720.98	Architecture—South America	NA1510.7-.73	720.95491	Architecture—Pakistan
			NA1512-.3	720.9591	Architecture—Burma
NA830-839	720.982	Architecture—Argentina	NA1514-.63	720.9597	Architecture—Vietnam
NA840-849	720.984	Architecture—Bolivia	NA1515-.3	720.9596	Architecture—Cambodia
NA850-859	720.981	Architecture—Brazil	NA1516-.3	720.9594	Architecture—Laos
NA860-869	720.983	Architecture—Chile	NA1521-1523	720.9593	Architecture—Thailand
NA870-879	720.9861	Architecture—Colombia	NA1525-.8	720.9595	Architecture—Malaysia
NA880-889	720.9866	Architecture—Ecuador	NA1526-.8	720.9598	Architecture—Indonesia
NA895	720.9881	Architecture—Guyana	NA1527-1529	720.9599	Architecture—Philippines
NA896	720.9883	Architecture—Surinam	NA1540-1549.6	720.951	Architecture—China
NA897	720.9882	Architecture—French Guiana	NA1540-1547	720.951	Pagodas
			NA1550-1559.6	720.952	Architecture—Japan
NA900-909	720.9892	Architecture—Paraguay	NA1560-1570.3	720.9519	Architecture—Korea
NA910-919	720.985	Architecture—Peru	NA1580-1599	720.96	Architecture—Africa
NA920-929	720.9895	Architecture—Uruguay	NA1581-1585.3	720.962	Architecture, Egyptian
NA930-939	720.987	Architecture—Venezuela	NA1586-.3	720.963	Architecture—Ethiopia
NA950-1455	720.94	Architecture—Europe	NA1588-.3	720.965	Architecture—Algeria
NA961-981	720.941	Architecture—Great Britain	NA1589-.3	720.9612	Architecture—Libya
			NA1590-.3	720.964	Architecture—Morocco
NA1001-1011.6	720.9436	Architecture—Austria	NA1591-.3	720.9611	Architecture—Tunisia
NA1012-1022	720.9439	Architecture—Hungary	NA1591.7-1596.6	720.968	Architecture—Southern Africa
NA1023-1034.5	720.9437	Architecture—Czechoslovakia			
			NA1597-.6	720.9676	Architecture—Africa, East
NA1041-1059	720.944	Architecture—France	NA1598-1599	720.966	Architecture—Africa, West
NA1061-1089	720.943	Architecture—Germany	NA1600-1605.3	720.994	Architecture—Australia
NA1091-1103	720.9495	Architecture—Greece	NA1606-1608	720.993	Architecture—New Zealand
NA1111-1123.3	720.945	Architecture—Italy			
NA1141-1153.3	720.9492	Architecture—Netherlands	NA1610-1613	720.99(5-6)	Architecture—Oceania
NA1161-1173.3	720.9493	Architecture—Belgium	NA1995	174.972	Architects—Professional ethics
NA1181-1199	720.947	Architecture—Russia			
NA1201-1293.3	720.948	Architecture—Scandinavia	NA2000-2320	720.71	Architecture—Study and teaching
NA1211-1223.3	720.9489	Architecture—Denmark			
NA1241-1253.3	720.94912	Architecture—Iceland	NA2335-2360	720.79	Architecture—Competitions
NA1261-1273.3	720.9481	Architecture—Norway			

LC	Dewey	Subject Heading	LC	Dewey	Subject Heading
NA2500	720.1	Architecture—Aesthetics	NA4470-4477	725.15	Courthouses
NA2542.7	720.473	Underground architecture	NA4490-4497	725.18	Police stations
NA2542.A73	720.9154	Architecture—Arid regions	NA4610-4710	726.1	Temples
NA2545	720.87	Architecture and the handicapped	NA4670	726.2	Mosques
			NA4690	726.3	Synagogue architecture
NA2545.P5	725.087	Public buildings—Access for the physically handicapped	NA4790-6113	726.5	Church architecture
			NA4790-5095	726.5	Church buildings
			NA4800-6113	726.7	Abbeys
NA2600-2635	720.222	Architecture—Designs and plans	NA4828.5	726.58(1-9)	Protestant church buildings
NA2700-2780	720.222	Architectural drawing	NA4830	726.6	Cathedrals
NA2750-2793	721	Architectural design	NA4850	726.7	Monasteries
NA2760	729.11	Architecture—Composition, proportion, etc.	NA4870	726.5	Chapels
			NA4910	726.4	Baptisteries
NA2790	720.22	Architectural models	NA5000	726.51	Church decoration and ornament
NA2794	729.28	Daylighting			
NA2800	729.29	Architectural acoustics	NA5060	726.5291	Altars
NA2835-3060	721	Architecture—Details	NA5070	726.5291	Fonts
NA2840-2841	729.1	Facades	NA6120-6199	726.8	Tombs
NA2850-2856	729.24	Interior architecture	NA6149-6199	726.809	Tombs—[By region or country]
NA2860-2875	721.3	Columns, Corinthian			
NA2860	721.3	Columns, Ionic	NA6210-6280	725.2	Commercial buildings
NA2880	721.41	Arches	NA6225	725.21	Shop fronts
NA2890	721.46	Domes	NA6230-6234	725.23	Office buildings
NA2900	721.5	Roofs, Open-timbered	NA6230-6234	720.483	Tall buildings
NA2920	721.5	Gables	NA6240-6245	725.24	Bank buildings
NA2930	721.5	Spires	NA6300-6307	725.39	Airport buildings
NA2930	721.5	Towers	NA6340-6343	725.35	Warehouses
NA2940-2942	721.2	Walls	NA6396-6589	725.4	Industrial buildings
NA2950	721.7	Ceilings	NA6396-6589	725.4	Factories
NA2970	721.6	Floors	NA6400-6589	725.4	Architecture, Industrial
NA3000-3030	721.823	Windows	NA6598	725.4	Employees' buildings and facilities
NA3010	721.822	Doorways			
NA3040	721.5	Chimneys	NA6600-6605	727.3	College buildings
NA3050-3055	721.8	Fireplaces	NA6750-6751	725.91	Exhibition buildings
NA3060	721.832	Stairs	NA6815	725.83	Auditoriums
NA3070	721.84	Balconies	NA6820-6846	725.822	Theater architecture
NA3310-4050	729	Decoration and ornament, Architectural	NA6820-6845	725.822	Theaters
			NA6845-6846	725.823	Motion picture theaters
NA3705	721.0443	Tiles	NA6860-7010	725.827	Stadiums
NA3750-3860	729.7	Pavements, Mosaic	NA6880-.5	725.91	Convention facilities
NA3750-3860	729.7	Mosaics	NA7100-7882	728	Architecture, Domestic
NA4125	721.0445	Concrete construction	NA7100-7884	728	Dwellings
NA4140	721.04496	Glass construction	NA7125	721.84	Porches
NA4145.A35	721.04422	Building, Adobe	NA7127-7135	728	Architecture, Domestic—Designs and plans
NA4170-5095	725	Public buildings			
NA4201-4385	725.09(4-9)	Public buildings—[By region or country]	NA7150	728	Brick houses
			NA7160	728	Concrete houses
NA4205-4228.3	725.0973	Public buildings—United States	NA7160	728	Stucco
			NA7175	728	Half-timbered houses
NA4410-4417	725.11	Capitols	NA7180	728	Steel houses
NA4411-4413	725.110973	United States—Capital and capitol	NA7195.A4	728.0846	Aged—Dwellings
			NA7201-7333	728.09(4-9)	Architecture, Domestic—[By region and country]
NA4415	725.1109(4-9)	[Other countries]—Capital and capitol			
			NA7520	728.312	Row houses
NA4430-4437	725.13	City halls	NA7531	728.370473	Earth sheltered houses
NA4430-4437	725.13	Municipal buildings	NA7551-7555	728.37	Cottages
NA4440-4447	725.17	Embassy buildings	NA7570-7572.5	728.091733	Suburban homes
NA4450-4457	725.16	Post office buildings	NA7574-7579	728.7	Vacation homes

LC	Dewey	Subject Heading	LC	Dewey	Subject Heading
NA7710-7786	728.82	Palaces	NB282-284	730.97285	Sculpture—Nicaragua
NA7710-7786	728.81	Castles	NB285-287	730.97287	Sculpture—Panama
NA7800-7853	728.5	Hotels	NB288-290	730.97284	Sculpture—El Salvador
NA7860-7863	728.314	Apartment houses	NB291-315	730.9729	Sculpture—West Indies
NA7910-7977	728.4	Clubhouses	NB300-302	730.97296	Sculpture—Bahamas
NA8200-8260	728.92	Farm buildings	NB303-305	730.97291	Sculpture—Cuba
NA8208-8210	728.6	Farmhouses	NB306-308	730.97294	Sculpture—Haiti
NA8230	728.922	Barns	NB309-311	730.97292	Sculpture—Jamaica
NA8240	728.92	Granaries	NB312-314	730.97295	Sculpture—Puerto Rico
NA8280	728.922	Dairy barns	NB320-439	730.98	Sculpture—South America
NA8348	725.38	Garages	NB330-339	730.982	Sculpture—Argentina
NA8370	728.927	Dovecotes	NB340-349	730.984	Sculpture—Bolivia
NA8375	728.93	Patios	NB350-359	730.981	Sculpture—Brazil
NA8390-8392	631.27	Fences	NB360-369	730.983	Sculpture—Chile
NA8470	728.73	Log cabins	NB370-379	730.9861	Sculpture—Colombia
NA8480	721.04497	Buildings, Prefabricated	NB380-389	730.9866	Sculpture—Ecuador
NA9000-9428	711.3	Regional planning	NB395	730.9881	Sculpture—Guyana
NA9000-9284	711	City planning	NB396	730.9883	Sculpture—Surinam
NA9050.5	725	Public architecture	NB397	730.9882	Sculpture—French Guiana
NA9053.B58	711.41	Blocks (City planning)	NB400-409	730.9892	Sculpture—Paraguay
NA9053.N	711.45	New towns	NB410-419	730.985	Sculpture—Peru
NA9070-9072	711.55	Plazas	NB420-429	730.9895	Sculpture—Uruguay
NA9101-9285	711.09(4-9)	City planning—[By region or country]	NB430-439	730.987	Sculpture—Venezuela
			NB450-955	730.94	Sculpture—Europe
NA9325-9355	725.94	Soldiers' monuments	NB461-481	730.941	Sculpture—Great Britain
NA9325-9330	725.94	War memorials	NB501-511.6	730.9436	Sculpture—Austria
NA9335-9355	725.94	Monuments	NB512-522.6	730.9439	Sculpture—Hungary
NA9360-9380	725.96	Triumphal arches	NB523-534.5	730.9437	Sculpture—Czechoslovakia
NA9400-9425	714	Fountains	NB541-553.3	730.944	Sculpture—France
			NB561-589	730.943	Sculpture—Germany
NB	730	Sculpture	NB591-603	730.9495	Sculpture—Greece
NB1	730.5	Sculpture—Periodicals	NB611-623.3	730.945	Sculpture—Italy
NB16-17	730.74	Sculpture—Exhibitions	NB641-653.3	730.9492	Sculpture—Netherlands
NB35	730.216	Sculpture—Catalogs	NB661-673.3	730.9493	Sculpture—Belgium
NB60-615	730.9	Sculpture—History	NB681-699	730.947	Sculpture—Russia
NB62-64	732.2	Sculpture, Primitive	NB701-793.3	730.948	Sculpture—Scandinavia
NB69-169	732.2	Sculpture, Ancient	NB711-723.3	730.9489	Sculpture—Denmark
NB69-169	732.2	Marble sculpture, Ancient	NB741-753.3	730.94912	Sculpture—Iceland
NB90-105	733.3	Sculpture, Greek	NB761-773.3	730.9481	Sculpture—Norway
NB115-120	733.5	Sculpture, Roman	NB781-793.3	730.9485	Sculpture—Sweden
NB135-143	731.456	Bronze sculpture	NB801-813.3	730.946	Sculpture—Spain
NB144	733.3	Marble sculpture, Classical	NB821-833.3	730.9469	Sculpture—Portugal
NB145-159	731.2	Terra-cotta sculpture	NB841-853.3	730.9494	Sculpture—Switzerland
NB170-180	734	Sculpture, Medieval	NB861-873.3	730.9561	Sculpture—Turkey
NB172	734.224	Sculpture, Byzantine	NB921-933.3	730.9498	Sculpture—Romania
NB185-198.5	735	Sculpture, Modern	NB941-953.3	730.9497	Sculpture—Yugoslavia
NB180	734.25	Sculpture, Gothic	NB955.F5	730.94897	Sculpture—Finland
NB190	735.21	Sculpture, Renaissance	NB955.P6	730.9438	Sculpture—Poland
NB193	735.21	Sculpture, Rococo	NB960-1070.3	730.95	Sculpture—Asia
NB201-1114	730.9(4-9)	Sculpture—[By region or country]	NB967-969	730.9567	Sculpture—Iraq
			NB970-972	730.9538	Sculpture—Saudi Arabia
NB205-238	730.973	Sculpture—United States	NB976.6-.8	730.95692	Sculpture—Lebanon
NB240-249.5	730.971	Sculpture—Canada	NB977-979	730.95694	Sculpture—Israel
NB250-259	730.972	Sculpture—Mexico	NB979.6-.8	730.95695	Sculpture—Jordan
NB260-290	730.9728	Sculpture—Central America	NB980-989	730.955	Sculpture—Iran
			NB989.6-.8	730.95691	Sculpture—Syria
NB273-275	730.97286	Sculpture—Costa Rica	NB992-.3	730.9581	Sculpture—Afghanistan
NB276-278	730.97281	Sculpture—Guatemala	NB992.4-999	730.957	Sculpture—Asiatic Russia
NB279-281	730.97283	Sculpture—Honduras	NB1001-1010.3	730.954	Sculpture—India

LC	Dewey	Subject Heading	LC	Dewey	Subject Heading
NB1010.6-.63	730.95493	Sculpture—Sri Lanka	NC	741	Drawing
NB1010.7-.73	730.95491	Sculpture—Pakistan	NC1	741.05	Drawing—Periodicals
NB1012-.3	730.9591	Sculpture—Burma	NC15-17	741.074	Drawing—Exhibitions
NB1014-.63	730.9597	Sculpture—Vietnam	NC30-33	741.074	Drawing—Private collections
NB1015-.3	730.9596	Sculpture—Cambodia			
NB1016-.3	730.9594	Sculpture—Laos	NC37-38.5	741.0294	Drawing—Catalogs
NB1021-1023	730.9593	Sculpture—Thailand	NC70-75	741.0902	Drawing, Medieval
NB1025-.8	730.9595	Sculpture—Malaysia	NC85	741.09024	Drawing, Renaissance
NB1026-.8	730.9598	Sculpture—Indonesia	NC86	741.09032	Drawing—17th century
NB1027-1029	730.9599	Sculpture—Philippines	NC87-.5	741.09033	Drawing—18th century
NB1040-1049.6	730.951	Sculpture, Chinese	NC90-.5	741.09034	Drawing—19th century
NB1050-1059.6	730.952	Sculpture, Japanese	NC95-.5	741.0904	Drawing—20th century
NB1060-1070.6	730.9519	Sculpture—Korea	NC101-377	741.09(4-9)	Drawing—[By region or country]
NB1080-1099	730.96	Sculpture—Africa			
NB1081-1085.3	730.962	Sculpture—Egypt	NC105-139.3	741.0973	Drawing—United States
NB1086.3	730.963	Sculpture—Ethiopia	NC141-143.3	741.0971	Drawing—Canada
NB1088.3	730.965	Sculpture—Algeria	NC144-146	741.0972	Drawing—Mexico
NB1089.3	730.9612	Sculpture—Libya	NC147-167	741.09728	Drawing—Central America
NB1090.3	730.964	Sculpture—Morocco	NC153-155	741.097286	Drawing—Costa Rica
NB1091.6	730.9611	Sculpture—Tunisia	NC156-158	741.097281	Drawing—Guatemala
NB1091.7-1096.6	730.968	Sculpture—Africa, Southern	NC159-161	741.097283	Drawing—Honduras
NB1097-.6	730.9676	Sculpture—Africa, East	NC162-164	741.097285	Drawing—Nicaragua
NB1098-1099	730.966	Sculpture—Africa, West	NC165	741.097287	Drawing—Panama
NB1100-1105.3	730.994	Sculpture—Australia	NC167	741.097284	Drawing—El Salvador
NB1106-1108	730.993	Sculpture—New Zealand	NC168-186	741.09729	Drawing—West Indies
NB1110-1113	730.99(5-6)	Sculpture—Oceania	NC171-173	741.097296	Drawing—Bahamas
NB1115	730.92	Sculptors	NC174-176	741.097291	Drawing—Cuba
NB1142.5	730.11	Sculpture—Appreciation	NC177-179	741.097294	Drawing—Haiti
NB1170-1195	731.028	Sculpture—Technique	NC180-182	741.097292	Drawing—Jamaica
NB1180-1185	731.42	Modeling	NC183-185	741.097295	Drawing—Puerto Rico
NB1190	731.452	Plaster casts	NC189-224	741.098	Drawing—South America
NB1199	731.48	Sculpture—Conservation and restoration	NC192-194	741.0982	Drawing—Argentina
			NC195-197	741.0984	Drawing—Bolivia
			NC198-200	741.0981	Drawing—Brazil
NB1208-1210	731.463	Stone carving	NC204-206	741.09861	Drawing—Colombia
NB1215	731.2	Concrete sculpture	NC207-209	741.09866	Drawing—Ecuador
NB1218	731.2	Marble sculpture	NC213-215	741.09892	Drawing—Paraguay
NB1220	731.2	Metal sculpture	NC216-218	741.0985	Drawing—Peru
NB1240.I75	731.2	Iron sculpture	NC219-221	741.09895	Drawing—Uruguay
NB1250	731.2	Driftwood sculpture	NC222-224	741.0987	Drawing—Venezuela
NB1265	731.2	Terra-cotta sculpture	NC225-312	741.094	Drawing—Europe
NB1270.G4	731.2	Glass sculpture	NC228-242	741.0941	Drawing—Great Britain
NB1270.G5	731.2	Fiberglass craft	NC246-248	741.0944	Drawing—France
NB1270.P3	731.2	Paper sculpture	NC249-251.6	741.0943	Drawing—Germany
NB1270.P5	731.2	Plastic sculpture	NC252-254	741.09495	Drawing—Greece
NB1280-1291	731.54	Bas-relief	NC255-257	741.0945	Drawing—Italy
NB1293-1310	731.82	Portrait sculpture	NC267-269	741.0947	Drawing—Russia
NB1300	731.74	Busts	NC270-284	741.0948	Drawing—Scandinavia
			NC273-275	741.09489	Drawing—Denmark
NB1310	731.75	Masks (Sculpture)	NC276-278	741.094912	Drawing—Iceland
NB1312-1313	731.81	Equestrian statues	NC279-281	741.09481	Drawing—Norway
NB1315	731.55	Mobiles (Sculpture)	NC282-284	741.09485	Drawing—Sweden
NB1330-1685	731.76	Monuments	NC285	741.0946	Drawing—Spain
NB1501-1685	731.7609(4-9)	Monuments—[By region or country]	NC288-290	741.09469	Drawing—Portugal
			NC291-293	741.09494	Drawing—Switzerland
NB1800-1895	736.5	Sepulchral monuments	NC294-296	741.09561	Drawing—Turkey
NB1930-1936	731.82	Figure sculpture	NC297-308	741.09496	Drawing—Balkan Peninsula
NB1940-1942	731.832	Animal sculpture			
			NC315-359	741.095	Drawing—Asia

LC	Dewey	Subject Heading	LC	Dewey	Subject Heading
NC318-320	741.0956	Drawing—Middle East	NC1300-1766	741.5	Caricatures and cartoons
NC320	741.095694	Drawing—Israel	NC1300	741.505	Caricatures and cartoons—Periodicals
NC321-323	741.0955	Drawing—Iran			
NC324.6	741.09581	Drawing—Afghanistan	NC1310-1312	741.5074	Caricatures and cartoons—Exhibitions
NC325	741.0957	Drawing—Asiatic Russia			
NC327-329	741.0954	Drawing—India	NC1400-1762	741.59(4-9)	Caricatures and cartoons—[By region or country]
NC330	741.095493	Drawing—Sri Lanka			
NC331	741.095491	Drawing—Pakistan			
NC334.C3	741.09596	Drawing—Cambodia	NC1470-1479	741.5942	English wit and humor, Pictorial
NC334.L3	741.09594	Drawing—Laos			
NC334.V5-.V55	741.09597	Drawing—Vietnam	NC1765-1766	741.58	Animated films
NC335	741.09593	Drawing—Thailand	NC1800-1850	741.674	Posters
NC336-338	741.09595	Drawing—Malaysia	NC1849.T68	741.674	Travel posters
NC339-341	741.09598	Drawing—Indonesia	NC1870-1879	741.683	Postcards
NC342-344	741.09599	Drawing—Philippines	NC1882-1883.3	741.66	Sound recordings—Album covers
NC348-350	741.0951	Drawing—China			
NC351-353	741.0952	Drawing—Japan	NC1920-1940	741.217	Drawing—Copying
NC353.6-.7	741.09519	Drawing—Korea			
NC360-368.6	741.096	Drawing—Africa	ND	750	Painting
NC361-365.6	741.0961	Drawing—Africa, North	ND34-38	759	Painting—Biography
NC363-.3	741.0962	Drawing—Egypt	ND40-45	750.294	Painting—Catalogs
NC365.7	741.0963	Drawing—Ethiopia	ND49-813	759	Painting—History
NC366-6	741.09676	Drawing—Africa, East	ND70-130	759.01	Painting, Ancient
NC367-.6	741.0966	Drawing—Africa, West	ND140-146	759.02	Painting, Medieval
NC368-.6	741.0968	Drawing—Africa, Southern	ND146	750.882971	Painting, Islamic
NC369-371	741.0994	Drawing—Australia	ND160-196	759.06	Painting, Modern
NC372-374	741.0993	Drawing—New Zealand	ND170-172	759.03	Painting, Renaissance
NC375-376	741.099(5-6)	Drawing—Oceania	ND180-182	759.04	Painting, Modern—17th century
NC390-670	741.071	Drawing—Study and teaching	ND186-188	759.04	Painting, Modern—18th century
NC703	745.4	Design	ND190-192	759.05	Painting, Modern—19th century
NC730-758	741.2	Drawing—Technique			
NC745	741.018	Proportion (Art)	ND195-196	759.06	Painting, Modern—20th century
NC749-750	742	Perspective			
NC755	742	Shades and shadows	ND204-1113	759.(1-9)	Painting—[By region or country]
NC760-783.8	743.49	Anatomy, Artistic			
NC765-778	743.4	Figure drawing	ND205-238	759.13	Painting—United States
NC770	743.42	Face	ND240-249.5	759.11	Painting—Canada
NC775	743.4	Drapery in art	ND250-259	759.972	Painting—Mexico
NC780-783.8	743.6	Animals in art	ND260-290	759.9728	Painting—Central America
NC790-800	743.836	Landscape drawing	ND273-275	759.97286	Painting—Costa Rica
NC825.E76	743.828	Erotic drawing	ND276-278	759.97281	Painting—Guatemala
NC845-915	741.2	Drawing instruments	ND279-281	759.97283	Painting—Honduras
NC850	741.22	Charcoal drawing	ND282-284	759.97285	Painting—Nicaragua
NC855-875	741.23	Crayon drawing	ND285-287	759.97287	Painting—Panama
NC870	741.23	Crayons	ND288-290	759.97284	Painting—El Salvador
NC880	741.235	Pastel drawing	ND291-315	759.9729	Painting—West Indies
NC890-895	741.24	Pencil drawing	ND300-302	759.97296	Painting—Bahamas
NC900-902	741.25	Silverpoint drawing	ND303-305	759.97291	Painting—Cuba
NC905	741.26	Pen drawing	ND306-308	759.97294	Painting—Haiti
NC910-.5	741.7	Silhouettes	ND309-311	759.97292	Painting—Jamaica
NC915.R8	760	Rubbing	ND312-314	759.97295	Painting—Puerto Rico
NC960-995.8	741.6	Illustration of books	ND320-439	759.98	Painting—South America
NC965.85	741.6	Picture books	ND330-339	759.982	Painting—Argentina
NC997-1003	741.6	Commercial art	ND340-349	759.984	Painting—Bolivia
NC997.A1	741.605	Commercial art—Periodicals	ND350-359	759.981	Painting—Brazil
			ND360-369	759.983	Painting—Chile
NC1000	741.6071	Commercial art—Study and teaching	ND370-379	759.9861	Painting—Colombia

LC	Dewey	Subject Heading	LC	Dewey	Subject Heading
ND380-389	759.9866	Painting—Ecuador	ND1091.7-1096.6	759.968	Painting—Africa, Southern
ND395	759.9881	Painting—Guyana	ND1097-.6	759.9676	Painting—Africa, East
ND396	759.9883	Painting—Surinam	ND1098-1099	759.966	Painting—Africa, West
ND397	759.9882	Painting—French Guiana	ND1100-1105.3	759.994	Painting—Australia
ND400-409	759.9892	Painting—Paraguay	ND1106-1108	759.993	Painting—New Zealand
ND410-419	759.985	Painting—Peru	ND1110-1113	759.99(5-6)	Painting—Oceania
ND420-429	759.9895	Painting—Uruguay	ND1115-1120	750.71	Painting—Study and teaching
ND430-439	759.987	Painting—Venezuela			
ND450-955	759.(2-8)	Painting—Europe	ND1142-1146	750	Pictures
ND461-481	759.2	Painting—Great Britain	ND1159	751.77	Small painting
ND501-511.6	759.36	Painting—Austria	ND1265	709.04042	Expressionism (Art)
ND512-522.6	759.39	Painting—Hungary	ND1267	700.4145	Primitivism in art
ND541-553.3	759.4	Painting—France	ND1290-1293	757	Figure painting
ND568-589	759.3	Painting—Germany	ND1300-1337	757	Portrait painting
ND591-603.3	759.3	Painting—Greece	ND1308	757.090(24-31)	Portrait painting—15th century
ND611-623.3	759.5	Painting—Italy			
ND681-699	759.7	Painting—Russia	ND1308	757.09031	Portrait painting—16th century
ND701-793.3	759.8	Painting—Scandinavia			
ND711-723.3	759.89	Painting—Denmark	ND1309.3	757.09032	Portrait painting—17th century
ND761-773.3	759.81	Painting—Norway			
ND781-793.3	759.85	Painting—Sweden	ND1309.4	757.09033	Portrait painting—18th century
ND801-813.3	759.6	Painting—Spain			
ND821-833.3	759.69	Painting—Portugal	ND1309.5	757.09034	Portrait painting—19th century
ND861-873.3	759.9561	Painting—Turkey			
ND955.F5	759.897	Painting—Finland	ND1309.6	757.0904	Portrait painting—20th century
ND960-1070.3	759.95	Painting—Asia			
ND967-969	759.9567	Painting, Iraqi	ND1311-.9	757.0973	Portrait painting—United States
ND970-972	759.9538	Painting—Saudi Arabia			
ND976.6-.8	759.95692	Painting—Lebanon	ND1313-1324	757.094	Portrait painting—Europe
ND977-979	759.95694	Painting—Israel	ND1314-.6	757.0941	Portrait painting—Great Britain
ND979-.8	759.95695	Painting—Jordan			
ND980-989	759.955	Painting—Iran	ND1316-.6	757.0944	Portrait painting—France
ND989.6-.8	759.95691	Painting—Syria	ND1317-.7	757.0943	Portrait painting—Germany
ND992-.3	759.9581	Painting—Afghanistan			
ND992.4-999	759.957	Painting—Asiatic Russia	ND1318-.6	757.0945	Portrait painting—Italy
ND999.P6	759.38	Painting—Poland	ND1319-.6	757.09492	Portrait painting—Netherlands
ND1001-1010.3	759.954	Painting—India			
ND1010.6-.63	759.95493	Painting—Sri Lanka	ND1320-.6	757.0947	Portrait painting—Russia
ND1010.7-.73	759.95491	Painting—Pakistan	ND1322-.6	757.0956	Portrait painting—Spain
ND1012-.3	759.9591	Painting—Burma	ND1325-1326.8	757.095	Portrait painting—Asia
ND1014-.63	759.9597	Painting—Vietnam	ND1328-1329	759	Portrait painting—Biography
ND1015-.3	759.9596	Painting—Cambodia			
ND1016-.3	759.9594	Painting—Laos	ND1329.8-1337	757.7	Portrait miniatures
ND1021-1023	759.9593	Painting—Thailand	ND1340-1367	758.1	Landscape painting
ND1025-.8	759.9595	Painting—Malaysia	ND1351-1367	758.109(4-9)	Landscape painting—[By region or country]
ND1026-.8	759.9598	Painting—Indonesia			
ND1027-1029	759.9599	Painting—Philippines	ND1351-.6	758.10973	Landscape painting—United States
ND1040-1049.6	759.951	Painting—China			
ND1050-1059.6	759.952	Painting—Japan	ND1352	758.109(71-8)	Landscape painting—America
ND1050-1059.6	759.952	Painting, Japanese			
ND1060-1070.3	759.9519	Painting—Korea	ND1353-1364	758.1094	Landscape painting—Europe
ND1060-1070.3	759.9519	Painting, Korean	ND1354-.6	758.10941	Landscape painting—Great Britain
ND1080-1099	759.96	Painting—Africa			
ND1081-1085.3	759.962	Painting—Egypt	ND1356-.6	758.10944	Landscape painting—France
ND1086-.3	759.963	Painting—Ethiopia			
ND1088-.3	759.965	Painting—Algeria	ND1357-.6	758.10943	Landscape painting—Germany
ND1089-.3	759.9612	Painting—Libya			
ND1090-.3	759.964	Painting—Morocco	ND1358-.6	758.10945	Landscape painting—Italy
ND1091-.3	759.9611	Painting—Tunisia			

LC	Dewey	Subject Heading	LC	Dewey	Subject Heading
ND1362-.6	758.10946	Landscape painting—Spain	NE830-835	760.28	Prints—Technique
ND1365-.96	758.1095	Landscape painting—Asia	NE880-885	769.12	Prints—Collectors and collecting
ND1370-1375	758.2	Marine painting	NE886	760.04	Engraving—Themes, motives
ND1380-1383	758.3	Animals in art			
ND1390-1400	758.4	Still-life painting	NE957-.3	769.437	Naval prints
ND1450-1452	754	Genre painting	NE960-.3	769.49796	Sporting prints
ND1505	751.4	Brushwork	NE965-.3	741.685	Business cards
ND1510	751.2	Pigments	NE1000-1325	761.2	Wood-engraving
ND1535	751.426	Acrylic painting	NE1000	761.205	Wood-engraving—Periodicals
ND1630-1662	751.6	Painting—Conservation and restoration	NE1010-1012	761.2074	Wood-engraving—Exhibitions
ND1700-2495	751.422	Watercolor painting	NE1030-1196.3	761.209	Wood-engraving—History
ND2110-2115	751.422071	Watercolor painting—Study and teaching	NE1050-1075	761.209024	Wood-engraving—15th century
ND2190-2192	751.42242	Figure painting	NE1050-1075	761.209031	Wood-engraving—16th century
ND2200-2202	751.42242	Portrait painting	NE1050-1075	761.209032	Wood-engraving—17th century
ND2240-2243	751.422436	Landscape painting	NE1085-1088	761.209033	Wood-engraving—18th century
ND2270-2272	751.422437	Marine painting			
ND2290-2305	751.422435	Still-life painting	NE1090-1093	761.209034	Wood-engraving—19th century
ND2460	741.26	Brush drawing	NE1095-1097	761.20904	Wood-engraving—20th century
ND2480	751.46	Encaustic painting			
ND2550-2877	751.73	Mural painting and decoration	NE1101-1196.3	761.209(4-9)	Wood-engraving—[By region or country]
ND2601-2877	751.7309(4-9)	Mural painting—[By region or country]	NE1410-1412	760.074	Engraving—Exhibitions
ND2880-2881	751.74	Panoramas	NE1638	760.09023	Engraving—14th century
ND2880-.5	751.74	Diorama	NE1655-1656	760.09024	Engraving—15th century
ND2885-2888	751.75	Scene painting	NE1665-1666	760.09031	Engraving—16th century
ND2889-3416	745.67	Illumination of books and manuscripts	NE1670-1690	760.09032	Engraving—17th century
			NE1710-1719	760.09033	Engraving—18th century
ND2893	745.67074	Illumination of books and manuscripts—Exhibitions	NE1720.5-1739	760.09034	Engraving—19th century
ND2910	745.670901	Illumination of books and manuscripts, Ancient	NE1740-1749	760.0904	Engraving—20th century
			NE1815-1816.5	766.2	Mezzotint engraving
ND2920-2980	745.670902	Illumination of books and manuscripts, Medieval	NE1843-1844	764.8	Serigraphy
ND2990	745.67090	Illumination of books and manuscripts—Renaissance	NE1850-1879	769	Color prints
			NE1940-2232.5	767.2	Etching
ND3001-3294.5	745.6709(4-9)	Illumination of books and manuscripts—[By region or country]	NE1950-1955	767.2074	Etching—Exhibitions
			NE1960	767.20294	Etching—Catalogs
			NE1980-2055.5	767.209	Etching—History
			NE1990-1992	767.209033	Etching—18th century
NE	760	Engraving	NE1994-1995	767.209034	Etching—19th century
NE	769	Prints	NE1997-1998	767.20904	Etching—20th century
NE1	769.05	Prints—Periodicals	NE2001-2096.3	767.209(4-9)	Etching—[By region or country]
NE20	769.03	Prints—Encyclopedias			
NE57-59	769.12	Prints—Private collections	NE2110	767.2092	Etchers
NE62	381.45769	Prints—Marketing	NE2220-2225	767.3	Dry-point
NE63-75	769.0294	Prints—Catalogs	NE2230	766.3	Aquatint
NE380	769.0288	Prints—Conservation and restoration	NE2250-2529	763	Lithography
			NE2272-2275	763.074	Lithography—Exhibitions
NE400-773	769.9	Prints—History	NE2280	763.0294	Lithography—Catalogs
NE501-794.5	769.9(4-9)	Prints—[By region or country]	NE2295-2396.3	763.09	Lithography—History
			NE2297	763.09034	Lithography—19th century
NE539.3.A35	769.08996073	Afro-American prints	NE2298	763.0904	Lithography—20th century
NE800	769.92	Engravers	NE2301-2396.3	763.09(4-9)	Lithography—[By region or country]
NE820	760.278	Engravers' marks			

LC	Dewey	Subject Heading	LC	Dewey	Subject Heading
NE2410	763.092	Lithographers	NK2117.B4	747.77	Bedrooms
NE2500-2529	764.2	Chromolithography	NK2117.D5	747.76	Dining room furniture
NE2690	748.62	Glass engraving	NK2117.D5	747.76	Dining rooms
NE2700-2710	765	Engraving (Metal-work)	NK2117.L5	747.75	Living room furniture
NE2800-2890	760	Engraving—Printing	NK2190-2192	747.86	Church decoration and ornament
NK	745.1	Antiques	NK2200-2750	749	Furniture
NK1-9	745.105	Antiques—Periodicals	NK2210-2211	747.074	Furniture—Exhibitions
NK28	745.103	Antiques—Encyclopedias	NK2220	749.074	Furniture—Private collections
NK30	745.103	Antiques—Dictionaries			
NK50-440	745.1071	Antiques—Study and teaching	NK2235	749	Furniture—Styles
			NK2401-2694.5	749.09(4-9)	Furniture—[By region or country]
NK492	745.5928	Miniature objects			
NK512-520	745.1074	Antiques—Exhibitions	NK2740	749.3	Shelving (Furniture)
NK530-570	745.1074	Antiques—Private collections	NK2775-2898	747.5	Rugs
			NK2775-2898	747.5	Carpets
NK610-685	745.0901	Art objects, Ancient	NK2790	747.5074	Rugs—Private collections
NK665-680	745.0938	Art objects, Classical	NK2808-2810	746.75095	Rugs, Oriental
NK801-1094.5	745.09(4-9)	Art objects—[By region or country]	NK2809.I8	746.70882971	Rugs, Islamic
			NK2910	749.3	Screens
NK839.3.A35	745.08996073	Afro-American decorative arts	NK2910	746.3	Wall hangings
			NK2975-3049	746.3	Tapestry
NK1125-1130	745.075	Art objects—Collectors and collecting	NK3175-3296.3	746.94	Drapery
			NK3375-3496.3	747.3	Wallpaper
NK1128	745.102872	Antiques—Reproduction	NK3600-3640	745.61	Lettering
NK1133-.26	745.0294	Art objects—Catalogs	NK3600-3640	745.61	Calligraphy
NK1135-1149.5	745	Arts and crafts movement	NK3649.5-.55	746.412	Basketwork
NK1160-1590	745.4	Design	NK3650-.5	745.582	Beadwork
NK1160-1590	745.4	Decoration and ornament	NK3685	745.5933	Candlesticks
NK1170	745.4071	Design—Study and teaching	NK3700-4695	738	Pottery
			NK3800-3855	738.0901	Pottery, Ancient
NK1177	745.441	Decoration and ornament, Primitive	NK3870-3885	738.0902	Pottery, Medieval
			NK4001-4184	738.09(4-9)	Pottery—[By region or country]
NK1180-1250	745.442	Decoration and ornament, Ancient			
			NK4200-4210	738.092	Potters
NK1260-1295	745.442	Decoration and ornament, Medieval	NK4230	738.075	Pottery—Collectors and collecting
NK1270-1275	745.442088297	Decoration and ornament, Islamic	NK4277	738.27	Blue and white transfer ware
NK1285	745.442	Decoration and ornament, Romanesque	NK4295-.5	738.37	Delftware
			NK4360-4367	738.3	Stoneware
NK1295	745.442	Decoration and ornament, Gothic	NK4370-4584	738.2	Porcelain
			NK4399.B58	738.27	Blue and white ware
NK1330	745.443	Decoration and ornament, Renaissance	NK4660	738.82	Hummel figurines
			NK4695.F6	738.8	Food warmers
NK1345	745.443	Decoration and ornament, Baroque	NK4695.T33	738.38	Ceramic tableware
			NK4870	745.594	Fans
NK1355	745.443	Decoration and ornament, Rococo	NK4890.C67	745.5942	Costume jewelry
			NK4891.3-4894.4	745.5923	Dollhouses
NK1652.25	745.442	Decoration and ornament, Byzantine	NK4891.3-4894.4	745.59221	Dolls
			NK4895	748.83	Drinking vessels
NK1676	745.40882943	Decoration and ornament, Buddhist	NK4997-5024	738.4	Enamel and enameling
			NK5100-5440	748	Glass
NK1700-3505	747	Interior decoration	NK5100-5440	748.2	Glassware
NK2000-2096.3	747.09(4-9)	Interior decoration—[By region or country]	NK5200-5205	748.6	Cut glass
			NK5300-5430	748.50282	Glass painting and staining
NK2115.5.D73	747.5	Drapery in interior decoration			
			NK5430	748.50285	Mosaics
NK2117.B33	747.78	Bathrooms	NK5439.E5	748.6	Enameled glass

LC	Dewey	Subject Heading	LC	Dewey	Subject Heading
NK5440.D75	748.83	Drinking glasses	NX528	700.97295	Arts—Puerto Rico
NK5440.D85	748.83	Dwarf ale glasses	NX530-541	700.98	Arts—South America
NK5440.P3	748.84	Paperweights	NX531	700.982	Arts—Argentina
NK5440.S49	748.8	Glass shoes	NX532	700.984	Arts—Bolivia
NK5561	736.20932	Scarabs	NX533	700.981	Arts—Brazil
NK5720-5722	736.222	Cameos	NX534	700.983	Arts—Chile
NK6020-6022	736.6	Bone carving	NX535	700.9861	Arts—Colombia
NK6200-6210	745.531	Leatherwork	NX536	700.9866	Arts—Ecuador
NK6400-8459	739	Art metal-work	NX538	700.9892	Arts—Paraguay
NK6400-8459	739	Metal-work	NX539	700.985	Arts—Peru
NK6600-6999	739.7	Weapons	NX540	700.9895	Arts—Uruguay
NK6700-6799	739.722	Swords	NX541	700.987	Arts—Venezuela
NK6808	739.752	Shields	NX542-571	700.94	Arts—Europe
NK7100-7695	739.23	Silverwork	NX543-547.6	700.941	Arts—Great Britain
NK7215-7230	739.2282	Chalices	NX548	700.9436	Arts—Austria
NK7234-7235	739.2383	Silver flatware	NX549	700.944	Arts—France
NK7300-7695	739.27	Jewelry	NX550-.6	700.943	Arts—Germany
NK7440-7459	739.2782	Rings	NX551	700.9495	Arts—Greece
NK7480-7499	739.3	Clocks and watches	NX552	700.945	Arts—Italy
NK7650-7690	739.27	Precious stones	NX554	700.9492	Arts—Netherlands
NK7658-7663	739.27	Diamonds	NX555	700.9493	Arts—Belgium
NK8360	749.63	Chandeliers	NX556	700.947	Arts—Russia
NK8400-8420	739.533	Pewter	NX557-561	700.948	Arts—Scandinavia
NK8440-.2	748.8	Mirrors	NX558	700.9489	Arts—Denmark
NK8470-8475	745.0228	Miniature objects	NX559	700.94912	Arts—Iceland
NK8475.A7	739.70228	Miniature weapons	NX560	700.9481	Arts—Norway
NK8500	738.5	Mosaics	NX561	700.9485	Arts—Sweden
NK8643	745.55	Shellcraft	NX562	700.946	Arts—Spain
NK8800-9505.5	746	Textile design	NX563	700.9469	Arts—Portugal
NK8800-9505.5	746.4	Needlework	NX564	700.9494	Arts—Switzerland
NK9100-9499	746.46	Patchwork	NX565	700.9561	Arts—Turkey
NK9200-9315	746.44	Embroidery	NX566-569	700.9496	Arts—Balkan Peninsula
NK9206.4.H56	746.44	Embroidery, Hmong	NX572-586	700.95	Arts—Asia
NK9510	745.74	Decalcomania	NX573-.7	700.956	Arts—Middle East
NK9600-9955	745.51	Woodwork	NX573.7	700.95694	Arts—Israel
NK9700-9799	736.4	Wood-carving	NX574	700.955	Arts—Iran
NK9900-.7	745.726	Lacquer and lacquering	NX575.6	700.9581	Arts—Afghanistan
			NX575.7	700.957	Arts—Asiatic Russia
NX	700	Arts	NX576	700.954	Arts—India
NX1-9	700.5	Arts—Periodicals	NX576.6	700.95493	Arts—Sri Lanka
NX70	700.3	Arts—Encyclopedias	NX576.7	700.95491	Arts—Pakistan
NX80	700.3	Arts—Dictionaries	NX578.6.C3	700.9596	Arts—Cambodia
NX501-596.3	700.9(4-9)	Arts—[By region or country]	NX578.6.L3	700.9594	Arts—Laos
			NX578.6.V5-.V55	700.9597	Arts—Vietnam
NX503-512.3	700.973	Arts—United States	NX578.7	700.9593	Arts—Thailand
NX513-.3	700.971	Arts—Canada	NX579	700.9595	Arts—Malaysia
NX514	700.972	Arts—Mexico	NX580	700.9598	Arts—Indonesia
NX515-522	700.9728	Arts—Central America	NX581	700.9599	Arts—Philippines
NX517	700.97286	Arts—Costa Rica	NX583	700.951	Arts—China
NX518	700.97281	Arts—Guatemala	NX584	700.952	Arts—Japan
NX519	700.97283	Arts—Honduras	NX584.6-.7	700.9519	Arts—Korea
NX520	700.97285	Arts—Nicaragua	NX587-589.8	700.96	Arts—Africa
NX521	700.97287	Arts—Panama	NX587.6-588.6	700.961	Arts—Africa, North
NX522	700.97284	Arts—El Salvador	NX588-.3	700.962	Arts—Egypt
NX523-529	700.9729	Arts—West Indies	NX588.7	700.963	Arts—Ethiopia
NX524	700.97296	Arts—Bahamas	NX588.8-.9	700.9676	Arts—Africa, East
NX525	700.97291	Arts—Cuba	NX589-.6	700.966	Arts—Africa, West
NX526	700.97294	Arts—Haiti	NX589.7-.8	700.968	Arts—Africa, Southern
NX527	700.97292	Arts—Jamaica	NX590	700.994	Arts—Australia

LC	Dewey	Subject Heading	LC	Dewey	Subject Heading
NX593	700.993	Arts—New Zealand	P128.M48	410.1	Metalanguage
NX595-596	700.99(5-6)	Arts—Oceania	P147	410.18	Functionalism (Linguistics)
NX600.D3	709.04062	Dadaism	P151-299	415	Grammar, Comparative and general
NX600.S9	709.04062	Surrealism			
NX636	702.874	Arts—Forgeries	P207	415	Language and languages—Grammars
NX650.E7	704.9428	Pornography			
NX688	704.9489	Arts, Islamic	P211-214	411	Alphabets
NX700-750	700.79	Arts—Endowments	P221-232	414.8	Phonetics
			P223	414.8	Tone (Phonetics)
P	400	Philology	P226	411	Transliteration
P1-410	400	Language and languages	P241-259	415	Morphemics
P1-10	405	Language and languages—Periodicals	P270-288	415	Parts of speech
			P301-.5	808	Rhetoric
P29	403	Language and languages—Dictionaries	P302-.87	401.41	Discourse analysis
			P305-.18	401.4	Vocabulary
P35	417.7	Linguistic paleontology	P307-310	418.020285	Machine translating
P37	401.9	Psycholinguistics	P311	808.1	Versification
P40	306.44	Sociolinguistics	P321-324.5	412	Language and languages—Etymology
P47	801.959	Criticism, Textual			
P51-59	407.1	Language and languages—Study and teaching	P325-.5	401.43	Semantics
			P325.5.H57	401.4309	Semantics, Historical
			P326	401.409	Historical lexicology
P53.44	407.1	Immersion method (Language teaching)	P361	413	Polyglot glossaries, phrase books, etc.
P87-96	302.2	Communication	P361	413	Dictionaries, Polyglot
P94.5.A37	302.2308996 + 073	Afro-Americans and mass media	P375-381	409	Linguistic geography
			P408	418	Colloquial language
P94.5.A37	302.2308996 + 073	Afro-Americans in mass media	P409-410	417.2	Slang
			P409	417.2	Jargon (Terminology)
P94.5.A37	302.2308996 + 073	Afro-American mass media	P501-769	410	Indo-European languages
			P501-769	410	Indo-European philology
P94.5.A37	302.20899607 + 073	Afro-Americans—Communication	P501	413.028	Indo-European philology—Periodicals
P94.5.M55	302.23089	Ethnic mass media	P505	410.6	Indo-European languages—Congresses
P95.8	302.2	Communication policy			
P95.8	302.23	Mass media policy	P575-769	415	Indo-European languages—Grammar, Comparative
P96.A38	305.26	Aged in mass media			
P96.A39	362.1969792	AIDS (Disease) in mass media			
			P583-610	414	Indo-European languages—Phonology
P96.A83	302.23	Audiences			
P96.C74	364	Crime in mass media	P611-627	415	Indo-European languages—Morphology
P96.D4	363.25092	Detectives in mass media			
P96.E29	370	Education in mass media	P631-663	415	Indo-European languages—Parts of speech
P96.F36	154.3	Fantasy in mass media			
P96.M6	567.9	Dinosaurs in mass media			
P96.S34	808.838762	Science fiction	P671-675	415	Indo-European languages—Syntax
P96.S48	305.3	Sexism in communication			
P96.S5	305.3	Sex role in mass media	P721-725	412	Indo-European languages—Etymology
P96.V5	303.6	Violence in mass media			
P99-.4	401.41	Semiotics	P761-769	413.028	Indo-European languages—Lexicography
P99.4.P72	401.9	Pragmatics			
P118-.7	401.93	Language acquisition	P943	499.93	Elamite language
P118.2	401.93	Second language acquisition	P945	491.998	Hittite language
			P1001	491.998	Anatolian languages
P121-149	410.92	Linguists	P1078	499.94	Etruscan language
P121-143.3	410	Linguistics			
P123	410	Comparative linguistics	PA	480	Classical languages
P140	417.7	Historical linguistics	PA1-199	480	Classical philology
P128.E94	417.24	Linguistics, Experimental			

LC	Dewey	Subject Heading	LC	Dewey	Subject Heading
PA31	480.03	Classical languages—Dictionaries	PA2001-2067	470	Latin philology
PA47	880.9	Criticism, Textual	PA2061-2067	470.71	Latin language—Study and teaching
PA111	485	Classical languages—Grammar, Comparative	PA2071-2310	475	Latin language—Grammar
PA201-1179	489.3	Greek language	PA2111-2131	475	Latin language—Phonology
PA231-241	489.3071	Greek language—Study and teaching	PA2133-2158	475	Latin language—Morphology
PA251-379	489.35	Greek language—Grammar	PA2161-2281	475	Latin language—Parts of speech
PA265-281	489.315	Greek language—Phonology	PA2285-2297	475	Latin language—Syntax
PA283-287	489.35	Greek language—Morphology	PA2300-2309	477	Latin language, Postclassical
PA303-361	489.35	Greek language—Parts of speech	PA2329-2340	871.6	Latin language—Metrics and rhythmics
PA367-379	489.35	Greek language—Syntax	PA2341-2350	472	Latin language—Etymology
PA401-407	889.309	Greek language—Style	PA2351-2390	473.028	Latin language—Lexicography
PA421-430	489.32	Greek language—Etymology	PA2361-2390	473	Latin language—Dictionaries
PA431-465	489.33028	Greek language—Lexicography	PA2420-2915	470	Italic languages and dialects
PA441-465	489.33	Greek language—Dictionaries	PA2510-2519	477	Latin language, Preclassical to ca. 100 B.C.
PA500-581	489	Greek language—Dialects			
PA530-539	480	Doric Greek dialect	PA2600-2748	477	Latin language, Vulgar
PA550-554	480	Aeolic Greek dialect	PA3001-3045	880.09	Classical literature—History and criticism
PA600-895	487.4	Greek language, Hellenistic (300 B.C.-600 A.D.)			
PA695-895	487.4	Greek language, Biblical	PA3013	880.01	Classical literature—Appreciation
PA813-857	487.45	Greek language, Biblical—Grammar	PA3019-3022	881.009	Classical poetry
PA881	487.43	Greek language, Biblical—Dictionaries	PA3024-3029	882.009	Classical drama—History and criticism
PA1000-1179	489	Greek language, Medieval and late	PA3051-4505	880	Greek literature
			PA3081-3084	880	Greek literature, Hellenistic
PA1000-1179	489.3	Greek language, Modern	PA3092-3125	881.009	Greek poetry
PA1031	489.33	Greek language, Modern—Dictionaries	PA3105-3107.5	881.03209	Epic poetry, Greek
PA1041-1049	489.3071	Greek language, Modern—Study and teaching	PA3131-3239	882.009	Greek drama
			PA3131-3159	882.051209	Greek drama (Tragedy)
			PA3161-3199	882.052309	Greek drama (Comedy)
PA1051-1099	489.35	Greek language, Modern—Grammar	PA3255-3273	888.08	Greek prose literature
			PA3265	808.0481	Rhetoric, Ancient
PA1061-1072	489.315	Greek language, Modern—Phonology	PA3285	398.2048	Folk literature, Greek
			PA3300-3516	880.8	Greek literature
PA1076	489.35	Greek language, Modern—Morphology	PA3301-3671	880.8	Classical literature
			PA3301-3371	091.09495	Manuscripts, Greek (Papyri)
PA1081-1089	489.35	Greek language, Modern—Parts of speech			
PA1091-1097	489.35	Greek language, Modern—Syntax	PA3431-3459	881	Classical poetry
			PA3437-3439	881.03208	Epic poetry, Greek
PA1111-1114.5	489.32	Greek language, Modern—Etymology	PA3461-3468	882	Greek drama
			PA3461-3466	882.008	Classical drama
PA1123-1145	489.33	Greek language, Modern—Dictionaries	PA3461-3463	882.051208	Greek drama (Tragedy)
			PA3465-3466	882.052308	Greek drama (Comedy)
PA1151-1159	489.37	Greek language, Modern—Dialects	PA3473-3475	888.08	Greek prose literature
			PA3479-3842	885.108	Oratory, Ancient
PA2001-2995	470	Latin language	PA3482	885.008	Funeral orations

LC	Dewey	Subject Heading	LC	Dewey	Subject Heading
PA3520-3564	880.9	Greek literature—Criticism, Textual	PB	491.6	Brythonic languages
			PB	491.67	Cornish language
			PB	491.62	Irish language
PA3527	880.9	Greek literature, Hellenistic—Criticism, Textual	PB73	418	Polyglot glossaries, phrase books, etc.
			PB331	413	Dictionaries, Polyglot
PA3537-3543	881.009	Greek literature, Hellenistic—Criticism, Textual	PB1001-1095	491.6	Celtic philology
			PB1001-1095	491.6	Celtic languages
PA5101-5167	880.9002	Byzantine literature	PB1011	491.6071	Celtic languages—Study and teaching
PA5150-5155	881.209	Byzantine poetry	PB1019-1071	491.6(2-8)5	Celtic languages—Grammar
PA5160-5163	882.209	Byzantine drama			
PA5165	888.08	Byzantine prose literature	PB1083-1085	491.6(2-8)2	Celtic languages—Etymology
PA5170-5198	880.8002	Byzantine literature			
PA5180-5189	881.208	Byzantine poetry	PB1087-1089	491.6(2-8)3028	Celtic languages—Lexicography
PA5190-5194	882.208	Byzantine drama			
PA5195-5196	888.08	Byzantine prose literature	PB1101-1113	491.6(2-3)	Gaelic philology
PA5201-5660	889	Greek literature, Modern	PB1111	491.6(2-3)071	Gaelic philology—Study and teaching
PA5230-5269	889.09	Greek literature, Modern—History and criticism	PB1187-1189	491.6(2-3)3028	Gaelic language—Lexicography
PA5259-5255	889.1009	Greek poetry, Modern	PB1201-1299	491.62	Irish language
PA5260-5263	889.2009	Greek drama, Modern	PB1211	491.62071	Irish language—Study and teaching
PA5265	888.08	Greek prose literature, Modern	PB1218	491.627	Irish language—To 1100
PA5280-5289	889.1008	Greek poetry, Modern	PB1218	491.627	Irish language—Middle Irish, 1100-1550
PA5290-5294	889.2008	Greek drama, Modern			
PA5295	889.808	Greek prose literature, Modern	PB1221-1273	491.625	Irish language—Grammar
			PB1283-1284	491.622	Irish language—Etymology
PA5301-5395	889.08001	Greek literature, Modern—1453-1800	PB1287-1295	491.623028	Irish language—Lexicography
PA6001-6098	870.9001	Latin literature—History and criticism	PB1299	491.627	Irish language—Slang
			PB1306-1449	891.62	Irish literature
PA6045-6063	871.09	Latin poetry	PB1321	891.6208001	Irish literature—To 1100
PA6067-6075	872.09	Latin drama—History and criticism	PB1321	891.621009	Fili (Irish poets)
PA6081-6095.5	878.08	Latin prose literature—History and criticism	PB1322	891.6208002	Irish literature—Middle Irish, 1100-1550
PA6101-6139	870.8001	Latin literature	PB1501-1599	491.6(2-3)	Gaelic language
PA6121-6135	871.08	Latin poetry	PB1511	491.6(2-3)071	Gaelic language—Study and teaching
PA6125	871.032108	Epic poetry, Latin			
PA6137	872.08	Latin drama	PB1521-1573	491.6(2-3)5	Gaelic language—Grammar
PA6138-6139	878.08	Latin prose literature			
PA8001-8595	870.900(3-4)	Latin literature, Medieval and modern	PB1583-1584	491.6(2-3)2	Gaelic language—Etymology
PA8050-8065	871.(3-4)09	Latin poetry, Medieval and modern—History and criticism	PB1587-1595	491.6(2-3)3028	Gaelic language—Lexicography
			PB1605-1709	891.63	Gaelic literature
PA8073-8079	872.(3-4)09	Latin drama, Medieval and modern	PB1801-1847	491.64	Manx language
			PB1851-1867	891.64	Manx literature
PA8081-8096	878.08	Latin prose literature, Medieval and modern—History and criticism	PB2001-2060	491.6	Brythonic languages
			PB2005	491.6(2-8)071	Brythonic languages—Study and teaching
PA8120-8133	871.(3-4)08	Latin poetry, Medieval and modern	PB2009-2015	491.6(2-8)5	Brythonic languages—Grammar
PA8135-8140	872.(3-4)08	Latin drama, Medieval and modern	PB2021	491.6(2-8)2	Brythonic languages—Etymology
PA8145-8149	878.08	Latin prose literature, Medieval and modern	PB2023	491.6(2-8)3028	Brythonic languages—Lexicography
			PB2101-2199	491.66	Welsh language
PB	491.6	Celtic languages			

LC	Dewey	Subject Heading	LC	Dewey	Subject Heading
PB2206-2499	891.66	Welsh literature	PC1571-1580	452	Italian language—Etymology
PB2501-2549	491.67	Cornish language	PC1620-1693	453.028	Italian language—Lexicography
PB2507	491.67071	Cornish language—Study and teaching	PC1620-1645	453	Italian language—Dictionaries
PB2511-2547	491.675	Cornish language—Grammar	PC1700-1977	457	Italian language—Dialects
PB2551-2621	891.67	Cornish literature	PC1851-1874	457	Gallo-Italian dialects
PB2800-2849	491.68	Breton language	PC1951-1977	457.09	Italian language—Slang
PB2807	491.68071	Breton language—Study and teaching	PC2001-3761	440	French language
			PC2001-2071	440	French philology
PB2811-2847	491.685	Breton language—Grammar	PC2065	440.71	French language—Study and teaching
PB2856-2932	891.68	Breton literature	PC2101-2400	445	French language—Grammar
PB3001-3029	491.6	Gaulish language			
			PC2113-2117	448.6	French language—Readers
PC	440	Romance languages	PC2131-2151	441.5	French language—Phonology
PC1-5	440.05	Romance languages—Periodicals			
PC35-39	440.071	Romance languages—Study and teaching	PC2171-2175	445	French language—Morphology
			PC2201-2321	445	French language—Parts of speech
PC601-872	459	Romanian philology	PC2571-2591	442	French language—Etymology
PC601-799	459	Romanian language			
PC619	459.071	Romanian language—Study and teaching	PC2620-2693	443.028	French language—Lexicography
			PC2700-3761	447	French language—Dialects
PC631-725	459.5	Romanian language—Grammar	PC2721-2746	445	French language—Grammar
PC761-767	459.2	Romanian language—Etymology	PC2761	442	French language—Etymology
PC775-784	459.3028	Romanian language—Lexicography			
PC785	459.11	Abbreviations, Romanian	PC2766	443.028	French language—Lexicography
PC799	459.7	Romanian language—Slang	PC2801-2896	447.0(1-2)	French language—To 1500
PC800-872	859	Romanian literature	PC2821-2873	447.0(1-2)5	French language—To 1500—Grammar
PC890	457.994972	Dalmatian language (Romance)	PC2883-2886	447.01(1-2)2	French language—To 1500—Etymology
PC901-949	459.9	Raeto-Romance language	PC2887-2895	447.0(1-2)3028	French language—To 1500—Lexicography
PC907	459.9071	Raeto-Romance language—Study and teaching			
			PC3081-3148	449	Franco-Provencal dialects
PC911-923	459.95	Raeto-Romance language—Grammar	PC3201-3299	449	Provencal language
PC931	459.92	Raeto-Romance language—Etymology	PC3219-3273	449.5	Provencal language—Grammar
PC937	459.93	Raeto-Romance language—Dictionaries	PC3283-3286	449.2	Provencal language—Etymology
PC941-949	459.97	Raeto-Romance language—Dialects	PC3287-3295	449.3028	Provencal language—Lexicography
PC949	459.97	Raeto-Romance language—Slang	PC3296	449.77	Provencal language—Dialects
PC951-986	859.9	Raeto-Romance literature	PC3299	449.7	Provencal language—Slang
PC1001-1977	450	Italian language	PC3301-3359	849	Provencal literature
PC1001-1977	450	Italian philology	PC3304-3330	849.104	Troubadours
PC1065	450.71	Italian language—Study and teaching	PC3371-3420	449	Langue d'oc
			PC3381-3420.5	849	Langue d'oc literature
PC1099-1400	455	Italian language—Grammar			
PC1300-1766	741.5945	Wit and humor, Pictorial	PC3801-3899	449.9	Catalan language

LC	Dewey	Subject Heading	LC	Dewey	Subject Heading
PC3819-3873	449.95	Catalan language—Grammar	PD1193	439.93	Gothic language—Dictionaries
PC3883-3886	449.92	Catalan language—Etymology	PD1270	439.9	Vandal language
PC3887-3895	449.93028	Catalan language—Lexicography	PD1501-5929	439.(5-6)	Scandinavian languages
			PD1501-1541	439.(5-6)	Scandinavian philology
PC3900-3976	849.9	Catalan literature	PD1535-1539	439.(5-6)071	Scandinavian languages—Study and teaching
PC4001-4977	460	Spanish language			
PC4001-4071	460	Spanish philology	PD1559-1701	439.(5-6)5	Scandinavian languages—Grammar
PC4065	460.71	Spanish language—Study and teaching			
			PD1801-1819	439.(5-6)2	Scandinavian languages—Etymology
PC4099-4400	465	Spanish language—Grammar			
			PD1823	439.(5-6)3028	Scandinavian languages—Lexicography
PC4571-4580	462	Spanish language—Etymology			
			PD1850-1893	439.(5-6)7	Scandinavian languages—Dialects
PC4620-4693	463.028	Spanish language—Lexicography			
			PD2201-2392	439.6	Old Norse language
PC4620-4645	463	Spanish language—Dictionaries	PD2201-2392	439.6	Old Norse philology
			PD2229-2331	439.65	Old Norse language—Grammar
PC4700-4941	467	Spanish language—Dialects			
			PD2361-2369	439.62	Old Norse language—Etymology
PC4951-4977	467.09	Spanish language—Slang			
PC5001-5498	469	Portuguese language	PD2376-2385	439.63028	Old Norse language—Lexicography
PC5001-5041	469	Portuguese philology			
PC5035-5039	469.0071	Portuguese language—Study and teaching	PD2387-2392	439.67	Old Norse language—Dialects
			PD2401-2447	439.69	Icelandic language
PC5061-5231	469.5	Portuguese language—Grammar	PD2407	439.69071	Icelandic language—Study and teaching
PC5301-5315	469.2	Portuguese language—Etymology	PD2411-2423	439.695	Icelandic language—Grammar
PC5320-5348	469.3028	Portuguese language—Lexicography	PD2431	439.692	Icelandic language—Etymology
PC5325-5348	469.3	Portuguese language—Dictionaries	PD2437	439.693	Icelandic language—Dictionaries
PC5350-5498	469.7	Portuguese language—Dialects	PD2447	439.697	Icelandic language—Slang
PC5411-5414	469.794	Galician dialect	PD2483-2489	439.67	Old Norse Language—Dialects
PC5498	469.709	Portuguese language—Slang	PD2483	439.699	Faroese language
			PD2501-2999	439.82	Norwegian philology
PD	430	Germanic languages	PD2571-2699	439.82	Norwegian language
PD1-9	430.05	Germanic languages—Periodicals	PD2611-2612	439.82071	Norwegian language—Study and teaching
PD51-60	437	Germanic languages—History	PD2619-2673	439.825	Norwegian language—Grammar
PD65-69	430.071	Germanic languages—Study and teaching	PD2683-2684	439.822	Norwegian language—Etymology
PD99-321	430.045	Germanic languages—Grammar	PD2687-2695	439.823028	Norwegian language—Lexicography
PD571-599	430.042	Germanic languages—Etymology	PD2688-2695	439.823	Norwegian language—Dictionaries
PD601-660	430.043028	Germanic languages—Lexicography	PD2696-2699	439.827	Norwegian language—Dialects
PD625-660	430.043	Germanic languages—Dictionaries	PD2699	439.827	Norwegian language—Slang
PD700-777	430.047	Germanic languages—Dialects	PD3001-3929	439.81	Danish language
			PD3001-3071	439.81	Danish philology
PD1101-1211	439.9	Gothic language	PD3065	439.81071	Danish—Study and teaching
PD1119-1167	439.95	Gothic language—Grammar			

LC	Dewey	Subject Heading
PD3101-3400	439.815	Danish language—Grammar
PD3571-3599	439.812	Danish language—Etymology
PD3601-3693	439.813028	Danish language—Lexicography
PD3625-3693	439.813	Danish language—Dictionaries
PD3700-3929	439.817	Danish language—Dialects
PD3901-3929	439.817	Danish language—Slang
PD5001-5929	439.7	Swedish language
PD5001-5071	439.7	Swedish philology
PD5065	439.7071	Swedish language—Study and teaching
PD5101-5400	439.75	Swedish language—Grammar
PD5571-5599	439.72	Swedish language—Etymology
PD5611-5693	439.73028	Swedish language—Lexicography
PD5625-5693	439.73	Swedish language—Dictionaries
PD5700-5929	439.77	Swedish language—Dialects
PE	420	English philology
PE101-299	429	English language— Old English, ca. 450-1100
PE101-123	429	English language—Old English, ca. 450-1100 —Philology
PE129-231	429.5	English language— Old English, ca. 450-1100 —Grammar
PE261-269	429.2	English language—Old English, ca. 450-1100—Etymology
PE274-285	429.3028	English language— Old English, ca. 450-1100—Lexicography
PE275-285	429.3	English language— Old English, ca. 450-1100—Dictionaries
PE287-299	429.7	English language— Old English, ca. 450-1100—Dialects
PE501-685	427.02	English language— Middle English, 1100-1500
PE524-531	427.02	English language— Middle English, 1100-1500—Philology
PE29-531	427.025	English language— Middle English, 1100-1500—Grammar
PE561-569	427.022	English language— Middle English, 1100-1500—Etymology
PE574-585	427.023028	English language— Middle English, 1100-1500—Lexicography
PE575-585	427.023	English language— Middle English, 1100-1500—Dictionaries
PE688	427.027	English language— Middle English, 1100-1500—Dialects
PE1001-3729	420	English language
PE1065-1069	420.71	English language—Study and teaching
PE1079-1087	427.9	English language—History
PE1079-1081	427.00903(1-2)	English language—Early modern, 1500-1700
PE1083	427.009033	English language—18th century
PE1085	427.009034	English language—19th century
PE1097-1105	425	English language—Grammar
PE1112	425	English language—Grammar— 1950-
PE1117-1130	428.6	Readers
PE1133-1168	421.5	English language—Phonology
PE1133	421.509	English language—Phonology, Historical
PE1144-1146	428.1	Spellers
PE1151	421	Phonetic alphabet
PE1151	421	Phonetic spelling
PE1171	425	English language—Morphology
PE1199-1359	425	English language—Parts of speech
PE1402-1497	808.042	English language—Rhetoric
PE1417	428.6	Readers
PE1425	820.8023	Narration (Rhetoric)
PE1427	820.8022	Description (Rhetoric)
PE1571-1599	422	English language—Etymology
PE1591	423.1	English language—Synonyms and antonyms
PE1601-1693	423.028	English language—Lexicography
PE1704	423	English language—Dictionaries
PE1700-3601	427	English language—Dialects
PE2101-2364	427.9411	Scots language
PE2801-3102	427.73	English language—United States
PE3701-3729	427.09	English language—Slang
PE3729.U	427	Pig Latin
PF	430	Germanic languages
PF1-979	439.31	Dutch language
PF1-979	439.31	Dutch philology
PF51-60	439.3109	Dutch language—History

LC	Dewey	Subject Heading	LC	Dewey	Subject Heading
PF65-69	439.31071	Dutch language—Study and teaching	PF3831-3931	437.015	German language— Old High German, 750-1050—Grammar
PF97	439.315	Dutch language—Grammar	PF3985-3991	839	German literature—Old High German, 750-1050
PF131-168	439.3115	Dutch language—Phonology	PF3992-4000	439.4	Old Saxon language
PF171-197	439.315	Dutch language—Morphology	PF4043-4350	437.02	German language—Middle High German, 1050-1500
PF199-335	439.315	Dutch language—Parts of speech	PF4061-4171	437.025	German language—Middle High German, 1050-1500—Grammar
PF410-497	808.043931	Dutch language—Rhetoric	PF4327-4345	437.023028	German language—Middle High German, 1050-1500—Lexicography
PF571-599	439.32	Dutch language—Etymology			
PF601-693	439.313028	Dutch language—Lexicography	PF4333-4345	437.023	German language—Middle High German, 1050-1500—Dictionaries
PF620-693	439.313	Dutch language—Dictionaries			
PF700-979	439.317	Dutch language—Dialects	PF4501-4596	437.090(1-2)	German language—Early modern, 1500-1700
PF861-884	439.36	Afrikaans language			
PF951-979	439.317	Dutch language—Slang	PF5000-5951	437	German language—Dialects
PF1001-1184	439.31	Dutch language			
PF1015	439.3109	Dutch language—History	PF5601-5844	439.4	Low German language
PF1019	439.31071	Dutch language—Study and teaching	PF5971-5999	437.09	German language—Slang
PF1033-1125	439.315	Dutch language—Grammar	PG	491.8	Slavic languages
PF1161-1167	439.312	Dutch language—Etymology	PG1-9198	491.8	Slavic languages
			PG1-41	491.8	Slavic philology
PF1175-1184	439.313	Dutch language—Dictionaries	PG35-39	491.8071	Slavic languages—Study and teaching
PF1401-1497	439.2	Frisian language	PG59-97	491.8045	Slavic languages—Grammar
PF1401-1411	439.2	Frisian language—Philology	PG301-319	491.8042	Slavic languages—Etymology
PF1501-1541	839.2	Frisian literature	PG320-335	491.8043028	Slavic languages—Lexicography
PF3001-5999	430	German language			
PF3051-3060	437	German language—History	PG331-335	491.83	Slavic languages—Dictionaries
PF3065-3069	430.71	German language—Study and teaching	PG350-400	491.877	Slavic languages—Dialects
PF3097-3400	435	German language—Grammar	PG400	491.877	Slavic languages—Slang
PF3131-3168	431.5	German language—Phonology	PG500-585	891.8	Slavic literature
PF3171-3197	435	German language—Morphology	PG601-698	491.81701	Church Slavic language
			PG661-698	491.817015	Church Slavic language—Grammar
PF3199-3335	435	German language—Parts of speech	PG700-716	891.81	Church Slavic literature
PF3410-3497	808.0431	German language—Rhetoric	PG801-993	491.81	Bulgarian language
			PG801-823	491.81	Bulgarian philology
PF3571-3599	432	German language—Etymology	PG831-925	491.815	Bulgarian language—Grammar
PF3601-3693	433.028	German language—Lexicography	PG975-984	491.813	Bulgarian language—Dictionaries
PF3620-3693	433	German language—Dictionaries	PG1000-1146	891.8109	Bulgarian literature
			PG1161-1164	491.819	Macedonian language
PF3801-3991	437.01	German language— Old High German, 750-1050	PG1201-1223	491.82	Serbo-Croatian philology
			PG1224-1399	491.82	Serbo-Croatian language
PF3801-3823	437.01	German language—Old High German, 750-1050—Philology	PG1229-1313	491.825	Serbo-Croatian language—Grammar
			PG1374-1384	491.823	Serbo-Croatian language—Dictionaries

LC	Dewey	Subject Heading	LC	Dewey	Subject Heading
PG1399	491.827	Serbo-Croatian language—Slang	PG6001-6790	491.85	Polish philology
			PG6625-6638	491.853028	Polish language—Lexicography
PG1650-.5	891.821009	Dalmatian poetry			
PG1654-.5	891.821008	Dalmatian poetry	PG6700-6790	491.857	Polish language—Dialects
PG1801-1899	491.84	Slovenian language	PG7001-7446	891.85	Polish literature
PG1801-1813	491.84	Slovenian philology	PG8201-8208	491.91	Prussian language
PG1819-1881	491.845	Slovenian language—Grammar	PG8206	491.913	Prussian language—Dictionaries
PG1887-1894.5	491.843028	Slovenian language—Lexicography	PG8501-8693	491.92	Lithuanian language
			PG8501-8693	491.92	Lithuanian philology
PG1888-1894.5	491.843	Slovenian language—Dictionaries	PG8701-8772	891.92	Lithuanian literature
			PG8801-8993	491.93	Latvian language
PG1900-1962	891.84	Slovenian literature	PG8801-8993	491.93	Latvian philology
PG2001-2847	491.7	Russian language	PG8998-9146	891.93	Latvian literature
PG2001-2069	491.7	Russian philology	PG9501-9599	491.991	Albanian language
PG2065-2069	491.7071	Russian language—Study and teaching	PG9501-9513	491.991	Albanian philology
			PG9601-9665	891.991	Albanian literature
PG2097-2127	491.75	Russian language—Grammar			
			PH	494.5	Finno-Ugric languages
PG2131-2161	491.715	Russian language—Phonology	PH1-11	494.5	Finno-Ugric philology
			PH11	494.5071	Finno-Ugric languages—Study and teaching
PG2171-2197	491.75	Russian language—Morphology			
			PH21-41	494.55	Finno-Ugric languages—Grammar
PG2199-2321	491.75	Russian language—Parts of speech			
			PH91-98	494.54	Finnic languages
PG2571-2591	491.72	Russian language—Etymology	PH101-293	494.541	Finnish language
			PH101-123	494.541	Finnish philology
PG2601-2693	491.73028	Russian language—Lexicography	PH131-225	494.5415	Finnish language—Grammar
PG2625-2693	491.73	Russian language—Dictionaries	PH300-405	894.54109	Finnish literature
			PH501-509	494.54	Karelian language
PG2700-2850	491.77	Russian language—Dialects	PH541-549	494.54	Veps language
			PH561-569	494.54	Votic language
PG2850	491.7709	Russian language—Slang	PH581-589	494.54	Livonian language
PG2900-3580	891.7	Russian literature	PH601-629	494.545	Estonian language
PG3801-3899	491.79	Ukrainian language	PH630-671	894.545	Estonian literature
PG3819-3881	491.795	Ukrainian language—Grammar	PH701-729	494.55	Lapp language
			PH731-735	894.55	Lapp literature
PG3887-3894.5	491.793028	Ukrainian language—Lexicography	PH751-779	494.56	Mordvin language
			PH781-785	894.56	Mordvin literature
PG3888-3894.5	491.793	Ukrainian language—Dictionaries	PH801-807	494.56	Mari language
			PH1001-1004	494.53	Permic languages
PG3900-3987	891.79	Ukrainian literature	PH1091-1097	493.111	Hieroglyphics
PG4001-4771	491.86	Czech philology	PH1251-1254	494.51	Ob-Ugric languages
PG4601-4771	491.86	Czech language	PH2001-2800	494.511	Hungarian language
PG4625-4693	491.863	Czech language—Dictionaries	PH2097-2410	494.5115	Hungarian language—Grammar
PG4700-4771	491.867	Czech language—Dialects	PH2601-2693	494.5113028	Hungarian language—Lexicography
PG5000-5146	891.86	Czech literature			
PG5201-5399	491.87	Slovak language	PH2625-2693	494.5113	Hungarian language—Dictionaries
PG5201-5223	491.87	Slovak philology			
PG5231-5325	491.875	Slovak language—Grammar	PH2800	494.5117	Hungarian language—Slang
PG5375-5384	491.873	Slovak language—Dictionaries	PH3001-3445	894.511	Hungarian literature
			PH5001-5259	499.92	Basque language
PG5400-5546	891.87	Slovak literature	PH5001-5022	499.92	Basque philology
PG5631-5698	491.88	Sorbian languages	PH5280-5490	899.92	Basque literature
PG5661-5698	891.88	Sorbian literature			
PG6001-6790	491.85	Polish language	PJ	490	Oriental languages

LC	Dewey	Subject Heading	LC	Dewey	Subject Heading
PJ65-69	490.071	Oriental languages—Study and teaching	PJ2401-2413	493.5	Cushitic languages
PJ120-171	490.5	Oriental languages—Grammar	PJ2405	493.55	Cushitic languages—Grammar
PJ183	490.2	Oriental languages—Etymology	PJ2409	493.52	Cushitic languages—Etymology
PJ187	490.3028	Oriental languages—Lexicography	PJ2413	493.53	Cushitic languages—Dictionaries
PJ306-489	895	Oriental literature	PJ2425-2594	493.57	Cushitic languages—Dialects
PJ371	895.2008	Oriental drama	PJ2465	493.5	Afar language
PJ990	492	Afroasiatic languages	PJ2531-2534	493.54	Somali language
PJ1001-1479	493.1	Egyptian language	PJ3001-9278	492	Semitic languages
PJ1001-1109	493.1	Egyptian philology	PJ3004	492.043	Semitic languages—Dictionaries
PJ1031	493.13	Egyptian language—Dictionaries	PJ3011-3013	492.04071	Semitic languages—Study and teaching
PJ1051-1109	493.111	Egyptian language—Writing	PJ3021-3041	492.045	Semitic languages—Grammar
PJ1091-1097	493.111	Egyptian language—Writing, Hieroglyphic	PJ3065	492.042	Semitic languages—Etymology
PJ1091	493.1	Hieroglyphics	PJ3071-3075	492.043028	Semitic languages—Lexicography
PJ1105	493.11	Egyptian language—Writing, Hieratic	PJ3081-3095	492.0411	Inscriptions, Semitic
PJ1107	493.111	Egyptian language—Writing, Demotic	PJ3097	892.009	Semitic literature
			PJ3101	492.1	Akkadian language
PJ1121-1201	493.15	Egyptian language—Grammar	PJ3191-3225	492.111	Cuneiform writing
PJ1350-1371	493.12	Egyptian language—Etymology	PJ3601-3953	892.1	Assyro-Babylonian literature
PJ1401-1439	493.13028	Egyptian language—Lexicography	PJ4001-4041	499.95	Sumerian language
PJ1423-1439	493.13	Egyptian language—Dictionaries	PJ4011-4025	499.955	Sumerian language—Grammar
PJ1481-1989	893.1	Egyptian literature	PJ4037	499.953	Sumerian language—Dictionaries
PJ1487	893.13	Egyptian fiction	PJ4045-4083	899.95	Sumerian literature
PJ1501-1921	493.111	Egyptian language—Papyri	PJ4051-4075	499.9511	Cuneiform inscriptions, Sumerian
PJ1501-1819	493.111	Egyptian language—Inscriptions			
PJ1571	893.12	Egyptian drama	PJ4121-4129	492.047	Semitic languages, Northwest
PJ1801-1921	493.1	Egyptian language—Demotic, ca. 650 B.C.-450 A.D.	PJ4149	496.35	Mossi languages
			PJ4150	492.67	Ugaritic language
			PJ4171-4187	492.6	Phoenician language
PJ2001-2187	493.2	Coptic language	PJ4501-4937	492.4	Hebrew language
PJ2019	493.2071	Coptic language—Study and teaching	PJ4501-4541	492.4	Hebrew philology
PJ2029-2113	493.25	Coptic language—Grammar	PJ4553-4731	492.45	Hebrew language—Grammar
PJ2161	493.22	Coptic language—Etymology	PJ4576-4583	492.415	Hebrew language—Phonology
PJ2181	493.23028	Coptic language—Lexicography	PJ4601-4677	492.45	Hebrew language—Morphology
PJ2190-2199	893.2	Coptic literature	PJ4801-4819	492.42	Hebrew language—Etymology
PJ2340-2349	493.3	Berber languages	PJ4820-4847	492.43028	Hebrew language—Lexicography
PJ2345	493.35	Berber languages—Grammar	PJ4825-4847	492.43	Hebrew language—Dictionaries
PJ2347	493.32	Berber languages—Etymology	PJ4855-4937	492.47	Hebrew language—Dialects
PJ2349	493.33	Berber languages—Dictionaries	PJ4901-4950	492.47	Hebrew language, Talmudic
PJ2369-2399	493.3	Berber languages			
PJ2377	493.3	Rif language			

LC	Dewey	Subject Heading	LC	Dewey	Subject Heading
PJ4911-4925	492.475	Hebrew language—Grammar	PJ6811-6820	492.77	Arabic language—Dialects—Syria
PJ4931-4933	492.42	Hebrew language—Etymology	PJ6821-6830	492.77	Arabic language—Dialects—Iraq
PJ4934-4937	492.43028	Hebrew language—Lexicography	PJ6841-6880	492.77	Arabic language—Dialects—Arabian Peninsula
PJ4935-4937	492.43	Hebrew language—Dictionaries	PJ7501-8518	892.7	Arabic literature
PJ5001-5060	892.4	Hebrew literature	PJ7541-7561	892.71009	Arabic poetry
PJ5007	892.4071	Hebrew literature—Study and teaching	PJ7565	892.72009	Arabic drama
			PJ7571-7577	892.7808	Arabic prose literature
PJ5016	892.409002	Hebrew literature, Medieval	PJ7580	398.204927	Folk literature, Arabic
					Inscriptions, Arabic
PJ5017-5021	892.409003	Hebrew literature, Modern	PJ7593-7600	492.711	
PJ5034.4-.9	492.411	Inscriptions, Hebrew	PJ7631-7661	892.71008	Arabic poetry
PJ5037	892.408002	Hebrew literature, Medieval	PJ7665	892.72008	Arabic drama
			PJ7671-7677	892.7808	Arabic prose literature
PJ5038	892.408003	Hebrew literature, Modern	PJ7680	398.204927	Folk literature, Arabic
PJ5048	398.204924	Folk literature, Hebrew	PJ8025-8190	892.7	Arabic literature—Asia
PJ5111-5119	439.1	Yiddish language	PJ8030-8129	892.7	Arabic literature—Middle East
PJ5115-5116.5	439.15	Yiddish language—Grammar			
			PJ8195-8390	892.7	Arabic literature—Africa
PJ5117	439.13	Yiddish language—Dictionaries	PJ8395-8490	892.7	Arabic literature—Europe
			PJ8500-8517	892.7	Arabic literature—America
PJ5120-5192	839.09	Yiddish literature	PJ8991-8999	492.8	Ethiopian languages
PJ5201-5329	492.2	Aramaic language	PJ9001-9087	492.81	Ethiopic language
PJ5208-5209	492.211	Inscriptions, Aramaic	PJ9090-9101	892.81	Ethiopic literature
PJ5271-5279	492.29	Samaritan Aramaic language			
			PK	491.1	Indo-Iranian languages
PJ5401-5411	492.3	Syriac philology	PK1-9201	491.1	Indo-Iranian languages
PJ5401	492.37	Mandailing dialect	PK1-17	491.1	Indo-Iranian philology
PJ5419-5471	492.35	Syriac language—Grammar	PK11-13	491.1071	Indo-Iranian philology—Study and teaching
PJ5483	492.32	Syriac language—Etymology	PK14	491.13	Indo-Iranian languages—Dictionaries
PJ5490-5493	492.33	Syriac language—Dictionaries	PK21-41	491.15	Indo-Iranian languages—Grammar
PJ5601-5695	892.3	Syriac literature	PK75-77	491.13	Indo-Iranian languages—Dictionaries
PJ5701-5809	492.3	Syriac language			
PJ6001-7144	492.7	Arabic language	PK80-85	891.1	Indo-Iranian literature
PJ6001-6071	492.7	Arabic philology	PK101-2899	491.(2-4)	Indo-Aryan languages
PJ6031	492.73	Arabic language—Dictionaries	PK101-119	491.(2-4)	Indo-Aryan philology
			PK119	491.(2-4)	Devanagari alphabet
PJ6065-6069	492.7071	Arabic language—Study and teaching	PK201-379	491.29	Vedic language
			PK231-313	491.295	Vedic language—Grammar
PJ6101-6599	492.75	Arabic language—Grammar			
			PK361-369	491.292	Vedic language—Etymology
PJ6123	492.711	Arabic alphabet			
PJ6172-6199	492.72	Arabic language—Etymology	PK375-379	491.293	Vedic language—Dictionaries
PJ6701-6901	492.77	Arabic language—Dialects	PK401-976	491.2	Sanskrit language
PJ6751-6760	492.77	Arabic language—Dialects—Spain	PK401-418	491.2	Sanskrit philology
			PK501-811	491.25	Sanskrit language—Grammar
PJ6771-6799	492.77	Arabic language—Dialects—Egypt	PK901-919	491.22	Sanskrit language—Etymology
PJ6805-6808	492.77	Arabic language—Dialects—Palestine	PK920-969	491.23028	Sanskrit language—Lexicography
PJ6810	492.77	Arabic language—Dialects—Lebanon	PK925-969	491.23	Sanskrit language—Dictionaries

LC	Dewey	Subject Heading	LC	Dewey	Subject Heading
PK1001-1095	491.37	Pali language	PK6443	891.55808	Persian prose literature
PK1001-1095	491.37	Pali philology	PK6871-6879	491.56	Dari language
PK1017-1073	491.375	Pali language—Grammar	PK7001-7070	491.499	Dardic languages
PK1083-1086	491.372	Pali language—Etymology	PK7021-7029	491.499	Kashmiri language
PK1087-1093	491.373028	Pali language—Lexicography	PK7031-7037	891.499	Kashmiri literature
			PK7045.M3	491.499	Maiya language
PK1089-1095	491.373	Pali language—Dictionaries	PK7070	491.499	Khowar language
			PK8001-8454	491.992	Armenian language
PK1201-1429	491.3	Prakrit languages	PK8451-8499	491.9927	East Armenian dialect
PK1206-1215	491.35	Prakrit languages—Grammar	PK8501-8835	891.992	Armenian literature
			PK8601-8661	891.992	Armenian literature—Europe
PK1223-1225	491.33	Prakrit languages—Dictionaries	PK8681-8689	891.992	Armenian literature—United States
PK1231-1239	491.1	Maharashtri language			
PK1501-2845	491.4	Indo-Aryan languages, Modern	PK9001-9201	499.96	Caucasian languages
			PK9051	499.962	Abkhazo-Adyghian languages
PK1511-1523	491.15	Indo-Aryan languages, Modern—Grammar	PK9051	499.964	Daghestan languages
PK1537	491.13	Indo-Aryan languages, Modern—Dictionaries	PK9051.5-.8	899.964	Daghestan literature
			PK9101-9151	499.969	Georgian language
PK1550-2899	491.4(1-9)	Indo-Aryan languages, Modern—Dialects	PK9106-9115	499.965	Georgian language—Grammar
PK1550-1599	491.451	Assamese language	PK9160-9169	899.969	Georgian literature
PK1651-1695	491.44	Bengali language	PK9201.A2	499.962	Abazin language
PK1821-1824	491.454	Magahi language	PK9201.A3	499.9623	Abkhaz language
PK1836	491.487	Divehi language	PK9201.A35-.A39	899.9623	Abkhaz literature
PK1841-1847	491.47	Gujarati language	PK9201.A45-.A49	899.9625	Adygei literature
PK1850-1888	891.47	Gujarati literature	PK9201.D3	499.964	Dargwa language
PK1931-1937	491.43	Hindustani language	PK9201.D35-.D39	899.964	Dargwa literature
PK1931-1939	491.43	Hindi language	PK9201.K3	499.9624	Kabardian language
PK1975-1987	491.439	Urdu language	PK9201.K35-.K39	899.9624	Kabardian literature
PK2030-2142	891.43	Hindustani literature			
PK2030-2058	891.439	Urdu literature	PL	494.35	Turkish language
PK2351-2378	491.46	Marathi language	PL	490	Oriental languages
PK2561-2569	491.45	Oriya language	PL	496	African languages
PK2591-2610	491.49	Pahari languages	PL1-9	494	Altaic languages
PK2595-2599	491.495	Nepali language	PL21-29	494.3	Turkic languages
PK2631-2639	491.42	Panjabi language	PL31	494.31	Old Turkic language
PK2701-2709	491.479	Rajasthani language	PL41-45	494.37	Turkic languages, Northeast
PK2781-2794	491.41	Sindhi language			
PK2896-2899	491.497	Romany language	PL51-56	494.357	Turkic languages, Southeast
PK2911	891.29	Vedic literature			
PK3591-4485	891.2	Sanskrit literature	PL61-65	494.37	Turkic languages, Northwest
PK4501-4681	891.37	Pali literature			
PK4990-5001.8	891.309	Prakrit literature	PL65.B2	494.38	Karachay-Balkar language
PK5003-5009	891.308	Prakrit literature	PL65.C74	494.388	Crimean Tatar language
PK6001-6996	491.5	Iranian languages	PL65.T3	494.387	Tatar language
PK6001-6996	491.5	Iranian philology	PL65.T35-.T39	894.387	Tatar literature
PK6101-6109	491.52	Avestan language	PL101-199	494.35	Turkish language
PK6121-6129	491.51	Old Persian language	PL201-272	894.35	Turkish literature
PK6128	491.5111	Old Persian inscriptions	PL221	894.352009	Turkish drama
PK6135	491.53	Iranian languages, Middle	PL237-238	894.352008	Turkish drama
PK6201-6399	491.55	Persian language	PL311-314	494.361	Azerbaijani language
PK6395	491.5511	Abbreviations, Persian	PL331-334	494.364	Turkmen language
PK6400-6599	891.55	Persian literature	PL364.Z9.D	494.332	Dolgan dialect
PK6416-6420	891.551009	Persian poetry	PL400-431	494.23	Mongolian languages
PK6421-6422	891.552009	Persian drama	PL401-409	494.23	Mongolian language
PK6423	891.55808	Persian prose literature	PL410-419	894.23	Mongolian literature
PK6426	398.2049155	Folk literature, Persian			

LC	Dewey	Subject Heading	LC	Dewey	Subject Heading
PL450	494.1	Tungus-Manchu languages	PL1077	495.17	Chinese language—To 600
PL451-459	494.1	Evenki language	PL1079	495.17	Chinese language—Ancient Chinese, 600-1200
PL471-479	494.1	Manchu language			
PL481.E92	494.1	Even language			
PL491-494	895	East Asian literature	PL1081	495.17	Chinese language—Middle Chinese, 1200-1919
PL495	494.6	Ainu language			
PL501-700	495.6	Japanese language	PL1083	495.17	Chinese language—Modern Chinese, 1919-
PL525-.6	495.67	Japanese language—Meiji period, 1868-1912			
PL525.2	495.67	Japanese language—To 794	PL1099-1241	495.15	Chinese language—Grammar
PL525.5	495.67	Japanese language—Edo period, 1600-1868	PL1201-1219	495.115	Chinese language—Phonology
PL531.3-532.5	495.65	Japanese language—Grammar	PL1281-1315	495.12	Chinese language—Etymology
PL674.5-677.6	495.63	Japanese language—Dictionaries	PL1401-1498	495.13028	Chinese language—Lexicography
PL700-889	895.6	Japanese literature	PL1420-1498	495.13	Chinese language—Dictionaries
PL726.12	895.609001	Japanese literature—To 794	PL1501-1940	495.17	Chinese language—Dialects
PL726.1185-.1186	895.609001	Japanese literature—To 1185	PL1731-1740	495.1727	Cantonese dialects
PL727-733	895.61009	Japanese poetry	PL1861-1870	495.17215	Hsiang dialects
PL734-739	895.62009	Japanese drama	PL1891-1900	495.1	Mandarin dialects
PL740-747	895.63009	Japanese fiction	PL1931-1940	495.172	Wu dialects
PL742-.83	895.6009	Japanese essays	PL2250-3207	895.1	Chinese literature
PL748-749	398.204956	Folk literature, Japanese	PL2280	895.1109	Chinese literature—To 221 B.C.—History and criticism
PL750-751	495.611	Inscriptions, Japanese			
PL755.12	895.608	Japanese literature			
PL757-763	895.61008	Japanese poetry	PL2283	895.10900(2-3)	Chinese literature—221 B.C.-960 A.D.—History and criticism
PL764-769	895.62008	Japanese drama			
PL770-777	895.63008	Japanese fiction			
PL772-.83	895.408	Japanese essays	PL2284.5	895.109002	Chinese literature—220-589—History and criticism
PL787-789	895.6108001	Japanese literature—Heian period, 794-1185			
PL790-792	895.608002	Japanese literature—1185-1600	PL2285	895.109002	Chinese literature—Three kingdoms, 220-265—History and criticism
PL793-799	895.608003	Japanese literature—Edo period, 1600-1868			
PL800-820	895.6080042	Japanese literature—Meiji period, 1868-1912	PL2286	895.109002	Chinese literature—Chin dynasty, 265-419—History and criticism
PL821-866	895.60800 + (44-5)	Japanese literature—Showa period, 1926-1989	PL2287	895.109002	Chinese literature—Liu Sung dynasty, 420-479—History and criticism
PL901-949	495.7	Korean language			
PL935-.6	495.73	Korean language—Dictionaries	PL2290	895.1090024	Chinese literature—Sui dynasty, 581-618—History and criticism
PL950-998	895.7	Korean literature			
PL959-961.4	895.71009	Korean poetry			
PL962-964	895.72009	Korean drama	PL2294	895.1090044	Chinese literature—Yüan dynasty, 1260-1368—History and criticism
PL965-967	895.73009	Korean fiction			
PL968.2-.4	398.204957	Folk literature, Korean			
PL969.2-.4	495.711	Inscriptions, Korean			
PL974-976.4	895.71008	Korean poetry	PL2296	895.1090046	Chinese literature—Ming dynasty, 1368-1644—History and criticism
PL977-979	895.72008	Korean drama			
PL980-981.5	895.73008	Korean fiction			
PL1001-2244	495.1	Chinese language			

LC	Dewey	Subject Heading	LC	Dewey	Subject Heading
PL2297	895.1090048	Chinese literature—Ch'ing dynasty, 1644-1912—History and criticism	PL8004	496.071	African languages—Study and teaching
			PL8008	496.5	African languages—Grammar
PL2306-2355.8	895.11009	Chinese poetry	PL8010-8014	896	African literature
PL2356-2393	895.12009	Chinese drama	PL8024.A33	496.361	Adamawa languages
PL2395-2413	895.14009	Chinese essays	PL8025	496.391	Bisa language
PL2415-2443	895.13009	Chinese fiction	PL8025	496.39	Bantu languages
PL2445-2446	398.204951	Folk literature, Chinese	PL8026.N44	496.3	Niger-Congo languages
PL2517-2565.8	895.11008	Chinese poetry	PL8041	496.5	Acoli language
PL2566-2603	895.12008	Chinese drama	PL8046.A63	496.3385	Akan language
PL2606-2623	895.14008	Chinese essays	PL8117	493.7	Daba language
PL2625-2653	895.13008	Chinese fiction	PL8123.5-.9	896.34	Dan literature
PL3521-3529	495	Sino-Tibetan languages	PL8127	496.5	Daza language
PL3551-4001	495.4	Tibeto-Burman languages	PL8131	496.5	Dinka language
PL3601-3651	495.4	Tibetan language	PL8134	496.32	Diola language
PL3651.D96	495.4	Dzongkha language	PL8141	496.3962	Duala language
PL3701-3775	895.4	Tibetan literature	PL8147	496.3642	Efik language
PL3881-3884	495.4	Naga languages	PL8161-8164	496.3374	Ewe language
PL3921-3969	495.8	Burmese language	PL8164.Z9	496.337	Fon dialect
PL3970-3988	895.8	Burmese literature	PL8167.F3	496.396	Fang language
PL4001.G2	495.4	Garo language	PL8167.F4	496.3385	Fanti language
PL4051-4054	495	Karen language	PL8181-8184	496.322	Fula language
PL4111-4251	495.91	Thai language	PL8191	496.3378	Ga language
PL4200-4209	895.911	Thai literature	PL8197	496.5	Gambai dialect
PL4281-4587	495.93	Austroasiatic languages	PL8201	496.3957	Ganda language
PL4301-4309	495.93	Mon-Khmer languages	PL8204	496.348	Gbandi language
PL4371-4379	495.922	Vietnamese language	PL8205	496.361	Gbaya language
PL4378	895.922	Vietnamese literature	PL8207.G55	496.395	Gisu language
PL4501-4509	495.95	Munda languages	PL8221	496.33	Grebo language
PL4601-4794	494.8	Dravidian languages	PL8541	496.1	Nama language
PL4601	494.8	Dravidian philology	PL8571-8574	496.5	Nubian languages
PL4627	494.82	Gadaba language (Dravidian)	PL8689	496.3977	Sotho language
PL4641-4649	494.814	Kannada language	PL8701-8704	496.392	Swahili language
PL4711-4719	494.812	Malayalam language	PL8771	496.397	Venda language
PL4751-4759	494.811	Tamil language	PL8801-8804	496.397	Yao language
PL4771-4779	494.827	Telugu language	PL8841-8844	496.3986	Zulu language
PL5021-6571	499.2	Austronesian languages			
PL5071-5079	499.221	Indonesian language	PM	497	North American language
PL5101-5129	499.28	Malay language	PM	499.99	Languages, Artificial
PL5161-5169	499.222	Javanese language	PM1-7356	497	Indians of North America—Languages
PL5170-5179	899.222	Javanese literature			
PL5221-5224	499.22	Balinese language	PM1-95	494.6	Hyperborean languages
PL5501-6135	499.21	Philippine languages	PM31-34	497.19	Aleut language
PL5530-5547	899.21	Philippine literature	PM50-94	497.1	Eskimo languages
PL6051-6059	499.211	Tagalog language	PM50-64	497.12	Inuit language
PL6058	899.211	Tagalog literature	PM600-609	497.3	Algonquian languages
PL6191-6195	499.52	Micronesian languages	PM635	497.354	Arapaho language
PL6201-6209	499.5	Melanesian languages	PM781-784	497.557	Cherokee language
PL6235	499.5	Fijian language	PM851-854	497.333	Ojibwa language
PL6401-6551	499.4	Polynesian languages	PM1001	497.5272	Crow language
PL6465	499.442	Maori language	PM1021-1024	497.5243	Dakota language
PL6515	499.444	Tahitian language	PM1343	497.57	Hokan-Coahuiltecan languages
PL6531	499.48	Tonga language (Tonga Islands)	PM1351	497.458	Hopi language
PL6601-6621	499.12	Papuan languages	PM1381-1384	497.55	Iroquoian languages
PL7001-7101	499.15	Australian languages	PM1881-1884	497.5542	Mohawk language
PL8000-8008	496	African languages	PM1885	497.344	Mohegan languge
			PM1971-1974	497.38	Muskogean languages

LC	Dewey	Subject Heading	LC	Dewey	Subject Heading
PM2006-2009	497.26	Navajo language	PN171.F6-.F7	098.3	Literary forgeries and mystifications
PM2175	497.45529	Pima languages			
PM2321	497.4574	Shoshonean languages	PN171.Q6	808.882	Quotation
PM2515	497.4576	Ute language	PN203	808	Style, Literary
PM2711	497.994	Zuni language	PN205	808.066	Exposition (Rhetoric)
PM3001-4566	497.9	Indians of Central America—Languages	PN441-595	809	Literature—History and criticism
PM3961-3969	497.42	Mayan languages	PN597	809.91	Literary movements
PM4061-4069	497.452	Nahuatl language	PN601	808.8012	Naturalism in literature
PM5001-7356	498	Indians of South America—Languages	PN603	808.80145	Romanticism
			PN611-630	809.01	Literature, Ancient
PM5071-5079	497	Indians of the West Indies—Languages	PN665-694	808.8002	Literature, Medieval
			PN683-687	398.20902	Legends
PM7171-7179	498.3829	Tupi languages	PN688-691	808.82	Poetry, Medieval
PM7801-7895	417.22	Pidgin languages	PN691	808.814	Lyric poetry
PM7801-7895	401.3	Lingua francas	PN695-779	808.800(3-4)	Literature, Modern
PM7831-7875	447.9	Creole dialects	PN715-749	808.80024	Renaissance
PM7875.G8	427.9	Sea Islands Creole dialect	PN750-759	808.80145	Romanticism
PM7891	427.9	Pidgin English	PN816	808.80145	Romance fiction
PM8001-9021	499.99	Languages, Artificial	PN836	839.3009	Germanic fiction
PM8008	401.3	Language, Universal	PN849.G	820	British literature
PM8201-8298	499.992	Esperanto	PN849.O26	899	Pacific Island literature
PM9001-9021	417.2	Languages, Secret	PN849.R9-.R92	891.708004	Soviet literature
			PN905-1008	398.209	Folk literature—History and criticism
PN	800	Literature	PN931-937	827	English wit and humor
PN1-9	805	Literature—Periodicals	PN1010-1525	808.1	Poetry
PN20-29	806	Literature—Societies, etc.	PN1031-1035	808.1	Versification
PN44	808.8024	Literature—Stories, plots, etc.	PN1039-1049	808.1	Poetics
			PN1101	808.81071	Poetry—Study and teaching
PN45	801.93	Literature—Aesthetics			
PN45	801	Literature—Philosophy	PN1105-1279	809.1	Poetry—History and criticism
PN48	808.8036	Nature in literature			
PN49	808.804291	Mysticism in literature	PN1301-1333	808.8132	Epic poetry
PN56.A5	808.8015	Allegory	PN1341-1347	398.2	Folk poetry
PN56.C6	808.80142	Classicism	PN1351-1389	808.14	Lyric poetry
PN56.M94	808.8015	Myth in literature	PN1441	808.882	Epigrams
PN56.M95	808.8037	Mythology in literature	PN1514	808.8142	Sonnet
PN56.R3	808.8012	Realism in literature	PN1530	808.8245	Monologue
PN56.R3	808.8012	Naturalism in literature	PN1551	808.8026	Dialogue
PN56.R7	808.80145	Romanticism	PN1560-1590	790.2	Performing arts
PN56.S87	808.801163	Surrealism (Literature)	PN1581	790.209	Performing arts—History
PN56.S9	808.8015	Symbolism in literature	PN1585-1589	725.83	Centers for the performing arts
PN57.D4	808.8038291 + 216	Devil in literature			
			PN1600-1861	808.2	Drama
PN59-72	807.1	Literature—Study and teaching	PN1660-1692	808.2	Drama—Technique
			PN1701	808.20071	Drama—Study and teaching
PN75-99	809	Literature—History and criticism	PN1707	809.2	Dramatic criticism
PN83	808.54509	Reading	PN1720-1861	809.2	Drama—History and criticism
PN101-249	808.02	Authorship			
PN154	174.98	Literary ethics	PN1761	809.2527	Mysteries and miracle-plays
PN161	381.45808	Authorship—Marketing			
PN161	381.45808	Queries (Authorship)	PN1910-1919	808.82527	Melodrama
PN162	808.027	Editing	PN1940-1949	808.825232	Farce
PN163	070.52	Literary agents	PN1960-1969	792.7	Music-halls (Variety-theaters, cabarets, etc.)
PN167-168	808	Plagiarism			
PN171.4-229	808	Rhetoric	PN1960-1969	792.7	Vaudeville

LC	Dewey	Subject Heading
PN1970-1979	791.53	Puppets
PN1979.S5	791.53	Shadow shows
PN1990-1992.92	384.54	Broadcasting
PN1991-.9	791.44	Radio broadcasting
PN1991.73	808.222	Radio plays—Technique
PN1991.8.C65	791.44617	Radio comedies
PN1991.8.E84	384.54089	Ethnic radio broadcasting
PN1991.8.S4	791.446	Soap operas
PN1992-.92	384.5532	Television programs
PN1992.4	791.45028092	Television actors and actresses
PN1992.8.C66	791.45617	Television comedies
PN1992.8.S4	791.456	Soap operas
PN1992.95	791.45	Video recordings
PN1993-1999	791.43	Motion pictures
PN1995	791.4375	Motion pictures—Reviews
PN1995.5	791.43682	Motion pictures—Religious aspects
PN1995.5	175	Motion pictures—Moral and ethical aspects
PN1995.9.D78	791.43655	Drugs in motion pictures
PN1995.9.E77	791.4092	Entertainers in motion pictures
PN1995.9.F67	791.43	Foreign films
PN1995.9.M86	791.43657	Musical films
PN1995.9.N4	791.4308996 + 073	Blacks in motion pictures
PN1995.9.S7	791.43028092	Stunt performers
PN1996-1997	791.437	Motion picture plays
PN1997.5	741.58	Animated films
PN2000-3299	792	Theater
PN2055	792.023	Acting—Vocational guidance
PN2056	174.97914	Actors—Professional ethics
PN2061-2071	792.028	Acting
PN2071.G4	792.3	Mime
PN2071.I5	792.028	Improvisation (Acting)
PN2091.A	792.028	Theaters—Accidents
PN2091.S8	792.025	Theaters—Stage-setting and scenery
PN2100-2193	792.09	Theater—History
PN2131-2145	792.0901	Theater—History—To 500
PN2152-2160	792.0902	Theater—History—Medieval, 500-1500
PN2171-2179	792.09033	Theater—History—18th century
PN2181-2193	792.09034	Theater—History—20th century
PN2205-2217	792.028092	Actors
PN2205-2217	792.028092	Actresses
PN2219.08	792.022	Theater, Open-air
PN2220-2298	792.0973	Theater—United States
PN2267	792.02230973	Little theater movement
PN2270.A35	792.08996073	Afro-American theater
PN2660-2668	792.09495	Theater—Greece
PN2870-2878	792.0951	Theater—China
PN2920-2928	792.0952	Theater—Japan
PN2924.5.K3	792.0952	Kabuki
PN3151-3171	792.0222	Amateur theater
PN3202-3299	791.62	Pageants
PN3203-3299	792.16	Passion-plays
PN3311-3503	808.3	Fiction
PN3329-3503	809.3	Fiction—History and criticism
PN3355-3383	808.3	Fiction—Technique
PN3373	809.31	Short story
PN3377.5.D4	809.3872	Detective and mystery stories—Technique
PN3378	809.924	Plots (Drama, novel, etc.)
PN3433-.8	808.838762	Science fiction
PN3441	809.381	Historical fiction
PN3448.A3	809.387	Adventure stories
PN3448.D4	809.3872	Detective and mystery stories
PN4001-4355	808.85	Oratory
PN4021-4055	809.5	Oratory—History
PN4096	809	Rhetorical criticism
PN4121-4130	808.851	Public speaking
PN4142	808.5	Speechwriting
PN4145-4151	808.54	Oral interpretation
PN4177-4191	808.53	Debates and debating
PN4199-4355	808.54	Recitations
PN4305.M6	808.8245	Monologues
PN4400	809.6	Letters
PN4500	808.4	Essay
PN4700-5650	070.4	Journalism
PN4700-5650	070.172	Press
PN4700-5650	050	Periodicals
PN4720	070.4074	Journalism—Exhibitions
PN4749	070.4	Journalism—Social aspects
PN4751	070.44932	Journalism—Political aspects
PN4778	070.41	Journalism—Editing
PN4781	070.43	Reporters and reporting
PN4784.A18	363.46	Abortion in the press
PN4784.D57	904	Disasters in the press
PN4784.E53	070.435	Electronic news gathering
PN4784.N5	070.175	Newsletters
PN4784.S6	070.449796	Sports journalism
PN4785-4823	070.4071	Journalism—Study and teaching
PN4823	070.4333092	War correspondents
PN4840-4900	071	American periodicals
PN4840-4899	051	American newspapers
PN4882.5	070.484	Afro-American press
PN4882.5	070.484	Afro-American newspapers
PN4888.A2	363.460973	Abortion in the press
PN4901-4920	051	Canadian periodicals
PN4930.5-4959	079.72	Journalism—West Indies
PN5000-5106	079.8	South American periodicals
PN5110-5355	073-078	European periodicals
PN5111-5130	052	English periodicals
PN5111-5129	072.(1-8)	English newspapers
PN5171-5790	054.1	French periodicals
PN5201-5220	053.1	German periodicals

LC	Dewey	Subject Heading	LC	Dewey	Subject Heading
PN5241-5250	055.1	Italian periodicals	PQ1-3999	840	French literature
PN5271-5280	059.9171	Russian periodicals	PQ51-65	840.71	French literature—Study and teaching
PN5280.5-5310	058	Scandinavian periodicals			
PN5281-5290	058.81	Danish periodicals	PQ151-221	840.(1-2)09	French literature—To 1500
PN5281-5289	078.489	Danish newspapers			
PN5317.P4	056.1	Spanish periodicals	PQ151-216	848.(1-2)08	French prose literature—To 1500
PN5321-5330	056.9	Portuguese periodicals			
PN5360-5449	079.5	Asian periodicals	PQ201-205	841.03209	Epic literature, French
PN5450-5499	079.6	African periodicals	PQ230-239	840.309	French literature—16th century
PN5510-5590	079.94	Australian periodicals			
PN6010-6078	808	Literature—Collections	PQ241-251	840.409	French literature—17th century
PN6010-6065	808.8	Anthologies			
PN6071.E7	808.803538	Erotic literature	PQ261-276	840.509	French literature—18th century
PN6080-6095	808.882	Quotations			
PN6081-6084	820.802	Quotations, English	PQ281-299	840.709	French literature—19th century
PN6086-6089	840.802	Quotations, French			
PN6090-6093	830.802	Quotations, German	PQ301-307	840.9109	French literature—20th century
PN6099-6110	808.108	Poetry—Collections			
PN6110.5-6120	808.82	Drama—Collections	PQ400-491	841.09	French poetry—History and criticism
PN6110.C4	398.8	Nursery rhymes			
PN6110.E6	808.8132	Epic poetry	PQ416-418	841.309	French poetry—16th century
PN6110.N17	808.813	Narrative poetry			
PN6110.O4	808.8143	Odes	PQ421-423	841.409	French poetry—17th century
PN6110.P3	808.87	Parodies			
PN6111-6120	808.820512	Tragedy	PQ426-428	841.509	French poetry—18th century
PN6119.9	792.0222	Amateur plays			
PN6120.95.A38	808.8387	Adventure stories	PQ431-439	841.709	French poetry—19th century
PN6120.95.S33	808.838762	Science fiction			
PN6120.F3	808.825232	Farces	PQ441-443	841.910	French poetry—20th century
PN6120.M9	808.82527	Detective and mystery plays			
			PQ601-657	848.08	French prose literature
PN6120.P3-.P4	792.3	Pantomimes	PQ631-671	843.009	French fiction
PN6120.R2	808.8222	Radio plays	PQ671	843.909	French fiction—20th century
PN6121-6129	808.85	Speeches, addresses, etc.			
PN6130-6140	808.86	Letters	PQ781-841	398.20441	Folk literature, French
PN6141-6145	808.84	Essays	PQ1121-1125	840.308	French literature—16th century
PN6147-6231	808.87	Wit and humor			
PN6147	808.87092	Humorists	PQ1126-1130	840.408	French literature—17th century
PN6149.P3	808.87	Parody			
PN6157-6162	817.008	American wit and humor	PQ1131-1135	840.508	French literature—18th century
PN6173-6175	827.008	English wit and humor			
PN6222.N	839.317008	Dutch wit and humor	PQ1136-1139	840.708	French literature—19th century
PN6222.S	839.367	Afrikaans wit and humor			
PN6231.B84	792.7	Burlesques	PQ1141	840.9108	French literature—20th century
PN6231.L5	808.8175	Limericks			
PN6231.S2	808.87	Satire	PQ1160-1193	841.08	French poetry
PN6259-6268	808.882	Anecdotes	PQ1211-1241	842.08	French drama
PN6269-6278	398.9	Aphorisms and apothegms	PQ1243-1279	848.08	French prose literature
PN6279-6288	808.882	Epigrams	PQ1261-1279	843.08	French fiction
PN6282	848.02	Epigrams, French	PQ1281-1283	845.08	Speeches, addresses, etc., French
PN6299-6308	398.9	Maxims			
PN6340-6348	808.851	Toasts	PQ1300-1595	840.(1-2)08	French literature—To 1500
PN6366-6377	793.24	Charades			
PN6366-6377	808.882	Riddles	PQ1300-1391	841.(1-2)08	French poetry—To 1500
PN6366-6377	793.73	Acrostics	PQ1341-1385	842.(1-2)08	French drama—To 1500
PN6400-6525	398.9	Proverbs	PQ3809	840	French literature—Foreign countries
PN6700-6790	070.444	Comic books, strips, etc.			
			PQ3810-3858	840	Belgian literature (French)
			PQ3870-3888	840	Swiss literature (French)
PQ	840	Romance literatures	PQ3900-3919.2	840	French-Canadian literature

LC	Dewey	Subject Heading	LC	Dewey	Subject Heading
PQ3940-3949	840	West Indian literature (French)	PQ7500-7509.2	860	Honduran literature
			PQ7510-7519.2	860	Nicaraguan literature
PQ3960-3979	840	Vietnamese literature (French)	PQ7520-7529.2	860	Panamanian literature
			PQ7530-7539.2	860	Salvadoran literature
PQ3980-3989.2	840	African literature (French)	PQ7600-7798.36	860	Argentine literature
PQ3998.5.N	840	New Caledonian literature (French)	PQ7801-7820	860	Bolivian literature
			PQ7900-8098.36	860	Chilean literature
PQ4001-5999	850	Italian literature	PQ8160-8180.36	860	Colombian literature
PQ4001-4199	850.9	Italian literature—History and criticism	PQ8200-8220.36	860	Ecuadorian literature
			PQ8210	861	Ecuadorian poetry
PQ4013-4023	850.71	Italian literature—Study and teaching	PQ8212	863	Ecuadorian fiction
			PQ8214-.5	861	Ecuadorian poetry
PQ4075	850.209	Italian literature—15th century	PQ8216.F5	863	Ecuadorian fiction
			PQ8250-8259	860	Paraguayan literature
PQ4079-4080	850.409	Italian literature—16th century	PQ8300-8498.36	860	Peruvian literature
			PQ8510-8519	860	Uruguayan literature
PQ4081-4082	850.509	Italian literature—17th century	PQ8530-8550.36	860	Venezuelan literature
			PQ8700-8899	860	Philippine literature
PQ4083-4084	850.609	Italian literature—18th century	PQ9000-9999	869	Portuguese literature
			PQ9008-9009.5	869.071	Portuguese literature—Study and teaching
PQ4085-4086	850.709	Italian literature—19th century			
PQ4087	850.9109	Italian literature—20th century	PQ9061-9081	869.109	Portuguese poetry
			PQ9083-9095	869.209	Portuguese drama
PQ4091-4131	851.09	Italian poetry	PQ9097-9119	869.80809	Portuguese prose literature
PQ4133-4160	852.09	Italian drama			
PQ4161-4185	858.0809	Italian prose literature	PQ9121-9128	398.20469	Folk literature, Portuguese
PQ4183.E8	854.09	Italian essays	PQ9149-9163	869.108	Portuguese poetry
PQ4183.L4	856.09	Italian letters	PQ9164-9170	869.208	Portuguese drama
PQ4186-4199	398.20451	Folk literature, Italian	PQ9172-9188	869.80808	Portuguese prose literature
PQ6001-8929	860	Spanish literature			
PQ6013-6020	860.71	Spanish literature—Study and teaching	PQ9421	869	Portuguese literature—Foreign countries
PQ6022-6167	860.9	Spanish literature—History and criticism	PQ9450-9469.2	869	Galician literature
			PQ9500-9699	869	Brazilian literature
PQ6057-6060	860.(1-2)09	Spanish literature—To 1500	PQ9900-9948	869	African literature (Portuguese)
PQ6063-6072	860.(2-3)09	Spanish literature—Classical period, 1500-1700			
			PR	820	English literature
PQ6075-6098	861.09	Spanish poetry	PR1-9680	820	English literature
PQ6099-6129	862.09	Spanish drama	PR1-978	820.9	English literature—History and criticism
PQ6131-6153	868.0809	Spanish prose literature			
PQ6138-6147	863.09	Spanish fiction	PR19	820.3	English literature—Dictionaries
PQ6155-6167	398.20461	Folk literature, Spanish			
PQ6174.95-6215	861.08	Spanish poetry	PR31-55	820.71	English literature—Study and teaching
PQ6217-6241	862.08	Spanish drama			
PQ6247-6264	868.0808	Spanish prose literature	PR57-78	820.9	English literature—Criticism, Textual
PQ6251-6257	863.08	Spanish fiction			
PQ7020-8921	860	Spanish literature—Foreign countries	PR87	820.0202	English literature—Outlines, syllabi, etc.
PQ7100-7298.36	860	Mexican literature	PR111-119	821.0099287	English poetry—Women authors
PQ7370-7390	860	Cuban literature			
PQ7400-7409.2	860	Dominican literature	PR111-119	820.99287	English literature—Women authors
PQ7402	861	Dominican poetry			
PQ7406	861	Dominican poetry	PR171-236	829.09	English literature—Old English, ca. 450-1100
PQ7420-7440	860	Puerto Rican literature			
PQ7480-7489.2	860	Costa Rican literature	PR201-217	829.109	English poetry—Old English, ca. 450-1100
PQ7490-7499.2	860	Guatemalan literature			

LC	Dewey	Subject Heading	LC	Dewey	Subject Heading
PR221-236	829.80809	English prose literature—Old English, ca. 450-1100	PR1110.C3	820.809222	English literature—Catholic authors
PR251-369	820.(1-2)09	English literature—Middle English, 1100-1500	PR1110.W6	820.809287	English literature—Women authors
PR311-369	821.(1-2)09	English poetry, Middle English, 1100-1500	PR1119-1131	820.(1-2)08	English literature—Middle English, 1100-1500
PR321-347	821.03209	Epic poetry, English	PR1119-1131	820.(2-4)08	English literature— Early modern, 1500-1700
PR401-439	820.(2-4)09	English literature—Early modern, 1500-1700	PR1134-1139	820.508	English literature—18th century
PR441-449	820.509	English literature—18th century	PR1143-1145	820.808	English literature—19th century
PR451-469	820.809	English literature—19th century	PR1149	820.908	English literature—20th century
PR471-479	820.909	English literature—20th century	PR1170-1227	821	English poetry
PR500-611	821.9	English poetry	PR1177	821.00809287	English poetry—Women authors
PR500-609	821.9	English poetry—History and criticism	PR1195.M2	782.43	Madrigals
PR521-549	821.(2-4)09	English poetry—Early modern, 1500-1700	PR1203	821.(1-2)08	English poetry—Middle English, 1100-1500
PR551-579	821.509	English poetry—18th century	PR1204-1213	821.(3-4)08	English poetry—Early modern, 1500-1700
PR581-599	821.809	English poetry—19th century	PR1215-1219	821.508	English poetry—18th century
PR601-609	821.909	English poetry—20th century	PR1221-1224	821.808	English poetry—19th century
PR621-739	822.09	English drama	PR1224-1227	821.9108	English poetry—20th century
PR631	822.052309	English drama (Comedy)	PR1241-1273	822.08	English drama
PR633	822.051209	English drama (Tragedy)	PR1248	822.052308	English drama (Comedy)
PR635.D45	822.09	Domestic drama, English	PR1257	822.051208	English drama (Tragedy)
PR641-644	822.(1- 2)09	English drama—To 1500	PR1260	822.(1-2)08	English drama—To 1500
PR646-658	822.(2-3)09	English drama—Early modern and Elizabethan, 1500-1600	PR1262-1263	822.(2-3)08	English drama—Early modern and Elizabethan, 1500-1600
PR671-698	822.409	English drama—17th century	PR1265.3-1266	822.408	English drama—17th century
PR701-719	822.509	English drama—18th century	PR1269	822.508	English drama—18th century
PR721-734	822.809	English drama—19th century	PR1271	822.808	English drama—19th century
PR736-739	822.909	English drama—20th century	PR1272	822.9108	English drama—20th century
PR750-888	828.08	English prose literature	PR1281-1300	828.08	English prose literature
PR767-769	828.08(2-3)09	English prose literature—Early modern, 1500-1700	PR1281-1309	823.08	English fiction
			PR1285	820.8022	Description (Rhetoric)
PR769	828.08509	English prose literature—18th century	PR1293-1295	828.08(2-3)	English prose literature—Early modern and Elizabethan, 1500-1600
PR821-888	823.09	English fiction	PR1297	828.085	English prose literature—18th century
PR881-888	823.9109	English fiction—20th century	PR1301-1304	820.808	English literature—19th century
PR901-907	825.09	Speeches, addresses, etc., English	PR1321-1329	825.08	Speeches, addresses, etc., English
PR908	828.03	English diaries	PR1330	828.03	English diaries
PR911-917	826.009	English letters	PR1341-1349	826.08	English letters
PR921-927	824.009	English essays	PR1361-1369	824.08	English essays
PR931-937	827.009	English wit and humor	PR1490-1508	829.1	English poetry—Old English, ca. 450-1100
PR951-981	398.2042	Folk literature, English			

LC	Dewey	Subject Heading	LC	Dewey	Subject Heading
PR2750-3112	822.33	Shakespeare, William, 1564-1616	PS208	810.(2-3)09	American literature—1783-1850
PR8500-8621	820.99411	English literature—Scottish authors	PS221-228	810.509	American literature—20th century
PR8510-8553	820.9	Scottish literature	PS306-.5	811.071	American poetry—Study and teaching
PR8561-8581	821.0089411	English poetry—Scottish authors	PS312	811.109	American poetry—Colonial period, ca. 1600-1775
PR8597-8607	828.08	English prose literature—Scottish authors	PS314	811.209	American poetry—Revolutionary period, 1775-1783
PR8631-8693	820.809411	English literature—Scottish authors	PS316-321	811.309	American poetry—19th century
PR8631-8644	820	Scottish literature	PS319	811.209	American poetry—1783-1850
PR8649-8663	821.00809411	English poetry—Scottish authors	PS324	811.509	American poetry—20th century
PR8672-8687	828.08	English prose literature—Scottish authors	PS330-351	812.09	American drama
PR8700-8821	820.99415	English literature—Irish authors	PS335	812.071	American drama—Study and teaching
PR8831-8893	820.809415	English literature—Irish authors	PS336.C7	812.052309	American drama (Comedy)
PR8848-8863	821.00809415	English poetry—Irish authors	PS336.T7	812.051209	American drama (Tragedy)
			PS360-379	818.0809	American prose literature
PR8900-8997	820.809429	English literature—Welsh authors	PS366	818.08109	American prose literature—Colonial period, ca. 1600-1775
PR8926-8932	821.00909429	English poetry—Welsh authors	PS367-369	818.08209	American prose—Revolutionary period, 1775-1783
PR8955-8969	821.00809429	English poetry—Welsh authors			
PR9320-.9	820	Guyanese literature	PS371-379	813.09	American fiction
PR9340-9408	820.9	African literature (English)	PS400-408	815.09	Speeches, addresses, etc., American
PR9342	821.09	African poetry (English)			
PR9343	822	African drama (English)	PS409	818.03	American diaries
PR9344	823	African fiction (English)	PS410-418	816.09	American letters
PR9346-.5	821.08	African poetry (English)	PS420-428	814.09	American essays
PR9347	822.08	African drama (English)	PS430-438	817.09	American wit and humor
PR9347.5	823.09	African fiction (English)	PS451-478	398.20973	Folk literature, American
PR9600-9619.3	820	Australian literature	PS508.N3	810.80896073	American literature—Afro-American authors
PR9632.2-.6	828.08	New Zealand prose literature	PS508.W7	810.809287	American literature—Women authors
PR9637.25-.92	828.08	New Zealand prose literature	PS589	811.00809287	American poetry—Women authors
PR9900.J	820.80952	English literature—Japanese authors	PS591.N4	811.0080896 + 073	American poetry—Afro-American authors
PS	810	American literature	PS623-635	812.08	American drama
PS	811	American poetry	PS642-659.2	818.08	American prose literature
PS147-151	810.99287	American literature—Women authors	PS660-668	815.08	Speeches, addresses, etc., American
			PS669	818.3	American diaries
PS153-490	810.9	American literature—History and criticism	PS670-678	816.08	American letters
PS153.N5	810.9896073	Afro-American authors	PS680-688	814.08	American essays
PS185-191	810.109	American literature—Colonial period, ca. 1600-1775	PT	830	German
			PT	839.31	Dutch
PS193	810.209	American literature—Revolutionary period, 1775-1783	PT	839.5	Scandinavian literatures
			PT1-1021	830	German literature
PS201-214	810.309	American literature—19th century	PT31	830.6	German literature—Congresses

LC	Dewey	Subject Heading	LC	Dewey	Subject Heading
PT41	830.3	German language dictionaries	PT1171-1173	831.708	German poetry—19th century
PT51-65	830.71	German literature—Study and teaching	PT1174-1175	831.908	German poetry—20th century
PT175-230	830.(2-3)	German literature—Middle High German, 1050-1500	PT1251-1299	832.08	German drama
			PT1271-1273	832.051208	German drama (Tragedy)
PT175-227	831.(2-3)09	German poetry—Middle High German, 1050-1500	PT1275-1277	832.052308	German drama (Comedy)
			PT1301-1340	838.08	German prose literature
PT183	830.109	German literature—Old High German, 750-1050	PT1314-1340	833.08	German fiction
			PT1315	833.608	German fiction—18th century
PT238-281	830.(4-5)09	German literature—Early modern, 1500-1700	PT1332	833.708	German fiction—19th century
PT285-321	830.609	German literature—18th century—History and criticism	PT1334	833.908	German fiction—20th century
PT341-395	830.709	German literature—19th century—History and criticism	PT1337-1340	833.0108	Short stories, German
			PT1344-1345	835.08	Speeches, addresses, etc., German
PT401-403	830.1099	German literature—20th century	PT1348-1352	836.08	German letters
			PT1354	834.08	German essays
PT412-418	839.69808	Icelandic prose literature	PT1375-1479	830.208	German literature—Middle High German, 1050-1500
PT500-597	831.009	German poetry			
PT525-531	831.(4-5)09	German poetry—Early modern, 1500-1700	PT1391-1429	831.(2-3)08	German poetry—Middle High German, 1050-1500
PT533-535	831.609	German poetry—18th century	PT1411-1418	831.03208	Epic poetry, German
PT541-547	831.709	German poetry—19th century	PT3808-3809	830	German literature—Foreign countries
PT551-553	831.909	German poetry—20th century	PT3830-3837.5	830	German literature—Czechoslovakia
PT605-709	832.09	German drama	PT3840-3848	830	Hungarian literature (German)
PT711-871	838.08	German prose literature			
PT741-772	833.09	German fiction	PT3860-3878	830	Swiss literature (German)
PT753-756	833.(4-5)09	German fiction—Early modern, 1500-1700	PT3900-3919	830	German American literature (German)
PT759	833.609	German fiction—18th century	PT4801-4897	839.4	Low German literature
			PT4803	839.4071	Low German literature—Study and teaching
PT763-771	833.709	German fiction—19th century	PT4813	839.4109	Low German literature—To 1500
PT772	833.909	German fiction—20th century	PT4817-4820	839.4109	Low German poetry
PT801	835.009	Speeches, addresses, etc., German	PT4821	839.4209	Low German drama
			PT4829-4830	398.204394	Folk literature, Low German
PT811	836.009	German letters			
PT831	834.009	German essays	PT4834-4836	839.41008	Low German poetry
PT881-951	398.20431	Folk literature, German	PT4837-4838	839.42008	Low German drama
PT1100-1479	830.8	German literature	PT5001-5980	839.31	Dutch literature
PT1121-1126	830.(4-5)08	German literature—Early modern, 1500-1700	PT5040-5044	839.31071	Dutch literature—Study and teaching
PT1131	830.608	German literature—18th century	PT5121-5137	839.3109	Dutch literature—To 1500
			PT5141-5165	839.31(2-4)09	Dutch literature—1500-1800
PT1136	830.708	German literature—19th century	PT5170-5175	839.31509	Dutch literature—19th century
PT1141	830.908	German literature—20th century	PT5180-5185	839.31609	Dutch literature—20th century
PT1151-1241	831.8	German poetry	PT5201-5245	839.31109	Dutch poetry
PT1163-1165	831.(4-5)08	German poetry—Early modern, 1500-1700	PT5250-5295	839.31209	Dutch drama
PT1167-1169	831.608	German poetry—18th century	PT5300-5336	839.31808	Dutch prose literature

LC	Dewey	Subject Heading	LC	Dewey	Subject Heading
PT5320-5336	839.31309	Dutch fiction	PT7741-7747	839.814	Danish literature—18th century
PT5346	839.31709	Dutch wit and humor	PT7751-7756	839.816	Danish literature—19th century
PT5351-5395	398.2043931	Folk literature, Dutch			
PT5470-5488	839.31108	Dutch poetry	PT7760	839.817	Danish literature—20th century
PT5490-5515	839.31208	Dutch drama			
PT5517-5547	839.31808	Dutch prose literature	PT7770-7795	839.811	Danish poetry
PT5520-5530	839.31308	Dutch fiction	PT7800-7832	839.81209	Danish drama
PT5539	839.31408	Dutch essays	PT7835-7862	839.81808	Danish prose literature
PT5541	839.31708	Dutch wit and humor	PT7835-7862	839.81309	Danish fiction
PT6000-6466.36	839.31	Flemish literature	PT7866	839.81609	Danish letters
PT6040	839.31071	Flemish literature—Study and teaching	PT7900-7930	398.2043981	Folk literature, Danish
			PT7975-7994	839.81108	Danish poetry
PT6140	839.31109	Flemish poetry	PT7999-8020	839.81208	Danish drama
PT6200-6230	398.2043931	Folk literature, Flemish	PT8021-8024	839.81808	Danish prose literature
PT6330-6348	839.31108	Flemish poetry	PT8022-8024	839.81308	Danish fiction
PT6350-6360	839.31208	Flemish drama	PT8030	839.81608	Danish letters
PT6365-6397	839.31808	Flemish prose literature	PT8301-9155	839.82	Norwegian literature
PT6500-6593.36	839.36	Afrikaans literature	PT8340-8344	839.82071	Norwegian literature—Study and teaching
PT6515	839.36109	Afrikaans poetry			
PT6520	839.36209	Afrikaans drama	PT8460-8490	839.82109	Norwegian poetry
PT6525	839.36309	Afrikaans fiction	PT8500-8534	839.82209	Norwegian drama
PT6525	839.36808	Afrikaans prose literature	PT8540-8567	839.82808	Norwegian prose literature
PT6540-6545	398.2043936	Folk literature, Afrikaans	PT8555-8567	839.82309	Norwegian fiction
PT6545	839.36108	Afrikaans poetry	PT8600-8635	398.2043982	Folk literature, Norwegian
PT6560	839.36108	Afrikaans poetry	PT8675-8695	839.82108	Norwegian poetry
PT6590	839.36808	Afrikaans prose literature	PT8699-8718	839.82208	Norwegian drama
PT6570	839.36808	Afrikaans prose literature	PT8719-8722	839.82808	Norwegian prose literature
PT6570	839.36308	Afrikaans fiction	PT8720-8722	839.82308	Norwegian fiction
PT6570	839.36208	Afrikaans drama	PT9000-9094	839.82	Norwegian literature (Nynorsk)
PT7001-9999	839.5	Scandinavian literature			
PT7035-7039	839.5071	Scandinavian literature—Study and teaching	PT9201-9999	839.7	Swedish literature
			PT9375-9405	839.7109	Swedish poetry
PT7088-7089	398.204395	Folk literature, Scandinavian	PT9415-9449	839.7209	Swedish drama
			PT9460-9499	839.7808	Swedish prose literature
PT7101-7338	839.6	Old Norse literature	PT9480-9492	839.7309	Swedish fiction
PT7135-7139	839.6071	Old Norse literature—Study and teaching	PT9509-9542	398.204397	Folk literature, Swedish
			PT9580-9599	839.7108	Swedish poetry
PT7170-7175	839.6109	Old Norse Poetry	PT9605-9625	839.7208	Swedish drama
PT7177-7211	839.6808	Old Norse prose literature	PT9626-9639	839.7808	Swedish prose literature
PT7181-7193	839.6309	Sagas	PT9627-9630	839.7308	Swedish fiction
PT7230-7252	839.6108	Old Norse poetry			
PT7255-7262	839.6808	Old Norse prose literature	PZ1	823.00809287	English fiction—Women authors
PT7261-7262	839.6308	Sagas			
PT7351-7550	839.69	Icelandic literature	PZ1-3	808.83872	Detective and mystery stories
PT7370-7373	839.69071	Icelandic literature—Study and teaching			
			PZ1	813	American fiction
PT7411	839.69209	Icelandic drama	PZ5-90	808.068	Children's literature
PT7413	839.69309	Icelandic fiction	PZ8	398.2	Fairy tales
PT7420-7438	398.20439691	Folk literature, Icelandic	PZ8.3	398.8	Nursery rhymes
PT7465-7467	839.69108	Icelandic poetry			
PT7470-7477	839.69208	Icelandic drama	Q	500	Science
PT7480-7495	839.69808	Icelandic prose literature	Q	500.2	Physical sciences
PT7485-7487	839.69308	Icelandic fiction	Q1-9	505	Science—Periodicals
PT7601-8260	839.81	Danish literature	Q10-99	506	Science—Societies, etc.
PT7640-7644	839.81071	Danish literature—Study and teaching	Q105	507.4	Science—Exhibitions
			Q123	503	Science—Dictionaries
PT7721-7737	839.811	Danish literature—To 1500	Q124.95	509.01	Science, Ancient
			Q124.97	509.02	Science, Medieval

LC	Dewey	Subject Heading	LC	Dewey	Subject Heading
Q124.6-127.2	509	Science—History	QA9.A7	511.34	Forcing (Model theory)
Q125.2	509.0(24-31)	Science, Renaissance	QA9.7	511.34	Model theory
Q127-.2	509.(4-9)	Science—[By region or country]	QA10-.3	511.324	Algebraic logic
			QA10.3	511.324	Algebra, Boolean
Q141-143	509.2	Scientists—Biography	QA11-20	510.71	Mathematics—Study and teaching
Q145	502.5	Scientists—Directories			
Q148-149	508	Scientific surveys	QA21-27	510.9	Mathematics—History
Q172.5.C45	003.857	Chaotic behavior in systems	QA22	510.901	Mathematics, Ancient
Q172.5.S95	539.725	Symmetry	QA22	510.935	Mathematics, Babylonian
Q174-175.32	501	Science—Philosophy	QA22	510.938	Mathematics, Greek
Q174-175.32	501	Science—Methodology	QA23	510.902	Mathematics, Medieval
Q175.5	303.483	Science—Social aspects	QA27	510.9(4-9)	Mathematics—[By region or country]
Q179	501.4	Science—Terminology			
Q179	501.4	Science—Nomenclature	QA27.C	510.931	Mathematics, Chinese
Q180	507.2	Research	QA28-29	510.92	Mathematicians
Q180.55.D57	509	Discoveries in science	QA32	510.902	Mathematics, Medieval
Q180.55.G7	001.40681	Endowment of research	QA49	513.23	Square root
Q181-183.4	507.1	Science—Study and teaching	QA51	513.23021	Factor tables
			QA55-59	512.922	Logarithms
Q182.3	507.8	Science projects	QA55	516.24021	Trigonometry—Tables
Q183-.4	507.2	Laboratories	QA71-90	510.284	Mathematical instruments
Q183.9	502.85	Science—Data processing	QA73	510.284	Slide-rule
Q184-185.7	502.84	Scientific apparatus and instruments	QA75	513.0284	Abacus
			QA75	510.284	Calculators
Q222	502.2	Scientific illustration	QA75.5-.95	004	Computers
Q295	003.01	System theory	QA76.9.D3	005.74	Database management
Q300-390	003.5	Cybernetics	QA76.15	004.03	Computers—Dictionaries
Q304	003.503	Cybernetics—Dictionaries	QA76.17	004.09	Computers—History
Q305	003.509	Cybernetics—History	QA76.5	005.13	EGPS (Computer program language)
Q316	003.5071	Cybernetics—Study and teaching			
			QA76.5	004.35	Multiprocessors
Q317-321	003.5	Bionics	QA76.5	004.35	Parallel computers
Q325-390	003.7	Self-organizing systems	QA76.54-.545	004.33	Real-time data processing
Q325.5-.78	006.31	Machine learning	QA76.55-.57	005.7	Online data processing—Downloading
Q325.6	006.31	Reinforcement learning (Machine learning)			
			QA76.575	006.7	Multimedia systems
Q327	006.4	Pattern perception	QA76.6-.66	004.1	Electronic digital computers—Programming
Q334-342	006.3	Artificial intelligence			
Q337	006.3	Distributed artificial intelligence	QA76.6-.66	005.1	Programming (Electronic computers)
Q350-390	003.54	Information theory	QA76.6	005.452	Interpreters (Computer programs)
Q387-.5	006.332	Knowledge representation (Information theory)			
			QA76.6	005.112	Modular programming
			QA76.6	005.45	Macro processors
QA	510	Mathematics	QA76.6.U84	005.43	Utilities (Computer programs)
QA1	510.5	Mathematics—Periodicals			
QA5	510.3	Mathematics—Dictionaries	QA76.63	005.115	Logic programming
			QA76.64	005.117	Object-oriented programming (Computer science)
QA8-10.5	510.1	Mathematics—Philosophy			
QA9-10.3	511.3	Logic, Symbolic and mathematical			
			QA76.7-.73	005.13	Programming languages (Electronic computers)
QA9	510.1	Metamathematics			
QA9	515.24	Infinite	QA76.75-.9	005.3	Computer software
QA9.4-.5	511.31	Nonclassical mathematical logic	QA76.758	005.1	Software engineering
			QA76.76.A65	005.5	Application software
QA9.5	511.35	Lambda calculus	QA76.76.C64	005	Software compatibility
QA9.54	511.36	Proof theory	QA76.76.C65	005.453	Compilers (Computer programs)
QA9.65	511.3	Decidability (Mathematical logic)			
			QA76.76.C68	005.84	Computer viruses

LC	Dewey	Subject Heading	LC	Dewey	Subject Heading
QA76.76.D49	005.713	Device drivers (Computer programs)	QA76.9.T48	005	Text processing (Computer science)
QA76.76.D63	005.3	Software documentation	QA76.9.U83	005.437	User interfaces (Computer systems)
QA76.76.E95	006.33	Expert systems (Computer science)	QA90	518.23	Nomography (Mathematics)
QA76.76.I59	006.7	Interactive multimedia	QA101-141.8	513	Arithmetic
QA76.76.O63	005.43	Operating systems (Computers)	QA113	513.211	Counting
QA76.76.O63	005.4476	Distributed operating systems (Computers)	QA115	513.211	Addition
			QA115	513.212	Subtraction
QA76.76.P76	005.8	Software protection	QA115	513.214	Division
QA76.76.S46	005.3	Shareware (Computer software)	QA115	513.213	Multiplication
			QA117	513.26	Fractions
QA76.76.S64	005.16	Software maintenance	QA119	513.23	Roots, Numerical
QA76.76.S95	005.43	Systems software	QA119	513.23	Square root
QA76.85	004.1	Fifth generation computers	QA135-139	513.26071	Fractions—Study and teaching
QA76.87	006.32	Neural computers	QA141-.8	513.5	Numeration
QA76.87	006.32	Neural networks (Computer science)	QA141.15	512.7	Number concept
			QA141.5	513.5	Duodecimal system
QA76.88	004.11	Supercomputers	QA141.8.S4	513.5	Sexadecimal system
QA76.89	004.16	Pen-based computers	QA150-272.5	512	Algebra
QA76.9.A25	005.8	Computer security	QA159	512.0071	Algebra—Study and teaching
QA76.9.A43	005.1	Computer algorithms			
QA76.9.A73	004.22	Computer architecture	QA161	512.94222	Equations, Quadratic
QA76.9.B32	005.86	Electronic data processing—Backup processing alternatives	QA161.B5	512.9422	Binomial theorem
			QA161.F3	512.923	Factors (Algebra)
			QA162	512.02	Algebra, Abstract
QA76.9.C55	004.36	Client/server computing	QA164-167.2	511.6	Combinatorial analysis
QA76.9.C64	004	Computer literacy	QA164.8	515.55	Generating functions
QA76.9.C65	003.3	Computer simulation	QA165	511.64	Combinations
QA76.9.D26	005.74	Database design	QA165	511.64	Magic squares
QA76.9.D3	005.758	Distributed databases	QA165	511.64	Permutations
QA76.9.D3	005.74	Database management	QA165	512.73	Partitions (Mathematics)
QA76.9.D314	005.8	Database security	QA166-.24	511.5	Graph theory
QA76.9.D32	005.74	Databases	QA171	512.4	Group extensions (Mathematics)
QA76.9.D32	006.33	Deductive databases			
QA76.9.D33	005.746	Data compression (Computer science)	QA171	512.3	Infinite groups
			QA171	512.32	Galois theory
QA76.9.D337	005.72	Electronic data processing—Data entry	QA171.5	512.7	Lattices, Distributive
			QA171.5	511.33	Lattice theory
QA76.9.D345	005.72	Electronic data processing—Data preparation	QA174-183	512.2	Group theory
			QA176	512.22	Representations of groups
			QA184	512.5	Algebras, Linear
QA76.9.D348	005.86	Data recovery (Computer science)	QA188-196	512.9434	Matrices
			QA190-201	512.5	Substitutions, Linear
QA76.9.D5	004.36	Electronic data processing—Distributed processing	QA191	512.9432	Determinants
			QA199.5	512.5	Multilinear algebra
			QA201	512.944	Forms (Mathematics)
QA76.9.D6	004	Electronic data processing documentation	QA211	512.32	Galois theory
			QA211-218	512.94	Equations, Theory of
QA76.9.F5	005.741	File organization (Computer science)	QA211-218	512.94	Equations
			QA214	512.32	Galois theory
QA76.9.F53	005.74	File processing (Computer science)	QA215	512.9422	Equations, Quartic
			QA215	512.25	Equations, Abelian
QA76.9.H85	004.019	Human-computer interaction	QA215	512.9422	Equations, Cubic
			QA221-224	512.924	Approximation theory
QA76.9.N38	006.35	Natural language processing (Computer science)	QA241-247.5	512.7	Number theory
			QA242	512.72	Diophantine equations

LC	Dewey	Subject Heading	LC	Dewey	Subject Heading
QA242	512.74	Diophantine analysis	QA308-311	515.4	Integrals
QA242	512.72	Numbers, Divisibility of	QA312	515.4	Integrals, Generalized
QA242	512.923	Factors (Algebra)	QA313	515.48	Ergodic theory
QA242	513.265	Decimal fractions	QA315-316	515.64	Calculus of variations
QA242-244	512.72	Congruences and residues	QA319-329.9	515.7	Functional analysis
QA243	512.944	Forms (Mathematics)	QA321.5	515.7248	Nonlinear functional analysis
QA244	512.74	Fermat's theorem	QA322	515.73	Linear topological spaces, Ordered
QA245	512.9422	Equations, Binomial	QA324	515.7	Theory of distributions (Functional analysis)
QA246	515.52	Euler's numbers			
QA246	512.723	Numbers, Prime	QA326	512.556	Operator algebras
QA246	512	Numerical functions	QA329.42	515.7242	Partial differential operators
QA247-.45	512.3	Algebraic fields			
QA247	512.4	Ideals (Algebra)	QA331-355	515.25	Functions
QA247	512.4	Rings (Algebra)	QA331	515.73	Analytic functions
QA247.35	513.6	Modular arithmetic	QA331.5	515.8	Functions of real variables
QA247.4	512.56	Difference algebra	QA331.7	515.92	Functions of complex variables
QA247.45	512.3	Division algebras			
QA248-.5	513	Arithmetic—Foundations	QA333-337	515.93	Riemann surfaces
QA251	512	Algebra, Universal	QA341	512.74	Algebraic functions
QA251.3	512.4	Dedekind rings	QA343	515.983	Elliptic functions
QA252.3	512.482	Lie algebras	QA351	515.56	Functions, Zeta
QA267-268.5	511.35	Machine theory	QA353.G3	515.52	Gamma functions
QA269-272.5	519.3	Game theory	QA353.G44	515.55	Generating functions
QA273	519.27	Games of chance (Mathematics)	QA355	518.53	Numerical differentiation
			QA360	515.9	Conformal mapping
QA273-274.8	519.2	Chance	QA370-380	515.35	Differential equations
QA273-274.8	519.2	Probabilities	QA372	515.354	Differential equations, Linear
QA273-281	519.537	Correlation (Statistics)			
QA273.6	519.24	Distribution (Probability theory)	QA372.5	512.56	Differential-algebraic equations
QA274-.8	519.23	Stochastic processes	QA373	515.38	Differential-difference equations
QA274.7-.76	519.233	Markov processes			
QA274.75	519.233	Diffusion processes	QA374-377	515.353	Differential equations, Partial
QA274.8	519.82	Queuing theory			
QA275	511.43	Error analysis (Mathematics)	QA381	515.37	Differential invariants
			QA381	515.37	Differential forms
QA275	511.42	Least squares	QA387	512.482	Lie groups
QA276-280	519.5	Mathematical statistics	QA402-.37	003	System analysis
QA276.17	310.92	Statistical consultants	QA402	003.83	Discrete-time systems
QA276.6	519.52	Sampling (Statistics)	QA402.2	518	Decomposition method
QA276.8	519.544	Estimation theory	QA402.3-.37	515.642	Control theory
QA278.5	519.5354	Factor analysis	QA402.35	515.642	Nonlinear control theory
QA278.6	519.535	Latent structure analysis	QA402.5	519.7	Programming (Mathematics)
QA278.65	519.535	Discriminant analysis			
QA278.8	519.5	Nonparametric statistics	QA403-.3	515.2433	Harmonic analysis
QA279-.2	519.538	Analysis of variance	QA403.3	515.2433	Wavelets (Mathematics)
QA279.4-.7	519.542	Decision-making	QA403.5-404.5	515.2433	Fourier analysis
QA280	519.55	Time-series analysis	QA405	515.53	Harmonic functions
QA295	515.26	Inequalities (Mathematics)	QA405	515.54	Mathieu functions
QA295	515.243	Partial sums (Series)	QA408	515.53	Hankel functions
QA295	515.24	Processes, Infinite	QA431	515.625	Difference equations
QA295	515.243	Series, Infinite	QA432	515.723	Laplace transformation
QA297-299.4	518	Numerical analysis	QA433	515.63	Vector analysis
QA297	518	Numerical calculations	QA440-699	516	Geometry
QA299.3-.4	518.54	Numerical integration	QA451-485	516.22	Geometry, Plane
QA299.82	515	Nonstandard mathematical analysis	QA451-469	516.21	Euclid's Elements
			QA457	516.23	Geometry, Solid
QA303-316	515	Calculus			
QA306	511.66	Maxima and minima			

LC	Dewey	Subject Heading	LC	Dewey	Subject Heading
QA465	516.15	Mensuration	QA907	532.25	Floating bodies
QA473-475	516.04	Geometry, Modern	QA911-930	530.42	Fluid dynamics
QA473	516.04	Inversions (Geometry)	QA911-930	532.5	Hydrodynamics
QA481	516.	Axioms	QA913	532.593	Wakes (Fluid dynamics)
QA482	516.154	Polygons	QA913	532.59	Turbulence
QA482	516.154	Triangle	QA913	532.051	Boundary layer
QA484	516.152	Circle	QA913	532.5	Kinematics
QA485	516.152	Parabola	QA913	532.5	Rotating masses of fluid
QA491	516.23	Geometry, Solid	QA925	532.59	Vortex-motion
QA491	516.156	Prisms	QA927	532.593	Nonlinear wave equations
QA501-521	516.6	Geometry, Descriptive	QA927	532.593	Wave-motion, Theory of
QA501-521	516.5	Projection	QA927	532.59	Gravity waves
QA531-538	516.24	Trigonometry	QA929	532.0525	Laminar flow
QA533	516.242	Plane trigonometry	QA930	533.62	Aerodynamics
QA535	516.244	Spherical trigonometry	QA930	533.2	Gas dynamics
QA551-563	516.3	Geometry, Analytic	QA931-939	531.381	Strains and stresses
QA564-609	516.35	Geometry, Algebraic	QA931-939	531.382	Elasticity
QA571-573	516.352	Surfaces	QA931-939	531.385	Plasticity
QA601-608	516.1	Transformations (Mathematics)	QA935-939	531.32	Vibration
QA608	516.2	Congruences (Geometry)	QA935	531.382	Elastic solids
QA608	516.183	Line geometry	QA935	531.382	Elastic plates and shells
QA611-614.97	514	Topology	QA935	531.382	Elastic waves
QA611.234	514.3	Hewitt-Nachbin spaces	QA935	531.33	Wave-motion, Theory of
QA611.28	514.325	Metric spaces			
QA611.5	514	Ergodic theory	QB	520	Astronomy
QA612.3-.77	514.23	Homology theory	QB1	520.5	Astronomy—Periodicals
QA613.6-.66	514.72	Differential topology	QB4-.9	522.1	Astronomy—Observations
QA613.62	514.72	Foliations (Mathematics)	QB6	520.216	Astrographic catalog and chart
QA614-.97	514.74	Global analysis (Mathematics)	QB6	523.80216	Stars—Catalogs
QA614.8	515.39	Differentiable dynamical systems	QB6	523.8	Stars—Observations
			QB7-9	528	Ephemerides
			QB8	528	Nautical almanacs
QA614.83	515.39	Hamiltonian systems	QB14	520.3	Astronomy—Encyclopedias
QA614.92	514.74	Index theorems	QB14.5	520.1	Astronomy—Philosophy
QA615-639	516.36	Geometry, Infinitesimal	QB15-34	520.9	Astronomy—History
QA631-638	516.36	Surfaces	QB15-26	523	Zodiac
QA641-672	516.36	Surfaces	QB16-22	520.901	Astronomy, Ancient
QA641-672	516.36	Geometry, Differential	QB17	520.931	Astronomy, Chinese
QA646	515.9	Conformal mapping	QB19	520.935	Astronomy, Assyro-Babylonian
QA689	514.3	Generalized spaces			
QA689	516.375	Finsler spaces	QB21	520.938	Astronomy, Greek
QA689	516.375	G-spaces	QB23-26	520.902	Astronomy, Medieval
QA801-871	531.01515	Mechanics, Analytic	QB25-26	520	Astrology
QA801-935	531.11	Motion	QB29	520.90(23-31)	Astronomy, Renaissance
QA821-835	531.12	Statics	QB35-36	520.92	Astronomers—Biography
QA821-835	531.12	Equilibrium	QB47	520.151	Astronomy—Mathematics
QA839	531.12	Moments of inertia	QB51.3.I45	522	Imaging systems in astronomy
QA841-842	531.112	Kinematics			
QA845-871	531.11	Dynamics	QB54	999	Life on other planets
QA851-855	531.16	Dynamics of a particle	QB61-62.7	520.71	Astronomy—Study and teaching
QA861-863	531.11	Dynamics, Rigid			
QA862.G9	531.34	Gyroscopes	QB63	523.1	Constellations
QA862.P4	531.324	Pendulum	QB65	529.223	Astronomy—Charts, diagrams, etc.
QA865-867.5	531.32	Oscillations			
QA871	515.392	Perturbation (Mathematics)	QB65	520.223	Stars—Atlases
			QB67	520.228	Astronomical models
QA871	515.392	Stability	QB81-84	522.29	Astronomical observatories
QA901-930	532	Fluids	QB84.5-115	522.2	Astronomical instruments

LC	Dewey	Subject Heading	LC	Dewey	Subject Heading
QB84.5-135	522	Lenses	QB384	523.463	Saturn (Planet)—Orbit
QB88	522.2	Reflecting telescopes	QB384	523.45	Jupiter (Planet)
QB88	522.2	Telescopes	QB384	523.46	Saturn (Planet)
QB105	522	Solar compass	QB387	523.47	Uranus (Planet)
QB105	522.4	Quadrant	QB388	523.481	Neptune (Planet)
QB107	522.5	Chronometers	QB391-399	523.3	Lunar theory
QB107	522.5	Astronomical clocks	QB399	523.3021	Moon—Tables
QB121-.5	522.63	Astronomical photography	QB401-407	523.98	Satellites
QB121	523.87	Stars—Photographic measurements	QB405	523.986	Saturn (Planet)—Ring system
QB135	522.62	Astronomical photometry	QB407	523.9881	Neptune (Planet)—Satellites
QB136	520	Space astronomy			
QB140-237	522.7	Spherical astronomy	QB421	523.841	Double stars
QB149	520.21	Statistical astronomy	QB450-.5	523.02	Cosmochemistry
QB155-156	522.9	Refraction, Astronomical	QB460-466	523.01	Astrophysics
QB163	522.9	Aberration	QB462.6	523.019	Molecular astrophysics
QB165	521.9	Nutation	QB462.7-.72	523.019	Plasma astrophysics
QB175-185	523.99	Eclipses	QB463-464.2	523.019	Nuclear astrophysics
QB175-185	523.9	Transits	QB465	522.67	Astronomical spectroscopy
QB201-205	526.6	Geodetic astronomy	QB470	522.683	Infrared astronomy
QB207	526.63	Azimuth	QB471.7.B85	522.6862	Gamma ray bursts
QB209-224	529	Time	QB472-473	522.6863	X-ray astronomy
QB213	529.7	Time measurements	QB475-479.55	522.682	Radio astronomy
QB214	529.7	Hour-glasses	QB479.2	522.682	Radio telescopes
QB215	529.7	Dialing	QB480	522.68	Radar in astronomy
QB215	529.7	Sundials	QB495-500.268	500.5	Space sciences
QB216	525.317	Sun—Rising and setting	QB500.267-.268	522.29	Orbiting astronomical observatories
QB217	529.1	Time, Equation of			
QB223	529.0218	Time—Systems and standards	QB500.5-785	523.2	Solar system
QB225-229.5	526.62	Longitude	QB509-513	523.423	Venus (Planet), Transit of
QB231-237	526.61	Latitude	QB516	523.44	Asteroids
QB275-343	526.1	Geodesy	QB516.F6	523.75	Solar flares
QB279	526.103	Geodesy—Encyclopedias	QB520-545	523.7	Sun
QB280.5	526.109	Geodesy—History	QB523	523.73	Sun—Rotation
QB291	526.30287	Arc measures	QB524-526	523.72	Solar activity
QB297	526.10285	Geodesy—Computer programs	QB525	523.75	Sunspots
			QB526.C9	523.73	Solar cycle
QB301-328	526.3	Surveys	QB529	523.58	Solar wind
QB303	526.3	Base measuring	QB529	523.75	Sun—Corona
QB311	526.33	Triangulation	QB531	523.72	Solar radiation
QB330-339	526.7	Gravity	QB539.I5	523.76	Sun—Internal structure
QB331	526.0284	Gravimeters (Geophysical instruments)	QB539.M23	523.72	Solar magnetic fields
			QB539.N6	523.72	Solar noise storms
QB341	526.7	Gravitation	QB541-545	523.78	Solar eclipses
QB349-421	521	Celestial mechanics	QB551	523.73	Sun—Rotation
QB355-357	521.3	Orbits	QB579	523.38	Lunar eclipses
QB357	523.63	Comets—Orbits	QB580-595	523.3	Moon
QB361-407	521.4	Perturbation (Astronomy)	QB591	523.3	Moon—Surface
QB361-389	523.4	Planetary theory	QB592	523.3	Lunar geology
QB362.F47	521.4	Few-body problem	QB592	523.3	Lunar soil
QB362.M3	521.4	Many-body problem	QB600-701	523.4	Planets
QB362.T9	521.4	Two-body problem	QB603.R55	523.4	Planetary rings
QB371	523.41	Mercury (Planet)	QB611	523.41	Mercury (Planet)
QB372	523.423	Venus (Planet)—Orbit	QB621	523.42	Venus (Planet)—Surface
QB372	523.42	Venus (Planet)	QB621	523.42	Venus (Planet)
QB374	523.7021	Sun—Tables	QB630-638.8	525	Earth
QB376	523.43	Mars (Planet)	QB630-638.8	525	Astronomical geography
QB377-379	523.44	Asteroids	QB632	523.12	Earth—Origin
			QB633	525.35	Earth—Rotation

LC	Dewey	Subject Heading	LC	Dewey	Subject Heading
QB637.2-.8	525.5	Seasons	QC	530	Physics
QB641	523.43	Mars (Planet)	QC1	530.06	Physics—Congresses
QB651	523.44	Asteroids	QC5	530.03	Physics—Encyclopedias
QB661	523.45	Jupiter (Planet)	QC5.56-6.4	530.01	Physics—Philosophy
QB671	523.46	Saturn (Planet)	QC6.9-9	530.09	Physics—History
QB681	523.47	Uranus (Planet)	QC15-16	530.092	Physicists
QB691	523.481	Neptune (Planet)	QC19.2-20.85	530.15	Mathematical physics
QB701	523.482	Pluto (Planet)	QC20.8-.82	530.15071	Mathematical physics—Study and teaching
QB717-732	523.6	Comets			
QB723.B5	523.6	Biela's comet	QC29	530.071	Physics—Vocational guidance
QB723.D	523.6	Donati's Comet			
QB723.E3	523.6	Encke's comet	QC30-48	530.071	Physics—Study and teaching
QB723.H2	523.642	Halley's comet			
QB738	523.51	Meteoroids	QC35-37	530.078	Physics—Laboratory manuals
QB740-753	523.51	Meteors			
QB754.8-759	523.51	Meteorites	QC51	530.072	Physical laboratories
QB754.8-759	551.397	Meteorite craters	QC53-55	530.7	Physical instruments
QB790-792	523.1125	Interstellar matter	QC53	530.7	Recording instruments
QB791	523.1125	Cosmic dust	QC72-73.8	531.6	Force and energy
QB791.3	523.1126	Dark matter (Astronomy)	QC73.8.C6	531.62	Energy conservation
QB799-903	523.8	Stars	QC81-114	530.81	Weights and measures
QB802	523	Zodiac	QC83-86	530.8109	Weights and measures—History
QB806	523.88	Stars—Formation			
QB806	523.88	Stars—Evolution	QC90.8-94	530.812	Metric system
QB807	522	Astrometry	QC90.8-94	530.812	Decimal system
QB810	523.83	Stars—Rotation	QC100-111	530.8	Testing
QB812	523.83	Stellar oscillations	QC100.5-.8	530.7	Measuring instruments
QB814	523.81	Stars—Masses	QC107	530.7	Scales (Weighing instruments)
QB817	523.82	Stars—Radiation			
QB821-830	523.841	Multiple stars	QC107	530.7	Weighing-machines
QB821-830	523.841	Double stars	QC111-114	531.14	Specific gravity
QB833-841	523.844	Variable stars	QC115-116	543.4	Electrochemical analysis
QB835.E4	523.8444	Eclipsing binaries—Orbits	QC120-168.86	530	Mechanics
QB841	523.88	Stars, New	QC122-168	531.11	Motion
QB843.A12	523.8	A stars	QC131	531.11	Equilibrium
QB843.B12	523.8	B stars	QC138-168.86	532	Fluids
QB843.B55	523.8875	Black holes (Astronomy)	QC141-159	532	Liquids
QB843.B55	523.8875	Kerr black holes	QC147	532.25	Floating bodies
QB843.D85	523.8446	Dwarf Novae	QC150-159	532.5	Fluid dynamics
QB843.D9	523.88	Dwarf stars	QC150-159	532.5	Hydrodynamics
QB843.E2	523.88	Early stars	QC157	532.593	Waves
QB843.N12	523.88	N stars	QC159	532.595	Vortex-motion
QB843.N4	523.8874	Neutron stars	QC161-166.5	533	Pneumatics
QB843.R4	523.88	Red dwarfs	QC161-166.5	533.6	Air
QB843.R42	523.88	Red giants	QC161-166.5	533	Gases
QB843.W5	523.887	White dwarfs	QC164	536.412	Expansion of gases
QB851-855.9	523.85	Stars—Clusters	QC166-.5	533.5	Vacuum
QB855.5	523.1135	Planetary nebulae	QC166	533.50284	Vacuum-gages
QB856-858.8	523.112	Galaxies	QC167.5-168.86	533.2	Gas dynamics
QB858	523.112	Dwarf Galaxies	QC168	533.61	Aerostatics
QB858.3	523.112	Active galaxies	QC168.85.D46	532.593	Detonation waves
QB860	523.115	Quasars	QC170-197	530	Matter
QB895	523.88	Stars, New	QC173	539.7	Atoms
QB980-991	523.1	Cosmology	QC173	539.6	Molecules
QB980-991	523.12	Cosmogony	QC173	539.7217	Photon beams
QB991.B54	523.18	Big bang theory	QC173	541.242	Atomic mass
QB991.E53	523.19	End of the universe	QC173.4.A87	539.14	Atomic structure
QB991.I54	523.18	Inflationary universe	QC173.4.C74	530.474	Critical phenomena (Physics)

LC	Dewey	Subject Heading	LC	Dewey	Subject Heading
QC173.45-.458.U54	530.41	Condensed matter	QC270-278.6	536.50287	Temperature measurements
QC173.5-.65	530.11	Relativity (Physics)			
QC173.59.S65	530.11	Space and time	QC270-278.6	536.50287	Thermometers
QC173.68-.75	530.14	Field theory (Physics)	QC276-277	536.57	High temperatures
QC173.96-174.52	530.12	Quantum theory	QC277	536.520287	Pyrometers
QC174.1	530.416	Tunneling (Physics)	QC277.9-278.6	536.56072	Low temperature research
QC174.17.B6	530.12	Bound states (Quantum mechanics)	QC281.5.E9	536.41	Expansion (Heat)
			QC284	536.4	Compressibility
QC174.17.D44	530.122	Density matrices	QC290-297	536.6	Calorimeters
QC174.17.H4	530.122	Heisenberg uncertainty principle	QC303	536.42	Fusion
			QC303	536.42	Solidification
QC174.17.P7	530.14	Few-body problem	QC304	536.44	Evaporation
QC174.17.P7	530.144	Many-body problem	QC310.15-319	536.7	Thermodynamics
QC174.17.S9	530.1423	Supergravity	QC318.M3	530.475	Mass transfer
QC174.17.S9	539.725	Symmetry (Physics)	QC319.8-338.5	536.2	Heat—Transmission
QC174.2-.26	530.124	Wave mechanics	QC350-467	535	Light
QC174.3-.35	530.122	Matrix mechanics	QC350-467	535	Optics
QC174.4-.43	530.133	Quantum statistics	QC367	535.0284	Optical measurements
QC174.45-.52	530.143	Quantum field theory	QC370.5-379	535.028	Optical instruments
QC174.52.D43	530.143	Degree of freedom	QC373.B55	681.4125	Binoculars
QC174.7-175.36	530.13	Statistical mechanics	QC375	666.156	Glass, Optical
QC175-.16	533.7	Kinetic theory of gases	QC385	535.323	Reflection (Optics)
QC175.16.P5	530.474	Phase transformations (Statistical physics)	QC385	535.324	Lenses
			QC391	535.220287	Photometry
QC175.2-.25	530.138	Transport theory	QC392-449.5	535.2	Physical optics
QC175.3-.36	532.5	Kinetic theory of liquids	QC402	535.12	Light, Corpuscular theory of
QC175.4-.47	530.42	Superfluidity	QC403	535.2	Coherence (Optics)
QC176-.9	531	Solid state physics	QC403	535.13	Light, Wave theory of
QC176.8.E9	530.416	Exciton theory	QC411	535.47	Interference (Light)
QC176.8.L3	530.411	Lattice dynamics	QC414.8-417	535.4	Diffraction
QC176.82-.9.R37	530.4175	Thin films	QC425	535.420284	Prisms
QC178	531.14	Gravitational fields	QC425	535.323	Reflection (Optics)
QC178	531.14	Gravitation	QC425	535.324	Refraction, Double
QC179	539.6	Molecules	QC431-435	535.4	Dispersion
QC183	530.475	Brownian movements	QC437	535.326	Absorption of light
QC183	530.427	Surface tension	QC440-446	535.52	Polarization (Light)
QC183	541.33	Adhesion	QC446.15-.3	535.2	Nonlinear optics
QC183	541.33	Cohesion	QC447.9-448.2	621.3692	Fiber optics
QC185	530.475	Diffusion	QC449-.3	774.0153	Holography
QC189-.2	531.1134	Viscosity	QC450-467	543.5	Spectrum analysis
QC191	531.382	Elastic solids	QC451	535.840284	Spectrum analysis—Instruments
QC191	531.382	Elasticity			
QC191	531.385	Plasticity	QC454.A8	535.84	Atomic absorption spectroscopy
QC191	531.382	Elastic waves			
QC197	531.1134	Friction	QC454.E46	535.84	Emission spectroscopy
QC220-246	534	Sound	QC454.L63	535.843	Light beating spectroscopy
QC228.3	534.0284	Sound—Equipment and supplies	QC454.R36	535.846	Raman effect
			QC457	535.842	Infrared spectra
QC231	534.5	Kinematics	QC457	535.842	Infrared spectroscopy
QC233	534.208	Absorption of sound	QC459-.5	535.014	Ultraviolet radiation
QC233	534.204	Echo	QC459-.5	535.844	Ultraviolet spectroscopy
QC235-241	534.5	Vibration	QC459.5	535.014	Far ultraviolet radiation
QC235	534.208	Sound-waves—Damping	QC465	535.84	Spectroscope
QC242-.5	534.23	Underwater acoustics	QC474-492	539.2	Radiation
QC243	534.0287	Sound—Measurement	QC476.4-480.2	535.35	Luminescence
QC243	534.208	Sound-waves—Damping	QC476.S6	539.2	Radiation sources
QC244	534.55	Ultrasonic waves	QC477-.4	535.352	Fluorescence
QC251-338.5	536	Heat	QC480-482.3	539.7222	X-rays
			QC480	535.357	Electroluminescence

LC	Dewey	Subject Heading	LC	Dewey	Subject Heading
QC482.S6	537.5352	X-ray spectroscopy	QC702.7.H42	539.7234	Heavy ions
QC484.3	539.7222	Bremsstrahlung	QC703.7	537.5	Exploding wire phenomena
QC484.8-485.9	539.7223	Cosmic rays	QC705	537.52	Electric arc
QC485	539.7223	Solar cosmic rays	QC715.15	537.54	Photoemission
QC485.8.S5	539.7223	Cosmic ray showers	QC717-.8	530.44	Plasma (Ionized gases)
QC494-496.9	535.6	Colors	QC718.5.M36	538.6	Magnetohydrodynamics
QC494-496.9	535.6	Color	QC750-776	538	Magnetism
QC501-721	537	Electricity	QC754.2.M33	538.4	Magnetic induction
QC514-515	537.092	Electricians	QC757	538.4	Magnets
QC527	537.0724	Electricity—Experiments	QC759.6-761.3	537	Electromagnetism
QC533-534	537.0724	Electricity—Experiments	QC760-.3	538	Electromagnets
QC535-537	537.0287	Electric measurements	QC761	538.0287	Magnetic measurements
QC541-543	541.372	Electrolytes	QC762	538.362	Nuclear magnetic resonance
QC541	537.072	Electric laboratories			
QC543-544	537.0284	Electric apparatus and appliances	QC762	538.362	Deuteron magnetic resonance spectroscopy
QC544.C3	537.0284	Cathode ray tubes	QC762.6.A25	538.362	Acoustic nuclear magnetic resonance
QC570-596.9	537.2	Electrostatics			
QC581.E4	537.21	Electric charge and distribution	QC763	538.364	Electron paramagnetic resonance
QC584-585.8	537.24	Dielectrics	QC770-798	539.7	Nuclear physics
QC584	537.240287	Dielectric measurements	QC771	538.42	Diamagnetism
QC596-.9	537.2448	Ferroelectricity	QC783.3-.4	621.4830285	Nuclear reactors—Computer programs
QC601-641	537.6	Electric currents			
QC610.3-635	537.62	Electric conductivity	QC785.5-787	539.770284	Radioactivity—Instruments
QC610.9-611.8	537.6226	Semiconductors	QC786.4-786.8	621.483	Nuclear reactors
QC611	537.62	Electric resistance	QC787.C6	539.77	Neutron counters
QC611	537.54	Photoelectricity	QC787.C6	539.77	Nuclear counters
QC611.8.D66	537.6223	Doped semiconductors	QC787.E39	539.73	Electron accelerators
QC611.8.M25	537.6223	Diluted magnetic semiconductors	QC787.E4	539.732	Electrostatic accelerators
			QC787.G4	539.774	Geiger-Muller counters
QC611.8.N35	537.6223	Narrow gap semiconductors	QC787.I6	539.772	Ionization chambers
			QC787.L5	539.733	Linear accelerators
QC611.8.07	537.6223	Organic semiconductors	QC787.P3	539.73	Particle accelerators
QC611.8.W53	537.6223	Wide gap semiconductors	QC787.S34	539.775	Scintillation counters
QC611.9-.98	537.623	Superconductivity	QC787.S83	539.736	Superconducting Super Collider
QC612.H3	537.6	Hall effect			
QC612.P5	537.54	Photoconductivity	QC787.S9	539.735	Synchrotrons
QC615	621.3743	Voltameter	QC789.7-790.8	539.762	Nuclear fission
QC621-625	537.65	Thermoelectricity	QC790.95-791.8	539.764	Nuclear fusion
QC623	537.6	Electric currents—Heating effects	QC791.7-.775	539.764	Controlled fusion
			QC791.9-792.8	539.7	Nuclear energy
QC630-648	537.6	Electrodynamics	QC793-.5	539.72	Particles (Nuclear physics)
QC641	537.6	Electric currents, Alternating	QC793.3.B4	539.73	Particle beams
			QC793.3.D4	539.752	Decay schemes (Radioactivity)
QC660.5-665	537.534	Electric waves			
QC661	621.381331	Wave guides	QC793.3.F5	530.1435	Gauge fields (Physics)
QC665.D5	539.2	Electromagnetic waves—Diffraction	QC793.3.S8	539.74	Nuclear structure
			QC793.3.S9	539.725	Symmetry (Physics)
QC665.E4	539.2	Electromagnetic fields	QC793.5.A22-.A229	539.7232	Alpha rays
QC665.P6	537.534	Radio waves—Polarization			
QC665.T7	539.2	Electromagnetic waves—Transmission	QC793.5.B425	539.7523	Beta decay
			QC793.5.E462-.E4629	539.72112	Electrons
QC669-675.8	537	Electromagnetic theory			
QC676-678.6	537.534	Radio waves	QC793.5.E62-.E629	537.56	Electron optics
QC679-680.5	530.1433	Quantum electrodynamics			
QC685-689.55	537.5	Quantum electronics	QC793.5.E628	539.72112	Electrons—Polarization
QC701.7-702.7	530.444	Ionization	QC793.5.F42-.F429	539.721	Fermions
QC7C02-721	530.44	Ionization of gases			

LC	Dewey	Subject Heading	LC	Dewey	Subject Heading
QC793.5.G322	539.7222	Gamma ray sources	QC851-999	551.5	Atmosphere
QC793.5.H32 -.H329	539.7216	Hadrons	QC851-999	551.6	Climatology
			QC851-999	551.5	Meteorology
QC793.5.L42- .L429	539.7211	Leptons (Nuclear physics)	QC851	551.505	Meteorology—Periodicals
			QC854.2	551.5014	Meteorology—Terminology
QC793.5.M42- .M429	539.72162	Mesons	QC855-857	551.509	Meteorology—History
			QC858	551.5092	Meteorologists—Biography
QC793.5.M42- .M429	539.72162	Kaons	QC875	551.63	Automatic meteorological stations
QC793.5.N42- .N429	539.7215	Neutrinos	QC875	354.37	Meteorological services
			QC875	551.63	Meteorological stations
QC793.5.N462- .N4622	539.7213	Neutrons	QC875.5-876.7	551.50284	Meteorological instruments
QC793.5.N4629	539.7213	Neutron sources	QC877.5	551.632	Weather reporting, Radio
QC793.5.P42- .P429	539.7217	Photons	QC877.5	551.632	Weather broadcasting
			QC877.5	551.632	Television weather casting
QC793.5.P72- .P729	539.72123	Antiprotons	QC879-.59	551.514	Atmosphere, Upper
QC793.5.Q252 -.Q2529	539.72167	Quarks	QC879	551.514	Atmosphere, Upper—Rocket observations
QC793.5.S72-.57 29	539.7216	Strange particles	QC879	551.5145	F region
			QC879.6-.85	551.511	Atmospheric chemistry
QC794	539.75	Annihilation reactions	QC880-.4	551.5	Dynamic meteorology
QC794.6.C6	539.757	Collisions (Nuclear physics)	QC880	551.5	Atmospheric density
QC794.6.E9	539.725	Spin excitations	QC880	551.50284	Densitometer (Meteorological instrument)
QC794.6.G7	530.142	Grand unified theories (Nuclear physics)	QC880.4.A5	551.5512	Air masses
QC794.6.S3	539.758	Scattering amplitude (Nuclear physics)	QC880.4.A8	551.517	Atmospheric circulation
			QC880.4.D5	551.515	Divergence (Meteorology)
QC794.6.S3	539.758	Scattering (Physics)	QC880.4.F7	551.5512	Fronts (Meteorology)
QC794.8.D57	539.76	Direct reactions (Nuclear physics)	QC880.4.F7	551.5512	Occluded fronts (Meteorology)
QC794.8.E4	539.7546	Electromagnetic interactions	QC880.4.S65	551.55	Squall lines
			QC880.4.S65	551.55	Squalls
QC794.8.P4	539.756	Photonuclear reactions	QC880.4.T5	551.52	Atmospheric thermodynamics
QC794.8.W4	539.7544	Weak interactions (Nuclear physics)	QC880.4.T8	551.55	Atmospheric turbulence
QC794.95-798	539.752	Radioactivity	QC881.2.D2	538.7672	D region
QC795.8.D4	539.752	Decay schemes (Radioactivity)	QC881.2.E2	551.5145	E region
			QC881.2.I6	551.5145	Ionosphere
QC795.8.E5	539.725	Energy levels (Quantum mechanics)	QC881.2.O9	551.5142	Ozone layer
			QC881.2.T75	551.513	Troposphere
QC795.8.H3	539.752	Half-life (Nuclear physics)	QC882	363.7392	Smaze
QC801-809	550	Cosmic physics	QC882.4-.46	363.7392	Aerosols
QC801-809	550	Geophysics	QC882.5	551.5113	Dust
QC809.C6	551.5276	Cosmic noise	QC882.6	363.7392	Smoke plumes
QC809.M25	538.7	Cosmic magnetic fields	QC883-.2	551.5	Weather, Influence of the moon on
QC809.M3	538.6	Magnetohydrodynamics	QC883.2.S6	551.5276	Cosmic physics
QC809.M35	538.766	Magnetosphere	QC883.2.A8	551.464	Atmospheric tides
QC809.T4	551.5272	Terrestrial radiation	QC883.7-.86	551.66	Micrometeorology
QC809.V3	538.766	Van Allen radiation belts	QC884-.2	551.69	Paleoclimatology
QC811-849	538.7	Geomagnetism	QC885-896	551.54	Atmospheric pressure
QC818-849	538.0287	Magnetic measurements	QC886-887	551.540284	Barometers
QC818	538.79	Geomagnetic observatories	QC901-912.2	551.525	Atmospheric temperature
QC822	538.70223	Geomagnetism—Maps	QC910.2-913.2	551.5271	Sunshine
QC835	538.744	Magnetic storms	QC910.2-911.82	551.5271	Solar radiation
QC845	538.748	Earth currents	QC912.3	551.5273	Atmospheric radiation

LC	Dewey	Subject Heading	LC	Dewey	Subject Heading
QC913-.2	551.5276	Atmospheric radioactivity	QC973.45-.8	551.6353	Radar meteorology
QC915-929	551.57	Moisture	QC973.8.W	551.6353	Weather radar networks
QC915-917	551.572	Evaporation (Meteorology)	QC974.5-976	551.56	Meteorological optics
QC915-917	551.571	Humidity	QC976.R2	551.567	Rainbow
QC915	551.57	Moisture index	QC980-999	551.6	Weather
QC915.5-.7	551.572	Evapotranspiration	QC980	551.605	Weather—Periodicals
QC920	551.57	Water	QC981.7.U7	551.691732	Urban climatology
QC920.7-924	551.576	Clouds	QC981.8.A5	551.5512	Cold waves (Meteorology)
QC921.6.C6	551.574	Condensation (Meteorology)	QC981.8.C5	551.5253	Climatic changes
			QC981.8.G56	551.5253	Global warming
QC921.6.C6	551.5741	Atmospheric nucleation	QC982.8-994.9	551.5253	Climatic changes
QC924.5-926.2	551.577	Rain and rainfall	QC983-984	551.6973	United States—Climate
QC926	551.5770284	Rain gauges	QC985-.5	551.6971	Canada—Climate
QC926	551.5770284	Precipitation gauges	QC986	551.6972	Mexico—Climate
QC926.6-928.74	551.68	Weather control	QC987	551.69729	West Indies—Climate
QC926.5-.57	551.5771	Acid precipitation (Meteorology)	QC988	551.698	South America—Climate
			QC989	551.694	Europe—Climate
QC926.5-.57	363.7386	Acid rain	QC990	551.695	Asia—Climate
QC928.6	551.68	Rain-making	QC991	551.696	Africa—Climate
QC929	551.577	Precipitation (Meteorology)	QC992	551.6994	Australia—Climate
			QC993.5	551.6913	Tropics—Climate
QC929.2-.28	551.5773	Droughts	QC993.6	551.69143	Mountain climate
QC929.2-.28	551.64773	Drought forecasting	QC993.7	551.69154	Arid regions climate
QC929.A8	551.307	Avalanches	QC993.83-994.9	551.65162	Marine meteorology
QC929.D5	551.5744	Dew	QC994.95-999	551.63	Weather forecasting
QC929.F7	551.575	Ice fog	QC996	551.634	Numerical weather forecasting
QC929.F7	551.575	Fog			
QC929.H15	551.5787	Hail	QC996.5	551.633	Statistical weather forecasting
QC929.H15	551.554	Hailstorms			
QC929.H6	551.38	Frost	QC997	551.6365	Long-range weather forecasting
QC929.S7	551.5784	Snow			
QC930.5-959	551.518	Winds	QC997.75	551.6362	Nowcasting (Meteorology)
QC931	551.6418	Wind forecasting	QC999	551.6365	Almanacs
QC935	551.5183	Jet stream			
QC935	551.518	Winds aloft	QD	540	Chemistry
QC939.F6	551.5185	Chinook winds	QD1	540.6	Chemistry—Societies, etc.
QC939.L37	551.5185	Sea breeze	QD4-5	540.3	Chemistry—Dictionaries
QC939.M7	551.5184	Monsoons	QD7	540.14	Chemistry—Nomenclature
QC939.M8	551.5185	Mountain wave	QD11-18	540.9	Chemistry—History
QC939.T7	551.5183	Trade winds	QD13	540.112	Alchemy
QC940.6-959	551.5513	Cyclones	QD21-22	540.92	Chemists
QC940.6-959	551.55	Storms	QD23.3-26.5	540.112	Alchemy
QC944-948	551.552	Hurricanes	QD40-49	540.71	Chemistry—Study and teaching
QC948	551.552	Typhoons			
QC948	551.68	Typhoon modification	QD43	540.724	Chemistry—Experiments
QC951	551.64513	Cyclone forecasting	QD51-64	540.72	Chemical laboratories
QC955-.5	551.553	Tornadoes	QD53-54	542	Chemical apparatus
QC957	551.553	Waterspouts	QD54.C4	542	Centrifuges
QC958-959	551.559	Dust storms	QD63.D6	542.4	Distillation
QC960.5-969	551.563	Atmospheric electricity	QD63.F5	542.6	Filters and filtration
QC966-.7	551.5632	Lightning	QD63.09	541.393	Electrolytic oxidation
QC966.7.A84	551.561	Atmospheric ionization	QD63.R4	541.393	Electrolytic reduction
QC968-.2	551.554	Thunderstorms	QD63.R4	541.393	Reduction (Chemistry)
QC970-972.5	538.768	Auroras	QD71-142	543	Chemistry, Analytic
QC972.6-973.8	551.635	Radio meteorology	QD71	543.05	Chemistry, Analytic—Periodicals
QC973.4.R35	551.51	Atmospheric radio refractivity			
			QD79.C45	543.85	Gas chromatography
QC973.4.M33	551.514	Magnetospheric radio wave propagation	QD79.E44	541.372	Electrophoresis
			QD79.T38	543.26	Thermal analysis

LC	Dewey	Subject Heading	LC	Dewey	Subject Heading
QD81-98	543	Chemistry, Analytic— Qualitative	QD281.P6	547.28	Polymerization
			QD281.R4	547.23	Electrolytic reduction
QD87	542.4	Blowpipe	QD305.H5-.H9	547.41	Hydrocarbons
QD95-96	543.5	Spectrum analysis	QD305.H8	547.413	Acetylene compounds
QD101-117	543.1	Chemistry, Analytic— Quantitative	QD305.H8	547.413	Acetylene
			QD320-327	547.78	Carbohydrates
QD111	543.24	Volumetric analysis	QD320-327	547.78	Sugars
QD117.C515	543.85	Gas chromatography	QD321	547.78	Fructose
QD117.E45	541.372	Electrophoresis	QD321	547.78	Dextrose
QD117.T4	543.26	Thermal analysis	QD321	547.78	Glucose
QD142	546.22	Water—Analysis	QD330-341	547.6	Aromatic compounds
QD146-197	546	Chemistry, Inorganic	QD341	547.2	Condensation products (Chemistry)
QD146	546.06	Chemistry, Inorganic—Societies, etc.			
			QD341.H9	547.611	Benzene
QD157	546.0284	Electric furnaces	QD341.H9	547.61	Hydrocarbons
QD169.W3	546.22	Water	QD341.P5	547.632	Phenols
QD161-169	546.7	Nonmetals	QD380-388	547.7	Polymers
QD165	546.73	Halogen compounds	QD399-406	547.59	Heterocyclic compounds
QD167	546.24	Inorganic acids	QD410-412.5	547.05	Organometallic compounds
QD171-172	543	Metals			
QD172.A4	546.38	Alkalies	QD412	547.62	Halogen compounds
QD172.R2	546.41	Earths, Rare	QD415-436	572	Biochemistry
QD172.R2	546.41	Rare earth metals	QD419-.7	547.8434	Gums and resins
QD172.T6	546.6	Transition metal compounds	QD421-.7	547.7	Alkaloids
			QD431-.7	547.75	Proteins
QD181.A6	546.753	Argon	QD431-.7	547.75	Amino acids
QD181.B1	553.6	Boron	QD431-.7	547.756	Peptides
QD181.C1	546.6812	Carbon dioxide	QD450-801	541	Chemistry, Physical and theoretical
QD181.C8	546.385	Cesium			
QD181.F1	546.731	Fluorine	QD450	541.06	Chemistry, Physical and theoretical—Societies, etc.
QD181.H1	546.212	Deuterium			
QD181.H1	546.2	Hydrogen			
QD181.H4	546.751	Helium	QD461	541.2	Atomic theory
QD181.H6	546.663	Mercury	QD461	541.22	Molecular structure
QD181.I1	546.734	Iodine	QD462-464	541.28	Quantum chemistry
QD181.N1	546.711	Nitrogen	QD463-464	541.242	Atomic weights
QD181.N1	546.7112	Ammonia	QD463-464	541.222	Molecular weights
QD181.N5	546.752	Neon	QD466-467	540	Chemical elements
QD181.O1	546.721	Oxygen	QD466	541.242	Atomic mass
QD181.O1	546.721	Active oxygen	QD466.5	541.388	Isotopes
QD181.P1	546.712	Phosphorus	QD467	546.8	Periodic law
QD181.R2	546.756	Radon	QD471	541.224	Radicals (Chemistry)
QD181.S3	546.716	Antimony	QD471	541.2252	Tautomerism
QD181.T7	546.678	Thallium	QD471	541.224	Free radicals (Chemistry)
QD181.U7	546.431	Uranium	QD461	541.2	Molecular theory
QD181.X1	546.755	Xenon	QD478	541.0421	Organic solid state chemistry
QD189-193	546.34	Salts			
QD191	546.34	Double salts	QD478	541.0421	Solid state chemistry
QD241-441	547	Chemistry, Organic	QD501-505.5	541.39	Chemical reaction, Conditions and law of
QD241	547.005	Chemistry, Organic— Periodicals			
			QD501	541.395	Catalysts
QD262	547.2	Organic compounds— Synthesis	QD501	541.392	Chemical equilibrium
			QD503	541.392	Phase rule and equilibrium
QD272.E43	541.372	Electrophoresis	QD505	541.395	Phase-transfer catalysts
QD273	541.37	Electrochemistry	QD505	541.395	Catalysis
QD277	541.370284	Electric furnaces	QD506-509	541.33	Surface chemistry
QD281.O9	547.23	Electrolytic oxidation	QD510-536	541.36	Thermochemistry
QD281.O9	547.23	Oxidation	QD515	541.3686	Cryochemistry
QD281.P6	547.28	Addition polymerization	QD516	541.361	Combustion

LC	Dewey	Subject Heading	LC	Dewey	Subject Heading
QD516	541.361	Explosions	QE260-288	554	Geology—Europe
QD516	541.361	Flame	QE289-319	555	Geology—Asia
QD517	541.364	Dissociation	QE320-339	556	Geology—Africa
QD535	542	Dewar flasks	QE340-348	559.4	Geology—Australia
QD536	541.3686072	Low temperature research	QE350	559.89	Geology—Antarctica
QD541-549	541.34	Solution (Chemistry)	QE351-399.2	549	Mineralogy
QD541-543	541.34	Activity coefficients	QE351	549.05	Mineralogy—Periodicals
QD543	541.342	Solubility	QE364.2.R3	549.528	Radioactive substances
QD543	541.3415	Osmosis	QE367-369	549.1	Mineralogy, Determinative
QD549	541.372	Electrolytes	QE371	549.13	Mineralogical chemistry
QD551-575	541.37	Electrochemistry	QE388	549.012	Minerals—Classification
QD553-585	541.372	Electrolytes	QE389.1	549.2	Native element minerals
QD561-562	541.3722	Ionization	QE389.4	549.4	Halide minerals
QD561-562	541.372	Ions	QE389.64	549.72	Phosphate minerals
QD562.I63	541.3723	Ion exchange	QE390.2.T85	549.74	Tungsten ores
QD562.I65	541.3722	Dissociation	QE391.D6	549.782	Dolomite
QD565	541.372	Electrolytes—Conductivity	QE391.F3	549.68	Feldspar
QD571-572	541.3724	Electrodes	QE391.G37	549.62	Garnet
QD581	541.0424	Plasma chemistry	QE391.I7	546.621	Iron
QD601-608	541.38	Nuclear chemistry	QE391.Q2	549.68	Quartz
QD601-608	541.38	Radiochemistry	QE391.T6	549.62	Topaz
QD625-655	541.382	Radiation chemistry	QE393	549.27	Diamonds
QD701-731	541.35	Photochemistry	QE394.07	549.68	Opals
QD901-999	548	Crystallography	QE394.T8	549.72	Turquoise
QD901-999	548.5	Crystallization	QE420-499	552	Petrology
QD911-919	548.7	Crystallography, Mathematical	QE420-499	552	Rocks
			QE420	552.005	Petrology—Periodicals
QD911-919	548.7	Lattice theory	QE444-445	552.00973	Petrology—United States
QD921-926	548.5	Crystal growth	QE445.5-446	552.00971	Petrology—Canada
QD945	548.842	Dislocations in crystals	QE446.5-.6	552.00972	Petrology—Mexico
			QE447	552.09728	Petrology—Central America
QE	551	Geology			
QE1	551.06	Geology—Societies, etc.	QE448	552.09729	Petrology—West Indies
QE7	551.014	Geology—Terminology	QE449	552.098	Petrology—South America
QE11-13	551.09	Geology—History	QE451	552.0094	Petrology—Europe
QE21-22	551.092	Geologists	QE452	552.095	Petrology—Asia
QE28.2	551	Physical geology	QE453	552.096	Petrology—Africa
QE28.3	551.09	Historical geology	QE453.5-454	552.0994	Petrology—Australia
QE36	551.0223	Geology—Maps	QE454.5-.6	552.0993	Petrology—New Zealand
QE39	551.468	Submarine geology	QE455	552.099(5-6)	Petrology—Oceania
QE40-48	551.071	Geology—Study and teaching	QE456	552.09981	Petrology—Arctic regions
			QE456.5	552.09989	Petrology—Antarctic regions
QE43	551.0228	Geological modeling			
QE48.8	551.0285	Geology—Computer programs	QE461-462	552.1	Rocks, Igneous
			QE461-462	552.23	Volcanic ash, tuff, etc.
QE49.5	550.284	Earth science instruments	QE461	552.22	Lava
QE51	551.074	Geological museums	QE462.D56	552.3	Diorite
QE61-350.62	551.0723	Geological surveys	QE462.G7	552.3	Granite
QE61-350	551.0723	Surveys	QE471-.15	552.5	Rocks, Sedimentary
QE70	559.8(1-2)	Geology—Arctic regions	QE471-.15	552.5	Sedimentology
QE71-217	557	Geology—North America	QE471.15.C3	552.58	Rocks, Carbonate
QE72-182	557.3	Geology—United States	QE471.15.D6	552.58	Dolomite
QE81-182	557.(4-9)	Geology—[United States, By state]	QE471.15.S25	552.5	Sandstone
			QE471.15.S5	552.5	Shale
QE185-199	557.1	Geology—Canada	QE471.3	552.5	Clay
QE201-203	557.2	Geology—Mexico	QE472	552.5	Sedimentary structures
QE210-217	557.28	Geology—Central America	QE475	552.4	Rocks, Metamorphic
QE220-226	557.29	Geology—West Indies	QE475.A2	552.4	Metamorphism (Geology)
QE230-251	558	Geology—South America	QE500-639.5	551.(2-3)	Geodynamics

LC	Dewey	Subject Heading	LC	Dewey	Subject Heading
QE500-511.7	550	Geophysics	QE738	560.1785	Paleontology—Oligocene
QE501.4.P3	551.7	Paleogeography	QE739	560.1787	Paleontology—Miocene
QE501.4.P35	538.727	Paleomagnetism	QE744	560.9981	Paleontology—Arctic regions
QE508	551.701	Earth—Age	QE746-747	560.973	Paleontology—United States
QE508	551.701	Geological time			
QE508	551.701	Radioactive dating	QE748	560.971	Paleontology—Canada
QE509	551.11	Earth—Internal structure	QE749	560.972	Paleontology—Mexico
QE509	551.12	Earth temperature	QE750	560.9729(9)	Paleontology—West Indies
QE511.4-.48	551.8	Plate tectonics	QE751	560.9728	Paleontology—Central America
QE511.7	551.136	Sea-floor spreading			
QE514-516.5	551.9	Geochemistry	QE752	560.98	Paleontology—South America
QE521.5-527.5	551.21	Volcanoes			
QE528	551.23	Hot springs	QE753-755	560.94	Paleontology—Europe
QE531-541	551.22	Seismology	QE756	560.95	Paleontology—Asia
QE531-541	551.22	Earthquakes	QE757	560.96	Paleontology—Africa
QE539	551.22	Elastic waves	QE758	560.994	Paleontology—Australia
QE541	551.220287	Seismometry	QE760	560.9989	Paleontology—Antarctic regions
QE545	551.23	Volcanic gases			
QE565-566	551.424	Coral reefs and islands	QE760.8-899.2	560	Animals, Fossil
QE570	551.302	Weathering	QE770-832	562	Invertebrates, Fossil
QE571-597	551.302	Erosion	QE815-832	565	Arthropoda, Fossil
QE571-597	551.303	Sedimentation and deposition	QE841-899	566	Vertebrates, Fossil
			QE862.D5	567.9	Dinosaurs
QE575-579	551.313	Glacial erosion	QE881-882	569	Mammals, Fossil
QE597	551.372	Wind erosion	QE882.C15	569.78	Cave bear
QE598-600.3	551.307	Earth movements	QE882.C5	569.5	Dolphins, Fossil
QE598-600.3	551.307	Mass-wasting	QE882.P7	569.8	Primates, Fossil
QE599	551.307	Debris avalanches	QE934	561.1998(1-8)	Paleobotany—Arctic regions
QE599	551.307	Landslides			
QE599	551.307	Rockslides	QE936-937	561.1973	Paleobotany—United States
QE604	551.8	Rock deformation			
QE606-.5	551.872	Faults (Geology)	QE938	561.1971	Paleobotany—Canada
QE606-.5	551.875	Folds (Geology)	QE939	561.1972	Paleobotany—Mexico
QE611-.5	551.88	Dikes (Geology)	QE940	561.19729	Paleobotany—West Indies
QE611-.5	551.88	Necks (Geology)	QE941	561.19728	Paleobotany—Central America
QE611-.5	551.88	Intrusions (Geology)			
QE611-.5	551.88	Veins (Geology)	QE942	561.198	Paleobotany—South America
QE640-699	551.7	Geology, Stratigraphic			
QE654-674	551.72	Geology, Stratigraphic—Paleozoic	QE943-945	561.194	Paleobotany—Europe
			QE946	561.195	Paleobotany—Asia
QE675-688	551.76	Geology, Stratigraphic—Mesozoic	QE947	561.196	Paleobotany—Africa
			QE948	561.1994	Paleobotany—Australia
QE690-699	551.78	Geology, Stratigraphic—Cenozoic	QE948.2	561.1993	Paleobotany—New Zealand
QE697-698	551.792	Glacial epoch	QE949	561.199(5-6)	Paleobotany—Oceania
QE701-996.5	560	Paleontology	QE950	561.19989	Paleobotany—Antarctic regions
QE701	560.5	Paleontology—Periodicals			
QE718	560.75	Fossils—Collection and preservation	QE975-978	561.5	Gymnosperms, Fossil
			QE980-983	561	Angiosperms, Fossil
QE721.2.E97	576.84	Extinction (Biology)	QE983	561.3	Dicetyledons, Fossil
QE724	560.171	Paleontology—Precambrian	QE991	561.16	Petrified forests
QE725-730	560.172	Paleontology—Paleozoic			
QE726	560.1723	Paleontology—Cambrian	QH	508	Natural history
QE728	560.174	Paleontology—Devonian	QH1-7	508.06	Natural history—Periodicals
QE731-734	560.176	Paleontology—Mesozoic			
QE733	560.1766	Paleontology—Jurassic	QH13	508.03	Natural history—Dictionaries
QE734	560.177	Paleontology—Cretaceous			
QE735-741.3	560.178	Paleontology—Cenozoic	QH26-35	508.092	Naturalists
QE737	560.1784	Paleontology—Eocene			

LC	Dewey	Subject Heading	LC	Dewey	Subject Heading
QH26-31	570.92	Biologists	QH135-178	578.094	Natural history—Europe
QH46	508.0222	Natural history—Pictorial works	QH179-193	578.095	Natural history—Asia
			QH194-195	578.096	Natural history—Africa
QH46.5	508.022	Natural history illustration	QH197	578.0994	Natural history—Australia
QH51-58	508.071	Natural history—Study and teaching	QH201-278.5	570.282	Microscopy
			QH211-212	570.282	Microscopes
QH51-58	508.071	Nature study	QH212.A25	502.82	Acoustic microscopy
QH68	635.9824	Terrariums	QH212.E4	570.2825	Electron microscopy
QH70	508.074	Natural history museums	QH212.E4	570.2825	Electron microscopes
QH75-77	508.072	Research natural areas	QH236.2	570.2827	Freeze fracturing
QH75-77	333.95	Biological diversity conservation	QH237	570.2827	Stains and staining (Microscopy)
QH75-77	333.95	Biosphere reserves	QH301-705	570	Biology
QH75-77	333.7816	Nature conservation	QH305-.2	570.9	Biology—History
QH75-77	333.91816	Wetland conservation	QH315-320	570.72	Biology—Research
QH75-77	578.68	Endangered species	QH315-320	570.71	Biology—Study and teaching
QH75-77	578.68	Endangered ecosystems	QH321-323.2	570.72	Biological laboratories
QH78	576.84	Extinction (Biology)	QH323.5	570.151	Biomathematics
QH83	508.014	Natural history—Terminology	QH324	570.284	Biological apparatus and supplies
QH84-198	578.09	Biogeography	QH324.2	570.285	Biology—Data processing
QH84.8	578.757	Soil biology	QH324.8	570.228	Biological models
QH87.3	578.768	Wetlands	QH324.9.C7	571.4645	Cryobiology
QH87.3	578.768	Marshes	QH325-349	570.1	Life (Biology)
QH87.3	578.768	Swamps	QH325	576.83	Spontaneous generation
QH87.5	578.738	Moors and heaths	QH327-328	571.0919	Space biology
QH87.7	578.748	Savannas	QH331	570.1	Biology—Philosophy
QH88	578.754	Desert biology	QH332	174.957	Bioethics
QH88	578.754	Deserts	QH343.7-344	577.14	Biogeochemistry
QH90-100	578.76	Aquatic biology	QH345	572	Biochemistry
QH90.8.P5	578.776	Plankton	QH351	571.3	Morphology
QH91-95.59	578.77	Marine biology	QH352	577.88	Population biology
QH91.6-.65	578.77072	Marine laboratories	QH353	577.18	Biological invasions
QH91.75	578.77	Marine parks and reserves	QH359-425	576.8	Evolution (Biology)
QH92-93.9	578.773	Marine biology—Atlantic Ocean	QH372	576.87	Coevolution
QH94-.7	578.775	Marine biology—Indian Ocean	QH375	576.82	Natural selection
			QH401-411	576.54	Variation (Biology)
QH95-.55	578.774	Marine biology—Pacific Ocean	QH426-470	576.5	Genetics
			QH432	591.35	Animal genetics
QH95.58	578.777	Marine biology—Antarctic Ocean	QH442-.6	660.65	Genetic engineering
			QH442.2	660.65	Cloning
QH95.8	578.7789	Coral reef biology	QH442.2	660.65	Molecular cloning
QH95.9	578.77	Brackish water biology	QH443-450.6	572.877	Genetic recombination
QH96-100	578.76	Freshwater biology	QH445.2	572.8633	Gene mapping
QH98	578.763	Lakes	QH447-.8	572.86	Genes
QH101-199	578.09(4-9)	Natural history—[By region or country]	QH447	572.86	Genomes
			QH450-.6	572.865	Genetic regulation
QH101-198	577.34	Cloud forest ecology	QH450.2	572.8845	Genetic transcription
QH104-105	578.0973	Natural history—United States	QH450.5	572.645	Genetic translation
			QH455	576.58	Population genetics
QH106-.2	578.0971	Natural history—Canada	QH460-468	576.549	Mutation (Biology)
QH107	578.0972	Natural history—Mexico	QH465-.5	576.549	Mutagens
QH108	578.09728	Natural history—Central America	QH471-489	571.8	Reproduction
			QH475-479	571.89	Reproduction, Asexual
QH109	578.09729	Natural history—West Indies	QH485	571.864	Fertilization (Biology)
			QH489	571.884	Generations, Alterating
QH111-130	578.098	Natural history—South America	QH499	571.889	Regeneration (Biology)
			QH504	154.72	Biomagnetism

LC	Dewey	Subject Heading	LC	Dewey	Subject Heading
QH505	571.4	Biophysics	QH546.3	577.83	Competition (Biology)
QH506	572.8	Molecular biology	QH548.3	577.852	Mutualism (Biology)
QH508	571.7	Biological control systems	QH573-671	571.6	Cytology
QH509	571.64	Biological transport	QH573-671	571.6	Cells
QH511	571.8	Growth	QH583-.2	571.6072	Cytology—Research
QH513	571.43	Biomechanics	QH585.2-.45	571.638	Cell culture
QH514.15.E27	577	Ecotones	QH595	571.66	Cell nuclei
QH517	572.437	Electrophysiology	QH600-.6	572.87	Chromosomes
QH521	572.4	Metabolism	QH601-602	571.64	Cell membranes
QH527	571.77	Biological rhythms	QH603.R5	571.658	Ribosomes
QH529	571.878	Aging	QH605-.3	571.844	Cell division
QH540-549.5	591.7	Animal ecology	QH605	571.845	Meiosis
QH540-549.5	577	Ecology	QH605.2	571.844	Mitosis
QH541.15.B56	333.95	Biological diversity	QH607	571.835	Cell differentiation
QH541.5.C5	577.38	Chaparral ecology	QH613	572	Histochemistry
QH541.5.C63	577.34	Cloud forest ecology	QH631-647	571.6	Cell physiology
QH541.5.C65	577.69	Coastal ecology	QH633	572.47	Cell respiration
QH541.15.E24	577	Ecological heterogeneity	QH634.5	572.4	Cell metabolism
QH541.15.M64	363.7063	Environmental monitoring	QH641	572.4358	Bioluminescence
QH541.15.S95	577.0723	Ecological surveys	QH651	571.63455	Light—Physiological effect
QH541.2-.264	577.071	Environmental education	QH652-.7	571.6345	Cells—Effect of radiation on
QH541.3	577.15	Biological productivity			
QH541.5.B63	577.687	Bog ecology	QH657	571.63435	Gravity
QH541.5.C6	577.56	Urban ecology (Biology)	QH671	571.939	Cell death
QH541.5.C7	577.789	Coral reef ecology	QH671	571.936	Death
QH541.5.D35	577.7	Deep-sea ecology			
QH541.5.D4	577.54	Desert ecology	QK	580	Botany
QH541.5.E8	577.786	Estuarine ecology	QK1	580.6	Botany—Societies, etc.
QH541.5.F6	577.3	Forest ecology	QK9	580.3	Botany—Dictionaries
QH541.5.F7	577.6	Freshwater ecology	QK10	580.14	Botany—Terminology
QH541.5.G37	577.554	Garden ecology	QK26-31	580.92	Botanists
QH541.5.H67	577.554	Household ecology	QK51-57	580.71	Botany—Study and teaching
QH541.5.L27	577.63	Lagoon ecology			
QH541.5.L3	577.63	Lake ecology	QK61	580.75	Plants—Collection and preservation
QH541.5.M3	577.68	Wetland ecology			
QH541.5.M4	577.46	Meadow ecology	QK62	580.723	Vegetation surveys
QH541.5.M6	577.38	Moor ecology	QK63	580.223	Vegetation mapping
QH541.5.P7	577.4	Grasslands	QK71-73	580.73	Botanical gardens
QH541.5.P7	577.4	Grassland ecology	QK75-77	580.74	Herbaria
QH541.5.P7	577.48	Savanna ecology	QK79-.5	580.74	Botany—Exhibitions
QH541.5.P7	577.44	Prairie ecology	QK86-.4	333.953	Plant conservation
QH541.5.R27	577.34	Rain forest ecology	QK86	581.68	Endangered plants
QH541.5.R3	577.4	Range ecology	QK91-97	580.12	Botany—Classification
QH541.5.R62	577.55	Roadside ecology	QK96	580.14	Botany—Nomenclature
QH541.5.S22	577.639	Salt lake ecology	QK98	580.222	Botany—Pictorial works
QH541.5.S26	577.583	Sand dune ecology	QK98.4	581.63	Plants, Useful
QH541.5.S35	577.69	Seashore ecology	QK98.5	581.632	Wild plants, Edible
QH541.5.S35	577.69	Tide pool ecology	QK98.5	581.632	Plants, Edible
QH541.5.S55	577.38	Shrubland ecology	QK98.7	581.636	Dye plants
QH541.5.S6	577.57	Soil ecology	QK99	581.634	Botany, Medical
QH541.5.S7	577.64	Stream ecology	QK99	581.634	Medicinal plants
QH541.5.S87	577.78	Sublittoral ecology	QK100	581.659	Poisonous plants
QH541.5.S9	577.68	Swamp ecology	QK101-474.5	581.9	Phytogeography
QH541.5.W3	577.6	Aquatic ecology	QK102-105	581.76	Aquatic plants
QH543-.2	577.22	Bioclimatology	QK105	581.76	Freshwater plants
QH543.2	578.42	Acclimatization	QK108-474.5	583	Dicotyledons
QH543.5-.6	577.277	Radioecology	QK108-474.5	581.7786	Estuarine plants
QH544	578.42	Phenology	QK108-474.5	581.73	Forest plants
QH546	578.4	Adaptation (Biology)	QK115-195	580.973	Botany—United States

LC	Dewey	Subject Heading	LC	Dewey	Subject Heading
QK145-195	580.97(4-9)	Botany—[United States, By state]	QK495.R98	583.77	Citrus
			QK495.S7	583.952	Eggplant
QK201-203	580.971	Botany—Canada	QK495.S7	583.952	Belladonna (Plant)
QK211	580.972	Botany—Mexico	QK495.U48	583.849	Dill
QK215-222	580.9728	Botany—Central America	QK495.V84	583.86	Grapes
QK225-231	580.9729	Botany—West Indies	QK504-635	586	Cryptogams
QK241-274	580.98	Botany—South America	QK520-532	587	Pteridophyta
QK281-339	580.94	Botany—Europe	QK532.4-563.87	588	Bryophytes
QK341-379	580.95	Botany—Asia	QK564-580.5	579.8	Algae
QK353	580.956	Botany—Middle East	QK569.P5	579.88	Brown algae
QK360-368	580.959	Botany—Asia, Southeastern	QK580.7-597.7	579.7	Lichens
			QK600-635	579.5	Fungi
QK376	581.9561	Botany—Turkey	QK600-635	579.6	Mushrooms, Hallucinogenic
QK381-424	580.96	Botany—Africa			
QK431-461	580.994	Botany—Australia	QK602	579.5135	Fungi—Genetics
QK474-.3	580.998	Botany—Arctic regions	QK617	579.6	Mushrooms, Edible
QK474.4	580.9989	Botany—Antarctica	QK617	581.659	Mushrooms, Poisonous
QK474.8-494	582.16	Trees	QK641-707	575	Botany—Anatomy
QK494-.5	585	Gymnosperms	QK644	575.54	Roots (Botany)
QK494	585	Conifers	QK645-650	575.49	Shoots (Botany)
QK494.5.C975	585.4	Eastern red cedar	QK648	581.47	Bark
QK494.5.P66	585.2	Douglas fir	QK649	575.57	Leaves
QK494.5.P66	585.2	Eastern hemlock	QK653-661	575.633	Flowers—Anatomy
QK494.5.P66	585.2	Fir	QK653-661	575.633	Flowers—Morphology
QK494.5.T3	585.5	Dawn redwood	QK653	575.6	Double flowers
QK495.A1	580	Angiosperms	QK658-659	575.6	Plants, Sex in
QK495.A12	583	Dicotyledons	QK658	571.845	Pollen
QK495.A26	584.352	Agave	QK710-899	575	Plant physiology
QK495.A484	584.34	Daffodils	QK725	571.7236	Plant cells and tissues
QK495.A6853	583.84	Ginseng	QK725	571.7236	Plant cell development
QK495.B4	583.627	Begonias	QK725	571.72366	Plant chromosomes
QK495.C74	583.99	Dandelions	QK728	572.82	Plant molecular biology
QK495.C74	583.99	Daisies	QK731-745	571.82	Growth (Plants)
QK495.C74	583.99	Big sagebrush	QK740	571.862	Germination
QK495.C9	583.64	Bok choy	QK750-751	577.27	Plants, Effect of pollution on
QK495.C98	583.94	Dodder			
QK495.E92	583.79	Coca	QK751	577.2752	Plants, Effect of acid precipitation on
QK495.F14	583.46	Durmast oak			
QK495.F14	583.46	English oak	QK751	577.276	Plants, Effect of air pollution on
QK495.G4	583.95	African violets			
QK495.G74	584.9	Deepwater rice	QK756	632.11	Plants—Frost resistance
QK495.G74	584.9	Durum wheat	QK761	571.772	Biological rhythms in plants
QK495.G74	584.9	Fescue			
QK495.G74	584.9	Grasses	QK761	571.782	Dormancy in plants
QK495.G74	584.9	Bamboo	QK776	581.498	Roots (Botany)
QK495.G74	584.92	Corn	QK825-830	575.6	Plants—Reproduction
QK495.G74	584.92	Crabgrass	QK827-830	575.6	Plants, Sex in
QK495.I75	584.38	Dwarf irises	QK828	571.8642	Fertilization of plants
QK495.L72	584.32	Daylilies	QK828	575.65	Pollination
QK495.L72	584.32	Easter lily	QK830	575.6	Plants, Flowering of
QK495.L9	583.76	Crape myrtle, Common	QK830	575.6	Double flowers
QK495.M27	583.685	Hibiscus	QK840	571.8892	Regeneration (Botany)
QK495.M73	583.45	Fig	QK845	572.4372	Electrophysiology of plants
QK495.M9	583.766	Eucalyptus	QK861-899	572.2	Botanical chemistry
QK495.M9	583.765	Guava	QK867-898	572.42	Plants—Nutrition
QK495.M98	584.39	Bananas	QK871	575.76	Plants—Absorption of water
QK495.N9	583.53	Bougainvillea			
QK495.P17	584.5	Date palm	QK871	575.75	Plants, Motion of fluids in
QK495.R78	583.73	Apples	QK873	575.8	Evapotranspiration

LC	Dewey	Subject Heading	LC	Dewey	Subject Heading
QK876	575.8	Gases from plants	QL101-345	590.9(4-9)	Zoogeography
QK881-897	572.42	Plants—Metabolism	QL105	590.98	Zoology—Arctic regions
QK882	572.46	Photosynthesis	QL112	591.73	Forest animals
QK891	572.472	Plants—Respiration	QL115.3-.5	591.74	Grassland fauna
QK898.E58	572.72	Plant enzymes	QL116	591.754	Desert animals
QK898.H67	571.742	Plant hormones	QL117	591.7584	Cave animals
QK898.P7	572.592	Plant pigments	QL120-149	591.77	Aquatic animals
QK900-938	577	Plants—Habitat	QL126	591.7732	Aquatic animals—Arctic Ocean
QK900-938	581.7	Plant ecology			
QK911	577.83	Plant competition	QL126.5	591.777	Aquatic animals—Antarctic Ocean
QK917	583.75	Carnivorous plants			
QK922	581.754	Desert plants	QL127-135	591.773	Aquatic animals—Atlantic Ocean
QK926	571.8642	Fertilization of plants by insects			
			QL137	591.775	Aquatic animals—Indian Ocean
QK926	571.8642	Pollination			
QK929	571.847	Spores (Botany)—Dispersal	QL138	591.774	Aquatic animals—Pacific Ocean
QK930-935	581.76	Aquatic plants	QL141-149	591.76	Freshwater animals
QK932-.7	581.76	Freshwater plants	QL155-339	590.9(4-9)	Zoology—[By region or country]
QK936	581.748	Tropical plants			
QK937	581.7538	Mountain plants	QL337.E25	590.72309676	Wildlife watching—Africa, Eastern
QK938.D4	581.754	Desert plants			
QK938.E	581.7786	Estuarine plants	QL360-599	592	Invertebrates
QK938.F6	581.73	Timberline	QL366-369.2	579.4	Protozoa
QK938.F6	581.73	Forest ecology	QL368.A5	579.432	Amoeba
QK938.F6	581.73	Forest plants	QL368.F5	579.82	Flagellata
QK938.M4	581.746	Meadow plants	QL370.7-374.2	593.4	Sponges
QK938.P7	581.74	Grasslands	QL375-379	593.5	Coelenterata
QK938.P7	581.744	Prairies	QL380-.8	593.8	Ctenophora
QK980-989	581.38	Plants—Evolution	QL381-385.2	593.9	Echinodermata
QK981.3	581.35	Plant biochemical genetics	QL386-394	592.3	Worms
QK981.4	581.35	Plant genetic regulation	QL391.A6	592.64	Earthworms
			QL401-445.2	594	Shellfish
QL	590	Zoology	QL401-432	591.477	Shells
QL1	590.6	Zoology—Societies, etc.	QL401-432	594	Mollusks
QL10	590.14	Zoology—Terminology	QL430.5.H34	594.32	Abalones
QL26-31	590.92	Ethologist	QL430.6-.7	594.4	Clams
QL26-31	591.5092	Zoologists	QL434-599.82	595	Arthropoda
QL46	590.222	Zoology—Pictorial works	QL435-445.2	595.3	Crustacea
QL51-58	590.71	Zoology—Study and teaching	QL444.C58	595.35	Barnacles
			QL444.M33	595.386	Blue crab
QL52.6	590.724	Zoology—Experiments	QL444.M33	595.386	Crabs
QL63	590.752	Taxidermy	QL444.M33	595.384	Crayfish
QL71	590.74	Zoological museums	QL444.M33	595.38	Decapoda (Crustacea)
QL73	590.73	Menageries	QL449.5-.55	595.62	Centipedes
QL76-77.5	590.73	Petting zoos	QL449.6-.65	595.66	Millipedes
QL76-77.5	590.73	Zoos	QL451-459.2	595.4	Arachnida
QL78-79	597.073	Aquariums, Public	QL461-599.82	595.7	Insects
QL78.5	597.073	Marine aquariums, Public	QL468.5	595.7072	Entomology—Research
QL81.5-84.7	333.95416	Wildlife conservation	QL505.5-.82	595.728	Cockroaches
QL81.5-84.77	578.68	Endangered species	QL508.A2	595.726	Desert locust
QL83.2	636.0832	Wildlife rescue	QL508.A2	595.726	Migratory locust
QL83.4	333.95416	Wildlife reintroduction	QL508.G8	595.726	Crickets
QL88-.15	560	Extinct animals	QL520-.42	595.733	Damselflies
QL89.2.C53	001.944	Champ (Monster)	QL520-.42	595.733	Dragonflies
QL89.2.S2	001.944	Sasquatch	QL541-562.4	595.789	Butterflies
QL100	591.65	Dangerous animals	QL544.6	638.5789	Butterfly gardens
QL100	591.6509162	Dangerous marine animals	QL561.L3	595.78139	Eastern tent caterpillar
QL100	591.65	Poisonous animals	QL561.S2	595.78	Ailanthus moth

LC	Dewey	Subject Heading	LC	Dewey	Subject Heading
QL561.T55	595.78	Clothes moths	QL678-695.5	598.09(4-9)	Birds—Geographical distribution
QL563-569.4	595.799	Bees			
QL568.A6	595.799	Honeybee	QL696.A52	598.41	Ducks
QL568.A6	595.799	Africanized honeybee	QL696.A52	598.415	Eider
QL568.A6	595.799	Bumblebees	QL696.C34	598.53	Emus
QL568.F7	595.796	Army ants	QL696.C63	598.65	Eared dove
QL568.F7	595.796	Ants	QL696.C67	598.65	Dodo
QL568.F7	595.796	Fire ants	QL696.F3	598.94	Buzzards
QL571-597.2	595.76	Beetles	QL696.F32	598.943	Bald eagle
QL596.S3	595.7649	Dung beetles	QL696.F32	598.942	African fish eagle
QL596.S35	595.76	Douglas fir beetle	QL696.F32	598.942	Eagles
QL605-739.8	596	Vertebrates	QL696.F33	598.92	Andean condor
QL605-739.8	596	Chordata	QL696.F34	598.96	Falcons
QL614-639.8	597	Fishes	QL696.G27	598.625	Pheasants
QL618	597.012	Fishes—Classification	QL696.P23	598.82	Creepers (Birds)
QL618.3	597.1788	Fish populations	QL696.P235	598.832	Dippers (Birds)
QL618.5-.55	597.072	Fishes—Research	QL696.P2367	598.864	Crows
QL618.7	597.165	Dangerous fishes	QL696.P2438	598.883	Dusky seaside sparrow
QL618.7	597.165	Poisonous fishes	QL696.P2438	598.883	Cardinals (Birds)
QL619-637	597.09(4-9)	Fishes—Geographical distribution	QL696.P2475	598.874	Cowbirds
			QL696.P288	598.842	Eastern bluebird
QL637.9.A5	597.43	Eels	QL696.P7	598.71	African gray parrot
QL638.9	597.36	Dogfish	QL696.P7	598.71	Cockatoos
QL638.95.S7	597.3	Hammerhead sharks	QL696.S473	598.47	Adelie penguin
QL638.99	597.135	Fishes—Genetics	QL696.S473	598.47	Emperor penguin
QL638.P4	597.75	Darters (Fishes)	QL697	598.147	Feathers
QL638.S2	597.554	Brook trout	QL698.5	598.1594	Birdsongs
QL638.S2	597.56	Chinook salmon	QL698.7	598.1479	Birds—Flight
QL638.S2	597.56	Coho salmon	QL698.8	573.87	Bird navigation
QL638.S9	597.6798	Dwarf sea horse	QL700-739.8	599	Mammals
QL639	597.1479	Fins	QL706.8-.83	599.168	Rare mammals
QL639	597.1477	Scales (Fishes)	QL707	569	Extinct mammals
QL639.2	597.562	Fishes—Spawning	QL708.6	599.1788	Mammal populations
QL639.4	597.1479	Fishes—Locomotion	QL737.C2	599.7	Carnivora
QL639.5	597.1568	Fishes—Migration	QL737.C2	599.77	Dogs
QL641-669.3	597.8	Amphibians	QL737.C22	599.775	Foxes
QL641-669	597.9	Reptiles	QL737.C23	599.756	Tigers
QL645.7	597.9165	Dangerous reptiles	QL737.C27	599.78	Bears
QL666.C584	597.92	Desert tortoise	QL737.C27	599.784	Brown bear
QL666.C925	597.984	Alligators	QL737.C423	599.5276	Bowhead whale
QL666.C925	597.982	Crocodiles	QL737.C432	599.53	Dolphins
QL666.L23	597.956	Chameleons	QL737.C434	599.53	Dall Porpoise
QL666.06-.694	597.96	Snakes	QL737.M242	599.336	Elephant shrews
QL666.064	597.96	Cobras	QL737.P63	599.79	Eared seals
QL666.064	597.9644	Coral snakes	QL737.P64	599.794	Elephant seals
QL666.069	597.96	Broad-banded copperhead	QL737.P9-.P968	599.8	Primates
QL666.069	597.963	Copperhead	QL737.P925	599.85	Capuchin monkeys
QL666.069	597.96	Eastern diamondback rattlesnake	QL737.P93	599.83	Demidoff's galago
			QL737.P96	599.88	Apes
QL668.E2-.E275	597.89	Frogs	QL737.P96	599.885	Chimpanzees
QL671-699	598	Ornithology	QL737.P96	599.884	Gorilla
QL671-699	598	Birds	QL737.P98	599.674	African elephant
QL676.5-.57	639.978	Bird attracting	QL737.P98	599.67	Elephants
QL676.5-.57	333.958	Bird refuges	QL737.R6	599.35	Dancing mice
QL676.5-.57	636.50831	Birdhouses	QL737.R632	599.37	American beaver
QL676.7	597.168	Rare birds	QL737.R634	599.3592	Guinea pigs
QL676.8	597.168	Extinct birds	QL737.R666	599.356	Hamsters
QL677.75	598.165	Dangerous birds	QL737.R638	599.356	Dwarf hamsters
QL677.8	598.073	Aviaries	QL737.R656	599.3596	Dormice

LC	Dewey	Subject Heading	LC	Dewey	Subject Heading
QL737.R656	599.3596	Edible dormouse	QL821	573.76	Bones
QL737.R66	599.35987	Desert kangaroo rat	QL825	573.78	Joints
QL737.R68	599.36	Abent squirrel	QL827	573.78356	Ligaments
QL737.R68	599.364	Eastern chipmunk	QL831	573.75	Muscles
QL737.T8	599.31	Aardvark	QL835-841	573.1	Cardiovascular system
QL737.U5	599.642	Elands	QL835	573.18	Blood-vessels
QL737.U5	599.642	Buffaloes	QL835	573.185	Arteries
QL737.U53	599.642	African buffalo	QL835	573.186	Veins
QL737.U53	599.64	Antelopes	QL838	573.17	Heart—Anatomy
QL737.U53	599.643	American bison	QL841	573.16	Lymphatics
QL737.U54	599.6362	Camels	QL845-855	573.2	Respiratory organs
QL737.U55	599.65	Deer	QL848	573.22	Lungs
QL737.U55	599.657	Elk	QL851	573.26	Diaphragm
QL737.U56	599.638	Giraffe	QL856-867	573.3	Digestive organs
QL737.U62	599.665	African wild ass	QL857	573.35	Mouth
QL737.U62	599.665	Asses	QL857	573.355	Lips
QL737.U62	599.665	Equus	QL858	573.356	Teeth
QL750-795	591.5	Animal behavior	QL861	573.359	Esophagus
QL752	591.788	Animal populations	QL862	573.36	Stomache
QL755	591.565	Hibernation	QL863	573.378	Duodenum
QL756-.15	591.564	Animals—Habitations	QL863	573.37	Intestines
QL756.15	591.5648	Animal burrowing	QL865-868	573.4	Glands
QL756.5-.57	591.5(3-4)	Animals—Food	QL866	573.377	Pancreas
QL756.57	591.53	Cannibalism in animals	QL867	573.38	Gallbladder
QL757	591.65	Parasitology	QL867	573.38	Bile ducts
QL757	591.65	Parasites	QL867	573.38	Liver
QL759	591.47	Animal defenses	QL868	573.4	Endocrinology, Comparative
QL761	591.562	Sexual behavior in animals			
QL761	591.562	Sexual selection in animals	QL868	573.4	Endocrine glands
			QL868	573.45	Pituitary gland
QL761.5	591.563	Familial behavior in animals	QL868	573.1555	Spleen
			QL872-881	573.49	Urinary organs
QL762	591.563	Parental behavior in animals	QL872-875	573.49	Excretory organs
			QL872	573.49	Bladder
QL763.2	591.563	Imprinting (Psychology)	QL873	573.496	Kidneys
QL763.5	591.563	Play behavior in animals	QL876-881	573.6	Generative organs
QL765	591.594	Animal sounds	QL878	573.65	Generative organs, Male
QL765	591.594	Sound production by animals	QL878	573.658	Prostate
			QL881	573.66	Generative organs, Female
QL765	591.594	Voice	QL881	573.665	Ovaries
QL767	591.472	Protective coloration (Biology)	QL881	573.667	Uterus
			QL921-939	573.8	Nervous system
QL768	591.479	Animal tracks	QL933-937	573.86	Medulla oblongata
QL775	591.56	Social hierarchy in animals	QL933-937	573.86	Meninges
QL776	591.59	Animal communication	QL937	573.86	Cerebellum
QL776	591.59	Human-animal communication	QL938.H56	573.86	Hippocampus (Brain)
			QL938.S6	573.869	Spinal cord
QL781	591.512	Instinct	QL939	573.85	Nerves
QL782	573.87	Animal navigation	QL939	573.85	Sympathetic nervous system
QL785-.27	591.5	Animal psychology			
QL785	591.513	Cognition in animals	QL940	591.47	Animal weapons
QL785	591.513	Animal intelligence	QL941-943	573.5	Dermis
QL785.3	591.5	Extrasensory perception in animals	QL941-943	573.5	Epidermis
			QL941-943	573.5	Skin
QL799-.5	571.3	Morphology (Animals)	QL942	573.58	Hair
QL801-950.9	571.3	Anatomy, Comparative	QL942	573.59	Nails (Anatomy)
QL807	571.5	Histology	QL942	573.59	Toenails
QL821-831	573.7	Musculoskeletal system	QL944	573.679	Mammary glands
QL821-827	573.76	Skeleton	QL945-949	573.87	Sense organs

LC	Dewey	Subject Heading	LC	Dewey	Subject Heading
QL946	573.357	Tongue	QM301-367	611.3	Digestive organs
QL948	573.89	Ear, External	QM301-367	611.3	Gastrointestinal system
QL948	573.89	Ear	QM306	611.317	Lips
QL948	573.89	Eustachian tube	QM306	611.31	Mouth
QL948	573.89	Middle ear	QM311	611.314	Teeth
QL948	579.89	Labyrinth (Ear)	QM325-371	611.316	Salivary glands
QL949	573.88	Eye	QM325-371	611.4	Glands
QL949	573.88	Eyelids	QM331	611.32	Esophagus
QL949	573.88	Optic nerve	QM331	611.32	Pharynx
QL949	573.88	Pupil (Eye)	QM331	611.32	Tonsils
QL949	573.88	Retina	QM341	611.33	Stomache
QL950.7	573.79	Leg	QM345	611.347	Colon (Anatomy)
QL951-991	571.86	Embryology	QM345	611.345	Appendix (Anatomy)
QL961	571.860724	Embryology, Experimental	QM345	611.341	Duodenum
QL975	571.86	Amniotic liquid	QM345	611.34	Intestines
QL981	571.876	Metamorphosis	QM351	611.36	Liver
			QM351	573.38	Bile ducts
QM	611	Human anatomy	QM352	611.36	Gallbladder
QM24	611	Human anatomy—Variation	QM353	611.37	Pancreas
QM25	611.0022	Human anatomy—Atlases	QM367	611.38	Peritoneum
QM34	611.0078	Human anatomy—Laboratory manuals	QM371	611.45	Adrenal glands
			QM371	611.4	Endocrine glands
			QM371	611.47	Pituitary gland
			QM371	611.41	Spleen
QM51	611.0074	Anatomical museums	QM371	611.44	Thyroid gland
QM100-170	611.7	Musculoskeletal system	QM401-413	611.61	Urinary organs
QM101-117	611.71	Human skeleton	QM404	611.61	Kidneys
QM101-117	611.71	Skeleton	QM411	611.62	Bladder
QM101-117	611.71	Bones	QM416-421	611.6	Generative organs
QM101	611.717	Clavicle	QM416	611.64	Penis
QM105	611.716	Jaws	QM416	611.63	Prostate
QM105	611.715	Skull	QM416	611.63	Generative organs, Male
QM111	611.711	Spinal canal	QM421	611.65	Fallopian tubes
QM111	611.711	Cervical vertebrae	QM421	611.65	Generative organs, Female
QM111	611.711	Vertebrae	QM421	611.65	Ovaries
QM111	611.711	Spine	QM421	611.66	Uterus
QM113	611.712	Ribs	QM451-471	611.8	Nervous system
QM117	611.718	Femur	QM455	611.81	Cerebellum
QM131-142	611.72	Joints	QM455	611.81	Hippocampus (Brain)
QM141	611.72	Ligaments	QM455	611.81	Hypothalamus
QM151-170	611.73	Muscles	QM455	611.81	Medulla oblongata
QM170	611.74	Tendons	QM465	611.82	Spinal cord
QM178-197	611.1	Cardiovascular system	QM469	611.81	Meninges
QM181	611.12	Heart—Anatomy	QM471	611.83	Nerves
QM181	611.11	Pericardium	QM471	611.83	Sympathetic nervous system
QM181	611.12	Myocardium			
QM191	611.13	Aorta	QM481-484	611.77	Skin
QM191	611.13	Blood-vessels	QM484	611.77	Dermis
QM191	611.13	Arteries	QM484	611.77	Epidermis
QM191	611.13	Pulmonary artery	QM488	611.78	Eyelashes
QM191	611.14	Veins	QM488	611.78	Hair
QM197	611.42	Lymphatics	QM488	611.78	Nails (Anatomy)
QM251-265	611.2	Respiratory organs	QM495	611.49	Breast
QM255	611.22	Epiglottis	QM495	611.49	Mammary glands
QM255	611.22	Glottis	QM501-511	611.8	Sense organs
QM255	611.22	Larynx	QM503	611.313	Tongue
QM261	611.24	Lungs	QM505	611.21	Frontal sinus
QM265	611.26	Diaphragm	QM505	611.21	Nasopharynx
QM301-367	611.3	Alimentary canal	QM507	611.85	Ear

LC	Dewey	Subject Heading	LC	Dewey	Subject Heading
QM507	611.85	Ear, External	QP82.2.N6	571.444	Noise—Physiological effect
QM507	611.85	Eustachian tube	QP82.2.N64	571.45	Nonionizing radiation
QM507	611.85	Middle ear	QP82.2.P6	571.49	Pollution—Physiological effect
QM507	611.85	Labyrinth (Ear)	QP82.2.P7	571.437	Atmospheric pressure—Physiological effect
QM511	611.84	Eye			
QM511	611.84	Eyelids			
QM511	611.84	Optic nerve	QP84	612.6	Human growth
QM511	611.84	Pupil (Eye)	QP84	612.6	Growth
QM511	611.84	Retina	QP84.4	612.661	Puberty
QM531-549	611.9	Anatomy, Surgical and topographical	QP84.6	571.77	Biological rhythms
			QP84.6	571.77	Sleep-wake cycle
QM535	611.92	Chin	QP85	612.68	Longevity
QM535	611.91	Head	QP86	612.67	Old age
QM535	611.93	Neck	QP87	571.939	Death
QM535	611.92	Face	QP88-.6	611.018	Tissues
QM535	611.92	Cheek	QP88.5	573.5	Dermis
QM535	611.32	Throat	QP88.5	573.5	Epidermis
QM540	612.9	Back	QP90.4	571.75	Homeostasis
QM543	611.95	Abdomen	QP91-99.5	612.11	Blood
QM548-549	611.9(7-8)	Extremities (Anatomy)	QP91	612.115	Fibrin
QM548	611.97	Arm	QP93.5-.7	612.115	Blood—Coagulation
QM548	611.97	Hand	QP93.5-.7	612.115	Blood coagulation factors
QM548	611.97	Forearm	QP96.5	612.1111	Hemoglobin
QM548	611.97	Fingers	QP98	612.11825	Blood groups
QM549	611.98	Toes	QP99	612.116	Blood plasma
QM549	611.98	Foot	QP101	612.14	Pulse
QM549	611.98	Leg	QP105-.4	612.14	Blood pressure
QM550-577.8	611.018	Histology	QP106.6	573.187	Capillaries
QM551-575	611.018	Tissues	QP107	612.2	Pulmonary circulation
QM561	611.77	Epidermis	QP108	612.17	Coronary circulation
QM563	611.74	Connective tissues	QP109	612.18	Vasomotor system
QM563	611.0182	Elastic tissue	QP111-114	612.17	Heart
QM563	611.74	Fasciae (Anatomy)	QP113.2	612.17	Myocardium
QM563	611.72	Ligaments	QP115	612.42	Lymphatics
QM565	611.01827	Adipose tissues	QP121-125	612.2	Lungs
QM567	611.0183	Cartilage	QP121-125	612.2	Respiratory organs
QM569	611.41	Bone marrow	QP121-125	612.2	Respiration
QM571	611.73	Muscles	QP121	612.2	Diaphragm
QM575	611.0188	Nerve tissue	QP135	612.01426	Body temperature
QM576	611.4	Endocrine glands	QP139	612.391	Thirst
QM601-695	611.013	Embryology, Human	QP141-185.3	612.3	Nutrition
QM611	611.013	Amniotic liquid	QP141	612.391	Hunger
			QP145-159	612.3	Digestion
QP	571	Physiology	QP146	612.315	Esophagus
QP1	571.05	Physiology—Periodicals	QP146	612.312	Tonsils
QP13	571.014	Physiology—Terminology	QP151-156	612.3	Gastrointestinal system
QP31-33	571.1	Physiology, Comparative	QP151	612.32	Stomache
QP34-38	612	Human physiology	QP156	612.33	Duodenum
QP34-38	612	Human biology	QP156	612.33	Intestines
QP39-47	571.071	Physiology—Study and teaching	QP159	612.46	Excretion
QP55	571.0284	Physiological apparatus	QP165	612.38	Absorption (Physiology)
QP81-87	570.1	Life (Biology)	QP165	612.38	Intestinal absorption
QP82-.2	578.4	Adaptation (Physiology)	QP171-177	612.39	Metabolism
QP82.2.A4	571.49	Altitude, Influence of	QP176	572.43	Energy metabolism
QP82.2.C5	571.49	Weather—Physiological effect	QP185	612.35	Gallbladder
			QP185	612.35	Liver
QP82.2.C6	571.464	Cold—Physiological effect			
QP82.2.G7	571.435	Gravity			

LC	Dewey	Subject Heading	LC	Dewey	Subject Heading
QP187-.6	612.4	Endocrinology, Comparative	QP406	612.82	Memory
QP187-.6	612.4	Endocrinology	QP425-427	612.821	Sleep
QP187-.6	612.4	Endocrine glands	QP431-495	612.8	Senses and sensation
QP187	612.41	Spleen	QP451	612.88	Touch
QP187.7	612.4	Exocrine glands	QP455-458	612.86	Chemical senses
QP188.A28	612.45	Adrenal cortex	QP456	612.87	Taste
QP188.A3	612.45	Adrenal glands	QP458	612.86	Odors
QP188.M3	612.664	Mammary glands	QP458	612.86	Nose
QP188.P26	612.34	Pancreas	QP458	612.86	Smell
QP188.P3	612.44	Parathyroid glands	QP460-471.2	612.85	Ear
QP188.P58	612.492	Pituitary gland	QP460-469.3	612.85	Hearing
QP186-246	612.4	Glands	QP461	612.854	Eustachian tube
QP190-246.5	612.4	Secretion	QP461	612.854	Middle ear
QP191	612.313	Saliva	QP471-.2	612.858	Labyrinth (Ear)
QP188.S2	612.313	Salivary glands	QP471	612.858	Vestibular apparatus
QP193	612.32	Gastric juice	QP474-495	612.84	Vision
QP193	612.32	Stomache—Secretions	QP475-495	612.84	Eye
QP195	612.34	Pancreas—Secretions	QP476	612.84	Pupil (Eye)
QP197	573.38379	Bile	QP477.5	612.846	Eye—Movements
QP211	612.46	Excretion	QP479	612.843	Retina
QP221	612.7921	Perspiration	QP501-801	572	Biochemistry
QP246	612.664	Lactation	QP517.P45	572.435	Photobiochemistry
QP247-250.8	612.46	Urinary organs	QP519.7-.9	572.36	Analytical biochemistry
QP249	612.463	Kidneys	QP527	541.224	Free radicals (Chemistry)
QP251-285	612.6	Generative organs	QP531-535	572.51	Bioinorganic chemistry
QP251-285	612.6	Reproduction	QP532	572.52	Metals in the body
QP251-285	612.6	Human reproduction	QP533	572.51	Minerals in the body
QP251-281	612.63	Conception	QP534	572.515	Trace elements in the body
QP253-257	612.61	Generative organs, Male	QP535.O1	572.53	Active oxygen in the body
QP255	612.61	Semen	QP535.C2	572.516	Calcium in the body
QP259-281	612.62	Generative organs, Female	QP535.C2	572.516	Calcium
QP301-336	612.7	Musculoskeletal system	QP535.H1	572.539	Water in the body
QP301-336	612.76	Human mechanics	QP535.N1	572.54	Nitrogen in the body
QP301-336	612.76	Locomotion	QP550-801	572	Bioorganic chemistry
QP301-336	613.71	Exercise	QP551	572.633	Amino acid sequence
QP301-310	612.76	Animal locomotion	QP551	613.282	Amino acids in nutrition
QP301-310	612.044	Exercise—Physiological aspects	QP552.C34	572.696	Carrier proteins
			QP552.P4	572.65	Peptides
QP303	613.7	Kinesiology	QP561-563	572.65	Amino acids
QP306	612.2	Larynx	QP561	613.282	Amino acids in human nutrition
QP306	612.78	Voice			
QP306	612.78	Speech	QP572.A27	573.46	Adrenaline
QP310.F5	573.798	Animal flight	QP572.A5	612.61	Androgens
QP311	612.92	Jaws	QP572.H9	612.8262	Hypothalamic hormones
QP321-322	612.74	Muscles	QP572.I5	612.34	Insulin
QP321	612.744	Fatigue	QP572.M44	612.02	Melatonin
QP330	612.83	Spine	QP572.P4	572.65	Peptide hormones
QP341	572.437	Electrophysiology	QP572.P7	612.405	Progesterone
QP351-430	612.81	Nervous system	QP572.P74	612.405	Prolactin
QP356.3	612.8042	Neurochemistry	QP572.S4	612.405	Hormones, Sex
QP360	152.1423	Pattern perception	QP572.T4	612.405	Testosterone
QP361-375.5	612.81	Nerves	QP572.V28	572.65	Vasoactive intestinal peptides
QP370-375	612.83	Spinal cord			
QP376-430	612.82	Brain	QP601-619	572.7	Enzymes
QP377	612.828	Medulla oblongata	QP609.D52	573.347	Digestive enzymes
QP379	612.827	Cerebellum	QP616.D56	572.86	DNA topoisomerase I
QP383-.17	612.825	Cerebral cortex	QP616.D56	572.86	DNA topoisomerase II
QP401	612.88	Pain	QP619.D53	572.86	DNA ligases
			QP620-625	572.8	Nucleic acids

LC	Dewey	Subject Heading	LC	Dewey	Subject Heading
QP623-.5	572.88	RNA	QR106-.5	579.177	Marine microbiology
QP623.5.M47	572.88	Messenger RNA	QR111-113	579.1757	Soil microbiology
QP623.5.T73	572.886	Transfer RNA	QR111	579.31755	Bacteriology, Agricultural
QP624-.75	572.86	DNA	QR115-129	664.001579	Food—Bacteriology
QP624.5.C57	572.86	Circular DNA	QR115-129	664.001579	Food—Microbiology
QP625.N89	572.8633	Nucleotide sequence	QR130	579.17	Space microbiology
QP670-671	572.59	Pigments (Biology)	QR151	579.562	Yeast
QP701-702	572.56	Carbohydrates	QR177	616.9041	Drug resistance in
QP702.S85	572.565	Sugar in the body			microorganisms
QP702.S85	572.565	Sugars	QR180-189.5	571.96	Immunology
QP751-752	572.57	Lipids	QR180-183.5	571.960724	Experimental immunology
QP752.B54	573.38379	Bile acids	QR184-.4	571.9648	Immunogenetics
QP752.C5	572.5795	Cholesterol	QR184.2	616.0796	Human immunogenetics
QP752.E84	572.57	Essential fatty acids	QR184.5	571.9638	Developmental
QP752.F35	572.57	Fatty acids in human			immunology
		nutrition	QR185.2	571.96	Natural immunity
QP752.F35	572.57	Fatty acids	QR185.8.C6	571.9688	Complement (Immunology)
QP801.A48	572.548	Amines in the body	QR185.8.T2	571.966	T cells
QP801.H7	573.44	Hormones	QR186-.3	571.964	Immune response
QP801.P38	571.49	Pesticides—Physiological	QR186.5-.6	571.9645	Antigens
		effect	QR186.6.B33	571.9645	Bacterial antigens
QP913.C1	612.22	Carbon dioxide—	QR186.7-.85	571.967	Immunoglobulins
		Physiological effect	QR186.82-.83	571.973	Autoantibodies
QP913.N2	572.5238224	Salt—Physiological effect	QR187-.3	571.9677	Antigen-antibody reactions
QP913.01	572.53	Oxygen—Physiological	QR187.5	571.9644	Interferon inducers
		effect	QR187.5	571.9644	Interferon
			QR188	571.972	Allergy
QR	579.3	Bacteriology	QR188.3	571.973	Autoimmunity
QR	579	Microbiology	QR188.35	571.974	Immunodeficiency
QR1	579.05	Microbiology—Periodicals	QR189-.5	615.372	Vaccines
QR11	579.014	Microbiology—Terminology	QR189.5.A33	615.372	AIDS vaccines
QR12	579.012	Microbiology—	QR189.5.B33	615.372	Bacterial vaccines
		Classification	QR189.5.E53	615.372	Enterobacterial vaccines
QR13	579.138	Microorganisms—	QR201	579.165	Pathogenic
		Evolution			microorganisms
QR21-22	579.09	Microbiology—History	QR201	579.3	Pathogenic bacteria
QR30-31	579.092	Microbiologists	QR201.A72	571.992562	Arbovirus infections
QR46-48	616.9041	Body,	QR201.B34	571.993	Bacterial diseases
		Human—Microbiology	QR201.E75	571.992	Epstein-Barr virus
QR46	616.9201	Medical bacteriology			diseases
QR46	616.9041	Medical microbiology	QR201.P26	571.992445	Papillomavirus diseases
QR53-.5	660.62	Industrial microbiology	QR201.P33	571.99247	Parvovirus infections
QR54	579.0222	Microbiology—Pictorial	QR201.S68	571.99353	Staphylococcal infections
		works	QR245-248	571.995	Pathogenic fungi
QR61-63	579.072	Microbiology—Research	QR251-255	616.96	Medical parasitology
QR64-.8	579.3072	Bacteriological	QR342-.2	579.26	Bacteriophages
		laboratories	QR343	579.27	Fungal viruses
QR65-69	579.3028	Bacteriology—Technique	QR351	579.28	Plant viruses
QR65-69	579.028	Microbiology—Technique	QR351	579.31755	Bacteriology, Agricultural
QR75-99.5	579.3	Bacteria	QR353.5.R4	571.99327	Rickettsia
QR77.35	571.629	Bacteria cell surfaces	QR355-502	579.2	Viruses
QR78	571.672	Flagella (Microbiology)	QR372.058	579.2569	Oncogenic DNA viruses
QR81.7	579.3138	Bacteria—Evolution	QR394.5	579.24	DNA viruses
QR82.B3	579.362	Bacillus (Bacteria)	QR395	579.25	RNA viruses
QR82.P78	579.332	Pseudomonas	QR398	579.2562	Arboviruses
QR82.S78	579.355	Streptococcus	QR406-.2	579.2445	Papovaviruses
QR89.5	579.3149	Anaerobic bacteria	QR408-.2	579.247	Parvoviruses
QR100-130	576.15	Microbial ecology	QR414.5-.6	579.2569	Retroviruses
QR105.5	579.176	Freshwater microbiology	QR414.6.H58	616.979201	HIV (Viruses)

LC	Dewey	Subject Heading	LC	Dewey	Subject Heading
			R651-654	610.96	Medicine—Africa
R	610	Medicine	R671-674	610.994	Medicine—Australia
R5-101	610.5	Medicine—Periodicals	R675-678	610.993	Medicine—New Zealand
R10-99.7	610.6	Medicine—Societies, etc.	R681-684	610.99(5-6)	Medicine—Oceania
R106	610.6	Medicine—Congresses	R692	610.82	Women physicians
R119.8	026.61	Archives, Medical	R695	610.8996073	Afro-Americans in
R120	610.222	Medicine—Pictorial works			medicine
R121	610.3	Medicine—Dictionaries	R695	610.8996073	Blacks in medicine
R123	610.14	Medicine—Terminology	R697.A4	610.737	Allied health personnel
R131-684	610.9	Medicine—History	R702	616.009	Diseases and history
R134-.5	610.92	Physicians—Biography	R707-.4	610.695	Physicians
R135-138.5	610.901	Medicine, Ancient	R711-713.97	610.695025	Physicians—Directories
R135	610.935	Medicine, Persian	R723-.5	610.1	Medicine—Philosophy
R141-144	610.902	Medicine, Medieval	R724-726	174.2	Medical ethics
R143	610.089927	Medicine, Arab	R726	179.7	Assisted suicide
R151-363	610.973	Medicine—United States	R726	179.7	Euthanasia
R155-363	610.97(4-9)	Medicine—[United States,	R726.5-.8	601.9	Medicine and psychology
		By state]	R726.8	362.1756	Hospices (Terminal care)
R461-464	610.971	Medicine—Canada	R726.8	616.029	Terminally ill
R465-468	610.972	Medicine—Mexico	R726.8	616.029	Terminal care
R469-472	610.9728	Medicine—Central	R727.3-.45	610.696	Physician and patient
		America	R727.43	615.5	Patient compliance
R473-476	610.9729	Medicine—West Indies	R727.5	362.172	Medical referral
R480-483	610.98	Medicine—South America	R729.5	610.6	Medicine—Practice
R484-575	610.94	Medicine—Europe	R728	651.3741	Medical secretaries
R486-498.4	610.941	Medicine—Great Britain	R728	610.6	Medical offices
R498.6-.9	610.9415	Medicine—Ireland	R728.8	610.737	Medical assistants
R499-502	610.9436	Medicine—Austria	R733	615.5	Alternative medicine
R504-507	610.944	Medicine—France	R735-845	610.711	Medical colleges
R509-512.5	610.943	Medicine—Germany	R735-845	610.71	Medicine—Study and
R513-516	610.9495	Medicine—Greece			teaching
R517-520	610.945	Medicine—Italy	R837.E9	616.075	Medicine—Examinations
R521-524	610.9493	Medicine—Belgium	R850-854	616.027	Medicine, Experimental
R526-529	610.9492	Medicine—Netherlands	R853.C55	615.50724	Clinical trials
R531-534	610.947	Medicine—Russia	R853.H8	615.50724	Human experimentation in
R535-538	610.9438	Medicine—Poland			medicine
R539-542	610.9489	Medicine—Denmark	R856-858	610.284	Medical instruments and
R543-546	610.94912	Medicine—Iceland			apparatus
R547-550	610.9481	Medicine—Norway	R856-857	610.28	Biomedical engineering
R551-554	610.9485	Medicine—Sweden	R857.U48	616.07543	Ultrasonics in medicine
R555-558	610.946	Medicine—Spain	R858-859.7	610.285	Medical informatics
R559-562	610.9469	Medicine—Portugal	R860-862	610.72	Medical laboratories
R563-566	610.9494	Medicine—Switzerland	R895-920	616.07575	Nuclear medicine
R581-644	610.95	Medicine—Asia			
R581	610.95	Medicine, Oriental	RA	614	Public health
R591-594	610.9538	Medicine—Saudi Arabia	RA10-388	353.606	Health boards
R601-604	610.951	Medicine—China	RA11-182	353.606073	Health boards—United
R603.T5	610.951	Medicine, Tibetan			States
R604.2-.5	610.95491	Medicine—Pakistan	RA15-182	353.60607(4-9)	Health boards—[United
R605-608	610.954	Medicine—India			States, By city]
R608.2-.5	610.95493	Medicine—Sri Lanka	RA184-186	353.606071	Health boards—Canada
R609-612	610.959(3-7)	Medicine—Indochina	RA187-188	353.606072	Health boards—Mexico
R614-617	610.9598	Medicine—Indonesia	RA191	353.6060728	Health boards—Central
R618-621	610.9599	Medicine—Philippines			America
R623-626	610.952	Medicine—Japan	RA198-235	353.60608	Health boards—South
R627-630	610.9519	Medicine—Korea			America
R631-634	610.955	Medicine—Iran	RA239-299	353.60604	Health boards—Europe
R635-638	610.957	Medicine—Asiatic Russia	RA303-340	353.60605	Health boards—Asia
R640-643	610.9561	Medicine—Turkey	RA345-352	353.60606	Health boards—Africa

LC	Dewey	Subject Heading	LC	Dewey	Subject Heading
RA371-372	353.606094	Health boards—Australia	RA639-641	614.43	Animals as carriers of disease
RA390-392	362.1	Missions, Medical			
RA404	614.4	Diseases—Reporting	RA639.3	614.43	Vector control
RA405	353.596	Death—Proof and certification	RA639.5	614.432	Insects as carriers of disease
RA407-409.5	610.21	Medical statistics	RA640	614.4323	Mosquitoes as carriers of disease
RA407.3-408	614.42	Health surveys			
RA410-415	338.473621	Medical economics	RA640	614.4323	Mosquitoes—Control
RA413-.7	362.104258	Health maintenance organizations	RA641.D6	614.56	Dogs as carriers of disease
RA413-.5	362.104258	Managed care plans (Medical care)	RA641.M5	614.433	Mites as carriers of disease
RA418.5.F3	613.04	Family—Health and hygiene	RA641.T5	614.433	Tick-borne diseases
			RA641.T7	614.4322	Tsetse flies
RA421-790	613	Medicine, Preventive	RA642.A5	616.9	Airborne infection
RA424.4-.5	613.092	Hygienists	RA642.B56	616.94	Bloodborne infections
RA427.5-.6	362.177	Medical screening	RA643-644	614.5	Communicable diseases
RA427.8	613	Health promotion	RA643-644	614.55	Parasitic diseases
RA440.85-.87	614.072	Public health—Research	RA644.A25	614.599392	AIDS-related complex
RA441.5	614.091724	Public health—Developing countries	RA644.A25	616.9792	AIDS (Disease)
			RA644.A6	614.5610947	Anthrax—Russia (Federation)—Epidemiology
RA442-558	614.09(4-9)	Public health—[By region or country]			
RA443-450	614.097	Public health—North America	RA644.A57	614.516	Amebiasis
			RA644.C3	614.514	Cholera
RA445-448.5	614.0973	Public health—United States	RA644.D4	614.58852	Dengue
			RA644.D6	614.5123	Diphtheria—Prevention
RA448.5.N4	362.108996073	Afro-Americans—Medical care	RA644.E52	614.59832	Epidemic encephalitis
			RA644.F5	614.5552	Filariasis
RA448.5.N4	613.08996073	Afro-Americans—Health and hygiene	RA644.H45	614.547	Herpes genitalis
			RA644.I6	614.518	Influenza
RA449-450	614.0971	Public health—Canada	RA644.M2	614.532	Malaria
RA451-452	614.0972	Public health—Mexico	RA644.M5	614.523	Measles
RA453-454	614.09728	Public health—Central America	RA644.P7	614.5732	Plague—Vaccination
			RA644.P8	616.241	Pneumonia
RA455-456	614.09729	Public health—West Indies	RA644.R3	614.563	Rabies
			RA644.R8	614.524	Rubella
RA457-482	614.098	Public health—South America	RA644.T7	614.542	Tuberculosis—Vaccination
			RA644.T7	614.542	Tuberculosis
RA483-523	614.094	Public health—Europe	RA644.T8	614.5112	Typhoid fever—Vaccination
RA525-541	614.095	Public health—Asia			
RA545-552	614.096	Public health—Africa	RA644.T8	614.5112	Typhoid fever
RA566.7	613.091732	Urban health	RA644.V4	614.547	Sexually transmitted diseases—Prevention
RA571	613.1	Soil pollution			
RA576	614.59	Smog	RA644.V4	614.547	Sexually transmitted diseases
RA577	615.91	Gases, Asphyxiating and poisonous			
			RA644.V55	614.57	Virus diseases
RA601.5	614.5	Foodborne diseases	RA644.W6	614.543	Whooping cough
RA615.2	629.1344	Aeronautics—Sanitation	RA644.Y4	614.541	Yellow fever
RA619-640	614.6	Dead	RA645.3-.37	362.14	Home care services
RA622-623.6	363.75	Undertakers and undertaking	RA645.5-.7	616.025	Emergency medical technicians
RA625-630	614.6	Burial	RA645.5-.9	362.18	Emergency medical services
RA626-630	363.75	Cemeteries			
RA631-636.7	614.6	Cremation	RA645.5-.8	616.025	Emergency medical personnel
RA636-.7	363.75	Crematoriums			
RA638	614.47	Vaccination	RA645.A44	614.5993	Allergy
RA639-641	614.56	Zoonoses	RA645.C47	614.59836	Cerebral palsy
			RA645.D5	614.59462	Diabetes

LC	Dewey	Subject Heading	LC	Dewey	Subject Heading
RA645.M82	614.59834	Multiple sclerosis	RA785	613.792	Relaxation
RA645.N87	614.5939	Nutrition disorders	RA785	613.79	Rest
RA645.N87	614.5939	Nutritionally induced diseases	RA786-.3	613.794	Sleep
			RA788	613.95	Hygiene, Sexual
RA645.N87	614.5939	Malnutrition	RA790-.95	362.2	Mental health services
RA648.5-654	614.4	Epidemics	RA790-.95	362.2	Mental health
RA648.5-653.5	614.4	Epidemiology	RA790.55	362.22	Community psychology
RA650-.9	614.42(4-9)	Epidemics—[By region or country]	RA791-954	616.988	Medical climatology
			RA791-954	614.42	Medical geography
RA650-.55	614.42(7-8)	Epidemics—America	RA793-954	613.287	Mineral waters
RA650.6	614.424	Epidemics—Europe	RA794-954	613.122	Health resorts
RA650.7	614.425	Epidemics—Asia	RA801-954	614.42(4-9)	Medical geography—[By region or country]
RA650.8	614.426	Epidemics—Africa			
RA650.9.A8	614.4294	Epidemics—Australia	RA804-807	614.4273	Medical geography—United States
RA652.2.P82	614.42	Public health surveillance			
RA655-758	614.46	Quarantine	RA809-810	614.4271	Medical geography—Canada
RA664-758	614.4609(4-9)	Quarantine—[By region or country]	RA811-812	614.4272	Medical geography—Mexico
RA664-677	614.46097	Quarantine—North America	RA813-814	614.42728	Medical geography—Central America
RA665-667	614.460973	Quarantine—United States	RA815-816	614.42729	Medical geography—West Indies
RA671	614.460971	Quarantine—Canada	RA817-844	614.428	Medical geography—South America
RA673	614.460972	Quarantine—Mexico			
RA675	614.4609728	Quarantine—Central America	RA845-887	614.424	Medical geography—Europe
RA677	614.4609729	Quarantine—West Indies	RA891-934	614.425	Medical geography—Asia
RA678-699	614.46098	Quarantine—South America	RA943-949	614.426	Medical geography—Africa
			RA951-952	614.4294	Medical geography—Australia
RA700-737	614.46094	Quarantine—Europe			
RA738-751	614.46095	Quarantine—Asia	RA952.5	614.4293	Medical geography—New Zealand
RA753-755	614.46096	Quarantine—Africa			
RA756	614.460994	Quarantine—Australia	RA953-954	614.429(5-6)	Medical geography—Oceania
RA758	614.46099(5-6)	Quarantine—Oceania	RA960-996	362.11	Hospitals
RA761-767	614.48	Fumigation	RA960-996	362.11	Public hospitals
RA761-767	614.48	Disinfection and disinfectants	RA960-993	362.12	Dispensaries
			RA960-993	362.16	Sanatoriums
RA766.G6	614.48	Glycerin	RA964	362.110902	Hospitals, Medieval
RA766.H9	614.48	Hydrogen peroxide	RA964.5	362.11072	Hospitals—Research
RA766.R2	614.48	Radiation sterilization	RA966	362.12	Clinics
RA766.S8	614.48	Steam as a disinfectant	RA971-.8	362.11068	Hospitals—Administration
RA770.5	613	Hygiene	RA972	610.695	Interns (Medicine)
RA771-.7	613.091734	Rural health	RA972	610.695	Residents (Medicine)
RA772.T7	363.125	Traffic accidents	RA974-.5	362.12	Hospitals—Outpatient services
RA773-790	613	Health			
RA776.75	612.68	Longevity	RA974-.5	362.12	Public hospitals—Outpatient services
RA780	613	Hygiene			
RA780	613.41	Baths	RA975	614.45	Isolation (Hospital care)
RA780.5	615.822	Massage	RA975.D57	362.11	Disaster hospitals
RA781-.85	613.71	Exercise	RA975.5.C6	362.1961204	Coronary care units
RA781.15	613.71	Aerobic exercises	RA975.5.E5	362.18	Hospitals—Emergency service
RA781.15	613.71	Low impact aerobic exercises			
RA781.17	613.71	Aquatic exercises	RA975.5.I56	362.174	Intensive care units
RA781.5	613.78	Posture	RA975.5.T83	362.18	Trauma centers
RA782	613.192	Breathing exercises	RA975.R87	362.11091734	Rural hospitals
RA783.5	613.68	Travel—Health aspects	RA980-993	362.1109(4-9)	Hospitals—[By region or country]
RA784	613.2	Diet			
RA784	613.2	Nutrition			

LC	Dewey	Subject Heading	LC	Dewey	Subject Heading
RA981-982	362.110973	Hospitals—United States	RA1231.R2	616.9897	Radioactive substances—Toxicology
RA983	362.110971	Hospitals—Canada			
RA985-989	362.11094	Hospitals—Europe	RA1242.S48	615.954	Seafood poisoning
RA986-988	362.110941	Hospitals—Great Britain	RA1242.S53	615.942	Poisonous snakes—Venom
RA990	362.11095	Hospitals—Asia			
RA990.5	362.1109174927	Hospitals—Arab countries	RA1245-1247	615.91	Gases, Asphyxiating and poisonous
RA991	362.11096	Hospitals—Africa			
RA992-.3	362.110994	Hospitals—Australia	RA1247.C17	615.91	Carbon monoxide
RA992.5-.7	362.110993	Hospitals—New Zealand	RA1247.M8	615.91	Mustard gas
RA993	362.11099(5-6)	Hospitals—Oceania	RA1258-1260	615.954	Food—Toxicology
RA995-996	362.188	Ambulance service			
RA996.5	362.188	Airplane ambulances	RB	616.07	Pathology
RA997-999	362.16	Long-term care facilities	RB1	616.0705	Pathology—Periodicals
RA997-999	362.16	Nursing homes	RB3	616.0706	Pathology—Congresses
RA997-998	362.16092	Volunteer workers in long-term care facilities	RB15-.2	616.0709	Pathology—History
			RB37-56.5	616.075	Diagnosis, Laboratory
RA1001-1171	614.1	Medical jurisprudence	RB43-.6	616.0758	Medical microscopy
RA1018.5-.56	614.1021	Medical jurisprudence—Statistics	RB45-15	616.07561	Blood—Analysis
			RB46.7	616.0758	Electron microscopic immunocytochemistry
RA1021-1022	614.109	Medical jurisprudence—History			
			RB48.5	616.047	Endocrine manifestations of general diseases
RA1027-.5	614.107	Medical jurisprudence—Study and teaching			
			RB52	616.0756	Body fluids—Analysis
RA1055.5	616.075	Disability evaluations	RB57	616.0759	Autopsy
RA1056.5	344.0411	Medical personnel—Malpractice	RB112.5	616.0756	Clinical biochemistry
			RB113	571.9	Physiology, Pathological
RA1057	614.12	Chemistry, Forensic	RB123-124	616.07071	Pathology—Study and teaching
RA1062	614.18	Dental jurisprudence			
RA1063-.5	616.078	Death	RB127	616.0472	Pain
RA1063	616.078	Death—Causes	RB128	616.8491	Headache
RA1063	616.078	Death, Apparent	RB128	616.84914	Tension headache
RA1063.3	616.078	Brain death	RB129	616.047	Fever
RA1063.4	614.1	Forensic pathology	RB131-.5	571.9379	Suppuration
RA1063.4	614.1	Autopsy	RB138	572.516	Calcification
RA1067	342.084	Abortion	RB140-.5	616.47	Growth disorders
RA1071-1082	617.18	Asphyxia	RB144-.5	616.1	Blood circulation disorders
RA1076	617.18	Drowning	RB144-.5	616.047	Edema
RA1085	617.11	Fires—Casualties	RB144-.5	616.157	Hemorrhage
RA1091	617.12	Electrical injuries	RB145	616.15027	Hematology, Experimental
RA1116	616.39	Starvation	RB147	616.3992	Acidosis
RA1121	617.1	Wounds and injuries	RB147	616.39	Metabolism—Disorders
RA1136-1137	616.858445	Suicide	RB150.A65	616.85262	Anorexia
RA1146	616.8582	Self-mutilation	RB150.A87	616.238	Asthma
RA1148	614.15	Psychology, Forensic	RB150.C6	616.849	Coma
RA1151-1152	614.15	Forensic psychiatry	RB150.F37	616.0478	Chronic fatigue syndrome
RA1190-1270	615.9	Poisons	RB150.S5	616.047	Shock
RA1190-1270	615.9	Toxicology	RB152	616.98	Environmentally induced diseases
RA1190-1270	615.9	Poisoning			
RA1198-.3	615.90071	Toxicology—Study and teaching	RB153-154	616.9	Infection
			RB155-.8	616.042	Medical genetics
RA1199-.5	615.90072	Toxicology—Research	RB155.5-.8	616.042	Human chromosome abnormalities
RA1199-.5	615.907	Toxicity testing			
RA1199.4.A38	615.907	Acute toxicity testing	RB155.5-.8	616.042	Genetic disorders
RA1221-1223	615.907	Analytical toxicology	RB155.8	616.042	Gene therapy
RA1224.5	615.908	Toxicological emergencies	RB156	616.044	Chronic diseases
RA1225	615.90083	Poisoning, Accidental, in children	RB170	541.224	Free radicals (Chemicals)
RA1226	615.902	Environmental toxicology	RC	616	Internal medicine
RA1229-.5	615.902	Industrial toxicology	RC31-80	616	Clinical medicine

LC	Dewey	Subject Heading	LC	Dewey	Subject Heading
RC41	616.003	Internal medicine—Dictionaries	RC121.A6	616.956	Anthrax
			RC124	616.82	Meningitis
RC48.6	618	Women—Diseases	RC125	616.914	Chickenpox
RC49-52	616.08	Medicine, Psychosomatic	RC126-134	616.932	Cholera
RC65	616.0751	Medical history taking	RC137	616.91852	Dengue
RC69	616.047	Symptomatology	RC138-.9	616.9313	Diphtheria
RC71-78.7	616.075	Diagnosis	RC140	616.935	Dysentery
RC71.5	616.075	Diagnosis, Differential	RC141.E6	614.832	Epidemic encephalitis
RC71.6	616.075	Diagnosis, Noninvasive	RC141.5	616.91	Epstein-Barr virus diseases
RC73-.2	616.0472	Pain			
RC73.2	615.892	Acupuncture points	RC142.5	616.9652	Elephantiasis
RC75	610.284	Medical thermometers	RC142.5	616.9652	Filariasis
RC75	616.0754	Body temperature	RC144.G3	616.047	Gas gangrene
RC76-.5	616.0754	Physical diagnosis	RC147.G6	616.91122	Mononucleosis
RC76.3	616.0754028	Stethoscopes	RC148	616.953	Rabies
RC77-.5	616.07547	Electrodiagnosis	RC150-.9	616.203	Influenza
RC78-.5	616.0757	Diagnosis, Radioscopic	RC150	616.203	Asian flu
RC78-.5	616.07572	Radiography, Medical	RC154-.9	616.998	Leprosy
RC78.7.D53	616.0754	Diagnostic imaging	RC156-166	616.936	Malaria
RC78.7.D86	616.07543	Duplex ultrasonography—Diagnostic use	RC168.M4	616.915	Measles
			RC168.M8	616.313	Mumps
RC78.7.E5	616.07545	Endoscopy	RC171-179	616.9232	Black death
RC78.7.F5	616.07572	Diagnosis, Fluoroscopic	RC171-179	616.9232	Plague
RC78.7.N83	616.07548	Magnetic resonance imaging	RC180-181	616.835	Poliomyelitis
			RC180.8	616.8350231	Poliomyelitis—Nursing
RC78.7.T6	616.0757	Tomography	RC182.R3	616.9244	Relapsing fever
RC78.7.U4	616.07543	Diagnosis, Ultrasonic	RC182.R4	616.991	Rheumatic fever
RC80	616.075	Prognosis	RC182.R8	616.916	Rubella
RC86-88.9	616.028	Critical care medicine	RC182.S12	616.927	Salmonellosis
RC86-88.9	616.025	Emergency medicine	RC182.S2	616.92987	Scarlatina
RC86-88.9	616.0252	First aid in illness and injury	RC183-.9	616.912	Smallpox
			RC184.T6	616.964	Echinococcosis
RC86-88.9	616.025	Medical emergencies	RC185	616.9318	Tetanus
RC87	615.025	Resuscitation	RC186.T82	616.9363	African trypanosomiasis
RC87	617.1	Wounds and injuries	RC187-197	616.9272	Typhoid fever
RC87.3	617.18	Asphyxia	RC199-.9	616.9222	Typhus fever
RC87.9	617.1806	Artificial respiration	RC200-203	616.951	Sexually transmitted diseases
RC87.9	616.1025	CPR (First aid)			
RC88.9.095	616.98	Outdoor medical emergencies	RC201-.9	616.9513	Syphilis
			RC203.H45	616.9518	Herpes genitalis
RC88.9.T47	613.6	Bioterrorism	RC204	616.204	Whooping cough
RC90	615.5	Iatrogenic diseases	RC206-216	616.91854	Yellow fever
RC103.A4	616.9893	Mountain sickness	RC226-248	616.96	Blood—Parasites
RC103.C3	616.9894	Decompression sickness	RC254-282	616.994	Tumors
RC103.M6	616.9892	Motion sickness	RC254-282	616.994	Oncology
RC106	616.9	Exanthemata	RC261-282	616.994	Cancer
RC108	616.044	Chronic diseases	RC266	616.9940231	Cancer—Nursing
RC109-216	616.9(01-6)	Communicable diseases	RC267	616.9940072	Cancer—Research
RC113.5	616.959	Zoonoses	RC268-.15	616.99405	Cancer—Prevention
RC114-.7	616.91	Virus diseases	RC268.4-.44	616.994042	Cancer—Genetic aspects
RC114.6	616.91	Slow virus diseases	RC268.48	616.994071	Cancer—Etiology
RC115-116	616.92	Bacterial diseases	RC268.5-.7	616.994071	Carcinogenesis
RC116.M8	616.92	Mycobacterial diseases	RC268.55	616.994	Radiation carcinogenesis
RC116.S8	616.92	Staphylococcal infections	RC268.57	616.994071	Viral carcinogenesis
RC117	616.969	Mycoses	RC268.6-.7	616.994071	Carcinogens
RC118.7	616.936	Protozoan diseases	RC270.8-271	616.99406	Cancer—Treatment
RC119-.7	616.96	Parasitic diseases	RC271.C5	616.99406	Antineoplastic agents
RC119.5	616.968	Ectoparasitic infestations	RC271.D68	616.994061	Doxorubicin
RC121.A5	616.936	Amebiasis	RC271.H55	616.99406	Cancer—Hormone therapy

LC	Dewey	Subject Heading	LC	Dewey	Subject Heading
RC271.I45	616.99406	Cancer—Immunotherapy	RC406.P3	617.58	Paraplegics
RC271.P54	616.99406	Plasma exchange (Therapeutics)	RC416	616.856	Neuritis
			RC420	616.856	Sciatica
RC271.R3	616.9940642	Cancer—Radiotherapy	RC422.C26	616.856	Carpal tunnel syndrome
RC280.A2	616.99495	Abdomen—Tumors	RC422.C4	616.73	Cervical syndrome
RC280.A2	616.99495	Abdomen—Cancer	RC423-428.8	616.855	Speech disorders
RC280.B6	616.9947	Osteosarcoma	RC423-428.8	616.85506	Speech therapy
RC280.B7	616.99481	Brain—Cancer	RC423-428.8	616.855	Communicative disorders
RC280.C6	616.994347	Colon—Cancer	RC423-428.5	616.855	Language disorders
RC280.D5	616.99434	Digestive organs—Cancer	RC424	616.8554	Stuttering
RC280.E2	616.99485	Ear—Tumors	RC424.7	616.855	Articulation disorders
RC280.E8	616.99432	Esophagus—Cancer	RC425-.7	616.8552	Aphasia
RC280.E8	616.99432	Esophagus—Tumors	RC425.5	616.8552	Agrammatism
RC280.H47	616.99419	Hematological oncology	RC435-571	616.89	Psychology, Pathological
RC280.L8	616.99424	Lungs—Cancer	RC439.2	616.891	Psychiatric day treatment
RC280.M37	616.99477	Melanoma	RC439.4	362.21	Violence in psychiatric hospitals
RC280.M6	616.99431	Mouth—Cancer	RC440	616.890231	Psychiatric nursing
RC280.N4	616.9948	Neuroblastoma	RC440.5	616.890092	Psychiatric aides
RC280.S5	616.99477	Basal cell carcinoma	RC440.7	616.89	Mental health care teams
RC280.S5	616.99477	Skin—Cancer	RC451.4.A5	362.20846	Aged—Mental health services
RC306-320.5	616.995	Tuberculosis	RC451.4.A5	618.9789	Geriatric psychiatry
RC309-.5	362.196995	Tuberculosis—Hospitals	RC451.5.N4	616.89008996 + 073	Afro-Americans—Mental health
RC311.2	616.995075	Tuberculin test			
RC311.3.C45	616.995061	Tuberculosis—Chemotherapy	RC455	362.22	Community psychiatry
RC311.D5	616.9950654	Tuberculosis—Diet therapy	RC455.2.A28	616.89140092	Psychotherapy patients—Abuse of
RC346-429	616.8(1-4)	Neurology	RC455.2.C4	616.89075	Mental illness—Classification
RC346-429	616.8(1-4)	Nervous system—Diseases			
RC348-349	616.804075	Neurologic examination	RC455.2.E8	616.8914	Psychotherapy—Moral and ethical aspects
RC350.N48	616.806	Neural stimulation			
RC350.N49	616.8028	Neurological intensive care	RC455.2.E8	174.2	Psychotherapists—Professional ethics
RC350.5	616.804231	Neurological nursing	RC455.2.E8	174.2	Psychiatric ethics
RC372-374.5	616.853	Epilepsy	RC455.2.M4	616.89001	Psychiatry—Methodology
RC374.5	616.853	Petit mal epilepsy	RC455.2.R43	362.172	Psychiatric referral
RC376	616.82	Meningitis	RC455.4.C6	616.89	Psychiatry, Comparative
RC377	616.834	Multiple sclerosis	RC455.4.L67	155.93	Loss (Psychology)
RC382	616.833	Parkinsonism	RC455.4.S67	302.14	Social adjustment
RC382	616.833	Parkinsonism, Symptomatic	RC455.4.S87	155.24	Adjustment disorders
RC386-395	616.8(1-4)	Brain—Diseases	RC466-.3	158.3	Mental health counseling
RC386.6.A45	616.8047547	Ambulatory electroencephalography	RC466.8-467.95	616.89	Clinical psychology
			RC469-473	616.89075	Psychodiagnostics
RC386.6.E43	616.8047547	Electroencephalography	RC469	616.89075	Mental illness—Diagnosis
RC386.6.U45	616.8047543	Ultrasonic encephalography	RC473.D43	155.2	Defense Mechanisms Inventory
RC388	616.836	Cerebral palsied	RC473.E36	154.2	Ego Function Assessment
RC388.5	616.81	Cerebrovascular disease	RC473.G7	155.282	Graphology
RC390	616.832	Chronic encephalitis	RC473.M5	616.89075	Minnesota Multiphasic Personality Inventory
RC391	616.858843	Hydrocephalus			
RC392	616.84913	Cluster headache	RC473.P7	616.890028	Projective techniques
RC392	616.8491	Headache	RC473.R6	616.89075	Rorschach Test
RC394.A5	616.85232	Amnesia	RC475-489	616.8914	Psychotherapy
RC394.C77	616.845	Convulsions	RC480.52	616.891	Psychiatry—Differential therapeutics
RC394.D35	616.8	Brain—Degeneration			
RC394.I5	616.81	Cerebral infarction	RC480.55	616.8914	Single-session psychotherapy
RC394.M46	616.83	Memory disorders			
RC394.W6	616.8553	Dyslexia	RC480.55	616.8914	Brief psychotherapy
RC400-406	616.856	Spinal cord—Diseases			

LC	Dewey	Subject Heading	LC	Dewey	Subject Heading
RC480.6	616.89025	Psychiatric emergencies	RC524	616.83	Senile dementia
RC480.6	362.2881	Psychiatric hospitals—Emergency service	RC525-527	616.861	Alcoholic psychoses
			RC526	616.861	Delirium tremens
			RC530-552	616.852	Neuroses
RC480.7	616.8910028	Interviewing in psychiatry	RC531	616.8522	Anxiety
RC481	616.8914	Client-centered psychotherapy	RC532	616.8524	Hysteria
			RC533	616.8584	Compulsive behavior
RC485	616.89122	Electroconvulsive therapy	RC533	616.85227	Obsessive-compulsive disorders
RC487	616.89165	Occupational therapy			
RC488-.6	616.89152	Group psychotherapy	RC535	616.85225	Phobias
RC488.5-.6	616.89156	Marital psychotherapy	RC535	616.85223	Panic disorders
RC488.5-.6	616.89156	Family psychotherapy	RC537-545	616.8527	Affective disorders
RC488.6	616.89156	Divorce therapy	RC537-545	616.8527	Depression, Mental
RC489.A7	616.891656	Art therapy	RC537.5	616.852700846	Depression in old age
RC489.A77	158.2	Assertiveness training	RC547-549	616.8498	Sleep disorders
RC489.B4	616.89142	Behavior therapy	RC548-.5	616.84982	Insomnia
RC489.B4	616.89142	Aversion therapy	RC549	616.8498	Narcolepsy
RC489.B48	615.8516	Bibliotherapy	RC552.A43	616.85225	Acrophobia
RC489.C6	616.89142	Cognitive-analytic therapy	RC552.A44	616.85225	Agoraphobia
RC489.C63	616.89142	Cognitive therapy	RC552.A5	616.85262	Anorexia nervosa
RC489.C68	616.8914	Countertransference (Psychology)	RC552.B84	616.85263	Bulimia
			RC552.C65	616.8526	Compulsive eating
RC489.D3	616.891655	Dance therapy	RC552.E18	616.8526	Eating disorders
RC489.D45	616.8914	Desensitization (Psychotherapy)	RC552.N5	616.8528	Neurasthenia
			RC552.O3	616.8521	Occupational neuroses
RC489.E24	616.8914	Eclectic psychotherapy	RC552.P67	616.8521	Post-traumatic stress disorder
RC489.E93	616.8914	Existential psychotherapy			
RC489.F27	616.8914	Psychotherapy—Failure	RC552.S4	616.8582	Self-mutilation
RC489.I45	616.8914	Impasse (Psychotherapy)	RC552.S66	616.8524	Somatization disorder
RC489.M85	616.8914	Multiple psychotherapy	RC553.A88	616.85882	Autism
RC489.N3	616.8918	Narcotherapy	RC553.D5	616.8523	Dissociative disorders
RC489.O24	616.8917	Object constancy (Psychoanalysis)	RC553.H3	616.8634	Hallucinations and illusions
RC489.O25	616.8917	Object relations (Psychoanalysis)	RC553.M36	616.85835	Masochism
			RC553.N36	616.85854	Narcissism
RC489.P68	616.8914	Problem-solving therapy	RC554-569.5	616.858	Personality disorders
RC489.P7	616.891523	Psychodrama	RC555	616.858	Antisocial personality disorders
RC489.R4	616.891653	Recreational therapy			
RC489.S86	616.8914	Supportive psychotherapy	RC556-560	616.8583	Psychosexual disorders
RC489.T45	616.8914	Psychotherapy—Termination	RC558-.5	616.8583	Homosexuality
			RC558.5	616.8583	Lesbianism
RC489.T7	616.89145	Transactional analysis	RC560.A97	616.8583	Autoerotic asphyxia
RC489.T73	154.2	Transference (Psychology)	RC560.C46	616.85836	Child sexual abuse
RC490-499	616.89162	Therapeutics, Suggestive	RC560.I45	616.85832	Impotence
RC490-499	154.7	Hypnotism	RC560.I53	618.9285836	Incest victims
RC499.D7	154.63	Dreams	nORC560.I53	616.85836	Incest
RC499.S92	153.736	Subliminal perception	RC560.R36	616.8521	Rape trauma syndrome
RC500-510	616.8917	Psychoanalysis	RC560.R36	362.883	Rape victims
RC550	616.85212	Combat—Psychological aspects	RC560.S23	616.85835	Sadomasochism
			RC560.S43	616.8583	Sex addition
RC550	616.8521	War neuroses	RC560.S45	616.8583	Sexual aversion disorders
RC510	616.8917	Group psychoanalysis	RC560.V68	616.8583	Voyeurism
RC512-528	616.89	Psychoses	RC563-568	616.86	Substance abuse
RC514	616.898	Schizophrenia	RC564.7-565.9	616.861	Alcoholism
RC514	616.898	Paranoid schizophrenia	RC566	616.8632	Narcotic habit
RC516	616.895	Manic-depressive psychoses	RC567	616.865	Tobacco—Physiological effect
RC521-524	616.83	Dementia	RC567	616.865	Nicotine
RC523-.2	616.831	Alzheimer's disease	RC567	616.865	Smoking

LC	Dewey	Subject Heading	LC	Dewey	Subject Heading
RC567	616.865	Tobacco habit	RC636	616.15027	Hematology, Experimental
RC567.5	616.8526	Coffee habit	RC641-.7	616.152	Anemia
RC567.5	362.299	Caffeine habit	RC641.C6	614.432	Cockroaches as carriers of disease
RC568.C2	616.8635	Hashish			
RC568.C2	616.8635	Cannabis	RC641.7.F36	616.152	Fanconi's anemia
RC568.C6	616.8647	Cocaine habit	RC641.7.R44	616.152	Renal anemia
RC568.C6	616.8647	Crack (Drug)	RC642	616.1572	Hemophilia
RC568.O58	616.8632	Opioid habit	RC643	616.99419	Acute leukemia
RC568.O6	616.8632	Morphine habit	RC643	616.99419	Chronic lymphocytic leukemia
RC568.O6	616.8632	Opium habit			
RC569	616.858445	Suicide	RC643	616.99419	Leukemia
RC569	616.858445	Suicidal behavior	RC643	616.99419	Lymphocytic leukemia
RC569.5.A53	152.47	Anger	RC644	616.99446	Hodgkin's disease
RC569.5.B67	616.85852	Borderline personality disorder	RC647.B5	616.15	Blood platelet disorders
			RC647.C55	616.157	Blood coagulation disorders
RC569.5.C55	616.858223	Child abuse			
RC569.5.C63	616.8619	Codependency	RC647.D5	616.157	Disseminated intravascular coagulation
RC569.5.C68	154.2	Complexes (Psychology)			
RC569.5.D47	155.232	Dependency (Psychology)	RC648-665	616.4	Endocrine glands—Diseases
RC569.5.E5	616.849	Enuresis			
RC569.5.F3	616.85822	Family violence	RC648-665	616.4	Endocrinology
RC569.5.F3	616.85822	Wife abuse	RC655-657	616.44	Thyroid gland—Diseases
RC569.5.G35	616.85841	Compulsive gambling	RC656-.3	616.442	Goiter
RC569.5.I46	616.8584	Impulsive personality	RC657	616.858848043	Cretinism
RC569.5.M8	616.85236	Multiple personality	RC657	616.444	Hypothyroidism
RC569.5.P75	616.858223	Psychological child abuse	RC657.5.G7	616.443	Graves' disease
RC569.5.P9	616.85843	Pyromania	RC658-.7	616.47	Pituitary gland—Diseases
RC569.5.S45	616.8582	Self-destructive behavior	RC658.3	616.47	Acromegaly
RC569.5.S48	616.8582	Self-injurious behavior	RC658.5	616.462	Diabetes
RC569.5.V55	616.8582	Violence	RC659	616.45	Adrenal glands—Diseases
RC569.7-571	616.8588	Mental retardation	RC659	616.45	Addison's disease
RC571	616.858842	Down's syndrome	RC660-662.18	616.462	Non-insulin-dependent diabetes
RC583-598	616.97	Allergy			
RC588.C45	616.97	Antiallergic agents	RC660-662.4	616.462	Diabetes
RC588.D53	616.9750654	Food allergy—Diet therapy	RC660.7	362.12	Diabetes clinics
RC589-596	616.202	Respiratory allergy	RC666-701	616.1	Cardiovascular system—Diseases
RC590	616.202	Hay fever			
RC591	616.238	Asthma	RC666.7-.72	616.10092	Cardiologists
RC596	616.975	Food allergy	RC670-.5	616.1075	Cardiovascular system—Diagnosis
RC598.D7	616.9758	Drug allergy			
RC600	616.978	Autoimmune diseases	RC674	616.10231	Cardiovascular system—Diseases—Nursing
RC606-607	616.979	Immunological deficiency syndromes			
			RC681-688	616.12	Heart—Diseases
RC607.A26	616.9792	AIDS (Disease)	RC683.5.A43	616.132075	Ambulatory blood pressure monitoring
RC620-627	616.39	Nutrition disorders			
RC622	616.39	Nutritionally induced diseases	RC683.5.A45	616.1207547	Ambulatory electrocardiography
			RC683.5.A5	616.1207572	Angiocardiography
RC623	616.39	Malnutrition	RC683.5.B63	616.12075	Body surface mapping
RC623.5-627	616.39	Deficiency diseases	RC683.5.E5	616.1207547	Electrocardiography
RC623.7	616.39	Avitaminosis	RC683.5.E94	616.12075	Treadmill exercise tests
RC627.5-632	616.39	Metabolism—Disorders	RC683.5.U5	616.1207543	Doppler echocardiography
RC627.8	616.39043	Metabolism, Inborn errors of	RC683.5.U5	616.1207543	Two-dimensional echocardiography
RC628-.5	616.398	Obesity	RC683.5.U5	616.1207543	Echocardiography
RC629-.5	616.3999	Gout	RC634	616.1206	Adrenergic alpha blockers
RC630	616.3992	Water-electrolyte imbalances	RC684.A35	616.1206	Adrenergic beta blockers
			RC684.C36	616.12028	Cardiac intensive care
RC632.L33	616.3998	Lactose intolerance	RC684.E4	616.120645	Electric countershock
RC633-647.5	616.15	Blood—Diseases			

LC	Dewey	Subject Heading	LC	Dewey	Subject Heading
RC684.P3	617.4120645	Cardiac pacing	RC776.F33	616.24	Farmer's lung
RC684.P3	617.4120645	Pacemaker, Artificial (Heart)	RC776.03	616.24	Respiratory organs—Obstructions
RC684.P3	617.4120645	Cardiac pacemakers	RC776.P85	616.249	Pulmonary embolism
RC685.A6	616.122	Angina pectoris	RC778	616.234	Bronchitis
RC685.A65	616.128	Arrhythmia	RC778	616.23	Bronchi—Diseases
RC685.A65	616.128	Palpitation	RC799-869	616.3	Digestive organs—Diseases
RC685.C173	616.123025	Cardiac arrest			
RC685.C18	616.12	Cardiogenic shock	RC799-869	616.33	Gastrointestinal system
RC685.C6	616.123	Coronary heart disease	RC804.A5	616.307572	Digestive organs—Radiography
RC685.E5	616.11	Endocarditis			
RC685.H8	616.132	Hypertension	RC804.G3	616.3307545	Gastroscopy
RC685.H8	616.132	Essential hypertension	RC804.D79	616.3407545	Duodenoscopy
RC685.H93	616.13	Hypotension	RC804.R6	616.3407572	Duodenum—Radiography
RC685.I6	616.1237	Myocardial infarction	RC811	616.31	Gastrointestinal system—Motility—Disorders
RC685.M9	616.124	Myocardium—Diseases			
RC685.M92	616.124	Myocarditis	RC815-.6	616.31	Mouth—Diseases
RC685.P5	616.11	Pericardium	RC815-.6	616.31	Oral medicine
RC685.V2	616.125	Heart valves—Diseases	RC815.2	616.332	Indigestion disorders
RC685.V2	616.125	Mitral valve insufficiency	RC815.2	616.32	Deglutition disorders
RC685.V43	616.128	Ventricular fibrillation	RC815.7	616.32	Esophagus—Diseases
RC687	616.12043	Congenital heart disease	RC815.7	616.32	Esophageal varices
RC691-701	616.13	Blood-vessels—Diseases	RC815.7	616.32043	Esophagus—Abnormalities
RC691-697	616.13	Arteries—Diseases	RC816-840	616.33	Stomache—Diseases
RC691	616.138	Aorta—Diseases	RC821	616.343	Peptic ulcer
RC691	616.135	Embolism	RC827	616.332	Indigestion
RC691.5-.6	616.13075	Blood-vessels—Diseases—Diagnosis	RC831	616.333	Gastritis
			RC840.G3	616.33	Gastroenteritis
RC691.6.A53	616.1307572	Angiography	RC845-848	616.362	Liver—Diseases
RC691.6.D87	616.1307543	Duplex ultrasonography—Diagnostic use	RC847-.5	616.362075	Liver function tests
			RC848.A42	616.3624	Alcoholic liver diseases
RC693	616.133	Aneurysms	RC848.C4	616.3623	Chronic active hepatitis
RC693	616.138	Aortic aneurysms	RC848.H42	616.3623	Hepatitis
RC693	617.413059	Dissecting aortic aneurysms	RC849-853	616.365	Gallbladder—Diseases
			RC851	616.3625	Jaundice
RC694	616.131	Peripheral vascular diseases	RC857-858	616.37	Pancreas—Diseases
			RC858.C95	616.37	Cystic fibrosis
RC694.5.I53	616.13	Arteritis	RC860-862	616.34	Colon—Diseases
RC694.5.I53	616.131	Vasculitis	RC861	616.3428	Constipation
RC695-697	616.143	Varicose veins	RC862.C6	616.3447	Colitis
RC695-697	616.14	Veins—Diseases	RC862.D5	616.3427	Diarrhea
RC696	616.142	Phlebitis	RC862.E5	616.344	Enteritis
RC701	616.1043	Cardiovascular system—Abnormalities	RC862.M3	616.399	Malabsorption syndromes
			RC864-866	616.35	Proctology
RC705-779	616.2	Respiratory organs—Diseases	RC865	616.352	Hemorrhoids
			RC866.D43	616.342	Fecal incontinence
RC734.P84	616.2075	Pulmonary function tests	RC866.D43	616.342	Defecation disorders
RC735.5	616.20231	Respiratory organs—Diseases—Nursing	RC867.5	618.7	Peritonitis
			RC870-923	616.6	Urology
RC735.H54	616.206	High-frequency ventilation (Therapy)	RC875-899.5	616.65	Andrology
			RC881.5-883.5	616.65043	Generative organs—Abnormalities
RC735.I5	615.836	Respiratory therapy			
RC737-.5	616.209	Apnea	RC883	616.694	Hermaphroditism
RC740	616.2	Respiratory infections	RC884	616.693	Climacteric, Male
RC746	616.201	Croup	RC889	616.6921	Infertility, Male
RC751	616.25	Pleurisy	RC889	616.692	Infertility
RC756-776	616.24	Lungs-Diseases	RC889	616.6922	Impotence
RC771-772	616.241	Pneumonia	RC892	616.62	Urethra—Diseases
RC776.E5	616.248	Emphysema, Pulmonary	RC896	616.66	Penis—Diseases

220

LC	Dewey	Subject Heading	LC	Dewey	Subject Heading
RC897	616.67	Scrotum—Diseases	RC981-986	616.98024	Medicine, Naval
RC899	616.65	Prostate—Diseases	RC1000-1020	616.98022	Submarine medicine
RC900-923	616.6	Urinary organs—Diseases	RC1030-1035	616.9802	Transportation medicine
RC901	616.6075	Urinary organs—Examination	RC1040-1045	613.69	Traffic accidents
RC901.75	616.6	Urination disorders	RC1050-1097	616.980213	Aviation medicine
RC901.8	616.6	Urinary tract infections	RC1076.J48	616.980213	Jet lag
RC902-918	616.61	Kidneys—Diseases	RC1120-1160	616.980214	Space medicine
RC902	616.61	Nephrology	RC1150-1151	612.0145	Space flight—Physiological effect
RC904-.5	616.61075	Kidneys—Diseases—Diagnosis	RC1151.B54	612	Biological rhythms—Effect of space flight on
RC907	616.612	Bright's disease	RC1200-1245	617.1027	Sports medicine
RC915	616.635	Uremia			
RC916	616.622	Urinary organs—Calculi	RD	617	Surgery
RC918.R38	616.132	Renal hypertension	RD33.5	617.05	Electrolysis in surgery
RC918.R4	616.614	Chronic renal failure	RD33.53	617.057	Endoscopic surgery
RC919-921	616.62	Bladder—Diseases	RD52.F59	615.854	Electrolyte therapy
RC924-.5	616.77	Connective tissues—Diseases	RD78.3-87.3	615.781	Anesthesia
RC925-935	616.7	Muscles—Diseases	RD78.3-87.3	615.781	Anesthetics
RC927-.5	616.723	Rheumatism	RD79-86	617.96	Ether (Anesthetic)
RC927.3	616.723	Fibromyalgia	RD86.C5	615.781	Chloroform
RC927.5.N65	616.723	Nonarticular rheumatism	RD96.15	617.1	Blunt trauma
RC930-931	616.71	Bones—Diseases	RD96.3	617.145	Gunshot wounds
RC931.F5	616.71	Fibrous dysplasia of bone	RD96.4-.55	617.11	Burn care teams
RC931.064	616.712	Osteitis	RD96.4-.55	617.11	Burns and scalds
RC931.067	616.7223	Osteoarthritis	RD96.45	617.11	Chemical burns
RC931.073	616.716	Osteoporosis	RD96.5	617.12	Electrical burns
RC933	616.722	Arthritis	RD98-.4	617.919	Surgery—Complications
RC933	616.7227	Rheumatoid arthritis	RD98.3	617.919	Surgical wound infections
RC935.A8	616.74	Muscular atrophy	RD98.4	617.919	Postoperative pain
RC935.B8	616.76	Bursitis	RD99-.35	617.0231	Surgical nursing
RC935.T4	616.76	Tendinitis	RD101-104	617.15	Fractures
RC936	617.51	Head—Diseases	RD101	617.15	Fractures, Spontaneous
RC941	617.54	Chest pain	RD103.B65	617.471	Bone wiring (Orthopedics)
RC941	617.54	Chest—Diseases	RD103.E88	617.471059	External skeletal fixation (Surgery)
RC944	617.55	Abdomen—Diseases	RD104.A95	617.15	Avulsion fractures
RC946	617.55	Pelvis—Diseases	RD104.S77	617.15	Stress fractures (Orthopedics)
RC951	617.585	Foot—Diseases			
RC951	617.58	Extremities (Anatomy)—Diseases	RD106	617.16	Dislocations
			RD110-.5	617.024	Ambulatory surgery
RC952-954.6	618.97	Aged—Diseases	RD111-114	617.024	Surgery, Minor
RC952-954.6	618.97	Geriatrics	RD113-.4	617.93	Bandages and bandaging
RC953.7	615.10846	Geriatric pharmacology	RD113-.4	617.93	Surgical dressings
RC953.8.E93	615.820846	Exercise therapy for the aged	RD118-120.5	617.952	Surgery, Plastic
			RD119.5.F33	617.520592	Facelift
RC954	618.970231	Geriatric nursing	RD120.6-129.8	617.954	Transplantation of organs, tissues, etc.
RC955-958	616.9881	Circumpolar medicine			
RC960-962	616.9883	Tropical medicine	RD121	617.4770592	Skin-grafting
RC963-969	616.9803	Work environment	RD123	617.4710592	Bone-grafting
RC963-969	616.9803	Medicine, Industrial	RD123.5	617.4410592	Bone marrow—Transplantation
RC963	613.62092	Industrial hygienists	RD127-128.5	362.1783	Tissue banks
RC963.4	616.075	Disability evaluations	RD128	362.1783	Musculoskeletal banks
RC965.P46	616.0088791	Entertainers—Diseases	RD129.5	362.1783	Donation of organs, tissues, etc.
RC967	613.62	Industrial hygiene			
RC967.5	158.7	Industrial psychiatry	RD129.5	362.1783092	Organ donors
RC968-969	613.62	Occupational health services	RD130	617.9	Prosthesis
RC970-971	616.98023	Medicine, Military	RD137-139	617.98	Children—Surgery

LC	Dewey	Subject Heading	LC	Dewey	Subject Heading
RD137	616.244	Respiratory organs—Foreign bodies	RD551-563	617.58059	Extremities (Anatomy)—Surgery
RD139	617.960083	Pediatric anesthesia	RD551-563	617.580592	Extremities (Anatomy)—Transplantation
RD145	617.97	Aged—Surgery	RD551-563	617.58044	Extremities (Anatomy)—Wounds and injuries
RD145	617.9600846	Geriatric anesthesia			
RD151-498	617.99	Surgery, Military	RD553	617.58059	Amputation
RD151-498	617.99	Surgery, Naval	RD553	617.58	Phantom limb
RD153	616.047	Gangrene	RD557.5	617.16	Shoulder joint—Dislocation
RD156	617.044	War wounds			
RD200-214	617.990973	Surgery, Military—United States	RD557	617.574059	Arm—Amputation
RD216	617.990971	Surgery, Military—Canada	RD558	617.157	Elbow—Fractures
RD221	617.990972	Surgery, Military—Mexico	RD561	617.5820592	Artificial knee
RD224-225	617.9909728	Surgery, Military—Central America	RD561	617.5820592	Total knee replacement
			RD562	617.584059	Excision of ankle
RD231-232	617.9909729	Surgery, Military—West Indies	RD563	617.5850592	Foot—Amputation
			RD563	617.5850592	Foot—Reimplantation
RD235-267	617.99098	Surgery, Military—South America	RD563	617.585075	Foot—Examination
			RD563	617.585044	Foot—Wounds and injuries
RD268-441	617.99094	Surgery, Military—Europe			
RD445-476	617.99095	Surgery, Military—Asia	RD563	617.585059	Foot—Surgery
RD481-489	617.99096	Surgery, Military—Africa	RD563	616.547	Nails, Ingrowing
RD493	617.990994	Surgery, Military—Australia	RD563	617.585	Podiatry
			RD572	617.463059	Castration
RD493.5	617.990993	Surgery, Military—New Zealand	RD580-581	617.462059	Bladder—Surgery
			RD585	618.145	Sterilization reversal
RD498	617.99099(5-6)	Surgery, Military—Oceania	RD585.5	617.463	Sterilization reversal
RD523-527	617.52059	Face—Surgery	RD585.5	617.463	Vasectomy
RD523	617.52044	Face—Wounds and injuries	RD590	617.463	Circumcision
			RD592.5-596	617.48059	Nervous system—Surgery
RD524	617.522	Cleft lip	RD592.5-596	617.48044	Nervous system—Wounds and injuries
RD529	617.155	Skull—Fractures			
RD529	617.514	Craniotomy	RD594-.15	617.481059	Brain—Surgery
RD533	617.482044	Spine—Wounds and injuries	RD594-.15	617.481044	Brain—Wounds and injuries
RD539.5	617.548044	Esophagus—Wounds and injuries	RD594-.15	617.481	Psychosurgery
			RD594.3	617.482059	Spinal cord—Surgery
RD539.5	617.548059	Esophagus—Surgery	RD596	610.7368	Neurological nursing
RD539.5	617.548	Esophagectomy	RD597-598.7	617.41	Cardiovascular system—Surgery
RD539.8	618.190592	Augmentation mammaplasty			
			RD598-.35	617.412	Heart—Surgery
RD539.8	618.19059	Mammaplasty	RD598.35.A78	617.4120592	Heart, Artificial
RD540-548	617.55	Acute abdomen	RD598.35.C35	617.412	Cardiac catheterization
RD540-548	617.55059	Abdomen—Surgery	RD598.35.C37	617.412	Cardiomyoplasty
RD540-548	617.55044	Abdomen—Wounds and injuries	RD598.35.C67	617.413	Coronary artery bypass
			RD598.35.T7	617.4120592	Heart—Transplantation
RD540-547	617.55059	Digestive organs—Surgery	RD598.5-.7	617.413	Blood-vessels—Surgery
RD540.5-.57	617.553059	Gastrectomy	RD598.5	617.413	Angioplasty
RD540.5-.57	617.553059	Stomache—Surgery	RD598.5	617.413	Arterial catheterization
RD540.5	617.553059	Gastrostomy	RD598.5	617.413	Dissecting aortic aneurysms
RD542	617.5545	Appendectomy			
RD546-547	617.5565	Gallbladder—Surgery	RD599.5.A37	617.44	Adrenalectomy
RD546-547	617.5567	Bile ducts—Surgery	RD599.5.P58	617.440592	Pituitary gland—Transplantation
RD549-.5	617.158	Pelvic bones—Fractures			
RD549	617.4720592	Artificial hip joints	RD621-626	617.559059	Hernia
RD549	617.4720592	Total hip replacement	RD628	616.047	Gangrene
RD551-563	617.158	Extremities (Anatomy)—Fractures	RD641	616.047	Abscess
			RD651-678	616.994059	Cancer—Surgery
			RD651-678	616.994	Tumors

LC	Dewey	Subject Heading	LC	Dewey	Subject Heading
RD663	616.9948	Nervous system—Tumors	RE26-30	617.709	Ophthalmology—History
RD663	616.99481	Brain—Tumors	RE31-36	617.70232	Ophthalmologists
RD667.5	616.99449059	Mastectomy	RE48	617.755	Eyestrain
RD680-688	617.47044	Musculoskeletal system—Wounds and injuries	RE48	617.7026	Ophthalmologic emergencies
RD684	617.471059	Bones—Surgery	RE48.2.C5	618.920977	Pediatric ophthalmology
RD688	616.74	Muscles—Diseases	RE51	617.75	Eyestrain
RD701-811	616.7	Orthopedics	RE56	617.70071	Ophthalmology—Study and teaching
RD701-789	617.47	Orthopedic surgery			
RD705-706	362.11	Orthopedic hospitals	RE73	617.700284	Ophthalmology—Instruments
RD705.5	362.110973	Orthopedic hospitals—United States	RE73	616.700284	Optical instruments
RD711	616.7005	Orthopedics—Periodicals	RE75-79	617.7075	Eye—Examination
RD725-726	616.709	Orthopedics—History	RE79.E39	617.707547	Electroculography
RD727-728	616.70232	Orthopedists	RE79.E4	617.707547	Electroretinography
RD733.2	617.300222	Orthopedics—Pictorial works	RE79.R3	617.707572	Eye—Radiography
RD734-.5	616.70754	Orthopedics—Diagnosis	RE80-87	617.7059	Eye—Surgery
RD736.M25	615.82	Manipulation (Therapeutics)	RE88	617.70231	Ophthalmic nursing
			RE89	362.1783	Eye banks
RD736.T7	617.9	Orthopedic traction	RE91-95	617.75	Vision disorders
RD750	616.7025	Orthopedic emergencies	RE91-95	617.712	Blindness
RD753	616.70231	Orthopedic nursing	RE91	617.712	Low vision
RD755-757	617.9	Orthopedic apparatus	RE95	617.712	Vision, Monocular
RD755.5-.7	617.470592	Orthopedic implants	RE96	617.74	Eye—Infections
RD756-.42	617.58	Artificial limbs	RE96	617.74	Eye—Inflammation
RD756	617.9	Crutches	RE121-155	617.771	Eyelids—Diseases
RD756.2-.22	617.574	Artificial arms	RE201-216	617.764	Lacrimal apparatus—Diseases
RD756.4-.42	617.58	Artificial legs			
RD757.S45	616.70284	Orthopedic shoes	RE310-326	617.773	Conjunctiva—Diseases
RD757.S5	617.9	Orthopedic slings	RE320	617.773	Acute hemorrhagic conjunctivitis
RD757.W4	617.9	Wheelchairs	RE321	617.773	Conjunctivitis
RD762	616.7	Posture disorders	RE328	617.719	Sclera—Diseases
RD763	616.71043	Skull—Abnormalities	RE336-340	617.719	Cornea—Diseases
RD768-771	616.73043	Spine—Abnormalities	RE336	617.7190592	Artificial corneas
RD771.B217	617.564	Backache	RE350-355	617.72	Uvea—Diseases
RD771.I58	616.73	Spine—Instability	RE401-461	617.742	Crystalline lens—Diseases
RD772	617.71043	Hip joint—Dislocation, Congenital	RE451	617.742	Cataract
RD775-789	616.71043	Extremities (Anatomy)—Abnormalities	RE501	617.746	Vitreous body—Diseases
			RE551-661	617.735	Retina—Diseases
RD778-.5	617.575059	Hand—Surgery	RE603	617.735	Retinal detachment
RD779-789	616.71043	Leg—Abnormalities	RE651	617.74	Thrombosis
RD781-789	617.585043	Foot—Abnormalities	RE661.D5	617.735	Diabetic retinopathy
RD781	617.585044	Foot—Dislocation	RE711	617.78	Eye-sockets—Diseases
RD786-789	617.585043	Toes—Abnormalities	RE725-780	617.732	Neuroophthalmology
RD925-927	616.74	Muscles—Diseases	RE731-780	617.762	Eye—Muscles
			RE731-780	617.762	Eye—Movement disorders
RE	617.7	Ophthalmology	RE738	617.762	Diplopia
RE1	617.7006	Ophthalmology—Societies, etc.	RE760	617.762	Eye—Paralysis
			RE831-840	617.713	Eye—Wounds and injuries
RE6	617.7005	Ophthalmology—Periodicals	RE835	617.74	Eye—Foreign bodies
			RE871	617.741	Glaucoma
RE11	617.7006	Ophthalmology—Congresses	RE906	617.7043	Eye—Abnormalities
			RE918-921	617.759075	Color vision—Testing
RE20	617.70014	Ophthalmology—Terminology	RE921	617.759	Color blindness
			RE925-939	617.755	Eye—Refractive errors
RE22	617.70025	Ophthalmologists—Directories	RE925-939	617.755	Eye—Accommodation and refraction
			RE932	617.755	Astigmatism

LC	Dewey	Subject Heading	LC	Dewey	Subject Heading
RE940-981	681.4092	Opticians	RF460-547	616.31	Throat—Diseases
RE940-981	617.75	Optometry	RF476	616.31075	Throat—Examination
RE940-981	617.7522	Eyeglasses	RF481-499	616.32	Tonsils—Diseases
RE961-962	617.7522	Ophthalmic lenses	RF481-499	616.32	Pharnyx—Diseases
RE977.C6	617.7523	Contact lenses	RF484.5	617.531059	Tonsillectomy
RE986-988	617.79	Eyes, Artificial	RF485	616.32	Pharyngitis
RE988	617.7524	Intraocular lenses	RF491	616.314	Tonsillitis
RE994	617.7061	Ophthalmic drugs	RF510-540	616.855	Voice disorders
RE994	617.7061	Ocular pharmacology	RF514-.5	616.2207545	Laryngoscopy
			RF516-517	617.533059	Larynx—Surgery
RF	617.51	Otolaryngology	RF517	617.533059	Tracheotomy
RF1	617.51006	Otolaryngology—Societies, etc.	RF526	616.22	Vocal cords—Diseases
			RF538	617.5330592	Artificial larynx
RF5-6	362.11	Hospitals, Ophthalmic and aural	RF545	616.32	Esophagus—Foreign bodies
RF6	362.1109(4-9)	Hospitals, Ophthalmic and aural—By region or country]	RF547	617.531044	Throat—Wounds and injuries
RF11	617.51005	Otolaryngology—Periodicals	RG	618.1	Gynecology
			RG	618.2	Obstetrics
RF16	617.51006	Otolaryngology—Congresses	RG1	618.1006	Gynecology—Societies, etc.
RF25-26	617.5109	Otolaryngology—History	RG12-16	362.11	Hospitals, Gynecologic and obstetric
RF28	617.510025	Otolaryngologists—Directories	RG26	618.1005	Gynecology—Periodicals
RF37-38	617.51092	Otolaryngologists	RG31	618.1006	Gynecology—Congresses
RF48-.5	617.51075	Otolaryngology—Diagnosis	RG32-33	618.10025	Gynecologists—Directories
RF48-.5	617.51075	Otolaryngologic examination	RG47	618.10014	Gynecology—Terminology
			RG51-67	618.1009	Gynecology—History
RF50	617.51044	Otolaryngology—Wounds and injuries	RG71-76	618.1092	Gynecologists
			RG77	618.07	Gynecologic pathology
RF51-52	617.51059	Otolaryngology, Operative	RG103.5	618.10019	Gynecology—Psychological aspects
RF52.5	617.80231	Otolaryngological nursing			
RF62	617.80071	Otolaryngology—Study and teaching	RG104-.7	618.145	Generative organs, Female—Surgery
RF110-320	617.8	Ear—Diseases	RG104.5	618.1059	Gynoplasty
RF110-320	617.8	Otology	RG105	618.10231	Gynecologic nursing
RF126-127	617.8059	Ear—Surgery	RG107-.5	618.1075	Gynecologic examination
RF210	617.85	Tympanic membrane—Diseases	RG107.5.E48	618.107543	Endoscopic ultrasonography
RF220-229	617.84	Middle ear—Diseases	RG107.5.L34	618.107545	Laparoscopy
RF230	617.86	Eustachian tube—Diseases	RG133	618.2	Conception
			RG133.5-135	618.178	Human reproductive technology
RF235	617.87	Mastoid process—Diseases	RG134	618.178	Artificial insemination, Human
RF260-275	617.882	Labyrinth (Ear)—Diseases			
RF286-320	617.8	Audiology	RG135	618.178059	Fertilization in vitro, Human
RF286-320	617.8	Deafness			
RF286-320	617.8	Hearing disorders	RG136-137.6	613.94	Contraception
RF286	617.8006	Audiology—Societies, etc.	RG136.5	613.9434	Natural family planning
RF293.5	617.8	Deafness, Noise induced	RG136.85	613.9432	Antifertility vaccines
RF294-.5	612.85	Audiometry	RG137-.6	613.9432	Contraceptives
RF298-310	617.800284	Audiology—Instruments	RG137.2	613.9435	Contraceptives, Vaginal
RF300-310	617.89	Hearing aids	RG137.2	613.9432	Spermicides
RF305	617.8820592	Cochlear implants	RG137.3	613.9435	Intrauterine contraceptives
RF341-437	616.21	Nose—Diseases	RG137.4-.6	613.9432	Contraceptive drugs
RF341	616.856	Smell disorders	RG137.5	613.94322	Oral contraceptives
RF345	616.21207545	Nasoscopy	RG138	618.12059	Sterilization of women
RF361	616.205	Cold (Disease)	RG138	618.12059	Sterilization reversal

LC	Dewey	Subject Heading	LC	Dewey	Subject Heading
RG155	618.20072	Obstetrics—Research	RG600-650	618.32	Perinatology
RG158	618.1025	Gynecologic emergencies	RG610-621	612.647	Fetus—Physiology
RG159-208	618.17	Endocrine gynecology	RG613	612.647	Fetus—Growth
RG161-186	618.172	Menstrual cycle	RG613.7	618.32	Fetus—Immunology
RG161-186	618.172	Menstruation disorders	RG615	618.326	Fetus—Metabolism
RG165	618.172	Premenstrual syndrome	RG618	618.3261	Perinatal cardiology
RG181	618.172	Dysmenorrhea	RG620	618.4	Fetus—Respiration and cry
RG186	618.175	Menopause			
RG201-205	618.178	Infertility, Female	RG626-629	618.32	Fetus—Diseases
RG261-266	618.16	Vulva—Diseases	RG626-629	618.32043	Fetus—Abnormalities
RG268-272	618.15	Vagina—Diseases	RG626-629	618.32043	Abnormalities, Human
RG301-391	618.14	Uterus—Diseases	RG627.6.D79	618.32	Fetus—Effect of drugs on
RG304-.5	618.1075	Uterus—Diseases—Diagnosis	RG627.6.M34	618.32	Fetal malnutrition
			RG628-.3	618.32075	Prenatal diagnosis
RG310-315	618.14	Cervix uteri—Diseases	RG628-.3	618.32075	Fetal monitoring
RG314	618.14	Cervix erosion	RG628.3.A48	618.3204275	Amniocentesis
RG316	618.1	Endometrium—Diseases	RG628.3.E34	618.326107543	Echocardiography
RG361	618.14	Uterus—Rupture	RG628.3.H42	618.3261075	Fetal heart rate monitoring
RG391	618.1453	Hysterectomy	RG628.3.U58	618.3207543	Fetus—Ultrasonic imaging
RG411	618.142	Pelvic inflammatory disease	RG629.G75	618.32	Fetal growth disorders
			RG629.G76	618.32	Fetal growth retardation
RG421-433	618.12	Fallopian tubes—Diseases	RG631-633	618.32	Perinatal death
RG483.P44	618.1	Pelvic pain	RG631-633	618.4	Stillbirth
RG484-485	616.62	Bladder—Diseases	RG631-633	618.32	Fetal death
RG491-499	618.19	Breast—Diseases	RG648	618.392	Miscarriage
RG504-505	618.20025	Obstetricians—Directories	RG649	618.397	Labor, Premature
RG509-510	618.2092	Obstetricians	RG651-791	618.4	Labor (Obstetrics)
RG511-518	618.209	Obstetrics—History	RG661-662	618.45	Natural childbirth
RG519-520	618.2	Uterus, Pregnant	RG661.5	618.4	Childbirth at home
RG527.5.U48	618.207543	Ultrasonics in obstetrics	RG662	618.4	Active childbirth
RG529	618.209	Obstetrics—Case studies	RG663	618.4	Underwater childbirth
RG545	618.200284	Obstetrics—Apparatus and instruments	RG671-693	618.42	Fetal presentation
			RG696-698	618.25	Multiple birth
RG551-591	618.2	Pregnancy	RG701-721	618.5	Labor (Obstetrics)—Complications
RG556.5	618.200835	Teenage pregnancy			
RG559	618.24	Pregnancy—Nutritional aspects	RG711	618.54	Uterine hemorrhage
			RG715	618.5	Placenta praevia
RG560	618.20019	Pregnancy—Psychological aspects	RG719	618.5	Umbilical cord—Prolapse
			RG725-791	618.8	Obstetrics—Surgery
RG563-564	618.2075	Pregnancy—Signs and diagnosis	RG732-733	617.9682	Anesthesia in obstetrics
			RG734-.5	363.46	Abortion services
RG567	618.25	Multiple pregnancy	RG734	618.4	Labor, Induced (Obstetrics)
RG571-591	618.3025	Obstetrical emergencies			
RG575-576	618.7	Toxemia of pregnancy	RG734	618.172	Menstrual regulation
RG576	618.7	Eclampsia	RG739	618.20284	Obstetrical forceps
RG580.A44	618.3	AIDS (Disease) in pregnancy	RG741	618.82	Obstetrical extraction
			RG761	618.86	Cesarean section
RG580.D5	618.326	Diabetes in pregnancy	RG781	618.88	Craniotomy
RG580.D76	618.3268	Drug abuse in pregnancy	RG801-871	618.7	Puerperal disorders
RG580.E64	618.3268	Epilepsy in pregnancy	RG801-871	618.7	Postnatal care
RG580.H47	618.3261	Blood diseases in pregnancy	RG821	618.54	Uterine hemorrhage
			RG831	618	Puerperal convulsions
RG580.H5	618.54	Uterine hemorrhage	RG850-852	618.76	Postpartum psychiatric disorders
RG580.M34	618.3	Malnutrition in pregnancy			
RG580.S75	618.3268	Substance abuse in pregnancy	RG851	618.76	Puerperal psychoses
			RG852	618.76	Postpartum depression
RG586	618.31	Ectopic pregnancy	RG861-866	618.71	Lactation disorders
RG591	618.34	Placenta	RG950	618.2	Midwives
RG600-650	618.32	Fetus	RG951	618.20231	Maternity nursing

225

LC	Dewey	Subject Heading	LC	Dewey	Subject Heading
			RJ296	618.92097773	Conjunctivitis, Infantile
RJ	618.92	Pediatrics	RJ301	618.92842	Paralysis
RJ	618.92	Children—Diseases	RJ312	618.922	Respiratory insufficiency in children
RJ1	618.920006	Pediatricians—Societies, etc	RJ320.S93	618.92	Sudden infant death syndrome
RJ16	618.920005	Pediatrics—Periodicals	RJ370	618.920025	Pediatric emergencies
RJ21	618.920006	Pediatrics—Congresses	RJ370	618.920028	Pediatric intensive care
RJ27-28	362.12	Pediatric clinics	RJ386-.5	618.9297	Allergy in children
RJ27.2-.3	362.110973	Pediatric clinics—United States	RJ386.5	618.92975	Food allergy in children
RJ29	618.9200025	Pediatricians—Directories	RJ386.5	618.92975	Food allergy in infants
RJ33.5-.8	618.920232	Pediatrics—Practice	RJ387.A25	618.929792	AIDS (Disease) in children
RJ36-42	618.920009	Pediatrics—History	RJ387.A25	616.979200835	AIDS (Disease) in adolescence
RJ43	618.9200092	Pediatricians	RJ387.A25	618.929792	AIDS (Disease) in infants
RJ47.3-.4	618.920042	Genetic disorders in children	RJ396	618.92395	Rickets
RJ47.5-.53	618.9200019	Pediatrics—Psychosomatic aspects	RJ399.M26	618.9239	Malnutrition in children
			RJ401-406	618.92925	Virus diseases in children
RJ52-53	615.542	Children—Diseases—Treatment	RJ406.B32	618.9292	Bacterial diseases in children
RJ53.A27	615.892083	Acupuncture for children	RJ411-416	618.9215	Pediatric hematology
RJ53.A27	615.8222083	Acupressure for children	RJ416.A25	618.9299419	Acute myelocytic leukemia in children
RJ53.D53	618.9200654	Diet therapy for children			
RJ53.E95	618.920062	Exercise therapy for children	RJ418-420	618.924	Pediatric endocrinology
			RJ420.A27	618.9245	Adrenal glands
RJ53.F5	618.9200653	Fluid therapy for children	RJ420.D5	618.92462083	Diabetes in youth
RJ61	618.9201	Infants—Care	RJ420.D5	618.92462083	Diabetes in children
RJ91	618.24	Prenatal influences	RJ420.D5	616.46200835	Diabetes in adolescence
RJ101-103	649.122	Infants—Care	RJ420.G65	618.92442	Endemic goiter in children
RJ125-137	612.0083	Children—Physiology	RJ420.P58	618.9247	Dwarfism, Pituitary
RJ128	618.92716	Children—Metabolism	RJ421-426	618.9212	Pediatric cardiology
RJ131-137	612.65	Child development	RJ423.5.D54	618.92107572	Digital subtraction angiography
RJ131-137	612.65	Children—Growth			
RJ134	612.654	Infants—Development	RJ423.5.U46	618.921207543	Echocardiography
RJ135	618.92	Failure to thrive syndrome	RJ431-436	618.922	Pediatric respiratory diseases
RJ140-145	612.661	Youth—Physiology			
RJ140	612.661	Teenagers—Growth	RJ434	615.542	Respiratory therapy for children
RJ145	612.662	Menarche			
RJ206-235	612.3	Children—Nutrition	RJ436.A8	618.92238	Asthma in children
RJ216	613.269	Breast feeding	RJ446-456	618.9233	Pediatric gastroenterology
RJ240	613.0432	Immunization of children	RJ456.D5	618.923427	Diarrhea Infantile
RJ245-247	618.9200231	Pediatric nursing	RJ456.E83	618.9232	Esophagus—Atresia
RJ250-.3	618.92011	Infants (Premature)	RJ456.F43	618.92342	Fecal incontinence in children
RJ251-325	618.9201	Neonatology			
RJ253.5	618.9201	Neonatal emergencies	RJ460-463	618.9231	Pediatric oral medicine
RJ253.5	618.9201	Neonatal intensive care	RJ466-478.5	618.926	Pediatric urology
RJ256	618.922	Asphyxia neonatorum	RJ476.5-478.5	618.92098	Sexual disorders in children
RJ267	618.9233	Colic			
RJ268.8	618.9201	Neonatal gastroenterology	RJ476.E6	618.92849	Enuresis
RJ269	618.3261043	Fetal heart—Abnormalities	RJ476.R46	618.92614	Acute renal failure in children
RJ269.5-271	618.9215	Neonatal hematology			
RJ272	618.923623	Hepatitis, Neonatal	RJ478-.5	618.92098	Adolescent gynecology
RJ274	618.922	Hyaline membrane disease	RJ482.B65	618.9271	Bone diseases in children
			RJ482.C65	618.9277	Connective tissue diseases in children
RJ275	618.929	Neonatal infections			
RJ276	618.923625	Jaundice, Neonatal	RJ482.D78	618.92748	Duchenne muscular dystrophy
R281	618.9201	Birth weight, Low			
RJ290-.5	618.928043	Nervous system—Abnormalities	RJ486-496	618.928	Pediatric neurology
			RJ496.A5	618.928553	Dyslexic children

LC	Dewey	Subject Heading	LC	Dewey	Subject Heading
RJ496.B7	618.928043	Brain-damaged children	RK3.5	362.1109(4-9)	Dental clinics—[By region or country]
RJ496.C4	618.92836	Cerebral palsied children			
RJ496.C7	618.92845	Febrile convulsions	RK16	617.6005	Dentistry—Periodicals
RJ496.E6	618.92853	Epilepsy in children	RK21	617.6006	Dentistry—Congresses
RJ496.E6	616.85300835	Epilepsy in adolescence	RK28	617.60014	Dentistry—Terminology
RJ496.P2	618.92842	Paralysis	RK29-34	617.60901	Dentistry—History
RJ496.S8	618.928554	Stuttering in children	RK31	617.60901	Dentistry, Ancient
RJ499-520	618.9289	Child psychiatry	RK37	617.60025	Dentists—Directories
RJ499-520	618.9289	Child psychopathology	RK52-.45	617.600723	Dental surveys
RJ499-507	618.9289	Child mental health	RK52-.45	614.5996	Dental public health
RJ500.2	618.9289027	Child psychopathology—Research	RK52.7	174.2	Dental ethics
			RK53	617.60019	Dentistry—Psychological aspects
RJ502.3	616.8900835	Adolescent psychiatric nursing	RK55.C5	617.645	Pedodontics
RJ502.5	616.890932	Infant psychiatry	RK57	617.60076	Dentistry—Examinations, questions, etc.
RJ503	616.8900835	Adolescent psychopathology	RK58-59.3	617.6023	Dentistry—Practice
RJ503	618.928917	Adolescent analysis	RK60-.5	617.60023	Dentistry—Vocational guidance
RJ503	616.891400835	Adolescent psychotherapy			
RJ503	616.8900835	Adolescent psychiatry	RK60.45	617.6008996 + 073	Afro-Americans in dentistry
RJ504-505	618.928914	Child psychotherapy			
RJ504.2	618.928917	Child analysis	RK60.5	617.60233	Dental auxiliary personnel
RJ505.D3	615.85155083	Dance therapy for children	RK60.7-.8	617.601	Dental prophylaxis
RJ505.T47	616.891400835	Adolescent psychotherapy—Termination	RK60.7-.8	617.601	Preventive dentistry
			RK60.7	617.601	Teeth—Polishing
			RK60.8	617.60071	Dental health education
RJ506.A58	618.9285223	Anxiety in children	RK61	617.601	Teeth—Care and hygiene
RJ506.A9	618.928982	Autism in children	RK71-231	617.60071	Dentistry—Study and teaching
RJ506.B44	618.92858	Behavior disorders in children			
RJ506.C48	616.85836	Child sexual abuse	RK80	617.60072	Dentistry—Research
RJ506.C65	618.9289	Conduct disorders in children	RK86-231	617.600710(4-9)	Dentistry—Study and teaching—[By region or country]
RJ506.D4	618.928527	Depression in infants	RK91-97	617.6071073	Dentistry—Study and teaching—United States
RJ506.D4	618.928527	Depression in children			
RJ506.D4	616.852700835	Depression in adolescence	RK301-493	617.63	Teeth—Diseases
RJ506.D68	618.92858842	Down's syndrome	RK305	617.63	Focal infection, Dental
RJ506.E18	616.852600835	Eating disorders in adolescence	RK308-310	617.630754	Teeth—Diseases—Diagnosis
RJ506.F73	618.928588	Fragile X syndrome	RK318-320	617.606	Dental therapeutics
RJ506.H9	618.928589	Attention-deficit hyperactivity disorder	RK320.E53	617.634	Dental enamel microabrasion
RJ506.M4	618.9285884	Mental retardation	RK328	617.6	Dental calculus
RJ506.P38	618.9285225	Phobias in children	RK328	617.6	Dental plaque
RJ506.S39	618.928582	Self-destructive behavior in children	RK328	617.6	Dental deposits
			RK331	617.67	Dental caries
RJ506.D4	618.928527	Affective disorders in children	RK340-341	617.634	Dental enamel—Diseases
			RK351-356	617.6342	Endodontics
RJ507.F47	155.4567	Feral children	RK351	617.63	Focal infection, Dental
RJ507.S49	618.9285836	Sexually abused children	RK361-450	617.645	Periodontics
RJ516.E35	618.92521	Eczema in children	RK361-450	617.632	Periodontal disease
RJ520.C64	618.9277	Collagen diseases in children	RK401-410	617.632	Gums—Diseases
			RK410	617.632	Gingivitis
RJ550	616.00835	Adolescent medicine	RK450.P4	617.632	Periodontitis
RJ560-570	615.1083(2-4)	Pediatric pharmacology	RK490-493	617.6044	Teeth—Wounds and injuries
RK	617.6	Dentistry	RK501-519	617.605	Dentistry, Operative
RK1	617.6006	Dentistry—Societies, etc.	RK503	617.605	Dentistry, Operative—Positioning
RK3-.5	362.11	Dental clinics			

LC	Dewey	Subject Heading	LC	Dewey	Subject Heading
RK510-512	617.9676	Anesthesia in dentistry	RL94	646.727	Manicuring
RK513	617.605	Dentistry, Operative—Complications	RL125	616.50231	Dermatologic nursing
			RL131	616.53	Acne
RK515	617.672	Dental drilling	RL155-.5	616.546	Baldness
RK515	617.672	Dental cavity preparation	RL221	616.523	Carbuncle
RK517-519	617.675	Fillings (Dentistry)	RL221	616.523	Furuncle
RK519.A4	617.675	Dental amalgams	RL231-241	616.5	Skin—Inflammation
RK520-528	617.643	Orthodontics	RL241	616.5	Occupational dermatitis
RK523	617.643	Malocclusion	RL242-249	616.5	Atopic dermatitis
RK527-528	617.643	Orthodontics, Corrective	RL244	616.51	Contact dermatitis
RK527-528	617.64300284	Orthodonic appliances	RL247	616.5	Photosensitivity disorders
RK529-535	617.605	Mouth—Surgery	RL251	616.51	Eczema
RK531-.5	617.66	Teeth—Extraction	RL283	616.523	Impetigo
RK533	617.60592	Teeth—Transplantation	RL321	616.526	Psoriasis
RK641-667	617.69	Prosthodontics	RL431	616.546	Hupertrichosis
RK652.5-655	617.695	Dental materials	RL435	616.544	Keratosis
RK652.7-.8	617.695	Dental cements	RL435	616.544	Ichthyosis
RK652.7-.8	617.695	Dental adhesives	RL451	616.544	Scleroderma (Disease)
RK652.7-.8	617.69	Dental bonding	RL471	616.544	Warts
RK653	617.675	Dental metallurgy	RL675	616.545	Bedsores
RK653	617.675	Gold alloys	RL701-751	616.5	Neurocutaneous disorders
RK653.5	617.675	Dental ceramic metals	RL764.S28	616.57	Scabies
RK655	617.675	Dental ceramics	RL780	616.57	Ringworm
RK656	617.69	Denture attachments	RL793	616.55	Mole (Dermatology)
RK656-666	617.692	Dentures, Immediate			
RK656-666	617.692	Overlay dentures	RM	615.5	Therapeutics
RK656-666	617.692	Dentures	RM1	615.506	Therapeutics—Societies, etc.
RK664-666	617.692	Partial dentures			
RK665	617.692	Partial dentures, Removable	RM16	615.505	Therapeutics—Periodicals
			RM21	615.506	Therapeutics—Congresses
RK666	617.692	Bridges (Dentistry)	RM38	615.5014	Therapeutics—Terminology
RK666	617.6922	Crowns (Dentistry)	RM40	616.0756	Clinical chemistry
RK667.I45	617.693	Implant dentures	RM41-47	615.509	Therapeutics—History
RK667.T57	617.69	Tissue-integrated prostheses	RM108-.5	615.5071	Therapeutics—Study and teaching
RK681-686	617.600284	Dental instruments and apparatus	RM111	615.5072	Therapeutics, Experimental
RK701-715	617.606	Dentistry—Formulae, receipts, prescriptions	RM138	615.14	Drugs—Prescribing
			RM139	615.14	Prescription writing
			RM147-180	615.6	Drugs—Administration
RL	616.5	Dermatology	RM149	615.855	Parenteral therapy
RL1	616.5006	Dermatology—Societies, etc.	RM149	615.855	Parenteral solutions
			RM161	615.836	Respiratory therapy
RL26	616.5005	Dermatology—Periodicals	RM162	615.6	Oral medication
RL31	616.5006	Dermatology—Congresses	RM163-176	615.6	Injections
RL39	616.50014	Dermatology—Terminology	RM169	615.6	Injections, Hypodermic
RL43	616.50025	Dermatologists—Directories	RM170-180	615.855	Intravenous therapy
			RM171-174	615.39	Blood—Transfusion
RL46	616.5009	Dermatology—History	RM171.4-.45	615.39	Blood products
RL46.2-.3	616.50092	Dermatologists	RM171.4	615.39	Recombinant blood proteins
RL55	616.500284	Dermatology—Apparatus and instruments	RM171.5	615.39	Blood coagulation factors
RL77	616.50071	Dermatology—Study and teaching	RM171.7	615.399	Blood plasma substitutes
			RM171.7	615.399	Blood substitutes
RL79	616.5027	Dermatology, Experimental	RM172	362.1784	Blood banks
			RM175-176	615.39	Plasma exchange (Therapeutics)
RL87	613.4	Skin—Care and hygiene			
RL91	616.546	Dandruff	RM177	615.39	Blood platelets—Transfusion
RL91	616.546	Beard			

LC	Dewey	Subject Heading	LC	Dewey	Subject Heading
RM182-190	617.414059	Veins—Puncture	RM325	615.7821	Barbiturates
RM184-.5	615.892	Acupuncture	RM325	615.782	Hypnotics
RM214-258	615.854	Dietetics	RM325	615.782	Sedatives
RM214-258	615.854	Diet therapy	RM328	615.7822	Narcotics
RM214-258	615.854	Diet in disease	RM330	615.782	Central nervous system depressants
RM219	641.563	Cookery for the sick			
RM221.D4	641.5631	Deglutition disorders	RM332-.3	615.78	Antidepressants
RM222.2	613.25	Low-calorie diet	RM332-.3	615.785	Stimulants
RM222.2	613.25	Reducing diets	RM333	615.7882	Tranquilizing drugs
RM226-228	613.25	Fasting	RM345-349	615.71	Cardiovascular agents
RM232	613.26	Egg-free diet	RM345-349	615.71	Cardiovascular pharmacology
RM234.5	613.26	Milk-free diet			
RM236	613.262	Vegetarianism	RM347	615.716	Myocardial depressants
RM237.5	613.26	Raw food diet	RM349	615.71	Cardiotonic agents
RM237.56	613.285	High-calcium diet	RM355-365	615.73	Gastrointestinal agents
RM237.58	613.283	Complex carbohydrate diet	RM357	615.732	Laxatives
RM237.59	613.283	High-carbohydrate diet	RM359	615.73	Emetics
RM237.6	613.263	High-fiber diet	RM365	615.73	Antacids
RM237.65	613.282	High-protein diet	RM370-373	615.37	Immunopharmacology
RM237.7	613.284	Low-fat diet	RM373	615.37	Immunosuppressive agents
RM237.73	613.283	Low-carbohydrate diet			
RM237.75	613.284	Low-Cholesterol diet	RM377	615.761	Diuretics
RM237.8	613.285	Salt-free diet	RM386	615.7669	Aphrodisiacs
RM237.85	613.26	Sugar-free diet	RM388-.7	615.72	Pulmonary pharmacology
RM237.87	613.26	Wheat-free diet	RM388-.7	615.72	Respiratory agents
RM259	615.328	Vitamin therapy	RM390	615.72	Expectorants
RM260-263	615.58	Chemotherapy	RM409	615.329	Antibacterial agents
RM265-267	615.329	Antibiotics	RM666.A4	615.321	Alkaloids
RM270-282	615.37	Immunotherapy	RM666.A68	615.3219	Aromatherapy
RM270-282	615.37	Serotherapy	RM666.A82	615.3137	Aspirin
RM278	615.37	Antitoxins	RM666.B2	615.329	Bacitracin
RM281	615.372	Vaccination	RM666.B375	615.36	Bee pollen
RM282.T7	615.37	Transfer factor (Immunology)	RM666.B4	615.323952	Belladonna (Drug)
			RM666.C266	615.7827	Cannabis
RM283-298	615.36	Hormone therapy	RM666.C375	615.32369	Castor oil
RM298.P5	615.39	Placental extracts	RM666.D5	615.711	Digitalis
RM300-671.5	615.1	Pharmacology	RM666.H33	615.321	Herbs—Therapeutic use
RM300-671.5	615.1	Drugs	RM666.L88	615.788	LSD (Drug)
RM301.25-.27	615.10724	Pharmacology, Experimental	RM666.M8	615.7822	Morphine
			RM666.O8	615.836	Oxygen therapy
RM301.25	615.19	Drug development	RM666.P35	615.3295654	Penicillin
RM301.27	615.1901	Drugs—Testing	RM666.T2	615.73	Tartar emetic
RM301.28	615	Clinical pharmacology	RM666.T6	616.865	Tobacco—Physiological effect
RM301.5	615.7	Pharmacokinetics			
RM301.56	615.7045	Drug activation	RM671-.5	615.1	Drugs, Nonprescription
RM302-.4	615.7045	Drug interactions	RM671-.5	615.1	Patent medicines
RM302.5	615.7042	Drugs—Side effects	RM695-951	615.82	Medicine, Physical
RM312	615.773	Musculoskeletal system—Effect of drugs on	RM695-931	615.82	Therapeutics, Physiological
			RM695-893	615.82	Physical therapy
RM312	615.773	Neuromuscular blocking agents	RM695	615.8206	Physical therapy—Societies, etc.
RM315-334	615.78	Neuropsychopharmacology	RM696	615.8206	Physical therapy—Congresses
RM315-334	615.788	Psychotropic drugs			
RM315-334	615.78	Psychopharmacology	RM697	615.82025	Physical therapists—Directories
RM315-334	615.78	Neuropharmacology			
RM316	616.86	Designer drugs	RM699.5-.7	615.82092	Physical therapists
RM316	615.78	Drugs of abuse	RM706-707	615.82071	Physical therapy—Study and teaching
RM319	615.783	Analgesics			
RM324.8	615.7883	Hallucinogenic drugs	RM719-727	615.82	Mechanotherapy

LC	Dewey	Subject Heading	LC	Dewey	Subject Heading
RM721-723	615.822	Massage	RS125-131.9	615.13	Medicine— Formulae, receipts, prescriptions
RM723.A27	615.8222	Acupressure			
RM724	615.82	Manipulation (Therapeutics)	RS139-141.9	615.11	Pharmacopoeias
			RS151.2-.9	615.13	Dispensatories
RM725-727	615.82	Exercise therapy	RS153-185	615.1	Materia medica
RM735-.7	615.8515	Occupational therapy	RS159	615.18	Drugs—Preservation
RM735.7.H35	615.85156	Handicraft—Therapeutic use	RS159.5	615.18	Drugs—Packaging
			RS160-167	615.321	Pharmacognosy
RM736.7	615.85153	Recreational therapy	RS164	615.32103	Medicinal plants—Encyclopedias
RM801-822	615.853	Hydrotherapy			
RM824-827	615.836	Aerotherapy	RS165.C3	633.88393	Quinine
RM827	615.836	Compressed air—Therapeutic use	RS165.C5	615.32379	Coca
			RS165.D5	615.711	Digitalis
RM835-844	615.831	Phototherapy	RS165.H3	633.79	Hashish
RM835-844	615.831	Light, Colored	RS165.P38	615.3295654	Penicillin
RM838	615.831	Light—Physiological effect	RS189-190	615.1901	Drugs—Analysis
RM840	615.8312	Color—Therapeutic use	RS189	615.10128	Drugs—Standards
RM843	613.193	Sun-baths	RS190.D77	615.78	Drugs of abuse
RM845-862.5	615.842	Radiotherapy	RS192-210	615.19	Pharmaceutical technology
RM845-862.5	615.842	Radiation—Dosage			
RM859	615.8423	Radium—Therapeutic use	RS199.5-210	615.19	Drug delivery systems
RM862.7	615.83	Ultrasonic waves—Therapeutic use	RS200-201	615.14	Drugs—Dosage forms
			RS201.B54	615.19	Bioadhesive drug delivery systems
RM862.E4	615.845	Electron beams—Therapeutic use	RS201.C3	615.19	Capsules (Pharmacy)
RM865-868.5	615.832	Thermotherapy	RS201.C64	615.19	Drugs—Controlled release
RM868-.5	615.832	Fever therapy	RS201.E4	615.19	Elixirs
RM869-890	615.845	Electrotherapeutics	RS201.E5	615.19	Emulsions (Pharmacy)
RM874	615.8323	Diathermy	RS201.O3	615.19	Ointments
RM886	615.845	Electrolysis in medicine	RS201.P37	615.19	Parenteral solutions
RM889	610.284	Electric apparatus and appliances	RS201.P5	615.19	Pills
			RS201.P8	615.19	Powders (Pharmacy)
RM930-950	617.03	Medical rehabilitation	RS201.S6	615.19	Solutions (Pharmacy)
RM950	617.03	Rehabilitation technology	RS201.S8	615.19	Syrups
			RS201.T2	615.19	Tablets (Medicine)
RS	615.1	Pharmacy	RS201.V43	615.19	Drugs—Vehicles
RS1	615.106	Pharmacy—Societies, etc.	RS210	615.19	Drug delivery devices
RS3	615.106	Pharmacy—Congresses	RS400-431	615.19	Pharmaceutical chemistry
RS21	615.105	Pharmacy—Periodicals	RS424	615.1	Drug stability
RS55	615.1014	Pharmacy—Terminology	RS431.D58	615.761	Diuretics
RS57	615.10151	Pharmaceutical arithmetic	RS431.E73	615.321	Exgot alkaloids
RS61-68	615.109	Pharmacy—History			
RS71-73	615.1092	Pharmacists	RT	610.73	Nursing
RS74-76	615.1025	Pharmacists—Directories	RT1	610.7306	Nursing—Societies, etc.
RS93	615.1078	Pharmacy—Laboratory manuals	RT3	610.7306	Nursing—Congresses
			RT4-17	610.7309(4-9)	Nursing—[By region or country]
RS100-.4	615.1068	Pharmacy management			
RS100.5	174.2	Pharmaceutical ethics	RT25	610.73025	Nurses—Directories
RS101-121	615.1071	Pharmacy—Study and teaching	RT31	610.7309	Nursing—History
			RT34-37	610.73092	Nurses
RS110-121	615.10710(4-9)	Pharmacy—Study and teaching—[By region or country]	RT48-.6	610.73069	Nursing assessment
			RT48.6	610.73069	Nursing diagnosis
			RT50.5	610.730285	Nursing—Data processing
RS122	615.10724	Pharmacy—Research	RT62	610.730693	Practical nursing
RS122.5	615.108996073	Afro-American pharmacists	RT71-81	610.730711	Nursing schools
			RT71-81	610.73071	Nursing—Study and teaching
RS122.95	615.1092	Pharmacy technicians			
RS123	615.1074	Pharmaceutical museums	RT81.5	610.73072	Nursing—Research
			RT82.8	610.730692	Nurse practitioners

LC	Dewey	Subject Heading	LC	Dewey	Subject Heading
RT83.5	615.7308996 + 073	Afro-American nurses	RV381-391	616.506	Dermatology
			RV431	615.53	Dispensatories, Eclectic
RT84	610.730698	Nurses' aides			
RT84.5	610.7301	Nursing—Philosophy	RX	615.532	Homeopathy
RT85	174.2	Nursing ethics	RX1	615.53206	Homeopathy—Societies, etc.
RT86	610.73019	Nursing—Psychological aspects	RX6-.5	362.11	Homeopathy—Hospitals and dispensaries
RT86.3	610.730699	Nurse and patient	RX11	615.53205	Homeopathy—Periodicals
RT86.4	610.730699	Nurse and physician	RX21	615.53206	Homeopathy—Congresses
RT86.7-.75	610.73069	Nursing—Practice	RX46	615.532025	Homeopathic physicians—Directories
RT87.T45	616.029	Hospice care			
RT87.T45	616.029	Terminal care	RX51	615.53209	Homeopathy—History
RT90-.3	615.507	Patient education	RX61-66	615.532092	Homeopathic physicians—Biography
RT90.5	610.73028	Team nursing			
RT90.7	610.733	Primary nursing	RX81	615.532	Homeopathy—Attenuations, dilutions, and potencies
RT97	610.734	Public health nursing			
RT98	610.7343	Visiting nurses	RX91-101	615.532071	Homeopathy—Study and teaching
RT98	610.7343	Community health nursing			
RT104	610.732	Private duty nursing	RX211	616.04706	Fever—Homeopathic treatment
RT108	610.7349	Disaster nursing			
RT120.E4	616.025	Emergency nursing	RX261.C3	616.99406	Cancer—Homeopathic treatment
RT120.I5	616.028	Intensive care nursing			
			RX281-301	616.806	Nervous system—Diseases—Homeopathic treatment
RV	615.53	Medicine, Eclectic			
RV1-9	615.53	Medicine, Botanic			
RV11-431	615.53	Medicine, Eclectic	RX311-316	616.106	Cardiovascular system—Diseases—Homeopathic treatment
RV15	615.5305	Medicine, Eclectic—Periodicals			
			RX321-326	616.206	Respiratory organs—Diseases—Homoopathic treatment
RV21	615.5306	Medicine, Eclectic—Congresses			
RV61	615.5309	Medicine, Eclectic—History	RX331-336	616.306	Digestive organs—Diseases—Homeopathic treatment
RV100-181	615.53071	Medicine, Eclectic—Study and teaching			
			RX336.D5	616.306	Diarrhea—Homeopathic treatment
RV211	616.04706	Fever—Eclectic treatment			
RV241-246	616.806	Nervous system—Diseases—Eclectic treatment	RX360	617.5406	Chest—Diseases—Homeopathic treatment
			RX366-376	617	Surgery, Homeopathic
RV251-256	616.106	Cardiovascular system—Diseases—Eclectic treatment	RX410-431	617.706	Eye—Diseases—Homeopathic treatment
RV261-266	616.206	Respiratory organs—Diseases—Eclectic treatment	RX451	617.52306	Nose—Diseases—Homeopathic treatment
			RX476	618.206	Obstetrics, Homeopathic
RV271-276	616.306	Digestive organs—Diseases—Eclectic treatment	RX501-531	618.9206	Children—Diseases—Homeopathic treatment
			RX561-581	616.506	Dermatology
RV291	617.5106	Head—Diseases—Eclectic treatment	RX601-675	615.532	Homeopathy—Materia medica and therapeutics
RV293	617.5406	Chest—Diseases—Eclectic treatment	RX671-675	615.532	Pharmacy, Homeopathic
RV297	617.5506	Pelvis—Diseases—Eclectic treatment	RZ	615.534	Chiropractic
			RZ	615.533	Osteopathic medicine
RV321-331	617.706	Eye—Diseases—Eclectic treatment	RZ201-275	615.534	Chiropractic
			RZ201	615.53406	Chiropractic—Societies, etc.
RV341-347	617.52306	Nose—Diseases—Eclectic treatment			
			RZ211	615.53405	Chiropractic—Periodicals
RV361-365	618.206	Obstetrics, Eclectic	RZ213	615.53406	Chiropractic—Congresses
RV375-377	618.9206	Children—Diseases—Eclectic treatment	RZ221-225	615.53409	Chiropractic—History

LC	Dewey	Subject Heading	LC	Dewey	Subject Heading
RZ231-232	615.534092	Chiropractors—Biography	S494.5.A47	630	Agropastoral systems
RZ233	615.534025	Chiropractors—Directories	S494.5.E5	631.37	Agriculture and energy
RZ237-238	615.534071	Chiropractic—Study and teaching	S494.5.E8	630.723	Agricultural surveys
			S494.5.P47	631.58	Permaculture
RZ237-238	615.534	Chiropractic schools	S494.5.P75	338.16	Agricultural productivity
RZ242	362.12	Chiropractic clinics	S494.5.U72	630.91732	Urban agriculture
RZ260-275	615.534	Diseases—Chiropractic treatment	S521	390.463	Farm life
			S530-539	630.7	Agricultural education
RZ265.S64	616.73062	Spinal adjustment	S531-539	630.71	Agriculture—Study and teaching
RZ270-275	617.1062	Wounds and injuries—Chiropractic treatment	S533-534	630.715092	County agricultural agents
			S533.F66	630.6	4-H clubs
RZ301-397.5	615.533	Osteopathic medicine	S537-539	630.711	Agricultural colleges
RZ301	615.53306	Osteopathic medicine—Societies, etc.	S539.5-542	630.72	Agriculture—Research
			S541-543	630.724	Agricultural experimental stations
RZ302-304	362.11	Osteopathic hospitals	S544-545	630.715	Agricultural extension work
RZ311	615.53305	Osteopathic medicine—Periodicals	S549	630.74	Agricultural museums
			S550-559	630.74	Agricultural exhibitions
RZ313	615.53306	Osteopathic medicine—Congresses	S560-575	630	Farms
			S560-572	630.68	Farm management
RZ321-325	615.53309	Osteopathic medicine—History	S565	630.289	Agriculture—Safety measures
RZ331-332	615.533092	Osteopathic physicians—Biography	S571-.5	381.41	Farm produce—Marketing
			S571.5	381.41	Roadside marketing
RZ333	615.533025	Osteopathic physicians—Directories	S583-587.5	631.41	Agricultural chemistry
			S587.45	631.86	Natural products in agriculture
RZ336	615.533023	Osteopathic medicine—Vocational guidance	S587.5.N5	631.84	Nitrogen in agriculture
			S589-.6	631.43	Agricultural physics
RZ337-338	615.5330711	Osteopathic schools	S589.8-.85	631.4	Potting soils
RZ337-338	615.533071	Osteopathic medicine—Study and teaching	S589.8	631.4	Plant growing media
			S590-599.9	631.4	Soils
RZ400-408	615.851	Mental healing	S590-599.9	631.4	Soil science
RZ403.S56	615.851	Silva Mind Control	S590-599.9	631.4	Land capability for agriculture
RZ407-408	615.851092	Healers			
RZ414	615.53	Medicine, Chronothermal	S590-592	631.4	Soil management
RZ414.6	615.8312	Color—Therapeutic use	S592.14-.147	631.47	Soil surveys
RZ420	615.532	Electrohomeopathy	S592.17.A73	631.49154	Arid soils
RZ422	615.8454	Magnetic healing	S592.17.D47	631.49154	Desert soils
RZ433-445	615.535	Naturopathy	S592.367	631.42	Clay soils
RZ440	615.535092	Naturopaths	S592.5-.6	631.41	Soil chemistry
			S592.57-.575	631.42	Acid soils
S	630-638	Agriculture	S592.575	631.42	Acid sulfate soils
S1-954	630-638	Agriculture	S592.575	631.42	Soil acidity
S1-19	630.5	Agriculture—Periodicals	S592.6.A34	631.41	Soils—Agricultural chemical content
S20	630.6	Agriculture—Societies, etc.	S592.7-.85	631.417	Soil biochemistry
			S592.85	631.826	Peat soils
S419-481	630.9	Agriculture—History	S593	631.4	Soils—Analysis
S421-431	630.901	Agriculture, Prehistoric	S594	631.62	Drain-gages
S431	630.945632	Agriculture—Rome	S594	631.432	Moisture index
S439-481	630.11	Agricultural systems	S594	631.432	Soil moisture
S439-481	630.9(4-9)	Agricultural geography	S595	631.42	Alkali lands
S439-481	333.7316	Green Revolution	S599-.9	631.49154	Desert soils
S441-482	577.55	Agricultural ecology	S599-.9	631.587	Soils, Irrigated
S441-451	630.723	Agricultural surveys	S600	630.2515	Meteorology, Agricultural
S494	636.082	Breeding	S600.7.H37	631.55	Harvesting time
S494	636.082	Inbreeding	S600.7.P53	631.53	Planting time
S494.5.A4	630.23	Agriculture—Vocational guidance			
S494.5.A45	634.99	Agroforestry			

LC	Dewey	Subject Heading	LC	Dewey	Subject Heading
S602.87	631.5818	Shifting cultivation	S723	631.27	Gates
S603	631.582	Crop rotation	S790-.3	631.27	Fences
S603.5	631.58	Intercropping	S900-954	333.72	Conservation of natural resources
S603.7	631.58	Double cropping			
S603.7	631.58	Multiple cropping	S946	333.72071	Environmental education
S604	631.5814	No-tillage			
S604	631.51	Tillage	SB	630	Crops
S604.33	630.911	Cold regions agriculture	SB1-13	630.5	Crops—Periodicals
S604.5-.64	631.451	Agricultural conservation	SB16	630.6	Crops—Congresses
S604.8-621.5	631.6	Reclamation of land	SB45.65	630	Crop science literature
S605.5	631.584	Organic farming	SB51-56	630.72	Crops—Research
S607	631.61	Clearing of land	SB106.B56	631.5233	Plant biotechnology
S612-619	630.9154	Arid regions agriculture	SB106.I47	631.52	Crop improvement
S612-619	631.587	Irrigation	SB106.O74	631.52	Crops—Evolution
S612-619	631.6	Desert reclamation	SB107-109	338.1	Botany, Economic
S612-619	631.587	Irrigation farming	SB108-109	631.523	Plant introduction
S621	631.62	Drainage	SB109.7	630.911	Cold regions agriculture
S621.5.P59	631.64	Plants for land reclamation	SB110	631.586	Dry farming
			SB111	631.913	Tropical crops
S621.5.S3	631.64	Sand dune planting	SB113.2-118.45	631.521	Seeds
S622-627	631.45	Soil conservation	SB113.2-118.45	631.521	Seed technology
S627.H5	631.455	Hillside planting	SB114	631.521	Seed adulteration and inspection
S627.P55	631.45	Plants for soil conservation	SB118.48-.75	635	Nurseries (Horticulture)
S627.P76	631.45	Soil conservation projects	SB119-124	631.52	Plant propagation
S631-667	631.8	Fertilizers	SB121	631.53	Planting (Plant culture)
S633	631.8	Garden fertilizers	SB121	631.536	Seedlings—Transplanting
S647	631.85	Phosphatic fertilizers	SB121	631.531	Sowing
S651-.3	631.84	Nitrogen fertilizers	SB123-.25	631.52	Selection (Plant breeding)
S651-.3	631.842	Nitrates	SB123-.5	631.52	Plant breeding
S654	631.86	Organic fertilizers	SB123.57	631.5233	Crops—Genetic engineering
S654	631.86	Organic wastes as fertilizer			
S655	631.861	Manures	SB123.57	631.5233	Transgenic plants
S654.5	631.847	Biofertilizers	SB123.57	631.5233	Plant genetic engineering
S655	631.861	Farm manure	SB123.65	631.54	Grafting
S657	631.869	Sewage	SB123.65	631.53	Budding (Plant propagation)
S659	631.85	Bone-meal	SB125	631.54	Disbudding
S661	631.874	Green manuring	SB126.5-.57	631.585	Hydroponics
S661	631.875	Compost	SB129	631.55	Harvesting
S661.2.M3	631.87	Marine algae as fertilizer	SB170-171	634.99	Tree crops
S661.5	631.451	Mulching	SB172	634.99	Multipurpose trees
S662-.5	631.8	Liquid fertilizers	SB175-177	635	Food crops
S671-760	631.3	Agricultural machinery	SB175	641.303	Food crops
S671-760	631	Agricultural engineering	SB183-187	633	Seed crops
S671-760	631.3	Farm equipment	SB185.8	631.53	Planting time
S675.3	631.3	Agricultural mechanics	SB185.8	631.55	Harvesting time
S676-.3	631.3	Agricultural implements	SB188-192	633.1	Winter grain
S676.5	631.3	Agricultural instruments	SB189-192	633.1	Grain
S683-685	631.3	Plows	SB191.B2	633.16	Barley
S683-685	631.3	Cultivators	SB191.M2	633.15	Corn
S687-689	631.3	Drill (Agricultural implement)	SB191.P64	635.677	Popcorn
			SB191.W5	633.11	Durum wheat
S695-697	631.3	Sickles	SB193-207	633.2	Forage plants
S695-697	631.3	Mowing machines	SB193-.55	633.202	Rangelands
S699-701	631.3	Threshing machines	SB195	633.2	Silage
S711-713	631.373	Farm trucks	SB197-202	633.2	Grasses
S711-713	631.372	Power transmission	SB199	633.202	Meadows
S711-713	631.372	Farm tractors	SB199	633.202	Pastures
S715.C64	631.37	Cotton-picking machinery	SB201.K4	633.21	Kentucky bluegrass

LC	Dewey	Subject Heading	LC	Dewey	Subject Heading
SB203-205	633.3	Legumes	SB401	634.61	Copra
SB205.A4	633.31	Alfalfa	SB401.M32	634.5	Macadamia nut
SB205.F3	633.3	Fava bean	SB403-450.87	635.9	Flower gardening
SB209-211	635.1	Root crops	SB403-450.87	635.9	Floriculture
SB211.C3	641.33682	Cassava	SB403-450.87	635.9	Plants, Ornamental
SB215-239	633.6	Sugar	SB403-450	635.9	Flowers
SB241-261	633.5	Fiber plants	SB409	635.9344	Dendrobium
SB261.M3	633.571	Abaca (Fiber)	SB410.9-411.7	635.933734	Roses
SB267	633.74	Cacao	SB411	635.933734	Rose gardens
SB269	633.73	Coffee	SB413.B4	635.933627	Begonias
SB273-278	633.71	Tobacco	SB413.B65	635.93353	Bougainvillea
SB281-283	633.58	Matwork plants	SB413.C3	635.93353	Carnations
SB285-287	633.86	Dye plants	SB413.D2	635.93399	Daisies
SB289-291	633.8952	Rubber plants	SB413.D12	635.93434	Daffodils
SB289-291	633.895	Gums and resins	SB413.D13	635.93399	Dahlias
SB292	633.898	Pesticidal plants	SB413.D4	635.93334	Delphinium
SB293-295	633.88	Mushrooms, Hallucinogenic	SB413.E27	635.97752	Eastern hemlock
SB293-295	633.88	Medicinal plants	SB413.G35	635.93379	Dwarf pelargoniums
SB295.A45	633.88	Aloe	SB413.H6	635.933685	Hibiscus
SB295.E63	633.8858	Ephedra	SB413.I8	635.93438	Dwarf irises
SB295.G5	633.88384	Ginseng	SB413.P17	635.9345	Palms
SB295.06	633.75	Opium	SB413.R43	633.28	Red fescue
SB295.065	633.75	Opium poppy	SB414.6-416.3	635.9823	Greenhouse plants
SB298-299	633.85	Oilseed plants	SB415-416.3	631.583	Greenhouses
SB299.S9	635.93399	Sunflowers	SB415-416.3	631.583	Solar greenhouses
SB301-303	633.81	Aromatic plants	SB415	635.9823	Greenhouse gardening
SB305-307	633.8(3-4)	Spice plants	SB415	635.986	Plants, Potted
SB317.C2	634.775	Cactus	SB418-.4	635.986	Container gardening
SB317.5-319.77	635	Horticultural crops	SB418-.4	635.986	Hanging baskets
SB320-353.5	635	Vegetable gardening	SB419-.3	635.965	Indoor gardening
SB320-353.5	635	Vegetables	SB419-.3	635.9678	Window gardening
SB325	635.31	Asparagus	SB419-.3	635.965	Indoor gardens
SB339	635.61	Melons	SB419-.3	635.965	House plants
SB341	635.25	Onions	SB419.5	635.9671	Balcony gardening
SB349	635.642	Tomatoes	SB419.5	635.9671	Roof gardening
SB351.C53	635.3	Bok choy	SB422	635.9312	Annuals (Plants)
SB351.E5	635.646	Eggplant	SB423	635.9674	Water gardens
SB351.H5	635.7	Herb gardens	SB423.7-.75	635	Beds (Gardens)
SB351.H5	635.7	Herbs	SB427.5	635.9525	Desert gardening
SB351.R65	635.1	Root crops	SB427.5	635.9525	Desert plants
SB353-.5	635.8	Fungi, Edible	SBS428.5	635.973	Everlasting flowers
SB354-399	634	Fruit	SB429	635.9373	Ferns, Ornamental
SB354-402	634	Orchards	SB431	635.975	Foliage plants
SB363-.6	634.11	Apples	SB431.7	635.9	Ornamental grasses
SB364	634.62	Date	SB432.7	635.93375	Carnivorous plants
SB364	634.62	Date palm	SB433-.34	635.9647	Lawns
SB365	634.37	Fig	SB433-.34	635.9642	Turfgrasses
SB369-370	634.304	Citrus	SB433.5	635.9772	Bonsai
SB369	634.3	Citrus fruits	SB433.5	635.9772	Gardens, Miniature
SB370.G7	634.32	Grapefruit	SB434	635.932	Perennials
SB379.B2	634.772	Bananas	SB434.7	635.9543	Gardening in the shade
SB381-386	634.7	Berries	SB434.7	635.9543	Shade-tolerant plants
SB386.B6	634.713	Blackberries	SB435-437	635.97713	Flowering woody plants
SB386.B7	634.737	Blueberries	SB435-437	635.977	Ornamental trees
SB387-399	634.8	Grapes	SB435-437	635.977	Tree planting
SB401	634.57	Cashew nut	SB435-.8	635.9772	Dwarf trees
SB401	634.5	Nuts	SB435	635.97715	Ornamental evergreens
SB401	634.61	Coconut	SB435	635.9775	Evergreens
			SB436	635.977	Trees in cities

LC	Dewey	Subject Heading	LC	Dewey	Subject Heading
SB437	635.976	Hedges	SB750	632.95042	Plants—Disease and pest resistance
SB438-.34	635.93356	Cactus	SB761	634.96	Forest insects
SB439-.26	719	Natural landscaping	SB767	632.2	Galls (Botany)
SB439-.26	635.951	Native plant gardening	SB818-945	632.7	Insect pests
SB439.8	635.9525	Drought-tolerant plants	SB922-998	591.6	Zoology, Economic
SB441-.75	635.9074	Flower shows	SB939	632.752	Scale insects
SB442.8-445	381.4159092	Florists	SB950-989	632.9	Pests—Control
SB447	635.973	Everlasting flowers	SB950-989	632.9	Plants, Protection of
SB449-450.87	745.92	Flower arrangement	SB950-.5	632.6	Agricultural pests—Control
SB449.3.D7	745.92	Dried flower arrangement	SB950.9-970.4	632.95	Pesticides
SB449.5.W4	745.926	Wedding decorations	SB951.145.B68	632.9	Botanical pesticides
SB450.9-467.8	635	Gardening	SB951.145.N37	632.95	Natural pesticides
SB450.9-467	635	Gardens	SB951.3	632.952	Fungicides
SB453.5	635.0484	Organic gardening	SB951.4	632.954	Herbicides
SB454.3.P7	635.043	Planting time	SB951.5-.54	632.9517	Insecticides
SB454.8	635.0284	Garden tools	SB952.B7	632.95	Bromides
SB459	635.9528	Alpine gardens	SB952.8-955	632.94	Pesticides—Application
SB459	635.9672	Rock gardens	SB953	632.94	Spraying and dusting in agriculture
SB469-476.4	712	Landscape architecture			
SB472.45	712	Landscape design	SB955	632.94	Fumigation
SB473	635	Backyard gardens	SB957	632.95042	Pesticide resistance
SB473.2	635.9671	Patio gardening	SB970-.4	344.04633	Pesticides—Government policy
SB473.5	645.8	Garden ornaments and furniture			
			SB975-989	632.96	Pests—Biological control
SB475.8	714	Water in landscape architecture	SB975	632.96	Biological pest control agents
SB475.9.F67	719.33	Forest landscape design	SB979.5-985	632.93	Plant quarantine
SB476	621.3229	Garden lighting	SB993.3-.34	591.609(4-9)	Zoology, Economic—[By region or country]
SB481-485	363.68068	Parks—Management			
SB481-485	363.68	Parks	SB993.3-32	591.60973	Zoology, Economic—United States
SB481-484	363.68	National parks and reserves			
			SB993.34	591.609(4-9)	Zoology, Economic—[Other countries]
SB482-483	363.680973	Parks—United States			
SB484-485	363.6809(4-9)	Parks—[Other countries or regions]			
			SB993.5-994	632.69	Mammal pests
SB599-1100	632.(6-7)	Pests	SB995-996	632.96	Beneficial birds
SB599-989	632.3	Plant diseases	SB995	632.68	Bird pests
SB599-999	632.(6-7)	Agricultural pests			
SB599.2	632.(6-7)06	Agricultural pests—Congresses	SD	634.9	Forests and forestry
			SD1	634.906	Forests and forestry—Societies, etc.
SB601	632	Plant parasites			
SB603.5	635.92	Garden pests	SD11-115	634.909(4-9)	Forests and forestry—[By region or country]
SB605	632.09(4-9)	Garden pests—[By region or country]			
			SD11-12	634.90973	Forests and forestry—United States
SB610-615	632.5	Weeds			
SB610-615	632.5	Weeds—Control	SD12	634.9097(4-9)	Forests and forestry—[United States, By state]
SB610-615	632.52	Parasitic plants			
SB733	632.4	Fungal diseases of plants			
SB733	632.4	Fungi in agriculture	SD250-381.5	634.9071	Forestry schools and education
SB741.D68	632.446	Downy mildew diseases			
SB741.M65	632.43	Mildew	SD356-.54	634.9072	Forests and forestry—Research
SB745	632.19	Crops—Effect of air pollution on			
			SD387.C58	634.92	Clearcutting
SB745	632.19	Crops—Effect of acid precipitation on	SD387.O43	333.75	Old growth forests
			SD387.S52	634.92	Short rotation forestry
SB745	632.19	Plants, Effect of air pollution on	SD387.W6	634.99	Woodlots
			SD388	634.90284	Forest machinery
SB745	632.19	Plants, Effect of acid precipitation on	SD391-535	634.9	Trees

LC	Dewey	Subject Heading	LC	Dewey	Subject Heading
SD391	634.9565	Tree planting	SF99.Y4	636.0855	Yeast as feed
SD392	634.95	Silvicultural systems	SF101-103.5	636.20812	Livestock brands
SD396.5	634.953	Forest thinning	SF101-103.5	636.20812	Cattle brands
SD397.C47	578.738	Chaparral	SF105-109	636.082	Animal breeding
SD397.C7	634.974	Conifers	SF105	636.082	Inbreeding
SD397.D37	634.9758	Dawn redwood	SF105.27-.275	636.082	Rare breeds
SD397.D7	634.9754	Douglas fir	SF105.5	636.08245	Artificial insemination
SD397.D87	634.9721	Durmast oak	SF140.B54	636.0821	Animal biotechnology
SD397.E27	634.9753	Eastern hemlock	SF140.P38	636.0845	Pastoral systems
SD397.E54	634.9721	English oak	SF170-180	636.0886	Working animals
SD397.E8	634.973766	Eucalyptus	SF180	636.0882	Draft animals
SD397.F5	634.9754	Fir	SF191-219	636.2	Cattle
SD397.R3	634.9758	Redwood	SF191-219	636.2	Cows
SD399.5	634.956	Forest genetics	SF198-199	636.2(2-8)	Cattle breeds
SD409	634.956	Afforestation	SF199.A3	636.28	Africander cattle
SD409	634.956	Reforestation	SF199.D38	636.226	Devon cattle
SD411-428	634.93	Forest protection	SF199.D4	636.225	Dexter cattle
SD411-428	634.9	Forest conservation	SF199.E2	636.23	East Prussian cattle
SD411	634.93	Forests and forestry—Safety measures	SF199.G8	636.224	Guernsey cattle
			SF207	636.213	Beef cattle
SD420.5-421.5	634.9618	Forest fires	SF208	636.2142	Dairy cattle
SD421	634.9618	Forest fire detection	SF211	636.226	Dual-purpose cattle
SD421	634.9618	Forest fires—Prevention and control	SF221-250	636.2142	Dairy farming
			SF221-250	636.2142	Dairy farms
SD421.375	634.93	Fire lookout stations	SF221-250	636.2142	Dairying
SD421.43	634.9618	Aeronautics in wildfire control	SF241-245	636.21420711	Dairy schools
			SF241-245	636.2142071	Dairying—Study and teaching
SD425	634.9617	Floods			
SD426-428	333.7511	Forest reserves	SF247	636.21420284	Dairying—Equipment and supplies
SD430-557	338.17498	Timber			
SD537-538.83	634.98	Logging	SF247	637.1240284	Milking machines
SD538-557	634.98	Lumbering	SF247	637.148	Cream-separators
SD543.3.U6	634.9870973	Non-timber forest products—United States	SF250	637.124	Milking
			SF250.5-275	637.14	Dairy processing
			SF250.5-275	637	Dairy products
SF	636	Animal culture	SF251-262.5	637.141	Milk
SF1-140	636	Livestock	SF255	637.12	Dairy inspection
SF41	636.082	Domestication	SF259	637.143	Dairy products—Drying
SF84.82-85.6	636.0845	Rangelands	SF259	637.143	Dried milk
SF84.82-98	636.0845	Range management	SF259	637.141	Milk—Pasteurization
SF94.5-99	636.085	Animal nutrition	SF259	637.141	Milk—Sterilization
SF94.5-99	636.0855	Feeds	SF259	637.141	Homogenized milk
SF94.5-99	636.084	Animal feeding	SF259	637.142	Condensed milk
SF97.7	636.0855	Feeds—Flavor and odor	SF261	636.21420681	Dairying—Accounting
SF98.A2	636.08557	Feed additives	SF261	381.417	Dairy products—Marketing
SF98.A5	636.08557	Antibiotics in animal nutrition	SF263-269.5	637.2	Butter
			SF266	637.148	Creameries
SF98.F	636.0852	Fiber in animal nutrition	SF270-274	637.3	Cheese
SF98.F	636.0855	Feeds—Fiber content	SF272.C5	637.354	Cheddar cheese
SF98.M4	636.08557	Medicated feeds	SF272.P3	637.354	Parmesan cheese
SF98.P46	636.0855	Pesticide residues in feeds	SF277-359.7	636.101	Foals
SF99.A37	636.08556	Agricultural wastes as feed	SF277-359.7	636.1	Horses
SF99.A5	636.0855	Alfalfa as feed	SF290-291	636.1	Horse farms
SF99.C59	633.255	Corn as feed	SF293.A5	636.13	American saddlebred horse
SF99.D5	636.0855	Distillers feeds			
SF99.F37	636.0855	Feathers as feed	SF293.M56	636.109	Miniature horses
SF99.F5	636.0855	Fish meal as feed	SF293.P5	636.13	Pinto horse
SF99.M33	636.0855	Marine algae as feed	SF293.S72	636.13	Standardbred horse
SF99.W34	636.0855	Organic wastes as feed	SF294.2-294.35	798	Horse sports

LC	Dewey	Subject Heading	LC	Dewey	Subject Heading
SF294.5-297.7	636.10811	Horse shows	SF411.5	636.0811	Pet shows
SF295.185-.187	636.10811	Show horses	SF414.2	636.0887	Pets—Housing
SF295.2	798.24	Show riding	SF414.3	636.0887	Pet boarding facilities
SF295.65	799.23	Hunt riding	SF421-440.2	636.7	Dogs
SF295.7	636.10811	Event horses	SF421-435	636.707	Puppies
SF296.R4	798.2028	Reining (Horsemanship)	SF422.7-.82	636.708	Dog owners
SF296.T75	798.23	Trick riding	SF422.7-.86	636.7082	Dog breeders
SF296.V37	798.25	Vaulting (Horsemanship)	SF423	636.70822	Dogs—Pedigrees
SF304.5-307	388.341	Driving of horse-drawn vehicles	SF425-.8	636.70811	Dog shows
SF304.5-307	388.341	Coaching	SF425.3	636.70811	Show dogs
SF309	798.2	Horsemanship	SF425.7	636.70811	Dogs—Obedience trials
SF309.27	798.23	Sidesaddle riding	SF427.15	636.70837	Dog collars
SF309.28	798.23	Trail riding	SF427.46	636.7083	Dog walking
SF309.3	798.23	Western riding	SF427.55	636.70833	Pet grooming salons
SF309.48-.658	798.23	Dressage	SF427.55	381.41670833	Dog grooming industry
SF309.65-.653	636.13	Dressage horses	SF428	636.70831	Kennels
SF309.9	636.10837	Bits (Bridles)	SF428.2	636.73	Working dogs
SF309.9	636.10837	Bridles	SF428.5	636.752	Bird dogs
SF309.9	636.13037	English saddles	SF428.55	636.70886	Rescue dogs
SF309.9	636.13037	Western saddle	SF428.6	636.70886	Livestock protection dogs
SF310-.5	798.2306	Riding clubs	SF428.7	636.70886	Sled dogs
SF310.4	798.23071	Riding schools	SF428.73	636.70886	Search dogs
SF311-.3	636.15	Draft horses	SF428.8	636.70886	Watchdogs
SF312	636.14	Coach horses	SF429.A4	636.7533	Afghan hounds
SF315	636.16	Ponies	SF429.B47	636.73	Bernese mountain dog
SF315.2.C4	636.16	Chincoteague pony	SF429.B78	636.7524	Brittany spaniel
SF321-359.7	798.4	Horse racing	SF429.B86	636.73	Bullmastiff
SF324-.4	798.40068	Racetracks (Horse-racing)	SF429.C3	636.755	Cairn terriers
SF338.7-345	798.46	Harness racing	SF429.D25	636.7538	Dachshunds
SF343	636.12	Harness racehorses	SF429.D3	636.72	Dalmatian dog
SF357.E67	798.400942	Epsom Derby, England (Horse race)	SF429.D33	636.755	Dandie Dinmont terrier
SF357.K4	798.4009 76944	Kentucky Derby, Louisville, Ky.	SF429.D6	636.736	Doberman pinschers
			SF429.E47	636.7524	English cocker spaniel
SF359-.7	798.45	Steeplechasing	SF429.E7	636.7524	English springer spaniels
SF359.7.G7	798.4509 42753	Grand National Handicap Steeplechase	SF429.E8	636.73	Eskimo dogs
			SF429.G75	636.73	Great Pyrenees
SF360.6-361.75	636.1	Domestic asses	SF429.H6	636.753	Hounds
SF361	636.182	Donkeys	SF429.S39	636.7532	Scottish deerhound
SF361	636.182092	Donkey breeders	SF429.S5	636.7526	Setters (Dogs)
SF362	636.183	Mules	SF431	636.70835	Dogs—Training
SF371-379	636.3	Sheep	SF434.5-435	381.4167	Dog industry
SF376.5	636.3	Lambs	SF439.5-440.2	798.8	Dog racing
SF379	636.30833	Sheep-shearing	SF440.15	798.83	Sled dog racing
SF380-388	636.39	Goats	SF440.2	798.8	Dog race betting
SF391-397.4	636.4	Swine	SF441-450	636.8	Cats
SF393.D9	636.483	Duroc Jersey swine	SF443	636.80822	Cats—Pedigrees
SF401.A45	636.292	American bison	SF446.6	636.80835	Cats—Training
SF401.C2	636.295	Camels	SF449	636.8	Cat breeds
SF401.D3	636.29401	Deer farming	SF449.A28	636.826	Abyssinian cat
SF401.E4	636.965701	Elk farming	SF449.C34	636.8	Calico cats
SF401.G85	636.93592	Guinea pigs	SF449.P4	636.832	Persian cat
SF402-405	636.9701	Fur farming	SF451-455	636.9322	Rabbits
SF403-405	636.97	Fur-bearing animals	SF455.D8	636.9322	Dutch rabbits
SF405.5-407	636.0885	Laboratory animals	SF455.D85	636.9322	Dwarf rabbits
SF405.M6	636.97662701	Mink farming	SF456-458.83	597.073	Aquariums
SF408-.6	636.9	Captive wild animals	SF457.1	597.177073	Marine aquariums
SF411-459	636.0887	Pets	SF459.C45	639.3956	Chameleons as pets
			SF459.H3	636.93560887	Dwarf hamsters as pets
			SF461	636.68	Cage birds

LC	Dewey	Subject Heading	LC	Dewey	Subject Heading
SF461	636.6	Aviculture	SF769	636.08960759	Veterinary autopsy
SF462.5	636.6	Captive wild birds	SF771-774	636.0896075	Veterinary
SF463-.7	636.68625	Canaries			medicine—Diagnosis
SF473.C63	636.6865	Cockatoos	SF774.5	636.089073	Veterinary nursing
SF481-513	636.5	Chickens	SF756.3-.37	636.0890711	Veterinary colleges
SF489.B2	636.5871	Bantams	SF778	636.0896025	Veterinary emergencies
SF490-.8	636.5142	Eggs—Production	SF778	636.0896028	Veterinary critical care
SF490-.8	636.5142	Eggs	SF780.3	636.0896014	Veterinary bacteriology
SF492-493	636.5082	Poultry—Breeding	SF780.4	636.08960194	Veterinary virology
SF494	636.508(4-5)	Poultry—Feeding and	SF780.9	636.08944	Veterinary epidemiology
		feeds	SF781-809	636.08969	Communicable diseases in
SF495	636.5082	Eggs—Incubation			animals
SF495-497	636.5082	Poultry—Hatcheries	SF787	636.0896956	Anthrax
SF502.8-503.52	636.63	Game fowl	SF799	636.089682	Meningitis
SF504.7-505.63	636.597	Ducks	SF810	636.089696	Domestic animals—
SF507	636.592	Turkeys			Parasites
SF508-510	636.63082	Game bird culture	SF810.H8	636.0896964	Echinococcosis
SF515.5.A44	639.3984	Alligator farming	SF811	636.089612	Veterinary cardiology
SF517-562	638	Beneficial insects	SF851-855	636.089639	Nutrition disorders in
SF518	638	Insect rearing			animals
SF521-539	638.1	Bee culture	SF887	636.08982	Veterinary obstetrics
SF521-539	638.12	Honeybee	SF910.5	636.08967	Veterinary orthopedics
SF539	638.16	Honey	SF910.T8	636.0896992	Veterinary oncology
SF539	638.16	Bee products	SF911-914.4	636.0897	Veterinary surgery
SF539	638.16	Bee pollen	SF914	636.089796	Veterinary anesthesia
SF541-560	638.2	Sericulture	SF914.3	636.08960252	First aid for animals
SF541-560	638.2	Silk	SF914.4	636.089715	Fractures in animals
SF541-560	638.2	Silkworms	SF914.5	636.0895892	Veterinary acupuncture
SF559.5-560	638.2	Silkworms, Non-mulberry	SF915-918	636.08951	Pharmacy
SF597.E3	639.75	Earthworm culture	SF916.5	636.08951	Veterinary prescriptions
SF600-1100	636.0896	Domestic animals—	SF918.A5	636.0895329	Antibiotics in veterinary
		Diseases			medicine
SF600-1100	636.0893	Animal health	SF918.V32	636.0895372	Veterinary vaccines
SF600-1100	636.0896	Animals—Diseases	SF959.C6	636.1089755	Colic in horses
SF600-1100	636.0896	Livestock—Diseases	SF961-967	636.20886	Cattle—Diseases
SF600-1100	636.089	Veterinary medicine	SF961-967	636.208969	Cattle—Infections
SF600-604	636.08906	Veterinary medicine—	SF962	636.208969	Blackleg in cattle
		Societies, etc.	SF967.E3	636.208969	East Coast fever
SF604.4-.7	636.089	Veterinary hospitals	SF969.E	636.308969	Epizootic catarrh in sheep
SF605	636.08906	Veterinary medicine—	SF977.P5	636.408969	Swine plague
		Congresses	SF985-986	636.80896	Cats—Diseases
SF610	636.089014	Veterinary medicine—	SF986.C37	636.808696	Cat flea
		Terminology	SF991.D5	636.70896	Distemper
SF611	636.089025	Veterinarians—Directories	SF991-992	636.70896	Dogs—Diseases
SF612-613	636.089092	Veterinarians	SF995-.4	636.50896	Poultry—Diseases
SF615-724	636.08909	Veterinary medicine—	SF996.45	333.95416	Wildlife rehabilitation
		History			
SF740	636.0894	Veterinary public health	SH	639.2	Fisheries
SF740	636.089456	Animals as carriers of	SH1	639.305	Fisheries—Periodicals
		disease	SH3	639.206	Fisheries—Congresses
SF740	636.0896959	Zoonoses	SH11	639.20973	Fisheries—United States
SF756.39	174.2	Veterinarians—	SH20	639.2092	Fish culturists
		Professional ethics	SH20.5-191	639.8	Aquaculture
SF756.5	636.0821	Domestic animals—	SH21	639.809	Aquaculture—History
		Genetic engineering	SH34-133	639.809(4-9)	Aquaculture—[By region
SF756.5	636.0821	Veterinary genetics			or country]
SF757.15	636.089448	Veterinary disinfection	SH138	639.8	Mariculture
SF761-767	636.0891	Veterinary anatomy	SH151-179	639.3	Fish-culture
SF768-.2	636.0892	Veterinary physiology	SH153	639.92	Fishways

LC	Dewey	Subject Heading	LC	Dewey	Subject Heading
SH157.8-.85	639.92	Fish habitat improvement	SH343.9	639.20289	Fisheries—Safety measures
SH157.85.A7	639.92	Artificial reefs	SH344-.8	639.20284	Fisheries—Equipment and supplies
SH171-179	639.964	Fishes—Pathogens			
SH171-179	639.96	Fish kills	SH344.6.T67	639.20284	Fish traps
SH171-179	639.964	Fishes—Diseases	SH344.8.H6	639.20284	Fishhooks
SH171-179	639.964	Fishes—Infections	SH344.8.N4	639.20284	Fishing nets
SH175	639.96	Fishes—Parasites	SH351.E4	639.2743	Eel fisheries
SH177.R4	639.964	Red tide	SH351.S3	639.2745	Sardine fisheries
SH177.R4	615.954	Paralytic shellfish poisoning	SH360-363	639.29	Sealing
			SH365-380.92	639.4	Shellfish culture
SH185	639.3789	Frog culture	SH365-367	639.409(4-9)	Shellfish culture—[By region or country]
SH211	639.209	Fisheries—History			
SH213-.77	639.209163	Fisheries—Atlantic Ocean	SH371-374.52	639.42	Mussel fisheries
SH214-215	639.209164	Fisheries—Pacific Ocean	SH371	639.41	Oyster fisheries
SH216-.55	639.209165	Fisheries—Indian Ocean	SH371.5-.52	639.4832	Abalone fisheries
SH221-222	639.20973	Fisheries—United States	SH371.5-.52	639.4832	Abalone culture
SH223-229	639.20971	Fisheries—Canada	SH372.5-.52	639.42	Mussels
SH231	639.20972	Fisheries—Mexico	SH375-377	639.412	Pearl fisheries
SH232	639.209728	Fisheries—Central America	SH377.5	639.412	Mother-of-pearl
			SH379.5	639.41	Oyster shell
SH233	639.209729	Fisheries—West Indies	SH380.4-.45	639.56	Crab culture
SH234-251	639.2098	Fisheries—South America	SH380.4-.45	639.56	Crab fisheries
SH253-293	639.2094	Fisheries—Europe	SH381-385	639.28	Whaling
SH255-260	639.20941	Fisheries—Great Britain	SH393	639.89	Seagrasses
SH261-262	639.209415	Fisheries—Ireland	SH399.C6	639.32	Coral fisheries
SH267-268	639.209489	Fisheries—Denmark	SH399.T9	639.392	Turtle fisheries
SH268.G83	639.209982	Fisheries—Greenland	SH400-.8	639.22	Seafood gathering
SH273-274	639.209495	Fisheries—Greece	SH400.4-.8	639.4	Shellfish gathering
SH275-276	639.209492	Fisheries—Netherlands	SH400.5.C53	639.44	Clamming
SH277-278	639.20945	Fisheries—Italy	SH400.5.C7	639.56	Crabbing
SH279-280	639.209481	Fisheries—Norway	SH401-691	799.12	Fishing
SH281-282	639.209469	Fisheries—Portugal	SH401	799.1205	Fishing—Periodicals
SH283-284	639.20947	Fisheries—Russia	SH403	799.1206	Hunting and fishing clubs
SH285-286	639.20946	Fisheries—Spain	SH414-415	799.1092	Fishers
SH287-288	639.209485	Fisheries—Sweden	SH421	799.109	Fishing—History
SH291-292	639.209561	Fisheries—Turkey	SH447-453	799.10284	Fishing tackle
SH295-307	639.2095	Fisheries—Asia	SH447-453	799.10284	Fishing—Equipment and supplies
SH297-298	639.20951	Fisheries—China			
SH301-302	639.20952	Fisheries—Japan	SH448	799.10284	Bait
SH302.5-.7	639.209519	Fisheries—Korea	SH451.3	799.10284	Fish decoys
SH317-318	639.20994	Fisheries—Australia	SH452-.2	799.10284	Fishing rods
SH318.5	639.20993	Fisheries—New Zealand	SH452.9.H	799.10284	Fishhooks
SH319	639.2099(5-6)	Fisheries—Oceania	SH452.9.K6	799.1028	Fishing knots
SH327.5	333.7	Fishery resources	SH454-.9	799.124	Casting (Fishing)
SH327.7	639.977	Fishery conservation	SH454.2	799.124	Fly casting
SH328-329	639.2068	Fishery management	SH455.4	799.122	Bait fishing
SH332-.2	639.2071	Fishery schools	SH455.6	799.122	Bottom fishing
SH332-.2	639.2072	Fishery research stations	SH456-.2	799.124	Fly fishing
SH334	338.3727	Fisheries subsidies	SH457-.5	799.16	Saltwater fishing
SH334.5-344.8	639.2028	Fishery technology	SH457.5	799.12	Big game fishing
SH334.9-336.5	664.94	Fishery processing	SH462	799.1097	Fishing—North America
SH335-337	664.94(1-8)	Fishery products—Preservation	SH463-565	799.10973	Fishing—United States
			SH571-572	799.10971	Fishing—Canada
SH335	363.1929064	Fish inspection	SH577-578	799.1209729	Fishing—West Indies
SH337.5	387.1	Fishing ports	SH681	799.1758	Bass fishing
SH343.4	338.372072	Fishery research vessels	SH684-686.7	799.1755	Salmon fishing
SH343.5	639.2072	Exploratory fishing	SH687-688	799.1755	Trout fishing
SH343.8	623.89	Fisheries navigation	SH691.E4	799.1743	Eel fishing

240

LC	Dewey	Subject Heading	LC	Dewey	Subject Heading
T57.35	670.21	Industrial engineering—Statistical methods	TA30-31	620.009728	Engineering—Central America
T57.72	658.544	Fatigue	TA32-33	620.009729	Engineering—West Indies
T57.74-.79	519.72	Linear programming	TA36-37	620.00982	Engineering—Argentina
T57.8-.825	519.76	Nonlinear programming	TA38-39	620.00984	Engineering—Bolivia
T57.85	658.4032	Network analysis (Planning)	TA41-42	620.00981	Engineering—Brazil
			TA43-44	620.00983	Engineering—Chile
T57.9	658.4034	Queuing theory	TA45-46	620.009861	Engineering—Colombia
T57.92	519.3	Game theory	TA47	620.009866	Engineering—Ecuador
T57.95	658.5036	Decision-making	TA48	620.009881	Engineering—Guyana
T58.8	658.515	Industrial efficiency	TA49	620.009883	Engineering—Surinam
T58.7-.8	338/670.42	Industrial capacity	TA50	620.009882	Engineering—French Guiana
T59-.2	658.562	Standardization			
T59.5	670.427	Automation	TA51	620.009892	Engineering—Paraguay
T60.4-.47	658.5421	Time study	TA52	620.00985	Engineering—Peru
T60.7	658.542	Motion study	TA53	620.009895	Engineering—Uruguay
T61-173	607.1	Technical education	TA54	620.00987	Engineering—Venezuela
T65	607.2	Research	TA57-64	620.00941	Engineering—Great Britain
T71-170	607.10(4-9)	Technical education—[By region or country]	TA65-.2	620.009436	Engineering—Austria
			TA65.3-.4	620.009437	Engineering—Czechoslovakia
T174	601.12	Technological forecasting			
T174.3	338.926	Technology transfer	TA65.5-66	620.009439	Engineering—Hungary
T174.5	303.483	Technology assessment	TA67-68	620.009493	Engineering—Belgium
T174.7	620.5	Nanotechnology	TA69-70	620.009489	Engineering—Denmark
T175-178	607.2	Research, Industrial	TA71-72.5	620.00944	Engineering—France
T201-342	608	Patents	TA73-74.5	620.00943	Engineering—Germany
T201-339	608	Inventions	TA75-76	620.009495	Engineering—Greece
T221-323.7	608.7	Patents—History	TA77-78	620.009492	Engineering—Netherlands
T324	608.0228	Models (Patents)	TA79-80	620.00945	Engineering—Italy
T325	602.75	Trademarks	TA81-82	620.009481	Engineering—Norway
T351-385	604.2	Mechanical drawing	TA83-84.5	620.009469	Engineering—Portugal
T352	604.2068	Drawing-room management	TA85-86	620.00947	Engineering—Russia
			TA87-88	620.00946	Engineering—Spain
T352	604.24	Drawing-room practice	TA88.5	620.00948	Engineering—Scandinavia
T355	604.2	Structural drawing	TA89-90	620.009485	Engineering—Sweden
T359	604.2	Freehand technical sketching	TA91-92	620.009494	Engineering—Switzerland
			TA95.A2	620.009496	Engineering—Balkan Peninsula
T362-369	604.245	Projection			
T369	604.245	Perspective	TA95.F5	620.0094897	Engineering—Finland
T375-377	604.20284	Drawing instruments	TA95.Y8	620.009497	Engineering—Yugoslavia
T379	604.25	Blueprints	TA101-102	620.00951	Engineering—China
T385	006.6	Computer graphics	TA103-104	620.00954	Engineering—India
T391-999	607.34	Exhibitions	TA104.5-.6	620.0095491	Engineering—Pakistan
			TA104.7-.8	620.0095493	Engineering—Sri Lanka
TA	620	Engineering	TA105-106	620.00952	Engineering—Japan
TA	624	Civil engineering	TA107-108	620.00955	Engineering—Iran
TA1-4	620.005	Engineering—Periodicals	TA109-110	620.00957	Engineering—Asiatic Russia
TA5	620.006	Engineering—Congresses			
TA9	620.003	Engineering—Dictionaries	TA111-112	620.009561	Engineering—Turkey
TA11	620.00148	Engineering—Notation	TA113.I55	620.009598	Engineering—Indonesia
TA12	620.0025	Engineering firms—Directories	TA113.I7	620.009567	Engineering—Iraq
			TA113.I75	620.0095694	Engineering—Israel
TA15-19	620.009	Engineering—History	TA113.P6	620.009599	Engineering—Philippines
TA21-127	620.009(4-9)	Engineering—[By region or country]	TA115-119	620.0096	Engineering—Africa
			TA117-118	620.00962	Engineering—Egypt
TA23-25	620.00973	Engineering—United States	TA121-122	620.00994	Engineering—Australia
			TA122.5-.6	620.00993	Engineering—New Zealand
TA26-27	620.00971	Engineering—Canada			
TA28-29	620.00972	Engineering—Mexico	TA123-124	620.0099(5-6)	Engineering—Oceania

LC	Dewey	Subject Heading	LC	Dewey	Subject Heading
TA125-.5	620.00998	Engineering—Arctic regions	TA416-417	620.0072	Engineering laboratories
			TA417.2-.55	620.1127	Non-destructive testing
TA139-140	620.0092	Engineers—Biography	TA417.4	620.11274	Ultrasonic testing
TA157-158.3	620.0023	Engineers	TA417.6	620.11232	Deformations (Mechanics)
TA157	620.008996073	Afro-American engineers	TA418.12	620.11295	Photoelasticity
TA157	174.962	Engineering ethics	TA418.16	620.1126	Brittleness
TA157	620.006	Engineering firms	TA418.22	620.11233	Materials—Creep
TA160-.6	620.0072	Engineering—Research	TA418.42	620.1126	Hardness
TA165	629.8	Automatic control	TA418.45	620.1126	Hard materials
TA165	620.00284	Engineering instruments	TA418.58	620.1121	Thermal stresses
TA167	621.3984	Man-machine systems	TA418.74-.76	620.11223	Corrosion and anti-corrosives
TA168	620.001171	Systems engineering			
TA171	363.7064	Environmental testing	TA418.76	667.9	Protective coatings
TA174	620.0042	Engineering design	TA418.9.C6	620.118	Composite materials
TA177	620.00228	Engineering models	TA419-424.6	620.12	Timber
TA177.4-185	620.00681	Engineering economy	TA426-428	691.2	Building stones
TA180-182	620.00212	Engineering—Specifications	TA432-433	691.4	Bricks
TA180-181	620.00212	Specifications	TA439	620.136	Expansive concrete
TA191	620.0044	Engineering inspection	TA439-446	620.136	Concrete
TA190-194	620.0068	Engineering—Management	TA447	620.14	Drain-tiles
			TA450	620.144	Glass
TA213-215	620.00284	Engineering—Equipment and supplies	TA455.F5	620.143	Fire-clay
			TA455.P5-.P55	620.1923	Plastics
TA216-217	620.006	Engineering firms	TA455.P58	620.192	Polymers
TA329-348	620.00151	Engineering mathematics	TA459-492	620.160287	Metals—Testing
TA337-338	620.00728	Engineering—Graphic methods	TA460	620.166	Metals—Fatigue
			TA473	620.176	Steel—Fatigue
TA340	620.00727	Engineering—Statistical methods	TA472-473	620.17	Steel, Galvanized
			TA474-475	620.17	Cast-iron
TA345	620.00420285	Computer-aided engineering	TA478	620.18	Nonmetallic steel
			TA479.3	620.18	Nonferrous metals
TA347.D45	620.00151	Differential equations	TA479.C37	620.17	Carbon steel
TA347.F5	620.00151535	Finite element method	TA479.S7	620.16	Steel, Stainless
TA350-359	620.1	Mechanics, Applied	TA480.A6	620.186	Aluminum, Structural
TA354.5	620.1126	Penetration mechanics	TA480.A6	620.186	Aluminum alloys
TA357-359	620.106	Fluid dynamics	TA480.C7	620.182	Copper
TA357.5.C38	620.1064	Cavitation	TA480.N6	620.188	Nickel
TA357.5.M43	620.10640287	Fluid dynamic measurements	TA480.S5	620.18923	Silver
			TA480.T5	620.185	Tin
TA357.5.M59	620.1064	Mixing	TA480.T54	620.18932	Titanium
TA357.5.M84	620.1064	Multiphase flow	TA486	620.16	Corrosion resistant alloys
TA357.5.U57	620.1064	Unsteady flow (Fluid dynamics)	TA492.G5	624.17723	Girders
			TA492.S25	624.1779	Sandwich construction
TA365-367	620.2	Acoustical engineering	TA501-625	526.9	Surveying
TA368	620.00218	Standards, Engineering	TA515-531	526.9	Surveyors
TA401-492	620.11	Materials	TA535-538	526.9071	Surveying—Study and teaching
TA401-492	620.110287	Testing			
TA401-492	620.1(2-9)	Building materials	TA562-581	526.90284	Surveying—Instruments
TA401	620.1105	Materials—Periodicals	TA579-581	526.90284	Measuring-tapes
TA402	620.1103	Materials—Dictionaries	TA579	526.90284	Surveyors' chains
TA404.2	620.11072	Materials—Research	TA583	526.33	Triangulation
TA405	620.112	Strength of materials	TA590	526.3	Topographical surveying
TA409	620.1126	Fracture mechanics	TA592-593.9	526.982	Photographic surveying
TA410-417.7	620.112	Strength of materials	TA593	526.982	Photogrammetry
TA410	620.112	Buckling (Mechanics)	TA597	526.63	Azimuth
TA413-.5	620.11260287	Fatigue testing machines	TA611	526.9	Surveys—Plotting
TA413-.5	620.11260287	Testing-machines	TA616	526.98	Topographical drawing
TA416-417	620.0072	Engineering experiment stations	TA625	526.9	Route surveying
			TA630-901	624.1	Structural engineering

LC	Dewey	Subject Heading	LC	Dewey	Subject Heading
TA630	624.105	Structural engineering—Periodicals	TA1015	629.0409	Transportation engineering—History
TA638.2	624.1072	Structural engineering—Research	TA1021-1127	629.0409(4-9)	Transportation engineering—[By region or country]
TA641	624.10285	Structural engineering—Computer programs	TA1023-1025	629.040973	Transportation engineering—United States
TA645-656.5	624.171	Structural analysis (Engineering)	TA1163	629.04071	Transportation engineering—Study and teaching
TA648.2	624.172	Dead loads (Mechanics)			
TA652	620.11233	Plastic analysis (Engineering)	TA1205-1207	388.4	Urban transportation
			TA1225	388.47	Terminals (Transportation)
TA654-656.5	624.176	Structural dynamics	TA1250	629.040289	Signal lights
TA654.4	624.172	Snow loads	TA1501-1820	621.36	Photonics
TA654.6	624.1762	Earthquake engineering	TA1570	621.362	Infrared technology
TA656.5	624.10289	Safety factor in engineering	TA1570	621.362	Infrared sources
			TA1637	621.367	Image processing
TA658-.8	624.1771	Structural design	TA1660	621.3693	Integrated optics
TA658.44	624.1762	Earthquake resistant design	TA1671-1715	621.366	Lasers
			TA1690	621.3664	Dye lasers
TA660.F7-.F73	624.1773	Structural frames	TA1693	621.366	Free electron lasers
TA660.S6	624.1772	Slabs	TA1695	621.3663	Gas lasers
TA660.S67	624.17723	Steel I-beams	TA1705	621.366	Ruby lasers
TA660.T8	624.1773	Trusses	TA1750	623.7314	Electrooptical devices
TA665	624.183412	Prestressed construction	TA1770	621.3828	Acoustooptical devices
TA668	624.18923	Plastics in building			
TA670-683.94	624.183	Masonry	TC	621.2	Hydraulic engineering
TA680-683.94	624.1834	Concrete construction	TC1	621.205	Hydraulic engineering—Periodicals
TA680-683.94	624.1833	Portland cement			
TA683-683.94	624.18341	Reinforced concrete construction	TC9	621.203	Hydraulic engineering—Dictionaries
TA683.5.S4	624.1834	Shells, Concrete	TC15-20	621.209	Hydraulic engineering—History
TA683.5.W34	624.1834	Concrete walls			
TA683.9-.94	624.183412	Prestressed concrete construction	TC21-127	621.109(4-9)	Hydraulic engineering—[By region or country]
TA684-695	624.182	Building, Iron and steel	TC139-140	621.2092	Hydraulic engineers—Biography
TA684-695	624.1821	Steel, Structural			
TA703-705.4	624.151	Engineering geology	TC147	621.20422	Tidal power
TA705.2-.4	624.15109(3-4)	Engineering geology—[By region or country]	TC147	621.20422	Ocean wave power
			TC147	621.20422	Water-power
TA710-711.5	624.15136	Soil mechanics	TC157-.5	621.1071	Hydraulic engineering—Study and teaching
TA712	624.19	Underground construction			
TA715-772	624.152	Earthwork	TC158	621.2072	Hydraulic laboratories
TA725	624.1520284	Earthmoving machinery	TC160-179	532	Hydraulics
TA725	624.1520284	Scrapers (Earthmoving machinery)	TC167	627.4	Flood dams and reservoirs
			TC167	627.86	Reservoirs
TA730-748	624.152	Excavation	TC171-179	532.5	Hydrodynamics
TA735-747	621.865	Excavating machinery	TC172	532.59	Wave makers
TA740-747	624.152	Rock excavation	TC172	532.59	Water waves
TA745-747	621.952	Rock-drills	TC173	532.52	Water jets
TA748	624.1526	Blasting	TC173	532.52	Nozzles
TA760-772	624.162	Embankments	TC174	620.1064	Water hammer
TA760-772	624.164	Retaining walls	TC175-.2	532.54	Channels (Hydraulic engineering)
TA775-787	624.15	Foundations			
TA780-787	624.154	Piling (Civil engineering)	TC175.2	551.353	Sediment transport
TA800-820	624.19	Tunneling	TC177	532.510284	Flow meters
TA1001-1280	629.04	Transportation engineering	TC187-188	627.73	Dredging
TA1001-1004	629.0405	Transportation engineering—Periodicals	TC187	627.73	Dredging spoil
			TC188	627.73	Dredges

LC	Dewey	Subject Heading	LC	Dewey	Subject Heading
TC193	627.75	Underwater drilling	TC970	627.54	Ditches
TC195-201	627.7	Underwater construction	TC975	627.54	Marshes
TC198	624.157	Coffer-dams	TC1501-1800	620.4162	Ocean engineering
TC201	594.4	Shipworms	TC1501	620.416205	Ocean engineering—
TC203-327	387.1	Harbors			Periodicals
TC328	627.38	Marinas	TC1505	620.416206	Ocean engineering—
TC330-340	627.24	Shore protection			Congresses
TC333	627.24	Breakwaters	TC1662	623.8205	Remote submersibles
TC335	627.24	Sea-walls	TC1800	627.7	Underwater pipelines
TC337	627.24	Dikes (Engineering)			
TC337	627.24	Levees	TD	628	Sanitary engineering
TC337	627.24	Embankments	TD1-4	628.05	Sanitary engineering—
TC343-345	627.54	Reclamation of land			Periodicals
TC353-365	627.2	Harbors	TD12	628.025	Sanitary engineers—
TC355-365	627.31	Docks			Directories
TC357	627.31	Piers	TD15-20	628.09	Sanitary engineering—
TC357	627.31	Wharves			History
TC361	627.31	Dry docks	TD21-127	628.09(4-9)	Sanitary engineering—[By
TC363	623.83	Floating harbors			region or country]
TC375-381	627.922	Lighthouses	TD139-140	628.092	Sanitary engineers—
TC401-558	628.112	River engineering			Biography
TC401-558	628.112	Rivers	TD159-168	628	Municipal engineering
TC401-558	627	Water resources	TD169-171.8	628	Environmental protection
		development	TD172-193.5	628.5	Pollution
TC415-527	628.109(4-9)	River engineering—[By	TD178.5-.7	628.5072	Pollution—Research
		region or country]	TD179	628.509	Pollution—History
TC533	627.42	Embankments	TD179.5-191	628.509(4-9)	Pollution—[By region or
TC533	627.42	Levees			country]
TC540-558	627.8	Dams	TD180-181	628.50973	Pollution—United States
TC540-558	627.8	Flood dams and reservoirs	TD182-.4	628.50971	Pollution—Canada
TC540	627.8	Dams—Design and	TD182.6-.7	628.50972	Pollution—Mexico
		construction	TD185-.5	628.5098	Pollution—South America
TC542.5	627.8	Dams—Earthquake effects	TD186-.5	628.5094	Pollution—Europe
TC543	627.83	Earth dams	TD187-.5	628.5095	Pollution—Asia
TC547	627.8	Arch dams	TD188-.5	628.5096	Pollution—Africa
TC547	627.82	Concrete dams	TD189.5.N4	628.50993	Pollution—New Zealand
TC550	627.80684	Dam safety	TD189.5.A8	628.50994	Pollution—Australia
TC553	627.882	Sluice gates	TD190-.5	628.50998	Pollution—Arctic regions
TC555	627.883	Spillways	TD192	628.5028	Pollution control
TC601-791	623.89229	Inland navigation			equipment
TC601-791	627.13	Canals	TD193-.5	577.14	Environmental chemistry
TC601-791	627.1	Canals, Interoceanic	TD194.5-.58	363.7	Environmental impact
TC615-727	627.109(4-9)	Inland navigation—[By			statements
		region or country]	TD194.6	363.7	Environmental impact
TC759	627.133	Embankments			analysis
TC763	627.1353	Canals—Lifts	TD194.7	363.7	Environmental auditing
TC765	623.829	Canal-boats	TD195.A34	577.273	Agricultural pollution
TC769	623.89229	Canals—Steam-navigation	TD196.C45	628.16836	Chemical spills
TC771-772	625.39	Ship-railroads	TD201-500	628.1	Municipal water supply
TC791	627.1370962	Suez Canal (Egypt)	TD201-500	628.1	Water-supply
TC801-957	333.736153	Desert reclamation	TD215-220	628.109	Water-supply—History
TC801-937	627.5	Reclamation of land	TD221-327	628.109(4-9)	Water-supply—[By region
TC815-927	627.509(4-9)	Reclamation of land—[By			or country]
		region or country]	TD365-.5	628.16	Water quality
TC930-933	627.52	Irrigation canals and			management
		flumes	TD370-375	628.16	Water quality
TC933	627.52	Flumes	TD388-.5	628.13	Water conservation
TC970-978	627.5	Reclamation of land	TD388-.5	628.13	Water conservation
TC970-978	627.54	Drainage			projects

LC	Dewey	Subject Heading	LC	Dewey	Subject Heading
TD395-397	628.132	Reservoirs	TD788-.4	628.440973	Refuse collection—United States
TD395	628.13	Dew-ponds	TD789	628.4409(4-9)	Refuse collection—[Other countries]
TD396	628.132	Reservoir sedimentation			
TD398	628.15	Aqueducts	TD793.3	628.44072	Refuse and refuse disposal—Research
TD405-414	628.114	Wells			
TD412	628.114	Boring	TD793.95	628.44	Source reduction (Waste management)
TD412	628.114	Percussion drilling			
TD418	628.11	Rain-water (Water-supply)	TD794	628.442	Refuse collection
TD419-428	628.168	Water—Pollution	TD794.5	628.4458	Recycling (Waste, etc.)
TD426-.8	628.168	Groundwater—Pollution	TD795-.7	628.44564	Sanitary landfills
TD427.D4	628.1682	Detergent pollution of rivers, lakes, etc.	TD796-.2	628.4457	Incineration
			TD796.5	363.728	Compost
TD427.O7	628.1682	Organic water pollutants	TD800	628.16837	Petroleum waste
TD427.P4	628.16833	Oil pollution of water	TD812-.4	628.42	Radioactive waste disposal
TD427.R3	628.1685	Radioactive substances in rivers, lakes, etc.	TD813-870	628.44	Litter (Trash)
			TD813-870	628.46	Street cleaning
TD427.R3	628.1685	Radioactive pollution of water	TD815-849	628.4609(4-9)	Street cleaning—[By region or country]
TD427.V55	628.168	Viral pollution of water	TD860	628.460284	Street cleaning—Equipment and supplies
TD429	628.162	Water reuse			
TD429.5-477	628.162	Water—Purification	TD868-870	625.763	Snow removal
TD434	628.162	Water treatment plants	TD878-880	363.7396	Soil pollution
TD441-449	628.164	Filters and filtration	TD878-880	628.5	Soil protection
TD458	628.165	Water—Aeration	TD879.P37	628.55	Soils—Pesticide content
TD478-480.7	628.167	Saline water conversion	TD879.P4	628.55	Oil pollution of soils
TD479.6	628.16723	Nuclear saline water conversion plants	TD881-890	628.53	Air—Pollution
			TD883	628.53	Air quality
TD479.7	628.16725	Solar saline water conversion plants	TD884	614.59	Smoke
			TD884	628.532	Smoke prevention
TD480.4	628.16744	Saline water conversion—Reverse osmosis process	TD885	628.532	Flue gases
			TD885.5.G73	628.532	Greenhouse gases
			TD887.H3	628.532	Halocarbons
TD480.5	628.1674	Saline water conversion—Electrodialysis process	TD887.R3	628.535	Radioactive pollution of the atmosphere
TD481-493	628.144	Water—Distribution	TD891-893.6	620.23	Noise pollution
TD485-487	628.144	Pumping stations	TD891-893	620.23	City noise
TD489	628.13	Water towers	TD892	620.23	Noise barriers
TD491	628.15	Water-pipes	TD893.6.T7	620.23	Transportation noise
TD491	628.15	Electrolytic corrosion	TD895	628.51	Factory sanitation
TD511-780	628.3	Sewerage	TD896-899	628.51	Factory and trade waste
TD515-520	628.309	Sewerage—History	TD899.M5	628.42	Acid mine drainage
TD521-627	628.309(4-9)	Sewerage—[By region or country]	TD899.P4	628.16836	Petroleum waste
			TD920-931	628.7	Sanitation, Rural
TD657-.5	628.21	Urban runoff	TD927	628.72	Water-supply, Rural
TD665	628.212	Storm sewers	TD929-930.4	628.742	Sewerage, Rural
TD678-688	628.2	Sewer design	TD929-930.4	628.744	Refuse and refuse disposal, Rural
TD682	628.2	Sewers, Concrete			
TD730-737	628.3	Sewage	TD929-930.4	628.742	Sewage disposal, Rural
TD741-780	628.36	Sewage disposal	TD929	628.742	Drainage, House
TD745-758.5	628.3	Sewage—Purification	TD930.2	628.16846	Feedlot runoff
TD746.5	628.351	Sewage lagoons			
TD760	628.3623	Sewage irrigation	TE	625.7	Highway engineering
TD769.7	628.364	Sewage sludge—Conditioning	TE1-4	625.705	Roads—Periodicals
			TE5	625.706	Roads—Congresses
TD770-.3	628.37	Sewage sludge—Incineration	TE15-19	625.709	Roads—History
			TE21-127	625.709(4-9)	Roads—[By region or country]
TD778	628.742	Septic tanks			
TD785-812.5	628.44	Refuse and refuse disposal			

LC	Dewey	Subject Heading	LC	Dewey	Subject Heading
TE175	625.725	Roads—Design and construction	TF197	625.19	Railroads—Models
TE176.5	625.7	Traffic circles	TF200-320	625.1	Railroads—Design and construction
TE177	625.77	Roadside improvement	TF205	625.10021	Railroad engineering—Tables
TE178.8	625.77	Roadside rest areas			
TE180	625.70212	Roads—Specifications	TF210-217	625.11	Railroads—Surveying
TE191	625.7071	Roads—Study and teaching	TF220-226	625.12	Railroads—Earthwork
			TF240-268	625.14	Railroads—Track
TE200-205	625.8	Road materials	TF258-262	625.15	Railroads—Rails
TE206-209.5	625.7	Roads—Location	TF262	625.15	Railroads—Continuous rails
TE208-.5	625.732	Soil surveys			
TE209-.5	625.723	Roads—Surveying	TF263	625.163	Railroads—Crossings
TE210-212	625.733	Roads—Foundations	TF300-308	625.18	Railroad terminals
TE210.5.B5	625.85	Bitumen	TF340-499	625.100284	Railroads—Equipment and supplies
TE213	625.7342	Culverts			
TE215	625.734	Road drainage	TF371-499	625.2	Railroads—Cars
TE220-.63	625.76	Roads—Maintenance and repair	TF413	625.21	Draft-gear
			TF420-430	625.25	Air-brakes
TE221	625.85	Bituminous materials	TF455-461	625.23	Railroads—Passenger-cars
TE223-227	625.70284	Road machinery	TF457	625.23	Pullman cars
TE223-227	625.70284	Road-rollers	TF459	625.23	Sleeping-cars (Railroads)
TE228	625.794	Electronic traffic controls	TF470-481	625.24	Railroads—Freight-cars
TE229-.9	625.7091734	Rural roads	TF477	625.24	Refrigerator cars
TE229.5	625.709152	Forest roads	TF485	625.22	Cabooses (Railroads)
TE229.8	625.709143	Mountain roads	TF530-548	625.100288	Railroads—Maintenance and repair
TE230	625.74	Roads, Earth			
TE233	625.82	Roads, Gravel	TF542	625.100288	Railroads—Snow-plows
TE243	625.86	Roads, Macadamized	TF542	625.22	Snow removal
TE245	625.83	Roads, Plank	TF590-593	625.18	Railroads—Yards
TE250-278.8	625.8	Pavements	TF592	625.163	Railroads—Switching
TE253	625.83	Pavements, Wooden	TF610	625.100289	Railroads—Safety measures
TE255	625.82	Roads, Brick			
TE266-276	625.85	Pavements, Asphalt	TF615-640	625.165	Railroads—Signaling
TE278-.8	625.84	Pavements, Concrete	TF653	385.22	Railroads—Passenger traffic
TE278-.8	625.84	Roads, Concrete			
TE279.3	625.889	Driveways	TF656	625.23	Railroads—Baggage handling
TE280-295	625.88	Sidewalks			
TE298	625.888	Curbs	TF662-667	625.24	Railroads—Freight
TE301	625.88	Bicycle trails	TF670-1124	385.5/625.(4-6)	Railroads, Local and light
TE303	625.88	Trails	TF675	385.52	Railroads, Narrow-gage
TE304	625.88	Trails	TF677	385.54	Railroads, Industrial
TE305	796.72068	Racetracks (Automobile racing)	TF694	625.103	Monorail railroads
			TF701-1124	625.66	Street-railroads
			TF830	625.66	Horse railroads
TF	625.1	Railroad engineering/ Railroads	TF835	625.5	Railroads, Cable
			TF840-841	625.44	Railroads, Elevated
TF1-4	625.1005	Railroads—Periodicals	TF845-851	625.42	Subways
TF5	625.1006	Railroads—Congresses	TF857	625.19	Electric railroads, Miniature
TF6	625.10074	Railroad museums			
TF12	625.10025	Railroads—Directories	TF858-859	621.33	Railroads—Electrification
TF15-20	625.1009	Railroads—History	TF863-952	621.33	Electric railroads—Design and construction
TF16	625.1	Horse railroads			
TF21-127	625.1009(4-9)	Railroads—[By region or country]	TF872	625.15	Electric railroads—Rails
			TF880-900	621.33	Electric railroads—Wires and wiring
TF139-140	625.10092	Railroad engineers			
TF171-183	625.10072	Railroads—Research	TF890	625.15	Electric railroads—Third rail
TF193	625.11299	Railroads—Design and construction—Costs			
			TF920-952	625.2	Electric railroads—Cars
TF195	625.100212	Railroads—Specifications			

LC	Dewey	Subject Heading	LC	Dewey	Subject Heading
TF920-952	621.330284	Electric railroads—Equipment and supplies	TH21-127	690.09(4-9)	Building—[By region or country]
TF930	621.33	Electric controllers	TH23-25	690.0973	Building—United States
TF935	621.33	Electric railway motors	TH165-213	690.071	Building—Study and teaching
TF949.B7	625.25	Electric railroads—Brakes	TH425	692.3	Buildings—Specifications
TF970	385.24	Electric railroads—Freight	TH434-437	692.5	Building—Estimates
TF975	625.263	Electric locomotives	TH443	690.22	Building—Accidents
TF980	625.263	Electro-diesel locomotive	TH845-895	690.21	Strains and stresses
TF1021-1127	621.3309(4-9)	Electric railroads—[By region or country]	TH895	690.21	Snow loads
TF1600	625.4	Magnetic levitation vehicles	TH900-915	690.0284	Construction equipment
			TH915	690.0284	Building—Equipment and supplies
TG	624.2	Bridges	TH1061-1093	693.82	Building, Fireproof
TG1-4	624.205	Bridges—Periodicals	TH1061-1093	693.82	Fireproofing
TG5	624.206	Bridges—Congresses	TH1065	693.82	Fire resistant materials
TG15-20	624.209	Bridges—History	TH1077-1083	693.3	Tile construction
TG21-127	624.209(4-9)	Bridges—[By region or country]	TH1095	693.852	Buildings—Earthquake effects
TG260-270	624.25	Structural analysis (Engineering)	TH1097	693.854	Building, Bombproof
TG260	624.257	Structural frames	TH1097	690.5	Air raid shelters
TG265-267	624.252	Strains and stresses	TH1098	693.97	Modular construction
TG265-267	624.25	Moments of inertia	TH1098	693.97	Buildings, Prefabricated
TG265	624.252	Flexure	TH1199-1301	693.1	Masonry
TG265	624.252	Buckling (Mechanics)	TH1201	693.1	Building, Stone
TG300-304	624.25	Bridges—Design and construction	TH1301	693.21	Building, Brick
TG304	624.252	Snow loads	TH1421	690.8370473	Earth construction
TG315	624.20288	Bridges—Maintenance and repair	TH1431	693.91	Building, Ice and snow
			TH1461-1501	693.5	Concrete construction
TG320	624.284	Bridges—Foundations and piers	TH1491	693.5	Concrete blocks
TG325	624.28	Bridges—Abutments	TH1501	693.54	Reinforced concrete construction
TG325	624.257	Retaining walls	TH1560	693.96	Glass construction
TG325.6	624.283	Bridges—Floors	TH1610-1635	693.71	Building, Iron and steel
TG327-340	624.225	Bridges, Arched	TH1715-1718	621.4024	Insulation (Heat)
TG330	624.225	Bridges, Brick	TH1725	693.834	Factories—Soundproofing
TG330	624.225	Bridges, Stone	TH1725	693.834	Soundproofing
TG335-340	624.22	Bridges, Concrete	TH2025-3000	690.1	Building—Details
TG350-362	624.21	Girders	TH2060	690.1	Buildings—Joints
TG355	624.21	Girders, Continuous	TH2101	690.11	Foundations
TG365-370	624.2	Trestles	TH2170-.7	690.146	Domes
TG365	624.218	Bridges, Wooden	TH2180	690.15	Towers
TG375-380	624.217	Bridges, Truss	TH2201-2251.5	690.12	Walls
TG375	624.218	Bridges, Wooden	TH2235-2238.7	690.12	Exterior walls
TG385	624.219	Bridges, Cantilever	TH2243	690.12	Brick walls
TG400	624.23	Suspension bridges	TH2245	690.12	Concrete walls
TG413-416	624.21	Bridges, Continuous	TH2249	690.12	Stone walls
TG420	624.24	Drawbridges	TH2252-2253	690.13	Columns
TG450	624.24	Pontoon bridges	TH2261-2276	690.1823	Windows
			TH2274	628.922	Fire-escapes
TH	690	Building	TH2276	690.182	Blinds
TH1-4	690.05	Building—Periodicals	TH2278	690.1822	Fire doors
TH5	690.06	Building—Congresses	TH2278	690.1822	Screen doors
TH12-13	690.025	Building—Directories	TH2278	690.1822	Doors
TH15-19	690.09	Building—History	TH2279	690.1822	Door fittings
			TH2279	683.32	Locks and keys
			TH2281-2288	697.8	Flues
			TH2281-2288	690.15	Chimneys
			TH2301-2311	694.2	Framing (Building)

LC	Dewey	Subject Heading	LC	Dewey	Subject Heading
TH2391-2495	690.15	Roofs	TH6025	648	Electronics in sanitary engineering
TH2409	690.15	Flat roofs			
TH2416-2417	690.15	Roofs, Shell	TH6057.T23	690	Tall buildings
TH2431-2459	690.15	Roofing	TH6101-6729	696.1	Plumbing
TH2521-2529	690.16	Flooring	TH6485-6500	696.182	Bathrooms
TH2531-2533	690.17	Ceilings	TH6492	696.182	Showers (Plumbing fixtures)
TH3000	643.5	Attics			
TH3000.B36	643.5	Basements	TH6493	696.182	Bathtubs
TH3351-3361	690.24	Buildings—Maintenance	TH6498	696.182	Toilets
TH3401-3411	690.24	Buildings—Remodeling for other use	TH6551-6568	696.6	Hot-water supply
			TH6561	696.6	Water heaters, Gas
TH3401-3411	690.24	Buildings—Repair and reconstruction	TH6571-6675	696.13	Drainage, House
			TH6681-6685	696.10288	Plumbing—Repairing
TH4224	690.61	Pagodas—Design and construction	TH6703-6729	696.2	Pipe fitting
			TH6880	696.2	Gas-burners
TH4311-4315	690.52	Commercial buildings—Design and construction	TH6840	696.2	Gas-fitting
			TH7005-7699	697	Heating
			TH7140	697.07	Fluidized-bed furnaces
TH4451-4499	690.535	Warehouses—Design and construction	TH7400	697.07	Furnaces
			TH7413-7414	697.78	Solar heating
TH4461	690.53	Granaries—Design and construction	TH7414	697.78	Solar houses
			TH7421-7434.7	697.1	Fireplaces
TH4511-4591	690.54	Factories	TH7435-7458	697.22	Stoves
TH4511-4591	690.54	Factories—Design and construction	TH7437-7441	697.22	Stoves, Wood
			TH7443-7446	697.22	Stoves, Coal
TH4532	690.54	Distilleries	TH7450.5	697.24	Kerosene heaters
TH4541	690.54	Drug factories	TH7453-7457	697.043	Gas—Heating and cooking
TH4581-4591	690.54	Power-plants	TH7454-7457	697.043	Stoves, Gas
TH4805-4890	690.8	House construction	TH7461	697.03	Heating plants
TH4805-4890	690.8	Dwellings	TH7466.06	697.044	Oil burners
TH4816.2	690.24	Buildings—Additions	TH7480-7495	697.507	Radiators
TH4818.A3	690.8370473	Earth houses	TH7511-7549	697.4	Hot-water heating
TH4819.E27	690.8370473	Earth sheltered houses	TH7538	697.07	Boilers
TH4819.P7	643.2	Prefabricated houses	TH7561-7599	697.5	Steam-heating
TH4835	690.872	Vacation homes	TH7570-7578	697.5	Steam-heating, Low pressure
TH4840	690.873	Log cabins			
TH4911-4935	690.892	Farm buildings	TH7588	697.507	Boilers
TH4920	690.86	Farmhouses	TH7601-7635	697.3	Hot-air heating
TH4930	690.8922	Dairy barns	TH7638	697.3	Heat pumps
TH4935	690.892	Silos	TH7647-7699	697.92	Ventilation
TH4970	690.893	Decks (Architecture, Domestic)	TH7684.F2-.F3	697.9354	Factories—Air conditioning
			TH7687-7688	697.93	Air conditioning
TH5101	624.152	Excavation	TH7688.H6	697.938	Dwellings—Air conditioning
TH5201	690.11	Foundations			
TH5281	624.152	Shoring and underpinning	TH7694	620.86	Clean rooms
TH5311-5701	693.1	Masonry	TH7700-7975	621.32	Lighting
TH5401-5440	693.1	Stonemasonry	TH7703	729.28	Lighting, Architectural and decorative
TH5501	693.1	Bricklaying			
TH5601-5695	694	Carpentry	TH7910-7970	621.324	Gas-lighting
TH5611	694.1	Carpentry drafting	TH7960-7967	621.3240284	Gas-fixtures
TH5618	694.0284	Miter-gages	TH8135-8139	693.6	Plaster
TH5640-5695	694.6	Finish carpentry	TH8251-8275	698.5	Glazing
TH5662-5663	694.6	Joinery	TH8441	698.6	Paperhanging
TH5667-5680	690.1832	Staircases	TH8461-8463	676.2848	Wallpaper
TH6010-6013	696-697	Building fittings	TH9031	693.892	Dampness in buildings
TH6014-7696	648	Sanitation, Household	TH9031	693.892	Waterproofing
TH6014-6085	697	Buildings—Environmental engineering	TH9057-9092	693.898	Lightning protection
			TH9057-9092	693.898	Lightning-conductors
			TH9111-9599	693.82	Fire prevention

LC	Dewey	Subject Heading	LC	Dewey	Subject Heading
TH9111-9599	628.925	Fire extinction	TJ254.7	621.43	Combustion chambers
TH9120	628.922072	Fire prevention—Research	TJ255-265	621.4025	Heat-engines
TH9128	363.37092	Fire fighters—Physical training	TJ262	621.4025	Heat pumps
TH9271-9275	628.9225	Fire alarms	TJ265	621.4021	Thermodynamics
TH9271	628.9225	Fire detectors	TJ266-267.5	621.406	Turbines
TH9311-9334	628.9252	Fire extinction—Water-supply	TJ266-267.5	621.406	Turbomachines
			TJ268-748	621.1	Steam engineering
TH9332-9334	628.9252	Water towers	TJ268-280.7	621.1	Steam
TH9336	628.9252	Fire sprinklers	TJ281-393	621.183	Steam-boilers
TH9338	628.9254	Fire extinction—Chemical systems	TJ290-291	621.194	Boiler-plates
			TJ320-358	621.183	Furnaces
TH9362	628.9254	Fire extinguishers	TJ350-357	621.1830289	Steam-boilers—Safety appliances
TH9365	628.9252	Hydrants	TJ370-372	621.185	Pressure gages
TH9371-9377	628.9259	Fire engines	TJ395-444	621.312132	Steam power plants
TH9375	628.9259	Chemical fire engines	TJ415-444	621.185	Steam-pipes
TH9391	628.9259	Fireboats	TJ427	621.185	Steam-pipe coverings
TH9448-9449	628.92	Fires	TJ461-740	621.1	Steam-engines
TH9701-9745	643.16	Burglary protection	TJ533	621.84	Pistons
TH9735	683.32	Locks and keys	TJ557-565	621.197	Condensers (Steam)
TH9739	643.16	Burglar alarms	TJ563	621.197	Cooling towers
			TJ603-695	625.26	Locomotives
TJ	621	Mechanical engineering	TJ619-.7	625.266	Diesel locomotives
TJ	621.8	Machinery	TJ735-740	621.165	Steam-turbines
TJ1-4	621.05	Mechanical engineering—Periodicals	TJ751-805	621.43	Internal combustion engines
TJ5	621.06	Mechanical engineering—Congresses	TJ778	621.433	Gas-turbines
TJ11-13	621.025	Mechanical engineers—Directories	TJ779	621.4335	Free piston engines
			TJ787	621.437	Carburetors
TJ14	621.01	Mechanical engineering—Philosophy	TJ795	621.436	Diesel motor
TJ15-20	621.09	Mechanical engineering—History	TJ807-830	621.042	Renewable energy sources
			TJ809-812.8	621.47	Solar energy
TJ21-127	621.09(4-9)	Mechanical engineering—[By region or country]	TJ811-.5	621.47072	Solar energy—Research
			TJ812	621.472	Solar collectors
TJ139-140	621.092	Mechanical engineers—Biography	TJ812.5	621.473	Solar engines
			TJ820-828	621.45	Wind power
TJ148	621.80287	Machinery—Testing	TJ823-828	621.453	Windmills
TJ158-159	621.071	Mechanical engineering—Study and teaching	TJ836-935	621.2	Hydraulic machinery
			TJ840-890	621.21	Water-power
TJ163.6-.95	621	Power (Mechanics)	TJ843	621.20424	Oil hydraulic machinery
TJ164	621.3121	Power-plants	TJ844	621.20424	Hydraulic fluids
TJ177	621.81	Machinery—Vibration	TJ855-857	621.2	Hydraulic motors
TJ181-210	621.81	Mechanical movements	TJ859	621.21	Water mills
TJ181.5	621.81	Wheels	TJ860-880	621.21	Water-wheels
TJ183	621.825	Couplings	TJ898.5	388.57	Coal slurry pipelines
TJ184-204	621.833	Gearing	TJ899-927	621.69	Pumping machinery
TJ192	621.8333	Gearing, Spiral	TJ901	621.6	Ejector pumps
TJ193-196	621.8332	Gearing, Bevel	TJ915	621.65	Reciprocating pumps
TJ200	621.8333	Gearing, Worm	TJ917	621.66	Rotary pumps
TJ210	621.824	Springs (Mechanism)	TJ930-934	621.8672	Pipelines
TJ210.2-211.49	629.892	Robots	TJ940-.5	621.55	Vacuum technology
TJ210.2-211.49	629.892	Robotics	TJ940.5	621.55	Vacuum pumps
TJ212.2-225	629.8	Automatic machinery	TJ950-1030	621.51	Pneumatic machinery
TJ216	629.83	Feedback control systems	TJ981-1009	621.51	Compressed air
TJ217.5	629.89	Intelligent control systems	TJ990-992	621.51	Air-compressors
TJ227-240	621.815	Machine design	TJ990-992	621.51	Compressors
TJ250-255	621.4	Engines	TJ1005-1007	621.904	Pneumatic tools
			TJ1045-1119	621.85	Power transmission
			TJ1061-1073.7	621.822	Bearings (Machinery)

LC	Dewey	Subject Heading	LC	Dewey	Subject Heading
TJ1071-1073	621.822	Ball-bearings	TK165-213	621.3071	Electric engineering—Study and teaching
TJ1071	621.822	Roller bearings			
TJ1073.R8	621.822	Rubber bearings	TK275-399	621.37	Electric measurements
TJ1075-1081	621.89	Lubrication and lubricants	TK301-399	621.373	Electric meters
TJ1081	621.890284	Oil filters	TK321	621.3743	Voltmeter
TJ1100-1119	621.852	Belts and belting	TK331	621.3744	Voltameter
TJ1103	621.85	Pulleys	TK393	621.373	Recording instruments
TJ1165	670.420151	Shop mathematics	TK401	621.37	Electric testing
TJ1180-1313	621.902	Machine-tools	TK431	621.30221	Electric drafting
TJ1180-1313	621.9	Tools	TK454.2	621.3192	Electric networks, Active
TJ1193	621.9	Diamonds, Industrial	TK454.2	621.3192	Electric network topology
TJ1201.H3	621.973	Hammers	TK454.2	621.3192	Electric networks, Passive
TJ1205-1210	621.91	Planing-machines	TK1001-1841	621.3121	Electric power production
TJ1218-1222	621.942	Lathes	TK1001-1841	621.31	Electric power
TJ1225-1227	621.91	Milling-machines	TK1041-1078	621.3121	Cogeneration of electric power and heat
TJ1230-1240	621.93	Cutting machines			
TJ1233-1255	621.934	Saws	TK1078	621.483	Nuclear power plants
TJ1233	621.93	Hacksaws	TK1081-1083	621.312134	Hydroelectric power plants
TJ1260-1270	621.952	Drilling and boring	TK1081	621.312134	Tidal power-plants
TJ1260	621.952	Drill presses	TK1085-1087	621.31244	Solar power plants
TJ1280-1298	621.92	Grinding and polishing	TK1141-1168	621.31913	Electric currents, Alternating
TJ1290	621.923	Emery-wheels			
TJ1320-1340	621.88	Fasteners	TK1191-1841	621.3121	Electric power-plants
TJ1330-1333	621.882	Bolts and nuts	TK1545	621.31244	Solar power plants
TJ1335	621.984	Taps and dies	TK1751	621.3126	Electric substations
TJ1338-1340	621.882	Screws	TK1831	621.31210287	Electric power-plants—Testing
TJ1345	621.914	Crushing machinery			
TJ1350-1383	621.862	Hoisting machinery	TK2000-2891	621.31042	Electric machinery
TJ1363-1365	621.87	Cranes, derricks, etc.	TK2271	621.31042	Eddy currents (Electric)
TJ1363-1365	621.873	Electric cranes	TK2411-2491	621.313	Electric generators
TJ1365	621.873	Gantry cranes	TK2435	621.46	Electric motors—Design and construction
TJ1370-1380	621.877	Elevators			
TJ1376	621.8676	Escalators	TK2441	621.3132	Gramme dynamos
TJ1385-1418	621.867	Conveying machinery	TK2477	621.316	Armatures
TJ1435	621.2	Hydraulic jacks	TK2484	621.316	Brushes, Carbon
TJ1465	621.98	Pneumatic presses	TK2511-2541	621.46	Electric motors
TJ1480-1496	631.3	Agricultural machinery	TK2551	621.314	Electric transformers
TJ1482	631.510284	Cultivators	TK2611-2699	621.3132	Electric machinery—Direct current
TJ1501-1519	646.2044	Sewing machines			
TJ1560	629.82	Vending machines	TK2681	621.46	Electric motors
TJ1570	688.752	Slot machines	TK2699	621.3815322	Electric inverters
			TK2711-2799	621.3133	Electric machinery—Alternating current
TK	621.3	Electric engineering			
TK1-4	621.305	Electric engineering—Periodicals	TK2781-2789	621.46	Electric motors, Alternating current
TK5	621.306	Electric engineering—Congresses	TK2781-2789	621.46	Electric motors
			TK2796	621.313	Electric current converters
TK6	621.3074	Electric engineering—Museums	TK2796	621.313	Rotary converters
			TK2821-2846	621.317	Electric switchgear
TK9	621.303	Electric engineering—Dictionaries	TK2842	621.317	Electric circuit-breakers
			TK2851	629.8043	Electric controllers
TK12	621.3025	Electric engineering—Directories	TK2851	621.317	Electric rheostats
			TK2861	621.317	Electric contactors
TK15-18	621.309	Electric engineering—History	TK2861	621.317	Differential relays
			TK2896-2986	621.31242	Electric batteries
TK21-127	621.309(4-9)	Electric engineering—[By region or country]	TK2896	621.3124	Direct energy conversion
			TK2931	621.312429	Fuel cells
TK139-140	621.31924092	Electricians	TK2941	621.31242	Storage batteries
TK153	621.31	Electric power factor			

LC	Dewey	Subject Heading	LC	Dewey	Subject Heading
TK2960	621.31244	Solar cells	TK5104-.2	621.3825	Artificial satellites in telecommunication
TK3001-3521	621.3192	Electric circuits			
TK3001-3521	621.319	Electric power distribution	TK5105-5865	621.383	Telegraph
TK3001-3521	621.319	Electric power transmission	TK5105-.42	621.38216	Data transmission systems
TK3001-3511	621.31	Electric power	TK5105	621.38216	Packet switching (Data transmission)
TK3091	621.319	Electric power failures			
TK3111	621.31912	Electric power distribution—Direct current	TK5105.5-.9	004.6	Computer networks
			TK5105.7-.85	004.68	Local area networks (Computer networks)
TK3141-3171	621.31913	Electric power transmission—Alternating current	TK5105.73	004.692	Electronic mail systems
			TK5105.87-.888	004.67	Wide area networks (Computer networks)
TK3141-3171	621.31913	Electric power distribution—Alternating current	TK5105.875.I57	004.678	Internet (Computer network)
TK3144	621.31913	Electric power distribution—High tension	TK5105.9	005.3	Communications software
			TK5107	621.38305	Telegraph—Periodicals
TK3201-3261	621.3192	Electric lines	TK5301-5481	384.15	Telegraph lines
TK3201-3285	621.31933	Electric wiring	TK5601-5681	384.1	Cables, Submarine
TK3226	621.3192	Electric networks	TK5700-5865	621.3842	Telegraph, Wireless
TK3226	621.31921	Transients (Electricity)	TK5811-5865	621.3842	Telegraph, Wireless—Marconi system
TK3242-3243	621.3192	Electric lines—Poles and towers			
			TK5981-5990	621.3828	Electro-acoustics
TK3251-3261	621.31923	Underground electric lines	TK5984	621.38234	Magnetic tapes
TK3271-3285	621.31933	Electric wiring, Interior	TK5986	621.38284	Electrostatic microphone
TK3301-3351	621.3193	Electric conductors	TK6001-6571.5	621.385	Telephone
TK3301-3351	621.31934	Electric cables	TK6001	621.38505	Telephone—Periodicals
TK3301-3351	621.31933	Electric wire	TK6011	621.385025	Telephone—Directories
TK3331-3441	621.31937	Electric insulators and insulation	TK6201-6285	621.38784	Telephone lines
			TK6381-6383	621.38784	Telephone wire
TK4001-9971	621.31	Electric power	TK6381-6383	621.38784	Telephone cables
TK4058-4059	629.2293	Electric driving	TK6391-6397	621.385	Telephone switchboards
TK4125-4399	621.32	Electric lighting	TK6397	621.3857	Telephone switching systems, Electronic
TK4134-4156	621.3209(4-9)	Electric lighting—[By region or country]			
			TK6401-6505	621.387	Telephone systems
TK4188	621.3229	Exterior lighting	TK6540-6571.5	621.384(1-5)	Radio
TK4198	621.320284	Electric light fixtures	TK6540	621.38405	Radio—Periodicals
TK4310-4399	621.32	Electric lamps	TK6553	621.38411	Radio—Interference
TK4311-4335	621.325	Electric lighting, Arc	TK6553	621.384 + (1-5)0288	Radio—Repairing
TK4321-4335	621.325	Electric lamps, Arc			
TK4341-4367	621.326	Electric lighting, Incandescent	TK6560-6565	621.384 + (1-5)0284	Radio—Equipment and supplies
TK4351-4367	621.326	Incandescent lamps	TK6561-6562	621.384131	Radio—Transmitters and transmission
TK4383	621.3275	Neon tubes			
TK4383	621.3275	Neon lamps	TK6563-6564	621.38418	Radio—Receivers and reception
TK4386	621.3273	Fluorescent lamps	TK6565.A55	621.38412	Amplifiers (Electronics)
TK4399.S6	621.3229	Electric signs	TK6565.A6	621.384135	Radio—Antennas
TK4601-4661	621.402	Electric heating	TK6565.O7	621.38412	Oscillators, Electric
TK4601	621.4028	Induction heating	TK6565.R426	621.384133	Electric resistors
TK4601	621.4028	Microwave heating	TK6565.V3	621.384132	Vacuum-tubes
TK4660	671.521	Electroslag welding	TK6570.C5	621.38454	Citizens band radio
TK4660	671.521	Electric welding	TK6573-6595	621.3848	Radar
TK4661	621.4028	Electric furnaces	TK6587	621.38483	Radar transmitters
TK5101-5105.9	621.382	Telecommunication	TK6592.D6	621.3848	Doppler radar
TK5101	621.38224	Random noise theory	TK6592.M67	621.3848	Moving target indicator radar
TK5103.59	621.3827	Optical communications			
TK5103.7-.8	621.382	Digital communications	TK6630-6720	621.388	Television
			TK6630.A1	621.388005	Television—Periodicals

LC	Dewey	Subject Heading	LC	Dewey	Subject Heading
TK6650-6655	621.38800284	Television—Equipment and supplies	TK7872.T7	621.314	Electronic transformers
			TK7872.V3	621.381512	Vacuum-tubes
TK6655.V5	621.38833	Videocassette recorders	TK7874-.8	621.395	Digital integrated circuits
TK6670	621.38804	Color television	TK7874	621.395	Linear integrated circuits
TK6676	621.38835	Television, Master antenna	TK7876	621.3813	Microwave devices
			TK7876	621.38131	Microwave transmission lines
TK6677	384.552	Direct broadcast satellite television	TK7878-7879.4	621.3810287	Electronic measurements
TK6678	621.38807	Digital television	TK7878.7	621.3815483	Cathode ray oscilloscope
TK6680	384.556	Closed-circuit television	TK7881.6	621.38932	Magnetic recorders and recording
TK6680.5-6687	621.388332	Digital video			
TK6685	384.558	Videodisc players	TK7881.65	621.3883	Digital audiotape recorders and recording
TK6687	006.7	Interactive video			
TK6710-7620	621.38235	Facsimile transmission	TK7881.75	621.38932	Compact disc players
TK7018-7301	643.6	Household appliances, Electric	TK7882.C56	621.3976	Compact discs
			TK7882.E2	621.38928	Electronic surveillance
TK7241	621.38928	Electric alarms	TK7882.S65	621.399	Speech synthesis
TK7800-8360	621.381	Electronics	TK7885-7895	621.39	Computer engineering
TK7800	621.38105	Electronics—Periodicals	TK7885-7895	621.39	Computers
TK7801	621.38106	Electronics—Congresses	TK7887	621.390288	Computers—Maintenance and repair
TK7825	621.3810728	Electronics—Graphic methods			
			TK7887.5	621.398	Computer interfaces
TK7855	621.381072	Electronics—Research	TK7887.55	621.3976	Data tape drives
TK7866	621.3810221	Electronic drafting	TK7887.6	621.39814	Analog-to-digital converters
TK7866	621.3810223	Electronics—Charts, diagrams, etc.			
			TK7887.8.M63	621.39814	Modems
TK7867-7868	621.3815	Electronic circuits	TK7887.8.T4	621.3985	Computer terminals
TK7868.I58	621.3981	Interface circuits	TK7888	621.3919	Electronic analog computers
TK7868.P7	621.381531	Printed circuits			
TK7868.S9	621.381537	Switching circuits	TK7888.3-.4	621.39	Electronic digital computers
TK7869-7872	621.3810284	Electronic apparatus and appliances			
			TK7888.4	621.395	Electronic digital computers—Circuits
TK7870	621.3810284	Electronic instruments			
TK7870	621.381	Electronic systems	TK7888.4	621.395	Logic circuits
TK7870	621.3810228	Miniature electronic equipment	TK7895.C39	621.39767	CD-ROMs
			TK7895.M4	621.397	Cache memory
TK7871.2-.58	621.381535	Transistor amplifiers	TK7895.M4	621.39767	Optical storage devices
TK7871.2-.58	621.381535	Amplifiers (Electronics)	TK7895.M4	621.3973	Random access memory
TK7871.58.B74	621.381535	Broadband amplifiers	TK7895.M4	621.3973	Read-only memory
TK7871.58.D5	621.381535	Direct current amplifiers	TK7895.M4	621.39732	Semiconductor storage devices
TK7871.6	621.3824	Antennas (Electronics)			
TK7871.7-.84	621.38151	Electron Tubes	TK8300-8360	621.381542	Photoelectric cells
TK7871.75	621.381334	Magnetrons	TK8314	621.381542	Photoelectric multipliers
TK7871.8-.84	621.381513	Gas tubes	TK9001-9401	621.48	Nuclear engineering
TK7871.85-.99	621.38152	Semiconductor wafers	TK9001-9401	621.48	Nuclear energy
TK7871.89.A94	621.381522	Diodes, IMPATT	TK9001	621.4805	Nuclear engineering—Periodicals
TK7871.89.S95	621.381522	Diodes, Switching			
TK7871.92	621.3815282	Junction transistors	TK9151.6-.7	621.4835	Remote handling (Radioactive substances)
TK7871.96.B55	621.381528	Bipolar transistors			
TK7871.99.M4	621.38152	Metal insulator semiconductors	TK9152-.16	621.480289	Radiation—Safety measures
			TK9152-.16	621.480289	Nuclear engineering—Safety measures
TK7872.F44	621.3815	Ferroelectric devices			
TK7872.I65	621.3815322	Electric inverters	TK9178-9183	621.480284	Nuclear power plants—Instruments
TK7872.L56	621.3815422	Liquid crystal displays			
TK7872.L64	621.395	Logic devices	TK9202-9230	621.483	Nuclear reactors
TK7872.M25	621.39763	Magnetic bubble devices	TK9203.B6	621.4834	Boiling water reactors
TK7872.O7	621.381533	Feedback oscillators	TK9203.B7	621.4834	Liquid metal fast breeder reactors
TK7872.R35	621.3137	Electric current rectifiers			
TK7872.S5	621.381548	Signal generators			

LC	Dewey	Subject Heading	LC	Dewey	Subject Heading
TK9203.H4	621.4834	Heavy water reactors	TL233-.8	629.2252	Farm tractors
TK9203.H4	621.483	Steam generating heavy water reactors	TL235.6-.7	388.34	All terrain vehicles
TK9203.S65	621.4834	Solid fuel reactors	TL235.8	629.22234	Ambulances
TK9203.S86	621.4834	Superheating reactors	TL236	629.228	Automobiles, Racing
TK9204	621.484	Fusion reactors	TL236.7	629.222	Dune buggies
TK9207	621.4833	Nuclear fuel rods	TL237-.2	629.221	Automobiles—Models
TK9212	621.48336	Nuclear reactors—Cooling	TL240-278	629.23	Automobiles—Design and construction
TK9230	621.485	Nuclear propulsion	TL245	629.231	Automobiles—Aerodynamics
TK9340	539.73	Particle accelerators	TL255-256.5	629.26	Automobiles—Bodies
TK9360	621.4833	Nuclear fuels	TL271-.5	629.2772	Automobiles—Heating and ventilation
TK9360	621.4838	Reactor fuel reprocessing			
TK9360	621.48335	Spent reactor fuels	TL272	629.2548	Automobiles—Electric equipment
TK9360	621.484	Thermonuclear fuels			
TK9956	621.38416	Amateur radio stations	TL272.5-.55	629.2549	Motor vehicles—Electronic equipment
TL	629.2	Motor vehicles	TL285-295	629.282	Automobiles—Testing
TL1-230.5	629.222	Automobiles	TL410-438	629.2272	Bicycles
TL1-5	629.22205	Automobiles—Periodicals	TL439-448	629.2275	Motorcycles
TL6	629.22206	Automobiles—Congresses	TL443	629.2275	Minibikes
TL7	629.222074	Automobiles—Museums	TL475-480	629.295	Roving vehicles (Astronautics)
TL9	629.22203	Automobiles—Encyclopedias			
TL12	629.2220294	Automobiles—Catalogs	TL480	629.295	Lunar surface vehicles
TL15	629.22209	Automobiles—History	TL500-4050	629.1	Aerospace engineering
TL21-127	629.22209(4-9)	Automobiles—[By region or country]	TL500-830	629.13	Aeronautics
			TL500-504	629.13006	Aeronautics—Societies, etc.
TL23-25	629.2220973	Automobiles—United States			
TL57-64	629.2220941	Automobiles—Great Britain	TL505	629.13006	Aeronautics—Congresses
			TL506	629.130074	Aeronautical museums
TL71-72.5	629.2220944	Automobiles—France	TL509	629.1300148	Aeronautics—Abbreviations
TL73-74.5	629.2220943	Automobiles—Germany	TL513	629.1300272	Aeronautics—Patents
TL85-86	629.2220947	Automobiles—Russia	TL515-532	629.13009	Aeronautics—History
TL105-106	629.2220952	Automobiles—Japan	TL521-532	629.13009(4-9)	Aeronautics—[By region or country]
TL139-140	629.222092	Automobile engineers—Biography			
			TL539-540	629.130092	Aeronautics—Biography
TL152-.2	629.287	Automobiles— Maintenance and repair	TL549	629.1300222	Aeronautics—Pictorial works
TL152.2	629.287	Automobiles— Conservation and restoration	TL553.5	629.1300289	Aeronautics—Safety measures
			TL553.5	363.124	Aircraft accidents
TL152.5-.55	629.283	Automobile driving	TL553.7	613.69	Survival after airplane accidents, shipwrecks, etc.
TL152.5-.55	629.283092	Automobile drivers			
TL153	629.286	Service stations			
TL154	629.283	Automobile parking	TL553.8	363.3481	Search and rescue operations
TL159.5	629.276	Air bag restraint systems			
TL200	629.2292	Automobiles, Steam	TL556-558	629.1324	Meteorology in aeronautics
TL210-.7	629.252	Automobiles—Motors			
TL214.P6	629.25	Automobiles—Pollution control devices	TL557.F6	629.1324	Fog—Control
			TL557.V5	629.136	Airports—Visibility
TL214.P6	629.25	Motor vehicles—Pollution control devices	TL566-568	629.130072	Aeronautical laboratories
			TL567.R47	629.130072	Research aircraft
TL230-.5	629.224	Trucks	TL570-578	629.13	Flight
TL230	629.2234	Vans	TL570-574	629.1323	Aerodynamics
TL230	629.224	Dump trucks	TL571.5	629.132306	Aerodynamics, Hypersonic
TL230.3	629.224092	Truck drivers	TL573	629.13230287	Aerodynamic measurements
TL232	629.22233	Trolley buses	TL574.B6	629.13237	Boundary layer
TL232.3	629.22233092	Bus drivers	TL574.F6	629.132362	Flutter (Aerodynamics)
TL233-.8	629.2252	Traction-engines	TL574.M6	629.132364	Rolling (Aerodynamics)

LC	Dewey	Subject Heading	LC	Dewey	Subject Heading
TL574.M6	629.132364	Yawing (Aerodynamics)	TL696.L33	629.1325213	Ground controlled approach
TL574.N6	629.1323	Aerodynamic noise			
TL574.S7	629.13236	Stability of airplanes	TL697.08	629.1344	Airplanes—Oxygen equipment
TL574.U5	629.13232	Unsteady flow (Aerodynamics)			
			TL701-704.7	629.13435	Airplanes—Motors
TL574.V5	629.132362	Vibration (Aeronautics)	TL704.7	629.134351	Airplanes—Fuel
TL586-589	629.13251	Navigation (Aeronautics)	TL705-708	629.13436	Propellers, Aerial
TL589-.5	629.135	Aeronautical instruments	TL708	629.134355	Airplanes—Nuclear power plants
TL589.2.A3	629.1352	Accelerometers			
TL589.2.C58	629.1352	Gyro compass	TL709-.5	629.134353	Airplanes—Jet propulsion
TL589.2.D7	629.1352	Drift indicator	TL709.3.T8	629.1343532	Airplanes—Turbine-propell er engines
TL589.2.06	629.1352	Optical gyroscopes			
TL589.5	629.1326	Automatic pilot (Airplanes)	TL709.3.T83	629.1343533	Airplanes—Turbojet engines
TL609-639	629.13322	Balloons			
TL620	629.13322	Balloon ascensions	TL709.5.C55	629.134353	Aircraft gas-turbines— Combustion chambers
TL638	629.13322	Hot air balloons			
TL650-668.1	629.13324	Airships	TL709.5.I5	629.134353	Airplanes—Turbojet engines—Air intakes
TL670-724	629.13334	Flying-machines			
TL670-723	629.13334	Airplanes	TL710-713.5	629.13252	Airplanes—Piloting
TL671.6	629.13431	Airframes	TL711.B6	629.1325214	Instrument flying
TL671.7	629.13453	Airplanes—Flight testing	TL711.H65	629.13252	Holding patterns (Aeronautics)
TL671.7	629.13452	Airplanes—Inspection			
TL672-673	629.13432	Airplanes—Wings	TL711.L3	629.1325213	Airplanes—Landing
TL673.F6	629.13433	Flaps (Airplanes)	TL711.N5	629.1325214	Night flying
TL673.S9	629.13432	Airplanes—Wings, Swept-back	TL711.S8	629.1325071	Student flying
			TL711.T3	629.1325212	Airplanes—Take-off
TL677.E6	629.13433	Elevators (Airplanes)	TL712-.8	629.1325071	Flight training
TL681.A5	629.13442	Airplanes—Air conditioning	TL712	629.13252	Air pilots
TL681.C3	629.13445	Aircraft cabins	TL716-.9	629.133352	Helicopters
TL681.P7	629.13442	Airplanes—Pressurization	TL720.7	387.744	Aeronautics, Commercial—Freight
TL682-683	629.134381	Airplanes—Landing gear			
TL684-.3	629.133347	Seaplanes	TL721	629.13	Aeronautics—Flights
TL684.4	629.133343	Biplanes	TL725-733	629.136	Airports
TL685	629.13335	Vertically rising aircraft	TL725-733	387.72	Airways
TL685.3	623.746	Airplanes, Military	TL725.3.B8	629.136	Airport buildings
TL685.3	623.7464	Fighter planes	TL725.3.C64	629.1366	Airport control towers
TL685.7	623.7465	Jet transports	TL725.3.R8	629.1363	Runways (Aeronautics)
TL685.7	623.7465	Supersonic transport planes	TL725.3.T7	629.1366	Air traffic control
			TL725.6	629.1361	Seaplane bases
TL686.B36	629.13334	Beechcraft (Airplanes)	TL726.15	629.136	International airports
TL686.D65	629.13334	Douglas airplanes	TL732	623.441	Catapults (Aeronautics)
TL686.D65	629.13334	Douglas transport planes	TL750-758	629.134386	Parachuting
TL686.G	629.133340422	Lear jet aircraft	TL750-758	629.134386	Parachutes
TL690-691	629.1354	Electricity in aeronautics	TL753	629.134386	Parachutes—Rigging
TL692-696	629.135	Aeronautics— Communication systems	TL759-.7	629.13332	Kites
			TL760-769	629.13333	Gliders (Aeronautics)
TL693.R2	629.1355	Airplanes—Radio equipment	TL778	745.592	Paper airplanes
			TL780-785.8	629.475	Rockets (Aeronautics)
TL693-696	629.1355	Airplanes—Electronic equipment	TL783.5	629.4753	Nuclear rockets
			TL783.54-.63	629.4755	Electric rocket engines
TL693-696	629.1355	Radio in aeronautics	TL783.57	629.4754	Photon rockets
TL694.T35	629.437	Aerospace telemetry	TL783.6	629.4755	Plasma rockets
TL695-696	629.135	Avionics	TL783.63	629.4755	Ion rockets
TL695-696	629.1351	Aids to air navigation	TL784.C63	629.47522	Liquid propellant rocket—Control systems
TL696.B4	621.384191	Radio beacons			
TL696.C7	629.1352	Radio compass	TL784.C63	629.433	Rockets (Aeronautics)— Guidance systems
TL696.D5	629.1352	Radio direction finders			
TL696.L3	629.1351	Landing aids (Aeronautics)	TL784.E4	629.470284	Electronics in rocketry
			TL785	629.47524	Solid propellants

LC	Dewey	Subject Heading	LC	Dewey	Subject Heading
TL787-4050	629.4	Astronautics	TN5	338.206	Mineral industries—Congresses
TL789-790	629.455	Interplanetary voyages	TN6	338.2074	Mineral industries—Exhibitions
TL789-.6	001.942	Unidentified flying objects			
TL789.8	629.409(4-9)	Astronautics—[By region or country]	TN9-10	338.203	Mineral industries—Dictionaries
TL790	629.41	Space flight	TN12	338.2025	Mineral industries—Directories
TL794.3	629.40724	Astronautics—Experiments			
TL795-.5	629.47	Space ships	TN15-124	338.209	Mineral industries—History
TL795.7	629.442	Space colonies	TN21-127	622.09(4-9)	Mines and mineral resources—[By region or country]
TL796.5.U6D	629.434	Discoverer (Artificial satellite)			
TL796-798	629.46	Artificial satellites	TN23-25	622.0973	Mines and mineral resources—United States
TL797	629.442	Space stations			
TL797	338.0999	Space industrialization	TN26-27	622.0971	Mines and mineral resources—Canada
TL798.G4	629.46	Geodetic satellites	TN28-29	622.0972	Mines and mineral resources—Mexico
TL799.J8	629.4555	Space flight to Jupiter			
TL799.M3	629.4553	Space flight to Mars	TN30-31	622.09728	Mines and mineral resources—Central America
TL799.M6	629.454	Space flight to the moon			
TL799.V45	629.4552	Space flight to Venus			
TL844	621.43560228	Rockets (Aeronautics)—Models	TN32-33	622.09729	Mines and mineral resources—West Indies
TL845-848	629.4071	Astronautics—Study and teaching	TN36-37	622.0982	Mines and mineral resources—Argentina
TL867	363.124	Space vehicle accidents	TN38-39	622.0984	Mines and mineral resources—Bolivia
TL869	629.40212	Space vehicles—Specifications			
TL943	629.455	Planetary quarantine	TN41-42	622.0981	Mines and mineral resources—Brazil
TL945	629.4774	Space vehicles—Sterilization			
TL950-954	629.472	Space vehicles—Materials	TN43-44	622.0983	Mines and mineral resources—Chile
TL1050-1060	629.4	Astrodynamics			
TL1065-1080	629.453	Navigation (Astronautics)	TN45-46	622.09861	Mines and mineral resources—Colombia
TL1070	629.453	Astronautical charts			
TL1082	629.474	Astronautical instruments	TN47	622.09866	Mines and mineral resources—Ecuador
TL1085	629.45071	Space flight training			
TL1090-1095	629.458	Space vehicles—Piloting	TN48	622.09881	Mines and mineral resources—Guyana
TL1098	629.450284	Space tools			
TL1100-1102	629.474	Space vehicles—Electric equipment	TN49	622.09883	Mines and mineral resources—Surinam
TL1102.B3	629.47445	Space vehicles—Batteries	TN50	622.09882	Mines and mineral resources—French Guiana
TL1500-1575	629.477	Life support systems (Space environment)			
TL1530	629.477	Space cabin atmospheres	TN51	622.09892	Mines and mineral resources—Paraguay
TL1550	629.4772	Space suits	TN52	622.0985	Mines and mineral resources—Peru
TL1565	629.4773	Space vehicles—Water-supply			
TL3000-3285	629.474	Space vehicles—Electronic equipment	TN53	622.09895	Mines and mineral resources—Uruguay
TL4000-4050	629.478	Ground support systems (Astronautics)	TN54	622.0987	Mines and mineral resources—Venezuela
TL4030	629.437	Space vehicles—Tracking	TN57-64	622.0941	Mines and mineral resources—Great Britain
TL4030	629.457	Space vehicles—Tracking			
TN	622	Mining engineering	TN65-.2	622.09436	Mines and mineral resources—Austria
TN	622.2	Mines and mineral resources	TN65.3-.4	622.09437	Mines and mineral resources—Czechoslovakia
TN1-4	338.205	Mineral industries—Periodicals	TN65.5-66	622.09439	Mines and mineral resources—Hungary

LC	Dewey	Subject Heading	LC	Dewey	Subject Heading
TN69-70	622.09489	Mines and mineral resources—Denmark	TN117-118	622.0962	Mines and mineral resources—Egypt
TN71-72.5	622.0944	Mines and mineral resources—France	TN121-122	622.0994	Mines and mineral resources—Australia
TN73-74.5	622.0943	Mines and mineral resources—Germany	TN122.5-.6	622.0993	Mines and mineral resources—New Zealand
TN75-76	622.09495	Mines and mineral resources—Greece	TN123-124	622.099(5-6)	Mines and mineral resources—Oceania
TN77-78	622.09492	Mines and mineral resources—Netherlands	TN125-.5	622.0998	Mines and mineral resources—Arctic regions
TN79-80	622.0945	Mines and mineral resources—Italy	TN139-140	622.092	Mining engineers
TN81-82	622.09481	Mines and mineral resources—Norway	TN165-213	622.071	Mining schools and education
TN83-84.5	622.09469	Mines and mineral resources—Portugal	TN260	553	Geology, Economic
			TN263.5	333.79	Energy minerals
TN85-86	622.0947	Mines and mineral resources—Russia	TN264	333.8509162	Marine mineral resources
			TN270-271	622.18	Prospecting
TN87-88	622.0946	Mines and mineral resources—Spain	TN271.P4	622.1828	Petroleum—Prospecting
			TN273	622.14	Mine surveying
TN88.5	622.0948	Mines and mineral resources—Scandinavia	TN277	622.8	Quarries and quarrying—Safety measures
TN89-90	622.09485	Mines and mineral resources—Sweden	TN277	622.292	Quarries and quarrying
			TN278	622.2927	Hydraulic mining
TN91-92	622.09494	Mines and mineral resources—Switzerland	TN279-281	622.23	Rock-drills
			TN279	622.23	Percussion drilling
TN95.A2	622.09496	Mines and mineral resources—Balkan Peninsula	TN279	622.23	Blasting
			TN281	622.24	Boring
			TN281.5	622.23	Rotary drilling
TN95.F5	622.094897	Mines and mineral resources—Finland	TN283	622.25	Shaft sinking
			TN285	622.26	Tunneling
TN95.Y8	622.09497	Mines and mineral resources—Yugoslavia	TN289	622.28	Mine timbering
			TN291	622.292	Strip mining
TN101-102	622.0951	Mines and mineral resources—China	TN295	622.8	Coal mines and mining—Safety measures
TN103-104	622.0954	Mines and mineral resources—India	TN297	622.89	Mine rescue work
			TN297	622.80284	Gas masks
TN104.5-.6	622.095491	Mines and mineral resources—Pakistan	TN301-306	622.42	Mine ventilation
			TN305-306	622.82	Firedamp
TN104.7-.8	622.095493	Mines and mineral resources—Sri Lanka	TN305-306	622.82	Mine gases
			TN307	622.473	Safety-lamps
TN105-106	622.0952	Mines and mineral resources—Japan	TN307	622.473	Electric lamps, Portable
			TN306.5-309	622.47	Mine lighting
TN107-108	622.0955	Mines and mineral resources—Iran	TN311-320	622.8	Coal mine accidents
			TN311-320	622.8	Mine accidents
TN109-110	622.0957	Mines and min. resources—Asiatic Russia	TN313-315	622.82	Combustion, Spontaneous
			TN313	622.82	Mine explosions
TN111-112	622.09561	Mines and mineral resources—Turkey	TN315	622.82	Mine fires
			TN318	622.5	Mine water
TN113.I55	622.09598	Mines and mineral resources—Indonesia	TN336	622.66	Mine railroads
			TN338	622.66	Gasoline locomotives
TN113.I7	622.09567	Mines and mineral resources—Iraq	TN342	622.6	Shuttle cars (Mine haulage)
TN113.I75	622.095694	Mines and mineral resources—Israel	TN343	622.48	Electricity in mining
			TN345-347	622.0284	Mining machinery
TN113.P6	622.09599	Mines and mineral resources—Philippines	TN400-580	622.34	Metals
			TN400-580	622.34	Ores
TN115-119	622.096	Mines and mineral resources—Africa	TN400-409	622.341	Iron mines and mining
			TN410-439	622.342	Precious metals
			TN410-429	622.3422	Gold mines and mining

LC	Dewey	Subject Heading	LC	Dewey	Subject Heading
TN420-429	622.3422	Gold ores	TN880-884	622.3385	Gas wells
TN422	622.3422	Gold dredging	TN880-884	622.3385	Gas engineering
TN430-439	622.3423	Silver mines and mining	TN880-884	622.3385	Natural gas
TN440-449	622.343	Copper mines and mining	TN880.5	665.744	Natural gas pipelines
TN450-459	622.344	Lead ores	TN885	622.339	Amber
TN470-479	622.3453	Tin mines and mining	TN890	622.3668	Sulphur
TN470-479	622.3453	Tin ores	TN895-897	669.725	Alkalies
TN490.B6	622.347	Bismuth ores	TN900-909	622.3632	Salt mines and mining
TN490.C6	622.3483	Cobalt ores	TN900-909	622.3632	Salt
TN530	622.77	Magnetic separation of ores	TN911	622.364	Nitrates
			TN913-914	622.364	Phosphate mines and mining
TN550-580	669.92	Assaying			
TN565	669.92	Metallurgical analysis	TN917	622.3633	Borax
TN600-799	669	Metallurgy	TN919	622.3636	Potassium salts
TN600-605	669.05	Metallurgy—Periodicals	TN923-929.7	622.373	Mineral waters
TN615-620	669.09	Metallurgy—History	TN930	622.3672	Asbestos
TN621-655	669.09(4-9)	Metallurgy—[By region or country]	TN933	622.3674	Mica
			TN939	622.3622	Sand and gravel plants
TN672	669.8	Precipitation hardening	TN939	622.3622	Sand
TN675.3	669.071	Metallurgy—Study and teaching	TN941-943	622.367	Fire-clay
			TN941-943	622.361	Clay
TN677-.5	669.0282	Smelting furnaces	TN945	622.368	Cement
TN677-.5	669.0282	Blast furnaces	TN946	622.3635	Gypsum
TN677-.5	669.0282	Metallurgical furnaces	TN948.D5	622.36	Diatomaceous earth
TN681-687	669.0284	Electrometallurgy	TN948.P5	622.3662	Pigments
TN686.5.E4	669.0284	Electroslag process	TN950-997	622.35	Stone
TN687	669.028	Electric furnaces	TN957	622.353	Sandstone
TN688	669.0283	Hydrometallurgy	TN967	622.3516	Dolomite
TN689-693	669.95	Metallography	TN970	622.352	Granite
TN690	669.9	Physical metallurgy	TN980-997	622.38	Precious stones
TN690	669.95	Alloys	TN990-994	622.382	Diamonds
TN695-697	671.37	Powder metallurgy	TN997.A35	622.387	Agates
TN710	669.1413	Cast-iron	TN997.E5	622.386	Emeralds
TN713-718	669.1413	Blast furnaces	TN997.G3	622.387	Garnet
TN736-738	669.1423	Bessemer process	TN997.S24	622.384	Sapphires
TN740-742	669.1422	Open-hearth furnaces			
TN755	669.142	Steel-works	TP	660	Chemistry, Technical
TN756-757	669.141	Iron alloys	TP1	660.05	Chemistry, Technical—Periodicals
TN758-799	669.(2-7)	Nonferrous metals			
TN760-769	669.22	Gold—Metallurgy	TP5	660.06	Chemistry, Technical—Congresses
TN775	669.722	Aluminum—Metallurgy			
TN780	669.3	Copper—Metallurgy	TP9	660.03	Chemistry, Technical—Encyclopedias
TN799.9-844.7	622.334	Coal			
TN799.9-844.7	622.334	Coal mines and mining	TP15-20	660.09	Chemistry, Technical—History
TN820-823	622.335	Anthracite coal			
TN850	622.33	Bitumen	TP149	660.2804	Chemicals—Safety measures
TN853	622.337	Asphalt			
TN858-859	662.3383	Oil shales	TP155-156	660	Chemical engineering
TN860-879	622.3382	Petroleum	TP155.5-.6	660.28	Chemical plants
TN870	622.338	Oil fields—Production methods	TP155.7-.75	660.281	Chemical processes
			TP156.C57	667.9	Coating processes
TN871	622.3382	Gushers	TP156.D5	660.28425	Distillation
TN871	622.3382	Oil reservoir engineering	TP156.E6	660.294514	Emulsions
TN871.2-.3	622.3381	Oil well drilling	TP156.E8	660.284248	Extraction (Chemistry)
TN871.27	622.3381	Drilling muds	TP156.F5	660.284245	Filters and filtration
TN871.3	622.33819	Oil well drilling, Submarine	TP156.F65	660.284292	Fluidization
TN871.37	622.3382	Secondary recovery of oil	TP156.P6	668.92	Polymerization
TN871.5	622.3381	Oil well drilling rigs	TP157-159	660.283	Chemical engineering—Equipment and supply
TN879.5-.6	665.544	Petroleum pipelines			

LC	Dewey	Subject Heading	LC	Dewey	Subject Heading
TP159.C3	660.2995	Catalysts	TP375-414.5	664.1	Syrups
TP165-183	660.072	Chemical engineering laboratories	TP390-391	664.123	Beet sugar
			TP415-416	664.2	Starch
TP187-197	660.072	Research, Industrial—Laboratories	TP434-435	664.756	Cereals, Prepared
			TP435.C67	664.724	Corn products
TP200-248	661	Chemicals	TP443-444	664.805	Vegetables—Drying
TP213-217	661.2	Acids	TP480-482	621.56	Low temperature engineering
TP213-217	661.2	Inorganic acids			
TP222-223	661.03	Alkalies	TP490-497	621.56	Refrigeration and refrigerating machinery
TP237-238	661.65	Nitrates			
TP240	661.63	Sulphites	TP496-497	621.57	Refrigerators
TP242-244	665.(7-8)	Gases	TP500-660	663	Beverages
TP245.C25	661.0385	Cesium	TP544-559	663.2	Wine and wine making
TP245.C4	661.0681	Carbon	TP555	663.224	Champagne (Wine)
TP245.F6	661.0731	Fluorine	TP559.P8	663.223	Madeira wine
TP245.H4	665.822	Helium	TP559.P8	663.223	Port wine
TP245.O9	661.0721	Oxygen	TP568-587	663.42	Beer
TP245.U7	661.0431	Uranium	TP568-587	663.3	Brewing
TP247-248	661.8	Organic compounds	TP569-587	663.3	Breweries
TP247.2	661.86	Organic acids	TP589-618	663.5	Liquors
TP247.5	661.807	Solvents	TP593	663.1	Alcohol
TP248.13-.65	660.6	Biotechnology	TP599	663.53	Brandy
TP248.25.M45	660.28424	Membrane reactors	TP605	663.52	Whiskey
TP248.25.M46	660.28424	Membrane separation	TP607.R9	663.59	Rum
TP248.27.M53	660.6	Microbial biotechnology	TP611	663.55	Liqueurs
TP248.3	660.63	Biochemical engineering	TP628-636	663.62	Carbonated beverages
TP248.6	660.65	Genetic engineering	TP645	663.93	Coffee
TP248.65.F66	664.024	Food—Biotechnology	TP669-699	664.3	Oils and fats
TP250-261	660.297	Electrochemistry, Industrial	TP669-695	665.1	Waxes
			TP676	664.34	Lard oil
TP265-267	660.2961	Fire	TP676	665.2	Fish oils
TP267.5-301	662.2	Explosives	TP678	638.17	Beeswax
TP268-299	623.452	Explosives, Military	TP680-684	665.3	Vegetable oils
TP272	662.26	Gunpowder	TP684.C275	665.353	Castor oil
TP276	662.26	Guncotton	TP684.C7	665.355	Coconut oil
TP285	662.27	Dynamite	TP684.M3	664.32	Margarine
TP297	662.20289	Explosives—Safety measures	TP685-699	665.4	Mineral oils
			TP690-692.5	665.53	Petroleum—Refining
TP300-301	662.1	Firecrackers	TP690-692.5	665.5	Petroleum
TP300-301	662.1	Fireworks	TP690-692.5	665.5	Petroleum products
TP310	662.5	Matches	TP690.4	665.533	Cracking process
TP315-360	662.6	Fuel	TP690.4	665.533	Catalytic cracking
TP323	662.65	Briquets (Fuel)	TP692.2	662.66	Gasoline, Synthetic
TP324	662.65	Fuelwood	TP692.2	665.53827	Gasoline
TP331	662.74	Charcoal	TP692.4.K4	665.5383	Kerosene
TP343	665.5384	Diesel fuels	TP692.5	665.542	Oil storage tanks
TP345-350	665.75	Gas as fuel	TP692.5	665.542	Petroleum—Storage
TP350	665.7	Natural gas	TP700-764	665.7	Gas manufacture and works
TP355	665.5	Petroleum as fuel			
TP358	662.6692	Alcohol as fuel	TP700	665.7	Gas
TP358	662.6692	Gasohol	TP751-764	665.7	Gas
TP359.B48	665.776	Biogas	TP757	665.744	Gas distribution
TP371.44	664.024	Fermented foods	TP757	665.744	Gas-pipes
TP371.8	664.0288	Radiation preservation of food	TP759	665.772	Coal gasification
			TP759	665.773	Oil gasification
TP372.2	664.02852	Cold storage	TP785-842	666.3	Pottery
TP372.3	664.02853	Frozen foods	TP811	666.3	Clay
TP375-414.5	664.1	Sugar—Manufacture and refining	TP812	666.427	Glazes
			TP823	666.427	Glazes

LC	Dewey	Subject Heading	LC	Dewey	Subject Heading
TP826-833	666.737	Brickmaking	TP1180.P6	668.4225	Polyesters
TP826-833	666.737	Bricks	TP1180.S7	668.4233	Styrene
TP839	666.733	Drain-tiles	TP1183.F6	668.493	Plastic foams
TP841-842	666.43	Kilns	TP1183.L3	668.492	Laminated plastics
TP845-869	666.1	Glass manufacture			
TP859	666.122	Glass blowing and working	TR	770	Photography
TP865-868	666.19	Glassware	TR1	770.5	Photography—Periodicals
TP866	666.192	Bottles	TR5	770.6	Photography—Congresses
TP866	663	Bottling	TR6	770.74	Photography—Exhibitions
TP867	681.428	Mirrors	TR9	770.3	Photography—
TP870	666.86	Artificial minerals			Encyclopedias
TP873-.5	666.88	Precious stones, Artificial	TR15	770.9	Photography—History
TP873.5.D5	666.88	Diamonds, Artificial	TR21-127	770.9(4-9)	Photography—[By region
TP885	666.894	Concrete products			or country]
TP885.C7	666.894	Concrete blocks	TR22-25	770.973	Photography—United
TP890-933	677	Textile chemistry			States
TP890-929	667.2	Dyes and dyeing—	TR26-27	770.971	Photography—Canada
		Chemistry	TR28-29	770.972	Photography—Mexico
TP894-895	667.14	Bleaching	TR30-31	770.9728	Photography—Central
TP897-929	667.2	Dyes and dyeing			America
TP901	686.2316	Silk-printing	TR32-33	770.9729	Photography—West Indies
TP990-992.5	667.1	Cleaning compounds	TR36-37	770.982	Photography—Argentina
TP932-.6	667.12	Dry cleaning	TR38-39	770.984	Photography—Bolivia
TP934-945	677.02825	Finishes and finishing	TR41-42	770.981	Photography—Brazil
TP934-937.5	667.6	Paint	TR43-44	770.983	Photography—Chile
TP934-937.5	667.29	Pigments	TR45-46	770.9861	Photography—Colombia
TP940	667.72	Polishes	TR47	770.9866	Photography—Ecuador
TP946-950	667.4	Ink	TR51	770.9892	Photography—Paraguay
TP953	661.803	Coal-tar	TR52	770.985	Photography—Peru
TP958-959	661.806	Essence and essential oils	TR53	770.9895	Photography—Uruguay
TP967-970	668.3	Glue	TR54	770.987	Photography—Venezuela
TP967-970	668.3	Adhesives	TR55-95	770.94	Photography—Europe
TP973	668.2	Glycerin	TR57-64	770.941	Photography—Great
TP977-979.5	665.332	Turpentine			Britain
TP977-979.5	668.374	Gums and resins,	TR59-60	770.9415	Photography—Ireland
		Synthetic	TR65-.2	770.9436	Photography—Austria
TP977-979.5	668.37	Gums and resins	TR71-72.5	770.944	Photography—France
TP983-986	668.55	Cosmetics	TR73-74.5	770.943	Photography—Germany
TP990-992.5	668.12	Soap	TR75-76	770.9495	Photography—Greece
TP993	665.1	Candles	TR77-78	770.9492	Photography—Netherlands
TP995-996	658.567	Waste products	TR79-80	770.945	Photography—Italy
TP1101-1185	668.4	Plastics	TR81-82	770.9481	Photography—Norway
TP1101	668.406	Plastics—Societies, etc.	TR85-86	770.947	Photography—Russia
TP1103	668.405	Plastics—Periodicals	TR87-88	770.946	Photography—Spain
TP1105	668.406	Plastics—Congresses	TR89-90	770.9485	Photography—Sweden
TP1110	668.403	Plastics—Encyclopedias	TR91-92	770.9494	Photography—Switzerland
TP1114	668.4027	Plastics—Patents	TR99-113	770.95	Photography—Asia
TP1116-1118	668.409	Plastics—History	TR101-102	770.951	Photography—China
TP1127-1129	668.4071	Plastics—Study and	TR103-104	770.954	Photography—India
		teaching	TR105-106	770.952	Photography—Japan
TP1135	668.41	Plastics machinery	TR107-108	770.955	Photography—Iran
TP1150	668.412	Plastics—Molding	TR109-110	770.957	Photography—Asiatic
TP1160	668.415	Plastics—Welding			Russia
TP1175.E9	668.413	Plastics—Extrusion	TR111-112	770.9561	Photography—Turkey
TP1180.A33	668.423	Acetal resins	TR115-119	770.96	Photography—Africa
TP1180.C5	668.44	Celluloid	TR117-118	770.962	Photography—Egypt
TP1180.C6	668.44	Cellulose	TR121-122	770.994	Photography—Australia
TP1180.E6	668.374	Epoxy resins	TR122.5-.6	770.993	Photography—New
TP1180.P57	668.423	Polycarbonates			Zealand

LC	Dewey	Subject Heading	LC	Dewey	Subject Heading
TR123-124	770.99(5-6)	Photography—Oceania	TR729.W54	778.932	Wildlife photography
TR139-140	770.92	Photography—Biography	TR755	778.34	Infrared photography
TR139	770.92	Photographers	TR785	623.72	Photography, Military
TR148	778.8	Trick photography	TR800	778.73	Underwater photography
TR151	770.21	Photography—Tables	TR810	778.35	Aerial photography
TR161	770.71	Photography—Study and teaching	TR818	371.897	School photography
			TR820	070.49	Photojournalism
TR183	770	Photography, Artistic	TR820.5	070.49	Documentary photography
TR196-199	771	Photography—Equipment and supplies	TR821	070.49796	Photography of sports
			TR824-835	686.4	Photocopying
TR210-212	771.5	Photographic chemistry	TR835	302.23	Microfilm readers
TR212	771.5	Photographic chemicals	TR845-899.5	778.53	Cinematography
TR225	771.47	Photography—Wastes, Recovery of	TR855	778.53	Wide-screen processes (Cinematography)
TR250-265	771.3	Cameras	TR858	778.5345	Cinematography—Special effects
TR256	771.33	Digital cameras			
TR262	771.32	35mm cameras	TR882.3	384.558	Camcorders
TR267	775	Digital photography	TR886.7	791.4302	Dubbing of motion pictures
TR268	771	Photography, Pinhole			
TR269	770	Instant photography	TR893.5	778.53859	Wildlife cinematography
TR270-271	771.352	Photographic lenses	TR897.5-.75	778.5347	Animation (Cinematography)
TR281	771.5322	Photography—Plates			
TR283	771.5324	Photography—Films	TR899-.5	778.535	Motion pictures—Editing
TR287-500	772.774	Photography—Processing	TR905	771.44	Photography—Enlarging
TR290-312	771.43	Photography—Negatives	TR920-923	686.4	Photographic reproduction of plans, drawings, etc.
TR295	771.49	Photography—Developing and developers	TR921	686.42	Blueprinting
TR330-333	772.774	Photography—Printing processes	TR925-997	686.232	Photomechanical processes
TR340	771.44	Photographs—Trimming, mounting, etc.	TR930-937	686.2325	Collotype
			TR940-950	686.2325	Photolithography
TR365	772.12	Daguerreotype	TR970-977	686.2327	Photoengraving
TR400	772.16	Kallitype	TR975	686.2327	Photoengraving—Halftone process
TR415	686.42	Blueprinting			
TR465	770.288	Photographs—Conservation and restoration	TR980	686.2327	Photogravure
			TR1010	686.22544	Phototypesetting
TR470	686.45	Photostat	TR1035-1050	686.44	Electrophotography
TR475	771.44	Photography—Enlarging			
TR504-508	778.2	Slides (Photography)	TS	670	Manufactures
TR510-545	778.6	Color photography	TS23-25	670.973	United States—Manufactures
TR550-581	771.1	Photography—Studios and dark rooms	TS26-27	670.971	Canada—Manufactures
TR575-581	778.92	Portrait photography	TS28-29	670.972	Mexico—Manufactures
TR590-620	778.72	Photography—Lighting	TS30-31	670.9728	Central America—Manufactures
TR593	778.37	Photography, High-speed			
TR600	778.72	Photography—Artificial light	TS32-33	670.9729	West Indies—Manufactures
TR610	778.719	Night photography	TS36-37	670.982	Argentina—Manufactures
TR640-688	770	Photography, Artistic	TS38-39	670.984	Bolivia—Manufactures
TR656.5	778.935	Still-life photography	TS41-42	670.981	Brazil—Manufactures
TR659	778.94	Architectural photography	TS43-44	670.983	Chile—Manufactures
TR659.5	778.71	Outdoor photography	TS45-46	670.9861	Colombia—Manufactures
TR660-.5	778.936	Landscape photography	TS47	670.9866	Ecuador—Manufactures
TR661	778.36	Photography, Panoramic	TS48	670.9881	Guyana—Manufactures
TR670-.5	778.937	Marine photography	TS49	670.9883	Surinam—Manufactures
TR680-681	778.92	Portrait photography	TS50	670.9882	French Guiana—Manufactures
TR693-696	526.982	Photogrammetry			
TR713	778.35	Space photography	TS51	670.9892	Paraguay—Manufactures
TR721-733	778.93	Nature photography	TS52	670.985	Peru—Manufactures

LC	Dewey	Subject Heading	LC	Dewey	Subject Heading
TS53	670.9895	Uruguay—Manufactures	TS215	671.0284	Metal-working machinery
TS54	670.987	Venezuela—Manufactures	TS225	671.332	Forging
TS57-64	670.941	Great Britain—Manufactures	TS227-228.96	671.52	Welding
			TS228.9	671.529	Pressure welding
TS65-.2	670.9436	Austria—Manufactures	TS228.97-239	671.2	Founding
TS65.3-.4	670.9437	Czechoslovakia—Manufactures	TS228.99-240	671.2	Founding
			TS250	671.823	Sheet-metal
TS65.5-66	670.9439	Hungary—Manufactures	TS253	621.984	Dies (Metal-working)
TS67-68	670.9493	Belgium—Manufactures	TS283	681.76041	Pressure vessels
TS69-70	670.9489	Denmark—Manufactures	TS300-360	672	Steel-works
TS71-72.5	670.944	France—Manufactures	TS320	671.36	Tempering
TS73-74.5	670.943	Germany—Manufactures	TS340	671.32	Roll-mill
TS75-76	670.9495	Greece—Manufactures	TS380-.4	683.82	Cutlery
TS77-78	670.9492	Netherlands—Manufactures	TS400-455	683	Hardware
			TS519-531	683.3	Locksmithing
TS79-80	670.945	Italy—Manufactures	TS519-531	683.32	Locks and keys
TS81-82	670.9481	Norway—Manufactures	TS532-537.5	683.4	Firearms
TS83-84.5	670.9469	Portugal—Manufactures	TS535-.4	683.4	Gunsmithing
TS85-86	670.947	Russia—Manufactures	TS536.6.B6	683.422	Rifles, Bolt action
TS87-88	670.946	Spain—Manufactures	TS537	683.436	Revolvers
TS88.5	670.948	Scandinavia—Manufactures	TS540-549	681.11(3-4)	Horology
			TS540-549	681.11(3-4)	Clock and watch making
TS89-90	670.9485	Sweden—Manufactures	TS540-549	681.11(3-4)	Clocks and watches
TS91-92	670.9494	Switzerland—Manufactures	TS551-552	669.72	Light metals
			TS564-589	673.3	Brass
TS95.A2	670.9496	Balkan Peninsula—Manufactures	TS570	673.3	Bronze
			TS653-719	671.7	Metals—Finishing
TS95.F5	670.94897	Finland—Manufactures	TS662-693	671.732	Plating
TS95.Y8	670.9497	Yugoslavia—Manufactures	TS670-693	671.732	Electroplating
TS101-102	670.951	China—Manufactures	TS720-770	739.2782	Rings
TS103-104	670.954	India—Manufactures	TS740-770	739.27	Jewelry making
TS104.5-.6	670.95491	Pakistan—Manufactures	TS747-770	739.27	Gems
TS104.7-.8	670.95493	Sri Lanka—Manufactures	TS753-.5	739.27	Diamonds
TS105-106	670.952	Japan—Manufactures	TS800-915	674	Lumber
TS107-108	670.955	Iran—Manufactures	TS850-851	674.0284	Saws
TS109-110	670.957	Asiatic Russia—Manufactures	TS850	674.2	Sawmills
			TS869	674.835	Laminated wood
TS111-112	670.9561	Turkey—Manufactures	TS870	674.834	Plywood
TS113.I55	670.9598	Indonesia—Manufactures	TS870	674.83	Veneers and veneering
TS113.I7	670.9567	Iraq—Manufactures	TS880	684.14	Desks
TS113.I75	670.95694	Israel—Manufactures	TS880	684.13	Tables
TS113.P6	670.9599	Philippines—Manufactures	TS880	684.13	Chairs
TS115-119	670.96	Africa—Manufactures	TS880-889	684.1	Furniture
TS117-118	670.962	Egypt—Manufactures	TS880-889	684.1	Furniture making
TS121-122	670.994	Australia—Manufactures	TS886.5.C74	645.4083	Cribs (Children's furniture)
TS122.5-.6	670.993	New Zealand—Manufactures	TS890	674.82	Coopers and cooperage
			TS900	674.82	Crates
TS123-124	670.99(5-6)	Oceania—Manufactures	TS932-934	674.386	Wood—Chemistry
TS155-194	658.5	Factory management	TS940-1047	675	Leather
TS155-194	658.5	Production management	TS940-1047	675.23	Tanning
TS156-.6	658.562	Quality control	TS967	675.2	Hides and skins
TS161	658.7	Materials management	TS989-1025	685.31	Shoes
TS192	670.288	Plant maintenance	TS989-1025	685.31	Boots
TS195-198.8	688.8	Packaging	TS1030-1035	685.1	Saddlery
TS197.5	688.8	Containers	TS1060-1070	675.3	Fur
TS200-770	671	Metal-work	TS1080-1268	676	Papermaking
TS200	671.05	Metal-work—Periodicals	TS1080-1268	676	Paper
TS213	671.732	Plating	TS1080-1268	676	Paper products
TS214	363.7288	Scrap metals	TS1090-1096	676.09	Papermaking—History

LC	Dewey	Subject Heading	LC	Dewey	Subject Heading
TS1118.F5	676.235	Paper coatings	TS2270	688.42	Tobacco-pipes
TS1118.F5	676.234	Paper finishing	TS2301.B8	679.6	Brooms and brushes
TS1171-1177	676.12	Wood-pulp	TS2301.T7	688.7221	Dolls
TS1228-1268	676.2823	Stationery			
TS1262-1266	681.6	Pens	TT	745.5	Handicraft
TS1300-1865	677	Textile fabrics	TT1	745.505	Handicraft—Periodicals
TS1480-1487	677.02822	Spinning	TT6	745.5074	Handicraft—Exhibitions
TS1485-1487	676.02821	Carding	TT9	745.503	Handicraft—Encyclopedias
TS1488	677.028	Sizing (Textile)	TT15-127	745.509(4-9)	Handicraft—[By region or country]
TS1490-1500	677.028242	Weaving			
TS1493	677.02854	Looms	TT151	745.50288	Repairing
TS1510	677.02825	Textile finishing	TT152-153.7	684.08	Workshops
TS1520	677.682	Waterproofing of fabrics	TT154-.5	688.1	Models and modelmaking
TS1540-1549	677	Textile fibers	TT161-170.7	373.246	Manual training
TS1542	677.21	Cotton	TT174-.5	745.592	Toys
TS1545-1548	677.3	Animal fibers	TT175-.7	745.59221	Dolls
TS1546	677.39	Silk	TT175.3	745.5923	Dollhouses
TS1547	677.31	Wool	TT175.5	745.5923	Doll furniture
TS1548.7.P58	677.4743	Polyester fibers	TT175.7	745.5922	Doll clothes—Patterns
TS1550-1590	677.02862	Yarn	TT180-203.5	745.51	Woodwork
TS1590	677.02862	Thread	TT194-199.4	684.1	Furniture making
TS1600-1631	677.02862	Yarn	TT194-199.4	684.104	Furniture
TS1600-1631	677.31	Woolen and worsted manufacture	TT197	684.16	Cabinetwork
			TT197	684.16	Chests
TS1640-1688	677.39	Satin	TT197.5.D4	684.14	Desks
TS1640-1688	677.39	Silk	TT197.5.D5	684.13	Dining room furniture
TS1675	677.617	Velvet	TT197.5.09	684.18	Outdoor furniture
TS1680	677.617	Plush	TT197.5.T3	684.13	Tables
TS1688	677.46	Rayon	TT199	684.100288	Furniture—Repairing
TS1688	677.4	Synthetic fabrics	TT199	684.130288	Chair caning
TS1700-1735	677.11	Flax	TT199.75	745.5936	Decoys (Hunting)
TS1760-1770	677	Dry-goods	TT205-273	745.56	Metal-work
TS1772-1779.5	677.643	Carpets	TT267	745.56	Brazing
TS1780	677.64	Tapestry	TT270-273	745.73	Stencil work
TS1783	677.77	Embroidery	TT273	686.2316	Screen process printing
TS1784-1787	677.71	Cordage	TT288	745.58	Bone carving
TS1784-1787	677.71	Rope	TT290	745.531	Leatherwork
TS1825	677.6(2-3)	Felt	TT297-.5	745.572	Plastics craft
TS1828	677.6	Nonwoven fabrics	TT300-380	667.6	Painting, Industrial
TS1870-1935	678.2	Rubber industry and trade	TT310	667.0283	Paint mixing
TS1891	678.24	Vulcanization	TT320-324	698.1	House painting
TS1912	678.32	Tires, Rubber	TT360	667.6	Sign painting
TS1920	678.35	Rubber bands	TT360	745.61	Lettering
TS1925-1927	678.72	Rubber, Artificial	TT390	646.21	Drapery
TS1927.S55	668.4227	Silicone rubber	TT490-695	687	Clothing trade
TS1950-1982	664.9	Animal products	TT490	646.05	Clothing trade—Periodicals
TS1960-1967	664.9029	Slaughtering and slaughter-houses	TT498	687	Clothing factories
TS1980-1981	664.34	Lard	TT500-560	687.112	Dressmaking
TS2001-2035	688.6	Carriage and wagon-making	TT507	687	Clothing and dress
			TT509	741.672	Fashion drawing
TS2120-2159	664.7207	Flour-mills	TT520	687.043	Garment cutting
TS2120-2159	664.7207	Meal	TT525	685.24	Fur garments
TS2120-2159	664.7207	Flour	TT530-535	687.147	Cloaks
TS2158	664.76	Feed mills	TT530	687.142	Coats
TS2160	685.4	Gloves	TT550	646.408	Clothing and dress—Alteration
TS2220-2283	679.7	Tobacco industry			
TS2255	679.7	Nicotine	TT570-630	687.044	Tailoring
TS2260	679.72	Cigars	TT570-630	646.402	Men's furnishing goods

LC	Dewey	Subject Heading	LC	Dewey	Subject Heading
TT583	648.1	Pressing of garments	TT973	646.724	Hair—Dyeing and bleaching
TT590	687.043	Garment cutting			
TT595-600	687.141	Coats	TT975	646.7247	Braids (Hairdressing)
TT603	646.40608341	Boy's clothing	TT975	646.724	Hairweaving
TT605	687.113	Trousers	TT975	646.7248	Wigs
TT616	687.19	Neckties	TT980-999	648.1	Laundries
TT626	687.16	Livery			
TT635-645	646.406	Children's clothing	TX	640	Home economics
TT637	646.4060832	Layettes	TX1	640.5	Home economics—Periodicals
TT650-665	687.42	Millinery			
TT657	687.19	Kerchiefs	TX5	640.6	Home economics—Congresses
TT669-678	687.2	Underwear			
TT669-670	687.22	Lingerie	TX11	640.3	Home economics—Encyclopedias
TT675	687.21	T-shirts			
TT677	687.22	Foundation garments	TX15-19	640.9	Home economics—History
TT679-695	687.3	Hosiery	TX21-127	640.9(4-9)	Home economics—[By region or country]
TT699-854.5	746	Textile crafts			
TT700-845	746.4	Needlework	TX147	647	Institution management
TT700-715	646.2	Sewing	TX151-162	641.5	Recipes
TT713	646.2044	Machine sewing	TX165-286	640.71	Home economics—Study and teaching
TT720-730	646.2	Clothing and dress—Repairing			
			TX298-299	640.284	Home economics—Equipment and supplies
TT740-897	746.4	Fancy work			
TT769-778	746.44	Embroidery	TX311-317	645	Interior decoration
TT778.C24	746.44	Candlewicking (Embroidery)	TX324	648.5	House cleaning
TT778.C3	746.442	Canvas embroidery	TX331-334	640.46	Domestics
TT778.C65	746.442	Counted thread embroidery	TX335	640.73	Consumer education
			TX340	646.3	Clothing and dress
TT800-810	746.22	Lace and lace making	TX341-641	641.3	Food
TT819-829	746.432	Knitting	TX341-641	363.8	Nutrition
TT820-829	746.434	Crocheting	TX341-357	641	Groceries
TT835	746.46	Quilting	TX356	641.31	Marketing (Home economics)
TT835	746.46	Coverlets			
TT840.S66	746.44	Smocking	TX364-365	363.8071	Nutrition—Study and teaching
TT840.T38	746.436	Tatting			
TT847	746.12	Hand spinning	TX369	641.302	Natural foods
TT848-849.2	746.14	Hand weaving	TX371-389	641.36	Meat
TT850	746.73	Rugs, Braided	TX385-388	641.392	Seafood
TT850.2	746.3	Wall hangings	TX385	641.392	Fish as food
TT852.5	746.662	Batik	TX391	641.35	Vegetable juices
TT853-854.5	746.6	Dyes and dyeing	TX392-.8	613.262	Vegetarianism
TT860	745.582	Beadwork	TX393	641.331	Flour
TT862	745.55	Shellcraft	TX393	641.331	Cereals as food
TT870	736.982	Origami	TX394.5	641.822	Pasta products
TT877.5	746.41	Palm frond weaving	TX395	641.331	Cereals, Prepared
TT879.B3	746.412	Basket making	TX401.2.S69	641.35655	Tofu
TT890-894	745.5943	Artificial flowers	TX406-407	641.3383	Spices
TT896.7	745.5944	Egg decoration	TX406-407	641.657	Herbs
TT900.E2	745.59416	Easter decorations	TX407.C	641.3384	Chili powder
TT900.P3	745.5941	Party decorations	TX415	641.357	Herbal teas
TT900.V34	745.59416	Valentine decorations	TX415	641.3373	Coffee
TT926	745.5941	Balloon decorations	TX501-597	363.192064	Food adulteration and inspection
TT950-979	646.724	Barbering			
TT950-979	646.7042	Beauty culture	TX551-560	641.563	Diet
TT967	646.724	Electric shavers	TX551-560	641.563	Dietaries
TT967	646.7240284	Razors	TX551	613.23	Food—Caloric content
TT969	646.7240284	Hair preparations	TX552	641.612	Canned foods
TT969	646.7240284	Shampoos	TX553.A3	641.3	Food additives
TT970	646.724	Shaving			

LC	Dewey	Subject Heading	LC	Dewey	Subject Heading
TX553.C28	613.283	Food—Carbohydrate content	TX740.5	641.819	Garnishes (Cookery)
			TX743-759.5	641.36	Food of animal origin
TX553.C43	613.284	Food—Cholesterol content	TX747	641.692	Cookery (Fish)
TX553.F53	613.263	Fiber in human nutrition	TX747	641.692	Cookery (Seafood)
TX553.S8	613.283	Sugars in human nutrition	TX749-.5	641.66	Cookery (Meat)
TX553.V5	613.286	Vitamins	TX750-.5	641.665	Cookery (Poultry)
TX555-556	641.36	Meat	TX761-799	664.02	Bakers and bakeries
TX556.B4	641.362	Beef	TX761-778	664.02	Baking
TX556.B8	641.36292	Buffalo meat	TX769-770	641.815	Bread
TX556.M5	641.37143	Dried skim milk	TX769	641.815	Crackers
TX558.L4	641.6565	Legumes as food	TX770.B55	641.815	Biscuits
TX558.R5	641.3318	Rice	TX770.B55	641.815	Scones
TX560.H7	641.38	Honey	TX770.M83	641.8157	Muffins
TX599-613	641.4	Food—Preservation	TX770.P34	641.815	Pancakes, waffles, etc.
TX599-612	641.4	Canning and preserving	TX770.P56	641.815	Pita bread
TX599-612	641.4	Food preservatives	TX771-.2	641.8653	Cake
TX609	641.44	Drying apparatus—Food	TX771	641.8659	Coffee cakes
TX609	641.44	Dried foods	TX771.2	641.86539	Cake decorating
TX609	641.44	Food—Drying	TX772	641.8654	Cookies
TX610	641.453	Frozen foods	TX773	641.86	Desserts
TX612.F5	641.494	Fishery products—Preservation	TX773	641.8659	Pastry
			TX773	641.8644	Puddings
TX631-641	641.013	Gastronomy	TX773	641.8653	Cheesecake (Cookery)
TX642-840	641.5	Cookery	TX783-793	641.853	Candy
TX645	641.509	Cookery—History	TX783-799	641.853	Confectionery
TX649	641.5092	Cooks	TX795	641.86(2-3)	Ice cream, ices, etc.
TX653-655	643.3	Kitchens	TX801-807	641.65	Cookery (Vegetables)
TX657.E35	641.589	Eggbeaters	TX807	641.83	Salads
TX657.064	641.5882	Microwave ovens	TX809.M17	641.822	Cookery (Pasta)
TX657.S3-.S8	641.5028	Stoves	TX809.N65	641.822	Noodles
TX661-669	641.5071	Cookery—Study and teaching	TX813.C7	641.675	Cookery (Eggs)
			TX815-817	641.87	Beverages
TX685	641.731	Boiling (Cookery)	TX817.C5	641.877	Cocoa
TX686	641.77	Braising (Cookery)	TX818	641.84	Sandwiches
TX687	641.76	Broiling	TX819	641.814	Sauces
TX689.5	641.774	Stir frying	TX819	641.3382	Condiments
TX690	641.71	Roasting (Cookery)	TX819.S27	641.814	Salad dressing
TX691	641.73	Steaming (Cookery)	TX820	641.57	Quantity cookery
TX693	641.821	Casserole cookery	TX821	641.612	Cookery (Canned foods)
TX693	641.73	Stews	TX823	641.578	Outdoor cookery
TX716.M4	641.5972	Cookery, Mexican	TX825	641.585	Chafing dish cookery
TX719-.2	641.5944	Cookery, French	TX825.5	641.589	Clay pot cookery
TX721	641.5943	Cookery, German	TX827	641.586	Stoves, Electric
TX724.5.C	641.589	Wok cookery	TX832	641.5882	Microwave cookery
TX724.5.J3	641.5952	Cookery, Japanese	TX837-838	641.5636	Vegetarian cookery
TX727-739.2	642	Menus	TX837-838	641.5636	Vegetarianism
TX731-739	642.4	Entertaining	TX840.B3	641.5784	Barbecue cookery
TX733	641.52	Breakfasts	TX840.C65	641.58	Convection oven cookery
TX735	641.53	Luncheons	TX840.F6	641.5892	Food processor cookery
TX737	641.54	Dinners and dining	TX840.P7	641.587	Pressure cookery
TX739-.2	641.568	Holiday cookery	TX840.W65	641.589	Wok Cookery
TX739.2.C45	641.5686	Christmas cookery	TX851-885	642.(6-8)	Entertaining
TX739.2.E37	641.568	Easter cookery	TX855-859	643.4	Dining rooms
TX739.2.H35	641.5676435	Hanukkah cookery	TX871-885	642	Table
TX739.2.P37	641.5676437	Passover cookery	TX871-885	642.7	Table setting and decoration
TX739.2.T45	641.568	Thanksgiving cookery			
TX740	641.812	Appetizers	TX885	642.6	Carving (Meat, etc.)
TX740	641.82	Entrees (Cookery)	TX901-946.5	338.47	Food service
TX740	641.83	Salads		+ 64795	

LC	Dewey	Subject Heading	LC	Dewey	Subject Heading
TX901-946	910.46	Hotels	U167.5.A35	355.4	Advanced guard (Military science)
TX901-941	910.466	Tourist camps, hostels, etc.	U167.5.E57	355.422	Envelopment (Military science)
TX901-921	642.4	Caterers and catering	U167.5.H3	355.824	Flexible weapons (Hand-to-hand fighting)
TX901-910	647.95	Coffeehouses			
TX907-910	910.466	Youth hostels	U167.5.J8	355.423	Jungle warfare
TX911.3.M27	338.47 + 64795 + 068	Food service management	U167.5.L5	355.422	Lightning war
			U167.5.R34	355.422	Raids (Military science)
TX911.3.P4	910.460683	Hotels—Personnel management	U167.5.W5	355.423	Winter warfare
			U168	355.411	Logistics
TX911.3.P4	647.950683	Restaurants—Personnel management	U168	355.411	Integrated logistic support
			U173	355.350973	United States. Army—Field service
TX945-.5	647.95	Restaurants			
TX951	641.874	Bartending	U173.5	355.350975	Confederate States of America. Army—Field service
TX951	641.874	Cocktails			
TX951	641.874	Martinis			
TX951	641.2	Beverages	U190-195	355.422	Guard duty
TX955	647	Building management	U190	355.413	Scouts and scouting
TX957-959	647.92	Apartment houses	U200	355.422	Landing operations
TX1100-1105	643.29	Mobile home living	U205	355.423	Stream crossing, Military
			U210	355.422	Skirmishing
U	355	Military art and science	U215	355.422	Rearguard action (Military science)
U	355.02	War			
U1-145	355.0092	Soldiers	U220	355.413	Military reconnaissance
U7	355.006	Military art and science—Congresses	U225	355.4	Combat survival
			U230	355.351	Riots
U11	355.309730216	United States. Army—Registers	U240	355.0218	Guerrilla warfare
			U241	355.0218	Counterinsurgency
U13	355.0074	Military art and science—Exhibitions	U250-255	355.4	Military maneuvers
			U253	355.40973	United States. Army—Maneuvers
U13	355.0074	Military museums			
U21	355.0213	Militarism	U260	355.46	Combined operations (Military science)
U22	355.123	Morale			
U22.3	355.0019	Psychology, Military	U260	366.46	Unified operations (Military science)
U24-26	355.003	Military art and science—Dictionaries			
			U261	355.46	Amphibious warfare
U27-43	355.009	Military art and science—History	U262	355.422	Commando troops
			U262	356.16	Special operations (Military science)
U29-35	355.00901	Military art and science—History—To 500			
			U262	356.160973	Special forces (Military science)—United States—History
U51-55	355.0092	Military art and science—Biography			
U51-55	355.0092	Generals	U263	355.0217	Nuclear warfare
U56-59	355.3460973	United States—Armed Forces—Officers' clubs	U263	355.0217	Nuclear crisis stability
			U264	355.825119	Nuclear weapons
U110-115	355.5	Military art and science—Soldiers' handbooks	U264	355.0217	No first use (Nuclear strategy)
U113	355.5470973	United States. Army—Handbooks, manuals, etc.	U280-285	355.4(8)	Staff rides
			U290-295	355.5	Military training camps
U130-135	355	Military art and science—Officers' handbooks	U300-305	355.5	Bombing and gunnery ranges
			U310	355.480285	Computer war games
U161-163	355.4	Operational art (Military science)	U310	355.48	War games
			U310	355.480285	AGATE (Computer war game)
U161-163	355.42	Strategy			
U162.6	355.0217	Deterrence (Strategy)	U313	355.48	Imaginary wars and battles
U164-167.5	355.42	Tactics	U320-325	355.5	Physical education and training, Military
U167	355.422	Friendly fire (Military science)			
U167	355.422	Ambushes and surprises			

LC	Dewey	Subject Heading	LC	Dewey	Subject Heading
U323	355.50973	United States. Army—Physical training	U875	355.8241	Ballista
			U875	355.8241	Catapult
U350-365	355.17	Military ceremonies, honors, and salutes	U877-878	355.8241	Bow and arrow
U350-355	355.17	Weddings, Military	UA	355.31	Armies
U370-375	355.35	Garrisons	UA	355.75	Armories
U390-395	355.07	Military research	UA10	355.0213	Militarism
U400-714	355.0071	Military education	UA10.7	355.45	Civilian-based defense
U407-714	355.00710(4-9)	Military education—[By region or country]	UA11	355.0335	Military policy
			UA11.5	355.0215	Limited war
U408-439	355.0071073	Military education—United States	UA12	355.031	Mutual security program, 1951-
U408.3	355.50973	Experimental Volunteer Army Training Program	UA12.5	327.1747	Disarmament—Inspection
			UA12.8	355.35	Guard troops
U409	355.007107(4-9)	Military education—[United States, By state]	UA13	355.37	Militia
			UA14	355.352	Armies, Colonial
U410.E9	355.0071073	Hazing	UA16	355.032	Military missions
U440-444	355.0071071	Military education—Canada	UA17	355.622	Armies, Cost of
			UA17	355.622	War, Cost of
U445-449	355.0071072	Military education—Mexico	UA17.5	355.22	Manpower
U450-454	355.00710728	Military education—Central America	UA18	355.26	Industrial mobilization
			UA19	355.0021	Military statistics
U455-459	355.00710729	Military education—West Indies	UA23.2-.6	355.60973	United States. Dept. of Defense
U465-499	355.007108	Military education—South America	UA24-39	355.30973	United States. Army
			UA23-25	355.30973	United States. Army—History
U505-630	355.007104	Military education—Europe	UA23	355.450973	United States—Defenses
U510-549.3	355.0071041	Military education—Great Britain	UA24-39	355.30973	United States. Army
			UA24.A7	355.30973	United States. Army—Appropriations and expenditures
U550-554	355.00710436	Military education—Austria	UA28-29	356.10973	United States. Army. Infantry
U570-574.54	355.0071043	Military education—Germany	UA30-31	357.10973	United States. Army. Cavalry
U635-660	355.007105	Military education—Asia	UA32-33	358.120973	United States. Army—Artillery
U640-644	355.0071051	Military education—China	UA34.S64	356.160973	United States. Army. Special Forces—History
U645-649	355.0071054	Military education—India			
U650-654	355.0071052	Military education—Japan			
U655-659	355.0071055	Military education—Iran	UA42-560	355.370973	United States—National Guard
U670-695	355.007106	Military education—Africa			
U700-704	355.0071094	Military education—Australia	UA42-560	355.370973	United States—Militia
			UA42-560	355.370973	United States—Armed Forces—Reserves
U715-717	355.5071	Soldiers—Education, Non-military	UA45	355.3480973	United States—Armed Forces—Women's reserves
U750-773	355.0092	Soldiers			
U800-897	623.4409	Armor	UA50-549	355.37097(4-9)	United States—Armed Forces—Reserves, [United States, By state]
U800-897	355.8	Weapons			
U804	623.441074	Armor—Exhibitions			
U805	623.4410901	Armor, Ancient	UA50-59	355.3709761	Alabama—National Guard
U818-823.5	623.44109(4-9)	Armor—[By region or country]	UA60-69	355.3709798	Alaska—National Guard
			UA70-79	355.3709791	Arizona—National Guard
U825	355.81	Helmets	UA80-89	355.3709767	Arkansas—National Guard
U850-872	355.8241	Swords	UA90-99	355.3709794	California—National Guard
U850-863	355.8241	Sabers	UA100-109	355.3709746	Connecticut—National Guard
U865	355.4	Swordplay			
U872	623.441	Lances			

LC	Dewey	Subject Heading	LC	Dewey	Subject Heading
UA110-119	355.3709751	Delaware—National Guard	UA520-529	355.3709754	West Virginia—National Guard
UA120-129	355.3709753	Washington (D.C.)—National Guard	UA530-539	355.3709775	Wisconsin—National Guard
UA140-149	355.3709759	Florida—National Guard	UA540-549	355.3709787	Wyoming—National Guard
UA150-159	355.3709758	Georgia—National Guard	UA580-585	355.30975	Confederate States of America. Army
UA159.1-.9	355.3709969	Hawaii—National Guard	UA580-585	355.450975	Confederate States of America—Defenses
UA160-169	355.3709796	Idaho—National Guard			
UA170-179	355.3709773	Illinois—National Guard	UA830	355.03305	East Asia—Strategic aspects
UA180-189	355.3709772	Indiana—National Guard			
UA190-199	355.3709777	Iowa—National Guard	UA835	355.00951	China—Armed Forces
UA200-209	355.3709781	Kansas—National Guard	UA910-915	355.28	Armed forces—Mobilization
UA210-219	355.3709769	Kentucky—National Guard			
UA220-229	355.3709763	Louisiana—National Guard	UA926-929	363.35	Civil defense
UA230-239	355.3709741	Maine—National Guard	UA940-945	355.85	Communications, Military
UA240-249	355.3709752	Maryland—National Guard	UA985-997	355.47	Military geography
UA250-259	355.3709744	Massachusetts—National Guard	UA985-997	355.47	Maps, Military
UA260-269	355.3709774	Michigan—National Guard	UB	355.6	Military administration
UA270-279	355.3709776	Minnesota—National Guard	UB1	355.605	Military administration—Periodicals
UA280-289	355.3709762	Mississippi—National Guard	UB15	355.609	Military administration—History
UA290-299	355.3709778	Missouri—National Guard			
UA300-309	355.3709786	Montana—National Guard	UB23-25	355.60973	United States—Armed Forces—Management
UA310-319	355.3709782	Nebraska—National Guard			
UA320-329	355.3709793	Nevada—National Guard	UB73-74	355.60943	Germany—Armed Forces—Management
UA330-339	355.3709742	New Hampshire—National Guard			
UA340-349	355.3709749	New Jersey—National Guard	UB85-86	355.60947	Russia—Armed Forces—Management
UA350-359	355.3709789	New Mexico—National Guard	UB101-102	355.60951	China—Armed Forces—Management
UA360-369	355.3709747	New York (State)—National Guard	UB105-106	355.60952	Japan—Armed Forces—Management
UA370-379	355.3709756	North Carolina—National Guard	UB163	355.60973	United States. Army—Records and correspondence
UA380-389	355.3709784	North Dakota—National Guard			
			UB210	355.33041	Command of troops
UA390-399	355.3709771	Ohio—National Guard	UB210	355.33041	Leadership
UA400-409	355.3709766	Oklahoma—National Guard	UB233	355.306073	United States—Armed Forces—Headquarters
UA410-419	355.3709795	Oregon—National Guard	UB240-245	355.685	Military inspectors general
UA420-429	355.3709748	Pennsylvania—National Guard	UB243	355.6850973	United States. Army—Inspection
UA430-439	355.3709745	Rhode Island—National Guard	UB250-271	355.3432	Military intelligence
			UB265	355.3432	Military interrogation
UA440-449	355.3709757	South Carolina—National Guard	UB270-271	355.3432092	Spies
			UB271.G	327.1243	Espionage, West German
UA450-459	355.3709783	South Dakota—National Guard	UB275-277	355.3434	Psychological warfare
			UB280-285	355.113	Military passes
UA460-469	355.3709768	Tennessee—National Guard	UB320-345	355.223	Recruiting and enlistment
UA470-479	355.3709764	Texas—National Guard	UB320-338	355.2236	Advertising—Recruiting and enlistment
UA480-489	355.3709792	Utah—National Guard			
UA490-499	355.3709743	Vermont—National Guard	UB320-325	355.22362	Military service, Voluntary
UA500-509	355.3709755	Virginia—National Guard	UB323	355.2230973	United States. Army—Recruiting, enlistment, etc.
UA510-519	355.3709797	Washington (State)—National Guard			
			UB340-355	355.22363	Draft
			UB341-342	355.224	Conscientious objectors

LC	Dewey	Subject Heading	LC	Dewey	Subject Heading
UB350-355	355.225	Draft	UB810-815	355.13325	Corporal punishment
UB356-375	362.1608697	Veterans	UB820-825	355.13323	Military police
UB356-359	331.52	Veterans—Employment	UB850-857	343.0143	Courts-martial and courts of inquiry
UB356-359	371.82697	Veterans—Education			
UB360-366	362.408697	Veterans, Disabled			
UB368-369.5	362.108697	Veterans—Medical care	UC	358.25	Transportation, Military
UB370-375	331.25291355	Military pensions	UC15	355.28	Requisitions, Military
UB380-385	362.1608697	Soldiers' homes	UC40-44	355.620973	United States. Army—Commissariat
UB390-395	355.7	Military reservations			
UB400-405	355.12	Military dependents	UC70-75	355.640973	United States. Army—Pay, allowances, etc.
UB408-.5	355.3320973	United States—Armed Forces—Warrant officers			
			UC85-86	355.620975	Confederate States of America. Army—Commissariat
UB410-415	355.332	Armies—Officers			
UB412-414	355.3320973	United States. Army—Officers	UC90-93	355.80971	Canada—Armed forces—Supplies and stores
UB418.B69	355.3308351	Boys as soldiers			
UB430-435	355.134	Military decorations	UC94-97	355.80972	Mexico—Armed forces—Supplies and stores
UB430-435	355.1342	Decorations of honor			
UB433	355.13420973	Distinguished Service Cross (U.S.)	UC98-99	355.809728	Central America—Armed Forces—Supplies and stores
UB433	355.13420973	Medal of Honor			
UB435.G	355.13420941	Distinguished Conduct Medal (Great Britain)	UC106-154	355.8098	South America—Armed Forces—Supplies and stores
UB461-736	343.(4-9)01	Military law—[By region or country]			
UB505-509	343.7101	Military law—Canada	UC158-233	355.8094	Europe—Armed Forces—Supplies and stores
UB510-514	343.7201	Military law—Mexico			
UB515-519	343.72801	Military law—Central America	UC180-183	355.80943	Germany—Armed Forces—Supplies and stores
UB520-524	343.72901	Military law—West Indies			
UB530-589	343.801	Military law—South America	UC184-187	355.80941	Great Britain—Armed Forces—Supplies and stores
UB530-534	343.8201	Military law—Argentina			
UB545-549	343.8301	Military law—Chile	UC234-245	355.8095	Asia—Armed Forces—Supplies and stores
UB550-554	343.86101	Military law—Colombia			
UB585-589	343.8701	Military law—Venezuela	UC241	355.80952	Japan—Armed Forces—Supplies and stores
UB590-684	343.401	Military law—Europe			
UB615-619	343.4401	Military law—France	UC247-253	355.8096	Africa—Armed Forces—Supplies and stores
UB620-624	343.4301	Military law—Germany			
UB630-634	343.49501	Military law—Greece	UC255-256	355.80994	Australia—Armed Forces—Supplies and stores
UB640-644	343.4501	Military law—Italy			
UB650-654	343.46901	Military law—Portugal			
UB655-659	343.4701	Military law—Russia	UC260-267	355.62137	Surplus military property
UB660-664	343.4601	Military law—Spain	UC260-267	355.8	Military supplies
UB685-710	343.501	Military law—Asia	UC260-267	355.62120973	United States—Armed Forces—Procurement
UB690-694	343.5101	Military law—China			
UB695-699	343.5401	Military law—India	UC260	355.6212	Armed forces—Procurement
UB700-704	343.5201	Military law—Japan			
UB715-729	343.601	Military law—Africa	UC263	355.62120973	United States. Army—Procurement
UB730-734	343.9401	Military law—Australia			
UB735-736	343.9(5-6)01	Military law—Oceania	UC270-360	358.25	Transportation, Military
UB780-789	355.1334	Military offenses	UC273	358.250973	United States. Army—Transportation
UB787	355.1334	Mutiny			
UB788	355.1334	Desertion, Military	UC300-305	358.25	Pack transportation
UB789	355.1334	Insubordination	UC320-325	355.83	Transports
UB790-795	343.014	Military discipline	UC330-335	355.83	Airlift, Military
UB800-805	365.48	Military prisons	UC330-335	355.83	Airdrop
UB803	365.480973	Prisoners of war—United States	UC340-345	355.83	Motorization, Military
			UC400-440	355.71	Barracks

LC	Dewey	Subject Heading	LC	Dewey	Subject Heading
UC410	355.71	Soldiers—Billeting	UE15	357.09	Cavalry—History
UC460-465	355.81	Armies—Equipment	UE21-124	357.09(4-9)	Cavalry—[By region or country]
UC480-485	355.14	Military uniforms			
UC523	355.80973	United States. Army—Equipment	UE23-25	357.0973	Cavalry—United States
			UE26-27	357.0971	Cavalry—Canada
UC530-535	355.14	Insignia	UE28-29	357.0972	Cavalry—Mexico
UC533	355.13420973	United States. Army—Medals, badges, decorations	UE30-31	357.09728	Cavalry—Central America
			UE32-33	357.09729	Cavalry—West Indies
			UE34-54	357.098	Cavalry—South America
UC570-575	355.81	Tents	UE36-37	357.0982	Cavalry—Argentina
UC590-595	355.15	Standards, Military	UE43-44	357.0983	Cavalry—Chile
UC590-595	355.15	Guidons	UE45-46	357.09861	Cavalry—Colombia
UC590-595	355.15	Flags	UE54	357.0987	Cavalry—Venezuela
UC600-695	357.2	Horses	UE55-95	357.094	Cavalry—Europe
UC600-695	357.2	Remount service	UE57-64	357.0941	Cavalry—Great Britain
UC700-780	355.62	Armies—Commissariat	UE71-72	357.0944	Cavalry—France
UC720-735	641.57	Cookery, Military	UE73-74	357.0943	Cavalry—Germany
UC723	355.3410973	United States—Armed Forces—Messes	UE75-76	357.09495	Cavalry—Greece
			UE79-80	357.0945	Cavalry—Italy
UC750-755	355.341	Canteens (Establishments)	UE83-84	357.09469	Cavalry—Portugal
			UE85-86	357.0947	Cavalry—Russia
UD	356.1	Infantry	UE86.5	357.0948	Cavalry—Scandinavia
UD1	356.106	Infantry—Societies, etc.	UE87-88	357.0946	Cavalry—Spain
UD15	356.109	Infantry—History	UE99-113	357.095	Cavalry—Asia
UD23	356.10973	United States. Army. Infantry	UE101-102	357.0951	Cavalry—China
			UE103-104	357.0954	Cavalry—India
UD157-302	356.1154	Infantry drill and tactics	UE105-106	357.0952	Cavalry—Japan
UD310-315	356.114	Marching	UE115-119	357.096	Cavalry—Africa
UD330-335	356.114	Sharpshooting (Military science)	UE121-122	357.0994	Cavalry—Australia
			UE123-124	357.099(5-6)	Cavalry—Oceania
UD330-335	356.114	Sniping (Military science)	UE157-302	357.184	Cavalry drill and tactics
UD330-335	356.11547	Shooting, Military	UE420-425	357.0482	Sabers
UD340-345	356.118241	Bayonets	UE420-425	357.048241	Swords
UD370-375	356.118	Infantry—Equipment	UE440-445	357.04144	Cavalry—Uniforms
UD380-415	356.1182	Firearms	UE460-475	357.2	War horses
UD383.5	355.82420975	Confederate States of America. Army—Firearms	UE460-475	357.2	Horses
			UE460-475	357.2	Horsemanship
UD390-395	356.1182425	Assault rifles			
UD390-395	356.1182425	Rifles	UF	358.12	Artillery
UD390	356.1182	Firearms—Sights	UF1	358.12006	Artillery—Societies, etc.
UD395.E	356.1182425 + 973	Enfield rifle	UF6	358.12074	Military museums
			UF9	358.1203	Artillery—Dictionaries
			UF15	358.1209	Artillery—History
UD395.M17	356.1182425 + 0973	M1 carbine	UF21-124	358.1209(4-9)	Artillery—[By region or country]
UD400	356.118241	Bayonets	UF23-25	358.120973	Artillery—United States
UD410-415	356.1182432	Pistols	UF23	358.120973	United States. Army—Artillery
UD410-415	356.1182436	Revolvers			
UD420-425	356.118241	Swords	UF26-27	358.120971	Artillery—Canada
UD460-465	356.164	Mountain warfare	UF28-29	358.120972	Artillery—Mexico
UD460-465	356.4	Military maneuvers	UF30-31	358.1209728	Artillery—Central America
UD470-475	356.164	Ski troops	UF32-33	358.1209729	Artillery—West Indies
UD480-485	356.166	Parachute troops	UF34-54	358.12098	Artillery—South America
UD483	356.1660973	United States—Armed Forces—Airborne troops	UF36-37	358.120982	Artillery—Argentina
			UF43-44	358.120983	Artillery—Chile
UD483	356.1660973	United States—Armed Forces—Parachute troops	UF45-46	358.1209861	Artillery—Colombia
			UF54	358.120987	Artillery—Venezuela
UE	357	Cavalry	UF55-95	358.12094	Artillery—Europe
UE1	357.06	Cavalry—Societies, etc.	UF57-64	358.120941	Artillery—Great Britain

LC	Dewey	Subject Heading	LC	Dewey	Subject Heading
UF71-72	358.120944	Artillery—France	UG	358.22	Military engineering
UF73-74	358.120943	Artillery—Germany	UG1	358.2206	Military engineering—
UF75-76	358.1209495	Artillery—Greece			Societies, etc.
UF79-80	358.120945	Artillery—Italy	UG5	358.2206	Military engineering—
UF83-84	358.1209469	Artillery—Portugal			Congresses
UF85-86	358.120947	Artillery—Russia	UG15	358.2209	Military engineering—
UF86.5	358.120948	Artillery—Scandinavia			History
UF87-88	358.120946	Artillery—Spain	UG21-124	358.2209(4-9)	Military engineering—[By
UF99-113	358.12095	Artillery—Asia			region or country]
UF101-102	358.120951	Artillery—China	UG127-128	358.22092	Tank engineers
UF103-104	358.120954	Artillery—India	UG157	358.22071	Military engineering—
UF105-106	358.120952	Artillery—Japan			Study and teaching
UF115-119	358.12096	Artillery—Africa	UG330	623.62	Military roads
UF121-122	358.120994	Artillery—Australia	UG335	623.67	Military bridges
UF122.5	358.120993	Artillery—New Zealand	UG335	623.67	Pontoon bridges
UF123-124	358.12099(5-6)	Artillery—Oceania	UG340	623.68	Tunneling
UF157-302	358.124	Artillery drill and tactics	UG345	623.63	Armored trains
UF160-162	358.1240973	United States. Army—	UG345	623.63	Military railroads
		Artillery—Drill and tactics	UG360-390	358.22	Military field engineering
UF340-345	358.125	Target practice	UG370	358.23	Demolition, Military
UF400-445	358.12	Artillery, Field and	UG375	358.22	Obstacles (Military
		mountain			science)
UF450-455	358.16	Artillery, Coast	UG400-442	623.1	Fortification
UF470-475	358.12822	Howitzers	UG403	623.1	Fortification, Field
UF520-780	358.1282	Ordnance	UG403	623.1	Intrenchments
UF523-563	355.80973	United States. Army—	UG405.15	623.1	Bunkers (Fortification)
		Ordnance and ordnance	UG410-442	355.45	Coast defenses
		stores	UG443-449	355.44	Siege warfare
UF540-545	355.7	Arsenals	UG446	355.44	Intrenchments
UF560-565	358.128	Ordnance, Rapid-fire	UG446.5	358.1883	Centurion (Tank)
UF560-565	358.1282	Howitzers	UG446.5	358.1883	M1 (Tank)
UF563.A77	358.1282	Trench mortars	UG446.5	358.1883	Armored personnel
UF620	358.1282	Machine-guns			carriers
UF625	358.1382	Antiaircraft guns	UG446.5	358.1883	Half-track vehicles,
UF625	358.174	Surface-to-air missiles			Military
UF628	358.12	Antitank weapons	UG446.5	358.1883	Tanks (Military science)
UF656	358.1282	Recoilless rifles	UG447-.5	358.34	Gases, Asphyxiating and
UF700-770	358.1282	Ammunition			poisonous—War use
UF740-745	358.128255	Cartridges	UG447-.65	358.34	Chemical warfare
UF750-770	358.1282513	Projectiles	UG447.5-.65	358.3482	Chemical weapons
UF765	358.1282	Grenades	UG447.5.M8	358.34	Mustard gas
UF767	358.128251	Projectiles, Aerial	UG447.7	355.41	Smoke screens
UF767	358.1282356	Rockets (Ordnance)	UG447.8	358.38	Biological warfare
UF780	358.1282	Electric detonators	UG447.8	358.38820947	Biological weapons—Soviet
UF800-805	623.55	Gunnery			Union
UF820-840	623.51	Ballistics	UG448	355.45	Coast defenses
UF820	623.51021	Ballistics—Tables	UG449	355.41	Camouflage (Military
UF830	623.510284	Ballistic instruments			science)
UF845	358.128	Telescopes	UG470-474	623.71	Maps, Military
UF848-856	623.558	Fire control (Gunnery)	UG476	623.72	Photographic
UF849	623.5580284	Fire control (Gunnery)—			interpretation (Military
		Optical equipment			science)
UF850-857	623.46	Range-finding	UG478	355.40285	Military art and
UF853	623.46	Position-finders			science—Automation
UF854	623.46	Firearms—Sights	UG480	623.76	Electricity in military
UF855	623.46	Telescopic sights			engineering
UF860-880	623.452	Military fireworks	UG485	623.043	Electronic
UF890	358.1280287	Ordnance testing			counter-countermeasures

LC	Dewey	Subject Heading	LC	Dewey	Subject Heading
UG485	623.043	Electronic countermeasures	UG1233	358.4383	Apache (Attack helicopter)
			UG1240-1242	358.4183	Airplanes, Military
UG485	623.043	Electronics in military engineering	UG1240	385.4183	Stealth aircraft
			UG1242.A25	358.4283	Antisubmarine aircraft
UG487	623.042	Infrared radiation—Military applications	UG1242.A28	358.4283	Dive bombers
			UG1242.A28	358.43	Attack planes
UG490	623.45115	Mines (Military explosives)	UG1242.A28	358.42	Dauntless (Dive bomber)
UG570-613.5	358.24	Signals and signaling	UG1242.B6	358.42830973	B-52 bomber
UG582.H4	623.7312	Heliograph	UG1242.D7	623.7469	Drone aircraft
UG590-613.5	623.732	Military telegraph	UG1242.F5	358.4303	Night fighter planes
UG590-610.5	623.73 (2-3)	Military telecommunication	UG1242.F5	358.4383	Fighter planes
			UG1242.R4	358.45	Reconnaissance aircraft
UG611-.5	623.7341	Radio, Military	UG1282.N48	358.428251	Neutron bomb
UG612-.5	623.7348	Radar—Military applications	UG1312.B34	358.1754	Ballistic missiles
			UG1312.C7	358.42	Cruise missiles
UG615-620	623.7472	Automobiles, Military	UG1312.I2	358.1754	Intercontinental ballistic missiles
UG615-620	623.7472	Tracked landing vehicles			
UG622-1425	358.4	Air forces	UG1500-1530	358.8	Space surveillance
UG622	358.4006	Air forces—Societies, etc.	UG1530	358.8	Space warfare
UG623	358.4006	Air forces—Congresses			
UG625	358.4009	Air forces—History	UH	355.345	War—Relief of sick and wounded
UG626-.2	358.40092	Air pilots, Military			
UG626-.2	358.43092	Fighter pilots	UH20-25	355.347	Chaplains
UG626.2.D66	358.40092	Generals—United States – Biography	UH40-45	781.599	Music in the army
			UH40-45	781.599	Military calls
UG630-670	358.4	Aeronautics, Military	UH40-45	781.599	Trumpet-calls
UG630-635	623.746	Airplanes, Military—Turrets	UH80-85	355.693	Postal service
UG630	358.4	Air warfare	UH87-100	355.8	Animals—War use
UG633-634.5	358.400973	United States. Air Force	UH201-551	355.345	War—Relief of sick and wounded
UG633	358.400973	United States. Air Force—History	UH201-515	355.345	Medicine, Military
UG633	356.16	Special forces (Military science)	UH205	355.34506	Medicine, Military—Congresses
UG635	358.4009(4-9)	Air forces—[Other countries]	UH215-325	355.345021	War—Casualties (Statistics, etc.)
UG700-705	358.434	Fighter plane combat	UH215-324	355.34509	Medicine, Military—History
UG700	358.41422	Air interdiction	UH223-224	355.3450973	Medicine, Military—United States
UG703	358.430973	Fighter plane combat—United States			
			UH226-227	355.3450971	Medicine, Military—Canada
UG730-735	358.414	Airborne warning and control systems	UH228-229	355.3450972	Medicine, Military—Mexico
UG730-735	358.414	Air defenses	UH230-231	355.34509728	Medicine, Military—Central America
UG740-745	358.171	Ballistic missile defenses			
UG760-765	358.45	Aerial reconnaissance	UH232-233	355.34509729	Medicine, Military—West Indies
UG763	358.450973	Aerial reconnaissance, American	UH234-254	355.345098	Medicine, Military—South America
UG765.G	358.450941	Aerial reconnaissance, British	UH236-237	355.3450982	Medicine, Military—Argentina
UG823	358.413380973	United States. Air Force—Non-commissioned officers—History	UH243-244	355.3450983	Medicine, Military—Chile
			UH245-246	355.34509861	Medicine, Military—Colombia
UG854.A4	363.34810973	Search and rescue operations—United States	UH254	355.3450987	Medicine, Military—Venezuela
UG1180-1185	358.414	Air forces—Insignia			
UG1230-1235	358.4383	Attack helicopters	UH255-295	355.345094	Medicine, Military—Europe
UG1232.T72	358.4483	Chinook (Military transport helicopter)			
			UH257-264	355.3450941	Medicine, Military—Great Britain
UG1232.T72	358.4483	Choctaw (Military transport helicopter)			

LC	Dewey	Subject Heading	LC	Dewey	Subject Heading
UH271-272	355.3450944	Medicine, Military—France	V175	359.350973	United States. Navy—Field service
UH273-274	355.3450943	Medicine, Military—Germany	V179	359.411	Logistics, Naval
UH275-276	355.34509495	Medicine, Military—Greece	V190	359.413	Naval reconnaissance
			V210-214.5	359.93	Submarine warfare
UH279-280	355.3450945	Medicine, Military—Italy	V214.5	359.93	Submarine boat combat
UH283-284	355.34509469	Medicine, Military—Portugal	V214-.5	359.93	Anti-submarine warfare
			V215	359.41	Warships—Camouflage
UH285-286	355.3450947	Medicine, Military—Russia	V215	359.41	Camouflage (Military science)
UH286.5	355.3450948	Medicine, Military—Scandinavia	V230	359.7	Navy-yards and naval stations
UH287-288	355.3450946	Medicine, Military—Spain	V245	359.41	Naval maneuvers
UH299-313	355.345095	Medicine, Military—Asia	V245	359.410973	United States. Navy—Maneuvers
UH301-302	355.3450951	Medicine, Military—China			
UH303-304	355.3450954	Medicine, Military—India	V250	359.48	War games, Naval
UH305-306	355.3450952	Medicine, Military—Japan	V253	359.48	Imaginary wars and battles
UH315-319	355.345096	Medicine, Military—Africa	V263	359.50973	United States. Navy—Physical training
UH321-322	355.345094	Medicine, Military—Australia			
UH323-324	355.345099 (5-6)	Medicine, Military—Oceania	V280-285	623.8561	Signals and signaling
			V300-305	359.15	Flags
UH341-347	355.345092	Medicine, Military—Biography	V303-304	359.150973	Flags—United States
			V305	359.1509(4-9)	Flags—[Other countries]
UH398-399	355.345071	Medicine, Military—Study and teaching	V310	359.17	Naval ceremonies, honors, and salutes
UH400	355.345092	Physicians	V383	359.00289	United States. Navy—Safety measures
UH420-425	355.345	Pharmacy, Military			
UH440-445	355.88	Medical supplies	V390-395	359.07	Naval research
UH460-485	355.72	Military hospitals	V396-.5	359.8	Military oceanography
UH490-495	355.345	Military nursing	V400-695	359.0071	Naval education
UH500-505	355.83	Transportation, Military	V411-695	359.00710(4-9)	Naval education—[By region or country]
UH535-537	361.77	Red Cross			
UH600-629.5	355.345	Military hygiene	V411-437	359.0071073	Naval education—United States
UH650-655	355.345	Veterinary service, Military			
UH750-769	306.27	Military social work	V415	359.0071073	Midshipmen
			V435-436	359.50973	Training-ships
V	359	Naval art and science	V437	359.9709073	United States. Coast Guard
V	359	War			
V1-5	359.005	Naval art and science—Periodicals	V438	359.0071075	Naval education—Confederate States of America
V7	359.006	Naval art and science—Congresses			
			V440-444	359.0071071	Naval education—Canada
V13	359.0074	Naval museums	V445-449	359.0071072	Naval education—Mexico
V23-24	359.003	Naval art and science—Dictionary	V450-453	359.00710728	Naval education—Central America
V23-24	359.003	Naval art and science—Terminology	V455-458	359.00710729	Naval education—West Indies
V25-55	359.009	Naval art and science—History	V465-496	359.007108	Naval education—South America
V46	359.3220948	Viking ships	V500-623	359.007104	Naval education—Europe
V61-65	359.0092	Naval biography	V510-530	359.0071041	Naval education—Great Britain
V123	359.3320973	United States. Navy—Petty officers' handbooks			
V133	359.3320973	United States. Navy—Officers' handbooks	V570-574.54	359.0071043	Naval education—Germany
			V625-650	359.007105	Naval education—Asia
V143-144	359.3380973	United States. Navy—Sailors' handbooks	V630-634	359.0071051	Naval education—China
			V635-639	359.0071054	Naval education—India
V160-165	359.42	Naval strategy	V640-644	359.0071052	Naval education—Japan
V167-178	359.42	Naval tactics	V645-649	359.0071055	Naval education—Iran

272

LC	Dewey	Subject Heading	LC	Dewey	Subject Heading
V660-680	359.007106	Naval education—Africa	VB32-33	359.609729	Naval art and science—West Indies
V690-694	359.0071094	Naval education—Australia	VB34-54	359.6098	Naval art and science—South America
V750-995	359.32	Warships	VB36-37	359.60982	Naval art and science—Argentina
V795	358.32	Ships of the line			
V799-800	359.32	Armored vessels	VB43-44	359.60983	Naval art and science—Chile
V810	623.888	Damage control (Warships)			
V815-.5	359.8352	Battleships	VB45-46	359.609861	Naval art and science—Colombia
V820-.5	359.3253	Battle cruisers			
V825-.5	359.3254	Destroyers (Warships)	VB55-96	359.6094	Naval art and science—Europe
V830-840	359.3258	Torpedo-boats			
V850-855	359.82517	Torpedoes	VB57-64	359.60941	Naval art and science—Great Britain
V856-.5	623.26	Mines and minelaying			
V857-859	359.933	Submarines (Ships)	VB71-72	359.60944	Naval art and science—France
V857-859	359.9383	Submarine boats			
V857.5	359.93834	Nuclear submarines	VB73-74.5	359.60943	Naval art and science—Germany
V858	359.9330973	United States. Navy—Submarine forces	VB75-76	359.609495	Naval art and science—Greece
V865	359.985	Naval auxiliary vessels	VB79-80	359.60945	Naval art and science—Italy
V874-875	359.9435	Aircraft carriers			
V880	359.3220973	United States. Navy—Boats	VB83-84	359.609469	Naval art and science—Portugal
V880	359.83	Motor vehicles, Amphibious	VB85-86	359.60947	Naval art and science—Russia
V880	359.82	Steel boats	VB87-88	359.60946	Naval art and science—Spain
V890	359.32	Floating batteries			
V990-995	359.981782	Fleet ballistic missile weapons systems	VB99-113	359.6095	Naval art and science—Asia
			VB101-102	359.60951	Naval art and science—China
VA	359	Naval districts			
VA20-25	359.6229	Navies, Cost of	VB105-106	359.60952	Naval art and science—Japan
VA37-42	359	Navies			
VA45	359.37	Naval reserves	VB115-119	359.6096	Naval art and science—Africa
VA49-395	359.30973	United States. Navy—Organization	VB121-122	359.60994	Naval art and science—Australia
VA53	359.6220973	United States. Navy—Appropriations and expenditures	VB123-124	359.6099(5-6)	Naval art and science—Oceania
VA66	359.70973	Navy-yards and naval stations—United States	VB190	359.331	Admirals
VA393-395	359.30975	Confederate States of America. Navy—Ordnance and ordnance stores	VB223	359.6850973	United States. Navy—Inspection
			VB230-250	359.3432	Intelligence service
VA402	359.370971	Naval militia—Canada	VB250	359.3432092	Spies
VA460	359.370941	Navy-yards and naval stations—Great Britain	VB258	359.610973	United States. Navy—Personnel management
VB	359.6	Naval art and science	VB260-275	359.2236	Recruiting and enlistment
VB21-124	359.609(4-9)	Naval art and science—[By region or country]	VB263	359.22360973	United States. Navy—Recruiting, enlistment, etc.
VB23-25	359.60973	Naval art and science—United States	VB280-285	362.86	Military pensions
VB26-27	359.60971	Naval art and science—Canada	VB308	359.3320973	United States—Armed Forces—Warrant officers
VB28-29	359.60972	Naval art and science—Mexico	VB310-315	359.332	Navies—Officers
			VB313-314	359.3320973	United States. Navy—Officers
VB30-31	359.609728	Naval art and science—Central America	VB330-335	359.1342	Military decorations
			VB333	355.13420973	Navy Cross (Medal)
			VB350-785	343.019	Naval law

LC	Dewey	Subject Heading	LC	Dewey	Subject Heading
VB800-807	343.0143	Courts-martial and courts of inquiry	VE55-96	359.963094	Marines—Europe
			VE57-64	359.9630941	Marines—Great Britain
VB840-845	343.014	Naval discipline	VE71-72	359.9630944	Marines—France
VB850-880	359.1334	Naval offenses	VE73-74.5	359.9630943	Marines—Germany
VB860-867	359.1334	Mutiny	VE79-80	359.9630945	Marines—Italy
VB870-875	359.1334	Desertion, Naval	VE85-86	359.9630947	Marines—Russia
VB880	359.1334	Insubordination	VE86.5	359.9630948	Marines—Scandinavia
VB890-895	365.48	Military prisons	VE87-88	359.9630946	Marines—Spain
VB910	359.13325	Corporal punishment	VE99-113	359.963095	Marines—Asia
VB920-925	359.13323	Military police	VE105-106	359.9630952	Marines—Japan
			VE115-119	359.963096	Marines—Africa
VC	359.83	Transportation, Military	VE121-122	359.9630994	Marines—Australia
VC20-65	359.80973	United States. Navy	VE122.5	359.9630993	Marines—New Zealand
VC50-65	359.80973	United States. Navy— Pay, allowances, etc.	VE150-155	359.9633	Marines—Handbooks, manuals, etc.
VC184-187	359.80941	Great Britain. Royal Navy	VE160-162	359.9650973	United States. Marine Corps—Drill and tactics
VC260-267	359.62120973	United States. Navy—Procurement	VE345	359.961342	Marines—Insigna
VC263	359.80973	United States. Navy— Supplies and stores	VE350-390	359.96824	Marines—Firearms
			VE400-405	359.9614	Marines—Uniforms
VC300-345	359.81	Military uniforms	VE420-425	359.9671	Marines—Barracks and quarters
VC345	359.1342	Insignia			
VC370-375	641.57	Cookery, Marine	VE430-435	359.965	Military training camps
VC423	359.710973	United States. Navy— Barracks and quarters	VF	359.82	Ordnance, Naval
VC503	359.6220973	United States. Navy—Accounting	VF1	359.8206	Ordnance, Naval—Societies, etc.
VC530-535	359.985	Military sealift	VF6	359.82074	Naval museums
VC550-580	359.985	Transportation, Military	VF15	359.8209	Ordnance, Naval—History
VC553	359.9850973	United States. Navy—Transportation	VF21-124	359.8209(4-9)	Ordnance, Naval—[By region or country]
			VF23-25	359.820973	Ordnance, Naval—United States
VD	359.0092	Sailors	VF26-27	359.820971	Ordnance, Naval—Canada
VD15	359.0092	Sailors—History	VF28-29	359.820972	Ordnance, Naval—Mexico
VD21-124	359.0092	Sailors—[By region or country]	VF30-31	359.8209728	Ordnance, Naval—Central America
VD23-25	359.009	Sailors—United States	VF32-33	359.8209729	Ordnance, Naval—West Indies
VD150-155	359.3380973	United States. Navy—Sailors' handbooks	VF34-54	359.82098	Ordnance, Naval—South America
VD360-390	359.824	Firearms	VF36-37	359.820982	Ordnance, Naval—Argentina
VD360-390	359.8240973	United States. Navy—Firearms			
VD370	359.82425	Rifles	VF43-44	359.820983	Ordnance, Naval—Chile
VD390	359.82432	Pistols	VF45-46	359.8209861	Ordnance, Naval—Colombia
VD390	359.82436	Revolvers			
VD403	359.310973	United States. Navy—Small-boat service	VF55-96	359.82094	Ordnance, Naval—Europe
			VF57-64	359.820941	Ordnance, Naval—Great Britain
VE	359.96	Marines	VF71-72	359.820944	Ordnance, Naval—France
VE15	359.9609	Marines—History	VF73-74.5	359.820943	Ordnance, Naval—Germany
VE21-124	359.96309(4-9)	Marines—[By region or country]	VF79-80	359.820945	Ordnance, Naval—Italy
VE23-25	359.9630973	United States. Marine Corps	VF83-84	359.8209469	Ordnance, Naval—Portugal
VE26-27	359.9630971	Marines—Canada	VF85-86	359.820947	Ordnance, Naval—Russia
VE28-29	359.9630972	Marines—Mexico	VF86.5	359.820948	Ordnance, Naval—Scandinavia
VE30-31	359.96309728	Marines—Central America			
VE32-33	359.96309729	Marines—West Indies	VF87-88	359.820946	Ordnance, Naval—Spain
VE34-54	359.963098	Marines—South America			

LC	Dewey	Subject Heading	LC	Dewey	Subject Heading
VF101-113	359.82095	Ordnance, Naval—Asia	VG100-475	359.345	Medicine, Naval
VF105-106	359.820952	Ordnance, Naval—Japan	VG121-224	359.34509(4-9)	Medicine, Naval—[By region or country]
VF111-112	359.8209561	Ordnance, Naval—Turkey			
VF115-119	359.82096	Ordnance, Naval—Africa	VG123-125	359.3450973	Medicine, Naval—United States
VF121-122	359.820994	Ordnance, Naval—Australia			
			VG126-127	359.3450971	Medicine, Naval—Canada
VF122.5	359.820993	Ordnance, Naval—New Zealand	VG128-129	359.3450972	Medicine, Naval—Mexico
			VG130-131	359.34509728	Medicine, Naval—Central America
VF310-315	359.547	Target practice			
VF347	359.820973	United States. Navy—Weapons systems	VG132-133	359.4509729	Medicine, Naval—West Indies
VF347	359.98170973	AEGIS (Weapons system)	VG134-154	359.345098	Medicine, Naval—South America
VF347	359.98170973	United Staes. Navy— Fire control technicians (Missile)	VG155-196	359.345094	Medicine, Naval—Europe
			VG157-164	359.3450941	Medicine, Naval—Great Britain
VF350-420	359.8240973	United States. Navy—Firearms	VG171-172	359.3450944	Medicine, Naval—France
VF353-420	359.80973	United States. Navy—Ordnance and ordnance stores	VG173-174.5	359.3450943	Medicine, Naval—Germany
			VG179-180	359.3450945	Medicine, Naval—Italy
VF410	359.82424	Machine-guns	VG185-186	359.450947	Medicine, Naval—Russia
VF410.G2-.G24	359.82424	Gardner machine-gun	VG186.5	359.3450948	Medicine, Naval—Scandinavia
VF410.G3-.G34	359.82424	Gatling guns			
VF440	359.32	Warships—Turrets	VG187-188	359.3450946	Medicine, Naval—Spain
VF440	359.820973	Ridgway's revolving battery	VG199-213	359.345095	Medicine, Naval—Asia
VF480-500	359.8251	Projectiles	VG205-206	359.3450952	Medicine, Naval—Japan
VF509	359.8251	Depth charges	VG215-219	359.345096	Medicine, Naval—Africa
VF520-530	359.422	Fire control (Naval gunnery)	VG221-222	359.3450994	Medicine, Naval—Australia
VF540	359.80287	Ordnance testing	VG222.5	359.3450993	Medicine, Naval—New Zealand
VF550	623.51021	Ballistics—Tables			
VF550	359.422	Range-finding	VG226-228	359.345092	Medicine, Naval—Biography
VG	359.345	Medicine, Naval	VG230-235	359.345071	Medicine, Naval—Study and teaching
VG	359.94	Naval aviation			
VG20-25	359.347	Chaplains, Military	VG270-275	359.345	Pharmacy, Military
VG23	359.3470973	United States. Navy—Chaplains	VG280-285	359.345	Dentistry, Naval
			VG290-295	359.88	Medical supplies
VG30-35	781.599	Military music	VG410-450	359.72	Hospitals, Naval and marine
VG33	782.421599	United States. Navy—Songs and music	VG457	361.77	Red Cross
VG50-55	359.984	Coastal surveillance	VG470-475	359.345	Naval hygiene
VG53	359.970973	United States. Coast Guard	VG500-505	359.342	Journalism, Military
			VG503	359.3420973	Journalism, Military—United States
VG60-65	359.34	Postal service			
VG63	359.340973	United States. Navy—Postal service	VG803	359.3380973	United States. Navy—Machinist's mates
VG70-85	623.8567	Communications, Military	VG903	359.3380973	United States. Navy—Yeomen
VG73	359.9830973	United States. Navy—Communication systems	VG913	359.3380973	United States. Navy—Draftsmen
VG86-88	359.984	Underwater demolition teams	VG953	359.3380973	United States. Navy—Boatswains
VG87	359.9840973	Underwater demolition teams—United States	VG1020	359.34320973	United States. Navy—Intelligence specialists
VG90-95	359.94	Naval aviation			
VG90-95	359.94834	Airplanes, Military—Turrets	VK	359.83	Ships
VG93	359.940973	United States. Navy—Aviation	VK	387.5	Merchant marine

VK1-4	387.505	Merchant marine—Periodicals
VK5	387.506	Merchant marine—Congresses
VK15-20	387.509	Merchant marine—History
VK21-124	387.509(4-9)	Merchant marine—[By region or country]
VK23-25	387.50973	Merchant marine—United States
VK139-140	387.5092	Merchant mariners—Biography
VK149	387.54044	Seafaring life
VK160	387.5023	Merchant marine—Vocational guidance
VK200	623.890289	Navigation—Safety measures
VK200	623.888	Merchant marine—Safety measures
VK205	387.5092	Ship captains
VK221	359.32092	Ships—Manning
VK221	387.5092	Merchant marine—Officers
VK235-237	387.245	Ships—Cargo
VK235	387.544	Cargo handling
VK235	387.544	Stowage
VK237	387.544	Load-line
VK321-369.8	387.1	Harbors
VK321	387.12	Roadsteads
VK361-365	387.54044	Mooring of ships
VK361-365	387.15	Docks
VK361	387.54044	Coaling
VK369-.8	387.1	Harbors of refuge
VK369-.8	387.15	Marinas
VK371-378	623.8884	Collisions at sea—Prevention
VK371	623.8884	Rule of the road at sea
VK381-397	623.8561	Signals and signaling
VK381-397	387.54	Merchant marine—Signaling
VK381-397	387.155	Aids to navigation
VK388	623.8938	Sonar
VK397	623.85642	Telegraph, Wireless—Installation on ships
VK397	623.8932	Radio—Installation on ships
VK397	623.8932	Radio in navigation
VK401-529	623.89071	Navigation—Study and teaching
VK525-529	623.880971	Nautical training-schools
VK541-547	623.88	Seamanship
VK543	623.88203	Sailing
VK549-587	527	Nautical astronomy
VK560-561	623.8932	Loran
VK560	623.89	Hyperbolic navigation
VK560	623.89	Decca navigation
VK560	623.893	Electronics in navigation
VK560	623.8938	Sonar

VK562	623.893	Artificial satellites in navigation
VK563-567	527.021	Navigation—Tables
VK563-567	523.3021	Moon—Tables
VK563	527	Azimuth
VK565-567	527.2	Longitude
VK565	527.1	Latitude
VK570	387.52	Optimum ship routing
VK571	387.52	Great circle sailing
VK572	527.015308	Mile, Nautical
VK573-587	623.89(2-3)	Nautical instruments
VK577	623.8932	Radio compass
VK577	623.8932	Gyro compass
VK577	623.8932	Compass
VK581	623.890284	Logs (Nautical instruments)
VK583	623.890284	Sextant
VK583	623.890284	Quadrant
VK583.5	623.89	Inertial navigation systems
VK584.A7	527.0284	Artificial horizons (Nautical instruments)
VK584.S6	623.8938	Echo sounding
VK584.S6	623.8938	Sounding and soundings
VK588-597	551.4607	Hydrographic surveying
VK798-997	623.8922	Pilot guides
VK798	623.8922	Notices to mariners
VK804-997	623.892216 (3-7)	Pilot guides—[By place]
VK810-880	623.89223	Pilot guides—Atlantic Ocean
VK815-818	623.8922336	Pilot guides—North Sea
VK819-821.8	623.8922334	Pilot guides—Baltic Sea
VK839-844	623.8922336	Pilot guides—English Channel
VK853-874	623.892238	Pilot guides—Mediterranean Sea
VK885-901	623.89225	Pilot guides—Indian Ocean
VK915-956	623.89224	Pilot guides—Pacific Ocean
VK917	623.892244	Pilot guides—North Pacific Ocean
VK925	623.892248	Pilot guides—South Pacific Ocean
VK947-948	623.89223(4/6)	Pilot guides—United States
VK1000-1249	387.155	Aids to navigation
VK1000-1249	623.8944	Beacons
VK1000-1246	623.8943	Lightships
VK1000-1246	623.8942	Lighthouses
VK1000-1246	623.8944	Buoys
VK1015	623.894209	Lighthouses—History
VK1021-1124	623.894209 (4-9)	Lighthouses—[By region or country]
VK1023-1025	623.89420973	Lighthouses—United States
VK1025.D	623.894209 + 16347	Drum Point Lighthouse (Md.)

VK1025.H	623.894209751	Harbor of Refuge Lighthouse
VK1026-1027	623.89420971	Lighthouses—Canada
VK1150-1246	623.8944	Buoys—[By region or country]
VK1250-1299	363.123	Steamboat disasters
VK1250-1299	363.123	Shipwrecks
VK1250-1294	623.8886	Ships—Fires and fire prevention
VK1259	363.3481	Refloating of ships
VK1265	363.123	Submarine disasters
VK1270-1294	363.12309(4-9)	Shipwrecks—[By region or country]
VK1300-1481	623.8887	Life-saving
VK1315	623.888709	Life-saving—History
VK1321-1424	623.888709 (4-9)	Life-saving—[By region or country]
VK1460-1481	623.8887	Life-saving apparatus
VK1473	387.29	Life-boats
VK1477	623.865	Life-preservers
VK1479	623.865	Line-throwing rockets
VK1481.L55	623.865	Line-throwing guns
VK1491	387.55	Salvage
VK1500-1661	623.8922	Pilots and pilotage
VK1515	623.892209	Pilots and pilotage—History
VK1521-1624	623.892(2-9) + (4-9)	Pilots and pilotage—[By region or country]
VM	623.81	Ships
VM	623.81	Naval architecture
VM17	623.821	Ships, Medieval
VM101	623.810951	Junks
VM142-144	623.8184	Ships, Wooden
VM146-147	623.81821	Ships, Iron and steel
VM146	623.81821	Marine steel
VM148	623.81833	Ships, Concrete
VM155	623.810287	Ships—Measurement
VM157	623.81	Displacement (Ships)
VM159	623.81	Stability of ships
VM165-276	623.81071	Naval architecture—Study and teaching
VM298	623.8201	Ship models
VM298	623.8201043	Sailing ships—Models
VM298.3	745.5928	Ship models in bottles
VM298.5-301	338.4762382	Shipbuilding industry
VM299.5-.7	623.820681	Shipbuilding subsidies
VM308	623.84	Figureheads of ships
VM311.C27	623.821	Caravels
VM311.C3	623.822	Catamarans
VM311.C33	623.8203	Catboats
VM317	623.8728	Nuclear ships
VM320-361	623.843	Steel boats
VM320-361	623.82	Boatbuilding
VM325	623.85641	Radio on boats
VM325	623.8504	Boats and boating—Electronic equipment
VM331-333	623.82023	Yachts
VM331	623.8226	Skipjacks

VM335	728.78	Houseboats
VM340-349	623.81	Motorboats
VM340-349	623.81	Launches
VM341-349	623.84	Planing hulls
VM341	623.8231	Cigarette boats
VM345-347	623.8726	Electric boats
VM351-361	623.8223	Sailboats
VM352	623.8202	Rafts
VM353	623.8202	Dugout canoes
VM362	623.8204	Hydrofoil boats
VM365-367	623.8257	Submarines (Ships)
VM371	623.8226	Dhows
VM381-383	623.8243	Passenger ships
VM391-395	623.8245	Cargo ships
VM393.B7	623.8245	Bulk carrier cargo ships
VM393.R64	623.8245	Roll-on/roll-off ships
VM396	623.82436	Inland waterway vessels
VM451	623.828	Ice-breaking vessels
VM453	623.8226	Oceanographic research ships
VM453	623.828	Deep-sea drilling ships
VM455	623.8245	Tankers
VM455.3	623.8245	Chemical carriers (Tankers)
VM457	623.8245	Ore carriers
VM459	623.8245	Refrigerator ships
VM460	623.82436	Lake steamers
VM461-.5	623.82436	River boats
VM461-.5	623.82436	River steamers
VM464	623.8232	Tugboats
VM464	623.8232	Towboats
VM466.B3	623.829	Barges
VM466.035	623.826	Offshore support vessels
VM471-479	623.8503	Ships—Electric equipment
VM480-.5	623.8504	Ships—Electronic equipment
VM481-482	623.853	Ships—Heating and ventilation
VM485	623.8535	Marine refrigeration
VM485	623.8535	Cold storage on shipboard
VM491-493	623.852	Ships—Lighting
VM493	623.852	Search-lights
VM503-505	623.8542	Ships—Water-supply
VM505	623.854	Seawater—Distillation
VM505	623.854	Distilled water
VM531-533	623.862	Masts and rigging
VM531-533	623.88	Marlin spike seamanship
VM532	623.862	Sails
VM533	623.8882	Knots and splices
VM595-989	623.87	Marine engineering
VM615-619	623.809	Marine engineering—History
VM621-724	623.809(4-9)	Marine engineering—[By region or country]
VM725-728	623.8071	Marine engineering—Study and teaching
VM731-779	623.87	Marine engines
VM741-750	623.8722	Steam-boilers, Marine

VM753-757	623.873	Propellers
VM770	623.87236	Marine diesel motors
VM774-777	623.8728	Nuclear ships
VM774-777	623.8728	Marine nuclear reactor plants
VM779	623.874	Ships—Fuel
VM781-861	623.86	Ships—Equipment and supplies
VM781	623.86	Deck machinery
VM791	623.862	Anchors
VM801	623.86	Davits
VM811	621.864	Windlasses
VM811	621.864	Capstan
VM815	623.852	Ships' lights
VM821	623.8501	Marine compressors
VM831	623.86	Davits
VM841-845	623.862	Steering-gear
VM965	623.8432	Underwater welding and cutting
VM987	623.827	Diving bells
Z	686.2	Printing
Z	020	Library Science
Z40-104.5	652.1	Writing
Z41-42	929.88	Signatures (Writing)
Z41-42.5	929.88	Autographs
Z43-45	745.61	Calligraphy
Z43-45	652.1	Penmanship
Z48	686.4	Copying processes
Z48	686.4	Fluid copying processes
Z49-50.5	652.3	Typewriters
Z53-104.5	653	Shorthand
Z102.5-104.5	652.8	Cryptography
Z105-115.5	411.7	Paleography
Z116.A2-265.5.A5	686.2	Printing
Z122-.5	686.071	Printing—Study and teaching
Z124-242	686.09	Printing—History
Z231-234	686.2092	Printers
Z231.5.L5	070.592	Small presses
Z235-236	686.20278	Printers' marks
Z240-241.5	092	Block books
Z242.9-264	686.225	Printing
Z244	686.2	Print finishing processes
Z245	686.20299	Printing industry—Estimates
Z246	686.2252	Printing—Layout
Z247	676	Paper
Z247	667.4	Printing ink
Z249-.4	681.62	Printing-press
Z249	686.20284	Paper-cutting machines
Z250	686.224	Printing—Specimens
Z252	686.221	Electrotyping
Z252.5.N46	686.233	Nonimpact printing
Z253	686.22542	Monotype
Z253	686.22542	Linotype
Z253.5	686.2252	Magazine design
Z253.53-.532	686.22544416	Desktop publishing
Z254	686.2255	Proofreading

Z256	686.20284	Rollers (Printing)
Z258	686.23042	Color-printing
Z265-.5	686.43	Documents on microfilm
Z265	686.43	Micrographics
Z266-276	686.3	Bookbinding
Z269-.3	686.30092	Bookbinders
Z272	686.3	Endpapers
Z278-550	381.45002	Booksellers and bookselling
Z278-550	070.5	Publishers and publishing
Z286.D47	686.22544416	Desktop publishing
Z286.S37	070.594	Scholarly publishing
Z289-550	070.509(4-9)	Publishers and publishing—[By region or country]
Z549	070.5	Book clubs
Z551-656	351.824	Copyright
Z649.T7	346.0482	Copyright—Transfer
Z657-659	323.445	Book burning
Z662-664	027	Libraries
Z665-720	020	Library science
Z674.2-.5	025.52	Information services
Z674.7-.83	021.65	Library information networks
Z675.A2	026	Special libraries
Z675.A5	026.62913	Aeronautical libraries
Z675.B8	027.69	Business libraries
Z675.C5	027.67	Church libraries
Z675.C8	027.5	Public libraries
Z675.D28	026.3046	Demographic libraries
Z675.D3	026.6176	Dental libraries
Z675.D4	025.26	Depository libraries
Z675.G7	027.5	Government libraries
Z675.H7	027.662	Hospital libraries
Z675.P8	027.665	Prison libraries
Z675.P85	027.2	Proprietary libraries
Z675.R4	027.3	Rental libraries
Z675.S3	027.8	School libraries
Z675.U5	027.7	Academic libraries
Z675.V7	027.091734	Rural libraries
Z678-.88	025.1	Library administration
Z678.9-.93	025.3132	Libraries—Automation
Z678.93.D85	025.3132	Dynix (Computer system)
Z682-.4	023.2	Librarians
Z682.4.A45	023.4	Library administrators
Z682.4.C65	023.2	Library consultants
Z683-.2	025.11	Library finance
Z683	027.0021	Library statistics
Z688.A7	025.277	Acquisition of art catalogs
Z688.M4	025.2761	Acquisition of medical literature
Z689-.5	025.21	Book selection
Z689-.8	025.2	Acquisitions (Libraries)
Z692.D38	025.284	Acquisition of databases
Z692.M3	025.286	Acquisition of maps
Z692.S5	025.28305	Acquisition of serial publications
Z693-695.83	025.32	Descriptive cataloging
Z695.83	025.31	Catalogs, Union

Z699-.5	025.3132	Machine-readable bibliographic data
Z700.9-701.5	025.7	Books—Conservation and restoration
Z701.3.D4	025.84	Books—Deacidification
Z702	025.82	Book thefts
Z704	025.56	Library rules and regulations
Z710	025.31	Library catalogs
Z711	028.7	Reference books
Z711.2	025.56	Library orientation
Z711.3	027.0021	Library statistics
Z711.3	025.58	Library use studies
Z720	020.92	Librarians
Z721-871	027.009	Libraries—History
Z987-997.2	026.1	Book collecting
Z998-1000.5	017.4	Catalogs, Booksellers'
Z1001-9000	010	Bibliography
Z1003-.5	028	Books and reading
Z1008	070.5	Book clubs
Z1030	096.2	Vellum printed books
Z1201-4980	015	Bibliography, National
Z1215-1363	015.73	Bibliography, National—United States
Z1365-1401	015.71	Bibliography, National—Canada
Z1411-1431	015.72	Bibliography, National—Mexico
Z1501-1595	015.729	Bibliography, National—West Indies
Z1601-1939	015.8	Bibliography, National—South America
Z2000-2959	015.4	Bibliography, National—Europe
Z3013-3028	015.56	Bibliography, National—Middle East
Z3126-3415	015.5	Bibliography, National—Asia
Z3221-3415	015.59	Bibliography, National—Asia, Southeastern
Z3366-3370	015.55	Bibliography, National—Iran
Z3401-3409	015.47	Bibliography, National—Asiatic Russia
Z3461-3465	015.4756	Bibliography, National—Armenia
Z3466-3470	015.5692	Bibliography, National—Lebanon
Z3476-3480	015.5694	Bibliography, National—Israel
Z3481-3485	015.5691	Bibliography, National—Syria
Z3501-3975	015.6	Bibliography, National—Africa
Z4001-4439	015.94	Bibliography, National—Australia

About the Author

After working in the fields of teaching and counseling, Ms. Scott earned her Masters in Library and Information Sciences summa cum laude from Catholic University, specializing in library automation.

In Federal Libraries, Ms. Scott has been the Head of Cataloging at the U.S. Bureau of the Census Library, Systems Librarian at the Judges' Library for the U.S. Court of Appeals in Washington, and Head of Technical Services and Systems at the NASA Goddard Space Flight Center Library. She also directed cataloging projects for the National Library of Medicine, National Oceanic and Atmospheric Administration, and NASA Langley.

Ms. Scott automated the library at the Harvard Center for Hellenic Studies, and a special military library at Ft. Belvoir, Virginia, and organized a digitization project for the architectural drawings used in the Pentagon Renovation Program.

Ms. Scott's interests are in providing information to users remotely through digitization and automation, and the arrangement of materials in manners most useful to the end user. Reflecting these interests, she provided access to needed materials for a special military library's branch sites scattered around the country utilizing a website, a customized web-based OPAC with pre-configured searches, and linking fields in cataloging records. She also developed a classification system reflecting the Agency's information needs and the type of materials in a special collection within the military library.